DINKUM DICTIONARY

Lenie (Midge) Johansen was born in Sale, Victoria, in 1950 and was a primary-school teacher in the Melbourne inner suburb of North Fitzroy from 1969 to 1979. It was there, through her contact with the mainly immigrant population, that her obsession with Aussie English was born. Now a resident of Queensland's Gold Coast, Lenie Johansen is a poet, potter and sculptor – and an inveterate collector of everything from flying ducks to stuffed snakes. It took her ten years to amass the colourful and often humorous expressions that make up *The Dinkum Dictionary*.

For Marcus, my 'other half', who supported my 'foinsapping' and tolerated my infernally bleeping and buzzing computer into the wee hours of many mornings.

THE DINKUM DICTIONARY

A ripper guide to Aussie English

Lenie (Midge) Johansen

Illustrated by Ken Maynard

LIFETIME DISTRIBUTORS
"The Book People"

Produced by Penguin Books Australia for
Lifetime Distributors
Unit 1, 22 Oramzi Street
Girraween NSW 2145

This edition published 1993

ISBN 0 670 90728 6

Printed and bound in Australia
by Australian Print Group

Contents

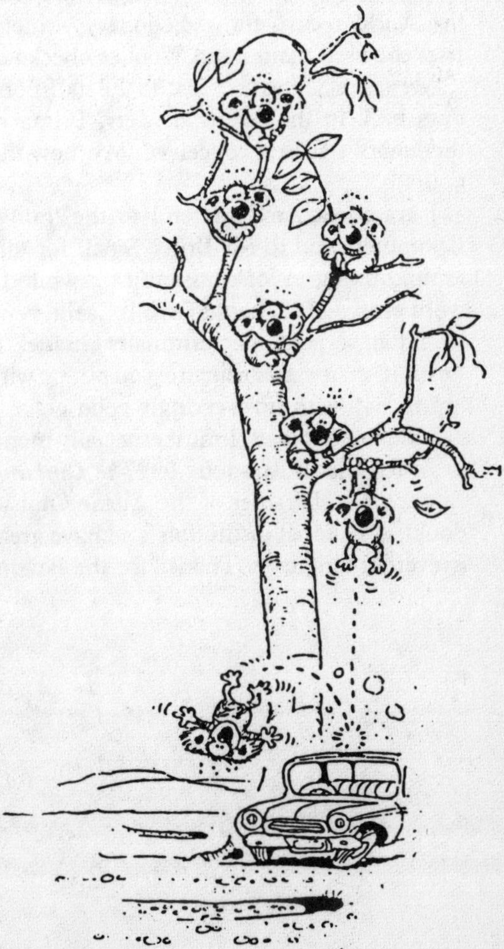

Acknowledgements

A great many people gave me invaluable help with the compiling, editing and processing of *The Dinkum Dictionary*. First on my list must be my husband, without whose support I would have starved.

Many thanks to all you friends and characters out there with whom I spent so many enjoyable hours of fun and hilarity over the years, picking your brains and scribbling madly on whatever was available. At one stage I must have had the world record for a dictionary written on the back of empty cigarette packets, used tissues and Woolies checkout dockets.

My appreciation goes also to the staffroom friends of my old school-teaching days back in the 1970s at Merri Primary School, where the idea for this dictionary was first conceived. My, how the years have flown! I still think of you all.

I am particularly grateful to the 'nutty professors' and staff of Eracom Computers and to Mr Bruce Small for tolerating my presence as I sneaked around trying to look insignificant while I used his computers, printers and word processors. Thanks Dr Bill Caelli — without you, my computer terminal would have sent me terminally insane! Thank you Barry Johnstone, my 'print it' man extraordinaire: you put up with my harassment to 'print this' and 'print that' with unswervingly good grace.

Last, but not least, I must especially mention cartoonist Ken Maynard, who provided the illustrations for *The Dinkum Dictionary*. His cartoons, which capture the character of the Aussie Outback so well, have become, without doubt, a 'national institution' and have greatly added to the amusement of an irreverent language. Thanks for the laughs, Ken!

Introduction

Is there a 'fair dinkum' Australian language? After all, everyone knows that Australians speak English. Moreover, they speak the same English across the nation — there are no regional dialects and only minor idiomatic and semantic variations between the States. Australians understand each other as easily as they understand a person from another country who speaks English.

Why is it then that English-speaking visitors to Australia have enormous trouble understanding Australians even after they have attuned their ears to the twang and the blending of words and consonants that form the Aussie accent? The answer to this question gradually revealed itself to me in the course of many hours spent entertaining overseas visitors at that most entrenched and indigenous of Australian institutions: the backyard 'barbie'. On several occasions we had the lot — my pet kangaroo, a friend and his talking cockatoo, smoke blowing wherever we sat, 'the girls' on one side 'chewing the rag', 'the boys' on the other talking sport, a variety of 'bangers', 'snags' and 'mystery bags', and more smoke — not to mention the 'mossies', 'midges' and 'blowies' and the requisite Esky stuffed with ice and beer. The number of ordinary Australian words that our visitors didn't understand provided a continual source of hilarity and amazement on both sides. They didn't even know what 'chooks' were — and I had assumed that everybody used the word! And who would have thought that simple everyday words like 'whinge', 'snags', 'stubbies', 'arvo', 'beaut', 'bludge', 'blue' and 'bugger' would not be understood by everybody?

Clearly here was a major problem. Non-Australians are simply not familiar with the Australian penchant for inventing and using colloquialisms for every facet of life — a habit that is now carrying over to the printed word. Colloquialisms by definition belong to speech rather than to the printed word, but these days the distinction is becoming blurred. Increasingly newspapers are resorting to the colloquial. It is this extensive use of idiomatic expressions (idiotic expressions many foreigners would say) in the printed as well as the spoken word which astonishes most non-Australians — much to the puzzlement of Aussies who think their language is simple enough for any 'nong' to understand.

A further difficulty with Australian English also became apparent at these social gatherings. A particular word may have several quite different meanings. It may change its meaning according to the context. Or its sense may be dependent upon the intonation of the speaker. Take this hypothetical, highly exaggerated discussion between two mates at the local 'boozer':

'Bugger me dead! Get a load of the knockers on that sheila — what a knockout!'

'Well I'll be buggered! That's Lucy Looselegs. Wonder who she's knockin' around with now?'

'Wouldn't mind if it were me. Bet she knocks like a Mack truck.'

'You've hit it right on the knocker, but you'd be a silly bugger if you tried to knock her off!'

'C'mon now — don't knock it till you've tried it. Yer always knockin' it fer fear of gettin' a knock-back!'

'No, I'm serious! I'll give yer the drum — you'd get bugger-all from her except trouble. Bit of a knock-about, she is. Used to run that swisho knock-shop called — gees, bugger it! Can't think of the name now!'

'Well I'll be buggered! You don't mean the one where that poor bugger got knocked off last year?'

'Yep! That's the one! Rumour has it that Lucy got knocked up by this bloke she was buggerising around with, and her pimp boyfriend — real heavy — did his block. Told her to tell the bloke to bugger off or he'd knock his block off. Lucy must've told the heavy to knock it off or somethin', and then he really got mad. Waited for Lucy to knock off one night, knocked up some sort of knock-out bomb and while she was out to it, waited for this other poor bugger to arrive. Knocked him off. Blew him to buggery with a twenty-two.'

'Bugger me dead! What happened to 'im — the boyfriend?'

'Buggered if I know. They never found 'im. Buggered up his chances of stayin' so he knocked off Lucy's car and shot through somewhere.'

'Well I'll be buggered!'

'Speakin' of which — feelin' a bit buggered meself. Think I'll knock off the slops fer tonight and shoot through to the little missus.'

'Get orff! You've knocked yerself out yappin' yer head off. Done bugger-all work today and complainin' of being knocked up! Knock back yer glass and have anotherie — my shout.'

'Cripes! Can't knock that offer back. Here's mud in yer eye!'

Nearly every one of those 'knocks' and 'buggers' has a different meaning!

Similarly, if an Aussie calls a friend a 'stupid old bastard', he may just be telling him that he's liked and accepted. On the other hand, if a stranger looks someone in the eye and calls him a 'stupid old bastard', it's probably meant, and my advice to the latter would be either to 'P.O.Q.' (piss off quick) or to give the stranger a 'fist full of fives', perhaps followed by a 'knuckle sandwich'.

Australians seem to take exceptional delight in the art of 'knocking' (criticising) or giving praise in a back-handed manner. However, much of what sounds cutting, abusive, unkind, spiteful or lewd is intended to be taken in fun, and Australians expect their friends, loved ones and acquaintances to 'cop it sweet' when they utter such jocular insults as:

'Look what the cat dragged in!'

'Your eyes look like two piss-holes in the snow.'

'If you get any thinner you'll have to run around under the shower to catch the drops.'

The difficulties of coping with an intractable language are not restricted to tourists. We are a nation of migrants and many foreigners who come to Australia come to stay. My own experience is in some senses 'typically Australian'. Although I'm a 'dinkum Aussie' born in 'Oz' my 'oldies' (parents) migrated after the Second World War, speaking very little English and absolutely no 'Australian'. Back in those days they were 'bloody wog galahs' who couldn't understand 'plain English'. It took them a long time to realise that their rudimentary textbook English wasn't going to help them work out 'what the blazes' those 'flamin' Aussies' were 'yapping about'. Of course much of that has changed now. The 'old cheese' 'swears like a trooper' if she burns the 'tucker', and the 'old man' 'raps' with the best of them at 'smoko'. Their pronunciation may be coloured by their continental accent, but their idiom is unmistakably Australian.

Made sensitive to the distinctiveness of the Australian vernacular by the difficulties of my family and overseas friends, I became more and more convinced of the need for a dictionary that recorded the variety and subtleties of the English spoken by Australians. *The Dinkum Dictionary* is the result. In it I hope I have captured Australians' quickness for inventing new ways of saying what they mean: ways that are hilarious, serious, cynical, amusing, disrespectful — and often vulgar and profane.

Let me point out here that not all Aussies use all the words and sayings in this dictionary as part of their everyday vocabulary. Lots of Aussies don't swear (much!) or use the more vulgar sayings, and a very few, if you'll pardon the expression, 'wouldn't say shit for a shilling'. But the fact that so much Aussie English is punctuated by crude and often vulgar words and expressions justifies the inclusion of them in a dictionary such as this. Many authors of works on Australian slang and idiom have ignored the cruder sayings, or their publishers for the sake of propriety have refused to print them. The truth is that Aussie English has little or no regard for propriety, preferring the direct, the down-to-earth, the colourful and the profane.

In any case, many words considered by some people to be rude, crude or lewd are quite acceptable to others. As freedom in society has grown, so too has a tolerance of language that was once considered vulgar. However, grossly indecent speech is uncommon in the home and in front of children, old people and women (unless delivered by other women). With exceptions, a form of instinctive and unanimous censorship applies that prevents the coarser and more vulgar parts of our colloquial speech being uttered in mixed company. Instead of 'pig's arse' you might hear 'pig's bum', or 'bullshit' shortened to 'bull', or 'cunning as a lavvy rat' instead of 'cunning as a shithouse rat'.

Many of these modified versions are used by women. In fact, the slang and expressions used by women have, to a great extent, been overlooked by the male authors of existing dictionaries of Australian colloquialisms. I have included as many of these expressions as I could collect (as well as those that I recollect from my own experiences as a member of the 'fairer sex'). For example, 'hubby', 'lippie', 'cardie', 'step-ins', 'nightie', 'flatties', 'put one's face on', 'powder one's nose', be 'on the rags', 'have kittens' and 'he only thinks of his belly and what hangs on the end of it', seem to me to be essentially female expressions.

I have attempted to include in *The Dinkum Dictionary* as many of the widely accepted definitions for a particular word or expression as possible. In general, I have preferred to include slang and colloquial speech that still have currency in Australia today, omitting those sayings that have faded into obscurity, as there is ample documentation of these elsewhere. However, there are many old expressions that are still heard and used. It is difficult to explain why some colloquial sayings go out of date while others remain immortal. Although the Bondi tram has long since stopped rattling through Sydney, you will still hear of people 'shooting through' like that proverbial vehicle. Decimal currency was introduced into Australia in 1966, yet imperial terms still abound in colloquial sayings like 'he's not the full quid's worth', 'the penny finally dropped' and 'he's as silly as a two-bob watch'.

It was difficult to decide whether the more uncommon expressions should be included, but where they could be verified by other people I have added them. Sayings that have a regional origin are used more widely than one might expect. For example, 'Albany doctor', 'back o' Bourke', 'Buckley's chance', 'doesn't know whether it's Pitt Street or Christmas' and 'more front than Myers', are universally used.

I had no difficulty in deciding whether or not to include sayings that are not strictly Australian in origin — I simply collected them all. I felt that too many dictionaries of the Australian vernacular ignore those words in frequent use that have been borrowed from other countries. A good deal of our slang is imported, then adapted to our own needs. Australian colloquial speech, now more than ever, uses not only words from other English-speaking countries, but non-English words as well: 'schemozzle' (disorder) is Yiddish, 'ciao' (farewell) is Italian and 'skol' (a toast) is Danish.

Interestingly, Australians have also, for reasons unknown, rejected some overseas terms. Although there are many New Zealanders now living in Australia, you won't hear Aussies using 'Kiwi' sayings such as 'bach' (holiday house), 'section' (block of land) or 'dairy' (milk-bar).

Finally, I have not documented the origins of the entries because of the enormity of the primary task of collection and recording. This, I admit, is sad, for greater insight and understanding are attained if words are accompanied by etymological explanation. Perhaps a later, revised edition will include research into the origins of the words and terms in the present collection, together with new additions to the language.

With such a future, revised edition in mind, I would be most interested and grateful to receive any additional words or phrases that readers might care to contribute to the dictionary.

Note to the revised edition

When I wrote these words in 1988 I could not have anticipated the enthusiastic response *The Dinkum Dictionary* would receive. I have had dozens of letters from all over Australia and as far away as Leningrad written by readers who revelled in the language captured in the book and had suggestions for further entries.

Because colloquial Australian has moved on so quickly, and because inevitably some expressions were missed in the first edition, I have now revised and updated the book to include 500 new or enduring words and phrases for the 1990s.

And, yes, I would still be very pleased to receive further suggestions for entries from readers, sent to P.O. Box 51, Mudgeeraba, Queensland 4213.

Parts of the body: 1

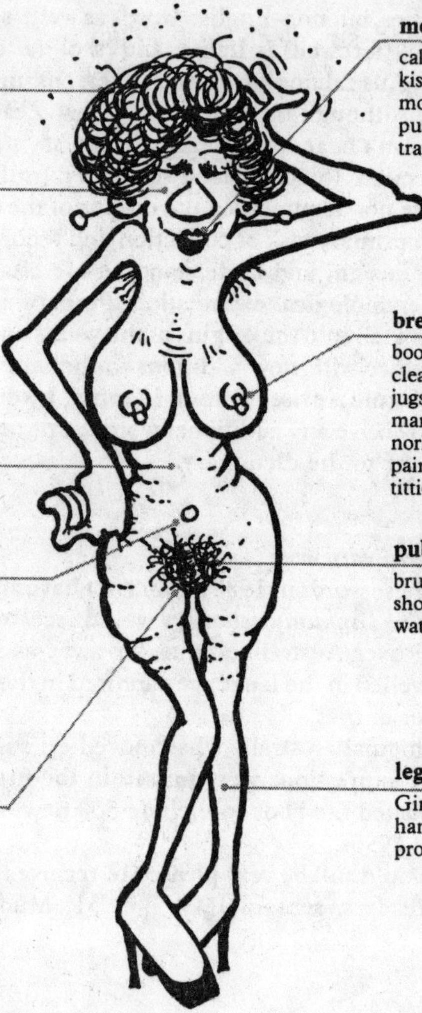

hair
fuzz, hair-do, mop

face
countenance, dial, features, kisser, moosh, mug, puss

mouth
cake-hole, chops, gob, hole, kisser, laughing gear, moosh, north-and-south, puss, rattle-trap, smacker, trap, yap

breasts
boobs, bristols, charlies, cleavage, dugs, fun-bags, jugs, knockers, lungs, mammaries, montezumas, norks, nubbies, nungers, pair, rose-buds, set, tits, titties

waist
middle, spare tyre

navel
belly-button

pubic hair
brush, bush, fuzz, pubes, short and curlies, watch-springs

pudendum
bearded clam, beaver, black badger, box, cherry, crack, cunt, date, dot, doughnut, fanny, flange, front-bum, fur-burger, gash, golden doughnut, growler, gutted rabbit, hair pie, hole, honeypot, Joe Hunt, man-hole, meat, michael, mick, mickey, monkey, muff, nasty, pussy, quim, slash, slit, slot, snatch, twat

legs
Ginger Meggs, ham and eggs, pegs, pins, props, shanks, stumps

Parts of the body: 2

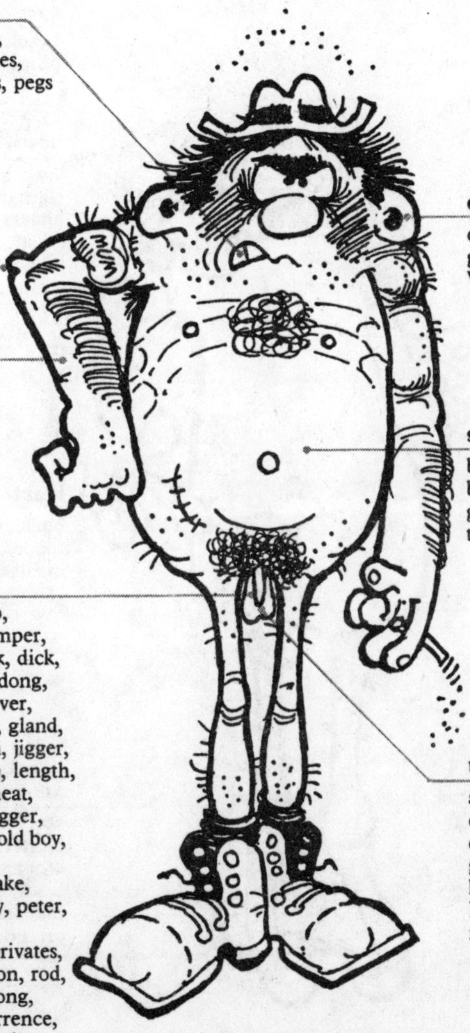

teeth

chompers, choppers, clackers, fangs, ivories, pearlies, pearly gates, pegs

elbow

funny-bone

arm

fin, Warwick Farm, warwick, wing

penis

beef bayonet, bishop, blue-vein junket-pumper, blue-vein steak, cock, dick, dickory dock, ding, dong, donger, doodle, doover, dork, dragon, ferret, gland, hoffman brick, horn, jigger, joy-stick, kerp, knob, length, man's best friend, meat, member, mutton dagger, nasty, nob, noodle, old boy, old feller, one-eyed trouser-snake, organ, pecker, percy, peter, pink oboe, pizzle, pork sword, prick, privates, prong, pyjama-python, rod, roger, sausage, schlong, stalk, stiff, tassel, terrence, thing, tonk, tool, tossle, vital organ, walloper, whistle, wick, wife's best friend, willie, zube, zubrick

ear

ear'ole, Germaine Greer, ginger-beer, lug, taxi door, Williamstown pier, wingnut

stomach

bay window, bingie, breadbasket, breadbin, gut, guts, pinny, pot, puku, tummy

testicles

agates, balls, bollocks, cobblers, cods, crown jewels, dim-sims, family jewels, giblets, gonads, goolies, kanakas, knackers, Niagara Falls, niagaras, nuts, orchestra stalls, pills

Parts of the body: 3

head

bean, block, conk, crown, cruet, crumpet, dome, loaf, lolly, melon, nob, nog, noggin, noodle, nut, onion, sconce, scone, skull

eyes

headlamps, mince-pies, peepers, whites, winkers

nose

beak, bracket, bugle, button, cherrypicker, conk, honk, honker, hooter, Lionel Rose, nozzle, schnoz, schnozzle, snoot, snot-box, snout, snoz, snozzle

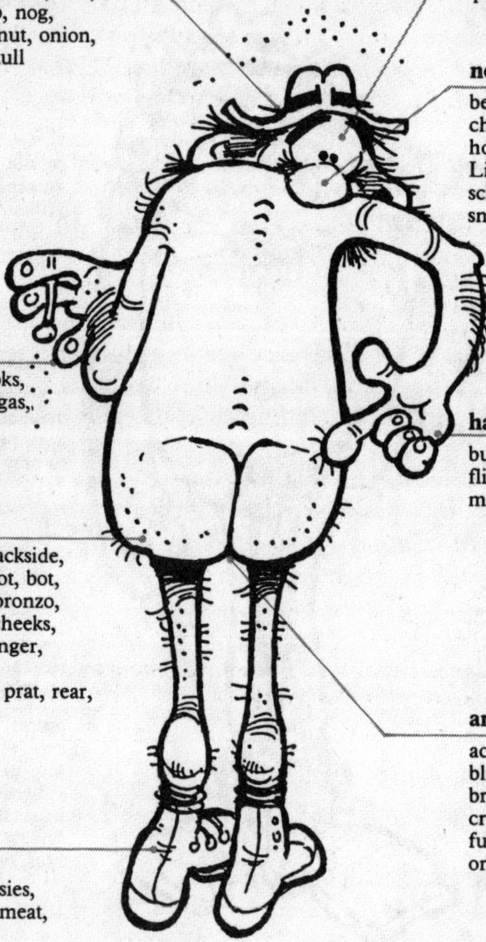

fingers

claws, digits, hooks, onkas, onkaparingas, pinkies

hand

bunch of fives, dook, duke, flipper, German band, mauler, mitt, paw

bum

ace, acre, arse, backside, beam, behind, blot, bot, bottom, bronze, bronzo, buns, butt, can, cheeks, derriere, ding, dinger, ginger, khyber, Khyber Pass, ort, prat, rear, rump, tail, tush

anus

ace, arsehole, back passage, blurter, breezer, bronze, bronzo, brown-eye, coit, crack, date, freckle, fundament, ginger, hole, ort, quoit, ring, ring-piece

feet

beetle-crushers, clodhoppers, footsies, hooves, plates of meat, tootsies

How to use the dictionary

All head words and phrases appear in **bold** and are followed by a brief explanation of their meanings. They are listed alphabetically, which in the case of the head phrases means that they are listed alphabetically by their first word. For example, 'why keep a dog and bark oneself?' will be found in the **why** entries.

However, the wording of some sayings varies slightly with usage. 'Why keep a dog and bark oneself?' is sometimes expressed as 'it's no use having a dog and doing its barking'. In instances such as this, if the saying, in the form in which you know it, is not found listed alphabetically under its first word, look up the key word of the phrase (**dog**). Under the head word you will find, in addition to its definitions, a sub-heading *See also* followed by a list of all the phrases in the dictionary which include the key word. In the present example, the head word **dog** has three definitions and a lengthy list of phrases under *See also*, including 'why keep a dog and bark oneself?'.

Where two or more phrases that follow each other alphabetically have the same meaning, they have been listed one after the other in bold, then given a common definition.

To demonstrate the range and inventiveness of the Australian language, where subjects of national preoccupation such as drinking are concerned, the dictionary also provides a number of alphabetical lists of words and phrases under subject headings. These are found at the end of the dictionary, after the main alphabetical entries.

The following abbreviations have been used throughout the dictionary:

abbrev.	abbreviated
cap.	word begins with a capital
caps	each word in the name or phrase begins with a capital
derog.	derogatory term
joc.	jocular use
vulg.	vulgar use

In the list of new words at the end of the book, recent variants or additional definitions of head words in the dictionary are cross-referred back to the main entry.

A
(see: give someone the big A)

a big deal
anything serious, important, noteworthy: e.g. This new project is going to be a big deal. (see also: big deal)

a bit gone
mad; silly; insane: e.g. He's a bit gone since his wife died.

a bit hot
1. unjustifiably, unfairly expensive.
2. rather excessive, unfair.

a bit more choke and you would have started
joc. statement to someone who has farted loudly in company.

a bit much
excessive, rude behaviour.

a bit rough/rugged
1. unfair; unjust: e.g. That court decision was a bit rough for such a minor offence.
2. unseemly; risque; lewd; indecent: e.g. That joke was a bit rough in front of the ladies.

a bit solid
harsh; unreasonable: e.g. That fine was a bit solid for such a minor offence.

a bit thick
1. too much to tolerate; unreasonable: e.g. Being expected to work late without pay is a bit thick.
2. (of a person) rather dumb.

a change is as good as a holiday
a break in one's usual routine is enough to revive the spirit.

a good few
quite a large amount: e.g. We didn't expect a large crowd, but a good few turned up for the meeting.

a good thing
1. something worthy, notable, admirable: e.g. That charity is doing a good thing for the aged and homeless.
2. just as well; for the better: e.g. It's a good thing you didn't burn those documents.

a man's home is his castle
home is a place of refuge, retreat, security.

A over T
(arse over tit) head over heels; fall heavily and clumsily; roll over: e.g. He stood on a banana skin and went A over T.

a pop
each: e.g. I paid two dollars a pop for those.

a pox on (someone)
a curse, disgust, ill-feeling directed at (someone).

a real . . .
an intensifier meaning very, extreme, absolute: e.g. He's a real galah; She's a real fool.

a real shit
a despicable person.

a throw
each: e.g. Those things cost me ten dollars a throw.

a wake-up
(of a person) to be fully aware of; to know the implications of a situation: e.g. I'm a wake-up to his tricks.

A.A.
(abbrev.) Alcoholics Anonymous.

ABC's
the main facts; rudiments of a subject: e.g. I want all the ABC's before I invest my money in that deal.

A.B.C.
(abbrev.) Australian Broadcasting Corporation.

Abo
Aborigine; Aboriginal. (sometimes, but not always, derogatory)

abortion
total failure: e.g. The party was a complete abortion.

about time!
finally!; at last!

about-face
reversal of opinion, policy, allegiance or loyalty: e.g. Alf used to vote for them but did an about-face and voted for the others.

above (oneself)
1. conceited; smug: e.g. He's a bit above himself since he made his fortune.
2. extremely excited or elated: e.g. He's going to be above himself when he hears about his big win in the lottery.

above the law
despotic; unauthorised; in a manner that defies incrimination.

above water
(see: all above water)

above-board
legal; without secrecy or concealment.

abso-bloody-lutely
positively; emphatically yes.

absolute steal
cheap; inexpensive; a bargain.

academy award
(try for an . . .) (Australian Rules football) a free kick.

accident
unplanned pregnancy: e.g. My second child was an accident.

ac-dc
bisexual.

ace
1. highly skilled; one who excels: e.g. He's an ace at athletics.
2. excellent; wonderful; very good: e.g. This car's ace to drive.
3. the anus, bum.
See also:
have/got an ace up (one's) sleeve
on (one's) ace

ace it up
stop it!

Achilles' heel
single point or area of weakness in a person.

acid
the hallucinogenic drug, LSD.
See also:
drop acid
put the acid on (someone)

acid test
conclusive test; final analysis.

acid-head
one addicted to taking LSD.

acquire
to steal; obtain without payment.

acquired taste
liking, developed over time for something previously considered distasteful: e.g. To many, eating oysters natural has been an acquired taste.

acre
buttocks; bum; anus.
See also:
six (or other number) axe-handles across the acre
wise-acre

acres of
large amounts of.

across-the-board
1. applying to all.
2. generally.

act
1. contrived or artificial behaviour: e.g. He's not for real, it's just an act.
2. display of bad temper: e.g. There's no need to bung on an act!
See also:
animal act
bit of an act
bung/stack/put on an act
caught in the act
get in on the act
get (one's) act together
hard act to follow

act like a clown
foolish, silly behaviour.

act of God
unforeseen circumstances brought about by the forces of nature.

act on the spur of the moment
impulsive behaviour.

act (one's/your) age
behave sensibly; (expression) grow up!: e.g. You'd think he'd act his age by now.

act the angora
behave in a foolish manner.

act the goat
behave in a foolish manner.

act up
1. misbehave; play up; take advantage of (someone).
2. to malfunction: e.g. My car's starting to act up.

action
1. event; happening; excitement: e.g. Where's the action?
2. members of the opposite sex, with the view to sexual pursuits: e.g. Seen/had any action lately?
See also:
get in on the action
piece of the action

action stations!
an order to get ready for a particular activity.

actor
person whose behaviour is often insincere, ostentatious, exaggerated.

ad
(abbrev.) advertisement.

ad lib
impromptu; improvised; without preparation.

Adam
(see: since Adam was a pup; wouldn't know someone from Adam)

Adam's ale
water.

Adam's apple
bump of cartilage at front of the throat.

add coal/fuel to the fire
to make a bad situation worse through word or action; aggravate.

add insult to injury
to compound or make worse a grievance already committed against someone.

add two and two together
be fully cognisant of the facts or real situation from available clues.

add up
make sense: e.g. It just doesn't add up.

admin
(abbrev.) administration.

advert
(abbrev.) advertisement.
See also:
it pays to advertise

aerial ping-pong
Australian Rules football.

aerialist
(Australian Rules football) exponent of the high mark.

affair
1. happening; event; party: e.g. New Year's Eve was a great affair.
2. scandal.
3. immoral sexual relationship.

afoot
happening; in progress.

afraid of (one's) own shadow
easily frightened; nervous.

African
cigarette. (rhyming slang — African nigger).

afro
curly, bushy and rounded hairstyle made popular by United States Blacks.

after a fashion
only average; so-so; mundanely: e.g. He did the job after a fashion, but it's not as good as I expected.

after darks
(rhyming slang) sharks.

after hours
(abbrev.: a/h) any time after normal work hours, usually after 5.30 p.m.

after (one's) own heart
to (one's) liking; appealing: e.g. He's a man after my own heart.

after (someone's) blood
seeking vengeance: e.g. Dad's after Fred's blood for getting me pregnant.

afternoon delight
sexual intercourse in the afternoon.

against the clock
quickly, in order to meet a deadline; in haste: e.g. We'll have to work against the clock to finish in time.

against the odds/tide/wind
with extreme difficulty; in the face of adverse conditions.

agates
testicles.

age of consent
age above which consent is recognised by law, particularly of a girl to sexual intercourse.

agent orange
chemical defoliant considered dangerous to human health.

ages
a long time.

aggro
aggressive; in the mood for trouble-making: e.g. Jim's a beaut bloke sober, but he gets aggro whenever he drinks too much.

aggy pipe
agricultural pipe used for drainage and landscaping.

aha!
exclamation which may mean several things, depending on how it is uttered and voice inflection, such as surprise, contempt, mockery, discovery.

ahead
in a favourable position.
See also:
get ahead

ahead of (one's) time
to have ideas and thoughts more advanced than those of the present time.

AIDS
(abbrev.) Acquired Immune Deficiency Syndrome, an often fatal condition.

ain't it the truth!
expression of sympathy, agreement.

air
(see: breath of fresh air; clear the air; dance on air; get some air; hot air; in the air; into thin air; off the air; on the air; out of thin air; put on airs; treading on air; up in the air; walking on air)

air and excercise
a prison sentence.

air between the ears
(to have . . .) dull-witted, not intelligent.

air was so thick you could cut it with a knife
pertaining to a morose, miserable or aggressive feeling between people in a room.

airs and graces
affected manner; haughtiness; assumed conceited behaviour: e.g. He's no better than the rest but he's always bunging on airs and graces.
See also:
put on airs

airtight
impermeable; without a weakness: e.g. He's got an airtight alibi.

airy-fairy
fanciful; vague.

Ajax
to clean a bath or sink etc. using an abrasive cleansing powder. (Trademark)

Akubra
typically Australian wide-brimmed felt hat. (Trademark)

Al Capone
(rhyming slang) phone.

Albany doctor
cool refreshing breeze. (taken from the W.A. town of Albany)

albatross around (one's) neck
a difficulty that persists.

Alf
1. the uneducated, average Australian male, showing no regard for women and preferring the company of male friends.
2. a stupid man.

Alfoil
aluminium foil. (Trademark)

Alice
(often: The Alice) Alice Springs, Northern Territory.

alive and kicking
1. in good health and spirits.
2. still alive as opposed to dead.

alkie
alcoholic; a heavy drinker. (also: alky)

all above water
legitimate; legal: e.g. The entire deal is all above water.

all alone like a country dunny
forlorn; without company; alone and dejected.

all along
all the time: e.g. I knew that all along.

all at once
suddenly; immediately: e.g. Everything happened all at once.

all at sea/sixes and sevens
perplexed; mixed up; floundering with a task, situation: e.g. He's all at sea when it comes to cooking.

all a-twitter
agitated.

all beer and skittles
easy task; easy going.

all broken/choked up
(sometimes used in a sarcastically mocking manner) distraught; emotionally upset: e.g. He's all broken up since his wife died.

all cush
all right; okay; without problems.

all cut up
distraught; emotionally upset.

all dolled up

all done up like a sore toe

all dressed up
dressed in one's best clothes.

all dressed up with nowhere to go
forlorn; lonely; having no friends and nothing to do.

all ears
1. listening attentively.
2. listening in or eavesdropping; prying.

all for (it)
in total agreement: e.g. The City Council is all for permitting high-rise development along the beach-front.

all for the good
in the best interests of — sometimes as a justification of an unpleasant task.

all froth and bubble
lacking substance.

all hands on deck
a call to begin work or activity.

all he thinks about is his belly and what hangs on the end of it
refers to the chauvinist male who has food and sex uppermost in his mind.

all heart
full of generosity, thoughtfulness and kindness.

all in
exhausted; tired: e.g. I'm going to bed early — I'm all in since starting work at daybreak.

all in a day's work
normal procedure in the pursuit of one's business (often ironic).

all in all
1. taken as a whole: e.g. All in all, it's a good idea.
2. one's sole purpose in life: e.g. She's my all in all.

all in the altogether
in the nude: e.g. They went swimming all in the altogether.

all in the family
confidentially; between ourselves.

all in the head
imaginary; not real: e.g. Her sickness is all in the head.

all laired/mockered up
(see: all dolled up)

all mouth
boasting; insincere; loquacious: e.g. He's all mouth.

all my eye and Betty Martin!
expression of disbelief.

all off
cancelled; finished: e.g. Our engagement's all off.

all one to (one)
of no particular consequence to (one); all the same to (one): e.g. I don't mind where we go for dinner — it's all one to me.

all (one's) Christmases have come at once
1. feel extremely elated.
2. have extreme good luck or fortune.
See also:
thought all (one's) Christmases had come at once

all out
exhausted; tired: e.g. I'm all out after all that work.
See also:
all-out

all over
1. finished; ended: e.g. The party's all over.
2. characteristically; typically: e.g. He's a dinkum footy fan all over.

all over (someone) like a rash
pay excessive and often (unwanted) amorous attention to (someone): e.g. She's been all over him like a rash since he walked in.

all over the place
in disorder, disarray: e.g. That company's books and files are all over the place.

all over the place like a madwoman's breakfast/ custard/knitting/lunch-box/ shit
complete disorder.

all over with
finished; ended: e.g. Their romance is all over with.

all pink on the inside
of dark-skinned women as sex objects.

all piss and wind
boastful, loquacious and insincere, especially when drunk.

all ponced up
dressed smartly; dressed in one's best.

all right!
a call, plea for attention, moderation.
See also:
it's all right for you!

all screwed up
1. mentally or emotionally disturbed; mixed up.
2. broken; damaged; impaired: e.g. Our television set is all screwed up.

all settled
finalised; agreed upon: e.g. The deal's all settled.

all shook up
emotionally upset, worried.

all show
pretence; ostentation; mere display: e.g. His bravado in front of the women was all show.

all Sir Garnet
all right; okay; doing well: e.g. Everything's all Sir Garnet.

all smiles
elated; happy; overjoyed: e.g. He's all smiles since he won the lottery.

all systems go
everything is ready to start, go ahead.

all that glitters is not gold
outward appearances may be deceptive.

all the best
expression of goodwill, farewell.

all the go/rage
fashionable; currently popular; trendy.

all the same to (one)
immaterial, not important to (one).

all there
1. of sound mind; sane: e.g. I don't think he's all there.
2. shrewd; intelligent: e.g. He's all there when it comes to business dealings.
See also:
not all there

all thumbs
clumsy with one's hands: e.g. He's all thumbs when it comes to carpentry.

all up
finished; at the point of failure or defeat: e.g. The game's all up for him and his cheating ways.

all washed up
1. complete failure: e.g. This company is all washed up.
2. exhausted; tired.

all wind and water
boastful; loquacious; insincere.

all wool and a yard wide
sincere; honest; scrupulous; authentic: e.g. Perry's all wool and a yard wide when he's sober, but all piss and wind when drunk.

all work and no play makes Jack a dull boy
one who concentrates too much on work and not enough on leisure becomes boring and tiresome.

all-day sucker
large, round, flat, candy-striped confection or lolly on a stick.

allergic/allergy to
antipathy to; dislike for: e.g. He's got an allergy to any sort of work.

alley
1. playing marble.
2. an organised two-up game or school.
See also:
blind alley
make (one's) alley good
right up (one's) alley
tin-pan alley
toss in (one's) alley
up (one's) alley

alley up
pay back (a debt); pay up (a bet).

all-out
1. complete; utter; total: e.g. It was an all-out failure.
2. involving all one's strength, energy and determination: e.g. We went all-out to win the race.
3. at full speed: e.g. We drove all-out for 6 hours to get there on time.
See also:
all out

all-rounder
person adept at many tasks.

all's fair in love and war
declaration that no rules, morals or ethics apply — that any action is acceptable.

all-time
outstanding; absolute: e.g. He's an all-time crook!

all-up
total; in total: e.g. 1. What do I owe all-up? 2. The all-up price was over ten thousand dollars.

almighty
1. very big; extreme; very: e.g. What an almighty mess this is.
2. (cap.) God: e.g. Who does he think he is — the Almighty?

almond rocks
(rhyming slang) socks.

also-ran
a failure; second-rate: e.g. He's an also-ran — none of his business ventures have been a success.

alternative life-style
(see: back to nature)

altogether
(see: in the . . .)

always in the shit — it's just the depth that varies
to always seem to be in trouble, or in someone's bad books.

always looking down (one's) nose at
regard with disdain; scoff, sneer at.

always on the go
busy; hyperactive.

always the bridesmaid, never the bride
to always be below one's desired goal, level of achievement.

amber, amber fluid/liquid
beer: e.g. Hubby's at the pub downing a few glasses of the amber with his mates.

Amex
American Express credit card. (Trademark)

ammo
ammunition.

amount to the same thing
equal; parallel; comparable: e.g. It might only have been a minor offence, but it still amounts to the same thing — he broke the law and has to be punished.

amp
amplifier.

an apple a day keeps the doctor away
saying in praise of the health benefits of apples.

an axe to grind
1. to have a particular purpose to pursue.
2. to have a grudge or grievance to work out (with someone).

an eye for an eye
revenge; repayment in kind.

an it
1. castrated animal: e.g. My cat's an it.
2. person of indeterminate sex.

anchors
brakes: e.g. I nearly went through the windscreen when he slammed on the anchors.
See also:
hit the anchors
throw out the anchors

ancient history
facts that are either well known or no longer relevant.

and a half
adding to the importance or exceptional qualities of: e.g. She's a woman and a half.

and all that (jazz)
etcetera; and so on; and all that sort of thing: e.g. He's really into drugs, sex, rock and roll and all that jazz.

and how!
certainly; very much; indeed: e.g. He can drink, and how!

and so on (and so forth)

and what have you and what have you not
etcetera; and anything else: e.g. I want all those books, papers, documents, magazines and what have you and what have you not stacked in the corner over there.

and then some
and more so: e.g. I'll tell you how much he lost — hundreds of dollars, and then some!

angel
innocent; kind; free from corruption. (often sarcastic)
See also:
be an angel
Hell's Angel
no angel

angel dust
highly dangerous, hallucinogenic drug. (P.C.P. — Phencyclidine)

angle
1. method; scheme; point of view.
2. action that is devious, self-interested.

angle for
attempt to gain through scheming, deception: e.g. His kindness is out of character — I think he's angling for something.

angle of the dangle
pertaining to an erection of the penis.

angry young man
young man, usually in the field of arts or literature, who is outspoken in his dissatisfaction with the Establishment.

animal
completely contemptible person.

animal act
a contemptible action: e.g. Betraying his friends was a real animal act.

animal magnetism
hypnotic charm, power exerted by a person (particularly a physically attractive one).

ankle
a contemptible, despicable person (an ankle is 3 foot lower than a cunt).

ankle-biters
children, particularly young babies or tots; the nippers.

another feather in (one's) cap
an honour, credit or mark of distinction.

another good man down the drain
pertaining to a man about to be married.

another mouth to feed
pertaining to an added member of the family (whether a person or animal, pet etc.) that would constitute a financial difficulty.

anotherie (just like the otherie)
another one — especially a glass of alcohol: e.g. I'll have anotherie.
See also:
tell us anotherie!

answer back
retaliate with an impertinent remark.

answer to (one's) prayers
person or thing that solves a problem for one: e.g. This kitchen gadget has been the answer to my prayers.

answer to the whip
obey immediately and without question; respond to a domineering person.

anti
opposed to: e.g. She's anti sex before marriage.

ants in (one's) pants
(to have . . .) impatient; unable to sit still: e.g. My kids have all got ants in their pants.

ant's pants
(see: the ant's pants)

any
sexual intercourse: e.g. Did you get any last night?
See also:
getting any?

any tick of the clock
1. soon: e.g. He'll be here at any tick of the clock.
2. at a time unknown: e.g. That bomb could go off at any tick of the clock.

anybody
person of little significance: e.g. I don't want to speak to just anybody — get me the boss!

anybody's guess
an uncertainty; unknown: e.g. It's anybody's guess who's going to win this contest.

anyone who's anyone
important people: e.g. Anyone who's anyone will be at the opening of the Casino.

anyone would think it/money grew on trees
there is not enough money and it is being spent too freely.
See also:
money doesn't grow on trees

anything
(see: like anything)

anything goes
a situation where anything is acceptable and there are no rules.

ANZAC/Anzac
1. Australian and New Zealand Army Corps.
2. an Australian or New Zealand soldier.
See also:
bronzed Anzac

A.O.
adults only.

A-okay
all right; working perfectly; very good; no problems.

A-one
(also: A-1) first class; first rate; working perfectly.

A.O.T.
arse over tit ; upside down; fall over heavily: e.g. I broke my leg when my horse went A.O.T.

APC
a quick, perfunctory wash of the body — armpits and crotch.

ape
1. large, uncouth man.
2. copy; mimic.
See also:
go ape over
go ape-shit over

apple
(see: Adam's apple; an apple a day keeps the doctor away; bad apple; Big Apple; could eat an apple through a paling fence; rotten apple; upset the apple-cart)

Apple Isle
Tasmania.

apple of (someone's) eye
anything held very dear: e.g. His cute little daughter, Cody Lee, is the apple of Gary's eye.

apple-pie
orderly; organised; satisfactory: e.g. Everything is apple-pie.

apples
1. okay; all right; very well: e.g. Everything's apples down on the farm.
2. (rhyming slang — apples and pears) stairs.
See also:
how's them apples?!
she'll be apples
she's apples

April fool
unsuspecting victim of a practical joke played by someone on April 1st.

apron strings
emotional dependence on a person, as of a child with its mother: e.g. He still hasn't let go the apron strings.
See also:
tied to (someone's) apron strings

are you a man or a mouse?
accusation directed towards a man's masculinity, bravery etc.

are you with me?
1. do you understand what I am saying?
2. are you loyal to me?; are you in agreement with what I am doing?; are you going to stand by me?

argue the toss
disagree; dispute a decision.

argy-bargy
tedious, argumentative talk.

aristotle
(rhyming slang) bottle.

arm
(see: chance one's arm; cost an arm and a leg; do it with one arm tied behind one's back; give one's right arm for; have/got short arms and long pockets; shot in the arm; twist someone's arm; up in arms; with open arms)

arm in arm
closely together: e.g. They're working arm in arm on that project.

armchair (mechanic, soldier etc.)
person not really adept at the practical side of his profession and depending too much on theory; remote from the reality of the job.

armchair ride
1. easy passage.
2. (Australian Rules football) easy game for a rover because of hit-outs from the ruckman.

armed to the teeth
fully armed (with weapons); fully prepared or equipped to handle a situation.

arm's length
nearly within reach.

around
approximately: e.g.
1. He'll be here at around midnight. 2. That will cost around fifty dollars.
See also:
been around

around the bend
(also: round . . .) crazy; mad; insane; increasingly irritable: e.g. The kids are driving me around the bend since the holidays started.

around the clock
constantly; for many hours: e.g. We've been working around the clock to get finished on time.

around the traps
(also: round . . .) pertaining to an intimate familiarity with and knowledge of the places where people gather, news is spread, decisions are made etc., such as pubs, clubs etc.
See also:
been around the traps

around the twist
(also: round . . .) crazy; mad; insane; increasingly irritable: e.g. I'll go around the twist if I don't have a holiday soon.

arras
bottles. (rhyming slang: aristotle — bottle)

arse
1. buttocks; bum; bottom.
2. cheek; impudence: e.g. Don't give me any arse!
3. nonsense; rubbish; foolish talk: e.g. What a lot of arse!
4. despicable person: e.g. I think he's an arse.
5. a woman as a sex object: She's a nice bit of arse.
6. daring; effrontery; self-confidence; brazenness: e.g. Jamie's got enough arse to be successful in any venture.
See also:
as long as (one's) arse points to the ground
bare as a bat's arse
bit of arse
chew the arse off (someone)
chew the arse out of a rag doll
crawl up (someone's) arse
died in the arse
doesn't give a rat's arse
down on (one's) arse
fart-arse
get (one's) arse in a sling
get (one's) arse into gear
get the arse
give (someone) the arse
hair like a bush pig's arse
have/got (one's) arse in (one's) hands

head down arse up
kick up the arse (give someone a . . .)
kiss my arse!
lick (someone's) arse
make an arse of (oneself)
more arse than class
need a kick up the arse
pain in the arse
pig's arse!
screw the arse off (someone)
shiny-arse
short-arse
sit (someone) on his arse
slack-arse
smart-arse
so tight you couldn't drive a pin up (his/her) arse with a sledgehammer
sparrows (doves or geese) flying out of (one's) arse
stick it up your arse!
suck-arse
tear the arse out of (someone)
tear-arse
thinks the sun shines out of his arse
tight as a fish's arse
tight-arse
tin-arse
up your arse!
wouldn't know (one's) arse from a hole in the ground
wouldn't know (one's) arse from a hole in a flower-pot
wouldn't know (one's) arse from (one's) elbow

arse about/around
1. fool around; waste time. 2. illogical order; back to front: e.g. 1. You've got your jumper on arse about. 2. He did it arse about.

arse about face
back to front; turned around; change in direction.

arse has dropped out of
a failed situation, especially in commerce, business, finance, real-estate: e.g. The arse has dropped out of the real-estate market because of the difficulty in getting finance.

arse knows no bounds!
exclamation referring to extreme good luck.

arse off
depart.

arse out of (one's) pants
(to have one's . . .) impoverished; poor: e.g. He's had his arse out of his pants since he lost his fortune gambling.

arse over apex/kettle/tit/turkey
1. fall heavily, clumsily, ungracefully: e.g. My horse stumbled at the last jump and we both went arse over apex.
2. upside down.
3. in a complete shambles, state of disorganisation.

arsed out
fired, dismissed unceremoniously: e.g. He was arsed out of his job because he was incompetent and lazy.

arsehole
1. anus.
2. despicable person or thing.
3. throw out unceremoniously; evict; sack; fire: e.g. He wasn't doing his job so we arseholed him quick smart.
See also:
from arsehole to breakfast time
talking through (one's) arsehole
ugly as a hatful of arseholes

arsehole about
waste time; fool about.

arsehole off
depart quickly.

arseholes!
1. rubbish! nonsense!
2. an expression of anger, frustration.

arse-licker
sycophantic, obsequious person.

arse'ole
(abbrev.) arsehole.

arse-paper
1. despicable person or thing.
2. second-rate; no good.

arse-up
1. fall heavily: e.g. I tripped and went arse-up.
2. upside down: e.g. A huge wave turned the boat arse-up.
3. ruined; in total disorder; a failure: e.g. Their whole business is arse-up at present.

arsey
unusually lucky.

artist
(in combination: e.g. bull artist, con artist) person noted for a particularly despicable or notorious characteristic.

arty-crafty
pretentiously artistic.

arty-farty
pretentiously interested in the arts.

arvo
afternoon.

as a rule
generally; usually.

as . . . as the next bloke
characteristically; as applied to normal, average people: e.g. He's as dishonest as the next bloke.

as . . . as they come
the utmost example of; characteristically: e.g. He's as gay as they come.

as good as
tantamount to: e.g. He's as good as dead now that he knows he's got cancer.

as good as (one's) word
reliable; dependable.

as good as they come
the best: e.g. For a carpenter, he's as good as they come.

as it were
so to speak.

as long as (one's) arse points to the ground
always; forever: e.g. Fleeb will tinker with crazy inventions as long as his arse points to the ground.

as luck would have it
by chance: e.g. As luck would have it, I lost my fortune on that gamble.

as much chance as pushing shit uphill

as much chance as pushing shit uphill with a rubber fork
very little or no chance at all.
See also:
easy as pushing shit uphill with a pointed stick/rubber fork

as near as damn it
as close as possible to: e.g. We came as near as damn it to winning the finals.

For other 'as . . . as . . .' entries see alphabetical listing for word following initial 'as': e.g. 'as mad as a meat-axe' is listed under 'mad as a meat-axe'.

as the actress said to the bishop
a stock remark to someone who has said something innocent or innocuous that could be taken as a sexual innuendo having a double, lewd meaning.

as the crow flies
in a straight, direct line: e.g. We live fifty kilometres away as the crow flies.

as ye sow, so shall ye reap
life will return as much pleasure or pain as one puts into it oneself.

A.S.A.P.
as soon as possible.

Ashes
(the . . .) trophy (urn containing a burnt stump) representing victory in test cricket played between Australia and England.

ask for the world
demand, expect too much.

ask me no questions and I'll tell you no lies
stock reply when someone asks too many personal questions.

ask (someone) out
invite (someone) to a social engagement.

asking a bit much
demanding, expecting too much: e.g. He's asking a bit much if he expects us to work for no pay.

asking for it
inviting trouble: e.g. You're asking for it if you do that.

asking price
price of an item set by the seller and often subject to bargaining: e.g. The asking price was 4000 dollars but I got it for 3500 dollars.

asleep
1. inattentive; idle or lazy at one's work: e.g. If I find you asleep on the job again, you're fired!
2. numb, as of a foot or arm, from inactivity.

asleep on the job
not doing one's proper share of the work.

Aspro
a prostitute.

ass
fool; stupid person.

astronomical
very large in number: e.g. My power bill was astronomical.

at
doing; engaged or occupied in: e.g. What's he at these days?
See also:
get at
keep at (someone)
this is where it's at

at a loose end
having nothing to do; idle; bored.

at a loss
1. uncertain; bewildered; confused: e.g. He's at a loss when it comes to running the business.
2. emotionally upset, unstable: e.g. She's been at a loss ever since he left.

at a pinch
under difficult circumstances if necessary; in an emergency: e.g. We might be able to help out at a pinch.

at a price
at a heavy cost, financial or otherwise: e.g. He'll do it for you, but it'll be at a price.

at a push
under difficult circumstances if absolutely necessary: e.g. We can arrange more finance at a push if you really need it.

at a rate of knots
very fast; quickly.

at any cost/price
at whatever cost; on any terms: e.g. He's determined to become famous and wealthy at any cost.

at any rate
anyway; in any case.

at any tick of the clock
1. at any moment; very soon: e.g. He'll be here at any tick of the clock.

2. at an unknown time: e.g. That bomb could go off at any tick of the clock.

at arm's length
at a distance: e.g. She's rather reserved and keeps everybody at arm's length.

at crack of dawn
at first light; daybreak.

at cross purposes
to have conflicting aims; to misunderstand (each other).

at death's door
gravely ill.

at each other's throats
in conflict; arguing bitterly: e.g. Pat and Rick used to be at each other's throats so often that we called them Pick and Rat.

at every turn
constantly: e.g. I'm sick of him complaining at every turn.

at first crack/light
at daybreak, dawn.

at full tilt
at full speed.

at hand
near: e.g. The end of the world is at hand in the opinion of some religious groups.

at heart
in one's feelings; in reality: e.g. He's a softy at heart.

at home with
accustomed to; familiar, comfortable with: e.g. He's as much at home in the kitchen as he is in the workshop.

at it again
behaving characteristically (usually in a manner frowned upon): e.g. He's been at it again (drinking) since he lost his job.

at large
free; escaped; at liberty.

at loggerheads
in dispute, disagreement.

at long last
finally, after much delay.

at odds
in disagreement; arguing: e.g. They've been at odds over how to do the job.

at once
1. immediately.
2. at the same time: e.g. Don't all speak at once.

at one time
in the past; formerly: e.g. He used to be wealthy at one time.

at (one's) beck and call
obedient to the slightest wish of (one); under (one's) power, authority to obey immediately: e.g. Ever since they got married he's been at her beck and call.

at (one's) best
performing to the best of (one's) ability: e.g. He's at his best when there's an audience.

at (one's) feet
devoted to (one); under (one's) power; at (one's) beck and call: e.g. I've finally got him at my feet.

at (one's) fingertips
1. readily and easily available: e.g. She's got a huge fortune at her fingertips.
2. just within reach.

at (one's) wit's end
totally perplexed or at a loss: e.g. I've been at my wit's end trying to fix this thing.

at opposite ends of the poles
at cross purposes; conflicting.

at panic stations
chaotic; extremely busy: e.g. The staff have been at panic stations since the sale started.

at rest
1. dead.
2. unworried; not anxious: e.g. My mind's at rest over the matter.

at sixes and sevens
confused; mixed up; perplexed: e.g. I'm at sixes and sevens when it comes to changing a tyre on the car.

at (someone)
criticising; accusing; harassing: e.g. He's always at me for one thing or another.

at (someone's) beck and call
obedient to the slightest wish of (someone).

at sparrow-fart
at dawn.

at that
besides; as well; additionally: e.g. He's a gambler and a good one at that.

at the cross-roads
a stage at which a critical decision is vital as to which course of action to take.

at the drop of a hat
immediately; on the spur of the moment; without much provocation: e.g. The wharfies go on strike at the drop of a hat.

at the end of (one's) rope/tether
1. exasperated; irritated; annoyed.
2. at the end of (one's) endurance, tolerance.

at the end of (one's) wits
totally perplexed or at a loss.

at the mercy of
in the power of; subject to; defenceless: e.g. The boat was at the mercy of the storm.

at the outside
the limit; the most possible: e.g. You'll get

50,000 dollars for the house at the outside.

at the point of
on the verge of, brink of.

at the same time
nevertheless.

at the top of (one's) lungs
as loudly as possible.

at the wheel
in control, power or command.

at your peril
at your risk, responsibility.

atmosphere so thick you could have cut it with a knife
(see: air so thick . . .)

attaboy!
exclamation of approval, urging, encouragement.

attempt the impossible
try to do something that is doomed to failure.

au naturel
1. naked; in the nude: e.g. We went swimming au naturel.
2. uncooked; natural.

auntie
(also: aunty) Australian Broadcasting Corporation (A.B.C.).

Aus/Aussie
1. Australia: e.g. Paul Hogan had tremendous success overseas promoting Aussie as the best place to come to for a holiday.
2. an Australian: e.g. Hoges (Paul Hogan) is considered by many to be a typical Aussie.
3. Australian: e.g. Paul Hogan has been a successfull Aussie ambassador overseas.

Aussie battler
the ordinary working-man earning a living against many odds.

Aussie Rules
Australian Rules football.

Aussie salute
the characteristic waving of the hand to chase away flies that continually and annoyingly buzz around one's face.

Aussie-land
Australia.

Australian adjective
(the great . . .) the word 'bloody' — notably Australia's greatest adjective because of its extensive use, signifying either approval or disapproval.

Australian as a meat pie
distinctively Australian in character.

Australian salute
(see: Aussie salute)

Australiana
collectable items of historical interest originating in Australia.

autumn leaf
(racing) jockey who continually falls.

available
single, unattached person assumed to be therefore interested in finding a partner: e.g. Since her divorce she's been available.

'Ave a go ya mug!
(cricket) cry directed at a slow batsman.

avant-garde
1. innovators in art.
2. affectedly modern, innovative.

avoid (someone) like the plague
to avoid meeting, speaking with (someone) at all costs and in a very obvious manner.

awake
(see: a wake-up)

away
1. having started and doing well: e.g. His business is away now.
2. in full flight: e.g. The suspect was up and away before the police could catch him.
See also:
do away with
get away
get away from it all
give something away
having it away with
make away with

away with the birds/fairies/pixies
1. not concentrating; day-dreaming; in a confused state of mind.
2. under the influence of drugs or alcohol.

awful
very great: e.g. He has an awful lot of money.

awfully
very: e.g. That was awfully nice of him.

awkward as a bull in a china shop
extremely clumsy.

AWOL
(abbrev.) Absent Without Official Leave.

axe
1. dismissal; the sack; to terminate, dismiss: e.g. 1. The network has decided to axe the programme due to unfavourable ratings. 2. He was given the axe.
2. musical instrument, especially a guitar.
3. to reduce prices, costs, expenditure sharply.
See also:
an axe to grind
battle-axe
get the axe
the axe

axe-handle
(joc.) unit of measure: e.g. A woman with a large backside or hips could be said to be two axe-handles across the acre.

B
bastard: e.g. He's such a B, nobody likes him.

b and d
1. brandy and dry-ginger.
2. Black and Decker brand of power tool.
3. bondage and discipline — the sexual practice of tying up one's sexual partner.

babble
1. idle incessant chatter; foolish, incoherent talk.
2. reveal a confidence; thoughtlessly reveal a secret: e.g. I'll murder you if you babble a single word to anyone.

babbler
1. person known not to be able to keep a secret.
2. (rhyming slang: babbling brook) cook.

babbling brook
(rhyming slang) cook.

babe
1. girl; young woman.
2. affectionate name for girl or lover.

babe in the woods
inexperienced novice, newcomer.

baby
1. girl; young woman; girl-friend.
2. invention, object or idea of which one is very proud: e.g. His latest baby is a yacht he's building in his back yard.
3. pamper; behave over-protectively: e.g. His mother still babies him even though he's over thirty.
4. coward: e.g. Don't be such a baby, you can do it.
5. small; diminutive: e.g. baby grand (piano).
See also:
leave someone holding the baby
like taking candy from a baby
throw the baby out with the bath-water

baby batter
sperm.

baccy
tobacco. (also: backy, bakky)

baching
(also: batching)
1. living alone (particularly of men).
2. keeping house alone during absence of partner (particularly of men not used to the task).

back
(see: behind one's back; break the back of; carry someone on one's back; do one's back in; get back at; get off my back Scobie; get off one's back!; get on someone's back; get one's back up; have/got one's back to the wall; knife in the back; on one's back; out the back; pat on the back; pay someone back; put one's back into; scratch my back and I'll scratch yours; see the back of someone; slap on the back; stab in the back; turn one's back on)

back country
the remote outback regions of Australia.

back door
pertaining to secretive, clandestine and underhanded dealings: e.g. He entered politics through the back door.

back down
retreat from an argument or opinion: e.g. He won't back down now.

back o' Bourke
1. any remote, sparsely populated country area: e.g. He lives on a farm out the back o' Bourke somewhere.
2. the suburbs, considered remote from the centre of activity in a city: e.g. Since they moved to the back o' Bourke I don't visit them often any more.

back of beyond
1. any remote, inaccessible and sparsely populated area: e.g. He got sick of the city rat-race and

moved out to the back of beyond somewhere.
2. the Australian outback: e.g. He's out touring the back of beyond before he takes a trip overseas.

back off
withdraw; cease argument; stop (harassing).

back on deck
a return to work or task after an absence: e.g. It was a great holiday but we're back on deck now.

back on (one's) feet

back on the rails
successful return from misfortune, illness, poverty etc.

back out of
retreat, withdraw from argument, opinion, a deal etc.

back passage
the anus.

back seat
inferior, subordinate position: e.g. He doesn't have any power — he's only in the back seat of the organisation.

back (someone) up
provide encouragement; support.

back to base one/home base
return to the start, beginning.

back to nature
pertaining to the practice of turning one's back on civilisation and its trappings of technology and materialism in order to lead a more simple life in appreciation of nature; pertaining to the alternative life-style.

back to square one

back to taws

back to the drawing board
begin again with a fresh approach; return to the start, beginning (often intimating that all that happened in the meantime was lost, pointless or irrelevant).

back to the grindstone
return to laborious, monotonous work: e.g. There's only a short holiday before it's back to the grindstone.

back to the wall
(to have one's . . .) to be in a precarious, disadvantageous position or predicament.

back up
support: e.g. He'll back you up even if you're wrong.

backbiting
speaking derogatively about someone in his absence; slander.

backblocks
1. remote, sparsely populated country area.
2. outer suburbs, considered remote from the centre of activity within a city.

backbone
strength of character; courage: e.g. He hasn't got the backbone to do it.

backbreaking
difficult or strenuous.

backchat
impertinence; impudence; rude answer: e.g. 1. Don't give me any backchat. 2. Children often backchat when parents try to administer discipline.

backdoor
clandestine; secret; illicit: e.g. The shop is just a front for a backdoor S.P. betting agency.

backdoor bandit
a homosexual man.

backdoor operation
clandestine, secretive and underhanded business or dealing.

backed into a corner
forced into a precarious, difficult or dangerous situation.

backflip
(see: do a backflip)

backhanded
indirectly insulting; opposite in meaning.

backhander
1. indirectly insulting comment.
2. a bribe: e.g. He got off lightly because he slipped the judge a backhander.

backing the wrong horse
supporting the losing team, side, person etc.

back-pedal
try to moderate or make less severe one's argument.

backroom boys
people working behind the scenes who desire to remain anonymous.

back-scratcher
one who offers a service expecting a favour in return.

backscuttle
1. to perform anal sexual intercourse.
2. to perform sexual intercourse from behind.

back-seat driver
1. passenger who continually interferes with the driver of a vehicle, offering instructions and advice.
2. person who interferes and offers unwanted advice.

backside
buttocks; bum.

back-slapper
obsequious person; crawler.

back-slapping
hearty mateship, friendship (especially between men): e.g. The election victory ended

with a lot of back-slapping.

back-stabbing
harmful and malicious verbal attack on someone's character or reputation; talking maliciously behind a person's back; betrayal.

backstage
behind the scenes; secret.

backstop
1. reliable person or thing to fall back on when all else fails.
2. (cricket) wicketkeeper.

back-street
underhanded; illicit; illegal: e.g. They run a back-street gambling den.

backtrack
1. retrace one's steps, procedures.
2. withdraw from a stand or opinion.

backward
retarded; slow; behind in progress.
See also:
bend/fall/lean over backward for
know (it) backward
not backward in coming forward

backwater
1.unsophisticated; retarded; out of date: e.g. The city's backwater politics are severely restricting its progress.
2. an unsophisticated place.

backwoods
1. remote and sparsely populated area: e.g. He's living in the backwoods somewhere now.
2. unsophisticated; rustic: e.g. His backwoods thinking won't get him far in politics.

backy
tobacco. (also: baccy)

backyard
1. (in combination: e.g. backyard mechanic) tradesman who operates from his place of residence.
2. unqualified; illegal; illicit: e.g. Backyard abortionist.

backyard job
illicit; illegal; improper; without proper authority; without the trappings of red tape.

bacon
(see: bring home the bacon; save one's bacon; save someone's bacon)

bad
(see: from bad to worse; in bad with; in the bad; in the bad books; not bad)

bad apple
1. one (person or thing) out of the group worse than the rest.
2. reprehensible, immoral person.

bad blood
hate, long-standing grudge: e.g. There's always been bad blood between the two brothers.

bad break
misfortune; bad luck: e.g. That was a bad break when her husband lost his job.

bad case
1. reprehensible, dishonest person.
2. person weighed down by misfortune, bad luck, emotional instability etc.

bad case of the trots
diarrhoea.

bad dog
an outstanding debt.

bad egg
reprehensible, dishonest, undesirable person.

bad form
breach of good manners: e.g. That joke was in bad form in front of the ladies.

bad loser
one who does not accept defeat with good grace.

bad lot
reprehensible, dishonest, troublesome person; a failure in life: e.g. He's a bad lot, that one.

bad luck!
1. an expression of sympathy at someone's misfortune.
2. an expression of scornful spite for someone's misfortune that went in your favour.

bad mixer
person who does not get on well with others socially.

bad news
person or thing likely to cause trouble, problems or misfortune: e.g. 1. Don't go out with him — he's bad news! 2. That car has been nothing but bad news.

bad patch
an awkward or unpleasant moment or situation.

bad penny
undesirable, unwanted person or thing that keeps returning: e.g. He keeps coming back into her life like a bad penny.

bad scene
extremely distasteful situation: e.g. The fight at the pub was a bad scene.

bad trot
series of misfortunes and bad luck: e.g. I've had a bad trot at the races lately.

bad turn
sudden change for the worse, particularly in health.

baddie
villain (of story or film).

badger
annoy; harass; nag.
See also:
black badger

badly done by
victimised by bad luck, misfortune or dishonest

people: e.g. 1. The farmers were badly done by the storm that ruined all their crops. 2. He's been badly done by since he started working for that new boss.

badly off
poor; financially destitute.
See also:
not badly off

badmouth
1. person who speaks ill of, always criticises: e.g. He's such a badmouth when it comes to religion.
2. criticise scathingly; speak ill of: e.g. One shouldn't badmouth politicians if one doesn't vote.

baffle (someone) with bullshit
1. convince, deceive, trick (someone) with irrelevant material or lies.
2. to avoid an issue by the use of jargon or language and terminology that is difficult to understand.

bag
1. ugly, disagreeable woman: e.g. She's such a bag.
2. chosen occupation; favourite pursuit: e.g. Sailing's not his bag — he'd rather go fishing.
3. a measure of marijuana: e.g. How much does a bag cost?
4. breathalyser — instrument used by police to test the level of alcohol a person has consumed.
5. to capture, arrest: e.g. The police finally bagged him.
6. criticise scathingly: e.g. He's always bagging politicians.
7. (cricket) a number of wickets taken.
See also:
blow in the bag
clagged the bag
flea-bag
in the bag
leave (someone) holding the bag
mixed bag
mystery bags
paper-bag job
pull something out of the bag
two-bagger

bag of bones
emaciated; thin.

bag of fruit
(rhyming slang) suit: e.g. He wore his best bag of fruit to the wedding.

bag of misery
morose, unhappy person.

bag of tricks
1. tools of trade: e.g. Bring your bag of tricks when you start work tomorrow morning.
2. any miscellaneous collection of articles.
3. resourceful person; one who is never at a loss: e.g. Mal's a real bag of tricks when it comes to making money.

bag of wind
verbose, loquacious person.

bag over the head job
a woman with whom a man will have sexual intercourse, but whose face he considers unattractive.

bag test
breathalyser examination by the police.

baggage
morally loose woman; impudent woman.

bagged
caught; captured; apprehended by the law: e.g. I got bagged for speeding.

baggies
baggy trousers.

bagging
severe criticism: e.g. The art show got a bagging by the critics.

bagman
1. tramp; swagman.
2. bookmaker.

bagman's gazette
graffiti; a fictitious publication containing rumours.

bags
1. lots of (particularly money): e.g. He can afford it, he's got bags of money.
2. elect to go first or have the first choice: e.g. I bags the red one.
See also:
rough as bags

bags under the eyes
showing signs of tiredness; exhaustion indicated by darkening of skin around the eyes.

bail
(see: I'll go bail; jump bail)

bail out
(also: bale out)
1. parachute out of an aeroplane.
2. retreat, withdraw from a situation that has become unsatisfactory: e.g. Her marriage is on the rocks so she's going to bail out.

bail (someone) out
rescue (someone) from a dangerous situation.

bail up
1. to delay and bore with tedious conversation: e.g. He bailed me up for hours at the party.
2. to rob at gunpoint.

bait
torment, tease, goad someone (usually to the point of anger) for amusement.
See also:
jump to the bait
take the bait

baker's dozen
thirteen.

baking
very hot, sweltering (weather).

bakky
(see: baccy)

bald as a badger/bandicoot/ beach-ball/billiard ball/golf ball
very bald; having no hair.

bald eagle
bald person.

bald tyres
tyres without a safe amount of tread left.

baldy
1. bald-headed.
2. a tyre without tread.

bale out
(see: bail out)

ball
(see: behind the eight-ball; blackball; get on the ball; get the ball rolling; have a ball; have/got the ball at one's feet; keep on the ball; keep one's eye on the ball; keep the ball rolling; no ball; oddball; on the ball; play ball; start the ball rolling; that's the way the ball bounces; whole new ball game)

ball and chain
1. (the old . . .) the wife.
2. anything that causes restraint, restriction: e.g. Paying off the house is a real ball and chain.

ball of muscle
physically strong, sturdy.

ball up
(Australian Rules football) bounce down.

balling
(of men) having sexual intercourse: e.g. Who's he been balling lately?

balls
1. testicles.
2. nonsense; rubbish; foolish talk: e.g. 1. What a lot of balls! 2. Balls.
3. courage; bravado; strength: e.g. He hasn't got the balls!
See also:
bet (one's) balls
do (one's) balls over
grab (someone) by the balls
great balls of fire!
have (someone's) balls
have/got the balls to
have/got (someone) by the balls
lover's balls
she's got balls

balls and all
enthusiastically; aggressively.

balls around
fool around and waste time.

ball's in (one's/someone's) court
opportunity or obligation to act or react lies with (one/someone): e.g. She committed adultery, now the ball's in his court.

balls to you too!
exclamation of scorn, ridicule, contempt etc.

balls up
make a mess of; make a bad mistake: e.g. If you balls up this time, you're fired!

balls-up
state of confusion; messy mistake; error: e.g. What a balls-up!

ball-tearer
anything exciting, wonderful, creating admiration.

ballyhoo
1. outcry; confusion; noise.
2. misleading or sensational publicity.

balmy
(see: barmy)

baloney
nonsense.

Balt
person originating from Central or Eastern Europe.

Bamboo Curtain
pertaining to China.

bamboozled
confused; puzzled.

banana chair/lounge
folding chair/lounge used outdoors.

banana republic
1. (caps) Queensland.
2. any backward, retarded country or area of unstable politics and economy.

Banana-bender
Queenslander.

Banana-land
Queensland.

bananas
1. crazy; mad; insane: e.g. He's a bit bananas.
2. (go . . .) become very angry: e.g. He'll go bananas when he finds out what you've done.
3. excited; enthusiastic: e.g. Everyone went bananas at the last concert.

band moll
(see: groupie)

Band-aid
small adhesive dressing for minor wound. (Trademark)

bandicoot
(in combination: e.g. poor as a bandicoot) an intensifier, suggesting extremity, loneliness, misery, poverty etc.
See also:
bald as a bandicoot
bandy as a bandicoot
barmy as a bandicoot
like a bandicoot on a burnt ridge
lousy as a bandicoot
miserable as a bandicoot
poor as a bandicoot

bandwagon
popular, favourite, winning cause or side.
See also:
climb/jump on the bandwagon

bandy as a bandicoot
very bandy-legged.

bandy-legged
having crooked legs (particularly when both bow outwards).

bang
1. marijuana; Indian hemp. (also: bhang)
2. sexual intercourse; to fornicate: e.g. 1. Did you get a bang last night? 2. Did you bang my wife?
3. person regarded as a sexual object: e.g. She'd be a good bang.
4. right; exactly: e.g. Bang on time.
See also:
gang bang
right slap-bang in the hey-diddle-diddle
whole bang lot
with a bang

bang goes (something)
that's the end of (something): e.g. bang goes my life of luxury! I didn't win the lottery!

bang in the middle
dead centre.

bang (something) up/over
to do (something) easily, quickly.

banged up
pregnant.

bangers
sausages.

bang-on
correct; right on mark; dead centre: e.g. He shot his arrow into the target bang-on that time.

bangs like a dunny door (in a gale)

bangs like a tappet
extremely promiscuous (particularly of women).

banjo
1. shovel; spade.
2. shoulder of mutton.
3. frying pan.
4. (cap.) the nickname of author A. B. Paterson.

bank haul/job
robbery of a bank.

bank on
depend, rely, count on.

bantam-weight
1. small; insignificant; of little importance.
2. (boxing) weight division.

bar
except: e.g. All bar two people arrived at the meeting.
See also:
bar-on
no holds barred
won't have a bar of

barbed tongue
sarcastic wit.

barbie/barby
barbecue.

Barcoo rot
festering skin disease.

Barcoo salute
(see: Australian salute)

bardie/bardy
Bardistus cibarius, an edible wood grub.
See also:
starve the bardies!

bare as a baby's bottom/ bat's arse
devoid of any covering.

bare bones
essential facts of a matter; relevant details only: e.g. I want the bare bones before I invest my money.

barefaced
impudent; shameless: e.g. That's a barefaced lie.

barf
vomit: e.g. Bronnie must have eaten something funny to make her barf all over the bed like that.

barf-bag
bag carried during travel in which one may vomit in an emergency case of travel-sickness.

barfly
habitual drinker at pubs.

bargain for
expect: e.g. He got much more than he bargained for.

bargain with the devil
enter freely into a risky or dangerous relationship.

barge
old, cumbersome boat.
See also:
wouldn't touch it with a barge-pole

barge in
interrupt.

bark/bark at the lawn
to vomit: e.g. He drank too much and barked all over the place.

bark is worse than his bite
(of dogs or people) to sound or look much more aggressive, dangerous than one really is.

barker
person who solicits customers for business by standing outside the premises and calling to them.

barking up the wrong tree
pursuing the wrong purpose; have the wrong idea about something.

barley!
call for a truce; plea for respite.

barmy (as a bandicoot)
crazy; mad; insane; stupid.

barney
noisy fight or argument.

barnyard
slovenly, untidy place of abode.

bar-on
an erection of the penis.

barra
barramundi.

barrack for
support: e.g. He barracks for his home footy team.

barrel
defeat; beat in a contest; physically beat or knock down.
See also:
have/got (someone) over a barrel

'When Dad started 'er up this morning he said th' engine was missing. I forgot to tell him it was in th' back of th' truck!'

When an engine is missing it is still there (although one probably wishes it wasn't!). A missing engine could be on the blink, bung, buggered, clapped out, clagged, crook, history, jiggered, kaput, onkus, rat-shit, rooted, stuffed, up the duff, up the putt. Or the engine may have had it — had the dick, gong, Richard or sword. In actuality it may simply have run out of petrol!

like shooting fish in a barrel
lock, stock and barrel
over a barrel
scrape the bottom of the barrel

barrel along
move extremely fast: e.g. The police caught him barrelling along the highway at 160 kilometres an hour!

barrel of fun/laughs
extremely amusing: e.g. He's a barrel of fun at parties.

base
(see: back to base one; back to home base; get to first base)

base over apex
head over heels; fall over heavily or clumsily.

bash
1. attempt; have a go: e.g. Have a bash at it.
2. drinking spree or wild party: e.g. We're having a bash at our place next week.
See also:
dud bash
ear-bash
give it a bash
have a bash

bash (someone's) ear
talk incessantly; bore with incessant talk.

bashing
1. (in combination: e.g. poofter-bashing; police-bashing) indulgence in excessive criticism; hate.
2. (in combination) excessive indulgence in: e.g. Bible-bashing is excessive and zealous promotion of the Bible or one's religious beliefs.
See also:
Bible-bashing
ear-bashing
poofter-bashing

bashing (one's) brains out
expending a great deal of time and energy in some form of mental pursuit (often in vain).

basket
euphemism for bastard: e.g. What's that silly basket doing?

basket case
person who is seriously upset; mentally disturbed.

bastard
1. despicable, reprehensible person: e.g. That bastard would sell his own mother.
2. friendly, jocular term for person: e.g. Gidday you old bastard.
3. any person: e.g. What's that bastard doing over there?
4. compassionate term for person: e.g. 1. Jim's not a bad old bastard but the grog has got to him a bit. 2. Poor bastard hasn't got two bob to his name since he lost his job.
5. (exclamation) an oath meaning: damn!; curses!
6. misfortune; bad situation: e.g. What a bastard! I didn't know his wife had died.
7. anything despised or unpleasant: e.g. I've been trying to fix this bastard all day and it still won't work!
See also:
every bastard and his dog
happy as a bastard on Father's Day
pommy bastard

bastard file
file with rough teeth for coarse filing.

bastard of a thing
terrible; unpleasant (thing, situation etc.).

bastardly
despicable.

bastardry
injustice; obnoxious and despicable behaviour.

bat
1. ugly, unattractive woman.
2. silly, foolish person.
See also:
blind as a bat
didn't bat an eyelid
like a bat out of hell
off (one's) own bat

bat on a sticky-wicket
(of men) to follow after someone else has had intercourse in a group sex activity.

bat (one's) eyelids at (someone)
flirt; make eyes at (someone).

bat the breeze
indulge in idle talk, chatter, gossip.

batching
(see: baching)

bathers
swimming costume; swimming togs.

bathroom
toilet: e.g. I've been dying to go to the bathroom all day.

bats
crazy; insane; mad; silly: e.g. The old bloke's bats.

bats in the belfry
(to have . . .) to be crazy, insane, mad or silly; to be lacking in intelligence.

batten down the hatches
prepare; be ready.

battle
struggle for a livelihood, living: e.g. We've had to battle for years to get this far.

battle of the bulge
fight against obesity; constant dieting to lose weight.

battle royal
extremely hard fight or heated argument.

battle-axe
unpleasant, ugly or domineering woman.

battler
1. conscientious person working against many odds for a living; one whose life is a constant struggle.
2. prostitute.
See also:
Aussie battler

battle-stations!
call to get ready for work or action immediately.

battling
struggling for a living: e.g. He's been battling for years to support his family.

batty
crazy; insane; mad; silly; stupid.

bawl (someone) out
berate, scold severely.

bay window
stomach, especially a paunch.

Bazza
nickname for a person whose name is Barry.

Bazzaland
Australia — coined from Barry McKenzie, the name of the character created by Barry Humphries.

BB gun
type of air-rifle.

BBQ
barbecue.

be a devil
dare to do it.

be a pal
plea for help: e.g. Would you be a pal and mind the kids for a couple of hours?

be a sport
1. agree to the rules; play fair.
2. plea (to someone) to be a help, be reasonable.
3. agree to, grant a request.

be an angel
(see: be a pal)

be blowed
1. (exclamation) no!; I refuse!
2. (curse) be damned: e.g. Be blowed if I'll ever help him again after what he did to me!
See also:
I'll be blowed!

be cruel to be kind
take harsh action that appears to be cruel but has benefits in the long run.

be good — if you can't, be careful!
a warning with sexual overtones.

be grateful for small mercies
be grateful, appreciative of whatever you can get, no matter how trifling.

be in it
be part of a venture; be willing to take part: e.g. I'll be in it as long as there's no trouble.

be in (someone's) shoes
be in (someone's) position, situation, predicament etc.; exchange places with (someone): e.g. I'd hate to be in his shoes with all the trouble he's in.

be on (someone's) bad/good side
be out of/in favour with (someone).

be on the safe side
take necessary precautions: e.g. Just to be on the safe side we'll all wear our life-jackets today.

be (one's) own boss
be independent; make (one's) own decisions; be self-employed.

be rough on (someone)
treat harshly, severely, unmercifully: e.g. He's really rough on her sometimes.

be sold a pup
be cheated, hoodwinked, conned or tricked.

be the death of (someone)
be the ruin, downfall of: e.g. He'll be the death of me if he doesn't get a job soon.

be there with bells/knobs on
arrive with enthusiasm.

be with you in a tick!
attend to you shortly, in a moment, without delay: e.g. Hold the line (telephone), he'll be with you in a tick.

be your age!
behave sensibly, reasonably, like an adult!

beach bum
one who spends a great deal of time on the beach, thereby considered a lazy good-for-nothing.

beak
1. nose.
2. policeman.
3. private investigator.
4. magistrate.

be-all and end-all
1. the ultimate conclusion or final aim.
2. the best; the ultimate: He's a creep but he thinks he's the be-all and end-all.

beam
bum; backside.
See also:
off the beam

bean
1. the head: e.g. I got hit on the bean by a flying beer-can.
2. a single cent: e.g. I haven't got a bean to my name so I can't afford that.
3. hit; strike; bash: e.g. I'll bean him if he comes here again!
See also:
full of beans
give (someone) beans
know how many beans make five
not worth a row of beans
spill the beans
yippie-beans

beanfeast
lavish feast or celebration.

beanie
close-fitting knitted cap, often with a pompom on top.

bean-pole
tall, lanky person.

bear
1. pertaining to declining prices on the stock exchange: e.g. bear market (unfavourable).
2. clumsy, irritable or rude person.
See also:
like a bear with a sore head

bearded clam
female pudendum, genitals.
See also:
spear the bearded clam

bear-hug
strong, affectionate embrace.

bears
1. police (in the jargon of long-distance truck drivers).
2. (cap.) Brisbane VFL football team.
3. (cap.) North Sydney N.S.W. Rugby League football team.

beast
1. despicable person.
2. pet name for one's car (usually a dilapidated one).

beat
1. exhausted; tired; worn out.
2. defeated.

beat about/around the bush
avoid the main issue by quoting irrelevant details; speak without getting to the point.

beat hell out of
(see: beat the hell out of)

beat it
1. go away!; get lost!
2. leave; depart: e.g. We're going to beat it before it gets dark.

beat (someone) down
haggle for a lower price: e.g. I beat him down to 5000 dollars.

beat (someone) hands down
defeat soundly and without effort.

beat the hell out of
1. severely punish; thrash; physically attack.
2. use roughly, carelessly: e.g. He beats the hell out of all his cars.
3. (see: beats the hell out of)

beat the living daylights out of
1. severely punish; thrash; physically and violently attack.
2. defeat soundly.
3. use roughly; abuse.

beat the meat
to masturbate (particularly of men).

beat the stuffing/tripe out of
1. severely punish; thrash; physically and violently attack.
2. defeat soundly: e.g. Labor beat the stuffing out of the Opposition in the last election.

beat to the punch
gain an advantage over: e.g. He was beaten to the punch by a complete newcomer who won 52 per cent of the votes.

beaten before (one) starts
at a serious disadvantage owing to circumstances detrimental to (one's) success: e.g. I'll be beaten before I start if I can't raise the money.

beating a dead horse

beating (one's) head against a brick wall
pursuing a futile course of action: e.g. Getting him to donate money is like beating your head against a brick wall!

beatnik
(1950s term for) person who defies conventional standards of dress and behaviour.

beats me!
I don't know!
See also:
what beats me

beats the heck/hell out of
better than; more acceptable than: e.g. Living in Queensland and soaking up the sunshine beats the hell out of freezing in Melbourne!

beat-up
dilapidated; worn-out: e.g. He drives a beat-up old Holden.

beaut
1. anything exceptional, excellent: e.g. What a beaut house he has right on the beach!
2. pertaining to reproval or reproach: e.g. You're a beaut! Now look what you've done!
See also:
you beaut!
you little beaut!
you-beaut
shaping up a beaut

beautiful people
people considered as fashionable, trendy, jet-setting, wealthy and attractive: e.g. Princess Diana is one of the beautiful people.

beauty
1. an exclamation of approval: e.g. Beauty! We'll all go to the pub and celebrate.
2. an exceptional example: e.g. The antique side-board was a beauty.
3. advantage: e.g. The beauty of this job is the company car I get to drive.
See also:
bewdy Newk!
no raving beauty

beauty sleep
much-needed sleep and rest.

beauty spot
mole on the skin.

beaver
female pudendum, genitals.

beaver show
(of women) pornography, but not as explicit as: split-beaver show.

bed
have sexual intercourse with: e.g. I'd love to bed him!
See also:
get out on the wrong side of bed
go to bed with
hop into bed with
hotbed
jump in and out of bed
so crooked (one) couldn't lie straight in bed
you made your bed — you lie in it!

bed of roses
an easy task; an extremely good situation: e.g. It's no bed of roses being married to a boozer.

beddable
sexually attractive.

beddy-byes
in children's speech — time to go to bed, sleep.

bed-fellows
close companions or associates (often in an underhanded, clandestine sense).

bed-hopping
promiscuity; promiscuous.

bed-worthy
sexually attractive.

bee in (one's) bonnet
1. (to have a . . .) an obsession: e.g. He's got a bee in his bonnet when it comes to saving for that car.
2. crazy notion; agitated attitude: e.g. He's had a bee in his bonnet all week.

beef
1. gripe; complaint: e.g. What's your beef?
2. to complain: e.g. What are you beefing about?

beef bayonet
the penis.

beef up
increase: e.g. It's about time they beefed up the number of buses from the city to the airport.

beefcake
photographs in magazines etc. of men posed to display their bodies and emphasising their sexual attributes.

beefed
physically exhausted.

beefy
solid; heavy; fat.

beehive
crowded place of great activity.

beeline
direct course: e.g. They made a beeline for the pub.

been and gone
done that already: e.g. She's been and gone with the housework and now she's started on the gardening.

been around
1. vastly experienced in life: e.g. He's been around so you won't be able to fool him.
2. (derog.) sexually experienced or promiscuous: e.g. If he finds out how much she's been around he'll drop her like a hot potato.

been around the traps
1. vastly experienced in life: e.g. He's been around the traps so long that you can't fool him.
2. searched or visited every possible place (pub, street, club etc.): e.g. I've been around the traps and I couldn't find a trace of him.
See also:
around the traps

been done/had
been overcharged, tricked, duped or cheated: e.g. He's just been done by that crooked car-dealer.

been sucking lemons
pertaining to a sour-faced, miserable expression.

been taken (for a ride)
(see: been done)

been there, done that!
expression of boredom, indicating that what was just suggested has already been tried or done.

been through the mill
been through a trying, difficult time: e.g. She's been through the mill since her husband left her.

been to hell and back
been through a trying, difficult time and come out unscathed, unhurt.

beeper
mechanical device for paging a person (carried on the person).

beer
(see: bones in one's beer; champagne taste on a beer income; crying in one's beer)

beer and skittles
pleasurable; fun: e.g. Being married to Fleeb hasn't all been beer and skittles, but Ruth still loves him.

beer gut
paunch; distended stomach caused by too much beer-drinking.

beer money
fund saved for leisure or miscellaneous purposes; pocket money (particularly of husbands).

beer pot
(see: beer gut)

beer-up
wild drinking party.

bee's dick
anything small or insignificant; the smallest measure of something: e.g. That was a bee's dick away from a collision!

bee's knees
(the . . .) the greatest; the best.

beetle
Volkswagon car (first model), so named because of its shape.

beetle along
move, go swiftly: e.g. We were beetling along the road when the police pulled us up and booked us for speeding.

beetle-browed
1. having large, bushy, overhanging eyebrows.
2. scowling; frowning.

beetle-crushers
feet or shoes.

before (one's) very eyes
in front of (one); in (one's) presence.

beg yours?
beg your pardon?; could you repeat that?

beggar
1. (joc.) rogue: e.g. My kids are little beggars, but I love them.
2. one who is over-keen or zealous: e.g. He's a beggar for work.

beggar for punishment
person who continually exerts himself to his limits (often to the detriment of his mental or physical health).

beggars can't be choosers
1. people with nothing have to take what they can get.
2. people who cadge, sponge off others or borrow with no intention of repayment have no right to complain or demand better.

beggars-in-the-pan
small type of bread or damper (also: beggars-on-the-coals; devils-on-the-coals).

behind
1. buttocks; bum: e.g. Mike's got a sexy behind.
2. (Australian Rules football) one point: e.g. Mike's team won by kicking a behind in the last few minutes.

behind closed doors
secretly; privately.

behind (one's/someone's) back
secretly; deceitfully: e.g. She did it behind my back.

behind the eight-ball
at a disadvantage; not up-to-date.

behind the scenes
out of view; in secret; not public: e.g. I'd love to know what goes on behind the scenes at the local massage parlour.

behind the times
old-fashioned; not up-to-date.

behind the wheel
in control of a vehicle (car); driving: e.g. The police want to know who was behind the wheel when the accident occurred.

believe nothing of what you hear and only half of what you see
remain sceptical and open-minded.

bell
telephone call: e.g. I'll give you a bell tomorrow.
See also:
be there with bells on
clear as a bell
hell's bells!
ring a bell
saved by the bell
sound as a bell

belly thinks me (my/your/his) throat's cut
I'm hungry.

belly-ache
1. to complain: e.g. I wish you wouldn't belly-ache all the time!
2. a complaint: e.g. What's your belly-ache?

belly-buster
poorly (and often painfully) executed dive in which the stomach hits the water first.

belly-button
navel.

bellyful
more than enough of anything: e.g. I've had a bellyful of her and her whingeing.

belly-whacker
(see: belly-buster)

belong
fit in socially; have the right social qualifications: e.g. She doesn't belong.

below (one)
not worthy of consideration: e.g. 1. She thinks everyone is below her. 2. I wouldn't do that to a friend — it's below me.

below the belt
underhanded; unfair: e.g. That comment was a bit below the belt.

belt
(see: below the belt; pull one's belt in; tighten the belt; under one's belt)

belt along
move swiftly: e.g. The police came belting along the highway, followed by an ambulance.

belt in the lug
a bash, punch in the ear.

belt into
begin quickly; act quickly, vigorously.

belt out
sing, play (musical instrument) loudly, with gusto: e.g. Greg can really belt out a song.

belt (someone) one
punch, bash, hit (someone): e.g. I'll belt him one if he doesn't shut up!

belt the living daylights out of
1. beat up; thrash; physically attack.
2. defeat soundly: e.g. Our team will belt the living daylights out of them in the game next week.
3. use, handle carelessly; abuse; treat roughly.

belt up
1. shut up!; be quiet!
2. put safety-belt on: e.g. If everyone belted up there would be fewer fatal accidents.

belting
1. thrashing; physical beating.
2. sound defeating (as in a contest).
3. rough treatment; abuse.

belting a tin
boasting; skiting.

bend
(see: around the bend; the bends)

bend over backwards
go to a great deal of effort and trouble: e.g. I'd bend over backwards to help him if he got into trouble.

bend (someone's) ear
talk incessantly at (someone); harangue.

bend the elbow
drink excessively (usually beer): e.g. Shane's been bending the elbow with his mates all afternoon.

bend the rules
deviate from the rules to suit the occasion: e.g. That judge has been known to bend the rules for people he knows.

bend the truth
tell lies; pervert the truth.

bend with the wind
have flexible attitude; go along with current trends: e.g. His business will fail if he doesn't bend with the wind a bit.

bender
1. wild drinking spree.
2. homosexual man.

benefit of the doubt
assumption of innocence rather than guilt: e.g. The judge gave him the benefit of the doubt and set him free.

benny
Benzedrine tablet, pill — an amphetamine.

bent
1. crazy; mad; insane.
2. behaving in an abnormal, unorthodox or deviant manner (of a drug addict, lesbian etc).
3. dishonest; corrupt: e.g. bent politician.
4. knack or skill for; particular interest: e.g. 1. Wayne's bent is antique cars. 2. Merridy's got a bent for pottery.

bent as a scrub tick
crazy; insane; foolish.

berk
a fool; disliked person.

berko
1. crazy; mad; insane.
2. berserk; exceptionally angry.

berley
1. vomit, as a result of sea-sickness.
2. good-humoured teasing.
3. bait scattered over the water to attract fish.

beside (oneself)
overcome with emotion: e.g. She's been beside herself since he went into hospital.

beside the point
inconsequential; not relevant.

Besser (block)
concrete-moulded building block (from Trademark): e.g. They built their home with Bessers.

best
1. get the better of; defeat.
2. one's best clothing: e.g. Wear your best to the ball.
See also:
all the best
at (one's) best
get the best of
make the best of

best bet
most advantageous course of action: e.g. Your best bet would be to go inland rather than up the coast.

best bib and tucker
best, finest clothes.

best man
bridegroom's attendant.

best of both worlds
the finest points, advantages or benefits of two separate and opposite situations or sets of circumstances: e.g. We've got the best of both worlds, living on a 4 hectare farmlet in the country with all that Surfer's Paradise has to offer only 15 minutes away.

best of British luck
an expression of good-will.

bet each way
1. cover all contingencies.
2. (racing) back a horse for a win and a place.

bet London to a brick
be absolutely certain: e.g. You can bet London to a brick that it'll rain tomorrow.

bet on two flies walking up the wall
to be a compulsive gambler.

bet (one's) balls

bet your boots on (it)

bet your bottom dollar

bet your life
be absolutely certain.

betcha
contraction of bet you: e.g. I'll betcha the favourite wins.

better
(see: think better of)

better half
one's wife or husband: e.g. Where's your better half?

better it
do better than (it).

better late than never
1. it is better to be late for an appointment rather than to risk one's life getting there in a hurry.
2. philosophical expression about a belated gift, card etc.

better oneself
improve oneself socially, educationally, intellectually etc.

better than a poke in the eye with a blunt/burnt stick

better than a poke in the eye with a pointed/sharp stick
sardonic expression of pleasure; view that things could be worse.

better the devil you know (than the one you don't)
when one is confronted by two options, both of which seem unpleasant or bad, it is safer to choose the more familiar.

better to be safe than sorry
attention to details and careful planning in the beginning can save one problems later.

between a rock and a hard place
in a predicament or vulnerable position with no apparent escape.

between the sheets
in bed with reference to sexual activity: e.g. Do you think those two have got it together between the sheets yet?

between two fires
under attack from all sides.

between wind and water
(see: between a rock and a hard place)

between you, me and the gate-post
confidential; confidentially.

bewdy
adulterated form of: beauty. (see: beauty, 1. and 2.)

bewdy Newk!
great!; terrific!; wonderful!

beyond a joke
intolerable; socially unacceptable: e.g. What he did was beyond a joke!

beyond help
having no possibility of redemption, saving.

beyond the Black Stump
(see: back o' Bourke)

beyond the pale
socially unacceptable; unbelievable.

B-grade
second-rate; inferior: e.g. That was a B-grade movie.

bhang
marijuana; Indian hemp.

bi
bisexual; person taking sexual partner of either sex.

bib and tucker
one's (best) clothes: e.g. Wear your best bib and tucker to the dinner party.

bib in
to interfere.
See also:
keep (one's) bib out
stick (one's) bib in

bibful
an embarrassing disclosure of a confidence: e.g. He let go a bibful in front of everybody.

Bible
the ultimate reference or authority on a subject: e.g. This book's the Bible on ceramic glaze recipes.
See also:
could have sworn on a stack of Bibles
swear on the Bible

Bible-basher
1. excessively zealous religious person.
2. clergyman; priest.

Bible-bashing
excessively and zealously promoting one's religious beliefs.

bickies
1. biscuits: e.g. Do you want some tea and bickies?
2. money: e.g. I'll bet that car cost a lot of bickies.
See also:
big bickies
not the full packet of bickies

biddy
old woman; foolish old woman.

bide (one's) time
wait for a favourable opportunity.

biff
1. hit; punch; strike: e.g. You'll get a biff in the ear if you don't shut up.
2. discard; throw away: e.g. Biff those — I don't want them.

big
very important: e.g.
1. This situation's big.
2. He's big in politics.
See also:
in big with
made it big
Mr Big
talk big
think big

big A
(see: get the big A; the big A)

Big Apple
New York.

big bang theory
theory that the origin of the universe started with an explosion of matter.

big bickies
a lot of money.

big bin
prison.

big boys
the most influential or powerful people.

Big Brother
1. person in power who behaves like a dictator, seemingly benevolent, but trying to control people's actions, thoughts and morals.
2. the authorities, such as the Government, who have the control of power.

big C
cancer.

big daddy
most influential; largest; leader in one's/its field; the boss: e.g. 1. Who's the big daddy around here? 2. That's the big daddy of cane-toads if I ever saw one!

big deal
1. exclamation of contempt, scorn, cynicism etc.: e.g. Big deal! I don't care what he said!
2. commotion; fuss: e.g. Don't make such a big deal of it.
3. important, significant matter: e.g. Doing that was a big deal for him.

big dipper
roller-coaster at an amusement park.

big dollars
a large amount of money.

big ears
(to have . . .) to eavesdrop; listen in: e.g. He's got big ears so watch what you say.
See also:
big-ears

big fish
the most influential, powerful person(s): e.g. He's a big fish in that organisation.

big gun
1. the boss; very important and influential person.
2. something important that will enable one to gain an advantage; main item of impact.

big head
(to have a . . .) to be vain and conceited.

big is beautiful
catchphrase of the overweight.

big league
top level of any pursuit: e.g. He's in the big league since his promotion.

big mob
large number of people, items etc.

big mother
something large, outstanding; a large example of its kind: e.g. That spider was a big mother!

big mouth
(to have a . . .)
1. to brag and boast in a conceited manner.
2. to have a tendency to reveal secrets or confidential matters: e.g. Don't tell her anything — she's got such a big mouth.
See also:
big-mouth
shut (one's) big mouth

big nob/noise
very important person; prominent and influential person in business, politics etc.

big on
1. knowledgeable: e.g. He's big on fixing cars.
2. full of enthusiasm for: e.g. He's big on model aeroplanes.
3. infatuated, in love with: e.g. He's big on her.

big ones
dollars: e.g. That cost me 5000 big ones.

big quid
plenty of money: e.g. He earns a big quid.

big set of boots
exceptionally wide set of tyres on a car.

big shot
very important and influential person.

big smoke
the city: e.g. We moved away from the big smoke into the country.

big spit
(go for the . . .) to vomit.

big talk
boasting; exaggeration: e.g. He's so full of big talk I don't know what to believe.

big talker
person given to boasting and exaggeration.

big time
the top level of any pursuit; pertaining to success, fame and fortune: e.g. Australian entertainers often go to the U.S.A. to make the big time.
See also:
break into the big time
hit the big time
made it big/to the big time

big top
the circus; the main tent of a circus.

big turn-out
large attendance: e.g. We had a big turn-out at our party.

big wheel
very important, influential person; the boss.

big yawn
something or someone extremely boring, tedious.

big-ears
eavesdropper.

bigger they are the harder they fall
the more one has the more one stands to lose.

biggie
a big person or thing.

bighead
conceited, vain person.

bigheaded
conceited; vain.

big-hearted
generous.

big-mouth
1. a garrulous, over-talkative, boastful person.
2. boast; skite: e.g. He's always big-mouthing about how good he is at fighting.
3. praise: e.g. He's full of big-mouthing for his new car.

big-note
to inflate one's achievements, talents or status.
See also:
come the big-note

bigwig
very important and influential person.

bike
1. bicycle; motorcycle.
2. promiscuous woman: e.g. She's a real bike.
3. prostitute.
See also:
get off (one's) bike
go through on the padre's bike
town bike
village bike

bike moll
female member of a bikie gang.

biker
person who rides a motorcycle (not a member of a gang as in: bikie).

bikie
member of a motorcycle gang, characterised by leather jackets, hidden weapons, unruly and violent behaviour and generally held in fear and contempt by society.

bikkies
(see: bickies)

bilge
nonsense; rubbish.

billies
children (rhyming slang: billy lids — kids).

billy
1. tin container used for boiling water, making tea etc. when out camping.
2. a bong — used for smoking marijuana (from rhyming slang: billabong).
See also:
boil the billy

billycart
small, homemade cart steered by ropes attached to movable front wheel axle.

billygoat
1. (rhyming slang) tote; TAB.
2. incompetent, silly person; fool.

billyo
1. (go to . . .) get lost!; go away!
2. (like . . .) with gusto, enthusiasm; speed, haste: e.g. 1. We laughed like billyo all through the show. 2. The car went like billyo down the steep hill.
3. (gone to . . .) a long way away; gone to a remote, far-away place; disappeared: e.g. He must have gone to billyo — I haven't seen him for two weeks.

bimbo
a homosexual man.

bin
prison.
See also:
big bin
loony bin

bind
nuisance: e.g. It's such a bind doing the housework.
See also:
in a bind

binder
1. hearty, solid meal; a feast.
2. cheese.
See also:
reaper and binder

binge
a period of excessive indulgence in activities such as drinking, spending.

binghi
an Aborigine.

bingie
stomach; tummy: e.g. I've got a pain in the bingie since eating those prawns. (also: bingy, binjy)

bingle
an accident in a car; to have a minor accident: e.g. 1. We had a bingle in our new car. 2. Dad bingled the new car.

bingo!
an exclamation of success, achievement.

bingy/binjy
(see: bingie)

bint
girl; woman (often a foolish one).

bird
1. young attractive woman; girlfriend.
2. strange, eccentric person: e.g. He's a weird bird.
3. (horse-racing) a certainty to win.
4. an aeroplane.
5. a prison sentence; a prison.
See also:
away with the birds
box of birds
dead bird
early bird catches the worm
for the birds

gaol-bird
kill two birds with one stone
like a bird
little bird told me
strictly for the birds

bird-brain
frivolous, scatter-brained person.

birdie
1. small bird; affectionate name for a bird.
2. one stroke under par in golf.

birds and the bees
the details of sexual behaviour: e.g. Many parents find it difficult to tell their children about the birds and the bees.

birds of a feather
people with similar ideas or tastes: e.g. Birds of a feather stick together.

bird's-eye view
seen from above.

birdwatcher
man who keenly watches attractive young women.

Biro
ballpoint pen. (Trademark)

birthday suit
pertaining to nakedness; in the nude: e.g. We went swimming in our birthday suits.

bishop
the penis.
See also:
bury the bishop

bit
1. sexual intercourse: e.g. Did you get a bit last night?
2. young woman as a sex object: e.g. She's not a bad bit.
3. an intensifier meaning very: e.g. a bit rough; a bit much.
4. a sum of money: e.g. She was left a bit after he died.
See also:
chafing at the bit
do (one's) bit
take the bit between (one's) teeth
thrilled to bits
tickled to bits

bit by bit
slowly; gradually.

bit much
excessive, rude behaviour: e.g. It was a bit much when Victor farted at the dinner table.

bit of all right
exciting; admirable; excellent, especially in a sexual sense: e.g. She's a bit of all right.

bit of an act
insincere behaviour: e.g. Her tears and sorrow were a bit of an act because she never really liked him.

bit of arse/crumpet/fluff/skirt
woman as a sex object.

bit on the nose
smelly: e.g. These prawns are a bit on the nose.

bit on the side
1. extra-marital affair: e.g. I bet he has a bit on the side when he goes away on business.
2. something extra apart from the usual.

bit part
1. minor part to play in a theatrical act or movie.
2. an unimportant role.

bit solid
harsh; unreasonable; unjust.

bitch
1. malicious woman.
2. derogatory term for a woman.
3. nuisance; cursed: e.g. This bitch of a thing doesn't work!
4. a complaint: e.g. What's your bitch?
5. complain; nag; whinge: e.g. What are you bitching about now?

bitchy
1. malicious; uncooperative.
2. angry; irritable.

bite
1. person from whom one expects an easy loan: e.g. He's a good bite.
2. response or reaction: e.g. Any bites at your land sale yet?
3. food; small meal: e.g. We had a bite at the last road-house.
4. tangy taste: e.g. That wine has a real bite to it.
5. cadge; request a loan: e.g. I'll bite Dad for ten bucks.
6. react emotionally or angrily to (teasing): e.g. Don't bite, he's only teasing.
See also:
put the bite on (someone)
raise a bite

bite at the cherry
share in the proceedings, action, profits etc.

bite off more than (one) can chew
endeavour to do, take on a project that is too difficult to complete or pursue.

bite (one's) lip
to suffer anxiety.

bite (one's) tongue
refrain from answering or commenting: e.g. I had to bite my tongue while he Bible-bashed all night.

bite (someone) for a loan
to cadge.

bite (someone's) ear
annoy, nag, harass, harangue (someone).

bite the bullet
face an unavoidable or unpleasant task bravely.

bite the dust
1. fall heavily and clumsily: e.g. He tripped and bit the dust.

2. fall dead; die (especially after combat).
3. fail: e.g. His latest venture bit the dust.

bite the hand that feeds (one)
act without loyalty.

bite your bum!
shut up!; be quiet!

bitie
any creature (such as insect, spider, snake) that might bite or be dangerous.

biting
1. troubling; worrying: e.g. What's biting him?
2. sarcastic: e.g. A biting remark.

bits
genitals: e.g. All the bits are showing in the latest centrefold.

bitser
person or animal (but particularly a dog) of mixed blood or stock.

bitten
cheated; tricked: e.g. I think I've been bitten for quite a sum.
See also:
once bitten, twice shy

bitter pill to swallow
disappointing or unfavourable fact: e.g. Getting only a few thousand dollars from that lengthy court case was a bitter pill to swallow.

bitumen blonde
1. Aboriginal woman.
2. brunette, dark-haired woman.

biz
(abbrev.) business: e.g. 1. Show biz. 2. That's none of your biz.

bizzo
1. nonsense; foolish, irrelevant details or matters: e.g. He's into religion and all that bizzo.
2. term for an object of which one does not know the actual name: e.g. Pass me that bizzo on the table.

blab/blabber
1. person who discloses secrets or confidential information indiscreetly.
2. to disclose secrets or confidential information indiscreetly.

blabbermouth
1. indiscreet person.
2. person who talks too much.

black
1. gloomy; dismal; sinister; evil; terrible: e.g. It was a black Christmas for Darwin when Cyclone Tracy hit.
2. dark-skinned person; of or pertaining to the dark-skinned races.
See also:
in the black
paint a black picture of

black and blue all over
discoloured, as from bruising.

black and tan
drink made with beer and stout.

black and white
pertaining to a limited range of options with contrasts clearly defined; opposite extremes.
See also:
in black and white

black art
witch-craft; magic.

black as the ace of spades
1. very dark.
2. pertaining to dark-skinned peoples.

black badger
female pudendum, genitals.

black ban
refusal of suppliers or producers to supply; refusal of consumers to purchase; refusal of a group to supply services in a dispute.

black book
private note-book of names of associates in business, sex, crime etc.
See also:
in (someone's) black books

black box
any invention, device, experiment etc. where the operation, workings are kept secret.

black cat
symbol of bad luck, misfortune.

black Friday
Friday 13th, considered to be unlucky.

black gold
oil.

black humour
humour that has underlying pessimism or tragedy.

black list
anybody's list of unreliable or suspicious people, firms, customers etc.

black magic
evil practice or involvement in the occult.

black maria
vehicle for the purpose of transporting prisoners to and from prison.

black mark
notice of failure or censure: e.g. I had a black mark against my name all through school.

black market
illegitimate trade in scarce or officially controlled goods or commodities: e.g. The authorities can't seem to stop the black market activities of the heroin dealers.

black mass
the ceremony performed by devil-worshippers.

black money
money gained illicitly, illegally.

black out
to faint.

black peter
a prison cell.

black power
movement advocating the advancement of the dark-skinned races, usually through violence.

black prince
a type of cicada.

black sheep (of the family)
failure, scoundrel, outcast, disreputable member of a family or group.

Black Stump
1. an imaginary division, area: e.g. He's the biggest crook this side of the Black Stump.
2. outback; remote, imaginary place; last post of civilisation.

black taxi
government-funded car providing free transport for politicians, public servants etc.

black tie
formal mode of dress associated with bow tie and dinner jacket: e.g. Her party was a real black tie event.

black velvet
dark-skinned girl viewed as a sex object.

blackball
1. vote against; reject.
2. ostracise.

blacken (someone's) name
defame; speak maliciously of.

blackfellow
(also: . . . fella; . . . feller) an Aborigine; a dark-skinned person.
See also:
do a blackfeller

blackfellow's picnic
an idle, lazy or easy time: e.g. Digging the garden in the hot sun was no blackfellow's picnic.

blackout
1. temporary fainting fit.
2. failure of, or deliberate extinguishing of, power and lights.

Blacks
Aborigines; dark-skinned peoples.
See also:
give it back to the Blacks

blah blah blah
1. incessant talk.
2. nonsense.
3. etcetera, etcetera, etcetera.

blank
euphemism for a vulgar word: e.g. He told me to blank off!
See also:
draw a blank
fire blanks

blank cheque
having no restraints; a free hand to do as one wishes.

blanket
attempt to hide, conceal the facts.

blanky
euphemism for bloody, damned: e.g. You can blanky well starve for all I care!

blarney
effusive flattery; cajoling talk.

blast
1. noisy, boisterous party, social occasion or drinking spree.
2. verbally berate and abuse: e.g. 1. I'll blast him for staying out so late. 2. I got blasted for staying out so late.
3. exclamation of frustration; damn!
See also:
give (someone) a blast
full blast

blast hell out of (someone)
severely scold, reprimand, abuse.

blasted
1. drunk; very intoxicated: e.g. Hubby's at the pub getting blasted with his mates.
2. intensifying adjective for annoyance, anger, frustration: e.g. This blasted thing won't work!

blatt
1. a newspaper: e.g. The daily blatt's full of bad news these days.
2. printed sheet of information, instructions etc.: e.g. Where's the blatt on how to operate this thing?
3. fast drive in a car; test drive in a car: e.g. We went for a blatt around the block in his new car.

blatting along
travelling at speed in a car.

blaze a trail
pioneer new ground or areas.

blazes
1. euphemism for hell, somewhere far-away: e.g. Go to blazes! (dismissal; get lost!)
2. an intensive for anger, frustration etc.: e.g. What the blazes are you doing!

bleary-eyed
suffering from the after-effects of alcohol, drugs or tiredness.

bleed (someone) dry/white
extort from; borrow continually excessive amounts from (someone).

bleeder
1. abusive term for a person: e.g. What's that bleeder doing with my car?
2. person; bloke; fellow: e.g. He's not such a bad little bleeder.

bleeding
euphemism for bloody: e.g. 1. He took the whole damned bleeding lot! 2. What a bleeding idiot!

bleeding like a stuck pig
bleeding profusely.

blessed
euphemism for cursed, damned: e.g. He spent every blessed penny!

blessing in disguise
something that looks bad in the first place, but has hidden advantages.

blew
(see entries for: blow)

blew it
1. lost the opportunity: e.g. I forgot to go for the job interview and really blew it.
2. made a mess of; ruined: e.g. He blew it through stupidity.

blighter
1. person; bloke; fellow.
2. despicable, annoying person.

blimey!
exclamation of surprise or amazement (also: gorblimey).

blimp
fat, obese person.

blind
1. drunk; intoxicated: e.g. He came home from the pub blind.
2. drinking spree; excessive indulgence in alcohol: e.g. He's been on a blind all week.
See also:
nod is as good as a wink to a blind man
rob (someone) blind
talk (someone) blind

blind alley
hopeless position or situation offering no escape or progress.

blind as a bat
1. very blind.
2. not seeing or perceiving the obvious.

blind date
social engagement made without having previously seen one's partner.

Blind Freddie
imaginary person used as a standard of extreme incompetence, obtuseness: e.g. Even Blind Freddy could see that!

blind leading the blind
pertaining to incompetent leaders.

blind man on a galloping horse would be glad to see it
a reassurance given to someone who has made a mistake or small error in a piece of work that doesn't seriously affect the quality of the work.

blind spot
1. area in a vehicle from which one cannot see due to some obstruction such as a window column.
2. an area or matter about which one has no knowledge or is ignorant, or which one refuses to acknowledge.

blind turn
(Australian Rules football) evasive manoeuvre.

blinder
1. excessive drinking spree.
2. very fast: e.g. That ball he bowled was a blinder.

blink and you'll miss it
expression signifying the smallness and insignificance of something: e.g. It's the kind of town that blink and you'll miss it!
See also:
don't blink or you'll miss it

blinking
euphemism for blasted, confounded, damned: e.g. I can't get this blinking thing to work!

Blinky Bill
Australian story-book character of a koala.

blithered
drunk; intoxicated.

blithering idiot
1. excessively talkative person.
2. complete fool; clumsy oaf.

blob
1. fool; idiot.
2. lazy person.
3. fat person.
4. (cricket) no score; nought: e.g. He was out for a blob.

block
the head: e.g. I'll knock his block off!
See also:
do (one's) block
off (one's) block

block and tackle
system of pulleys and weights used for lifting heavy objects.

blockbuster
anything large, lavish or spectacular: e.g. The latest movie is a real blockbuster.

blockhead
stupid person; fool.

blockie
1. person living on some land as opposed to one living in town.
2. small farmer.

bloke
fellow; man: e.g. He's a real good bloke.

blonde bombshell
sexually attractive blonde woman.

blondes have all the fun
belief that blonde ladies are more sexually attractive.

blood
(see: after someone's blood; bad blood; blue blood; can't get blood out of a stone; curdle the blood; draw first blood; flesh and blood; fresh blood; in cold blood; in one's blood; like squeezing blood out of a stone; make one's blood boil/curdle/run

cold; new blood; out for blood; sweat blood and tears)

blood and blister
(rhyming slang) sister.

blood and guts
excessive violence, bloodshed.

blood is thicker than water
pertaining to the loyalty among family members.

blood is up
(someone's . . .) to be very angry or aggressively ready for action: e.g. After what he did, my blood is really up.

blood money
1. a small payment for great and taxing effort.
2. compensation paid to victim or relatives of slain victim.

bloodbath
1. massacre; particularly violent fight or argument.
2. (cap.) (Australian Rules football) 1945 Grand Final.

bloodhouse
hotel or public house with a reputation for brawling.

blood-oath!
expression of agreement; emphatically yes!

Bloods
originally the South Melbourne VFL football team, but now the Sydney Swans.

blood's worth bottling
anyone whose blood's worth bottling is an exceptionally good or praiseworthy person.

bloodsucker
person who continually borrows without paying back; extortionist.

bloody
1. considered to be 'the Great Australian Adjective' because of its prolific use and ability to signify approval or disapproval: e.g. This bloody nong drove right up the bloody back of me bloody car and wiped the whole bloody back end off! Bloody ripper! Now I can claim on me bloody insurance and get a bloody brand new car!
2. euphemism for damned: e.g. He's a bloody idiot.
3. very; extremely: e.g. She's bloody gorgeous!

bloody galah
silly, foolish person; dolt.

bloody hell!
expression of frustration, anger, amazement.

bloody jew
person who is mean, stingy, tight with money.

bloody nong
silly, foolish person; dolt; someone who makes many errors.

bloody Nora!
mild oath of frustration, anger, amazement, wonder etc.

bloody oath!
expression of complete agreement; emphatically yes!

bloody pom
any person from England, but especially one held in contempt for being lazy and continually complaining.

bloody yank
any person from the United States, but especially one held in contempt for his garrulous personality.

bloody-minded
uncooperative; stubborn.

bloomer
an embarrassing, laughable mistake, person or situation.

bloomers
women's underpants; knickers.

blooming
euphemism for bloody, damned: e.g. He's a blooming idiot!

blooper
(see: bloomer)

blot
1. bum; backside; posterior: e.g. He sits on his blot all day doing nothing.
2. bad mark against or blemish on someone's personality.

blotto
very drunk; completely intoxicated.

blow
1. misfortune; bad luck: e.g. What a blow that was.
2. (of a man) ejaculate.
3. short rest after hard work: e.g. Have a blow for a few minutes.
4. depart; go; leave: e.g. We'd better blow before the cops arrive.
5. squander money; spend freely: e.g. I blew my whole pay at the casino.
6. fail; mess up; ruin, especially an opportunity: e.g. He blew it again.
7. boast: e.g. He's got nothing to blow about.
8. (horse-racing) lengthen the odds: e.g. Bookmakers blew the odds to 20 to 1.
9. cocaine.
See also:
I'll be blowed!
be blowed!
come to blows

blow a blue dog off its chain
pertaining to very windy weather.

blow a fuse/gasket
become very angry; lose one's temper.

blow a mint
spend or waste a great deal of money.

blow hot and cold
change the mind constantly; vacillate.

blow in
arrive, especially unexpectedly for a visit: e.g. All the relatives blew in over the weekend.

blow in the bag
to undergo a test on the breathalyser.

blow it!
1. scornful rejection or refusal: e.g. Blow it! I won't do it.
2. expression of frustration, anger.

blow it wide open
reveal the hidden facts of a situation to the public: e.g. This court case is likely to blow the whole drug scene wide open.

blow me down!
expression of amazement, surprise, disbelief.

blow (one) out
surprise, amaze, delight, astound (one): e.g. That new show will blow you out.

blow (one's) brains out
1. commit suicide through shooting.
2. astonish, amaze, overwhelm (one).

blow (one's) cool
1. lose (one's) temper.
2. lose (one's) face or prestige: e.g. Even though she tripped she didn't blow her cool in front of the judges.

blow (one's) cover
expose (one's) disguise.

blow (one's) gasket
lose (one's) temper; become very angry.

blow (one's) mind
1. achieve a state of euphoria when using drugs: e.g. This grass will really blow your mind.
2. become enthralled, enraptured: e.g. The concert really blew my mind.

blow (one's) own trumpet
to boast about oneself.

blow (one's) stack/top
lose (one's) temper; become very angry.

blow (one's) trumpet
boast; extol (one's) virtues; praise (oneself) enthusiastically.

blow over
cease; soon be forgotten: e.g. I'll wait for the trouble to blow over before I see him.

blow shit out of (someone)

blow (someone) up
scold, deride, abuse, reprimand (someone) severely.

blow that!
(see: blow it!)

blow the whistle on (someone)
tell a secret, inform on (someone).

blow through
1. leave, depart, go.
2. evade responsibility by secretly leaving: e.g. He blew through without paying the rent.

blow up
lose control of one's temper; become very angry suddenly.

blower
telephone.

blow-hard
effusive, garrulous talker.

blowies
blow-flies.

blow-in
casual arrival, particularly an uninvited guest.

blowing
fraudulent soliciting of business over the telephone — especially the sending of accounts for services that have not been rendered, such as the placing of advertisements in non-existing magazines.

blow-job
orgasm through oral or manual stimulation; fellatio: e.g. Do you know a massage parlour that gives good blow-jobs?

blown to smithereens
ruined; wrecked; completely destroyed as by an explosion or forceful wind.

blown-out
1. amazed; pleased; astonished; delighted.
2. horrified.

blow-out
1. burst tyre (especially when driving at speed).
2. lavish party, social gathering, meal, entertainment.

blow-up
suddent argument or outburst of temper.

blow-wave
to style the hair using a hand-held hair-drier; the hairstyle so obtained.

blowy
windy.

blub/blubber
weep; cry: e.g. What are you blubbing about?

bludge
1. do nothing; be lazy, idle, inactive; evade work or responsibilities (verb or noun): e.g. 1. He bludged all weekend, drinking beer with the mates. 2. He's going to have a good bludge this weekend.
2. borrow, take, cadge with no intention of paying back; impose on others: e.g. 1. Can I bludge a fag off you? 2. He's always bludging off his parents.
3. an easy job which entails a minimum of work: e.g. This job's a good bludge.

See also:
on the bludge

bludger
1. lazy, unconstructive person; loafer; shirker (generally held in contempt).
2. person who gains profit with no effort, work or risk (generally held in contempt).
3. affectionate term for a friend, mate or person: e.g. G'day you old bludger!
See also:
dole-bludger
pack of bludgers

blue
1. a fight or unfriendly argument: e.g. I had a blue with my boyfriend last night.
2. a mistake, blunder or error: e.g. I made a real blue on my exam paper and failed.
3. depressed in spirit; melancholy; sad: e.g. He's feeling blue today.
4. pertaining to obscenity or indecency: e.g. We watched a blue movie on video.
5. affectionate name for a friend, red-haired person, dog etc.
See also:
bolt out of the blue
boys in blue
cop the blue
like a blue-arsed fly
once in a blue moon
out of the blue
scream blue murder
stack on a blue
till (one) goes blue in the face
true blue

blue blood
royalty; of noble birth: e.g. There's no blue blood in our family.

blue duck
venture that has failed; a flop.

blue meanies
hallucinogenic mushrooms.

blue metal
crushed rock used for road base.

blue movie
pornographic movie (generally for the home video market or shown illegally).

blue murder
serious trouble: e.g. You're going to get blue murder when you get home.
See also:
get away with blue murder
scream blue murder

bluebottle
1. policeman.
2. stinging jellyfish.
3. large blue or green blow-fly.

blue-chip
valuable; having outstanding quality or value compared to others.

blue-collar
pertaining to manual workers such as factory, shop etc. as opposed to white-collar: e.g. The blue-collar work-force is in line for a pay rise.

blue-eyed
1. innocent; free of guilt or blame: e.g. What are you looking so blue-eyed about?
2. favourite; darling; pet: e.g. He's his mother's blue-eyed boy.

bluegrass
traditional country music derived from southern states of America.

blue-nosed wowser
teetotaller; killjoy.

blue-print
detailed plans: e.g. They want a blue-print before they go ahead with the deal.

blue-ribbon
pertaining to a winner; the best: e.g. Blue-ribbon wine.

blue-rinse set
old or middle-aged women with trivial pursuits or conservative and old-fashioned outlooks and opinions (particularly those with hair coloured blue or silver).

blue-vein junket-pumper

blue-vein steak
the penis.

blues
1. feeling of depression or melancholy: e.g. He's got the blues today.
2. style of melancholy music, jazz originating with the United States Blacks.
3. amphetamines (see: speed).
4. (cap.) Carlton VFL football team.

blue-singlet
pertaining to the working classes.

bluestocking
woman of literary and intellectual bent.

Bluestone College
Pentridge Prison (Melbourne).

bluey
1. summons issued by police: e.g. I got a bluey for speeding.
2. cattle-dog; kelpie.
3. nick-name for a friend, mate, red-haired person.
4. swag, blanket carried by the travelling swaggie (obsolete).
5. a ten-dollar note.
See also:
hump (one's) bluey
slap a bluey on (someone)

Bluey and Curly
Australian 'digger' cartoon characters by A. Gurney — now used as standard

Aussie characters in the telling of jokes.

blunder
gross error or mistake.

blunderbuss
1. stupid, clumsy person.
2. type of old-fashioned gun with wide muzzle.

blurb
announcement or advertisement found on book flaps, record-covers, instruction manuals, advertising mail etc.

blurt out
say without thinking; disclose unintentionally.

blurter
1. emission of wind from the anus; fart.
2. a gross mistake or error; blunder.
3. backside; bum; posterior: e.g. He sits around on his blurter all day at the office.

blusher
brush-on cosmetic rouge.

blushing bride
newly-wed woman, bride.

B.O.
unpleasant body odour.

board
floor of the woolshed where sheep are shorn.
See also:
go by the board
sweep the board
tread the boards

board shorts
type of swimming trunks made popular by surfers.

boardie
surfboard-riding enthusiast; surfie.

boarding-house reach
someone with long arms who can reach things easily.

boat
(see: boy/man in the boat; burn one's boats; don't rock the boat; in the same boat; little man in the boat; missed the boat)

boat people
term coined for the South-East Asian refugees making for Australia in small over-crowded boats.

boat race
1. situation in which the outcome has been secretly rigged, especially in horse-racing.
2. form of drinking competition; alcoholic drinking race.

boater
straw, flat-topped hat.

boatie
boat enthusiast or owner.

bob
a shilling in pre-decimal days, but still used in many sayings and phrases: e.g. Silly as a two-bob watch.
See also:
get (one's) two-bob's worth
haven't got two bob to rub together
mad as a two-bob watch
not short of a bob
not the full two-bob's worth
not worth two bob
only eighteen bob in the pound
put (one's) two-bob's worth in
so help me bob!
worth a few bob

Bob Hope
(rhyming slang) soap; dope — marijuana.

bobby
uniformed policeman (British).

bobby pin
hair pin or clip for fastening the hair.

bobby-dazzler
1. excellent, praiseworthy person or thing: e.g. His new car is a real bobby-dazzler.
2. person who has just done something extremely favourable: e.g. You little bobby-dazzler!

bob-in
a collection of money whereby all participants contribute a specified amount and drinks are purchased from this pool.

Bob's your uncle
expression indicating that everything is perfect, going extremely well, as planned and expected.

bod
1. body: e.g. Deb's got a nice bod.
2. person: e.g. Karl's not a bad bod.

bodgie
1. term from the 1950s for a man who dressed in a particular style, behaved in a wild and uncouth manner with little regard for the Establishment.
2. worthless; counterfeit; inferior.

bodgie job
inferior, unskilled, second-rate work performed on something.

bodgie name
false name; alias.

body and soul
completely amd utterly.

body language/talk
conveyance of thoughts, feelings and messages through gestures of the body such as a wink, a look, a touch etc.

bodywork
the outer shell of a car.

boffin
person involved in research, particularly technical research.

bog
1. defecation; excrement.
2. to defecate: e.g. I have to go and have a bog.
3. the toilet: e.g. Where's the bog?

'Wut's your explanation for doin' the ton through a built-up area?'

Our alert and ever-watchful speed-cops have many devices for apprehending the wayward motorist. Before you go lairising or hooning around the streets, you would be wise to familiarise yourself with all their devious devices, such as radar and red-light cameras, concealed fuzz-wagons ready for pursuit, on-the-spot blueys, and booze buses, RBT and bag tests.

4. car panel filler used in repair.

bog in
1. eat heartily and energetically.
2. begin a task energetically.
See also:
two, four, six, eight, bog in don't wait

bogarting
subconsciously, selfishly, unwittingly smoking a marijuana cigarette to the exclusion of other people (from Humphrey Bogart's habit of having a cigarette).

bogey
(see: bogie)

bogey-man
(also: bogieman; bogyman; boogie-man) evil spirit fabricated to frighten children.

bogged down
inundated with a heavy work load.

boggle
stare unashamedly.

boghouse
the toilet, especially an outside one.

bogie
1. hardened waste matter emitted from the nose; snot. (also: boogie)
2. swim, bathe: e.g. After a hard day's work, the men had a bogie in the river. (also: bogey)

boil
become increasingly angry; simmer with anger.

boil the billy
make a cup of tea or refreshments.

boiled shirt
pompous, pretentious man.

boiler
1. an aged fowl that requires boiling in order to be made palatable.
2. (derog.) an old woman.

boiling point
the peak of a situation or emotion: e.g. Industrial relations between the unions and the employers is at boiling point.

boil-over
an unexpected result in horse or dog racing, such as the favourite not winning.

boils down to
the essence or crux of the matter: e.g. It all boils down to the fact that she doesn't love him any more.

bold as brass
impudent; forward in manner.

bollocks
1. testicles, balls.
2. rubbish, nonsense: e.g. What a load of bollocks!
3. ruin; bungle; make a mess of: e.g. He bollocksed everything!

bollocky
nude, naked: e.g. We went swimming in the bollocky.

boloney
(see: baloney)

bolshie
1. (cap.) a Bolshevik.
2. having communist or left-wing views.

bolt it down
drink or eat quickly.

bolt it in
win by a large margin.

bolt out of the blue
any sudden and unexpected happening.

bolt upright
stiffly upright: e.g. He sat bolt upright all through the show.

bolter
an outsider who unexpectedly wins, especially in horse-racing.

bomb
1. an old, dilapidated car.
2. a failure: e.g. The show was a complete bomb.
3. a drug (usually a capsule or pill) for sleep or pain.
See also:
go like a bomb

bombed
drunk, intoxicated; drugged: e.g. He's bombed on booze and grass nearly all the time now.

bombed out
1. failed: e.g. I bombed out in my exams.
2. heavily under the influence of alcohol or drugs.

bomber
parking officer who records parking infringements.
See also:
brown bomber

Bombers
Essendon VFL football team.

bombora
submerged reef.

bomb-out
a failed situation; disaster; mistake.

bombs away!
expression signalling the enthusiastic start of something.

bombshell
1. physically attractive and well-endowed woman.
2. sudden, profound action or event: e.g. It was quite a bombshell when he got the sack as he didn't expect it.
See also:
drop a bombshell

bone
(see: bare bones; bury the bone; close to the bone; feel it in one's bones; have/got a bone to pick with; make no bones about; near to the bone; on the bones of one's bum; point the bone at)

bone of contention
situation or matter which causes disagreement.

bone up on
study and acquire information.

bone-chilling
terrifying.

boned out
exhausted.

bone-dry
1. very thirsty.
2. very dry.

bone-idle
very lazy.

bone-on
an erection of the penis.

boner
1. a glaring mistake.
2. an erection of the penis.

bones in (one's) beer
(to have . . .) to feel that (one's) beer is not palatable.

boney
very thin; emaciated.

boneyard
cemetery.

bonfire
a large fire in an open, outside place.

bonfire night
large public celebration (Guy Fawkes) with an open fire and fireworks, but fading into obscurity due to legal restrictions on the use of fireworks.

bong
1. hit, bash, dong (on the head).
2. special water-pipe used for smoking marijuana.

bong on
to participate in a heavy marijuana smoking session using a bong or water-pipe.

bonk
to have sexual intercourse.

bonkers
crazy; mad; insane.

bonza/bonzer
excellent; terrific; very good.

boo
1. jeer, deride, mock: e.g. The crowd booed at the competitor who tripped his opponent on purpose.
2. an exclamation to frighten someone.
See also:
wouldn't say boo to a goose

boob
1. woman's breast: e.g. She's got big boobs.
2. fool; dunce; stupid person.
3. prison: e.g. He's been in the boob for five years.

boo-boo
error; mistake; make an error or mistake: e.g. 1. He made a boo-boo on his exam paper. 2. He boo-booed again.

boob-tube
1. women's elasticised summer top without shoulders or sleeves.
2. the television, viewed as a mindless form of entertainment.

booby
stupid, ineffective person.

booby prize
consolation prize given with good-natured ridicule to the worst performance.

booby trap
device or situation that catches one off guard.

boodle
money: e.g. He's got oodles of boodle.

boofhead
1. stupid person; fool.
2. person with a large head.

boogie
evil spirit (see: bogey-man).

boogie board
type of surf-board for riding the waves.

boogie-man
(see: bogey-man)

boogie-woogie
type of instrumental blues using melodic variations over a repeated bass rhythm.

boohoo
to cry, weep: e.g. What's she boohooing about?

book
(of police) to record an offender's name for possible prosecution for a minor offence: e.g. I got booked for speeding again.
See also:
black book
by the book
can't judge a book by its cover
closed book
cook the books
fiddle the books
heard every excuse in the book
in (one's) book
in (someone's) bad books
in (someone's) good books
in the bad books
open book
read (someone) like a book
take a leaf out of (someone's) book
the Good Book
throw the book at (someone)
turn-up for the books
use every trick in the book

book (something) up
obtain on credit.

booked
to have one's name recorded by a police officer for the purpose of prosecution: e.g. I was booked for speeding the other day.

bookie
(racing) professional betting man who accepts the bets of others; a bookmaker.

bookworm
avid reader, or one who always studies hard.

boombaloomba!
remark of admiration (by a man) for an attractive woman.

boomer
1. something notably large.
2. something popular, successful, excellent.

boomerang
1. dishonoured cheque.
2. an object that is expected to be returned to the owner by the borrower.
3. a scheme that backfires, goes awry.
See also:
could sell boomerangs to the Blacks

booming
doing extremely well; successful: e.g. His business is booming.

boong/boori
(derog.) an Aborigine or black man.

boot
1. dismissal; the sack: e.g. He finally got the boot.
2. an electric shock: e.g. Our electric fence has quite a boot.
3. the sharp stimulating effect of drugs or alcohol.
See also:
bet your boots
get the boot
give (someone) the boot
heart in (one's) boots
in your boot!
Japanese riding boots
lick (someone's) boots
order of the boot
put in the boot
put the boots into
sink the boot
splash (one's) boots
stick the boots in
to boot
too big for (one's) boots

booties
knitted shoes for a baby.

bootleg
any illegally traded, smuggled or manufactured goods, but especially alcohol.

bootlicker
sycophant; obsequious person; toady.

boots and all
to do something using all one's strength, energy and know-how: e.g. He really went into it, boots and all.

boot's on the other foot
position in which the advantage or situation has reversed.

booze
alcoholic drinks.
See also:
on the booze

booze artist/hound
heavy drinker of alcohol.

booze bus
vehicle used for random breath testing to apprehend drivers under the influence of alcohol.

boozed
intoxicated; drunk.

boozer
1. local pub, hotel.
2. an immoderate, regular or heavy drinker of alcohol.

booze-up
1. excessive drinking spree.
2. a wild party with copious amounts of alcohol.

boozy
1. intoxicated; drunk.
2. pertaining to large amounts of alcohol: e.g. It was a boozy party.

bop
1. dance to rock or pop music; the dance performed.
2. to hit, punch: e.g. Bop him if he gives any cheek!

bo-peep
a look: e.g. Have a bo-peep at this!

borack
(see: poke borack at)

border-line case
1. person who is not quite normal.
2. verging on being obscene or indecent.

bore
(see: full bore; give it the full bore)

bore it up (someone)
verbally attack, criticise (someone) severely.

bore the pants off (someone)
bore (someone) immensely.

bored shitless/stiff/to tears
very bored.

born
(see: wasn't born yesterday; were you born in a tent?)

born and bred in
have an intimate knowledge of (subject or town being discussed): e.g. He was born and bred in the world of racing.

born loser
one who never seems to succeed or do well.

born on the wrong side of the tracks
to have originated from the poor side of town; not born into the wealthy sector.

born with a silver spoon in (one's) mouth
born into a wealthy family and having no need to work hard for a living.

born with a wooden spoon in (one's) mouth
the opposite to: born with a silver spoon . . .

born-again Christian
zealous convert to religion, Christianity.

bosh!
nonsense, rubbish!

bosker
excellent; very good; pleasing.

boss
1. employer; person in charge.
2. (joc.) wife; mistress of the house.
See also:
be (one's) own boss

boss-cocky
employer; someone in authority; leader.

bossy
domineering.

bot
1. person who borrows persistently with no intention of repaying.
2. bottom; bum.
3. a fly that infests cattle.
4. to cadge, borrow with no real intention of repayment.
See also:
how are the bots biting?
on the bot

botch up
make a mess of; ruin through poor effort; bungle or spoil.
See also:
make a botch of

botch-up
poor, clumsy effort; a mess; failure.

botchy
poor; badly done; unsatisfactory; second-rate.

bottie
1. euphemism for bum, bottom.
2. (in baby's speech) bottle.

bottle
(see: chief cook and bottle washer; hit the bottle; on the bottle; spin the bottle)

bottle baby
baby fed from a bottle rather than the breast.

bottle fed
not independent; pampered and sheltered to the detriment of one's independence.

bottle shop
store, part of an hotel where alcohol may be purchased to take away.

bottle up
to hide and restrain one's feelings.

bottleneck
obstruction, obstacle (in a road).

bottle-o(h)
collector of empty bottles; used-bottle merchant.

bottler
a person or thing of excellence, worthy of admiration.
See also:
little bottler

bottom
bum; backside.

bottom of (one's) world has dropped out
feeling acutely depressed and miserable due to a crushing turn of events.

bottomless pit
1. one who never seems to be able to satisfy his hunger or desires: e.g. He's a bottomless pit when it comes to food.
2. a seemingly never-ending supply: e.g. My wife seems to think my wallet is a bottomless pit.

bottom-of-the-harbour
pertaining to tax-evasion schemes of selling and re-selling companies in order to obscure tax-records.

bottoms up!
a call to finish one's drink in one gulp.

bought a lemon
purchased an item (usually a car) that is totally unreliable.

bought for a song
purchased very cheaply.

bought in
entered into; became involved (usually with unfavourable consequences).

bought it
died; was killed: e.g. He bought it at the hands of the Mafia.

bought off
bribed: e.g. Some politicians can be easily bought off.

bounce of the ball
(Australian Rules football) luck of the game; way the cookie crumbles.

bounced
1. pertaining to a cheque that could not be honoured: e.g. The cheque I got from him bounced.
2. beaten; bashed: e.g. He got thoroughly bounced at the pub last week.
3. caught in the act of doing something illegal: e.g. We were milking petrol from a car and got bounced by the fuzz.

bouncer
person employed to evict undesirables or trouble-makers.

bouncy cheque
a dishonoured cheque.

bound up
euphemism for being constipated.

bouquets or brickbats
praise or criticism.

bourbon-voiced
having a deeply resonant, gravelly voice.

bow
(see: drawing a long bow; full up to pussy's bow; second string to one's bow)

bow and scrape

bow down to
act obsequiously; be servile, submitting.

bow out
1. abstain or retreat from further involvement.
2. retire; go, leave, depart.

bowels turn to water
(to have one's . . .) to lose courage; suffer intense fear.

bowerbird
person who collects an astonishing array of sometimes useless objects.

bowl (someone) over
1. knock down; fight and defeat.
2. disconcert, upset, surprise, shock, dumbfound (someone).

bowling
moving very quickly (usually in a car): e.g. We were bowling down the highway when the police pulled us up for speeding.

bowser
1. petrol pump.
2. pet name for a dog.

bow-wow
dog (in children's speech).

bowyangs
straps or strings around the trousers just below the kneecaps.

box
1. female pudendum; vagina.
2. television set: e.g. What's on the box tonight?
3. an unimaginative, modern, cheaply built house.
See also:
glued to the box
nothing out of the box
one out of the box
put (someone) in his box
something out of the box

box of birds
pertaining to happiness, elation, good spirits: e.g. He's been like a box of birds since he won the lottery.

box office
1. ticket booth.
2. pertaining to the success of a show; drawing large crowds: e.g. This film will be a huge box office hit.

box seat
advantageous position; height of success: e.g. He's in the box seat compared with the other candidates for this election.

boxed in
surrounded; over-crowded.

boy!
exclamation of surprise, wonder, admiration.
See also:
old boy

boy in the boat
clitoris: e.g. She'll climax if you tickle her boy in the boat.

boy scout
serious, earnest and honest person.

boy-oh-boy!
exclamation of surprise, wonder, admiration.

boys
a man's friends, mates: e.g. Hubby's gone to the pub with the boys.
See also:
little boys
little boys'
one of the boys

boys in blue
policemen (wearing blue uniforms).

bra
brassiere — a supporting garment for a woman's breasts.

bracelets
handcuffs.

bracer
stimulating drink, usually alcoholic.

bracket
the nose.

brain
1. a smart, intelligent person.
2. bash, hit on the head: e.g. I'll brain him if he says any more.
See also:
bashing (one's) brains out
bird-brain
blow (one's) brains out
go off (one's) brain
hasn't got a brain in his head
hasn't got enough brains to give himself a headache
have/got no brains
have/got shit for brains
have/got (something) on the brain
if brains were dynamite
if brains were shit
if you had a brain it would be lonely
lame-brain
no brain, no pain
pea-brain
pick (someone's) brains
rack (one's) brains
shit for brains
tap (someone's) brain
water on the brain

brain-bucket
safety-helmet worn by motorcycle riders, horse riders etc.

brainchild
the end result or product of one's own work or idea.

brain-drain
the steady flow of the most intelligent and educated workers, researchers etc. from their place of origin to other countries or places.

brainless
stupid.

brain-power
organising ability; intelligence.

brains
the person who does the organising, thinking: e.g. Who's the brains around here?

brainstorm
a sudden wonderful idea or inspiration.

brainwash
indoctrinate.

brainwave
sudden wonderful idea or inspiration.

brainy
smart; clever; intelligent.

branded for life
to be left with a bad stigma or memory.

brand-spanking
completely new, unused.

brasco/braska
a toilet.

brass
1. money: e.g. I haven't got any brass on me.
2. management; senior organisers: e.g. All the big brass are having a meeting tonight.
3. senior, high-ranking military officers.
4. to cheat, defraud or swindle: e.g. That con-man would brass his own mother.
5. excessive brazenness, impudence.
See also:
bold as brass
top brass

brass monkey weather
very cold weather.
See also:
freeze the balls off a brass monkey.

brass razoo
money, especially in relation to having none, or being worthless: e.g. 1. I haven't got a brass razoo. 2. It's not worth a brass razoo.

brass tacks
main points; basic facts; realities: e.g. It's time we got down to brass tacks instead of avoiding the issues.

brassed
cheated: e.g. Watch you don't get brassed by that con-man.

brassed off
bad-tempered; annoyed; disillusioned.

brassy
1. brazen.
2. overdone; gaudy; tasteless.

brat
a child, but particularly an impudent one.

brave it out
1. defy gossip, suspicion etc.
2. endure pain, danger or difficult circumstances against all odds.

breach of promise
withdrawal from a promise to marry.

bread
money; earnings: e.g. He's got no bread to pay for that.
See also:
break bread
greatest thing since sliced bread

bread buttered on both sides
pertaining to having the best of both or opposing ways: e.g. To have a wife and a mistress is really having your bread buttered on both sides.
See also:
know which side (one's) bread is buttered on

bread-and-butter
the means by which one makes a living: eg 1. What's he do for his bread-and-butter? 2. To make a decent living out of pottery you need to have a bread-and-butter line that sells well.

breadbasket/breadbin
the stomach.

breadline
subsistence level; poor: e.g. Since he lost his job his family has been living on the breadline.

bread-winner
the one who works to support a family: e.g. The husband is usually the bread-winner.

break
1. chance; opportunity: e.g. Winning the Pools was a real break for that poor family.
2. pertaining to a very expensive cost that could (joc.) be the ruination of one: e.g. This new car is really going to break me.
See also:
bad break
give me a break!
give (someone) a break
make a break
make one or break one

break a bit off
to defecate.

break bread
share food.

break even
neither win nor lose.

break into
1. enter premises forcibly.
2. enter into a new venture or activity: e.g. I'd like to break into pottery.

break into the big time
achieve renowned success in business or some other venture.

break it down!
expression of disbelief or disagreement; plea for moderation.

break new ground
venture into a new or different activity; make advances in something.

break (one's) neck
attempt something dangerous or hazardous: e.g. I nearly broke my neck getting the cat out of the tree.

break (one's) word
renege, or go back on (one's) promise.

break open a coldie
have a drink, usually a can or bottle of beer.

break out
1. sudden erruption of pimples or acne: e.g. I wanted to look my best that day but my face broke out the night before.
2. produce refreshments, especially alcohol: e.g. Come back to our place — we'll break out the wine and celebrate!

break (someone's) heart
1. disappoint or hurt in love.
2. disappoint or cause great sorrow.

break square
(see: break even)

break the back of
1. to achieve or complete the most difficult part of a task.
2. to overburden to the point of ruin.

break the habit
cease a habit: e.g. I've tried everything to stop smoking but can't seem to break the habit.

break the ice
to break through a barrier of reserve or formality: e.g. He cracked a few jokes to break the ice at the meeting.

break the ties
severing of relationships, particularly of marriage.

break up
1. separate; sever a relationship, such as that of lovers or husband and wife.
2. collapse with uncontrollable laughter: e.g. He's so funny, I break up every time he opens his mouth.
3. (of a school) disband for term holidays.

break wind
emit wind from the anus; fart.

breakdancing/breaking
physical and athletic form of street dancing that started on the gang-ravaged streets of New York city's Bronx district where it was used as a peaceful means of settling disputes.

breaking and entering
trespass with criminal intent.

breaking point
the point at which any person or thing gives way under stress: e.g. Their marriage is at breaking point.

breaks
(see: that's the breaks!; those are the breaks!)

breaks me up
makes me collapse with laughter.

break-up
a separation, as of lovers or a marriage.

break-up party
end of term celebration.

breast (someone)
approach (someone) about something.

breath
(see: don't hold your breath; hold one's breath; save one's breath to cool one's porridge; take one's breath away; under one's breath; waste one's breath)

breath of fresh air
person with a fresh new positive approach and personality.

breath test
breathalyser test — a police test on the exhaled breath of drivers to measure alcohol content. The test is conducted by requesting the person to breathe or blow into a special bag.

breathe a word to
reveal a confidence; tell a secret: e.g. If you breathe a word about this to anybody I'll murder you!

breathe down (someone's) neck
stand over or watch (someone's) every move: e.g. I'm glad to work at home because I can't stand the boss breathing down my neck.

breathe easy/freely
relax; feel released from anxiety and worry.

breathe (one's) last
to die.

breather
a short rest.

breathing space
opportunity to pause for a rest or a think.

breed like rabbits
have many children.

breeze
an easy task or job.
See also:
bat the breeze
put the breeze up (someone)

breeze along
move quickly and easily.

breeze through
perform something without effort: e.g. He breezed through his exams.

breezer
1. the anus.
2. a fart; emission of wind from the anus.

brekkie/brekky
breakfast.

brew
beverage — either beer or tea.

brewer's droop
(of a man) inability to raise an erection after drinking too much alcohol: e.g. Louise got cranky when Kurt got a case of brewer's droop on their anniversary.

brewing
happening; forming; concocting.

brick
1. good, honest, reliable person: e.g. He's not a bad old brick.
2. formerly ten pounds, but now twenty dollars.
3. an amplifier.
4. prison sentence of ten years.
See also:
beating (one's) head against a brick wall
bet London to a brick
built like a brick (shithouse)
descend upon (someone) like a ton of bricks
drop a brick
fall for it like a ton of bricks
like a ton of bricks
like talking to a brick wall
shit bricks
thick as a brick
up against a brick wall

brick short of a load
(be a . . .) lacking in intelligence; dull-witted; simple-minded.

brickbat
unkind but often warranted criticism.

brickfielder
a sudden dust-bearing wind. (from the N.S.W. town of Brickfield Hill)

brickie
a bricklayer.

bride
(see: always the bridesmaid, never the bride; blushing bride)

bridge
(see: burn one's bridges; cross one's bridges when one comes to them; water has flowed under the bridge; water under the bridge)

bridge the gap
to make amends, compensate.

brigalow
remote country supporting a species of *Acacia* of the same name.

bright as a button
1. smart; quick-witted; intelligent.
2. happy; cheerful.

bright spark
1. alert; happy; cheerful.
2. (sarcastically) a fool: e.g. You're a bright spark! Now look what you've done!

bright-eyed and bushy-tailed
full of health, zest, vigour and happiness; ready for anything.

bring a ticket to get in
pertaining to the practice of bringing one's own alcohol to a function.

bring home the bacon
provide financial support.

bring home to (someone)
make perfectly understood: e.g. You've got to bring home to him the seriousness of the matter.

bring in the heavy artillery
approach a matter or project in earnest; become serious; provide necessary backing or support for a project, argument etc.

bring it off
successfully conclude; achieve an end: e.g. When he went into business we didn't think he'd be able to bring it off, but he did.

bring on the dancing girls
expression designed to induce cheer and vitality.

bring (someone) down a peg or two
humble (someone).

bring (someone) into line
chastise, make (someone) conform.

bring (someone) off/on
excite sexually and induce to orgasm: e.g. Karen says that the quickest way to bring hubby off is to wear leather boots in bed.

bring (someone) round
1. convince (someone) to agree to your views or opinions.
2. revive (someone) after unconsciousness.

bring (someone) to heel/his knees
cause (someone) to submit; defeat (someone); cause the downfall of (someone).

bring (someone) undone
cause (someone) to submit, admit defeat; cause (someone's) downfall: e.g. I'll bring him undone after I let the world know a few secrets about him.

bring (someone) up to date
inform (someone) of all the relevant facts of a matter to date: e.g. It's time someone brought him up to date about his wife's playing up.

bring (someone) up with a jolt
cause (someone) to stop, think and re-appraise.

bring the house down
create tremendous merriment, hilarity or uproar: e.g. He brought the house down with his ribald jokes.

bring to light
reveal; uncover; disclose; expose.

bring up
1. vomit: e.g. He got so drunk he brought his pizza up all over the place.
2. raise a subject for discussion: e.g. I wish you wouldn't bring that up all the time as I'm sick of talking about it!

bring up the rear
follow behind.

bring your own (grog)
bring your own alcohol to a function — abbreviated to B.Y.O. or B.Y.O.G.

brinnie/brinny
small stone or pebble.

briny
the sea, ocean.

Brissie
Brisbane. (also: Brizzie)

bristling
visibly hostile and angry.

bristols
(rhyming slang: Bristol city — titty) breasts, boobs, tits.

Brit
an Englishman.

britches
trousers.
See also:
too big for (one's) britches

britts
(see: have got the britts; have got the britts up)

brm brm
a car.

broad
woman: e.g. She's not a bad-looking broad.

broad accent
the peculiar Australian pronunciation of the English language.

broad around the beam
referring to very large hips or bottom (particularly of women).

broad between the ears
not very intelligent; witless.

broad joke
indecent joke.

broad-minded
liberal-minded; free from prejudice or bias; not easily shocked by indecent speech or action.

broadside
a strong verbal attack.

broke
penniless; having no money: e.g. I'm really broke this week.
See also:
flat broke
go for broke

broke me up
caused great hilarity, amusement.

broken down
1. grief-stricken; crushed by despair.
2. (of machinery etc.) rendered useless: e.g. My car's finally broken down.

broken English
imperfectly spoken, but able to be understood.

broken home
home in which the parents have separated or divorced.

broken up
distressed; worried; appalled: e.g. He's really broken up about that particular incident.
See also:
all broken up

broken-hearted
distressed; grief-stricken.

brolly
umbrella.

bronze
anus; bum.

bronzed Anzac
pertaining to the image of the healthy, suntanned, out-door, athletic Australian male.

bronzer
a homosexual man.

bronzo
anus; bum.

brood
children of family.

broody
1. moody; depressed.
2. wanting to bear children.

broom
(see: new broom sweeps clean)

brothel
any disreputable or messy room or place: e.g. Her bedroom's a real brothel.

brothel boots
sneakers or other shoes with soft, quiet soles.

brother!
oath, curse of frustration, scorn etc.
See also:
Big Brother

brow-beat
bully and intimidate with words.

brown as a berry
very suntanned.

brown bomber
N.S.W. parking police officer.

brown (someone) off
annoy, upset, bore (someone).

browned off
annoyed, upset, bored, discontented.

brown-eye
the anus, particularly when exposing it to someone as a gesture of contempt: e.g. When he gave the crowd a brown-eye, the police booked him for indecent exposure.

brownie
1. junior member of the Girl Guides.
2. bottle of beer.

Brownlow (medal)
best and fairest award in VFL.
See also:
come on Brownlow

brown-nose
1. obsequious person: e.g. He's such a brown-nose when the boss is around.
2. behave in an obsequious, fawning manner.

brown-trouser job
frightening, scary: e.g. That movie was a real brown-trouser job.

bruiser
bully; tough person.

brumby
1. wild horse.
2. person(s) with wild, unruly attributes: e.g. What a brumby lot they are!

brummy
cheap, shoddy, useless: e.g. I can't get this brummy thing to work properly!

brunch
meal that makes do as both breakfast and lunch.

brunch coat
light dressing-gown for women.

brush
1. girl, woman (also plural) viewed as a sex object.
2. female pubic hair.
3. a noisy fight or brawl.
4. to come into contact with or have (unpleasant) association with: e.g. He's had a few brushes with the police already.
See also:
tarred with the same brush
touch of the tar-brush

brush (someone) off
dismiss or rebuff rudely and quickly.

brush up on
revise one's knowledge: e.g. I'll have to brush up on my maths before I give that lecture.

brush-off
rude dismissal or rebuff: e.g. He asked me for a date but I gave him the brush-off.

brute
selfish, despicable person.

bub
1. baby.
2. derogatory term of address for someone younger: e.g. Listen here bub!

bubba
baby.

bubble and squeak
left-over meat and vegetables fried together.

bubble has burst
good, profitable times are over: e.g. The real-estate bubble finally burst and many investors went broke.

bubble over
be exuberant.

bubbly
1. champagne: e.g. We celebrated with a bottle of bubbly.
2. having an effervescent, bright personality.

bubs grade
grade or class one of an infant school.

buck
1. dollar: e.g. It cost a thousand bucks.
2. handsome, sexy young man.
3. object strongly: e.g. You can't always buck at progress.
See also:
buck-passing
buck's party
fast buck
pass the buck

buck the system
rebel against; object to or strongly resist the Establishment.

buck up
1. hurry up.
2. become cheerful.

bucket
to criticise, disparage, slander, accuse: e.g. That reporter always buckets politicians.
See also:
kick the bucket
tip the bucket on (someone)

bucket of nuts and bolts
dilapidated car.

bucket-brigade
pertaining to slander, scandalous accusations and severe criticism: e.g. It doesn't take long for politicians on opposing sides to bring out the bucket-brigade.

bucketing
severe criticism, verbal abuse.

bucket-mouth
person given to strong and vicious criticism.

buckle
(see: get buckled)

buckle down to
apply oneself to work or a task vigorously: e.g. It's about time he stopped fooling around and buckled down to his studies.

buckle under
give in to pressure; yield.

Buckley's
very slim, poor chance; little hope: e.g. You've got Buckley's of getting there on time in peak-hour traffic.

Buckley's and none
two chances that really amount to no chance at all.

Buckley's chance/hope
(see: Buckley's)

buck-passing
not accepting the responsibility or blame but trying to shift it to someone else: e.g. I tried to get some information about it from the council but all I got was buck-passing.

bucks
dollars.

buck's party/turn
party held by the friends of a bridegroom on the eve of his wedding, often ribald and accompanied by pornographic movies, wild pranks and excessive

drinking. Their women are excluded.

bucktoothed
having protruding top teeth.

bud
1. friend; brother.
2. derogatory term of address: e.g. Listen here bud!
See also:
nip it in the bud

Buddha stick
marijuana sold in a pre-rolled stick (originating from Asia).

buddy
friend, mate.

buddy-buddy
1. (often derog.) pertaining to a very close relationship or friend.
2. sycophantic; obsequious: e.g. He's so buddy-buddy whenever the boss walks in.

budgie
budgerigar.

buff
fanatical enthusiast: e.g. movie buff; camera buff; wine buff.
See also:
in the buff

buffer
old-fashioned, foolish or pompous man.

bug
1. an illness or viral infection: e.g. He's in bed with the bug.
2. an obsession: e.g. He's got a real bug about it.
3. defect or problem: e.g. The car has a few bugs in it but it goes all right.
4. hidden microphone used to tap information: e.g. The phone had a bug secretly installed in it.
5. to annoy or harass: e.g. I wish she wouldn't bug me all the time.
6. to install a bug device in a room, phone etc.
See also:
bug-rake

bug off!
go away!

bugbear
any cause for fright, fear, anxiety or annoyance.

bug-eyed
having eyes that appear to protrude when surprised, amazed.

bugger
1. contemptible and despicable person.
2. affectionate and jocular term of address: e.g. What are you up to you old bugger?
3. a nuisance or difficulty: e.g. That sewing-machine's a real bugger! What a bugger of a job!
4. ruin or spoil: e.g. Now look what you've done! You've buggered it!
5. render incapacitated: e.g. You'll bugger yourself if you keep that pace up.
6. exclamation of annoyance, frustration, disgust or contempt: e.g. Bugger! Now look what's happened!
See also:
give a bugger
little buggers
play funny-buggers
play silly-buggers

bugger about/around
mess, fool around; waste time: e.g. Get on with the job and don't bugger around all the time.

bugger it!
exclamation of exasperation, annoyance, frustration or contempt.

bugger me dead!
exclamation of amazement.

bugger off
1. depart; leave.
2. go away! get lost!

bugger (something) up
ruin; spoil; cause to fail: e.g. He'll just bugger things up if you let him do it.

bugger you Jack, I'm all right!
expression of contempt for someone else's selfish behaviour or complacency.

bugger-all
nothing; very little; meagre: e.g. 1. He gets bugger-all for all the work he does. 2. He's done bugger-all today.

buggered
1. broken; ruined; spoiled: e.g. This thing's buggered.
2. tired; exhausted: e.g. I'm buggered after all that work.
3.euphemism for damned: e.g. Be buggered if I do him a favour again!
See also:
I'll be buggered!

buggered if I know!
expression of ignorance.

buggered up
ruined; broken; spoiled.

buggerise about/around
waste time; fool around; behave ineffectually.

buggerlugs
affectionate term of address used with mock annoyance: e.g. Listen here buggerlugs!

buggery
1. very much: e.g. That hurt like buggery.
2. euphemism for hell: e.g. Go to buggery!
3. a remote, far-away place: e.g. He lives somewhere out to buggery.

buggy
car; off-road vehicle: e.g. beach-buggy.

bugle
nose.
See also:
on the bugle

bug-rake
a comb.

build castles in the air
to daydream, or to have unrealistic notions or ideas.

built
(of a woman in particular) well-endowed physically: e.g. She's really built!

built for
suitable: e.g. She's built for teaching.

built like a brick shithouse
1. very strong physically.
2. pertaining to an extremely large, obese or unattractive person.

built like a streak of pelican shit/weasel piss

built like a yard of pump-water
pertaining to an unattractively thin, tall person.

built like the side of a house
1. (of a person) extremely large, obese or unattractive.
2. (of a person) very strong, robust.

bulk
a lot of; a large amount: e.g. There were bulk people at the party.

bull
1. nonsense; excessive exaggeration: e.g. Stop talking a lot of bull!
2. police officer.
3. (as an exclamation) contempt or disbelief for what has been said. (shortened form of: bullshit)
4. deceive, trick or dupe: e.g. I think he's trying to bull me.
See also:
charge like a wounded bull
cock and bull
doesn't know B from a bull's foot!
get the bull by the horns
like a bull at a gate
like a bull in a china shop
stand/stick out like tits on a bull
strong as a mallee bull
take the bull by the horns
useful as tits on a bull
within a bull's roar

bull artist
one whose talk is excessively boastful, exaggerated and unreliable.

Bullamakanka
any remote, backward place — similar to: Woop-Woop.

Bulldogs
1. Footscray VFL football team.
2. Canterbury-Bankstown N.S.W. Rugby League football team.

bulldoze
coerce, intimidate.

bulldust
1. fine dust: e.g. Outback roads are booby-trapped with holes full of bulldust.
2. exaggerated, unreliable talk: e.g. He's full of bulldust.
3. (as an exclamation) nonsense!
4. to exaggerate: e.g. Stop bulldusting and tell the truth!

bullet
dismissal; the sack: e.g. If he won't do the work required, give him the bullet.
See also:
bite the bullet

bull-headed
1. obstinate; stubborn.
2. stupid.

bullocky
bullock-team driver.

bullocky's joy
treacle or golden syrup.

bullseye!
exclamation of success, triumph, attaining an exact target.

bullshit
(see: bull, 1., 3. and 4.)
See also:
baffle (someone) with bullshit
if bullshit was music . . .

bullshit artist
(see: bull artist)

bullswool
1. nonsense; exaggerated, unreliable talk: e.g. He's full of bullswool!
2. exclamation of disbelief, disgust, scorn etc.

bully for you!
exclamation of contempt or scorn.

bully-beef bomber
the Douglas Dakota C-47 Army cargo plane, so named because it was used to drop rations of corned or tinned meat to troops.

bum
1. loafer; tramp; no-hoper; down and out person.
2. mean, disagreeable person.
3. poor quality; worthless: e.g. What a bum gadget this is!
4. to borrow with no real intention of paying back; cadge: e.g. Can I bum a cigarette?
5. sponge on others for a living: e.g. He's been bumming off his parents for years.
See also:
beach bum
bite your bum!
bum's rush
do (one's) bum
need a kick up the bum
on the bones of (one's) bum
ram it up (one's) bum
up your bum!
(see also entries listed under: arse)

bum a ride
obtain a free ride in a car, truck etc.

bum around
1. do nothing in particular; be idle.
2. lead an idle life at the expense of other people.

bum sniffers
those who play Rugby League football.

bum steer
incorrect or false information.
See also:
give (someone) a bum steer
set on a bum steer

bum to mum
an order for football players to abstain from sexual activity on the eve of a match.

bum-bandit
a homosexual man.

bumbled
mismanaged; spoiled; ruined; handled inefficiently.

bumface
derogatory term of address for someone.

bumfluff
first growth of hair, usually on the face.

bum-fodder
1. toilet-paper.
2. any written material considered worthless.

bum-freezer
very short dress, coat etc.

bummer
disappointing turn of events; a failure.

bum-nuts
eggs.

bump and grind
1. rotation of the pelvis in sexual play or dance.
2. sexual intercourse.

bump into
meet by chance: e.g. You'll never guess who I bumped into at the supermarket!

bump off
kill; murder: e.g. He got bumped off by the Mafia.

bump up
to increase prices dramatically: e.g. They've bumped up the price of petrol again!

bumper
1. big; giant: e.g. This month's magazine will be a bumper issue.
2. an excessively large amount: e.g. Bumper crop.
3. a cigarette end.
See also:
not worth a bumper

bumper-to-bumper
(of traffic) moving very slowly.

bumping (one's) gums
talking excessively; gossiping.

bum's rush
abrupt dismissal, denial or rejection: e.g. He was given the bum's rush when he asked for a raise.

bumsucker
sycophantic, obsequious person.

bun
(see: do one's bun)

bun fight
1. noisy argument.
2. any crowd or gathering of noisy people: e.g. The sale at Myer was a real bun fight.

bun in the oven
(have a . . .) pregnant e.g. It won't be too long before she's got a bun in the oven.

bunch
group of people: e.g. They're not such a bad bunch.

bunch of fives
1. the fist or hand.
2. threat of beating, punching: e.g. If he doesn't shut up I'll give him a bunch of fives.

bunch of no-hopers
group of people held in low esteem.

bundle
1. a large sum of money.
2. to carry, cart off hastily.
See also:
cost a bundle
drop a bundle
drop (one's) bundle
lose a bundle

bundle of nerves
very nervous, anxious person.

bundle up
to dress warmly.

bundy
1. Bundaberg rum: e.g. I'll have a bundy and coke.
2. time-clock for employees.
See also:
punching the bundy

bung
1. broken; damaged; impaired: e.g. This can-opener's bung.
2. put, place without much care: e.g. Bung it on the table over there.
See also:
go bung

bung it on
1. behave excessively and temperamentally: e.g. Children often bung it on in front of their parents, yet are perfect angels in front of strangers.
2. stage; behave affectedly; put on airs and graces.

bung it on (someone)
tell, reveal, request something difficult.

bung on
1. put on, prepare or arange something on short notice: e.g. We managed to bung on some tucker for all of them.
2. stage; behave affectedly: e.g. She always bungs on airs and graces in front of him.

bung on an act
stage; behave falsely to either gain attention or deceive; behave

temperamentally or excessively; become bad-tempered.

bung on side
behave in an over-bearing, pompous, haughty manner.

bunger
large and noisy fire-work, now generally banned from sale due to its dangerous nature.

bunghole
cheese.

bunk
1. utter nonsense.
2. sleep in temporary bedding or arrangements: e.g. You can bunk on the couch tonight.
See also:
do a bunk

bunkum
utter nonsense and insincere talk.

bunk-up
help to climb on to something, given by a person who supports (one) or gives (one) a leg-up e.g. I need a bunk-up to get on to that tall horse.

bunny
1. rabbit.
2. someone who is prepared to shoulder the responsibility.
3. a fool; person with no mind or conviction of his own.
4. hostess dressed in sexy rabbit costume.
See also:
jungle-bunny

bunny-rug
baby's blanket.

buns
euphemism for arse: e.g. We worked our buns off all weekend.

bunyip
creature in Aboriginal legends which haunts billabongs and water-holes.

burble
(see: give it a burble)

bureaucratic bumbling
governmental or official inefficiency or mismanagement resulting from the cumbersome procedures and red tape of public service routine.

burg
town, city.

burgered out
stoned, under the influence of drugs.

buried up to the neck
inundated with or overwhelmed by something, such as debts, work, worries etc.

burl
1. attempt; have a go at; try: e.g. Why don't you have a burl?
2. to move fast, as in a car or vehicle: e.g. We were burling down the road when the police stopped us.
3. a drive; a test run; a demonstration: e.g. I took his car for a burl up the hill.
See also:
give it a burl

burn
1. a joyride or unofficial trial of a vehicle: e.g. We took it for a burn down the main drag and were very impressed.
2. to feel extreme emotion or passion: e.g. He was burning with anger by the time I got home.
3. to die in the electric chair: e.g. I hope the judge sentences him to burn for what he did.
See also:
do a slow burn

burn a hole in (one's) pocket
pertaining to great expense: e.g. Feeding a large family really burns a hole in a man's pocket these days.
See also:
money burns a hole in (one's) pocket

burn off
to race unofficially in a car or motorcycle, often starting from a set of traffic lights: e.g. Let's burn that Porsche off.

burn (one's) boats/bridges
to eliminate or destroy every possible avenue of retreat or choice, thereby committing oneself to a course of action from which there is no turning back: e.g. He doesn't want to burn all his bridges — that's why he keeps several girlfriends going at once.

burn (one's) fingers
suffer the consequences of rash action or involvement: e.g. He'll get his fingers burnt if he keeps associating with those criminals.

burn (oneself) out
mentally and physically exhaust (oneself).

burn rubber to get there
travel with excessive speed (in a car or vehicle).

burn the midnight oil
to stay up very late working or doing something.

burning
anxious; feeling extreme emotion or desire: e.g. I'm just burning to know what's in that box.

burning issue
a serious, most pressing problem.

burning question
the most pressing, serious question; the question that must be answered.

burning the candle at both ends
leading a strenuous and active life both day and night to the detriment of one's health and vitality.

burnt
(see: burn one's fingers; get burnt)

burnt offerings
an over-cooked or ruined meal.

burnt out
exhausted mentally and physically after pushing oneself too far.

burp
to belch, especially after food.

burry
(derog.) an Aborigine.

bursting at the seams
full to capacity — especially of food.

bury (one's) head in the sand
ignore a pressing matter or problem.

bury the bishop
(of a man) have sexual intercourse.

bury the bone/hatchet
forget a grievance; be reconciled.

bus
the car (often dilapidated): e.g. My old bus still gets me there and back.
See also:
missed the bus

bush
1. the country as opposed to the city: e.g. They live on a farm in the bush.
2. luxuriant growth of hair (especially female pubic).
See also:
beat about/around the bush
go bush
one in the bush is worth two in the hand
Sydney or the bush
take to the bush

bush band
Australian folk music group, characterised by instruments such as a tea-chest bass, violin, accordion and lagerphone.

bush carpenter
unqualified, amateur carpenter whose work is rough.

bush cure
a household remedy.

bush lawyer
one not qualified in law who offers a lot of free advice.

bush mile
a roughly estimated mile, considered to take into account the bends and hills encountered — usually arduous and underestimated.

bush oysters
testicles of castrated animals.

bush telegraph
(see: bush wireless)

bush week
protest or complaint against an imposition or an attempted deception: e.g. What do you think this is — bush week!?

bush wire/wireless
informally organised system of communication by which information and gossip are transmitted, (usually) by word of mouth from person to person: e.g. I found out that juicy bit of gossip over the bush wireless.

bushcraft
ability to survive in the wild with no or limited assistance or equipment.

bushed
1. tired; exhausted: e.g. I'm well and truly bushed.
2. lost; confused.

bushie
unsophisticated person who lives in the country.

bushman's clock
a kookaburra.

bushwhacked
1. ambushed and robbed.
2. amazed; astonished.
3. exhausted; tired.

bushwhacker
1. (obsolete) a highway robber.
2. generally unsophisticated person from the bush.

business
1. urination or defecation: e.g. I wish the cat would do its business in the Kitty Litter instead of on the floor.
2. prostitution: e.g. How long has she been in the business?
See also:
like nobody's business
mean business
monkey business

business is business
statement that attempts to justify an especially harsh business dealing or transaction: e.g. You may be a friend but business is business.

busman's holiday
leisure time spent doing the same thing as one does during working hours.

bust
1. an arrest, or to arrest, especially for possession of drugs.
2. broke; bankrupt: e.g. His business went bust.
3. to break and enter with the intention of theft: e.g. Thieves often try to bust houses in wealthy-looking areas.
4. spoil; wreck; ruin; destroy: e.g. I didn't mean to bust it!
See also:
go for bust

bust a boiler/foofer valve/gut
overdo; try too hard.

bust in
break and enter with intent to steal.

bust up
1. to quarrel, fight, argue and part with animosity.

2. to interrupt and disperse, spoil a meeting.
3. to break, wreck, destroy something.
See also:
bust-up

busted
1. caught out by a police raid: e.g. We got busted last week for growing marijuana.
2. broke; bankrupt: e.g. I can't pay my bills this week — I'm busted.
3. to have broken and entered with the intention of stealing.
4. broken; ruined; wrecked: e.g. Our television's been busted for weeks.
5. forced out of a card game by a card raising one's points higher than the bank.

buster
angry term of address for a male: e.g. Okay buster, what are you up to?
See also:
come a buster
southerly buster

busting to go
anxious to go to the toilet.

bust-up
1. separation — usually with animosity.
2. collapse or failure.
3. violent or noisy quarrel.
4. wild and noisy party; party to celebrate the end of a term.

busy as a bee

busy as a one-armed bill-poster in a gale

busy as a one-armed taxi-driver with crabs

busy as a one-eyed cat watching two rat holes

busy as Bourke Street

busy as Trimbole's travel agent
extremely busy, active, lively or harassed.

busybody
one who interferes or meddles.

but
however: e.g. We were going to have a barbecue — it rained but.
See also:
ifs or buts
no buts about it

butch
a lesbian, usually exhibiting masculine characteristics.

butcher
1. one who is guilty of cruel slaughter.
2. an inefficient, untidy surgeon; surgeon believed to use the knife unnecessarily.
3. to mess up; bungle; ruin: e.g. He really butchered that paint job on the car.
See also:
want to talk to the butcher, not the block

butchers (hook)
1. (rhyming slang: butcher's hook) look.
2. (rhyming slang) crook; angry.
See also:
go butchers (hook) at

butt
1. buttocks; bum: e.g. Get off your butt and do something!
2. remnant of smoked cigarette.

butt in
interrupt; interfere.

butter (someone) up
flatter (someone) grossly for some purpose or personal gain; cajole.

butter wouldn't melt in his/her mouth
assuming a demure or guileless demeanour.

butterfingers
clumsy person who continually drops things.

butterflies in the stomach
(to have . . .) to be extremely nervous.

buttinski
inquisitive, meddlesome person.

button
the nose.
See also:
bright as a button
not worth a button

button down
to restrain.

button your lip
be quiet; shut up; don't speak.

buttonhole (someone)
detain or corner in conversation.

buy
1. accept; believe: e.g. He won't buy that ridiculous story.
2. bribe; gain the support of (someone) through some form of payment: e.g. Some politicians can be bought at the right price.
3. a bargain: e.g. That house was a good buy!

buy a lemon
purchase an item that one later discovers has many faults: e.g. That car I bought was a real lemon.

buy back the Farm
political jargon — to redeem Australia from overseas investors.

buy in/into
become involved, join in (especially with reference to trouble): e.g. You'd be a fool to buy into any sort of business dealings with that con-man.

buy it
die; be killed: e.g. He bought it in a shoot-out with the police.

buy it for a song
purchase cheaply; get a bargain.

buy (someone) off
bribe into accepting an idea; pay or reward (someone) for not interfering: e.g. Those illegal gambling casinos operate because the police have been bought off.

buy (someone) out
to secure all the interest in a business venture from (someone).

buy (someone) the moon
to do anything for (someone).

buy trouble
to become involved against the better judgement of others.

buyer's market
a market situation that favours the buyer and not the seller.

buying power
purchasing ability: e.g. My wage doesn't seem to have the same buying power it had two years ago.

buzz
1. an exhilarating feeling induced by something, particularly drugs: e.g. 1. Try this marijuana — it'll give you the best buzz of your life. 2. I got a real buzz out of seeing that movie.
2. a rumour: e.g. What's the latest buzz?
3. telephone call: e.g. Give me a buzz tomorrow.
4. fly a light plane very low, often as a signal or greeting.

buzz around
move around quickly; do something actively: e.g. I'll buzz around and do the housework before they arrive.

buzz around like a blue-arsed fly
behave in a frenzied, hurried, erratic, harassed manner.

buzz off
1. leave; depart.
2. (as interjection) go away! get lost!

bwana
boss; person in command or authority.

by
(see: get by)

by a cat's whisker

by a hair
by a narrow margin: e.g. We missed crashing into that car by a hair.

by a long shot
by a large margin.

by a nose
by a narrow margin.

by all means
certainly; definitely; of course.

by and large
in general: e.g. By and large you can expect to pay a lot for even a second-hand Rolls Royce.

by cripes!
exclamation of surprise, amazement etc.

by ear
without the need for written music.

by fair means or foul
whatever the cost; under any circumstances.

by far
clearly; very much: e.g. He's by far the best.

by George/gum!
exclamation of surprise, amazement etc.

by half
by too much: e.g. He's too cheeky by half!

by halves
half-heartedly: e.g. He never does anything by halves — that's why he's so successful.

by hook or by crook
by any means, fair or foul: e.g. I'll win the contest by hook or by crook.

by inches
by a narrow margin: e.g. He escaped death by inches.

by jingo/jove!
exclamation of amazement, wonder, disbelief.

by the book
follow rules closely with no transgressions: e.g. A judge has no course of action other than to go by the book.

by the by
incidentally: e.g. By the by, where were you all night?

by the same token
similarly; moreover; incidentally.

by the skin of (one's) teeth
by a very narrow margin: e.g. He escaped serious injury by the skin of his teeth.

by the way
incidentally: e.g. By the way, where were you all night?

by word of mouth
information spread through speech from one person to another rather than by writing: e.g. He gets a lot of business just by word of mouth.

bye-bye
form of farewell; good-bye.

bye-byes
(in children's speech) sleep; the time to go to sleep.

B.Y.O.(G.)
1. abbreviation of: bring your own (grog).
2. restaurant with no licence to sell alcohol — patrons bring their own.

by-your-leave
apology or polite explanation: e.g. He left the party without so much as a by-your-leave!

'You kids are flamin' late home from school, again! Your mum has been expecting you since four o'clock — last Tuesday!'

Children — those cute, mischievous, endearing and innocent little tykes — are affectionately (or otherwise) known as ankle-biters, beggars, billy lids or billies, brats, horrors, imps, kids, littlies, monkeys, nippers, perishers, pipsqueaks, rug-rats, scone-gropers, terrors, toddlers, tots, youngies and whipper-snappers.

cab
taxi cab.
See also:
first cab off the rank

cabbage
1. paper money.
2. dull-witted person; person with no ambition or incentive.

cabbage patch
pertaining to Victoria — people from N.S.W. refer to Victoria as the 'cabbage patch' because of its small size.

cabbie
taxi-driver.

caboodle
all; the whole lot (also: the whole kit and caboodle) : e.g. When we were robbed they didn't just take a few things but the whole kit and caboodle.

cack
1. faeces; shit.
2. any muck and filth.
3. to defecate: e.g. Did you cack your pants?

cacked (one's) pants
1. became suddenly upset, angry, frightened or emotional as a result of some news or incident.
2. to be taken aback.

cack-handed
1. clumsy with the hands.
2. left-handed.

cackleberry
an egg.

cactus
1. ruined; spoiled; wrecked: e.g. Hubby had a go at fixing the car and it's really cactus now.
2. dead.
See also:
in the cactus

caff
cafeteria.

cagey
secretive; sly; wary.

cahoots
(in . . . with) partnership; dealing with; in close association with, often with illegal and clandestine intentions: e.g. I think he makes so much money because he's in cahoots with criminals.

cake
(see: can't have your cake and eat it; have one's cake and eat it; icing on the cake; piece of cake; slice of the cake; take the cake)

cake-hole
the mouth.

calculating bastard/bitch
scheming; two-timing; shrewd.

call
1. telephone conversation.
2. the act of telephoning: e.g. I'll give you a call tomorrow.
3. short visit or stopover: e.g. I'll call in tomorrow.
4. to broadcast a description of a horse or dog race.

call a spade a spade/ fucking shovel
speak bluntly; be honest.

call it a day
finish what is being done, either permanently or temporarily; stop work: e.g. It's time to call it a day and go to the pub.

call it quits
1. stop work.
2. break off a relationship.

call of nature
the need to urinate or defecate.

call off
stop; cancel; postpone: e.g. We had to call off the barbecue because of the rain.

call (someone's) bluff
to challenge, reveal (someone's) deceptive display of confidence.

call the shots/tune
be in charge; lead; be in authority; make the decisions: e.g. He calls the shots around here so we just have to do as he says.

called up
summoned to compulsory military service.

callgirl
prostitute.

calling card
mark or sign left behind, the owner of which is clearly recognisable: e.g. I know the cat was inside the house because it left its calling card on my nice clean carpet!

came in by the back door
entered into by using clandestine or underhanded tactics: e.g. He came in by the back door to become a politician.

came out like a shower of shit
very fast.

came over on the boat with Noah
pertaining to a very old person or thing.

For other entries beginning with 'came' see entries listed under 'come'.

camera-shy
embarrassed or unwilling to be photographed.

camp
1. (of a man) effeminate in nature; homosexual; (of a woman) lesbian.
2. group of people who share the same beliefs, doctrines etc.: e.g. The problem hasn't been solved yet as the council has split into two camps that argue at every meeting.
3. sleep: e.g. I'll camp on the sofa for the night.

camp as a row of tents
very obviously homosexual.

camp follower
person who follows but is not officially connected with a band, famous person, political group etc.

camp it up
display effeminate, homosexual mannerisms in an ostentatious way.

can
1. prison: e.g. He's in the can for murder.
2. toilet: e.g. I need to go to the can.
3. buttocks; bum.
4. to dismiss unfavourably; ridicule: e.g. My book got canned by the critics.
See also:
carry the can
in the can

can do
affirmative reply to a request.

can it!
be quiet! shut up!

can of worms
1. troublesome situation fraught with difficulties and problems.
2. (of a person) inability to be still and quiet.

can take it or leave it
an expression of indifference: e.g. As far as drinking is concerned, I can take it or leave it.

can you beat that?!
exclamation of astonishment, wonder, exasperation.

cancer stick
cigarette.

candidate
a likely prospect or subject: e.g. He's a candidate for cancer if he smokes three packets of fags a day.

candle
(see: burning the candle at both ends; like a candle in the wind)

candy
(see: like taking candy from a baby)

candy man
drug pusher, seller, especially to children and teenagers.

caning
1. a beating; physical attack: e.g. My dog got a real caning from the neighbour's Alsatian.
2. harsh rebuff or verbal abuse: e.g. The headmaster gave the boys a caning for their misbehaviour.
3. rough treatment; abuse: e.g. My son gives the car such a caning when he drives that I won't let him use it any more.
4. a sound defeating: e.g. Our team got a caning in the finals.

canned
1. drunk; intoxicated: e.g. He really got canned with the boys at the pub last night!
2. ridiculed; excluded; severely criticised: e.g. The critics canned my new book.

canned audience/laughter
pre-recorded; superimposed; not live.

cannonball run
an illegal and unauthorised car race through part of a country.

canoodle
indulge in sexual fondling and petting.

can't abide
cannot tolerate: e.g. I can't abide politics.

can't come at (something)
unwillingness to do or to participate or become involved in a particular activity: e.g. I've tried but I simply can't come at eating natural oysters.

can't find the handle
(Australian Rules football) can't pick up the ball.

can't get a word in edgeways
inability to speak over a voluble person or conversation: e.g. When his mother comes to visit I can't get a word in edgeways.

can't get blood out of a stone
cannot extract something (usually a moral quality) from someone/something that does not possess it in the first place: e.g. I knew it was too much to expect generosity from that old miser with his money — you can't get blood out of a stone!

can't get it up
(of a man) inability to have an erection of the penis.

can't grow grass on a busy street
stock answer for baldness.

can't hack the pace
inability to keep up with the task at hand: e.g. I'm not going to any more wild late-night parties — I can't hack the pace.

can't handle (someone/something)
to dislike (someone/something) intensely: e.g. I can't handle those two creeps!

can't have it both ways

can't have your cake and eat it too
pertaining to the necessity of having to make a choice between two equally desired but opposing options.

can't judge a book by its cover
one cannot make a valid assessment of a situation, person etc. simply from the often deceptive, outward appearances.

can't put one over (someone)
can't deceive, trick or fool (someone).

can't run with the hare and hunt with the hounds
(see: can't have it both ways)

can't see for looking
pertaining to the inability to see the obvious: e.g. The keys are exactly where I told you they were — you can't see for looking!

can't see past (one's) own nose
pertaining to the inability to see the obvious; an unwillingness to accept another's point of view: e.g. He can't see past his own nose so it's no use asking him for advice.

can't see the grass for the trees

can't see the trees for the forest

can't see the wood for the trees
to lack insight; able only to see, perceive or understand the less important detail, not the overall design etc. or the key facts.

can't stomach (someone/something)
detest; hate; despise.

can't take a joke
to be unable to see the humour.

can't take a trick
to be habitually unlucky.

can't take (someone) anywhere!
jocular remark to/about someone who has done something embarrassing or made a social blunder in public.

can't teach an old dog new tricks
pertaining to the generalisation that the older a person is, the more set in his ways he will be, and therefore the more difficult it will be for him to accept new ideas, methods or practices.

can't tell a book by its cover
(see: can't judge a book by its cover)

can't wear (someone/something) any more
can't abide, tolerate or put up with (someone/something): e.g. He came home drunk so often that I couldn't wear it any more, so I left him.

can't win!
exclamation of frustration over the fact that no matter what one does, it is unsatisfactory or wrong.

can't you understand plain English?!
exclamation of frustration over someone's inability to understand clearly what you have said.

For other possible entries beginning with 'can't' see entries listed under 'couldn't'.

Canuck
a Canadian (esp. French).

cap and gown
academic dress.

cap in hand
1. humbly: e.g. He went cap in hand to apologise.
2. obsequiously; in a fawning manner.

cap it off
finish; complete to perfection: e.g. I capped the meal off with a serving of Irish coffee and mints.

caper
1. activity; occupation: e.g. What caper is he in?
2. trick; deceitful action: e.g. I don't know what caper he's up to but I don't trust him.

capitalist
an accusation that someone has too much money and too much interest in making it.

cappo
(see: capitalist)

captain/Captain Cook
(rhyming slang) look: e.g. Have a captain at this!

Caramellos
Brisbane VFL football team (the Bears).

carbie
carburettor. (also: carby)

carboholic
person addicted to food high in carbohydrates.

carbon copy
(of a person) a duplicate in looks and mannerisms.

carby
(see: carbie)

carcass
person's body (not necessarily dead): e.g. Don't park your carcass on my clean bed!
See also:
shift (one's) carcass

card
likeable, funny, amusing person.
See also:
calling card
have/got a card up (one's) sleeve
lay (one's) cards down
lay (one's) cards on the table
on the cards
play (one's) cards close to (one's) chest
play (one's) cards right
put (one's) cards on the table
queer card

cardie
cardigan.

cards stacked against (one)
(to have the . . .) to have the odds against (one); to have a lot of opposition.

cardsharp
1. professional cheat at card games.
2. one with a passion for card games.

care
(see: couldn't care less; don't care a hoot)

care of
to the address of: e.g. Send it care of the business.

cark (it)
1. die: e.g. The old man carked it last night.
2. (of machinery etc.) break down; fail: e.g. Our lawn-mower finally carked.

carn!
come on! (sporting enthusiasts' cry): e.g. Carn the Roos! Carn ya mugs!

carnie
1. carnival.
2. a carnival worker.

carpet
to severely berate, criticise, chastise: e.g. The newspapers are going to carpet him for what he said.
See also:
on the carpet
red carpet

carpet burns
evidence of sexual activity, usually chafe marks on pertinent parts of the body such as elbows, knees, spine.

carpet grubs
children, especialy small babies.

carried away
behaved in an unconventional, out-of-character manner; swept into action beyond reason: e.g. She got a bit carried away and made a fool of herself after too much to drink.
See also:
get carried away

carried out feet first
1. to have died.
2. to have been soundly defeated.

carrot
anything that is a means of enticement: e.g. The carrot they dangled under his nose was the promise of a fortune far beyond his ordinary means.

carry a lot of weight
bear a great deal of responsibility or influence: e.g. He'd be the best person to go to for help as he carries a lot of weight in the organisation.

carry a torch (for someone)
to have (especially unreturned) love, admiration or infatuation for (someone).

carry on
1. behave in a foolish manner: e.g. Stop carrying on and get on with the job.
2. pet; fondle; flirt; indulge in sexual activity: e.g. They carried on in the back seat of the car all through the movie.

carry on like a pork chop
behave in a foolish manner.

carry (someone) on (one's) back
bear the burden of responsibility for (someone): e.g. You can't be expected to carry your children on your back forever.

carry (something) off
1. trick; act out a deception successfully.
2. handle a potentially difficult situation well; face consequences boldly.

carry the can
bear the responsibility; do the dirty work.

carry the day
be successful, triumphant.

carry the weight
(see: carry a lot of weight)

carry weight
have influence or importance: e.g. His suggestions always carry weight with the board of directors.

carrying
pregnant: e.g. Is she carrying again?

carryings-on/carry-on
foolish behaviour or events.

cart
to carry something with difficulty: e.g. You don't expect me to cart that log away by myself?
See also:
horse and cart
put the cart before the horse

carved up
1. soundly defeated, beaten: e.g. Our team got carved up in the finals of the season.
2. (of an estate, profits etc.) shared; distributed: e.g. His estate was carved up among his relatives when he died.

cas
casualty ward of a hospital.

case
unusual, peculiar, queer or hardened person: e.g. She's a weird case.
See also:
bad case
bad case of the trots
basket case
cot case
get off (one's) case
hard case
open-and-shut case

case (the joint)
1. to look over, survey, any premises prior to a crime.
2. to investigate a night club, party etc. for suitability or possible entry.

cash and carry
pertaining to a large supermarket — often a wholesaler to the trade only.

cash in hand
money paid to a worker in cash rather than by cheque or through the business records.

cash in on
gain profit or advantage from: e.g. Many astute people cashed in on the real-estate boom of the 1970s.

cash in (one's) chips
to die.

cash to splash
plenty of money.

cashback
the dubious offer of a discount in the form of money from a retailer.

cashed up
having plenty of money.

cask
wine packaged in an air-tight bag inside a cardboard box with a special tap for pouring.

Casket
(the Golden . . .) Queensland lottery.

cast from the same mould
alike, similar (often derogatory, referring to bad character).

cast the first stone
initiate, begin (particular rumour or nasty gossip).

cast-iron
strong; inflexible; sound (as of an alibi): e.g. 1. The witness has a cast-iron alibi. 2. He must have a cast-iron gut to eat that rubbish!

castles in the air
daydreaming; unrealistic ideas or notions: e.g. The Mayor is building castles in the air if he thinks the public will accept that proposal.

castrate
(of women) to deprive a man of his self-esteem and pride.

cat
1. spiteful, bitchy, malicious woman.
2. term for a person (especially in the jargon of musicians).
3. a catamaran.
4. a cat-o'-nine tails whip.
See also:
busy as a one-eyed cat watching two rat holes
by a cat's whisker
cat's pyjamas/whiskers
curiosity killed the cat
fat cat
fight like Kilkenny cats
flog the cat
fraidy-cat
game of cat and mouse
go like a cut cat
grin like a Cheshire cat
have/got too much of what the cat licks itself with
hellcat
innocent as a cat in a goldfish bowl
kick the cat
let the cat out of the bag
like a cat on a hot stove/tin roof
like a scalded cat
look what the cat dragged in!
looks like something the cat dragged in
looks like the cat that swallowed the mouse
mean as cat shit
nervous as a long-tailed cat in a room of rocking-chairs
no room to swing a cat
raining cats and dogs
scaredy-cat
set the cat among the pigeons
there are more ways of killing a cat than by drowning it
there are more ways than one to skin a cat
thinks he's/she's the cat's whiskers

weak as cat's piss
while the cat's away the mice will play
whip the cat
who's milking this cat!
wildcat
wildcat strike

cat got your tongue?
question directed at someone who refuses to speak.

cat-and-dog
pertaining to hostility and frequent quarrelling.

cat-and-mouse game
psychological manoeuvring between opponents in which one has the upper hand.

catcalling
heckling and interrupting to express disapproval.

catch
1. anybody considered to be a worthwhile proposition for marriage: e.g. He's a good catch for her.
2. a scheme or trick; a difficulty; hidden trap or problem: e.g. It sounds too good to be true — what's the catch?

catch as catch can
make do under the circumstances.

catch forty winks
have a nap, short restful sleep.

catch it
receive a severe scolding, berating, punishment.

catch on
1. understand; grasp the meaning of: e.g. He didn't catch on to a single thing that was said.
2. become popular, trendy.

catch (someone's) eye
gain (someone's) attention through eye contact.

catch 22
a no-win situation.

catch up on
1. revise; study; refamiliarise oneself.
2. make up arrears: e.g. I have to catch up on some sleep.

catch up with (someone)
1. pay (someone) a debt.
2. pursue for the purpose of exacting revenge: e.g. I'll catch up with him sooner or later and then he'll be sorry.

catch you later
form of farewell.

For other possible entries beginning with 'catch' see entries listed under 'caught'.

catching
1. infectious; contagious.
2. captivating; alluring.

catching flies
yawning; asleep with one's mouth wide open.

catchy
1. contagious.
2. easily remembered, as in a tune or jingle.

catfight
fight or argument between women.

cathouse
a brothel.

catnap
short, light sleep.

Cats
Geelong VFL football team.

cat's pyjamas/whiskers
(the . . .) terrific; great; excellent: e.g. He thinks he's the cat's whiskers.

cattle duffing
poaching; illegal theft and trading in the cattle industry.

cattle-tick
(derog.) a Catholic.

catty
malicious and spiteful (particularly of women).

caught between the devil and the deep blue sea
faced with having to choose between two equally distasteful alternatives.

caught in the act
1. discovered in the act of having sexual intercourse, or some other sexual act: e.g. Her husband caught her in the act and gave them both a beating.
2. discovered in the act of doing something incriminating.

caught it
1. got a severe beating or scolding: e.g. I really caught it from Dad when I got home so late.
2. got killed.

caught napping
1. suddenly found in a situation where one is at a disadvantage.
2. suddenly found being lazy or shirking one's duty.

caught off guard
at a disadvantage.

caught out/red-handed
surprised; found out; discovered in the act of doing something incriminating.

caught short
to be suddenly in a situation of lacking something such as money: e.g. I was caught short at the supermarket and had to return all the groceries I couldn't pay for.

caught the bug
1. became infected with a virus, cold, flu etc.
2. became very enthusiastic about a particular thing: e.g. I've caught the gambling bug.

caught the wog
became infected with a virus, cold, flu etc.

caught with (one's) hand in the till
discovered in the act of stealing money, embezzling funds etc.

caught with (one's) pants down
1. discovered in the act of doing something incriminating.
2. to be suddenly in a situation where one is at a disadvantage.

For other possible entries beginning with 'caught' see entries listed under 'catch'.

caulie
cauliflower.

cauliflower ears
ears that are deformed, particularly with reference to boxers.

cause a stir
create a disturbance, argument, trouble, sensation.

cavalry
help that arrives just in time.

cave in
to submit, yield to pressure.

CB radio
citizen's-band radio

cement shoes
(joc.) the means by which a criminal or murderer disposes of a body, cement shoes being a block of concrete set around the body's feet to create sufficient weight to drag the body to the bottom of a river, lake etc.

Centre
(the . . .) Central Australia.

cert
a certainty (especially in horse-racing): e.g. The grey's a cert to win tomorrow.

cesspool
any filthy or degenerate place, town etc.

chaff
money.

chaff-cutter
any vehicle that has an excessively or strangely noisy motor, such as a Volkswagon.

chafing at the bit
impatient; irritated.

chain around (one's) neck
anything that restricts, restrains or holds (one) back.

chained to (one's) desk
confined to tedious office-type procedure or work.

chained to the kitchen sink
(of women) confined to home and the tedious chores of house-work.

chain-smoker
person who continually smokes one cigarette after the other.

chairbound
having an office-type job rather than active, outdoors work.

chalk and cheese
(see: like chalk and cheese)

chalk up
1. score: e.g. Our team chalked up enough runs to win.
2. attribute to: e.g. That failure can be chalked up to inexperience.

chalkie
school-teacher.

chamber of horrors
any place that inspires horror or distaste.

champ
champion.

champ at the bit
be impatient, anxious to start.

champagne tastes on a beer income
extravagant desires and expenses that go far beyond one's means.

champers
champagne.

chance of a lifetime
the best opportunity you may ever get: e.g. Securing that job was the chance of a lifetime.

chance (one's) arm
take a risk.

chancy
risky; uncertain.

change
1. coins as opposed to notes.
2. dress oneself, usually into better clothes than what one is wearing: e.g. I'll shower and change when I get there.
See also:
a change is as good as a holiday

change hands
pass from one owner to another: e.g. The house changed hands.

change horses in mid-stream
alter one's course of action after the start; reverse one's allegiances, beliefs etc.

change of life
menopause in women.

change (one's) colours
reverse (one's) allegiances, beliefs, opinions etc.

change (one's) spots
alter (one's) basic personality, opinions etc.

change (one's) tune
modify or alter (one's) attitude or argument to a more humble one; to change (one's) allegiance.

chap/chappie
fellow; person.

character
an interesting, odd or eccentric person, usually well known: e.g. Old Fred's a real character.
See also:
out of character

charge
1. an alcoholic drink: e.g. I need a charge after all that work.
2. a thrill, high feeling of elation; kick: e.g. That drink gave me a real charge.

charge like a bull at a gate
act impetuously without thought in a rushed manner.

charge like a wounded bull

charge the earth
set prices that are excessive.

chariot
(joc.) a car.

charlie
girl; woman: e.g. Who's that nice-looking charlie over there?

charlies
breasts; boobs; tits.

charm the pants off (someone)
delight, please (someone) greatly.

charming!
statement uttered to show one's displeasure.

charts
current list of the most popular musical hits: e.g. That song went up the charts in a matter of days to become number one.

chase after (someone)
pursue a potential romantic interest: e.g. She's been chasing after him for years.

chase out a chocolate monster
to defecate.

chase up
obtain; locate; get: e.g. I need to go to the library to chase up a few books I need.

chaser
light drink (of water or beer) after a strong spirit.

chasing (one's) own tail
pursuing a course of action that gets (one) nowhere.

chasing the dollar
expending all one's time and energy in pursuit of money.

chassis
(of a woman) body; figure.

chasy
children's game of tag.

chat
slovenly person, woman.

chat (someone) up
1. talk to (someone) convincingly in order to get one's way: e.g. I'll chat the boss up at the party for a raise in salary.
2. flirt with (someone) with the aim of developing a romantic situation: e.g. Let's go out on the town and chat up some nice sorts.

chatterbox
very talkative person; a gossip.

chauvinistic pig
(of a man) excessively loyal to other men and displaying no respect for women (not to be confused with homosexuality).

cheap
(of a woman) vulgar; of low morals: e.g. She's nothing but a cheap tart.
See also:
dirt cheap
on the cheap

cheap and nasty
of poor and inferior quality; vulgar; imitation.

cheap as dirt
1. (of a woman) of low morals; vulgar; promiscuous.
2. inexpensive; at a bargain price.
3. anything of inferior quality; vulgar.

cheap at half the price
expression of satisfaction over the cost of something.

cheap drunk
person easily intoxicated after a small amount of alcohol.

cheapen
degrade.

cheapie
1. inexpensive item; a bargain.
2. inexpensive and inferior item.

cheapjack
shoddy; inferior; second-rate.

cheapskate
a mean, parsimonious person.

cheat on (someone)
to be sexually unfaithful to one's partner.

check
look at with interest, close scrutiny: e.g. Check the purple, spiky hair on that guy!

check it out
look into; investigate: e.g. I'd like to check it out before I have anything to do with it.

check you later
form of farewell; good-bye.

checking (one's) eyelids for holes
sleeping; having a nap.

checkout chick
cash-register operator at a supermarket, store.

cheeks
buttocks; bum.
See also:
tongue-in-cheek
turn the other cheek
with (one's) tongue in (one's) cheek

cheeky
impudent; brazen; audacious; rude.

cheer up
make or become happier.

cheerio
1. form of farewell; good-bye.
2. greeting sent to someone over the radio or television talk show.
3. small party sausage, saveloy.

cheers
salute to good health, usually with glass of alcohol held high.

cheese
(see: hard cheese; like chalk and cheese; old cheese; stiff cheese)

cheese and kisses
wife.

cheesecake
display of attractive female bodies in magazines, advertisements etc. with emphasis on sex-appeal.

cheesed off
annoyed; exasperated; bored.

cheesy grin
artificial or contrived smile.

chemistry
favourable interaction between two people; close relationship.

chequered career
varied personal history (sometimes with overtones of shadiness); life of ups and downs.

cherry
1. female pudendum, vagina; pertaining to virginity: e.g. 1. He plucked my cherry when I was sixteen. 2. I'd like to have a bite at her cherry.
2. pertaining to a profitable enterprise or opportunity: e.g. The real-estate market has been booming and everybody has been having a bite at the cherry while the going's good.
See also:
bite at the cherry
pluck (someone's) cherry
two bites at the cherry

cherrypicker
(joc.) a large nose.

chest
breasts: e.g. She's got a big chest.
See also:
get it off (one's) chest

chesty
1. (of women) having large breasts.
2. (of men) having a large chest.
3. suffering from a cold virus in the chest.

chevvy
Chevrolet (model of car).

chew and spew
1. any cheap cafe or restaurant serving take-away or fast-foods: e.g. We're eating at the local chew and spew tonight.
2. take-away food; fast-food; junk food.

chew it over

chew on it
discuss; work it out; think seriously about: e.g. I'll chew it over tonight and give you an answer tomorrow.

chew (someone's) ear
1. detain (someone) by talking at length; bore with incessant talk.
2. scold, reprimand, berate (someone).
3. cadge, borrow money from (someone).

chew (someone) out
scold, reprimand, berate, admonish (someone): e.g. Boy! Did I just get chewed out by the boss!

chew the arse off (someone)
1. severely scold, reprimand (someone).
2. beat (someone) up; assault, bash (someone).

chew the arse out of a rag doll

chew the crutch out of an Afghan camel-driver's jocks
to be extremely hungry: e.g. I'm so hungry I could chew the arse out of a rag doll.

chew the cud
reflect upon; think about; meditate upon.

chew the fat
talk; discuss; chat; gossip.

chew the rag
1. (see: chew the fat)
2. argue; brood; grieve.

chewie/chewy
1. chewing-gum: e.g. We used to stick our chewy under the desks at school.
2. tough eating: e.g. That steak was a bit chewy.

chewie on yer boot!
(Australian Rules football) expression shouted by barrackers to put off a footballer about to kick for goal.

chick
1. girl; girlfriend.
2. smart; fashionable.
See also:
pull a chick

chicken
1. a coward: e.g. I'm such a chicken when it comes to flying in small planes.
2. afraid; scared: e.g. He won't do it — he's too chicken.
See also:
don't count your chickens before they're hatched
play chicken
spring chicken

chicken out
withdraw, retire through cowardice, fear, tiredness etc.

chickenfeed
1. meagre, small amount of money: e.g. My pay is

chickenfeed compared to yours.
2. anything insignificant.

chicken-hearted/livered
cowardly; fearful; timid; apprehensive.

chickenshit
1. contemptible, unworthy person.
2. nonsense; rubbish; worthless talk.
3. nothing; nought; not much at all: e.g. He knows chickenshit about computers.

chief
the boss; leader: e.g. I asked the chief for a raise last week.
See also:
too many chiefs and not enough Indians

chief cook and bottle-washer
one who is not only in charge but does most of the manual labour as well.

children should be seen and not heard
catch-phrase used by an adult who is annoyed, irritated or interrupted by noisy children.

child's play
any easy or simple task.

chilled to the bone
1. very cold.
2. depressed; dispirited.

chiller
horror movie.

chime in
interrupt a conversation, especially to agree.

chin
(see: keep one's chin up; take it on the chin)

china
(rhyming slang: china plate — mate) mate, friend.

China syndrome
melting-down point of a nuclear reactor.

Chinaman's luck
uncanny or habitual good luck or fortune.

chin-chin
1. form of farewell; good-bye.
2. toast, salute drink to someone's good health.

chine
mate, pal, friend (from rhyming slang: china).

Chinese brothel
very untidy, dirty room or place of abode.
See also:
looks like a Chinese brothel (on a Sunday morning)

Chinese burn
the twisting of the skin on the forearm to cause a burning pain.

Chinese puzzle
anything difficult, tricky or complicated.

Chink
a Chinese person; Chinese.

chink in (one's) armour
vulnerable, weak spot or failing.

chinless wonder
person of weak character.

chin-up!
exclamation of encouragement.

chinwagger
gossip; person who talks too much and at length.

chinwagging
gossip; a lot of talk.

chip
piece of dried cow dung.
See also:
blue-chip

chip in
1. help; contribute; donate: e.g. They're passing the hat around for everyone to chip in for a going-away present for her.
2. interrupt; butt into a conversation.

chip off the old block
just like one's father or mother; person who has inherited marked characteristics from parents.

chip on (one's) shoulder
(to have a . . .) a grudge or grievance.

chip-chip
good-bye.

chipper
(see: looking chipper)

chippie
carpenter.

chips
money.
See also:
cash in (one's) chips
had (one's) chips
in the chips
shy of chips
spitting chips
when the chips are down

chirp up!
cheer up!

chirpy
happy; lively; cheerful.

chisel
cheat; defraud; swindle; trick: e.g. I've been chiselled by that car dealer.

chisel (one's) way in
win over through trickery, flattery or deceit.

chiseller
swindler; fraud; crook; cheat.

chit-chat
idle chatter; gossip; small talk.

chock of
fed up with; annoyed, irritated with: e.g. I'm chock of all this mess around the place!

chock-a-block/chockers
1. full; crowded; crammed in; packed: e.g. The local pub was chock-a-block last night.
2. intoxicated; drunk: e.g. My Dad got chockers at the pub last night.

chock-full
completely full; packed.

chockie bickies
chocolate biscuits.

chockies
chocolates.

chocko
(derog.) a dark-skinned person.

chocolate bandit
a male homosexual.

choice
vulgar; obscene: e.g. His language is a bit choice when he's had a few drinks.

choke a darkie
to defecate.

choked up
overcome with emotion: e.g. The boy was terribly choked up over the loss of his dog.
See also:
all choked up

chomp into
bite into; eat.

chompers
teeth.

choo-choo
baby talk for train.

choof off
depart; leave; go.

chook
1. a domestic fowl.
2. derogatory term for a woman; silly woman.
See also:
feed the chooks
have/got a face like a chook's bum
like a chook with its head cut off
may your chooks turn into emus . . .
nosey enough to want to know the ins and outs of a chook's bum

choom
an Englishman, used especially when addressing one.

choong
an example of onomatopoeia, denoting a swift action or sound: e.g. All of a sudden this thing went choong! and flew off.

choose
(see: you can choose your friends but you can't choose your relatives)

choosy
fastidious; fussy; hard to please.

chop
1. dismissal; the sack: e.g. My husband got the chop from work.
2. to dismiss; fire: e.g. I'm going to give him the chop.
See also:
carry on like a pork chop
get in for (one's) chop
in for (one's) chop
not much chop
rotten as a chop

chop and change
to change repeatedly.

chop-chop!
hurry up!

chopper
1. helicopter.
2. motorcycle — usually modified.

choppers
teeth.

chops
mouth: e.g. He needs a belt in the chops.
See also:
licking (one's) chops
slobber-chops

chosen
destined to be saved by God.

chow
1. a Chinese person; Chinese.
2. food: e.g. This chow is really good.

chow tucker
Chinese food.

Chrissie
Christmas.

Christ!

Christ almighty!
exclamation of frustration, annoyance, anger, wonder etc.

Christ help us (all)
exclamation of frustration, anger, despair.

christen
make use of for the first time, often in a grand manner: e.g. We've invited some people over to help us christen the new pool.
See also:
like a moll at a christening
serious as a whore at a christening

Christmas
(see: all one's Christmases have come at once; done up like a Christmas tree; lit up like a Christmas tree; thinks he's Christmas; what else did you get for Christmas?)

Christmas hold
handful of testicles, especially in a brawl or hold.

chrome dome
a bald man.

chromo
a prostitute.

chronic
terrible; bad; severe: e.g. I've got a chronic case of the munchies.

chuck
1. vomit: e.g. He chucked all over the place.
2. throw: e.g. You can chuck those things out.
3. to perform or do something with speed, force or flamboyance: e.g. Chuck a U-ie.

chuck a lefty
turn left (usually in a vehicle).

chuck a mental
display sudden anger.

chuck a seven
to die. (see: throw a seven)

chuck a spas
display sudden anger.

chuck a U-ie
turn around and go in the other direction (in a car).

chuck a willie/wobbly
(also: willy) display sudden anger.

chuck in
1. donate money to a cause; contribute to the cause of: e.g. We'll all chuck in ten dollars for some booze.
2. resign from: e.g. He chucked in his job and went overseas.

chuck it in
stop; give up; resign: e.g. I think I'll chuck it in for the day.

chuck off at (someone)
criticise (someone).

chuck (one's) weight around
bully; forcefully interfere; use (one's) influence or power unwelcomely.

chuck out
discard; throw away: e.g. What you don't want to take I'm going to chuck out.

chuck (someone) out
forcibly evict (someone).

chuck us
give me: e.g. Chuck us that hammer please.

chucker-outer
bouncer; person employed to evict troublemakers.

chucklehead
foolish or stupid person.

chuff off
go; depart.

chuffed
pleased; delighted.

chuffnuckle
affectionate name for a fool, friend.

chug-a-lug
1. encouragement to drink up.
2. hurry along.

chugging along
progressing slowly but surely.

chum
friend; mate.

chum up to (someone)
behave obsequiously towards (someone).

chum up with
strike up a friendship with.

chummy
sociable; intimately friendly.

chump
fool; dolt; idiot; pushover.

chunder
1. vomit.
2. to vomit.

chunderous
awful; horrible; unpleasant.

chunder room
toilet.

churn out
produce in quantity without regard to quality.

churned up
upset; anxious; agitated: e.g. He's churned up about the loss of his pet dog.

chute
a parachute.
See also:
in the chute

chuttie/chutty
chewing-gum.

chutzpah
impudence; gall.

ciao
good-bye; hello.

ciggie
cigarette.

cinch
certainty; sure or easy thing.

Cinderella
an ignored item; neglected or despised person.

circs
circumstances.

circulate
to move about and socialise with guests at a party or function.
See also:
out of circulation

circus
1. a rowdy, good time.
2. display of rowdy behaviour: e.g. The sale at Myer was a real circus as women fell over each other for the best bargains
3. a funny or entertaining person: e.g. He's a real circus when he's had a few drinks.
See also:
three-ring circus

cissy
(see: sissy)

city slicker
an ostentatious person well versed in the ways of city life.

cityite
city dweller; townie.

civvies
ordinary clothes as opposed to a uniform.

civvy
civilian.

clackers
teeth, especially false ones.

clagged out
1. tired; exhausted.
2. broken down; worn out; not functioning: e.g. My car's finally clagged out.

clagged the bag
1. ruined; broken; worn out.
2. dead; to have died.

clam
taciturn, silent person.
See also:
bearded clam

clam up
refuse to talk.

clamp down
become more strict: e.g. The police are going to clamp down on drunken driving.

clams
money: e.g. That's going to cost you a few clams!

clancy
any overflow, such as of water (from the poem 'Clancy of the Overflow', by A. B. Paterson).

clanger
a glaring or embarrassing mistake or remark: e.g. During his speech he dropped a real clanger.

clap
gonorrhoea; venereal disease: e.g. She's got the clap.

clap eyes on
catch sight of.

clapped in the clink
put into prison.

clapped out
1. broken down; in a state of disrepair; worn out: e.g. This car is clapped out.
2. tired; exhausted.

clappers
(see: go like the clappers)

claptrap
1. rubbish; nonsense; insincere talk.
2. car in a state of disrepair.

class
acceptable and approved style of manners, dress, behaviour; good style; elegance: e.g. He's got no class driving around in a bomb like that.

classy
acceptable; approved; elite; superior; stylish; elegant.

claws
fingers.

Claytons
any imitation, fraud, substitute. (Claytons is a non-alcoholic drink, and the company's advertising catch-phrase was: the drink you have when you're not having a drink)

Clayton's contract
a form of company tax-avoidance in which deals were made orally or by paying some form of deposit so there was no need to draw up documents which required the payment of stamp duty.

clean
1. virtuous; innocent; free from obscenity: e.g. She's not as clean as she makes out to be.
2. unarmed; without a weapon: e.g. The police frisked him and he was clean.
3. free from drug or alcohol addiction.
See also:
come clean
keep (one's) hands clean
keep the party clean!
squeaky-clean
take (someone) to the cleaners

clean as a nun's bum

clean as a whistle
1. extremely clean; tidy; neat.
2. (see: clean, 1.)

clean bill of health
assurance of good health, quality or condition: e.g. I took my car in for a check-up and it was given a clean bill of health.

clean fight
fight that is free of deplorable tactics.

clean forgot
to have forgotten entirely: e.g. I clean forgot about that meeting last night!

clean hands
free of guilt; a clear conscience: e.g. My hands are clean.

clean potato
law-abiding person free from guilt.
See also:
not the clean potato

clean slate
good record; having no criminal convictions; free from debt.

clean (someone) out
strip of all assets, money or possessions.

clean (someone) up
defeat soundly; beat by a large margin: e.g. 1. We cleaned up their team in the game last week. 2. He picked on the wrong bloke at the pub and got thoroughly cleaned up.

clean sweep
1. perfect execution of: e.g. We made a clean sweep of that job.
2. new, fresh start.

clean up
make large profits and gains: e.g. He really cleaned up in the lottery and now he's rich.

clean up (one's) own back yard
put (one's) own life and matters in order before (one) criticises other people.

clean up the dead wood
to get rid of the useless people in an enterprise, business or organisation.

clean-cut
wholesome; free from impropriety; neatly groomed.

cleaner-upper
a cleaner; person who has the job of tidying up after people.

clean-up
very large profit or gain.

clear
(see: in the clear)

clear as a bell
1. able to be heard perfectly.
2. able to be understood, comprehended perfectly.

clear as mud
confusing; not understood or comprehended.

clear off
go away; depart; disappear: e.g. I think we'd better clear off before the trouble starts.

clear (one's) name
to absolve (oneself) from guilt; prove (one's) innocence.

clear out
depart; go away: e.g. The tenants cleared out before they paid their bills.

clear the air
remove tension, anxiety, misunderstanding or ambiguity: e.g. The truth will clear the air once and for all.

clear the cobwebs
clear the head or mind of the effects of alcohol, drugs, sleep etc.; become lucid.

clear the decks
get ready for action.

clear-eyed
mentally acute; perceptive.

cleavage
the breasts; cleft or hollow between a woman's breasts.

clever
1. sly or cunning.
2. (sarcastically) not very smart or clever: e.g. That was clever of you — now look what you've done!

clever-dick
conceited, smug person.

click
1. fall into place; be understood: e.g. The identity of the murderer didn't click with the audience until the very end of the story.
2. form an immediate intimate or close relationship with: e.g. We clicked from the very first day we met.

clicks
kilometres. (also: klicks; k's)

clicky
(see: cliquey)

cliff-hanger
a contest so closely matched or a situation or story so suspenseful that the outcome is impossible to guess.

climax
orgasm.

climb down off (one's) perch
come down to earth and face reality.

climb mountains for
go to great lengths for; do anything for: e.g. She'd climb mountains for him but he treats her like dirt.

climb on the bandwagon
join the winning or most popular side; take advantage of a popular fashion or trend.

climb up the ladder
attempt to reach the successful top of the ranks in business or society.

climb up the wall
go mad, crazy with frustration, anger or irritation.

climber
person who strives to associate with and be like people socially superior.

clinging vine
person emotionally dependent on another.

clink
prison.

clip
the total amount of wool shorn in a season.

clip in the ear
sharp hit on the head.

clip (someone's) wings
restrain; restrict the freedom of.

clipjoint
nightclub or restaurant known for charging outrageous prices.

clipper
person or thing that is first-rate, classy, worthy of admiration.

cliquey
pertaining to a set or group of people with snobbish values or who are insular and unfriendly.

clit
clitoris.

cloak-and-dagger
pertaining to intrigue, suspense and espionage.

clobber
1. clothing or equipment: e.g. All my clobber is in the suitcase.
2. hit or bash severely: e.g. I'm going to clobber him.

clock
1. any piece of equipment with a dial for measuring, such as the speedometer of a car.
2. to hit, bash or strike: e.g. I'll clock you if you do that again!
See also:
against the clock
around the clock
like clockwork.

clock up
attain time, speed or distance: e.g. We clocked up quite a few kilometres on our first day.

clockwatcher
person who continually and impatiently checks the time.

clod
fool; stupid person.

clod-hoppers
1. foolish, clumsy people.
2. boots; footwear.
3. feet.

clog the works
hinder or encumber progress.

clonk
hit; strike; punch.

close
(see: too close for comfort)

close call
narrow escape.

close (one's) eyes to
refuse to see, understand or acknowledge: e.g. Many parents close their eyes to the misbehaviour of their children.

close shave
narrow escape.

close the tent flap
(joc.) shut the door.

close thing
narrow escape.

close to (one's) heart
dear to (one); something that means a great deal to (one).

close to the bone/knuckle
1. indecent; improper: e.g. That joke was a bit close to the bone.
2. (of a remark or statement) tactless; hurtful; uncomfortable revealing of the truth.

closed book
an item or matter that has been finished with and no longer to be discussed: e.g. As far as I am concerned that affair he had with her is a closed book.

closed mind
not open to suggestion; biased: e.g. My mother has such a closed mind when it comes to talking about sex.

closed shop
factory or business where permission to work or participate is restricted to members only: e.g. That gambling club is a closed shop.

close-down
strike or general stoppage of work.

close-fisted
miserly; mean; parsimonious.

close-knit
united and loyal: e.g. They're a very close-knit family.

closet
(see: come out of the closet; skeleton in the closet)

closet drinker
person who drinks alcohol in secret.

closet queen
a homosexual man who does not wish the fact to be made public.

closing time
the time when alcoholic drinks may no longer be legally sold in a pub or bar.

clot
fool; stupid person.

cloth
(see: cut from the same cloth; cut one's coat according to one's cloth)

clothes don't make the man
it's the inner qualities and not the outer trappings which determine the worth of a person.

clothes horse/peg
person who looks good and stylish in whatever is worn.

cloud
(see: every cloud has a silver lining; have/got one's head in the clouds; in cloudland; on cloud nine; under a cloud)

cloud the issue
attempt to confuse the real facts with irrelevant ones.

clouds on the horizon
trouble or problems on the way.

clout
influence; power; authority; importance: e.g. Ruth's got the clout to get things done properly.

clout down on
put a stop to; enforce restraints: e.g. The police are clouting down on drunken drivers.

clout in/on the earhole
a punch, hit in the ear or face.

clover
(see: four-leaf clover; in clover; rolling in clover)

clown
1. fool; idiot.
2. amusing or funny person.
3. rustic, unsophisticated person.

clown around
behave in a foolish manner; waste time with inconsequential activity.

club in
contribute one's share of expenses: e.g. If everyone clubbed in we wouldn't be in such a financial mess.

Club of Rome
the supposedly highly secret, international organisation composed of the richest and most powerful men in the world who actually control and manage world affairs.

clucky
feeling the maternal (or paternal) desire to have children.

clue (someone) in/up
give (someone) the facts; enlighten; explain.

clued-up
enlightened; informed.

clueless
stupid; ignorant.

cluey
extremely smart or intelligent; well-informed on a subject: e.g. He's pretty cluey about cars.

clumsy clot
awkward, fumbling person; maladroit.

clutch
(see: in someone's clutches)

clutch at straws
desperate and ineffectual attempts, measures, methods or resources: e.g. He's clutching at straws if he thinks those excuses are going to get him out of trouble.

coal to Newcastle
superfluous.

coast
make progress, act or do something with minimal exertion; aimlessly drift along; act without effort.

coast is clear
the danger is past; it is now safe.

coaster
aimless drifter; lazy person.

Coat-hanger
Sydney Harbour Bridge.

cobar
copper coins.

cobber
friend, mate, companion: e.g. Those two are the best of cobbers.

cobblers
1. testicles; balls.
2. nonsense, rubbish (especially in the phrase: load of old cobblers).

cock
1. penis.
2. friend; fellow; mate (usually: old cock).
3. nonsense; rubbish: e.g. That book is a lot of cock.
See also:
go off half-cocked
hands off cocks, on socks
hot cock
up and down like a honeymoon cock

cock a snook/snoot
to make a rude gesture of contempt with thumb to nose and fingers spread.

cock and bull
an incredible or unbelievable story; nonsense; rubbish: e.g. He tried to give me some cock and bull story about where he was last night.

cock up
ruin; spoil; make a mess of: e.g. You really cocked that up didn't you!

cock-a-doodle-do
the crow of a rooster; to crow.

cock-a-hoop
extremely elated, happy.

cockatoo
a sentry posted to keep watch during any illegal activity.

cockatoo gate
any rough make-shift fence or gate made of logs, branches etc.

cock-eyed
1. squinting; cross-eyed.
2. absurd; stupid; unbelievable; ridiculous: e.g. His plan to make a million is cock-eyed.
3. lopsided; askew; unbalanced; irregular: e.g. That beam on the roof looks a bit cock-eyed to me.
4. drunk; intoxicated: e.g. My old man got cock-eyed at the pub.

cockeyed bob
a storm. (W.A.)

cockie
1. cockroach.
2. (see: cocky)

cockles of the heart
innermost feelings and emotions: e.g. That movie warmed the cockles of my heart.

cocksucker
1. an obsequious, servile person; a crawler.
2. a homosexual man.

cock-sure
over-confident.

cock-teaser
woman who teases and leads men on sexually without submitting to the act of having sex.

cock-up
mess; failure; fiasco.

cocky
1. cockroach.
2. cockatoo.
3. a farmer: e.g. cow-cocky, wheat-cocky.
4. brash; cheeky; conceited; self-assertive.
See also:
boss-cocky
dip your left eye in hot cocky shit
mouth feels like the bottom of a cocky's cage

cocky's joy
golden syrup; treacle.

codger
1. fellow; chap.
2. mean, miserly or stingy person.
3. odd, eccentric or peculiar person.

cods
testicles; balls; scrotum.

codswallop
nonsense; rubbish: e.g. That's a load of old codswallop!

co-ed
co-educational.

coffin-nail
cigarette.

cog
an insignificant person in a large organisation.

coin a phrase
to use an acknowledged or hackneyed expression or cliche.

coin it
to make a lot of money quickly.

coit
bum; anus. (also: quoit)

coitus interruptus
avoiding conception by the withdrawal of the

penis before orgasm or ejaculation.

coke
1. (caps) Coca-Cola. (Trademark)
2. cocaine.

cold
(see: couldn't catch a cold; go cold on; in cold blood; in the cold; leave one cold; left cold; left out in the cold; out cold; throw cold water on)

cold as a witch's tit

cold as ice
1. very cold.
2. devoid of emotion, sympathy or affection.

cold comfort
almost no comfort or consolation at all.

cold enough to freeze the balls off a brass monkey
pertaining to very cold weather conditions.

cold feet
loss of nerve or courage: e.g. I always get cold feet when it comes to flying in small planes.

cold hard truth
the real facts.

cold reception
unfriendly greeting or attitude: e.g. I got a cold reception from the boss when I asked for a raise.

cold shoulder
deliberately unfriendly behaviour; to ignore: e.g. If he comes near me again I'm going to give him the cold shoulder.

cold turkey
1. blunt or candid comment or procedure.
2. sudden withdrawal of drugs as treatment for addiction.

cold-blooded
cruel; heartless; callous.

cold-hearted
lacking in sympathy; mean; unkind.

coldie
cold glass, can or bottle of beer.

collar
1. take over; monopolise: e.g. Organised crime syndicates have collared the market in hard drugs and prostitution.
2. take, especially without permission.
3. seize; detain (someone).
See also:
blue-collar
hot under the collar
white-collar

collect
1. win a bet, lottery or prize: e.g. I'd love to collect in the pools and become an instant millionaire.
2. smash into, collide with (especially in a motor vehicle): e.g. He backed his Mercedes down the narrow drive and collected the fence.

collect dust
lie idle and gather dirt through neglect: e.g. His model ships have been collecting dust since he became interested in other things.

college
prison.
See also:
Bluestone College

Collingwood six-footer
a 5 foot 11 inch Australian Rules footballer.

Collins Street farmer
Victorian business-man living in the city and having farming interests, usually as a tax dodge.

collywobbles
1. apprehensive feeling.
2. stomach-ache.

colossal
wonderful; splendid.

colour
(see: change one's colours; come through with flying colours; fly under false colours; horse of another colour; off-colour; show one's true colours)

colourful yawn
vomit; to vomit.

come
1. to have an orgasm: e.g. Did you come?
2. semen: e.g. The sheets are covered with come.
3. behave like: e.g. Don't come the idiot with me!
See also:
as . . . as they come
easy come, easy go

come a buster
1. fail, often due to misfortune rather than mismanagement.
2. fail due to shady or underhanded dealings.

come a clanger
fail; make an embarrassing blunder.

come a cropper/gutser
1. fall heavily and clumsily: e.g. He came a cropper on the slippery path and broke his ankle.
2. suddenly fail; be struck by sudden misfortune: e.g. He's going to come a cropper if he keeps investing money in that business.
3. have one's carefully laid plans fail.

come a stumer
suffer a major set-back, failure, especially financial.

come across
1. be understood; communicate successfully: e.g. His speech was so full of gobbledegook that it didn't come across.
2. own up or admit to something; pay up: e.g. If he doesn't come across with the money he owes me I'll take him to court.

'Let's be fair. If it stands on its edge, two out of three tosses, we'll go home!'

Although most Aussie men will probably swear black and blue that 'I'm not a gamblin' man meself!', they love to have a bet or wager. To exuberant cries of 'Toss ya for it!', 'You're on!', 'Double or nothing!' and 'Come in spinner!', many grave decisions and important issues are settled on the outcome of the toss of a coin. This quaint custom undoubtedly led to the development of Australia's national game: two-up.

3. to submit sexually: e.g. She flirts a lot but she never comes across.

come across with the goods
to submit sexually, especially of a woman.

come again?
repeat: e.g. I didn't hear what you said — would you come again?

come at
1. to rush at; attack: e.g. He came at me with a knife.
2. accept; do; undertake; attempt: e.g. He won't come at that.

come by
acquire; obtain (often illegally): e.g. No one knows how he came by so much money.
See also:
hard to come by

come clean
confess; tell the truth.

come down
lose the feeling of euphoria created by drugs.
See also:
didn't come down in the last shower

come down on (someone) like a ton of bricks
scold, berate (someone) severely.

come down to earth
be realistic; stop dreaming and see the facts as they really are.

come down with
become afflicted with a virus or disease: e.g. I came down with a bad case of the flu and had to stay in bed for a week.

come full circle
1. finalise; complete.
2. to end up where one started.

come good
to improve after a bad start: e.g. The business got off to a shaky start but it'll come good.

come hell or high water
no matter what happens: e.g. He's going to get to that meeting come hell or high water.

come in handy
be useful: e.g. This gadget might come in handy later.

come in on the grouter
take an unfair advantage of a situation, especially in a game of two-up where a bet is withheld until the odds are in one's favour.

come in spinner
the call for the tossing of the coins in the game of two-up.

come into
1. inherit: e.g. He'll come into a fortune when his father dies.
2. get; acquire: e.g. He'll come into a fortune if it works.

come into (one's) own
be able to show (one's) skill: e.g. He comes into his own when the conversation turns to computer technology.

come off
happen; succeed: e.g. After all that planning, the outdoor concert didn't come off because of bad weather.

come off it!
1. (as an exclamation) stop it!
2. (as an exclamation) stop talking nonsense, rubbish!
3. a plea to someone to moderate or cease his actions: e.g. Come off it Fred, you're acting like a fool!

come off second best
be defeated: e.g. When those two dogs have a fight it's usually the big one that comes off second best.

come off the grass!
an expression of disbelief; a plea to stop talking nonsense.

come on (a bit) strong
behave in an over-bearing manner.

come on Brownlow!
(Australian Rules football) ironic call to a Brownlow Medal winner who is not performing well.

come on real/too heavy
behave in an over-bearing or intolerable manner; become too serious: e.g. When you ask her for a date, don't come on too heavy or she'll knock you back.

come (one's) guts
to turn informer; betray.

come out in the wash
1. to be finally revealed, such as an indiscretion, secret or hidden fact.
2. to turn out all right in the end.

come out of hiding
be socially active again after an absence.

come out of (one's) shell
overcome (one's) shyness or reserve and become communicative.

come out of the closet
to admit to something previously hidden about one's nature or background.

come out of the woodwork
appear as if from nowhere, especially after a long absence.

come out on top
succeed; win; defeat the opposition.

come out with
reveal; tell; blurt out: e.g. She finally came out with the whole truth.

come over (someone)
to cause a change in (someone's) mood; affect:

e.g. What's come over her all of a sudden?

come round
1. eventually accept, agree: e.g. He'll come round after I have a talk to him about the truth of the matter.
2. regain consciousness.

come that on/with me
attempt to blatantly hoodwink, deceive, trick or cheat: e.g. Don't come that with me! I know the truth!

come the ...
behave like ...

come the big-note
inflate one's status or achievements; boast or exaggerate: e.g. He always comes the big-note in front of the boss.

come the crunch
when the show-down, crisis or decisive event finally happens: e.g. Come the crunch in that situation, I wouldn't know what to do either.

come the raw prawn (with someone)

come the uncooked crustacean
attempt to deceive, hoodwink or trick: e.g. Don't come the raw prawn with me!

come through with flying colours
be triumphantly successful.

come to a head
reach a climax, crisis.

come to a sticky end
to die violently.

come to blows
to start fighting, arguing strongly.

come to grips with
deal with; handle efficiently, successfully, satisfactorily.

come to light
be revealed, unearthed, found, as in a mystery or secret: e.g. It may take many years, but the truth will finally come to light.

come to (one)
be remembered; occur to (one's) mind: e.g. It didn't come to me for ages that I had met him before.

come to (one's) senses
become rational again.

come to pass
occur; happen.

come to the party
assist, particularly with money; agree to meet certain requirements: e.g. When we started the business the bank came to the party with a loan.

come under heavy fire
receive strong criticism.

come under the firing-squad
be subject to abuse, ridicule, criticism or verbal attack.

come undone/unstuck
lose credibility or rank; break down; collapse: e.g. He'll come unstuck when the police find enough evidence to arrest him.

come up for air
have a short rest or break.

come up to
reach; be equal to: e.g. I can't come up to him — he's too good.

come up trumps
end up a winner; succeed in the end.

come up with
1. supply; produce: e.g. Can you come up with enough money by the weekend to buy that car?
2. propose; suggest; bring to mind or attention: e.g. You'd better come up with some good ideas for the meeting.

For other possible entries beginning with 'come' see entries listed under 'came'.

come-as-you-are
casual dress as opposed to formal.

come-at-able.
accessible: e.g. Politicians never seem to be very come-at-able.

comeback
1. retort or retaliation.
2. grounds for complaint: e.g. You've got no comeback if you can't produce the receipt.
3. revival: e.g. The band made a successful comeback after a long absence.

comedown
humiliating downfall; let-down; disappointment.

come-on
lure; seductive ploy; inducement: e.g. If he gives me that come-on again I'll slap his face.

comeuppance
just reward for reprehensible behaviour; punishment that is well deserved.

comfort station
toilets — especially public.

comfy
comfortable.

comic-cuts
(rhyming slang) guts.

comics
comic cartoon strips in newspapers.

commie/commo
communist.

commit harakiri
to commit suicide or perform a suicidal act.

common as dishwater/dog-shit
1. coarse; vulgar; having low morals.
2. very common; nothing out of the ordinary.

common ground
agreement; empathy; compatability: e.g. Although those two politicians are in different parties, there's a lot of common ground between them.

common knowledge
information, facts etc. that most people know about.

communication gap
breakdown in communication, talk, discussion.

compare notes
to exchange ideas, views, opinions, experiences, information etc.: e.g. The girls are in the kitchen comparing notes about their past lovers.

compassionate as a starving shark
to have no sorrow or pity.

compo
compensation payment for injury received at work.

con
1. convict.
2. confidence trick; a swindle; deception; fraud.
3. to swindle, trick or cheat for the purpose of gain: e.g. He'll con you out of every cent you own.
4. entice; lure; seduce: e.g. I'll con him into coming to the party.
See also:
on the con

con artist/man
(see: con-man)

concert pitch
complete state of readiness for something.

conchie
conscientious objector; one who is conscientious to the extreme.

concrete jungle
city environment characterised by massive concrete structures with little greenery or trees.

condo
condominium; a block of high-rise apartments, flats.

cone
the cone-shaped receptacle in which marijuana is placed for smoking in a bong; the drug smoked in this way: e.g. Karl's already off his face because he's had six cones.

confounded
euphemism for damned: e.g. I can't get this confounded thing to work properly!

conk
1. the nose.
2. to hit or bash (especially on the head).
See also:
on the conk

conk out
1. (of an engine or machine) break down; fail.
2. collapse with exhaustion, tiredness.
3. die: e.g. The old man is just about ready to conk out.

con-man
1. confidence trickster; swindler; cheat.
2. one well-practised in the art of seduction, or of enticing people into doing his will.

connections
power through influential friends: e.g. He's got enough connections to have the charges dropped before he's taken to court.

conned
1. tricked; duped; deceived; swindled; cheated.
2. enticed; lured.

conscience money
money paid to relieve the conscience for something previously neglected.

conshie
(see: conchie)

contemplate (one's) navel
to daydream or waste time with idleness; do nothing in particular: e.g. Instead of getting on with the job, he's been sitting around all day contemplating his navel!

continental
(see: couldn't give a continental; give a continental)

contract
an agreement to have someone killed: e.g. The Mafia have a contract out on him.

contraption
strange device; odd machine or gadget.

cooee
(see: within cooee)

cook (someone's) goose
1. spoil, frustrate or ruin (someone's) plans.
2. severely scold, berate (someone).

cook the books
to illegally tamper with and falsify records, accounts.

cook up
fabricate; scheme; concoct; falsify: e.g. He's cooked up a pack of lies in an attempt to get him out of trouble.

cook up a storm
cause trouble.

cooked it!
spoiled, ruined, bungled, made a mess of: e.g. Now you've really cooked it!

cookie
person; fellow: e.g. He's a smart cookie.
See also:
that's the way the cookie crumbles
tough cookie

cooking
1. happening: e.g. What's cooking?
2. doing well: e.g. The

business is really cooking now.

cooking with gas/oil
going or happening satisfactorily; doing well.

cool
1. all right; okay; all's well: e.g. That's cool with me.
2. suave; smart; fashionable.
3. composure; self-possession; aloofness: e.g. He kept his cool even though he was provoked.
4. composed; self-possessed; level-headed: e.g. He remained cool even though he was provoked.
5. unfriendly; detached; lacking in warmth or enthusiasm: e.g. Even though I apologised she's still very cool with me.
6. without exaggeration: e.g. cool million.
See also:
blow (one's) cool
keep (one's) cool
lose (one's) cool
play it cool

cool as a cucumber
(see: cool, 4. and 5.)

cool, calm and collected
composed; self-possessed; confident; poised; unperturbed.

cool down/off
calm down; be reasonable.

cool it
1. (as an exclamation) plea or order to cease present action, behaviour or speech.
2. calm down; be reasonable.

cool (one's) heels
to be kept waiting.

cool the tinnies and warm the set
expression of the Aussie 'ocker' getting ready to watch sport on television while drinking copious amounts of beer.

cooler
prison cell.

Coolers
West Coast VFL football team (Western Australia).

Coolgardie safe
early outback food cooler, utilising wet sacking over a fly-proof container.

cool-headed
composed; self-possessed; reasoning; calm.

coon
(derog.) dark-skinned person.

coop
prison.
See also:
fly the coop

coot
1. man; fellow; person: e.g. What's that old coot doing?
2. fool; stupid person.

cop
1. policeman.
2. something profitable such as a job, position or particular situation: e.g. He's on a terrific cop since he started working for himself.
3. put up with; tolerate: e.g. I'm not going to cop any more of that sort of despicable behaviour from him.
4. get; receive: e.g. You're going to cop a belting if you get home late.
See also:
not much cop
on a good cop
sure cop
sweet cop

cop a blast
receive a severe reprimand; be strongly criticised.

cop a load
contract venereal disease.

cop a load of (that)
have a look at: e.g. Cop a load of the boobs on that sheila!

cop a serve
receive a severe reprimand; be strongly criticised: e.g. I copped a serve even though I didn't do anything wrong.

cop it
be punished; get into trouble for which one must face the consequences.

cop it rough
suffer unfairly: e.g. Many people have to cop it rough because they can't find employment.

cop it sweet
1. receive a lucky break; get a good deal; experience a profitable situation.
2. tolerate (something) with patience: e.g. If someone much bigger than you provokes you, it's probably safer to just cop it sweet.
3. accept with grace the consequences of one's own foolish actions or behaviour.

cop out
1. quit; give up; opt out: e.g. He's better off copping out now before he gets in any deeper and loses more money.
2. fail.

cop shop
police station.

cop some stick
receive a barrage of, be the recipient of severe and mocking criticism, sarcasm: e.g. He really copped some stick in the papers for what he said.

cop the backlash
receive a reaction that is excessive.

cop the blue
take the blame.

cop the flak
receive a barrage of heavy criticism or abuse.

cop the lot
1. receive, get everything.
2. get into severe trouble for one's actions: e.g. He'll cop the lot when the police catch up with him.
3. suffer the entire brunt of consequences.

cop this!
have a look at this!

cop you later
form of farewell, and a play on the words: copulate her.

cop-out
cowardly evasion of responsibility.

copped
caught (by police or others) for a crime.

coppers
police; policemen.

copter
helicopter.

copycat
one who copies or imitates rather than uses originality.

cor!
expression of amazement, surprise.

cords
corduroy trousers.

cork up!
shut up!
See also:
put a cork in it!

corked
drunk; intoxicated.

corker
astonishingly good thing or person.

corkie
cork (bruised) thigh in Australian Rules football: e.g. Peglegs got a corkie in last week's game so he may be out on Saturday.

corn
trite, hackneyed sentimentality.

cornball
hackneyed sentimentalist.

corner
detain at length; trap; force into an awkward situation or position.
See also:
backed into a corner
cut corners
drive (someone) into a corner
in a tight corner
just around the corner
round the corner

corner the market
to monopolise a commodity: e.g. Crime syndicates have cornered the market in drugs and prostitution.

cornflakes show
morning radio talk show.

cornstalk
someone born and raised in N.S.W.

corny
trite; sentimental; hackneyed; old-fashioned.

corpus delicti
attractive, shapely woman.

corroboree
any large and noisy gathering.

cosmic
fantastic; wonderful; mind-boggling.

cossie
bathing costume; swimming togs.

cost a bundle/packet/pretty penny/quid

cost an arm and a leg

cost the earth
cost a great deal of money; was extravagantly expensive.

cot
(see: hit the cot)

cot case
someone who is so sick, drunk or tired as to be confined to bed.

cotton between the ears
(to have . . .) to be lacking in intelligence; stupid.

cotton on (to)
1. understand; comprehend; perceive: e.g. We're giving him a surprise party and don't want him to cotton on.
2. discover; unearth; find out.

cotton on with
be friendly with; get on well with: e.g. He seems to have cottoned on well with the boss.

cotton up to (someone)
flatter; behave obsequiously towards.

cottonwool between the ears
(to have . . .) to be lacking in intelligence; stupid.

cough drop
fool; stupid person; simpleton.

cough up
give (unwillingly or reluctantly); hand over (especially money): e.g. I had to cough up a fortune in back taxes.

could eat a baby's bum through a cane chair

could eat a horse and chase the rider
an expression of one's extreme hunger.

could eat an apple through a paling fence
said of someone who has protruding buck teeth.

could have knocked me over with a feather
expression of amazement, complete surprise.

could have sworn on a stack of Bibles
expression of sincerity, utter belief: e.g. I could have sworn on a stack of Bibles that I paid him that money ages ago.

could kick a bullock up the arse and walk away with the hide
said of someone with exceptionally large feet.

could open a can of peaches with that nose
said of someone who has a large or hooked nose.

could sell boomerangs to the Abos/Blacks

could sell fridges to the Eskimos

could sell ham sandwiches to the synagogue
pertaining to a persuasive manner or personality.

could use her shit for toothpaste
expression of lust, desire.

couldn't care less
not to care at all; an expression of complete indifference.

couldn't catch a cold
incompetent.

couldn't drag the skin off a rice-pudding

couldn't fight (one's) way out of a wet paper bag

couldn't fight in a fit
1. physically weak; not strong.
2. incompetent.

couldn't drive a greasy stick up a dead dog's arse
totally ineffective, incompetent, especially in driving a car or vehicle.

couldn't get over it
expression of amazement, surprise, astonishment.

couldn't give a bugger

couldn't give a continental

couldn't give a damn

couldn't give a fuck

couldn't give a hang/hoot

couldn't give a shit/stuff

couldn't give two hoots/two stuffs
expression of total lack of concern or worry: e.g. I couldn't give a shit whether he comes back or not.

couldn't hack it (any more)
couldn't tolerate any longer.

couldn't hit a cow in the tit with a tin can
pertaining to either a bad aim, or ineffectual, useless and blundering behaviour.

couldn't hit the side of a barn
pertaining to bad aim.

couldn't knock the skin off a rice-pudding
(see: couldn't drag the skin off . . .)

couldn't lie straight in bed
pertaining to a crook, cad, cheat, ratbag, swindler etc.

couldn't make the kindergarten leftovers
pertaining to having no skill at a particular sport.

couldn't pull a greasy stick out of a dead dog's arse
to be totally ineffective, weak, incompetent.

couldn't raise a gallop
1. almost exhausted; just keeping going.
2. (of a man) pertaining to an inability to have an erection.

couldn't raise one
(see: couldn't raise a gallop, 2.)

couldn't run guts for a slow butcher
to be totally ineffective, incompetent, slow.

couldn't see (someone) for the dust
pertaining to a speedy departure.

couldn't stand/stomach (something)
couldn't tolerate or put up with.

couldn't talk if (one) lost (one's) arms
said of a person who gesticulates with hands and arms when speaking.

count
(see: don't count your chickens before they're hatched; out for the count)

count on (one's) fingers

count on the fingers of one hand
pertaining to a small amount: e.g. I could count on the fingers of one hand the times I've been out to dinner this year.

count (someone) in
include: e.g. You can count me in if you go.

count (someone) out
exclude: e.g. Count me out — I can't afford the tickets.

countenance
the face.

counter-jumper
person who works behind a counter, such as office worker, public servant, sales-person.

countrified
rustic; of a country nature; unsophisticated.

country bumpkin
unsophisticated, rustic person from the country.

country cousin
(rhyming slang) dozen.

country mile
1. a long way, distance or margin: e.g. He won the race by a country mile.
2. (see: bush mile)

court disaster
to risk danger or ruin by one's actions, behaviour.

cove
chap; person; fellow; bloke.

cover charge
an amount added to a bill of a restaurant, club or place of entertainment for services.

cover new ground
move into new areas of knowledge, information or subject matter.

cover (one's) tracks
leave no trace or clues for detection.

cover (oneself)
to insure (oneself) against risk, failure.

cover (something) up
keep secret; attempt to withhold or conceal the facts.

cover-up
fabrication; excuse (often a lie); an attempt to conceal the truth.

cow
1. bad-tempered or ugly woman.
2. term of abuse: e.g. Now look what you've done you stupid cow!
See also:
couldn't hit a cow in the tit with a tin can
dark as three feet up a cow's arsehole
fair cow
holy cow!
poor cow
sacred cow
talk till the cows come home
till the cows come home

cow cake/pat
the characteristically circular pile of cow dung.

cow juice
milk.

cow of a thing
anything exasperating, difficult, unpredictable or unpleasant.

coward's way out
easiest solution or course of action — not necessarily the best.

cow-banging
working or operating a dairy farm.

cow-cocky
dairy farmer.

cozzie
(see: cossie)

crab/crab apple
bad-tempered person.

crabby
irritable; bad-tempered; annoyed.

crabs
body lice, particularly in the pubic area.
See also:
busy as a one-armed taxi-driver with crabs
draw the crabs

crack
1. vagina.
2. the anus; bum.
3. an expert; skilled person: e.g. 1. He's a crack when it comes to fixing cars. 2. He's a crack mechanic.
4. cutting or witty remark: e.g. Any more cracks from you and I'll smack you one!
5. a highly addictive, purified or manufactured form of cocaine.
6. submit, yield to pressure or strain: e.g. The police will finally make him crack and admit his crimes.
7. (of a mystery) solve.
8. (of a safe) break into.
See also:
at first crack
have a crack at
wise-crack

crack a bottle
open a bottle of wine, beer etc.

crack a darkie
become suddenly angry, violent.

crack a fat
(of a man) have an erection of the penis.

crack a funny/joke
tell a joke.

crack a shitty
become suddenly angry, violent; lose one's temper.

crack a smile
smile unwillingly or suddenly.

crack down on
take severe disciplinary measures: e.g. The police are going to crack down on drunk-driving.

crack it
1. have sexual intercourse: e.g. Jacky must have cracked it last night — he's all smiles today.
2. be successful: e.g. After years of work he's finally cracked it and earning big money.

crack of dawn
first light of day.

crack on to
1. (someone) strike up a friendship, especially for the purpose of having sex.
2. (something) discover, find with enthusiasm.

crack the big time
be extremely successful: e.g. It took years of hard work to crack the big time.

crack the whip
an order to hurry up or get moving; incite to greater activity.
See also:
fair crack of the whip!

crack up
1. collapse under physical or mental strain.
2. collapse into fits of laughter, giggles.

crack-brained
stupid; crazy; ill-conceived.

cracked
crazy; mentally unsound.
See also:
not what it's cracked up to be

cracker
a firework.
See also:
haven't got a cracker
not worth a cracker

crackerjack
1. person of outstanding skill.
2. outstanding, excellent or first-class person or thing.

crackers
crazy; mentally unbalanced.

cracking
(see: get cracking)

cracking it
working as a prostitute.

crackpot
1. an eccentric or insane person.
2. eccentric; impractical: e.g. That's a crackpot idea.

cradle-snatcher
one who has romantic interests in someone much younger.

cramp (someone's) style
hinder (someone's) potential, especially in sexual pursuits.

crank
1. eccentric person obsessed with certain ideas or notions.
2. grumpy, ill-tempered person.
3. mixture of cocaine and amphetamines that can be highly lethal.

cranky
irritable; petulant; angry; ill-tempered.

crap
1. excrement; faeces; shit.
2. nonsense; rubbish; lies: e.g. Stop talking crap!
3. odds and ends; an assortment of junk, things, objects etc.: e.g. Get all that crap out of here.
4. to defecate.
See also:
cut the crap

crap artist
one given to excessive boasting, lies or talking nonsense.

crap on
boast excessively; talk nonsense; tell lies.

crap out
fail.

crap (someone) off
annoy, irritate, anger, disgust (someone).

crap up
bungle; make a mess of; ruin: e.g. He crapped that job up.

crapped off
annoyed; disgusted.

crapper
the toilet.

crappy
awful; disagreeable; second-rate; of poor quality.

crash
1. enter a party or function uninvited: e.g. I crashed the opening of the gallery and drank free wine all night.
2. fall into an exhausted sleep: He came home drunk and crashed in the car instead of getting into a comfortable bed.
3. stay for a short time: e.g. Where are you going to crash for the weekend?
4. fail, especially financially.
See also:
gate-crash

crash course/diet etc.
intensive and sudden course, diet etc.

crash on
pet; fondle; cuddle; indulge in sexual play: e.g. We used to crash on in the back seat of the FJ at the drive-in.

crash out
go to sleep (especially after exhaustion).

crash pad
sleeping quarters; bedroom.

crash-hot
excellent; first-rate; wonderful.

crashing bore
a complete and utter bore.

crate
car, vehicle or machine in a dilapidated state.

craters
pimples; acne; pock-marks on the skin.

crawl/crawl up (someone's) arse
behave ingratiatingly or obsequiously: e.g. I'm going to have to grow legs on my stomach and crawl to the boss for a raise.

crawl up the wall
be extremely annoyed, irritated, exasperated, frustrated.

crawler
1. ingratiating, obsequious person.
2. slow, unproductive worker.

cray
crayfish.

craze
fashion; popular thing or activity: e.g. The latest craze is green hair and gaudy make-up.

crazy
1. an insane or eccentric person: e.g. He's a real crazy.
2. intensely and outrageously eager or enthusiastic: e.g. He's crazy for motor-bikes at the moment.
See also:
like crazy

crazy about
infatuated or in love with: e.g. She's crazy about him.

cream
1. the best part of anything.
2. defeat; beat soundly in a fight or match: e.g. Our team will cream the opposition in next week's game.
3. to kill in a violent manner.

cream puff
a person who is weak physically or mentally, effeminate, homosexual or cowardly.

cream (one's) jeans
1. experience an orgasm in one's clothes.

2. become excited, sexually or otherwise.

creamed
1. soundly beaten in a fight or match.
2. killed in a violent or gory manner.

creamer
coward.

creature
contemptible, despicable person.

creature comforts
material trappings, such as a home, electrical appliances, food, alcohol etc. considered necessary for comfortable living: e.g. She likes her creature comforts too much to consider living in a caravan.

creek
(see: up the creek)

creep
1. unpleasant or despicable person.
2. sycophantic person.
See also:
make (one's) flesh creep
the creeps

creepy
1. unpleasant; frightening; weird; inspiring horror.
2. (of a person) obnoxious; unpleasant; inspiring fear.

creepy crawlies
1. obnoxious crawling insects.
2. sensation of fear, distaste or horror: e.g. That house gives me the creepy crawlies.

crème de la crème
the best part.

cretin
stupid person; a fool.

crew
company; friends; associates: e.g. Invite the whole crew to dinner.

crib
1. plagiarise; copy; cheat.
2. a petty theft.

cricket
(usually in the negative) fair play: e.g. His behaviour really wasn't cricket.
See also:
pissed as a cricket

crikes/crikey!
expression of astonishment; a mild oath.

crim
criminal.

crime ring
organised gang of criminals.

cripes!
expression of astonishment, surprise; a mild oath.

critter
creature.

croak
to die: e.g. He croaked last week.

croc
crocodile.

crock
old, inefficient and decrepit person.

crocodile tears
hypocritical and false show of sympathy, grief or emotion: e.g. She cried plenty of crocodile tears over her divorce.

crocodilian
hypocritical.

cronk
fraudulent; shoddy; deceptive; dishonest: e.g. That was a cronk deal he gave you. (also: kronk)

crook
1. lawless person; swindler; criminal; thief.
2. sick; ill; feeling bad: e.g. He's crook so he took the day off.
3. angry; ill-tempered; annoyed: e.g. He's crook over losing that money.
4. inferior; no good; second-rate: e.g. The weather's crook today.
5. broken; damaged; ruined: e.g. The telly's crook again.
See also:
feel crook
go crook

crook as Rookwood
(see: crook, 2., 4. and 5.) Rookwood is a cemetery in Sydney.

crooked
lawless; dishonest; fraudulent.
See also:
so crooked (one) couldn't lie straight in bed

crooked as a dog's hind leg
1. not straight; bent.
2. dishonest; unlawful; fraudulent.

crooked on
angry, upset with: e.g. I'm really crooked on her for not telling me sooner.

crookie
a failure; broken down and useless item.

crop up
turn up unexpectedly; arise: e.g. I hope no more problems crop up.

cropper
heavy fall: e.g. Everyone laughed when she came a cropper down the stairs.
See also:
come a cropper

cross
1. angry; annoyed.
2. an animal or plant of mixed breeding.
3. cheat; swindle: e.g. Watch he doesn't cross you.
See also:
double-cross
keep (one's) fingers crossed
the Cross

cross as two sticks
angry; annoyed; vexed; bad-tempered.

cross (one's) bridges when (one) comes to them
to act when a particular situation arises: e.g. There

are a few problems to sort out but we'll cross those bridges when we come to them.

cross (one's) heart (and hope to die)
promise; pledge; swear to the truth of.

cross (one's) mind
occur to (one), such as an idea: e.g. It never crossed my mind.

cross (one's) t's and dot (one's) i's
pay meticulous and often petty attention to detail.

cross (someone's) palm
to bribe (someone).

cross swords
argue; fight; do battle with — often verbally.

cross the floor
(politics) to vote with the opposition.

cross to bear
burden in life: e.g. He's become a heavy cross for her to bear since he became a quadraplegic.

crossbones
two bones illustrated crosswise, often over or below a skull, indicating danger or death.

cross-fire
heated exchange of words; insults: e.g. I was caught in the cross-fire and couldn't get a word in edgeways.

cross-grained
stubborn.

cross-paddock wrestlers
those who play Rugby League football.

crosspatch
ill-tempered person.

crotchety
irritable.

crow
1. an ugly, unattractive woman.
2. brag; boast.
See also:
as the crow flies
draw the crow
eat crow
starve/stiffen/stone the crows!
up with the crows
when the crow shits

crowd
urge by insistent nagging; annoy by urging, nagging or overwhelming presence: e.g. Don't crowd me — I'll do it when I'm ready!

crowd-pleaser
anything, such as a form of entertainment, that is popular with the masses of people.

crowd-puller
anything that acts as a drawcard or enticement for people to come or attend: e.g. His art is a good crowd-puller.

croweater
a South Australian; someone from South Australia.

crown
1. the head.
2. to bash or hit, especially on the head.

crown jewels
testicles.

crow's feet
wrinkles at the corners of the eyes.

crud
1. dirt; filth.
2. nonsense; rubbish; worthless talk: e.g. He's so full of crud.

cruddy
worthless; of poor quality; shoddy; second-rate.

cruel (the pitch)
spoil, ruin, especially someone else's chance of success.
See also:
be cruel to be kind

cruet
the head.

cruising
1. moving along, doing something, at a moderate, leisurely, successful pace.
2. the practice of male homosexuals looking for sexual encounters.

crumb
1. small, insignificant portion; paltry, trifling amount: e.g. The workers didn't get a crumb of the profits.
2. mean, lousy, parsimonious person: e.g. You lousy crumb!
3. loose ball in Australian Rules football.

crumb gatherer
(Australian Rules football) rover who is expert at getting the loose ball.

crummy
worthless; of poor quality; shoddy; inferior; second-rate.
See also:
feel crummy

crumpet
1. woman considered as a sexually attractive object: e.g. She's not a bad-looking bit of crumpet.
2. the head: e.g. Hit him in the crumpet if he gives any more cheek.
3. (of men) sexual intercourse: e.g. Get any crumpet last night?
See also:
go off (one's) crumpet
not worth a crumpet
off (one's) crumpet
soft in the crumpet

crunch
decisive event; the moment of crisis; show-down: e.g. When the crunch comes, he won't know what to do.
See also:
come the crunch

crush
1. an infatuation: e.g. She's got a real crush on him.

2. large crowded mass of people: e.g. The party was a real crush.
See also:
have/got a crush on (someone)

crust
livelihood; living; job: e.g. What's he do for a crust?
See also:
down to the last crust
upper crust

crutch
1. genital area of the human body; crotch.
2. anything heavily relied or depended on: e.g. He's been using her as a crutch and now that she's gone he's falling apart.
See also:
chew the crutch out of an Afghan camel-driver's jocks

cry
(see: enough to make a grown man cry; far cry from; in full cry)

cry crocodile tears
show false emotion or sympathy.

cry for the moon
to desire in vain; attempt something useless or doomed to certain failure.

cry Herb!
to vomit.

cry on (someone's) shoulder
show a need for sympathy: e.g. I've cried on his shoulder many times, and now that he needs someone he can have my shoulder to cry on.
See also:
need a shoulder to cry on

cry (one's) eyes out
to cry, shed tears profusely.

cry (one's) heart out
cry bitterly; feel emotionally crushed and dejected.

cry over spilt milk
to worry over or be upset about something which has happened and cannot be changed.

cry Ralph!/Ruth!
to vomit.

cry (someone) down
disparage or belittle (someone).

cry wolf
to give a false alarm, often as a joke or prank that backfires: e.g. He'd cried wolf so many times before that when he really needed help, no one came.

cry-baby
anybody who cries easily or shows hurt feelings without too much provocation.

crying in (one's) beer and pretzels
feeling dejected and sorry for oneself, particularly in a state of drunkenness.

crying shame
something that demands sympathy: e.g. It's a crying shame that both his boys were killed in that accident.

cubbyhole
snug, comfortable, confined spot or position; very small room or space.

cuckoo
crazy; silly; foolish: e.g. He's cuckoo!

cuey/cuie/cuke
cucumber.

cultural cringe
feeling that one's culture is inferior to someone else's.

cum
(see: come, 1. and 2.)

cunnilingus
oral stimulation of the female genitals.

cunning as a lavvy/shithouse rat
crafty; deceptive; shrewd.

cunt
1. vagina; female pudendum.
2. (vulg.) woman considered as a sexual object.
3. derogatory name for a person or thing considered despicable.
4. anything exasperating or annoying: e.g. This new gadget's a cunt — it won't work!
See also:
not worth a cunt full of cold water
useful as a cunt full of cold water

cunt of a thing!
expression of exasperation or annoyance.

cunt-face
derogatory insult to a despised person.

Cup
famous horse-race, the Melbourne Cup.

Cup Day
public holiday held for the running of the famous horse-race, the Melbourne Cup.

cup of tea
anything satisfactory, up to standard, pleasing, agreeable, to one's taste: e.g. Getting pissed with the boys at the pub is not my cup of tea!

cup runneth over
pertaining to extreme good fortune, well-being or comfort: e.g. My cup runneth over with love.

cupboard drinker
secret drinker; someone who drinks much more alcohol than he reveals.

cuppa
a cup of tea; tea-break.

curdle the blood
terrify; put fear into.

curiosity killed the cat
statement said to someone who is in trouble because of his curiosity.

curl (one's) lip up
express distaste, disdain: e.g. He curls his lip up every time I serve tripe for dinner.

curl the mo!
expression of wonder, amazement, admiration, pleasure.

curl up
1. lie down in comfort: e.g. I love curling up with a good book on rainy days.
2. have sexual intercourse: e.g. I wouldn't mind curling up with him!

curl up (one's) toes
1. to give up.
2. to die.

curly
difficult to deal with, handle or solve: e.g. Except for a few curly problems at the start, the business has been going well.

curry
(see: give someone curry)

curry favour
attempt to gain favour or personal gain by a show of flattery or kindness.

curse
(the . . .) menstruation: e.g. She didn't go to work today because she's got the curse.

curtains
1. the end, particularly in a predictive doomsday sense: e.g. It's curtains for him and his business if he can't raise enough money by next week.
2. death: e.g. It's curtains for him — he got the death sentence.
See also:
Iron Curtain

curvaceous/curvy
(of woman) shapely; sexually attractive.

cushy
(of a job etc.) easy; comfortable; without problems, difficulties or responsibilities: e.g. He's got a cushy job with the Government.
See also:
all cush

cuss
1. person, especially a mean and cranky one.
2. curse; swear; use obscene language.

customer
annoying person one has to deal with: e.g. If that customer comes to the door again with his Bible-bashing jargon, I'll throw him out.

cut
1. share of profits, gains; commission: e.g. His cut was five thousand dollars.
2. (of movie, film) edited; censored: e.g. The movie was cut to the extent that it was hard to follow the story.
3. absent oneself from: e.g. Students who don't stop cutting classes will fail their exams.
4. stop at once; quit: e.g. Cut that silly nonsense at once!
5. operate; perform surgery: e.g. There's no way I'll let that doctor cut me!
6. (of an animal) neutered; castrated.
7. drunk; intoxicated: e.g. He got so cut at the pub that he had to be carried home by his mates.
See also:
go like a cut cat
in for (one's) cut
mad/silly as a cut snake

cut a dash
show off; make a spectacle of oneself.

cut a fine figure
make an impression by one's behaviour or dress: e.g. He cut a fine figure up there on the stage in his graduation gown.

cut a long story short
be brief.

cut above the rest
better than; superior to: e.g. This horse is a cut above the rest and should win many races.

cut and dried
decisive; inflexible: e.g. His ideas are too cut and dried.

cut and run
abandon something and depart quickly: e.g. The gang decided to cut and run when the police arrived.

cut back
reduce, especially spending: e.g. If we don't cut back we'll go broke.

cut both ways
1. serve both sides: e.g. If we do it this way it cuts both ways and nobody gets upset.
2. beneficial in some ways and not in others: e.g. That deal cuts both ways and needs more thought before we sign.

cut corners
leave some things out, skimp on details in order to do a job more quickly, cheaply etc.

cut down on
reduce, especially spending.

cut from the same cloth
alike; akin; similar.

cut in
interrupt: e.g. I wish you wouldn't cut in every time I speak!

cut it fine
leave a very narrow margin for error.

cut it out
stop it; stop talking nonsense; stop acting that way.

cut loose
to swear, use abusive language in a sudden fit of anger.

cut lunch
a circumcised penis.

cut no ice with
achieve nothing; make no impression on: e.g. He cuts no ice with me — I can see through him and his ways.

cut off (one's) nose to spite (one's) face
severely injure or damage (one's) own interests through foolish and spiteful action or deed.

cut off (one's) right arm for
do anything for; expend tireless and unselfish energy for: e.g. He's done so much for me I'd cut off my right arm for him.

cut (one's) coat according to (one's) cloth
to live within the boundaries of (one's) means.

cut (one's) losses
abandon a project in which (one) has invested and lost so as not to incur any future losses.

cut (one's) own throat
to pursue a course of action that is detrimental to (oneself).

cut (one's) teeth on (something)
begin (one's) career; gain experience.

cut out for
qualified; well suited to: e.g. He's cut out for the job.

cut out for each other
well suited; compatible; able to co-exist.

cut out the funny business
behave; stop being silly; stop acting in a foolish manner.

cut (someone) down to size
berate; reduce in status; belittle.

cut (someone) short
interrupt.

cut the cackle!
be quiet; stop talking or laughing.

cut the crap!
stop talking nonsense; don't tell lies; don't exaggerate.

cut the ground from under (someone)
1. disconcert, belittle (someone); reduce (someone) in status.
2. disprove, invalidate (someone's) argument.

cut to ribbons/the quick
extremely hurt emotionally: e.g. He was cut to ribbons over the loss of his wife.

cut up
extremely distressed: e.g. He was really cut up over his dog being run over and killed.
See also:
all cut up

cut up rough
behave in an angry, upset manner.

cut-and-dried
matter-of-fact; businesslike; systematic; orderly.

cute
1. attractive; pretty; endearing.
2. smart; clever (often in a sarcastic manner): e.g. Who was the cute smart-alec who said that?

cutie
attractive, pretty or pleasing person or thing.

cutie-pie
attractive or pretty person, especially female.

cuts
corporal punishment, consisting of a strap on the palm of the hand, given at school: e.g. He got the cuts from the headmaster for stealing.

cuts me up
1. makes me laugh; causes hilarity: e.g. He really cuts me up when he starts telling jokes.
2. makes me very angry, upset: e.g. It cuts me up the way some parents mistreat their children.

cut-throat
murderous; intense and merciless: e.g. You have to be strong to survive in the cut-throat world of show-business.

D/Dee
a detective, especially a federal one: e.g. They'd hidden all the evidence before the D's arrived.

dab hand at
adept; skilled; good at: e.g. He's a dab hand at painting.

dack (oneself)
euphemism for shit (oneself): e.g. He dacked himself when he found out that he'd lost his wallet containing a thousand dollars.

dacka
(see: dakka)

dacks
(also: daks) trousers.

dad
father.

Dad 'n' Dave
1. (rhyming slang) shave.
2. pertaining to anything ludicrously rustic or unsophisticated: e.g. The dance in the hall will be a real Dad 'n' Dave affair.

daddy
1. father.
2. the most impressive or biggest of all: e.g. That giant, ugly cane-toad I saw was the daddy of them all.
See also:
big daddy
sugar-daddy

daddy-long-legs
1. type of spider with long, thin legs.
2. tall, lanky person with long legs.

Dad's Army
pertaining to anything old, worn-out or decrepit that is brought back into service or use.

daffy
silly; daft; crazy: e.g. That's a daffy idea.

dag
1. practical joker; lovable, odd or amusing person.
2. conservative person who lacks style and class.
3. untidy, dishevelled, slovenly person.
4. an untidy, dirty-looking lump of mud, excreta etc.
See also:
popular as a dag at a sheep show
rattle your dags!

dagger
the penis.
See also:
mutton-dagger
stare daggers

daggy
1. silly; idiotic; eccentric; amusing.
2. lacking in style, panache or appearance; conservative.
3. untidy; slovenly.

dago
(derog.) person of Latin origins; any foreign person.

dagwood sandwich
very large sandwich often with more than two slices of bread and a variety of fillings.

daily blatts
the daily newspapers.

daily grind
routine and often monotonous work.

daisy
(see: doozy)
See also:
fresh as a daisy
pushing up daisies

daisy chain
group sex performed by homosexual men linked anus to penis.

daisy cutter
(Australian Rules football) low, hard foot pass.

dakka
marijuana; pot; dope.

daks
(also: dacks) trousers.

damage
expense; cost: e.g. What's the damage for the repair of my car?

damaged goods
one who is no longer a virgin — especially a woman.

damn
very little or nothing: e.g. That's not worth a damn.
See also:
as near as damn it
don't give a damn

damn-all
nothing; very little: e.g. He knows damn-all about the business.

damn-bugger-bitch-bum!
expression of extreme frustration or annoyance.

damned
an intensive meaning extremely, very: e.g. What a damned shame!

dampen (one's) spirits
depress or deflate (one's) enthusiasm.

damper
1. type of outback bread cooked in a camp-fire.
2. depressing person or thing.
See also:
put a damper on (something)

damsel in distress
woman with a problem or difficult task with which she needs help, preferably from a man.

dance
(see: had someone dancing; lead someone a merry dance)

dance on air
to die by hanging.

dance on (someone's) grave
to wish (someone) dead: e.g. That man raped and killed my daughter and I'm going to dance on his grave when he gets convicted.

dance the night away
to celebrate all night.

dance to (one's/someone's) tune
to be under someone's power or control: e.g. Now that I'm the boss, he's going to dance to my tune.

dander
anger; fighting spirit: e.g. I really got my dander up at the last council meeting and gave them all a piece of my mind.

dandy
1. something that is fine, excellent or first-rate: e.g. His new car is a real dandy.
2. an effeminate, foppish man.
3. expression of sarcasm: e.g. That's just dandy, that is!

danger money
extra payment for work that is dangerous.

dangle
to die by hanging.
See also:
angle of the dangle

dangle a carrot (under someone's nose)
tempt; offer a bribe; make an offer that is irresistible.

Darby and Joan
pertaining to the devoted old married couple, living a life of placid matrimonial domesticity.

Darby and Joan club
any club or activity for elderly people.

dark
angry: e.g. What's the boss so dark about today?
See also:
get dark
in the dark
kept in the dark
leap in the dark
stab in the dark

Dark Ages
a state of ignorance and backwardness: e.g. He must be living in the Dark Ages if he thinks he can get away with that.

dark as a yard up a nigger's bum

dark as three feet up a cow's arsehole
very dark; complete absence of light.

dark clouds on the horizon
impending doom, disaster or trouble.

dark horse
person about whom little is known and whose capabilities might exceed expectations.

dark on (someone)
angry, annoyed with (someone): e.g. Dad's going to be dark on me for getting home so late.

darkie
1. (derog.) dark-skinned person.
2. excreta: e.g. I'm sick of dogs dropping darkies on my front lawn!
3. a fit of bad temper, anger: e.g. He really chucked a darkie when he found out.
See also:
choke/drop a darkie
crack a darkie
strangle a darkie

darl
darling.

Darling shower
(N.S.W.) dust storm.

darn!
euphemism for damn; a mild oath.
See also:
couldn't give a darn
don't give a darn

darned
1. euphemism for damned, bloody: e.g. This darned thing doesn't go properly!
2. very; extremely: e.g. That's darned good.
See also:
I'll be darned!

darnedest
1. most amazing, remarkable: e.g. That's the darnedest thing I've ever seen!
2. very best; try very hard: e.g. I'll do my darnedest to see that it gets there on time.

dart
cigarette: e.g. Throw me a dart.
See also:
Old Dart

Darwin shuffle
a company tax-avoidance scheme in which companies move shares around to avoid paying full duty on their transactions.

Darwin stubbie
very large beer bottle.

dash!
mild oath: e.g. Dash! Look what's happened now!
See also:
do a dash
done (one's) dash
dot and a dash

dashed (one's) chances
ruined (one's) chances or opportunity.

date
1. person of the opposite sex with whom one has a social outing.
2. female pudendum; vagina.
3. anus; bum; posterior: e.g. Get off your date and do something!
4. arrange a social appointment or outing, particularly with someone of the opposite sex: e.g. I'd like to date him.
See also:
up your date mate!

date roll
toilet paper.

dates
indicates that one is old-fashioned, out-of-date or obsolete: e.g. That suit dates him.

Dave and Mabel
(see: Dad 'n' Dave, 2.)

Davy Jones's locker
the sea, especially in regard to a grave: e.g. Scientists are trying to raise the *Titanic* from Davy Jones's locker.

day
that period of time when one's power or influence is at its best: e.g. He's had his day — it's time for someone else to take over now.
See also:
all in a day's work
call it a day
every dog has his day
field day
forever and a day
honest as the day is long
make (one's) day
many's the day
one of these days
rainy day
save the day
seen better days
that'll be the day!
the other day
those were the days
win the day
wouldn't give you the time of day

day in day out
for a long time; every day; interminably.

day of days
a best occasion.

day of reckoning
the time when one must atone or pay for one's actions or deeds.

day of rest
Sunday.

daydreamer
person who indulges in fanciful reverie to the detriment of productive work.

daylight
(see: beat/scare the living daylights out of; see daylight through someone's ears; starting to see daylight)

daylight robbery
unashamed swindling, cheating or robbery; charging of exorbitant prices: e.g. Making him pay that much for that old bomb was daylight robbery!

daylight saving
the setting forward of all clocks in order to give workers the benefit of usable extra sunshine hours.

days are numbered
time is limited and drawing closer to the end, death, or one's having to face up to responsibilities: e.g. His days in politics are numbered — the people will vote him out.

day-to-day
commonplace; ordinary: e.g. Housework is a day-to-day chore for most women.

dazzler
anything excellent, exceptionally good, brilliant.

D-day
the planned day for the start of any important event.

dead
1. exhausted; very tired: e.g. I feel dead today.
2. boring; unexciting: e.g. That was a dead party.
3. an adjective of emphasis: e.g. I'm dead sure.
4. slow; uneventful; quiet: e.g. Business has been dead this week.
See also:
bugger me dead!
drop dead!
enough to wake the dead
half dead
knock them dead
leave (someone) for dead
over my dead body!
play dead
wouldn't be seen dead at/in/with

dead and buried
1. dead.
2. an issue that is finished with; anything that one does not wish to discuss any more: e.g. As far as

I'm concerned that affair is dead and buried.

dead and won't lie down
pertaining to a person who is considered stupid, lacking in intelligence, or persistent against all hope.

dead as a dodo/doornail/ maggot
1. dead.
2. inanimate; broken down and not functioning; useless; worthless: e.g. This motor's as dead as a dodo.
3. unproductive, boring person without spirit or vigour.
4. boring, quiet function or event, lacking in vigour.

dead beat
exhausted; very tired: e.g. I'm dead beat today. (not to be confused with: deadbeat)

dead bird/cert
a certainty, especially in horse-racing.

dead drunk
totally inebriated.

dead duck
1. a failure; person or thing utterly without potential or promise; doomed to fail.
2. doomed; under threat of violence or revenge: e.g. Do that again and you're a dead duck!

dead from the neck up
person who is stupid, lacking in intelligence; a dunce.

dead give-away
obvious; revealing.

dead hand at
expert; skilled at.

Dead Heart
the arid centre of Australia.

dead heat
event where the competitors finish exactly together, having no outright winner.

dead horse
1. an outstanding debt: e.g. To work off a dead horse.
2. (rhyming slang) sauce.

dead loss
complete failure; totally worthless; hopeless: e.g. He's been a dead loss to the company.

dead marines
empty beer or wine bottles.

dead motherless broke
having no money at all.

dead on
correct; exactly right.

dead on (one's) feet
exhausted; tired.

dead on time
punctual: e.g. He arrived dead on time.

dead party
party that is boring, lacking in vigour.

dead right
absolutely correct.

dead ring/ringer for (someone/thing)
to look exactly like; replica: e.g. My husband's a dead ringer for Paul Newman.

dead set
(see: dead-set)

dead silence
absence of noise, particularly in a group of people and causing an embarrassing or uncomfortable atmosphere.

dead spit for (someone)
(see: dead ring . . .)

dead straight
1. absolutely straight; without curves.
2. law-abiding; without sin or guilt: e.g. He's dead straight since he's been out of prison.

dead sure
1. absolutely certain: e.g. I can't be dead sure but that's where I think it is.
2. arrogantly egotistical; confident: e.g. He's dead sure of himself.

dead to the world
1. fast asleep.
2. utterly exhausted.
3. drunk or under the influence of drugs.

dead wood
useless, unproductive people: e.g. The boss has decided to get rid of some of the dead wood — he's fired half the staff in the office.

deadbeat
1. person down on his luck; a down-and-out person.
2. vagrant, idle person; worthless, unproductive no-hoper.

dead-end
having no future prospects and leading nowhere.

dead-eye Dick
person whose aim is accurate, unerring.

dead-head
person lacking in intelligence or initiative.

dead-line
time-limit; latest possible time in which to complete something: e.g. The deadline for this assignment is tomorrow.

deadly
1. intense; intensely: e.g. I'm deadly serious.
2. accurate; unerring: e.g. His aim is deadly.
3. excessively: e.g. He's deadly boring.

deadpan
without expression or animation.

dead-set
truthful(ly); honest(ly); sure; certain: e.g. 1. Are you dead-set about giving up your new job? 2. Deadset! I didn't do it! 3. He's a dead-set bullshit artist.

'Actually, we get very few demands for no-hopers!'

The lack of demand for no-hopers has caused the queues outside the employment bureaus to grow longer and longer. This doesn't really worry the no-hopers as Australia has an amazing social benefits system that allows them to become professional dole-bludgers.

dead-shit
despicable, contemptible person.

deaf as a doornail/post
1. unable to hear; deaf.
2. refuse to listen: e.g. Dad's as deaf as a doornail when I ask for a loan of the car.

deal
1. mutually advantageous business arrangement or transaction that is often secret, underhanded or illegal.
2. measured quantity of marijuana: e.g. What did that deal cost?
See also:
a big deal
big deal!
fair deal
no deal
raw deal

deal (someone) the death blow
instigate an action that will cause the downfall, failure of.

dealer
trafficker of illegal drugs such as marijuana, heroin etc.

deaner
(see: deener)

dear
(see: old dear/dears)

dear Dorothy Dix
letter confessing some aspect of one's life and requesting advice or help in the matter.

dear John
letter terminating the relationship with one's lover — especially from a woman.

dearie
affectionate term of address.

death row
the place in a prison where condemned prisoners are kept before execution.

death seat
1. the front passenger seat in a car, considered dangerous in an accident.
2. (harness-racing) position behind the leader and boxed in on the outside by another.

death warrant
anything announcing complete failure and loss of hope.

death-knell
anything announcing a failure, ending or downfall; an omen of doom.

death's head
skull as a symbol of mortality.

death-trap
any dangerous situation.

debunk
expose false claims or pretentions ; deflate; mock; make fun of.

deck (someone)
knock (someone) to the ground: e.g. I'll deck him if he gives you any more trouble.
See also:
back on deck
clear the decks
hit the deck
not playing with the full deck
on deck

decked out in
dressed in: e.g. She was decked out in her finest clobber.

decko
(see: dekko)

declare (one's) hand
make known (one's) intentions, position or circumstances.

Dee
a detective. (also: D)

deejay
radio disc-jockey. (also: DJ)

deener
a shilling before decimal currency.
See also:
not worth a deener

deep
difficult to understand; abstruse; subtle: e.g. That book was too deep for my liking.
See also:
dig deep
dig in deeper
go off the deep end
in deep water
off the deep end

deep down
in one's innermost feelings: e.g. Deep down, he knew the truth.

deep throat
fellatio; oral stimulation of the penis.

deflower
(of a woman) deprive of virginity.

dekko
a look: e.g. Have a dekko at this!

deknackered
castrated.

deli
delicatessen. (also: dellie)

delight the taste buds
taste delicious.

delish
delicious.

deliver the goods
1. agree, consent to have sexual intercourse: e.g. She finally delivered the goods last night.
2. be true to one's promise; fulfil a promise or bargain.

dellie
delicatessen. (also: deli)

demo
demonstration: e.g. Make sure they give you a demo before you buy anything.

demo model
car used for demonstration or test-drive purposes.

demolish
eat or drink greedily or with great enjoyment.

demon
1. motorcycle policeman.
2. detective.

demon for work
one who is always an energetic and enthusiastic worker.

Demons
Melbourne VFL football team.

den of iniquity
squalid place; place where illegal things go on.

dense
stupid; lacking in intelligence: e.g. He's so dense.

dent (someone's) ego
deflate; mock; make fun of (someone).

departed
(the . . .) the dead.

dero
a derelict; a socially forsaken person; a homeless vagrant, characterised by slovenly, unkempt appearance and, in many cases, alcoholism. (also: derro)
See also:
pack of derros

derriere
bum; buttocks.

derro
(see: dero)

descend upon (someone) like a ton of bricks
1. make an unexpected visit on (someone).
2. make a sudden and hostile attack on (someone).

desperate
so willing to have sex as to go out with a very unattractive or ugly person in order to achieve it.

devil
1. sly, clever, mischievously energetic but likeable person: e.g. He's a cheeky little devil!
2. person in unfortunate circumstances: e.g. The poor devil's in hospital.
3. nerve; fighting spirit; energy: e.g. He's got a bit of devil in him.
See also:
bargain with the devil
be a devil
better the devil you know than the one you don't
caught between the devil and the deep blue sea
give the devil his due
let the devil take the hindmost
play the very devil with
raise the devil
side with the devil
speak/talk of the devil
trade with the devil

devil of a
very difficult; distasteful; unpleasant: e.g. That was a devil of a job.

devil to pay
serious trouble or consequences to face: e.g. You're going to have the devil to pay for staying out so late.

devil-may-care attitude
reckless; happy-go-lucky.

devil's advocate
an advocate of an opposing or bad cause; one who finds fault for the sake of argument.

devil's number
the number 87, which is 13 short of 100 in a sporting score.

devil's own job
difficult task: e.g. He's going to have the devil's own job convincing the court of his innocence.

devil's own luck
unusually good luck or fortune.

devils-on-the-coals
(see: beggars-in-the-pan)

dewy-eyed
1. naive; innocent; trusting.
2. close to tears.

dial
the face: e.g. He's got the ugliest dial I've ever seen.
See also:
wipe the smile off (someone's) dial

diamond anniversary
sixtieth wedding anniversary (sometimes the seventy-fifth), where a gift of diamonds is usual.

diamonds are a girl's best friend
(of a woman) mercenary attitude to friendship from a man.

dibs
marbles, pertaining to sanity: e.g. He's lost his dibs.
See also:
lose (one's) dibs
play for dibs

dice
1. reject; throw out or away: e.g. Dice what you don't want.
2. (motor-racing) situation where two cars jockey for position.
See also:
fair shake of the dice!
load the dice
no dice
whole box and dice

dice with death
to act dangerously.

dicey
risky; unreliable: e.g. This ladder feels a bit dicey.

dick
1. the penis.
2. a detective.
3. foolish, dislikeable person.
See also:
clever-dick
had the dick

dickens
1. euphemism for a mild oath; the devil; hell:

e.g. 1. What the dickens are you doing now! 2. You scared the dickens out of me!
2. (see: true dickens).

dick-head
fool; idiot; disliked person.

dick-headed
foolish; rash; stupid.

dickie
penis (particularly in children's speech).

dickory dock
(rhyming slang) cock; clock.

dicky
unsound; dicey; shaky; risky; difficult: e.g. He's in a dicky situation.

dicky-bird
bird (particularly in children's speech).

dicky-whacker
1. man who masturbates.
2. person who deceives himself by refusing to acknowledge the truth; a wanker.

did the sparks fly!
exclamation that a situation was very argumentative or that someone became very angry.

did you dip the wick?
(of a man) did you have sexual intercourse?

For other possible entries beginning with 'did' see entries listed under 'do'.

diddle
1. cheat; swindle: e.g. I think I got diddled by that shopkeeper.
2. tinker with: e.g. Don't diddle with it!

diddler
a cheat or swindler.

diddums
1. (in children's speech) did he/she/you?: e.g. Diddums wet your little pants?
2. used to express one's scorn at someone who is acting in a childish manner.
3. affectionate, pet name.

diddy
the toilet, lavatory.

didn't bat an eyelid
showed no emotion; didn't notice (or pretended not to): e.g. He didn't bat an eyelid when I took my clothes off.

didn't come down in/with the last shower
a claim that one is shrewder, smarter than one is given credit for.

didn't know what hit him/her
was taken completely unawares, causing confusion or dismay.

didn't know which way to look
suffered, felt embarrassed.

didn't see (someone) for the dust

didn't see (someone's) heels for the dust
pertaining to (someone) who has departed in great haste.

didn't touch the sides
(of a drink such as beer, tea) wasn't sufficient to quench the thirst, desire.

didn't turn a hair
showed no emotion or pretended not to notice.

For other possible entries beginning with 'didn't' see entries listed under 'wouldn't' or 'couldn't'.

die
1. suffer extreme embarrassment, remorse: e.g. I nearly died when my pants fell down in front of everybody.
2. (Australian Rules football) give up; run out of puff: e.g. The team died in the last quarter.
See also:
die-hard
do or die
dying for
never say die

die a thousand deaths
suffer severe embarrassment or mental anguish.

die hard
refuse to budge or yield; resist to the last: e.g. Some habits really die hard — like smoking.
See also:
die-hard

die laughing
laugh to a state of tears and exhaustion.

die on (someone)
1. to die, leaving someone with the burden of responsibilities arising from the death.
2. fall asleep in (someone's) company: e.g. We went to the party to have a ball and he died on me!

die trying
persist stubbornly; refuse to give up.

die with (one's) boots on
1. die violently.
2. to die suddenly or before expected.

died in the arse
1. failed completely: e.g. His latest scheme died in the arse.
2. became completely worn out or exhausted; lost vitality: e.g. The party just died in the arse.

die-hard
stubborn, conservative person.

diff
1. difference: e.g. What's the diff?
2. (of a motor-car) differential — arrangement of gears enabling driving wheels to revolve at different speeds.

different folks, different strokes
what is suitable for one person is not necessarily suitable for another.

different kettle of fish

different story again
another story, matter, thing, person, or situation altogether from the one being discussed.

dig
1. cutting or sarcastic remark: e.g. That was a nasty dig.
2. poke fun at; remark sarcastically: e.g. He always digs at me.
3. understand; comprehend: e.g. Do you dig?
4. like; admire: e.g. I used to really dig the Beatles' music.
5. take notice; look at: e.g. Did you dig the big boobs on her?
6. form of greeting, address among men (digger): e.g. G'day dig.
7. (cricket) an innings.
See also:
have a dig (at)
stand on (one's) dig

dig deep
1. donate money; find funds: e.g. I'm really going to have to dig deep to pay for this new car.
2. find out more information, particularly that which is secretive or concealed.

dig in deeper
become more stubborn, firm: e.g. Every time I try to reason with him he digs in deeper.

dig in/into
apply oneself vigorously and enthusiastically to work, food etc.

dig it in
persist with sarcasm or knowledge that is embarrassing or belittling: e.g. I know I made a mistake but you don't have to dig it in.

dig (one's) heels in
remain stubborn, firm.

dig (one's) own grave
cause (one's) own downfall, ruin.

dig out/up
discover; reveal.

dig up
1. find money for some purpose: e.g. I have to dig up a thousand dollars before tomorrow.
2. discover; find; reveal; bring to light: e.g. Did you dig up anything new to help our case?

dig up dirt
find out something scandalous or malicious to say about someone.

dig up the past
reveal, find out information or persistently disclose facts from the past: e.g. I wish she wouldn't always dig up the past when we argue.

digger
1. returned Serviceman — especially from World War 1.
2. an Australian.
3. term of friendly address among men; mate: e.g. G'day digger!

diggings/digs
lodgings; living quarters: e.g. His digs are on the other side of town.

digits
the fingers.

dike
(see: dyke)

dildo
artificial erect penis.

dill/dillpot
a fool; person who has good intentions but lacks intelligence.

dilly
1. terrific, amazing, excellent or first-rate: e.g. That's a dilly of an idea!
2. silly; crazy; mad.

dillybag
bag for carrying general purpose items.

dilly-dally
dawdle; waste time with indecision; vacillate.

dim
stupid; dumb: e.g. He's too dim to understand.
See also:
take a dim view of

dime a dozen
commonplace: e.g. These things are a dime a dozen.

dim-sim allowance
term coined for any restrictive work practice, and based on the case where workers on a building site near Sydney's Chinatown were paid extra because they objected to having to work with the smell of Chinese cooking in the air.

dim-sims
testicles; balls.

dimwit
stupid person.

din-dins
dinner; food: e.g. What's for din-dins?

dine at the Y
perform cunnilingus; oral stimulation of the vagina.

ding
1. minor accident between two vehicles: e.g. I had a slight ding at the supermarket car-park.
2. a dent in a car or vehicle: e.g. My car got a ding in it at the local car-park.
3. an argument: e.g. My parents had a ding last night again.
4. a fool: e.g. He's such a ding!

5. a successful and noisy party, happening or event (short for wing-ding): e.g. We went to a terrific ding last night.
6. the penis.
7. backside or bum.
8. to smash, break or damage: e.g. Don't ding the car!

dingaling
fool; idiot; silly, amusing or eccentric person.

dingbat
idiotic, foolish or peculiar person.

dingbats
idiotic; foolish; crazy; irrational.

ding-dong
1. noisy argument: e.g. We had a real ding-dong last night!
2. silly, foolish person.

dinger
backside; bum: e.g. I'll kick that dog in the dinger if it doesn't shut up!

dingo
1. term of contempt for a person considered to be treacherous.
2. an ugly woman.
See also:
dry as a dead dingo's dong
high as a dingo's howl
put on a dingo act
turn dingo

dink
carry someone as an extra passenger on a pushbike.

dinkum
1. genuine; real; authentic; cannot be faulted; the truth: e.g. He's a dinkum Aussie.
2. genuinely interested in a proposal: e.g. Are you dinkum about going overseas?
3. telling the truth: e.g. Are you dinkum?
4. an excellent, admirable example: e.g. 1. You little dinkum! You won! 2. That was a dinkum party!
See also:
fair dinkum

dinkum oil
reliable and truthful information or advice.

dinky
1. small; miniature.
2. neat; pretty; attractive: e.g. What a dinky little house they have.

dinky-di
1. really?; truthfully?; is that so?
2. really!; truthfully!; that's so!
3. (see: dinkum, 1., 2., 3.)

dinner
(see: do someone like a dinner; done like a dog's dinner; done up like a dinner)

dinnies
dinner; tea: e.g. What's for dinnies?

dip
short swim.

dip in
help financially; donate money towards: e.g. Everyone is dipping in for a present for the boss for Christmas.

dip into (one's) pocket
pay; donate money; spend.

dip into the piggy-bank
to take money somewhat unwillingly from a savings account to pay for something.

dip (one's) lid to
congratulate, salute or greet someone; show a gesture of respect.

dip (one's) wick
(of a man) have sexual intercourse.

dip out
1. fail: e.g. He dipped out badly in his exams.
2. stay neutral; refuse to become involved; renege; withdraw.
3. miss out on: e.g. I dipped out of the big prize by one number.

dip south
spend money; reach into one's pockets: e.g. I've had to dip south in a big way this week — all my bills seem to have come at once.

dip your left eye in hot cocky shit!
a rude remark of contempt, dismissal.

dippy
stupid; crazy; eccentric.

dipshit
(see: dipstick)

dipso
an alcoholic; a heavy drinker.

dipstick
a fool; crazy, mad or insane person; stupid person; person held in contempt.

dirt
1. anything or anyone vile, immoral, obscene or held in contempt.
2. malicious, scurrilous gossip; foul, obscene language.
3. property; a block or section of land.
See also:
cheap as dirt
dig up dirt
do (someone) dirt
eat dirt
treat (someone) like dirt

dirt cheap
inexpensive; a bargain: e.g. The house was dirt cheap.

dirt money
extra payment or wages for working under difficult and dirty conditions.

dirty
1. vile; mean; obscene; indecent; sordid; treacherous, despicable.
2. angry; annoyed; upset: e.g. He's been dirty all day.

3. adjective used to emphasise 'big': e.g. This dirty big bloke made my husband, who's six foot two, look like a mouse!
See also:
do the dirty on (someone)
do the dirty work
fight dirty
pull the dirty

dirty (book, movie etc.)
obscene; pornographic; lewd.

dirty deed
sexual intercourse (especially of men): e.g. Did you do the dirty deed with that girl you took home last night?

dirty ditty
lewd and vulgar song.

dirty dog
despicable person without principles or conscience.

dirty end of the stick
the worst or most unpleasant task or share of the work: e.g. I'm sick of being given the dirty end of the stick all the time!

dirty linen
scandalous facts about one's private life: e.g. Politicians always manage to find some dirty linen to air about their opponents.
See also:
wash (one's) dirty linen in public

dirty look
a look or expression of disgust or disapproval.

dirty mind
obsessively lewd, bawdy or obscene thinking.

dirty movie
pornographic movie; blue movie.

dirty old man
lascivious man, especially an older one.

dirty on (someone)
angry or annoyed with (someone).

dirty rotter
underhanded, treacherous and corrupt person.

dirty tricks
underhanded, corrupt and treacherous activities or tactics, designed to discredit or gain unfair advantage: e.g. I wouldn't vote for him — he's full of dirty tricks.

dirty weekend
weekend spent with a lover exploring lascivious delights.

dirty word
1. vulgar or obscene word; swear word.
2. any word, person, object or matter that is objectionable or unmentionable: e.g. Work is a dirty word as far as they are concerned.

dirty work
unpleasant task or job.
See also:
do (someone's) dirty work
do the dirty work

disappear
depart; leave; go: e.g. It's getting late — I think it's time we disappeared.

disappear into thin air
vanish; become lost; go without trace: e.g. I can't find it — it seems to have disappeared into thin air.

disaster area
1. any untidy, messy place, room, living quarters etc.
2. a person who is always experiencing trouble, difficulty or misfortune.

disc-jockey
radio music-show compere.

disco
pertaining to discothèques — places where people are able to dance to recorded music.

dish
1. sexually attractive man or woman: e.g. He's such a dish!
2. abandon; throw out; discard; sack or terminate: e.g. They've decided to dish that plan.

dish out
1. distribute; hand out: e.g. They stand on street corners dishing out pamphlets to the public.
2. pay money unwillingly or with a disgruntled attitude: e.g. We had to dish out an extra thousand dollars!
3. abandon; throw out; discard; sack: e.g. Dish out the things you don't want.

dish up
1. serve food.
2. say or do something that will be met with contempt or annoyance: e.g. I wish he wouldn't dish up all that nonsense at the meetings.

dish-licker
greyhound dog.

dish-water
pertaining to tea, soup, or any other drink or food that is weak looking or distasteful.
See also:
dull as dish-water

dishy
sexually attractive.

ditch
1. throw away; discard; give up; abandon: e.g. We're going to ditch that plan in favour of another.
2. make a forced landing of an aircraft, particularly at sea.
3. to break off a relationship: e.g. It's time I ditched him!
See also:
last-ditch effort

ditch-digger
common labourer seen as having no responsibilities or esteem.

dive
disreputable place of entertainment: e.g. That club is a dive.
See also:
take a dive

divvy
dividend, profit, especially at race meetings.

divvy up
share out; divide amongst: e.g. The prize was divvied up equally amongst the syndicate.

divvy-van
police van used to transport arrested people.

dixie-bashing
employed in a kitchen etc. washing dishes and pots — especially in the Army.

dizzy blonde
foolish, dumb or small-minded blonde-haired woman.

DJ
1. disc-jockey.
2. denim jacket.

do
1. party; celebration; event; happening: e.g. We're having a big do for his birthday.
2. a hairstyle: e.g. hair-do.
3. beat up; thrash; assault: e.g. I'll do him if I ever see his face around here again.
4. have sexual intercourse with: e.g. 1. He'd love to do her. 2. I'll bet he does her before the night's through.
5. cheat or swindle: e.g. 1. He'll do you if you're not careful. 2. I think I've been done over this car.
6. lose, forfeit, expend or consume completely: e.g. 1. You'll do all your money at the casino. 2. He did his dough on the pokies.
See also:
make do

do a backflip
demonstrate a strong emotion, such as anger, excitement, joy etc.: e.g. He's going to do a backflip when he finds out he won the lottery.

do a blackfella/blackfeller
shirk, avoid one's duties by disappearing, falling asleep etc.

do a bunk
(see: do a flit)

do a dash
depart in a hurry.

do a flit
1. elope; escape; run away, especially from a commitment or responsibility.
2. change one's place of residence quickly and secretly in order to avoid someone: e.g. They did a flit before the landlord could collect the rent they owed.

do a freeze
suffer from being very cold: e.g. I do a freeze every time I go to Melbourne.

do a job on (someone)
attack and severely slander, damage (someone's) reputation, good name, integrity.

do a line with (someone)
(of a man) flirt with a woman with a view to seduction.

do a Melba
the habit of returning from retirement to do 'farewell' performances.

do a moonlight flit
(see: do a flit)

do a perish
to die.

do a runner
flee; desert; abandon; walk out on: e.g. He did a runner before the police could catch him.

do a slow burn
smoulder with anger.

do a (someone)
copy, imitate (someone); behave or react as someone else would: e.g. Do a Cagney (imitate Cagney); Do a Bogart (imitate Bogart).

do a U-ee/U-ie
perform a U-turn in a car, vehicle.

do a world of good
be beneficial; help; do good.

do an about-face
1. turn around and go back the same way: e.g. We were half-way there but had to do an about-face because we forgot something.
2. change loyalties; retreat from one argument or opinion to the opposite: e.g. He did an about-face and voted for the others this time.

do as I say and not as I do
an instruction issued by adults to children (usually) to behave as they dictate, regardless of the fact that they themselves may be behaving differently.

do away with
1. discard; throw away: e.g. I'm going to do away with all the old clothes I don't wear.
2. kill: e.g. She did away with her husband by using poison.

Do bears shit in the woods? Is the Pope a Catholic?
stock reply to someone who asks a question to which the answer is obviously 'yes'.

do it
engage in sexual activity, intercourse: e.g. I can't imagine her doing it, can you?

do it for kicks
do something for the thrill, temporary pleasure, daring, fun or excitement.

do it on (one's) ear/head
do something with great ease and confidence.

do it on the off-chance
do something on the remote chance that it may succeed: e.g. I bought a lottery ticket just on the off-chance and could hardly believe it when I won.

do it standing on (one's) head
do something with great ease and confidence.

do it the hard way
choose a needlessly difficult manner of doing something.

do it with one arm tied behind (one's) back
do something with great ease and confidence.

do (one's) back in
injure (one's) back through mishap or strenuous activity.

do (one's) balls over
(of men) become infatuated or obsessed with: e.g. He's really done his balls over her.

do (one's) bit
contribute; participate; do (one's) share.

do (one's) block
become very angry; lose (one's) temper.

do (one's) bum
ruin (oneself) financially; go broke in a failed venture.

do (one's) bun/cruet
lose (one's) temper.

do (one's) business
to urinate or defecate.

do (one's) damnedest/ darnedest
try very hard; do (one's) best; excel.

do (one's) dough
squander, lose or waste (one's) money, especially on a gamble: e.g. He's always doing his dough on the pokies at the casino.

do (one's) homework
preparatory work in order to become familiar with any relevant facts prior to a meeting, interview, event or undertaking.

do (one's) level best
try very hard; excel; exert oneself.

do (one's) lolly/nana/narna/ nut
lose (one's) temper; become very angry.

do (one's) nuts over
(see: do one's balls)

do (one's) onion/quince/ scone
lose (one's) temper; become suddenly angry.

do (one's) stuff
show (one's) skills, abilities: e.g. He can really do his stuff when it comes to fixing the car.

do (one's) thing
pursue a favourite activity; act according to (one's) own beliefs; behave in a manner most satisfying to (oneself).

do (oneself) a mischief
to injure (oneself), especially of a man injuring his genitals.

do (oneself) in
commit suicide: e.g. He did himself in with a shotgun.

do or die
pertaining to a supreme last effort or chance.

do (someone) a good turn
do (someone) a favour.

do (someone) dirt
behave unfairly, unjustly, wrongly towards (someone).

do (someone) in
1. kill (someone): e.g. She did him in with a kitchen knife.
2. exhaust, tire, wear (someone) out: e.g. You'll do him in if you expect him to work all day in the sun.

do (someone) like a dinner
defeat (someone) soundly either physically, verbally, mentally or in some form of contest; get the better of (someone).

do (someone) out of
swindle, cheat or deprive (someone): e.g. She did him out of a fortune and ran off with another man.

do (someone) over
1. have sexual intercourse with (someone): e.g. He'd love to do her over.
2. beat up; assault; physically and violently defeat: e.g. He did Fred over in a pub brawl and put him in hospital.

do (someone) proud
treat lavishly.

do (someone's) dirty work
do an unpleasant task for someone.

do the dirty
use unfair tactics; cheat; behave unjustly and corruptly: e.g. It was bad enough when she cheated on him but she really did the dirty when she took all his money as well.

do the dirty work
do the most unpleasant tasks (often for no reward or thanks).

do the honours
to do delegated duties, chores that are usually pleasant.

do the messages
run errands.

do the right thing by
treat with respect and generosity: e.g. He did the

right thing by me when I was in trouble.

do the rounds
1. pay visits: e.g. We always do the rounds at Christmas.
2. perform tasks or allotted chores: e.g. It's our turn to do the rounds this week.
3. (of gossip) become generally known.

do the rounds of the kitchen
1. perform the usual duties in a kitchen; tidy up; housework.
2. lose one's temper; verbally abuse someone.

do the trick
achieve the desired result: e.g. Wear the sexy red dress — that'll do the trick.

do the world of good
be extremely beneficial: e.g. It'll do him the world of good to have a holiday for a few weeks.

do time
serve a prison term: e.g. He's doing time for murder.

do to death
do until hackneyed, commonplace or boring; over-do: e.g. That song's been done to death on the radio.

do up
renovate; restore: e.g. We're doing up our house.

do wees
urinate.

do without
refrain from having — often due to poverty.

For other possible entries beginning with 'do' see entries listed under 'done'.

dob
(Australian Rules football) kick a goal: e.g. He's dobbed that one.

dob in
contribute, especially money; donate: e.g. We all dobbed in for a present for the boss.

dob on (someone)
betray; tell on; inform on.

dob (someone) in
1. betray; inform on.
2. nominate someone for an unpleasant task, usually in that person's absence.

dobber
an informer.

dobbin
name for any large work-horse or aged, inferior horse.

doc
doctor.

doctor
1. to alter something to suit oneself; tamper with; falsify; modify; adulterate: e.g. This account has been doctored.
2. to castrate or spay an animal.
3. an expert; one who makes the decision: e.g. You're the doctor!
See also:
Albany doctor
an apple a day keeps the doctor away
Fremantle doctor
go for the doctor
just what the doctor ordered
play doctors and nurses

dodger
1. artful, elusive, shifty or dishonest person.
2. bread: e.g. All he had to eat was a hunk of stale old dodger.
3. a sausage: e.g. Throw another bunch of dodgers on the barbie.
4. a pamphlet that is distributed in the street to passers-by.

dodgy
tricky; difficult; unsure; deceitful: e.g. That deal sounds a bit dodgy to me.

dodo
dull-witted, dumb or stupid person.
See also:
dead as a dodo

doer
1. one who gets things done; an efficient person; a trier.
2. an eccentric, amusing or odd person: e.g. He's a bit of a doer, is old Alf.

doesn't give a hang/hoot/rat's arse/shit/stuff
doesn't care at all.

doesn't know B from a bull's foot!
pertaining to someone who is ignorant of the facts, stupid.

doesn't know whether (one) is Arthur or Martha

doesn't know whether it's Pitt Street or Christmas

doesn't know whether it's Tuesday or Bourke Street
pertaining to somebody who is stupid or always confused.

doesn't miss a trick
alert, never failing to miss an opportunity.

doesn't pull any punches
1. honest; direct; candid; outspoken.
2. harsh with opponents, having no mercy.

dog
1. woman considered extremely unattractive or ugly.
2. any despicable person.
3. pursue; hound; annoy: e.g. He's been dogging me all week for an answer.
See also:
bad dog
blow a blue dog off its chain
can't teach an old dog new tricks

common as dog-shit
couldn't drive a greasy stick up a dead dog's arse
couldn't pull a greasy stick out of a dead dog's arse
crooked as a dog's hind leg
dirty dog
done like a dog's dinner
every bastard/man and his dog
every dog has its day
go to the dogs
hair of the dog
happy as a dog with two tails
in the dogbox/doghouse
kill a brown dog
lame dog
lap dog
lead a dog's life
let sleeping dogs lie
like a greasy stick up a dead dog's arse
love me, love my dog
need (something) like a dog needs a flogging
not all (one's) dogs are barking
off like a robber's dog
old dog at
randy as a drover's dog
see a man about a dog
sick as a dog
sniffer dog
so hard a dog wouldn't sink a tooth in it
stand/stick out like dogs' balls
stink a dog off a gut-wagon
straight as a dog's hind leg
take (one's) dog for a walk
top dog
turn dog
two men and a dog
under-dog
why keep a dog and bark oneself?

dog days
the hottest part of the year.

dog tied up
(to have a . . .) to have an unpaid debt.

dogbox
1. train compartment without a corridor.
2. very small house; cramped living quarters.
See also:
in the dogbox

dog-collar
a stiff clerical collar.

dog-eared
pertaining to the corners of pages of a book which are turned down and tatty through constant use.

dog-eat-dog
pertaining to extreme competitiveness: e.g. Racing and gambling are real dog-eat-dog worlds.

dog-fight
a violent and noisy fight or argument.

dogger
dingo hunter.

doggie
small dog; nickname for a dog. (also: doggy)

doggie fashion
sexual intercourse performed on all fours — hands and knees — like an animal.

doggie-bag
special bag provided by restaurants to put left-over food in for customers to take home on request.

Doggies
Footscray VFL football team.

doggo
(see: lie doggo)

doggone
1. euphemism for damn, damned: e.g. Get that doggone thing out of here at once!
2. extremely; very; absolutely: e.g. He's so doggone wealthy!

dog-hairs
(see: hair of the dog)

do-gooder
a social reformer whose reforms are usually not popular; one who is a well-meaning activist.

dogs
1. greyhound racing: e.g. See you at the dogs next week.
2. (cap.) Footscray VFL football team.

dog's breakfast
any untidy mess.

dog's disease
a cold or the flu.

dog's eye
(rhyming slang) pie.

dog-tired
exhausted; worn out.

dog-tucker
(of an animal or food) fit only to be used as food for dogs.

doing
(see: nothing doing!; take some doing)

doing a roaring trade
doing extremely well and profitably.

doing a stint
doing an allotted amount of work; doing something for an allotted amount of time (such as serving a prison sentence): e.g. I'm doing a stint at the office this week because the secretary's sick.

doing over
1. a sound beating, bashing, defeat or scolding.
2. sexual intercourse: e.g. She's had a doing over by all the boys in town.
See also:
get done over
give (someone) a doing over

doing time
serving a prison sentence: e.g. He's doing time for murder.

doings
ingredients; necessary items: e.g. We've got all the doings to have a barbecue.

dole
social security benefits; a cheque from the government to support people who can't find employment.

dole-bludger
unemployed person held in contempt for receiving government benefits without making serious effort to find work.

doley
1. person receiving the dole.
2. (see: dole-bludger)

doll
sexually attractive man or woman.

dolled up
dressed smartly, sometimes too much so for the occasion: e.g. It's no use getting dolled up for a barbecue.

dollop
shapeless and messy lump of food.

Dolly Varden
woman's large, wide-brimmed hat, usually adorned with flowers.

D.O.M.
dirty old man.

dome
the head.

domestic
an argument with one's spouse at home or elsewhere: e.g. We had a bit of a domestic last night but we're fine now.

done
1. cheated; tricked; hoodwinked: e.g. I think I've been done!
2. socially acceptable: e.g. That's just not done!
3. agreed!
See also:
badly done by
get done
hard done by

done for
1. dead or close to death.
2. exhausted; worn out; tired.
3. in deep trouble: e.g. He's done for after what he did.
4. ruined; finished: e.g. It's no use trying to repair that — it's done for.

done in
exhausted; very tired: e.g. I'm really done in — think I'll rest.
See also:
get done in

done it now!
exclamation that the limits of patience or propriety have been breached: e.g. You've done it now! You're fired!

done like a (dog's) dinner
completely and utterly defeated.

done (one's) dash
to have lost (one's) chance or opportunity.

done (one's) dough
1. to have spent all (one's) money foolishly; to have lost (one's) money gambling.
2. to have been cheated of (one's) money.

done out of
cheated; treated unfairly and thereby incurring a loss: e.g. He was done out of his job for something he didn't do.

done over
1. beaten in a fight.
2. cheated; tricked; hoodwinked.
3. sexually molested; to have had sexual intercourse with: e.g. She's been done over by every bloke I know.

done the dirty deed
1. performed an unpleasant task.
2. had sexual intercourse: e.g. Has he done the dirty deed with her yet?

done thing
socially acceptable: e.g. Farting at the table isn't the done thing.

done to a T/turn
completed to perfection: e.g. The dinner's done to a T.

done to death
repeated until hackneyed; over-used; over-exposed: e.g. That song has been done to death over the radio.

done up like a Christmas tree

done up like a dinner

done up like a pet lizard

done up like a pox-doctor's clerk

done up like a sore finger/toe

done up like an organ-grinder's monkey

done up to the nines
1. dressed in one's best.
2. over-dressed for the occasion.

done with
1. finished with: e.g. Are you done with that book?
2. renounced: e.g. I'm done with him after the awful things he did to me.
3. ruined: e.g. After what he did, his business is done with.

dong
1. penis: e.g. He's got a dong like a horse! (also: donger)
2. hit; bash: e.g. I'm so mad I could dong him!

donga/donger
1. poor living quarters; tin shed; five or ten man hut used as temporary quarters for single male workers.

2. remote, country areas: e.g. He lives up the donga somewhere.

donk
engine: e.g. My car needs a new donk.

donkey
1. silly, obstinate or foolish person; fool.
2. a cigarette that is lit from another cigarette.

donkey vote
the insertion of preference numbers on a ballot paper in the same order as the listed candidates with no thought given to actual preferences.

donkey work
tedious work; drudgery.

donkey-lick
defeat soundly and easily, especially in horse-racing.

donkey's years
a long time.

donnybrook
a noisy fight or argument.

Dons
Essendon VFL football team.

don't all speak/talk at once
an expression used when confronted with silence.

don't bank on it
don't count, depend on it.

don't blink or you'll miss it
expression used when something (like a town) is so small as to be insignificant or easily missed.

don't bust a foofer valve/boiler
don't try too hard or over-exert yourself or you might cause yourself injury.

don't care a hoot/two hoots
not to care at all.

don't come the raw prawn/uncooked crustacean!
don't try to fool or deceive!

don't count your chickens before they're hatched
a warning not to expect or anticipate the outcome as things could quite conceivably turn out differently.

don't do anything I wouldn't do
jocular form of farewell and advice to someone going on a trip, holiday.

don't get your knickers in a knot/twist

don't get your tits in a tangle

don't get your toga in a knot
admonition not to get upset or angry so quickly.

don't give a bugger/continental/damn/darn/hoot/shit/stuff
not to care at all.

don't give me any of your lip
don't give cheek, answer back or be impertinent.

don't go in much for
show little enthusiasm for or interest in: e.g. I don't go in much for drugs or booze.

don't go nap on
to not favour, agree with, like: e.g. He never went nap on wine, but loved his beer.

don't hold with
don't agree with: e.g. I don't hold with any form of sexual violence as entertainment.

don't hold your breath
an expression indicating that something is going to take a long time.

don't knock it till you've tried it
don't criticise what you are not familiar with or what you haven't experienced personally.

don't know where (it's/someone's/etc.) been!
jocular exclamation of protest: e.g. I can't kiss him — I don't know where he's been!

don't let it throw you
don't be discouraged or put off by set-backs.

don't let the cat out of the bag
don't reveal a confidence or tell a secret.

don't let things get to you
don't be discouraged or put off by set-backs.

don't look a gift horse in the mouth
don't question the origins of gifts or favours or the motives of the giver; don't accept gifts ungraciously.

don't lose your head
1. don't get angry in haste; don't panic or act without thought.
2. don't become infatuated with someone.

don't make me laugh!
expression of disbelief, ridicule or disdain.

don't make waves
don't create problems or difficulties that may threaten the status quo.

don't pick your nose or your head will cave in
an insult to someone who is not very clever, lacking in intelligence.

don't push your luck
don't try to stretch your luck or fortune too far, or it may turn out badly for you.

don't put all your eggs in one basket
don't risk everything on one single enterprise.

don't put shit on me/someone
don't criticise, disparage or mock me/someone.

don't rock the boat
don't create problems or difficulties that may threaten the status quo.

don't spare the horses
hurry at all costs; act in utmost haste.

don't stand around like a bottle of stale piss
don't shirk your responsibilities by standing around and being idle.

don't strain yourself!
jocular or sarcastic remark to someone who is idle or not trying very hard at all.

doobrie/doobrieshankle/doodackie/doodad/doodah
1. any trifling ornament, decoration or trivial gadgetry.
2. any object for which one cannot remember the correct name immediately: e.g. Where's the doodad that's supposed to screw on to this thing here?

doodle
the penis.

doodlebob
(see: doobrie)

doodlebug
idle, ineffectual person.

doofer/doohickie
(see: doobrie)

dooks
hands: e.g. Put up your dooks and fight like a man! (also: dukes)
See also:
molly-dooker

DOOL
Days Of Our Lives — a popular, long-running television daytime soap opera.

doolackie
(see: doobrie)

doona
quilted eiderdown, filled with feathers or synthetic stuffing.

door
(see: behind closed doors; came in by the back door; lay it at someone's door; open doors; show someone the door; shut the door in someone's face)

doormat
subservient, spiritless person who meekly accepts bad treatment.

doormoney
admission fee.

door-to-door
canvassing or selling by visiting each house in a street.

doover
the penis.

doover/dooverlackey/dooverlackie
(see: doobrie)

doozy
anything excellent or first rate.

dope
1. marijuana; pot; grass; any narcotic.
2. idiot; fool; simpleton.
3. information; true facts: e.g. What's the latest dope on that case?

dopey
stupid; slow-witted.

dork
1. the penis.
2. stupid, dull-witted person.

dorky
stupid; corny.

Dorothy Dixer
question phrased in such a way that the answer is what one wanted to hear.

dos and don'ts
rules: e.g. Here's a list of dos and don'ts for the staff.

dose
venereal disease, particularly gonorrhoea: e.g. He got a dose while he was overseas.

dose of (one's) own medicine
an unpleasant treatment or experience given to (one) as a result of (one's) own nasty treatment of others.

dosh
money.

doss down
sleep in temporary bedding arrangements.

dosshouse
cheap boarding house for homeless men.

dot
1. the female pudendum.
2. hit: e.g. Dot him one if he bothers you again.
See also:
in the year dot
on the dot
sign on the dotted line

dot and a dash
pertaining to the female anus and genitals: e.g. That's not a bull calf — it's got a dot and a dash!

dot (one's) i's and cross (one's) t's
to be meticulous, fussy.

dots and carries one
walks with a limp.

dotty
silly; crazy; eccentric.

double
1. a ticket for two.
2. a bet on two horses in different races.
See also:
lead a double life
on the double

double back
retrace (one's) steps or route.

double or nothing/quits
a bet or gamble where the person betting stands to lose twice as much if he loses or be free of the original debt if he wins.

double take
delayed reaction, second look at a situation or person as its/his meaning or significance is grasped: e.g. He did a double take when she walked in because he thought she was dead.

double time
extra wages, usually double, paid for working on public holidays or after certain hours.

double-barrelled
1. having a double purpose, meaning or significance.
2. (of a surname) hyphenated.

double-bunk
sleep together in a single bed.

double-cross
1. an act of treachery: e.g. That was a double-cross.
2. deceive; betray; dupe; trick: e.g. He double-crossed me.

double-dealing
1. treachery; betrayal.
2. treacherous; devious.

double-decker
two layers of something: e.g. 1. We went for a tourist ride in a double-decker bus. 2. He ate a huge double-decker sandwich.

double-dink
to carry an extra person on a bicycle or horse.

double-dutch
nonsense; gibberish; talk which cannot be understood.

double-faced
hypocritical; dishonest.

double-jointed
having flexible joints allowing parts of the body to bend in extraordinary ways.

double-park
to park a car alongside another, often illegally.

double-talk
ambiguous speech: e.g. Many politicians are full of double-talk.

double-up
occupy a position with another person such as on a horse or bike.

doubting Thomas
a disbeliever who requires tangible proof.

dough
money.
See also:
do (one's) dough

doughnut
female pudendum, vagina.

doves flying out of (one's) arse
(to have . . .) to experience orgasm.

down
depressed, dejected, gloomy: e.g. I'm feeling down today.
See also:
come down
come down on (someone)
come down to earth
come down with
dress down
go down
go down badly/well
go down on (someone)
go down the wrong way
go downhill
live it down
look down on
put (someone) down
put-down
run (someone) down
sent down
take (someone) down
talk down to
went down like a lead balloon
went down like pork at a Jewish wedding

down a few
drinking expression: e.g. We're going to down a few at the pub after work if you want to join us.

down and out
destitute; without money, friends or future; having hopeless prospects: e.g. He's really down and out since he lost his job.

down at heel
shabby; poor; impoverished.

down in the dumps/mouth
depressed; miserable; gloomy; sad; dispirited.

down on
(have a . . .) have a feeling of hostility, dislike for; a grudge or prejudice against: e.g. I can't understand why he's got a down on me.

down on (one's) arse/luck/uppers
destitute; experiencing hard times or unfortunate circumstances.

down the boozer
at the pub: e.g. Hubby's down the boozer with his mates.

down the drain/gurgler/tube(s)
lost, failed or wasted through mismanagement, misuse or misadventure: e.g. 1. All my savings went down the drain when that company went broke.
2. His business went down the drain.

down the hatch
1. down the throat.
2. expression urging someone to eat or drink up quickly.

down the road
not far-away: e.g. They live just down the road.

down the tube(s)
(see: down the drain)

down time
lost time; unproductive time.

down to brass tacks
(get . . .) discuss, face realities, basic facts: e.g. If we want this to succeed we've got to get down to brass tacks.

down to (one's) bottom dollar
reached the end of (one's) finances.

down to the ground
completely: e.g. That arrangement suits me down to the ground.

down to the last crust
destitute; broke.

down to tin tacks
(see: down to brass tacks)

down tools
1. cease work: e.g. It's time to down tools and go to the pub.
2. begin a strike: e.g. The union bosses have decided to down tools.

Down Under
pertaining to Australia and its inhabitants; in Australia; Australian: e.g. Life is all beer and skittles Down Under. (sometimes: down-under)

downcast
dejected; despondent; sad.

downer
1. a tranquilliser: e.g. Valium is a downer prescribed by too many doctors.
2. a depressing state of mind or experience: e.g. The funeral was a terrible downer.

downfall
a fall from prosperity or power: e.g. The downfall of the present Government is inevitable.

down-hearted
despondent; dejected; discouraged.

downhill
failing; getting worse; deteriorating: e.g. 1. His health is going downhill. 2. He's on a downhill run with his business.

downright
absolute; thorough; blatant: e.g. He's a downright idiot!

downright highway robbery
blatant over-charging: e.g. The cost of that meal was downright highway robbery!

downswing
a decline or deterioration in business or prosperity.

down-to-earth
1. practical; realistic; natural; unaffected; matter-of-fact; honest.
2. coarse; mildly obscene; smutty; blunt; crude; ribald.

down-trodden
oppressed; tyrannised.

down-under
(see: Down Under)

downy
sly; canny; knowing: e.g. He's a downy bird.

dowser
a water-diviner.

dowsing
water-divining.

dozer
bulldozer — heavy earth-moving machine.

drab/drac/drack
untidy; slovenly; unattractive: e.g. 1. What a drack sort his wife is! 2. She's such a drack!

drack sack/sort
slattern; unattractive person, especially a woman.

dracky
untidy; slovenly; unattractive.

drag
1. tediously boring person, task, event etc.: e.g. The party was a terrible drag.
2. a puff, inhalation of a cigarette: e.g. Can I have a drag?
3. women's clothes worn by men; clothes of transvestites: e.g. My husband went to the fancy-dress party dressed in drag.
4. the main street in town: e.g. The pub's on the main drag.
5. a race between two cars from a standstill to see which can accelerate the fastest; to race as such: e.g. 1. Want a drag? 2. He tries to drag everybody off in his new Porsche.

drag (one's) feet
hang back deliberately; move slowly and laboriously.

drag queen
transvestite; man who dresses in women's clothes; male entertainer who dresses as a woman.

drag (someone's) name through the mud
to slander, speak ill of, make defamatory remarks about (someone), usually in that person's absence.

drag (someone) off
to race with (someone's) car from a standstill to see who can accelerate the fastest — this often takes place from a red traffic-light.

drag (something) up
to raise a topic for discussion that is unpleasant, embarrassing: e.g. I wish you wouldn't drag that up again!

drag the chain
1. try to get out of one's share of the work.
2. to lag behind, especially in a drinking round.

dragged
(Australian Rules football) changed for another player, taken off the field by the coach for a mistake.

dragged in
coerced into unwillingly: e.g. I was dragged into doing it by friends.

dragged screaming from the tart shop
pertaining especially to politicians who must face something — like an election — reluctantly, and who complain noisily.

dragged through the gutter/mud
slandered; defamed; spoken ill of: e.g. Although he was innocent

his name was dragged through the gutter by the press.

dragon
1. the penis.
2. ugly, severe, strict, tyrannical woman.
See also:
drain the dragon

Dragons
St George N.S.W. Rugby League football team.

drain
(see: down the drain)

drain the dragon/lizard/ potatoes/spuds
(of men) to urinate.

drat/drats!
mild oath, curse or exclamation of annoyance; bother!

dratted
euphemism for damned, confounded: e.g. That dratted fool!

draw a bead on
1. take aim at (with a gun).
2. look closely at; pay careful attention to: e.g. I think he's drawn a bead on that pretty blonde.

draw a blank
get no response; be unsuccessful: e.g. I drew a blank when I asked the bank for a loan.

draw a fine line
to come close to the limits of propriety, safety.

draw a veil over
avoid discussing or drawing attention to: e.g. The police have drawn a veil over the matter.

draw first blood
initiate the first move and gain an initial advantage.

draw out
prolong: e.g. That meeting was so drawn out it was boring.

draw (someone) out
persuade (someone) to talk openly: e.g. It's difficult to draw him out on that particular subject.

draw straws
select a winner, volunteer etc. by drawing lots (usually matches amongst which there is a short one) — the winner being the one who chooses the short piece.

draw the crabs/crow
1. attract undesirable, unwelcome attention or criticism.
2. receive the worst part of a bargain, allocation etc.

draw the line
1. stop; decline; put a stop to.
2. fix a limit to: e.g. I like sexy movies but I draw the line at hard-core pornography with animals.

draw the short straw
to be unlucky.

drawcard
something or someone that attracts a big audience or attendance: e.g. His paintings were the main drawcard for the exhibition.

drawing a long bow
1. to be acting on a minimal chance; a long shot.
2. unbelievable; hard to believe.

drawn and quartered
(sometimes: hung, . . .) punished severely: e.g. He should be (hung,) drawn and quartered for what he did.

dreaded lurgi/lurgy
any infectious illness, such as a cold, influenza.

dream
1. sexually attractive man or woman.
2. (in combination) ideal; perfect: e.g. dream-home, dream-boat.
See also:
go like a dream
stuff dreams are made of
wouldn't dream of it

dream up
invent; concoct; think up.

dream-boat
very attractive, sexy person.

dreamer
unrealistic person given to fanciful thinking.

dreaming
imagining, believing, in an unrealistic manner: e.g. I wish Warren would stop dreaming and make a positive move towards living in Australia.

dredge up
find, locate, with difficulty: e.g. Dredge up some money.

drench
to orally administer a medication to animals for the prevention of worms.

dress
(of a man) the side the genitals hang — to the left or right — for the purpose of tailoring pants, trousers.

dress down
severely reprimand, scold: e.g. She gets dressed down every time she comes home late.

dress up
1. put on one's best clothes: e.g. We're going to really dress up for the opening night.
2. put on fancy dress, costume or disguise.
See also:
all dressed up with nowhere to go

dressed in drag
wearing clothes in the manner of a transvestite.

dressed in (one's) Sunday best
dressed in (one's) best clothes.

dressed to beat the band

dressed to kill
dressed to have an irresistible and stunning effect on.

dressed (up) to the nines
1. dressed smartly in one's best clothes.
2. over-dressed for an occasion.

dressing down
a severe reprimand, scolding.

dribs and drabs
in small and irregular amounts: e.g. The people arrived in dribs and drabs.

drift
meaning: e.g. Get my drift?

drifter
1. a shiftless, aimless, itinerant person.
2. of no fixed abode; a wanderer; hobo; tramp.

drill
recognised procedure or routine: e.g. What's the drill?

drill (someone/thing) full of holes
shoot with a gun.

drink
1. the ocean: e.g. They threw his body in the drink.
2. any body of water, such as a swimming pool.
3. small informal party or gathering: e.g. I've invited a few people over for a drink.
4. to drink alcohol, especially to excess: e.g. Does he drink?

drink and be merry
expression of good cheer.

drink in
listen, absorb, understand with eagerness: e.g. Kids drink in anything their pop-idols have to say.

drink it out of an old sock
pertaining to thirst: e.g. I'm so thirsty I'd drink it out of an old sock!

drink like a fish

drink like it's going out of fashion
excessive indulgence in alcohol.

drink (someone) under the table
to be able to out-drink, out-last someone in an alcoholic drinking bout.

drink the piss from a brewer's horse
(he'd . . .) pertaining to an alcoholic, or one who thoroughly enjoys his alcohol.

drink too much
excessive indulgence in alcohol: e.g. He drinks too much.

drink with the flies
to drink (alcohol) alone, without company.

drink-driving
driving a vehicle whilst under the influence of alcohol.

drip
boring or dreary person; fool; simpleton.

dripping diamonds
wearing an extravagantly excessive amount of diamond jewellery: e.g. She went bankrupt, but she's still dripping diamonds.

drippy
boring; dreary; stupid: e.g. She's so drippy!

drive a hard bargain
be firm and unrelenting in one's dealings.

drive it home
make a very strong point; make fully understood: e.g. Going to prison will drive it home to him that crime doesn't pay.

drive (someone) around/round the bend/twist
to exasperate, annoy, irritate (someone): e.g. During the holidays the kids drive me round the bend.

drive (someone) into a corner
force (someone) into a position allowing little or no escape.

drive (someone) mental
annoy, irritate, exasperate (someone).

drive (someone) over the edge
persist with a situation beyond the limits of (someone's) tolerance or endurance.

drive (someone) up the wall
to exasperate, annoy, irritate (someone).

drone
1. lazy, idle person.
2. boring speaker.
3. freeloader; person who lives off other people.

drongo
stupid, dull-witted, unintelligent person; a fool.

droob
1. stupid, dull-witted person; hopeless, unattractive person.
2. minute, paltry, trifling amount: e.g. He didn't get a droob from his father's will.

drool at the mouth over
(see: drool over)

drool on (about something)
talk nonsense, rubbish, drivel.

drool over
show eager desire, pleasure or anticipation for: e.g. I wish he wouldn't drool over me every time we meet!

droopy-drawers
slow, lazy, idle, ineffective, incompetent person.

'We'll have to give Bert the three major prizes — his prize-winning cod is full of prize-winning trout and prize-winning redfin!'

Most Aussie men at some time or other have participated in the great outdoors sport of fishing, affectionately termed dangling a line or drowning some worms. The stories about 'the ones that got away', together with the copious supplies of Eskies, ice and beer included with the bait and tackle, make the whole shebang sound a bit fishy to the girls, who are rarely included in these outings.

drop
1. bring someone to the ground in a fight: e.g. I'll drop him if he gives any more cheek!
2. a small drink (of alcohol).
3. renounce or be done with a girlfriend or boyfriend: e.g. I'm going to drop him.
4. (Australian Rules football) drop-kick.
See also:
at the drop of a hat
get the drop on (someone)
have the drop on (someone)
nice little drop
long drop

drop a bombshell
make a startling announcement or disclosure.

drop a brick
make a glaring social blunder, error.

drop a bundle
1. give birth.
2. disclose some startling information: e.g. He really dropped a bundle at the last meeting.
3. lose a large sum of money (particularly in gambling).

drop a clanger
disclose something embarrassing or a piece of startling information, either intentionally or inadvertently.

drop a darkie
defecate: e.g. My dog dropped a darkie on his front lawn.

drop a fart
pass wind from the anus loudly or unexpectedly.

drop a hint
casually give a clue or reminder.

drop a U-ee (U-ie)
do a sudden U-turn in a car.

drop a wheelie
accelerate (in a car) from a standing position causing the tyres to screech: e.g. We dropped a wheelie at the lights and left the others for dead (left the others behind).

drop acid
take LSD : e.g. He's smoked marijuana but he's never dropped acid.

drop bears
imaginary dangerous koalas that drop on to people's shoulders and hug them to death — a tall story fabricated to dupe gullible American Servicemen during World War 2.

drop dead!
scornful exclamation of dismissal or rejection; go away!; get lost!: e.g. 1. He can drop dead for all I care! 2. Drop dead! You don't know what you're talking about.

drop in
casually visit: e.g. I dropped in on her the other day.

drop in the ocean
small, insignificant or trifling amount when all is taken into account.

drop it
desist, cease talking about or discussing the present matter.

drop like flies
sicken and/or die in great numbers: e.g. During the drought our sheep dropped like flies.

drop of rain
small or large amount of rain: e.g. 1. We only had a drop of rain yesterday. 2. We had quite a drop of rain yesterday.

drop off
1. fall asleep: e.g. Every time we go out to their place for a visit my husband drops off.
2. decline; decrease: e.g. Business has dropped off lately.
3. to die: e.g. The old man dropped off last week.

drop on your head!
an insult; derogatory remark of contempt, dismissal.

drop one
fart; emit wind from the anus: e.g. Who just dropped one?

drop (one's) bundle
1. lose (one's) nerve; give up.
2. (of a woman) give birth.

drop (one's) daks
let (one's) pants fall.

drop (one's) gear
get undressed.

drop (one's) lunch
fart; emit wind from the anus.

drop out
1. cease to participate; withdraw; renege: e.g. I'll have to drop out of the competition because of an injury.
2. fail: e.g. He dropped out of the course.
3. (see: drop-out)

drop (someone) a line
write (someone) an informal letter.

drop (someone) in
inform on (someone); betray: e.g. Someone dropped him in to the police.

drop (someone) off
drive (someone) to a particular destination.

drop test
(joc.) a method of either repairing or testing the durability of a device, item (by dropping it).

drop the hint
make known or fully understood one's feelings

or intentions in an obvious manner: e.g. I finally dropped the hint that I didn't want him around any more and he left.

drop the magic word
(see: say the magic word)

drop-in
1. too much alcohol: e.g. I can see you've had a drop-in!
2. a casual visitor; unannounced caller.

drop-kick
1. an obnoxious, disliked person.
2. (Australian Rules football) kick where a footballer drops the ball to the ground then kicks it as it comes up.

drop-out
1. person who turns his back on conventional society and opts for an alternative life-style.
2. one who is a failure at his life, education, job etc.
3. person who leaves, opts out or fails to maintain the entrance requirements of a class, club, group, job etc.

dropsies
clumsy dropping of things; inability to hang on to anything safely: e.g. I seem to have a bad case of the dropsies today — that's the second plate I've smashed!

drover's dog
anyone inconsequential or unimportant.

droves
(see: in droves)

drown (one's) sorrows
indulge in self-pity by drinking excessive amounts of alcohol.

drown some worms
go fishing.

druggie
habitual user of drugs; an addict.

drug-pushing/running
the business of dealing in illegal drugs.

drum
accurate, profitable, authentic information or advice: e.g. I'll give you the drum — that place is not worth going to.
See also:
give (someone) the drum
hump (one's) drum
not worth a drum
run a drum

drum it in
impart information by persistent repetition.

drum out
dismiss in disgrace, ignominy: e.g. He was drummed out of politics for cheating and lying.

drum (someone)
impart accurate, reliable, profitable, authentic information or advice to (someone).

drum up
obtain; get; acquire; procure: e.g. We'll drum up some people to help with that project.

drum up some business
solicit or obtain trade.

drumstick
the lower leg portion of cooked chicken, duck or turkey.

drunk
a drunken person; an alcoholic.

drunk as a lord/skunk/an owl
intoxicated; under the influence of alcohol: e.g. Marcus gets as drunk as a skunk every Friday night with the mates.

druthers
preference; choice: e.g. If I had my druthers I think I'd go for the pink one.

dry
1. dry ginger ale: e.g. brandy and dry.
2. (the Dry) prolonged period of no rain in the tropics: e.g. This year the Dry seems to be longer.
See also:
bleed (someone) dry

dry area
an area, vicinity, locality without hotels or liquor shops.

dry as a bone

dry as a dead dingo's dong

dry as a medieval monk's manuscript

dry as nun's cunt/nasty

dry as a pommy's towel

dry as a stone god

dry as a sun-struck bone

dry as a wooden chip/idol
1. extremely dry.
2. extremely thirsty.

dry horrors
(see: get the . . .)

dry out
undergo treatment to cure alcoholism, drug addiction etc.

dry rots
(rhyming slang) trots — diarrhoea.

dry run
try-out; test-run; rehearsal.

dry sense of humour
humorous in a sarcastic, unemotional way.

dry turn
a party or function without alcoholic drinks.

dry up
be quiet; shut up; a scornful rebuff.

D's
detectives.

D.T.'s
delirium tremens — excessive shaking and trembling due to excessive indulgence in drugs or alcohol.

dub in
donate, contribute (money).

dubbo
idiot; fool; simpleton; imbecile.

duchess
dressing-table (mainly Queensland).

duck
1. woman (derog.): e.g. What's that stupid duck doing?
2. plunge someone under water momentarily.
3. (cricket) no score (on the part of a batsman who is out before scoring).
See also:
blue duck
dead duck
holy snapping duck shit!
lame duck
like water off a duck's back
sitting duck
stuff a duck!
take to (something) like a duck to water
wood duck

duck in/out
go in/out momentarily: e.g. I'll duck in and buy some bread on the way home.

ducks and geese
(rhyming slang) police.

duck's disease
(of a person) short in stature: e.g. Wayne's no good for the basketball team — he's got duck's disease!

duck's nuts
(see: bee's knees)

duck-shoving
manipulative or unfair methods in order to attain a favourable or advantageous position.

ducky
(also: duckie)
1. delightful; wonderful; excellent.
2. term of endearment such as: dear, darling.

dud
1. counterfeit article.
2. person or thing that proves to be worthless, defective or a complete failure.
3. an empty bottle (of beer or alcohol).
4. to cheat, swindle (someone).

dud bash
someone who performs poorly sexually; an unsatisfactory partner in sexual intercourse.

duds
1. trousers; pants.
2. clothes in general.

duffer
1. stupid, inefficient person; a fool.
2. cattle or sheep thief.

duffle-coat
woollen overcoat with wooden toggles for buttons and a hood — made popular during the 1960s.

dugs
breasts; boobs; tits.

dukes
hands; fists. (also: dooks)

dull as dishwater
extremely boring.

Dullsville
any boring, tedious place or thing.

dumb-bell/bum/cluck

dumbo/dum-dum
stupid person; a dunce: e.g. He's such a dumb-cluck!

dumb Dora
stupid, dumb, silly woman.

dummy
1. stupid person; a dunce.
2. counterfeit article.
3. (Australian Rules football) to feint at the ball.
See also:
spit the dummy

dummy run
a trial, testing: e.g. We'll do a dummy run tonight to make sure everything is in working order for the weekend.

dump
1. inferior, decrepit, squalid place, town etc.
2. dispose of; reject; get rid of: e.g. Dump him if he's not a good worker.
See also:
down in the dumps

dumper
1. a strong wave in the surf.
2. a tip-truck.

dumpie/dumpy
garbage collector; garbo.

dunderhead
stupid, dull-witted person; a fool.

Dungeons and Dragons
a game of role-playing involving complex mythological characters and rules — popular among children and teenagers. (Trademark)

dunger
1. toilet.
2. awful; terrible; unpleasant: e.g. That's a dunger house they live in.

dung-hill
foul, vile, terrible, unpleasant place or person.

dung-puncher
a homosexual man.

dungy
awful; terrible; vile; unpleasant.

dunk
to dip biscuits into a cup of tea or coffee.

dunno
contraction of: don't know.

dunny
toilet, especially an outside one.

See also:
all alone like a country dunny

dunny paper
toilet paper.

dunnyman
one employed to empty lavatory cans, tins, where there is no sewer connected.

durrey
a hand-rolled cigarette.

dust
(see: bite the dust; couldn't/didn't see someone for the dust; lick the dust)

dust off
to bring (something) out of storage for use again: e.g. It's time to dust off the footy gear as the season starts in two weeks.

dusted
1. beaten; thrashed; bashed; soundly defeated: e.g. Our team got dusted last Saturday.
2. killed.

dusting
a beating, bashing or sound thrashing: e.g. Our team got a dusting.

dust-up
a fight, brawl, commotion.

Dutch
a situation in which each pays his own way: e.g. We go Dutch when we go out to a restaurant.
See also:
double-dutch

Dutch auction
sale in which the price is reduced until a buyer is found.

Dutch cap
diaphragm — contraceptive device worn in the vagina.

Dutch courage
courage, bravado, induced by alcohol.

Dutch gold
gold foil, plating, leaf.

Dutch oven
the practice of farting under the bed-covers, blankets.

Dutch treat
party or outing where each pays for his own share.

Dutch wife
a mattress.

dye
(see: of the blackest/deepest dye)

dyed-in-the-wool
absolute, complete, through and through: e.g. He's a dyed-in-the-wool Labor supporter.

dying for
to have a great desire or need for: e.g. I'm dying for a drink.

dying for a leak

dying to go to the loo
to have a great need to urinate.

dyke
1. toilet; dunny.
2. lesbian; female homosexual.

dynamite
1. exceptional, first-class, outstanding person or thing.
2. potentially dangerous person, thing or situation, likely to cause trouble.

dynamo
very energetic person.

eager beaver
enthusiastic, keen person.

eagle eyes
person with keen eyesight.
See also:
old eagle eyes

Eagles/Eags
West Coast VFL football team (Western Australia).

ear
(see: all ears; bash someone's ear; bend someone's ear; big ears; bite someone's ear; broad between the ears; by ear; chew someone's ear; cotton between the ears; do it on one's ear; easy on the ears; end up on one's ear; fall on deaf ears; flea in one's ear; get a lift under the ear; get an earful; get one's ears lowered; give someone a thick ear; goes in one ear and out the other; have one's ears burn; have/got an ear to the ground; in it up to one's ears; keep an ear to the ground; keep one's ears open; may your ears turn into arseholes . . .; music to one's ears; narrow between the ears; nothing between the ears; on one's ear; out on one's ear; pin someone's ears back; play it by ear; see daylight through someone's ears; smiling from one ear to the other; stand someone on one's ear; talk someone's ears off; thick between the ears; turn a deaf ear; up to one's ears; walls have ears; wet behind the ears)

earbash
harangue; talk incessantly; bore with tedious talk.

earbasher
boring, incessant talker.

earful
1. long, lengthy piece of unwanted advice or gossip.
2. lengthy tirade of abuse: e.g. I got an earful from the boss for arriving late for work.

earhole/ear'ole
the ear.

earlier in the piece
sooner: e.g. If you had seen me about it earlier in the piece, I may have been able to help you.

early bird
1. person who arrives before others.
2. person who rises early, gets up early in the morning.

early bird catches the worm
opportunities or advantages are gained by the person who acts early or first.

early in the piece
early; too soon: e.g. It's a bit early in the piece to know what's going to happen yet.

early off the mark
1. awake early.
2. too soon for something.

earmark
1. any identifying mark, sign or characteristic.
2. assign something (fund etc.) for a definite purpose: e.g. That money is earmarked for the new cultural centre.

earn a quid
earn money; work for a living: e.g. How does he earn a quid?

ears flapping
(have one's . . .) to be listening with great interest, especially when one is not supposed to hear what is being said: e.g. Be careful what you say — the children's ears are flapping.

ears like taxi doors/ wingnuts
pertaining to having big ears.

earshot
the distance or range of hearing: e.g. He's not within earshot.

ear-splitting
painfully harsh on the ears.

earth
a great deal: e.g. 1. This house cost the earth.
2. She wants the earth.
See also:
charge the earth
come down to earth
down-to-earth
expect the earth
haven't got an earthly
not an earthly
on earth
run it to earth
salt of the earth
to the ends of the earth
want the earth

earth-shattering
profound; important; vital: e.g. They made an earth-shattering discovery.

earthy
coarse; unrefined; blunt; direct; lewd.

earwig
eavesdropper.

ease off/up
1. slow down.
2. a plea to stop nagging; a plea to cease the present trend of discussion; reduce pressure, tension etc.

Easts
Eastern Suburbs N.S.W. Rugby League football team.

easy
1. having no firm preferences; carefree: e.g. I'm easy — I don't mind what we do.
2. (of a woman) having loose morals; willing to have sexual intercourse.
See also:
go easy on
go easy with
have/got it easy
I'm easy
on easy street

easy as falling off a log

easy as pie
very easy; simple task.

easy as pushing shit uphill with a pointed stick/rubber fork

easy as shoving butter up a porcupine's bum with a knitting-needle on a hot day

easy as spearing an eel with a spoon
not easy; extremely difficult.

easy come, easy go
pertaining to anything that is easily gained and just as easily lost — especially money.

easy does it
plea for moderation; be careful; handle carefully.

easy game
1. (of women) having loose morals; willing to have sexual intercourse.
2. (of people in general) easily tricked, duped or cheated.

easy lay
(of women) having loose morals; willing to have sexual intercourse.

easy mark/target/touch
(of people) easily tricked, duped or cheated.

easy may
(prison slang) a safe.

easy money
money obtained or earned without difficulty: e.g. I know a scheme that will make some easy money for us.

easy on!
slow down; plea for moderation.

easy on the ears
pleasant to listen to.

easy on the eyes
pleasant to look at: e.g. She's easy on the eyes.

easy score
(see: easy game)

easy street
(see: on easy street)

easy take/target/touch
(see: easy mark)

easy wicket
a comfortable, easy task, position or job: e.g. He's on an easy wicket with that new job.

easy-going
content; relaxed; nonchalant; not fussy: e.g. He's an easy-going type of person.

eat
perform cunnilingus or fellatio.
See also:
I'll eat my hat
what's eating (one/someone)?

eat a horse and chase the rider
(I could . . .) jocular declaration of one's hunger.

eat crow
to be forced to say or do something humiliating; to suffer the consequences and embarrassment of an idea, action or belief that has failed or backfired.

eat dirt
accept insults without comment or complaint.

eat fit to bust
eat heartily, a great deal.

eat humble pie
to be put into a humiliating position of forced apology.

eat like a bird/sparrow
eat sparingly or very little.

eat like a horse
eat a great deal; to have a voracious appetite.

eat (one's) heart out
1. pine, suffer in anxiety: e.g. I've been eating my heart out wondering where you've been all this time!
2. (as an exclamation) expression of scorn at someone else's envy: e.g. Eat your heart out! He's mine now!

eat (one's) words
take back or retract what one has said: e.g. I'll prove him wrong and make him eat his words!

eat (someone) out of house and home
to over-indulge on the hospitality and provisions of a household.

eat your heart out!
expression of scorn at someone's envy.

eating out of (one's) hand
be completely servile and trusting, often in a fawning or sycophantic manner: e.g. He'll do anything for her — she's got him eating out of her hand.

eau de cologne
(rhyming slang) phone, telephone.

eco
ecology: e.g. She's an eco freak.

edge
(see: get the edge on someone; have/got an edge against someone; have/got the edge on someone; on edge; over the edge; push someone over the edge; rough around the edges; thin edge of the wedge; two-edged)

edgy
irritable; nervous; apprehensive.

Eels
Parramatta N.S.W. Rugby League football team.

effing
euphemism for fucking: e.g. Get that effing idiot out of here!

egad!
exclamation of surprise, astonishment, dismay.

egg
(see: bad egg; don't put all your eggs in one basket; have/got egg on one's face; last one in is a rotten egg; lay an egg; sure as eggs; teach one's grandmother to suck eggs; tread on eggs; treading on eggs)

egg (someone) on
incite; provoke; urge (someone) to do: e.g. You shouldn't egg him on like that when he's drunk — you know he gets violent.

egg-beater
helicopter.

egghead
an intellectual.

egnishna
air-conditioner.

ego food
cocaine.

ego trip
behaviour designed to boost one's ego or self-esteem: e.g. Doing all that work for charity is a real ego trip for her.

either piss (in it) or get off the pot
do something constructive instead of complaining; don't be so indecisive.

Ekka
Brisbane's Agricultural Exhibition.

el cheapo
pertaining to anything that is cheap and inferior in quality, such as a camera, restaurant etc.: e.g. I know this camera is only an el cheapo but it still works well.

elbow
(see: bend the elbow; out at the elbow; raise one's elbow; rub elbows with; up to one's elbows)

elbow grease
vigorous hard work: e.g. Cleaning this kitchen is going to need some elbow grease.

elbow-room
1. sufficient space to work or move in: e.g. There's a lot of elbow-room in his workshop.
2. scope; freedom: e.g. He left that job because they didn't give him enough elbow-room.

elegant sufficiency
enough to eat.

elevenses
light, mid-morning refreshments; morning tea-break. (British)

eleventh hour
the last chance to be able to act or do anything.

'em
contraction of them: e.g. Bring 'em here. (non-standard use of English)

em-cee
(also: M.C.) master of ceremonies.

emma chisit
the Strine rendition of: how much is it?

empties
empty bottles (usually beer bottles).

empty
1. hungry: e.g. I'm so empty I could eat a horse.
2. foolish; not very intelligent: e.g. He's empty.
3. an empty bottle (beer, spirits).
4. emotionally drained.

empty-handed
without having gained or obtained what one had intended: e.g. They came back from the expedition empty-handed.

empty-headed
stupid; dull-witted; not very intelligent.

emu bob/parade
line of people employed to pick up rubbish in order to clean up an area quickly.

emu's breakfast
(joc.) a drink and a good look around.

end
(see: at a loose end; get one's end in; go off the deep end; keep one's end up; living end; make ends meet; no end; on the receiving end; tie up some loose ends)

end of the line/road
1. the finish; completion.
2. failure.

end of the world
emotional disaster: e.g. It's been the end of the world for him since his wife left.

end up
finish up; conclude; arrive at a final set of circumstances: e.g. He's so bad he'll end up in prison.

end up in smoke
fail; collapse; be a fiasco, flop.

end up on (one's) ear
finish up in trouble.

endless belt
a prostitute.

enough of a good thing
sufficient; ample.

enough on (one's) plate
(to have . . .) to have as much as (one) can satisfactorily cope with: e.g. He's got enough on his plate now without expecting him to do more work.

enough to drive one mad/ round the bend, twist/up the wall

enough to give (one) the shits

enough to make a grown man cry
expression of utter frustration over something that is intolerable.

enough to make (one's) blood curdle
frightening; terrifying.

enough to set (one's) teeth on edge
frightening; terrifying; extremely unpleasant.

enough to sink a battleship
more than enough; a great deal; too much: e.g. She's wearing enough jewellery and diamonds to sink a battleship.

enough to try the patience of Job
expression of frustration over something intolerable.

enough to wake the dead
very loud.

enough's enough!
expression signifying the end of one's tolerance.

enter the lion's den
to risk or face grave danger.

Enzed
New Zealand; N.Z.

Enzedder
New Zealander.

'er indoors
a man's wife.

Esky
highly successful portable ice-box for carrying beer and drinks to a party or barbecue. (Trademark)

E.S.P.
extra sensory perception; pertaining to extra powers of the mind, means of perception beyond the known senses.

establishment
1. (an . . .) euphemism for brothel or massage parlour.
2. (cap.) the social group that makes the rules and exercises authority and is resistant to change.

Estapol
a varnish for wood, now taken to mean the act of varnishing (Trademark): e.g. We Estapolled our old furniture.

etchings
(see: show someone one's etchings)

eternal triangle
complex sexual and emotional relationship involving three people.

ethnic
pertaining to a member of an ethnic group; migrant or descendant of a migrant to Australia (sometimes derog.).

ethno
(derog.) migrant or descendant of a migrant to Australia.

euchre
1. to outwit or defeat someone through scheming (from U.S. card game).
2. to spoil, ruin.

euchred
1. beaten; defeated; worn out; exhausted.
2. spoiled; ruined.

eureka!
exclamation of success, discovery: e.g. Eureka! We've finally found gold!

even
equal or on a par, especially after a debt or a score has been settled: e.g. I may have broken his leg, but we're even now — he broke my arm last year!
See also:
break even
evens
get even

even keel
steady; unruffled; calm and without problems: e.g. He's trying to keep his marriage on an even keel.

even the score
obtain revenge: e.g. I'll even the score with that bastard one day.

evens
1. (be . . .) (see even)
2. (horse-racing) even

money; a bet at odds that will double your money. *See also:* odds or evens?

even-stevens
1. equal in some form of competition; see: evens. 2. equal amounts, shares etc.: e.g. We split the lottery money even-stevens.

ever so
very; exceedingly: e.g. He's ever so big and strong.

evergreen
remaining popular through the years: e.g. Elvis Presley will always be an evergreen.

ever-loving
husband or wife: e.g. Where's your ever-loving this evening?

ever-so ever-so
pompous; haughty; stuck-up; snooty: e.g. She's ever-so ever-so since she went overseas.

every bastard and his dog
the general public; many people: e.g. Every bastard and his dog was there, yet it was supposed to be a secret.

every bit
in every respect: e.g. He's every bit as good as she is.

every cloud has a silver lining
pertaining to the belief that there is some good or benefit to be gained from every bad situation.

every dog has its day
eventually, opportunities come to each person.

every inch
in all respects; totally; completely: e.g. He's every inch a footy fan.

every inch of the way
for the duration; totally: e.g. We're going to fight every inch of the way.

every man and his dog
the general public; many people.

every man for himself
pertaining to the belief that one must look after one's own interests above others': e.g. When the ship sank it was every man for himself.

every man has his price
pertaining to the belief that every person is corruptible — one only needs to find the enticement that will do it.

every now and again/then

every once in a while

every so often
from time to time; occasionally: e.g. We go to the movies every now and again.

every Tom, Dick and Harry
the general public; many people: e.g. Every Tom, Dick and Harry was at that meeting.

every which way
in all directions; all over the place: e.g. The wind blew my newspaper every which way.

everybody who's anybody
everyone of importance.

everything but the kitchen sink
a lot of miscellaneous and often unnecessary items: e.g. She carries everything but the kitchen sink in that handbag.

everything's apples/rosy
all is well, under control, satisfactory, going well.

evil eye
1. the believed power of doing harm by a look. 2. a frowning look of disapproval: e.g. She gave me the evil eye when I walked in.

ex
former girl/boyfriend, wife, husband or lover: e.g. I never see my ex any more.

exam
examination; test.

exchange notes
to gossip: e.g. The girls are exchanging notes in the kitchen.

exciting as watching grass grow/paint dry
very boring.

excuse the French
an apology for swearing or using foul language: e.g. Excuse the French, but I think he's a shit.

exercise the ferret
(of a man) to have sexual intercourse.

expect the earth
to expect, desire, too much or more than is possible.

expecting
pregnant.

explore every avenue
try everything.

extra special
especially good.

extract the digit
stop being lazy, idle and start work; work harder and with more perseverance.

extra-curricular activities
illicit sexual activities; cheating on one's husband, wife or lover.

exy
expensive: e.g. hubby's drinking habits are becoming exy.

eye
(see: all my eye and Betty Martin; an eye for an eye; apple of someone's eye; before one's very eyes; better than a poke in the eye with . . .; catch someone's eye; clap eyes on; cry one's eyes out; easy on the eye; evil eye;

give someone the eye; go eyes out; had an eyeful; have/got an eye for; have/got eyes in the back of one's head; have/got eyes only for; in the blink of an eye; in the eyes of; in the public eye; keep an eye on; keep an eye out for; keep one's eyes open/peeled/skinned; knock one's eye out; lay eyes on; make eyes at; make someone open his eyes; more than meets the eye; mud in your eye!; open your eyes; pick the eyes out of; pinch the eye out of your cock if it wasn't stuck on; pull the wool over someone's eyes; run one's eye over; see eye to eye; see with half an eye; set eyes on; sheep's eyes; shut one's eyes to; sight for sore eyes; turn a blind eye to; up to the eyeballs; with an eye to; with one's eyes open; with the naked eye)

eye off
to stare at with desire or want (often with the intention of buying or stealing): e.g. Don't eye off another man's wife!

eyeball to eyeball
face to face, very close, in an aggressive attitude.

eyeful
1. remarkably attractive person: e.g. Isn't she an eyeful!
2. a good look at, especially at someone sexually provocative: e.g. Get an eyeful of that!

eye-opener
1. revelation; surprising fact: e.g. Finding out that he was married was a bit of an eye-opener!
2. alcohol, coffee or tea taken early in the morning before work or activity.

eyes bigger than (one's) stomach
(to have . . .) to want more than (one) can eat; to be greedy.

eyes fall out of (one's) head
(to have one's . . .) to show complete surprise, astonishment or wonder: e.g. His eyes fell out of his head when she walked in stark naked.

eyes glued to
(to have one's . . .) to watch keenly, stare openly at: e.g. He's got his eyes glued to the T.V. footy game for the day.

eyes in the back of the head
(to have . . .) to be keenly aware of everything; to appear to have the ability to see even what is going on behind one's back.

eyes like roadmaps

eyes like two holes burnt in a blanket

eyes like two piss-holes in the snow
bloodshot, red, tired-looking eyes.

eyes nearly pop out of (one's) head
(to have one's . . .) to show complete surprise, astonishment or wonder.

eyes on, hands off!
a warning that one may look but not touch.

eye-service
admiring looks: e.g. He gave you a lot of eye-service.

eye-sore
anything offensive to look at.

eyetie
(also: Itie) an Italian person or thing.

eyewash
nonsense; rubbish; bunkum.

f
(also: eff) euphemism for fuck; to swear by using this word: e.g. I told him to f off!

F.A.
(see: fuck-all; know sweet F.A.; sweet Fanny Adams)

fab
fabulous; marvellous; wonderful: e.g. That concert was fab.

face
well-known person; famous personality: e.g. He's a well-known face around town.
See also:
do an about-face
fall flat on (one's) face
fill (one's) face
have/got a face as long as a fiddle/wet week
have/got a face like a chook's bum
have/got egg on (one's) face
have/got (one's) face against the (pub) wall
have/got the face to
if he'd laugh his face would crack
keep a straight face
laugh on the other side of (one's) face
lie straight-faced
long face
look (someone) in the face
lose face
make faces
not just a pretty face
off (one's) face
on the face of it
pull faces
put on a good face
put (one's) face on
rearrange (someone's) face
rub (someone's) face in it
save face
show (one's) face
sit on my face
slap in the face
staring (one) right in the face
till (one) goes blue in the face
two-faced

face fungus
hair on the face such as a beard or moustache.

face like a festered pickle
(to have a . . .) to be suffering from acute acne or pimples.

face like a twisted sandshoe
(to have a . . .) to be extremely ugly.

face like a yard of tripe
(to have a . . .) to have a miserable countenance.

face like the back end of a truck

face like the north end of a south-bound bus/tram
(to have a . . .) to be extremely unattractive, ugly.

face the firing squad
deal with the (often unpleasant) consequences.

face the music
deal with the consequences bravely.

face to face with
confronted with: e.g. He came face to face with dying during his illness but pulled through against all odds.

face up
(cricket) be the batsman on strike.

face up to
deal with; to meet or deal with bravely, courageously: e.g. He's going to have to face up to the fact that his business is a failure.

face-ache
ugly or irritating person.

faceless men
men unaccountable and unknown to the public who wield power.

facts of life
1. the details of sexual behaviour: e.g. All parents should teach their children about the facts of life.
2. unchangeable realities in life that one must deal with: e.g. It's a fact of life that we all die some day.

fad
pet notion; a popular idea or fashion: e.g. The latest teenage fad is to dye the hair green and pink.

fading away to a shadow
getting thinner: e.g. Karen's fading away to a shadow since she's been on that diet.

fag
1. cigarette.
2. homosexual: e.g. He's nothing but a fag!
3. tire; exhaust: e.g. I'm really fagged after all that work.

fagged out
tired; exhausted.

faggot
a homosexual man.

faint-hearted
cowardly.

fair
complete; completely: e.g. 1. He's a fair idiot! 2. I was knocked fair off my feet by the explosion.

fair and square
1. honest; straightforward; equitably: e.g. When we were divorced we split everything up fair and square.
2. directly; accurately: e.g. He hit it fair and square in the middle of the target.

fair cow
anything exasperating, unpredictable or a nuisance: e.g. 1. She's a fair cow! 2. This thing's a fair cow!

fair crack of the whip!
plea for fair treatment, opportunity or reason.

fair deal
satisfactory, fair arrangement, transaction etc.

fair dink/dinks/dinkum
(see: dinkum, 1., 2. and 3.)

fair enough
1. statement of agreement; yes; all right.
2. acceptable; agreeable: e.g. I think that's fair enough.

fair game
1. single person seen as a suitable sex object: e.g. He's not fair game because he's married.
2. legitimate subject for attack or criticism: e.g. After what he said at the meeting tonight he's going to be fair game for the press.

fair go
1. an appeal or plea for fair treatment or reason: e.g. Fair go mate!
2. fair, equitable and just conditions: e.g. I don't think he was given a fair go.

fair hike
a long distance to travel, especially by walking.

fair play
just; honest; reasonable; equitable.

fair sex
pertaining to women.

fair shake of the dice!

fair suck of the sauce bottle/the sav!
(see: fair crack of the whip!)

fair to middling
average; so-so; tolerably satisfactory; feeling in average health or spirits.

fair's fair!
an exclamation pleading for fair play or just behaviour.

fair-weather friends
untrustworthy friends; people not to be counted on in a crisis.

fairy
homosexual; effeminate man.
See also:
off with the fairies
shoot a fairy

fairy godmother
benefactress: e.g. She's been like a fairy godmother to me.

fairytale
a lie; untruth.

fall apart at the seams
1. to drive oneself to physical and mental exhaustion.
2. to be shabby, tatty or dishevelled.
3. to be in a distressed state of anxiety, worry, nervousness.

fall down on (the job)
fail in: e.g. If he falls down on this job he'll get the sack.

fall flat
fail to have the desired effect: e.g. All his jokes fell flat.

fall flat on (one's) face/puss
to fail in an enterprise.

fall for
1. to become infatuated or captivated by someone: e.g. He's really fallen for her in a big way.
2. be deceived, tricked or hoodwinked by: e.g. You didn't fall for that con-man's tricks did you?

fall for it hook, line and sinker

fall for it like a ton of bricks
(see: fall for, 2.)

fall foul of
quarrel with; be on bad terms with: e.g. I've fallen foul of the boss for coming late to work.

fall guy
scapegoat; easy victim to cheat, hoodwink or deceive.

fall in a heap
1. disintegrate into tears and a state of self-pity.
2. collapse through exhaustion or over-work.

fall in with
1. become better acquainted with; join: e.g. I've fallen in with a beaut bunch of people at work.
2. meet by chance: e.g. You'll never guess who I fell in with at the supermarket!
3. agree with.

fall into
become the victim of a joke, trick, hoodwinker: e.g. I really fell into that one!

fall off the back of a truck
pertaining to something that has been stolen or of questionable origins: e.g. Don't ask where it came from — it fell off the back of a truck!

fall on deaf ears
pass unheeded; be ignored, usually on purpose: e.g. Every time I ask for a raise in salary it falls on deaf ears.

fall on hard times
suffer hardship, poverty, ill-fortune: e.g. The family has fallen on hard times since Father died.

fall on (one's) feet
emerge from a bad situation unscathed or without any serious problems: e.g. His first business went bust but he's fallen on his feet again with this new enterprise.

fall out (with)
quarrel with; disagree with: e.g. I fell out with my best friend over that silly incident.

fall over backwards for (someone)
go to a great deal of trouble and effort for.

fall over (oneself)
1. to show over-enthusiasm: e.g. He fell over himself when he learnt that he'd won the lottery.
2. to exhibit confusion and indecision when taking action.

fall short of
fail to meet the required standard or amount; disappoint: e.g. He really fell short of my expectations so I sacked him.

fall through
fail; come to nothing; collapse: e.g. The plans for the weekend have fallen through due to bad weather.

fall through the floor
expression of astonishment; surprise: e.g. I nearly fell through the floor when he told me he was gay!

fall to pieces
(see: fall apart at the seams, 1., 2. and 3.)

fall under
be classified with; be included in: e.g. He falls under the same category as me.

fall upon
find, discover by chance: e.g. We fell upon a fortune in old coins under the house.

fallen woman
woman who has lost her chastity.

falling-out
a quarrel or disagreement: e.g. We had a falling-out over that affair.

fall-out
1. (see: falling-out)
2. radio-active debris from nuclear explosion.

false step
an unwise or improper action or decision; a mistake or blunder.

false-hearted
treacherous; deceitful.

falsies
artificial teeth, breasts or eyelashes.

family
(see: in the family way; keep it all in the family; runs in the family)

family jewels
testicles; a man's genitals.

family skeleton
a sordid fact or scandal kept secret because of the shame it may cause.

famished
very hungry.

famous last words
an expression indicating one's doubt, disbelief, lack of faith in something someone says in a difficult or precarious situation.

fan
an enthusiast, follower or devotee.

fan the breeze
chat; gossip; indulge in idle talk, palaver.

fan the fire
encourage trouble; make matters worse than they are.

fancy
1. (of a man) a lover or Casanova; pursuer of women.
2. to desire, want, especially in a sexual context: e.g. I think he fancies you.
See also:
flight of fancy
take a fancy to
tickle (one's) fancy
whatever tickles your fancy

fancy duds
fashionable or best clothes.

fancy (oneself)
to hold an unduly high opinion of (oneself).

fancy woman
mistress or prostitute.

fancy-free
not encumbered by anything, especially a love relationship.

fancypants
1. a homosexual or effeminate man.
2. a smartie.

fandangle
1. nonsense; rubbish; trivia; baloney.
2. an elaborate and trivial piece of dangling ornament.

fandangled thing
annoying contraption: e.g. I can't get this fandangled thing to work properly!

fandangs
trivial ornaments or trinkets.

fanging for a feed
to be hungry.

fangs
teeth.
See also:
put the fangs in

fanny
woman's vagina; female genitals, pudendum.
See also:
sweet Fanny Adams
flash fanny at the Fowlers

fantabulous/ fantasmagorical/fantastic
wonderful; excellent; marvellous.

fantasy land
a dreamlike state of mind; daydreaming; not thinking realistically.

far and wide
over great distances.

far-away
detached; dreamy; not quite with it; remote: e.g. He's a bit far-away at the moment — he's got a lot of other things on his mind.

far cry from
very different; nothing like: e.g. He's a far cry from his father.

far gone
1. completely intoxicated or under the influence of drugs.
2. mad; crazy; insane.
3. in an advanced state of decay or ruin: e.g. This thing is too far gone to repair now.

far out
1. an exclamation of admiration, wonder, astonishment etc.
2. eccentric; non-conforming; strange; way out: e.g. She and her friends are all too far out for my liking.
See also:
far-out

far-fetched/flung
unbelievable; unlikely; implausible; exaggerated.

far-flung
remote; a long way: e.g. He lives in some far-flung town in the middle of the outback.

Farm
(the . . .)
1. in political jargon, 'Australia' — in the sense of buying it back from overseas investors: e.g. It's time the Government started buying back the Farm instead of selling out to interests overseas.
2. (Vic.) Monash University, as distinct from the University of Melbourne which is called the 'Shop'.
See also:
funny-farm

farmyard confetti
nonsense, rubbish; foolish talk.

far-out
1. avant-garde; unconventional; way out: e.g. She wears the most far-out clothes I've ever seen.
2. excellent; admirable: e.g. You should see the far-out house they live in.

fart
1. an emission of wind from the anus.
2. ineffectual, foolish, stupid person.
3. to emit wind from the anus.
See also:
full as a fart
going around like a fart in a colander wondering which hole to get out
like a fart in a bottle
pissed as a fart
piss-fart
spectacular as a fart in a bathtub
up at sparrow fart
wouldn't want (someone) to fart in my last pound of flour

fart a crowbar!
expression of amazement, annoyance, exasperation.

fart around
1. behave foolishly or ineffectually; waste time: e.g. Stop farting around and get to work!
2. tinker or tamper with: e.g. Don't you fart around with my things!

fart fodder
food likely to cause flatulence or farting.

fart sack
1. bed.
2. sleeping-bag used for camping.

fart-arse
waste time with inconsequential activity: e.g. I wish he wouldn't fart-arse around so much and get on with the job.

farts like a two-stroke
person with a noisy flatulence problem.

fashion plate
person always dressed in the latest styles.

fast
sexually promiscuous; having loose morals — especially of women.
See also:
in the fast lane

fast as a cut cat
very fast.

fast buck
money earned with little effort, often dishonestly: e.g. I know of a good scheme to earn a fast buck.

fast food
foods such as fish and chips, hamburgers and other fried items that are served without delay; junk food.

fast one
a trick; an unfair or deceitful act; a swindle: e.g. He tried to pull a fast one over me.

fast operator
con-man; swindler; cheat; fraud.

faster than instant coffee
very quickly.

fastie
(see: fast one)
See also:
pull a fastie
put over a fastie

fast-talk
irrelevant prattle designed to confuse or deceive.

fast-talker
1. person who is noted for his ability to con, coerce or deceive.
2. (of a man) a chaser of women; a Casanova.

fat
an erection of the penis: e.g. Crack a fat.
See also:
chew the fat
out of the fat and into the fire

fat cat
any member of the bureaucracy, Government or other department who expects special privileges and luxuries because of his position or wealth, and held in contempt by the public.

fat chance
very little or no chance: e.g. You've got fat chance of ever meeting the Queen in person.

fat lot of good/use (that is)
no good at all; useless: e.g. Asking him for help did a fat lot of good — he refused.

fat of the land
luxury; wealth; the best that the land can offer: e.g. He's living off the fat of the land.

fate played a hand
pertaining to a situation controlled by an irrevocable chain of predetermined events; destiny: e.g. Fate played a hand in his downfall.

fate worse than death
1. (joc.) rape.
2. a particularly awful or unpleasant situation (often joc.): e.g. Being married to her would be a fate worse than death!

fathead
stupid, ineffectual person; a fool.

fathom
work out; puzzle out.

fat's in the fire
the irrevocable step or action has been taken, often intimating that dire consequences have to be faced: e.g. The fat's in the fire after what he did to her.

fatso
fat, obese person.

fatties
1. obese people: e.g. Fatties are often jolly people.
2. large-tread tyres for a car.

fatty
fat, obese person.

favourite
most fancied horse in a race.

favourite haunt
a favourite meeting-place or place of entertainment, such as a night-club or bar.

favourite hobby-horse
a favourite topic or obsession: e.g. Arguing politics is his favourite hobby-horse.

favourite poison
preference in drink (especially alcoholic).

faze
intimidate; daunt; disturb; worry: e.g. Nothing seems to faze him.

feast or famine
(see: flood or famine)

feather
(see: haven't got a feather to fly with; in fine feather; in full feather; make the feathers fly; rooster one day and a feather duster the next; ruffle someone's feathers; tar and feather someone; you could have knocked me over with a feather)

feather in (one's) cap
something to (one's) credit.

feather (one's) own nest
providing for (one's) own wealth and comfort without thought to anyone else: e.g. Many politicians have been accused of simply feathering their own nests without worrying about the people who elected them.

feather-brained
dull-witted; ineffectual; irresponsible.

featherweight
a small and insignificant person or thing.

feature with (someone)
have sexual intercourse with (someone).

features
the face.

fed
policeman, especially a federal one.

fed up

fed up to the back teeth/ eyeballs/eye teeth/gills/neck
disgusted; bored; annoyed; frustrated: e.g. I'm fed up with the way he treats me!

feds
police, especially federal police.

feed
a meal: e.g. I haven't had a feed all day.
See also:
not worth feeding

feed (someone) some bullshit
tell (someone) anything to stall for time or to keep the peace for the time being: e.g. Just feed the crowd some bullshit until I get a proper report for them.

feed the chooks
1. (of a man) to masturbate.
2. give scraps of information to the press (phrase coined by Sir Joh Bjelke-Petersen, former Queensland Premier).

feed the fishes
1. be sea-sick.
2. to drown.

feeding time at the zoo
1. any disorderly, noisy event.
2. an enthusiastic meal-time.

feel
1. touch lasciviously.
2. a lascivious fondle: e.g. I saw my husband give her a feel at the party!
See also:
get the feel of

feel a bit off
feel ill, unwell.

feel at home
feel comfortable, at ease: e.g. 1. He makes me feel at home whenever I visit.
2. He feels at home with his computer after doing a course on how to operate it.

feel blue
feel sad, melancholy, depressed.

feel cocky
feel elated, confident.

feel cornered
feel uncomfortable in a situation from which there seems no escape.

feel crook
1. feel ill, unwell.
2. feel annoyed, angry: e.g. I can't help feeling crook after what he did!

feel crummy
1. feel ill, unwell.
2. feel regretful.

feel down
feel depressed, dejected, unhappy.

feel horny
feel sexually aroused.

feel it in (one's) bones
know intuitively: e.g. He's going to say no — I can feel it in my bones.

feel like
want; desire; have an inclination for: e.g. I feel like some chocolate.

feel like a gig
feel foolish, ashamed.

feel like a pick-pocket in a nudist camp
feel nervous, out of place, disoriented.

feel like a second-rate citizen
feel inferior, rejected, scorned, scoffed at.

feel (one's) oats
1. feel active, gay and lively.
2. test (one's) power or authority: e.g. The new boss is feeling his oats with the staff.

feel (oneself)
feel well; be in a state of well-being: e.g. She doesn't feel herself today so she didn't go to work.

feel (someone) out
find out more about (someone); test; assess: e.g. I'll feel him out for a while before I become more involved with him.

feel (someone) up
touch (someone) intimately, sexually, especially of a man to a woman.

feel the pinch
to be acutely aware of being short of money.

feel up to
feel able to cope with: e.g. I don't feel up to going for a long walk just now.

feeling chipper
feeling elated; having a sense of well-being.

feet
(see: at one's feet; carried out feet-first; dead on one's feet; drag one's feet; fall on one's feet; find one's feet; get back on one's feet; get cold feet; get one's feet wet; have/ got one's feet on the ground; itchy feet; keep one's feet; keep one's feet on the ground; land on one's feet; on one's feet; open one's mouth to change feet; put one's feet up; run off one's feet; set someone on his feet; stand on one's own two feet; sweep someone off his feet; take a load off one's feet; two left feet)

feet of clay
weakness; frailty; failing; cowardice.

feet planted firmly on the ground
(to have one's . . .) to be sensible and practical.

feet-first
impetuously; thoughtlessly; without thinking: e.g. He went

into it feet-first and now he's in trouble.

fell off the back of a truck
pertaining to something that has been stolen, or of questionable origins.

fell over (himself)
1. became confused and clumsy in (his) attempt.
2. showed excessive enthusiasm: e.g. He fell over himself when I told him he'd won the lottery.

For other possible entries beginning with 'fell' see entries listed under 'fall'.

fella/feller/fellow
1. man; person; bloke: e.g. He's not a bad fellow.
2. (aggressively) mate! you!: e.g. Listen here feller!
See also:
old fella

feminine wiles
the tactics peculiar to women to get what they want.

femme fatale
dangerously attractive and unfaithful woman.

fence
dealer in stolen goods.
See also:
on both sides of the fence
over the fence
rush (one's) fences
sit on the fence

fence-sitter
person who remains annoyingly neutral and refuses to voice his opinion.

Fergie/Fergy
an early model Ferguson tractor, usually grey in colour.

fernleaf
a New Zealander.

ferret
the penis.
See also:
exercise the ferret

Festival of Light
religious organisation devoted to guarding and enforcing the morals of society.

fetch up
1. to end up; reach a certain state as a final conclusion: e.g. He'll fetch up in trouble with the police.
2. to vomit.

few
(see: a good few; quite a few; the few)

few and far between
rare; not common.

fib
trivial lie, falsehood.

fibber
one who tells fibs; liar.

fibro
of or pertaining to that which is made from compressed asbestos and cement, especially a house: e.g. He lives in a little fibro on the beach.

fiddle
1. an artful trick or act of cheating.
2. interfere with illegally; gain by cheating; falsify: e.g. He fiddled the books to make it appear that the company was doing well while he embezzled the funds.
See also:
fit as a fiddle
have/got a face as long as a fiddle
on the fiddle
play second fiddle to

fiddle the books
falsify; interfere with or alter illegally the documents or account books of a firm.

fiddle-arse about
waste time with inconsequential activity.

fiddle-faddle
1. rubbish; nonsense.
2. trifle with; fidget aimlessly.

fiddler
a cheat, swindler, crook.
See also:
in and out like a fiddler's elbow

fiddlesticks
nonsense; rubbish.

fiddling
1. trivial.
2. awkward to use or handle: e.g. I can't do this fiddling zip up.

fiddly
awkward to do, use or handle: e.g. Fixing that tiny thing was so fiddly.

fiddly-dids
(rhyming slang) quids, formerly one pound notes but now taken to mean dollars, money: e.g. That fancy car must have cost a few fiddly-dids!

Fido
common name for a dog.

field berets
cow pats, dung.

field day
an occasion of exciting and unrestricted events or activities: e.g. He had a field day digging up antique bottles at the tip.

fierce
extreme; unfair; unreasonable: e.g. I thought the sentence that the judge gave him for such a small crime was a bit fierce.

fifth columnist
traitor; collaborator.

fifty to the dozen
fast; in haste; quickly.

fifty-fifty
equally; in equal amounts; half and half: e.g. If we win, we'll share the prize-money fifty-fifty.

fight
(see: couldn't fight in a fit; couldn't fight one's way out of a wet paper bag)

fight dirty
use unfair tactics.

'Cripes, Blue! When you said you were goin' to throw out the anchors, I thought you were joking!'

In Australia one stops the forward motion of a vehicle suddenly by 'chucking' or 'throwing' out 'the anchors'. Another tried-and-true method is to run into an unyielding object.

fight fire with fire
to use the same tactics as one's opponent.

fight like a trooper

fight like cat and dog
to constantly argue and bicker, especially of children, brothers and sisters.

fight like Kilkenny cats
to fight ferociously.

fight shy of
avoid on purpose.

fight tooth and nail
try hard with all one's resources and power; use extreme tactics to ensure victory or success: e.g. He's going to fight tooth and nail to win this election.

fighting a losing battle
to be in a position that offers little or no chance of victory or success.

fighting drunk
excessively and violently drunk.

fighting fit
healthy; extremely fit and well.

fighting mad
extremely angry: e.g. Dad's going to be fighting mad when he finds out what you've done!

fig-leaf
symbol of a covering for the genitals: e.g. We're going to the fancy-dress party as Adam and Eve and all we're wearing is a fig-leaf.

figure on
1. expect; take into consideration: e.g. I didn't figure on so many people coming.
2. count on; rely on: e.g. You can figure on him coming.

fill in time
occupy oneself in times of leisure or inactivity: e.g. Grandmother does tapestry to fill in time.

fill (one's) face
eat, especially with enthusiasm.

fill (someone) full of holes
shoot (someone).

fill (someone) in
inform more fully; elaborate; provide more information: e.g. Fill him in on what's happened while he's been away.

fill the bill
be satisfactory; be or do what is required: e.g. It will be difficult to find someone to fill the bill while he's away.

fill the hole in (one's) stomach
to satisfy (one's) hunger.

fill-in
a substitute; temporary replacement; stand-in.

filling/meat in the sandwich
pertaining to being caught in the centre of some argument or controversy, usually against one's will: e.g. That poor child is the filling in the sandwich in that divorce case.

filly
1. girl; young woman.
2. young female horse.

filthy
1. unpleasant: e.g. We had filthy weather for the holidays.
2. unfair; dishonest: e.g. 1. He's a filthy liar. 2. That was a filthy trick!

filthy look
expression of contempt, hatred, anger: e.g. His ex-wife gave me a filthy look when she came in.

filthy rich
extremely wealthy.

final straw
the ultimate or final act that led to or caused something else to happen: e.g. That was the final straw when he did that, so she left him.
See also:
straw that broke the camel's back

financial
having ready money: e.g. I'm not financial this week so I can't go to the concert with you.

find (one's) feet
to be able to act or do something independently, without the support or help of others: e.g. He'll eventually find his feet when he's a bit more mature.

find (one's) tongue
suddenly become verbose after a period of speechlessness.

find (oneself)
discover (one's) true abilities, potential, desires, vocation etc.: e.g. He's finally found himself with that new job.

find out the hard way
to discover, learn through a series of mistakes, often by ignoring the sound advice of others.

finders keepers (losers weepers)
an expression claiming the right to keep something one has just found.

fine and dandy
1. satisfactory; okay; good.
2. (sarcastically) not fine or satisfactory.

fine kettle of fish
pertaining to a troublesome, annoying, exasperating situation: e.g. That's a fine kettle of fish, that is!

fine line
little distinction: e.g. There's often a fine line between love and hate.

fine-spun
extremely subtle.

finger
(see: burn one's fingers; count on the fingers of

one hand; get one's fingers burnt; give someone the finger; have/got a finger in the pie; keep one's finger on the pulse; keep one's fingers crossed; lift a finger; more than one can poke a finger at; point the finger at; pull one's finger out; put one's finger on; slipped through one's fingers; snap one's fingers at; social finger; twist someone around one's little finger; wear/work one's fingers to the bone)

finger fuck
(of a man) to stimulate, touch erotically with a finger the genitals of a woman. (also: finger)

fingers crossed
(to have one's . . .)
1. to wish for good luck, success; maintain fervent hope: e.g. Keep your fingers crossed — we might win the prize.
2. to claim no responsibility or commitment to a promise (if one had one's fingers crossed when the promise was made).

finicky
excessively fastidious.

fink
contemptible person, especially one who reneges or goes back on an agreement or undertaking.

fins
the arms.

fire
sack; dismiss from a job.
See also:
add coal to the fire
between two fires
come under heavy fire
come under the firing-squad
fan the fire
fat's in the fire
fight fire with fire
get on like a house on fire
go through fire and water for
great balls of fire!
hang fire
in the firing-line
keep the home fires burning
light (someone's) fire
line of fire
play with fire

fire away
begin speaking or presenting one's argument.

fire blanks
(of a man) be impotent, sterile: e.g. She doesn't have to take contraceptives — her husband fires blanks.

fire from the hip
to act without thought, impulsively: e.g. He was firing from the hip when he said those terrible things during that argument.

fire (one's) mouth off
1. talk loudly and at length.
2. tell secrets; divulge confidences.

firebug
pyromaniac; arsonist.

fire-water
strong alcohol, spirits.

fireworks
display of anger; a noisy or violent argument: e.g. You should have seen the fireworks at their house last night!

firing
working at one's peak efficiency: e.g. He's really firing now that he's got the hang of it.

firm hand
authority; severity: e.g. He runs the school with a firm hand.

first cab off the rank
first to take advantage of an opportunity: e.g. He was hired because he was the first cab off the rank.

First Fleeter
person whose ancestry can be traced back to the convicts who arrived in Australia on the First Fleet in 1788.

first in best dressed/served
the best advantage or opportunity is gained by the first or earliest person.

first past the post
1. (of elections) candidate who gets the most votes wins.
2. the first person to do, complete something.

first thing
early in the morning; before anything else.

first up
at the first try or attempt: e.g. I missed the target first up, but I hit it every other time.

first up best dressed
(see: first in best dressed)

fish
person: e.g. He's a strange fish!
See also:
different kettle of fish
drink like a fish
feed the fishes
fine kettle of fish
like shooting fish in a barrel
not the only fish in the sea
other fish to fry
tight as a fish's arse
what's that got to do with the price of fish?

fish for
solicit, wheedle, cajole, coax, draw out by means of deception, trickery or indirect means: e.g. She's just fishing for compliments.

fish in troubled waters
one who turns a bad situation to his advantage.

fish out of water
uncomfortable and ill at ease in unfamiliar surroundings or circumstances.

fishwife
an abusive, coarse woman.

fishy
suspicious; dubious; shady; queer; odd: e.g. That deal sounds fishy to me.
See also:
smell fishy

fist
(see: hand over fist; make a good fist of)

fistful
troublesome; hard to control: e.g. That kid's a fistful!

fisticuffs
fight, bash or hit with the hands or fists: e.g. They're always having fisticuffs.

fit
angry show of temper.
See also:
in fits
nearly had a fit
take a fit
throw a fit

fit as a fiddle/mallee bull
extremely well, healthy and in good spirits.

fit for a king
suitable for the most discriminating tastes.

fit the bill
(see: fill the bill)

fit to be tied
very angry.

fits and starts
short spurts of activity: e.g. He built that boat in fits and starts over a period of ten years.

fits like a glove
fits extremely well; perfectly suitable.

five o'clock shadow
stubble of hair on the face as if one has not had a shave recently.

five-day week
the working days of one's occupation, usually from Monday to Friday: e.g. He does a five-day week.

five-finger discount/sale
shoplifting spree; an act of stealing: e.g. He got that watch at a five-finger sale.

fiver
formerly five pounds but now five dollars.

five-star
of excellent rating, such as a movie, motel or restaurant.

fix
1. dose of narcotic drug; shot of heroin.
2. any dishonest trick or act: e.g. He's always involved in some fix or other.
3. a predicament or troublesome situation from which there appears to be little chance of escape: e.g. He's in a real fix.
4. get even with; seek revenge: e.g. I'll fix him one day!
5. tamper with illegally or illicitly in order to secure a favourable outcome: e.g. He's been accused of fixing that race.
See also:
in a fix

fix (someone) up
1. pay back or settle any money matters: e.g. I'll fix you up for that fifty dollars I owe you next week.
2. attend to (someone's) wants or needs.

fix (someone's) wagon
get even with (someone); seek revenge upon (someone): e.g. I'll fix his wagon some day for cheating me!

fixed
illegally or dishonestly arranged or tampered with: e.g. That horse-race was fixed.
See also:
well-fixed

fizz
1. softdrink; effervescent drink.
2. champagne or effervescent alcoholic drink.
3. an informer, especially for the police or authorities.

fizz-bang
an old or vintage car.

fizzer
a failure; disappointing fiasco: e.g. The party was a fizzer.

fizz-gig
police informer.

fizzle out
fail feebly; peter out or come to nothing after what appeared to be a good start: e.g. The rally fizzled out due to lack of attendance.

fizz-out
(see: fizzer)

FJ
Australia's most popular, remembered model of the Holden car, made from 1953 to 1956, and now a collector's item.

flag
(see: flying the Australian flag; flying the flags; have/got the flags out; red flag)

flag-fall
the initial fee for hailing a taxi, registered on the meter before you start paying for your trip.

flag-pole
tall, thin and lanky person.

flag-waving
excessive and enthusiastic show of patriotism.

flak
barrage of heavy criticism, abuse or back-lashing: e.g. He's going to get a lot of flak through the press for what he said.
See also:
cop the flak
take the flak

flake
1. fillets of shark.
2. sleep, pass out, after physical exhaustion, drunkenness or excessive use of drugs.

flake out
(see: flake, 2.)

flame
lover, sweetheart.

flaming
euphemism for damned, bloody: e.g. He's a flaming idiot!

flange
female pudendum, genitals, vagina.

flap
(see: ears flapping; in a flap)

flap (one's) gums
talk at length: e.g. She's been flapping her gums for hours!

flare up
become suddenly angry.

flare-up
an angry outburst of temper; a sudden argument: e.g. Those two had another flare-up last night.

flash
1. gaudy; ostentatious; flamboyant; showy: e.g. That's a flash car he's driving now.
2. show or display something ostentatiously or proudly: e.g. She's been flashing her diamond engagement ring to everyone.
See also:
see (one's) life flash before (one's) eyes

flash a brown-eye
expose one's bare backside, anus, briefly and unexpectedly as a form of protest or insult.

flash fanny at the Fowlers
(of women) to urinate.

flash in the pan
of no significance or importance; here today, gone tomorrow: e.g. Many of today's pop-bands are just a flash in the pan.

flash (one's) nasty
expose, briefly and unexpectedly, (one's) genitals or private parts: e.g. That man over there just flashed his nasty.

flasher
1. man who exposes his genitals briefly in public.
2. person who runs suddenly and unexpectedly through a crowd naked.

flashy
1. ostentatious; gaudy; flamboyant; opulent: e.g. He drives a flashy Rolls.
2. pretentious; cheap; tawdry: e.g. I hate the flashy junk jewellery she wears.

flat
1. depressed; dejected: e.g. She's feeling a bit flat since her cat died.
2. a punctured tyre: e.g. We had a flat in the middle of nowhere!
3. lacking in bustline, breasts: e.g. She's too flat to wear that!
See also:
fall flat
fall flat on (one's) face
in nothing flat

flat as a tack
1. exhausted; tired; worn out.
2. (of a woman) lacking in bustline, breasts.

flat broke
having no money.

flat chat
as fast as possible; very quickly: e.g. We drove flat chat to get there on time.

flat out
1. extremely busy; having a full schedule: e.g. We're flat out this week and can't fit in another single appointment.
2. as fast as possible: e.g. They're working flat out to finish on time.
3. lying prone, prostrate: e.g. He's been flat out all week with the flu.

flat out like a lizard drinking
1. fast; busy; very active.
2. lying prone, prostrate; taking it easy.

flat spin
confusion; consternation; panic: e.g. Don't get into a flat spin until you know for sure what's happened!

flat stick/strap
(see: flat chat)

flat to the boards
1. very fast, active or busy.
2. travelling at top speed in a car, vehicle.

flatfoot
policeman.

flat-footed
1. uninspired; dull.
2. clumsy.

flathead
simpleton; dull-witted person; fool.

flatten
1. defeat soundly in a fight, match, contest etc.
2. astound; disconcert; dismay: e.g. He was flattened to hear that she wanted a divorce.

flattery will get you nowhere
rebuff to someone who is trying to corrupt, cajole, get something out of one through glib talk, flattery.

flattie/flatty
1. a flathead fish.
2. a punctured tyre.

flatties
low-heeled shoes.

flavour-of-the-month
popular fad or trend that is relatively short-lived.

flea in (one's) ear
(give someone/got/have/ put a . . .) pertaining to a sharp rebuke, hint.

flea-bag
1. a mangy dog.
2. slovenly, shabby-looking woman.
3. infested with fleas: e.g. That cat's a flea-bag.

flea-bitten
1. infested with fleas.
2. dirty; mangy; tatty; shabby.

flea-house
the cinema, picture theatre.

flea-market
market where people may sell second-hand goods; trash and treasure market.

flea-pit
1. the cinema, picture theatre.
2. any dirty, shabby, ill-kept house or dwelling.

fleece
cheat; swindle; strip of assets, money: e.g. He fleeced the company out of thousands of dollars.

flesh
(see: in the flesh; make one's flesh creep; pound of flesh)

flesh and blood
relatives; kin; offspring; family.

fleshpot
a carnal, sensual, sexy woman not averse to posing nude for photographs.

fleshpots
places providing luxurious and sensual pleasures.

flibbertigibbet
frivolous, gossiping or restless person — usually a young girl.

flick
a cinema film.

Flick Man
exterminator of household pests from the firm of the same name: e.g. I'm going to have to call the Flick Man to do something about all the cockroaches.

flick through
look quickly through a book, magazine etc.

flicks
1. cinema films.
2. the cinema: e.g. We're going to the flicks tonight.

flies
travels, moves fast: e.g. That car really flies.
See also:
bet on two flies walking up the wall
catching flies
drink with the flies
drop like flies
shut mouth catches no flies
there's no flies on (someone)

flight of fancy
indulgence in daydreaming and unrealistic notions.

flim-flam
light-hearted nonsense; deception; trickery.

fling
an unrestrained indulgence of one's desires, such as a party, a spending spree or a brief love affair.

flip
become enthusiastically excited, whether angrily or joyfully, depending on the situation: e.g. 1. The boss is going to flip when he finds out what you've done! 2. He's going to flip when he finds out he's won the lottery!

flip (one's) lid
become suddenly angry.

flip (oneself) off
(of a man) masturbate.

flip out
become suddenly angry; lose one's temper.

flip over (someone/ something)
1. fall madly in love with.
2. show extreme happiness, joy, desire, longing, admiration.

flip (someone) for it
toss a coin to decide the outcome or settle a disagreement between two people: e.g. I'll flip you to see who has to wash the dishes.

flippers
the hands.

flipping
euphemism for fucking; an adjective to describe annoyance, anger; very; absolute: e.g. He's a flipping idiot!

flipside
the side of a recording carrying the less popular song.

flit
(see: do a flit)

floater
1. a dead body found in the water.
2. vagrant; drifter; itinerant; person who doesn't stay in one place or job for long.
3. human faeces, shit, that floats rather than sinks to the bottom (of the toilet).
4. a cheque that is not honoured.
5. a meat pie in the middle of a plate of gravy or peas.

floating population
not fixed in numbers; population that changes constantly as in a holiday resort.

flog
1. sell; put up for sale: e.g. Flog the car for whatever you can get for it.
2. steal; pinch; pilfer; take without permission: e.g.

He didn't buy it, he flogged it.
3. use abusively; treat roughly or without respect: e.g. The way he flogs that car, it won't last very long.

flog the cat
to indulge in self-pity, regret and frustration, often by taking one's anger out on an innocent person.

flog to death
1. (see: flog, 3.)
2. overdo to the point of being mundane, hackneyed, crass or boring: e.g. That song has been flogged to death on the radio.

flogger
coloured streamers on a stick.

flogging a dead horse
attempting something useless, not worthwhile or of no value or interest to anyone; attempting to raise interest in matters no longer of value or interest.

flood or famine
pertaining to the concept that something is either too much or too little.

floor
1. the ground: e.g. He hit the floor like a bag of spuds after being kicked by that horse.
2. (see: floored, 1. and 2.)
See also:
cross the floor
fall through the floor
get in on the ground floor
have/got the floor
take the floor
wipe the floor with (someone)

floor show
any act (singing, dancing, comic etc.) in a nightclub or cabaret.

floored
1. knocked down, beaten soundly as in a fight: e.g. My husband floored him because he insulted me.
2. stunned; amazed; dismayed; baffled; nonplussed; staggered: e.g. I was floored by what he said.

floosie/floosy
promiscuous young woman.

flop
1. a failure; any person, thing or project that didn't succeed as expected: e.g. The party was a big flop because of poor attendance.
2. collapse; fail dismally: e.g. You'll flop in your exams if you don't study.
3. fall down comfortably into, as in a lounge chair: e.g. I think I'll flop in front of the telly for a while.
See also:
Foster's flop

flophouse
accommodation house — especially for homeless men.

flour bomb
any light container, such as folded paper, filled with flour and thrown at people in scorn, ridicule or contempt.

floury baker
a type of cicada with a covering that resembles white flour.

flower-child
a hippie.

flower-power
the doctrine of love and peace advocated by the hippies of the 1960s, and symbolised by the flower.

flowery
pertaining to an ostentatious way of speech; full of fine words: e.g. He talks all flowery in front of important or wealthy people in the hope of impressing them.

flown the coop
left home, especially of children living away from home for the first time.

flu
influenza.

flub
to botch, bungle, mess up or ruin.

fluff
1. an emission of wind from the anus; a fart.
2. a blunder, mistake or error, especially in speech.
3. young woman seen as a sex object: e.g. She's a nice bit of fluff.
4. to fart.
5. to make an error or mistake, especially in speech: e.g. He fluffed his lines in the play.

fluke
to do, gain or win by chance: e.g. I fluked a win in the lottery.

flukey/fluky
gained by chance, as opposed to skill: e.g. Hitting the target right in the middle was flukey as I've never done archery before.

flummoxed
bewildered or confused.

flunk
to fail, as in an examination or test: e.g. I flunked my driving test again!

flunk out
1. (see: flunk)
2. give up; withdraw; back out: e.g. I'll have to flunk out of classes for the rest of the year.

flunkey
lackey; servant; yes-man; servile slave to someone's commands and wishes.

flush (for money)
having plenty of money.

flutter (on the neddies)
(to have a . . .) to place a (small) bet or wager (on the horses).

flutterby
butterfly.

fly
1. an attempt; a try; a go: e.g. Let's give it a fly!
2. go very fast: e.g. That car can really fly!
3. leave, depart, especially in a hurry: e.g. Have to fly — I've got an appointment in ten minutes!
4. (Australian Rules football) go for a mark.
See also:
catching flies
drink with the flies
go fly a kite!
let fly
love to be a fly on the wall
only way to fly
pigs can/might fly!
run around like a blue-arsed fly
shut mouth catches no flies
Spanish fly
there are no flies on (someone)

fly a kite
1. pass a fraudulent cheque.
2. test public approval or opinion by spreading a rumour.
3. a rude rebuff or dismissal: e.g. Go fly a kite!

fly at (someone)
physically or verbally attack (someone).

fly cemetery
fruit cake or slice showing raisins or sultanas.

fly in the ointment
a problem, bother; someone or something that is troublesome: e.g. His mother-in-law was the fly in the ointment in their marriage.

fly off the handle
lose one's temper suddenly: e.g. Whenever I mention that, he flies off the handle.

fly off the handle at the drop of a hat
lose one's temper suddenly or quickly over minor things.

fly the coop
leave home; escape; get away: e.g. All parents must accept the fact that their children will fly the coop one day.

fly under false colours
deceive by behaving abnormally.

fly-blown
1. (of meat, sheep etc.) containing eggs laid by a fly.
2. tainted, corrupted.

flybog
jam.

fly-by-night
1. an unreliable person.
2. person who leads an active and gay night life.
3. in the habit of leaving secretly so as to avoid debts, consequences or responsibilities.

flying colours
triumphant success: e.g. He won the race with flying colours.
See also:
come through with flying colours

flying fox
cable-operated transport over difficult terrain or water.

flying high
1. in a state of bliss, euphoria induced by drugs.
2. following an ambitious path, desire that may be too difficult to attain: e.g. She's flying high if she thinks she'll get to the top of that organisation.

flying saucer
supposed ship or craft from outer space; a UFO.

flying start
great advantage over: e.g. He's got more money than you so he had a flying start.

flying the Australian flag
pertaining to someone's shirt-tails that are hanging out over the trousers.

flying the flags
(of women) to be menstruating.

foaming at the mouth
speechless with rage or anger.

fob (someone) off
treat (someone) rudely, unceremoniously, in an off-hand manner.

fogey
conservative, dull, old-fashioned person.

foggiest
(doesn't have, hasn't got, wouldn't have the . . .) not to have the least idea, any knowledge or a single clue: e.g. I haven't got the foggiest where it is.

foghorn
deep, loud voice.

foinsapping
Congratulations! You've been reading all that introductory stuff by the author at the beginning of the book! This word is not really Aussie slang — it's an in-house joke between my husband and myself. I saw it in a *Mad* mag — an onomatopoeic word denoting the sound of a person being slapped in the face with a carpenter's saw. I laughed so heartily that I couldn't get it out of my mind. Writing this dictionary was a bit like that — for weeks I'd have funny sayings on the brain. Whenever I worked on the dictionary, it became known as 'foinsapping'.

fold under pressure
(of a person) collapse, fail, withdraw due to strain, stress or pressure.

fold (up)
1. collapse, fail, as of a business or stage show.
2. close, shut down due to failure or unfortunate circumstances: e.g. We had to fold the business when the lease expired.
See also:
return to the fold

folding money/stuff/variety
paper money as opposed to coinage.

folkie
player or follower of folk-music.

folks
1. people in general.
2. one's family or relatives.

folksy
1. rustic.
2. sociable, informal, of the art and mores of the people rather than an elite.

follow
understand; comprehend: e.g. Do you follow?

follow in (someone's) footsteps
emulate (someone); be like, imitate (someone).

follow in (someone's) wake
1. copy or imitate another person.
2. be swept along by the success of someone else.

follow (one's) heart
act upon (one's) feelings rather than logic.

follow (one's) nose
find (one's) way as if by smell, intuition or instinct.

follow suit
conform to or imitate another's action or belief: e.g. When he walked out of the meeting a lot of others followed suit.

follow the bandwagon
conform to, follow, copy or imitate a currently popular trend, belief, idea or activity.

follower
1. supporter, especially of a particular football team.
2. person lacking in leadership qualities who follows in the footsteps of others.

food for thought
something worth thinking about.

foof 'em (for luck)
in card playing, a cut in the deck by someone poking the middle cards out with the thumb and placing them on top of the deck.

foofer valve
an undesignated part of the body or some machine or engine that is prone to breaking down.
See also:
bust a foofer valve
don't bust a foofer valve

fool and his money are soon parted
pertaining to a spendthrift or an unwise investor.

fool around
1. waste time with inconsequential activity.
2. philander with; cheat on or be unfaithful to one's spouse or partner: e.g. I know he's been fooling around with another woman.
3. indulge in sexual play, activity.

fool with
meddle, tamper, play with someone or something that may be potentially dangerous: e.g. 1. He shouldn't fool with those broken electrical appliances if he isn't qualified. 2. Don't fool with him or you'll be sorry.

foolproof
incapable of misuse or mistake; involving no risk; incapable of failing: e.g. 1. This is a foolproof way of making money. 2. This new thing is foolproof — anyone can work it!

fool's errand
useless, fruitless task.

fool's gold
metallic substance (iron pyrites) that looks similar to gold.

fool's paradise
happiness that is just a temporary illusion or based on false beliefs: e.g. He's living in a fool's paradise if he thinks his money can buy friends.

foot
(see: get off on the wrong foot; have/got one foot in the grave; my foot!; not put a foot wrong; put one's best foot forward; put one's foot down; put one's foot in it; set foot in; start off on the right foot; and see also entries under 'feet')

foot in (one's) mouth
(have, put one's . . .) make an embarrassing remark or statement.

foot it
to walk.

foot (someone) in the ring
kick (someone) in the backside, bum.

foot the bill
pay the costs, especially indignantly or unwillingly: e.g. I had to foot the bill when he bingled my car!

foot up
add up a column of figures.

foothold
a secure position.

foot-in-mouth disease
prone to saying the wrong thing all the time; given to making embarrassing statements.

footloose (and fancy-free)
free to do what one likes, unbound by a relationship or responsibilities; uncommitted and independent.

footsies
feet.
See also:
play footsies with (someone)

footslogger
member of the Army.

footslogging
hard, long-distance walking.

footy
football, especially Australian Rules, and invariably pronounced with a 'd' instead of the 't' — foody.

for
in agreement; interested in: e.g. 1. Who's for coffee? 2. Are you for the new plan or not?

for a song
very cheaply: e.g. He bought that car for a song.

for all (one) is worth
with all (one's) might, energy.

for all practical purposes
nearly; almost; all but.

for all the world
precisely; exactly: e.g. He looks for all the world like a derro, yet he's very wealthy!

for all to see
obvious; conspicuous.

for Christ's sake!

for crying out loud!
expression of annoyance, frustration, anger, the limit of one's tolerance: e.g. For crying out loud! Will you stop nagging!

for ever and a day
for a long time; always: e.g. She'll hate him for ever and a day.

for free
for no payment; without cost: e.g. I got it for free.

for fuck's sake!
expression of exasperation, annoyance, anger.

for fun
in jest; not seriously: e.g. We didn't mean to upset anybody — we did it just for fun.

for good (and all)
finally; for ever: e.g. It's time to settle this dispute for good and all.

for good measure
as an extra precaution; beyond the requirements: e.g. He took the gun with him for good measure.

for it
1. in dire trouble: e.g. You're really for it when he gets his hands on you!
2. interested in it; in agreement with it: e.g. We went to the boss with the idea and he's all for it.

for keeps
1. permanently: e.g. He's mine for keeps.
2. seriously: e.g. We're playing for keeps this time.
3. definite; sincere; actual; genuine: e.g. Is he for keeps?

for my money
in my opinion: e.g. For my money, I don't think it will work.

for my part
as far as I am concerned.

for next to nothing

for nothing
1. for free; at no charge.
2. to no avail; wasted: e.g. We did all that work for nothing!

for Pete's sake!
expression of frustration, exasperation, annoyance.

for real
definite; sincere; actual; genuine: e.g. Are you for real?

for sale
able to be bribed, corrupted: e.g. Some members of the police force are for sale.

for show
ostentation for effect or personal gain: e.g. His generosity was just for show so that people would vote for him.

for starters
in the first place: e.g. 1. For starters we're having the oysters and garlic prawns. 2. For starters, he wasn't even there, so how could he know what went on!

for the birds
of no consequence; trivial; not worthy of serious consideration: e.g. He thinks my hobby is for the birds!

for the hell of it
just for fun; for no particular reason: e.g. We went to the meeting just for the hell of it.

for the life of me
an expression indicating great effort in thought, and usually preceded by the negative can't: e.g. I can't for the life of me understand why he did what he did.

for the love of God/Mike!
expression of exasperation, annoyance, anger, the limit of one's tolerance: e.g. For the love of Mike! Would you be quiet!

for the nth/umpteenth time
1. for the last time: e.g. I've told you for the umpteenth time — no!
2. for a great amount of time: e.g. He's been told for the nth time how to do it but he keeps forgetting!

for the world
under any circumstances; on any account: e.g. I wouldn't do it for the world.

forbidden fruits
illicit, unlawful, out-of-bounds pleasures (especially sexual).

force (someone's) hand
compel (someone) to act unwillingly or prematurely.

foreman material
capable leader or organiser.

forever and a day
for a long time; always.

forget it
cease talking about it; drop the subject because it's closed; don't mention it.

forget (one's) head if it wasn't screwed on
to be extremely forgetful.

forget (oneself)
1. neglect one's interests or responsibilities.
2. say or do something improper or out of character.
3. act in a manner above or below (one's) usual status or social position.

forget the bullshit
get to the point without all the irrelevant details, explanations or excuses: e.g. Forget the bullshit and get on with the facts!

fork out/up
pay, donate or contribute one's share of money, usually unwillingly: e.g. I had to fork out for the rent this week.

fork out big bickies
pay a substantial amount of money, especially unwillingly.

fork over
1. pass or hand over something, usually money.
2. pay out on a bet one has lost.

form
1. a person's reputation or past behaviour: e.g. Going by his form, I wouldn't hire him for the job.
2. behaviour, usually impudent or cheeky: e.g. How's your form!
See also:
bad form
in good form

fortune hunter
person seeking wealth through marriage.

forty
scoundrel; petty criminal; thief. (from Ali Baba and the Forty Thieves)
See also:
wouldn't touch it with a forty-foot pole

forty winks
short nap or sleep: e.g. He's having forty winks on the couch.
See also:
catch forty winks

fossick
search for something in a haphazard manner, especially gold or precious stones.

fossil
an old, antiquated person.

Foster's flop
inability to achieve an erection of the penis due to an excessive indulgence in beer.

foul (one's) own nest
(see: shit in one's own nest)

foul play
underhanded, illegal, treacherous dealings often involving violence, crime, murder etc.: e.g. The police suspect foul play in his death.

foul up
ruin, spoil, make a mess of, bungle: e.g. Watch he doesn't foul up this job again.

foul-mouthed
using obscene language.

foul-up
a ruined situation; a mess; state of confusion.

four corners of the earth
all over the earth: e.g. This disease will spread to the four corners of the earth.

four-be/four-be-two

four-by/four-by-two
1. pre-cut timber, measuring four inches by two inches: e.g. I was hit on the head by a lump of four-be-two!
2. (rhyming slang) Jew.

four-eyes
person who wears prescription eye-glasses.

four-leaf clover
symbol of good luck.

four-letter word
1. any obscene, lewd, vulgar or offensive word having four letters, such as fuck, cunt, arse, shit.
2. anything considered distasteful or unpleasant: e.g. Work is a four-letter word in this house.

four-on-the-floor
(of a car) floor-shift gearbox as opposed to column-shift.

foursome
party of four people: e.g. We often go out as a foursome.

four-wheel drive
any on/off the road, jeep-like vehicle with power to all four wheels and designed to cope with rough terrain.

fox
1. cunning, sly person.
2. deceive; trick; puzzle.
See also:
outfox

foxie/foxy
1. cunning; sly; devious; scheming.
2. sophisticated; fashionable; with-it.
3. fox-terrier dog.

foxy lady
sophisticated, sexy woman.

fraidy-cat
coward (in children's speech).

frame
conspire to make an innocent person appear guilty: e.g. He was framed for that murder.

frame of mind
mood; temper; disposition; attitude: e.g. Ask him for a raise in salary when he's in a better frame of mind.

frame-up
conspiracy whereby the outcome has been illicitly, unlawfully pre-arranged; conspiracy whereby an innocent person has been made to appear guilty.

franger
contraceptive sheath for the penis.

frazzled (nerves)
edgy; nervous; worn-out; at the end of one's endurance or tolerance: e.g. By the end of the day many housewives with young children have frazzled nerves.
See also:
wear (oneself) to a frazzle

freak
1. a fanatic, believer, devoted follower, enthusiast: e.g. Jesus freak; dope freak; racing freak.
2. (see: freak out, 1., 2. and 3.)

freak out
1. to experience a strong emotional reaction to something (usually, but not necessarily, an adverse experience); to over-react: e.g. 1. Debbie freaked out when Richard threw a big hairy spider in her lap. 2. He'll freak out when he learns he's won the million-dollar lottery!
2. to experience an hallucination or trip whilst under the influence of drugs such as marijuana or LSD.
3. panic; become extremely nervous or agitated.

freaked out
1. upset; angry; frightened; nervous; panicky: e.g. He's so freaked out he can't think straight.
2. under the influence of drugs: e.g. He's been really freaked out since the last joint.

freak-out
1. strong emotional experience.
2. strong experience under the influence of drugs.
3. frightening, terrifying experience.

freckle
the anus.

freckle past a hair
stock answer to someone who asks what the time is (especially if one does not wear a watch).

fred
contraceptive sheath for the penis.

Fred Nurks
1. the average man in the street.
2. euphemism for anonymity.

free
(Australian Rules football) free kick.
See also:
for free
home free

free agent
an independent person having no restraints.

free and easy
spontaneous; casual; informal.

free hand
power or authority to do something without the fear of interference: e.g. He's got a free hand in the running of the business.

free love
pertaining to the belief in and practice of the individual having complete freedom in sexual relationships without the restraints and responsibilities associated with legal marriage.

free speech
the right to voice one's opinions without constraint in public.

freebase
cocaine prepared for smoking; to smoke cocaine.

freebie
something gained for no payment or without charge: e.g. Many shops give freebies in order to attract custom.

free-for-all
1. brawl, fight involving many people: e.g. The police were called to break up a huge free-for-all at the pub last night.
2. any event or occasion involving many people which becomes chaotic, disorganised and noisy.

free-loader
person who stays and eats without contributing to the costs.

free-wheeler
an independent person in action and speech.

freeze the balls off a brass monkey
pertaining to very cold weather: e.g. You could freeze the balls off a brass monkey in Melbourne through winter.

Fremantle doctor
cool and refreshing breeze (W.A.).

French
swear-word, obscene language that has been

uttered accidentally or without thought to what others may feel: e.g. Pardon my French, but I think he's a shit!
See also:
excuse the French
pardon the French

French kiss
the method of kissing whereby the tongue enters and explores the partner's mouth.

French leave
departure without permission or notice.

French letter

frenchie/frenchy
condom; contraceptive sheath for the penis.

Freo
Fremantle.

fresh
amorously impudent; cheeky; sexually presumptuous.

fresh as a daisy
alert; awake; well-rested; vigorous.

fresh blood
new people with new, fresh and original ideas.

fresh out of
lacking in; run out of (supplies, ideas etc.): e.g. I'm fresh out of coffee so you'll have to have tea.

fret and fume
be anxious, nervous, worried, upset, annoyed.

Freudian slip
an unintentional error in speech that is taken to reveal one's true subconscious feelings, thoughts, beliefs.

fridge/frig
refrigerator.

fried
1. severely sun-burned.
2. a severe reprimanding, scolding: e.g. He was really fried by the headmaster for wagging school.

fried eggs
flat breasts.

friend
euphemism for a lover, mate, partner, especially in circumstances where the exact nature of a relationship is unknown or hard to categorise.
See also:
man's best friend
with friends like that, who needs enemies!
you can choose your friends but you can't choose your relatives

friends
euphemism for menstruation: e.g. I won't come to the gym tonight — my friends have arrived.

friends in high places
influential friends.

frig
to masturbate.

frig around
1. behave foolishly, stupidly.
2. waste time; use one's time ineffectually.

frig around with
1. toy with; tamper with; interfere with: e.g. I wish he wouldn't frig around with the car.
2. have sexual intercourse with: e.g. If he's been frigging around with my wife I'll murder him!

frig it up
ruin; mess up; spoil; break; damage; confuse: e.g. He offered to fix the telly and really frigged it up.

frigged
ruined; broken; wrecked: e.g. 1. Look what you've done now — you've really frigged it! 2. The lawnmower's frigged.

frigging
1. masturbating: e.g. I caught him frigging in the shower.
2. an intensive, meaning damned, cursed; euphemism for fucking: e.g. This frigging thing won't work!

frightfully
very: e.g. He's frightfully handsome!

frigid digit
sexually unresponsive penis.

frig-up
ruined, failed situation; confusion; a mess.

frillie
frill-necked lizard. (also: frilly)

frills
1. extra benefits; perks; added advantages: e.g. There's quite a few frills attached to this job.
2. anything superfluous or useless; unnecessary elaboration.

frilly
(see: frillie)

fringe benefit
extra benefit; a perquisite.

fringe dweller
1. person who, through association, benefits from other people, groups, clubs etc. without actually contributing anything of value: e.g. There are many fringe dwellers in the field of politics.
2. Aborigine (or other) who lives on the edge of society without taking (or being permitted) an active part in that society.

fringe player
(Australian Rules football) player not picked for a team regularly.

frisk
to search for anything concealed, especially on the body: e.g. The police

frisked them for hidden weapons.

frisky
sexually aroused or eager.

frizzle
(of a meal) burn, spoil, over-cook.

frog
1. (cap.) a Frenchman.
2. condom; contraceptive sheath for the penis.
See also:
hit the frog and toad

frog in the throat
(to have a . . .) persistent, nagging hoarseness or breaking of the voice due to mucus at the back of the throat.

frog-march
to hustle someone forward, after seizing from behind and pinning the arms or seizing by the scruff of the neck and the back of the trousers: e.g. The teacher frog-marched the boy unceremoniously to the headmaster's office.

frogshit
nonsense; rubbish; insincere talk.

from a mile off
very obviously: e.g. You could tell he was a Kiwi from a mile off by his accent.

from A to Z
from beginning to end.

from all walks of life
from wide and varied parts of society: e.g. We get people coming to Alcoholics Anonymous for help from all walks of life.

from arsehole to breakfast-time
all over; completely: e.g. He was covered in mud from arsehole to breakfast-time.

from bad to worse
deteriorate further.

from go to whoa
from the beginning to the end: e.g. He's been nothing but a nuisance from go to whoa!

from head to foot
totally; thoroughly.

from here to Timbuktu
from here to a place very far-away (as a means of comparison): e.g. She's the best cook from here to Timbuktu.

from pillar to post
1. aimlessly from one place to another: e.g. He's been going from pillar to post all his life, but now he's found an interest in life that might settle him down.
2. from one predicament to another: e.g. That poor kid's been kicked from pillar to post because of the neglect of his parents.

from point A to point B
from one place to another: e.g. It's not such a bad car — at least it gets me from point A to point B.

from rags to riches
from being destitute to great wealth.

from scratch
from the beginning.

from the bottom of (one's) heart
sincerely.

from the start/top/word go
from the very beginning.

from the wrong side of the tracks
from the poor, least wealthy part of town or society.

from time to time
occasionally; sometimes.

from top to toe
totally; thoroughly.

front
anything that gives an air of respectability to illegal, illicit dealings: e.g. That shop is just a front for an illegal gambling den.
See also:
full frontal
more front than Myers
up front

front (up)
1. to appear before a court on a charge.
2. to put in an appearance, often in the face of adversity or discomfort: e.g. He didn't front for the test because he didn't study.

front man
figurehead (person) who gives an air of respectability to illegal dealings.

front-bum
female pudendum; vagina.

front-page
important; demanding of attention: e.g. That news is front-page stuff!

frostie/frosty
a cold bottle or can of beer.

froth and bubble
nonsense; idle, insincere, inconsequential talk.

froth at the mouth
1. talk nonsense.
2. (see: foaming at the mouth)

frug
an energetic disco dance.

fruit
1. crazy, mad person; eccentric or odd person.
2. a homosexual.
3. (as an exclamation) euphemism for fuck!; an expression of annoyance, anger, frustration, exasperation.
See also:
bag of fruit
forbidden fruits

fruit for the sideboard
extras; perks; a bonus; luxuries.

fruit of (one's) labours
rewards (not always good) of (one's) work and exertions.

fruitcake/fruit-loop
silly, nutty, irresponsible, foolish or crazy person.
See also:
nutty as a fruitcake

fruit-salad
mongrel; cat or dog of mixed, unknown breeding.

fubsy
fat; obese.

fuck
(vulg.)
1. the act of sexual intercourse: e.g. Did you get a fuck?
2. person as the object of sexual intercourse: e.g. She'd be a good fuck.
3. to have sexual intercourse (with): e.g. Did you fuck him?
4. to ruin, spoil, make a mess of, bungle or break: e.g. He seems to fuck everything he does.
5. an expletive, curse, oath of disgust, annoyance, anger, frustration.
6. exclamation of amazement, wonder, admiration.
See also:
couldn't give a fuck
for fuck's sake!
get fucked!
give a fuck
good fuck
he'd fuck anything on two legs
I'll be fucked!
lousy fuck
the fuck
what the fuck!

fuck a duck!
exclamation of surprise, astonishment, wonder etc.

fuck a town down and shake her arse at the ruins
(of a woman) a slut; promiscuous.

fuck about/around
behave stupidly; waste time; act the fool.

fuck around with
tamper with; interfere with; handle or fiddle with in an unsystematic way: e.g. Don't fuck around with the knobs on that!

fuck me dead/gently!
exclamation of surprise, amazement, wonder, disbelief, annoyance etc.: e.g. Fuck me dead! I didn't know Greg could sing!

fuck off
1. depart; leave: e.g. We have to fuck off.
2. offensive way of telling someone to get lost, go away.

fuck (someone) around
annoy; cause inconvenience to; waste (someone's) time; deceive; thwart; frustrate.

fuck (something) up
ruin; spoil; make a mess of; break; bungle.

fuck you!
expression of dismissal, contempt, rejection.

fuck-all
nothing; zero; nought: e.g. 1. He's done fuck-all work today! 2. He knows fuck-all about fixing cars.
See also:
know sweet fuck-all
sweet fuck-all

fucked
1. (of a person) mad; silly; crazy; insane.
2. (of a person) incoherent; confused; bewildered; suffering from stress or anxiety.
3. (of a person) in dire trouble; in bad circumstances.
4. (of a person) tired; exhausted; worn out.
5. ruined; spoiled; wrecked; broken; useless: e.g. The telly's fucked.
6. deceived; cheated; conned; tricked: e.g. I was fucked by a used-car salesman.
See also:
get fucked!

fucked if I know
proclamation of ignorance: e.g. Fucked if I know where he went.

fucked in the head
(see: fucked, 1. and 2.)

fucked up
1. (see: fucked, 1., 2., 5.)
2. made a total mess of or mistake with: e.g. He really fucked that up!

fucker
stupid, incompetent person; person held in contempt.

fucking
1. another 'great Australian adjective', akin to 'bloody' but considered more offensive and vulgar: e.g. fucking idiot; fucking wonderful; fucking pom; fucking terrific.
2. an intensive, meaning very much, extreme, extremely: e.g. He's such a fucking fool!

fucks like a rattlesnake
is extremely active and inventive during sexual intercourse.

fuck-truck
panel-van or other enclosed van or wagon-type vehicle.

fuck-up
a mess; disastrous situation; a failure; state of confusion; mistake: e.g. That meeting was a huge fuck-up!

fuck-wit
stupid person; fool; dolt; idiot.

fuddy-duddy
old-fashioned, conservative or fussy person.

full
drunk; intoxicated: e.g. He came home from the pub full again.

See also:
in full cry
in full force
in full swing
not the full quid
not the full two-bob's worth

full as a boot/bull/bull's bum

full as a fairy's phone-book/fart/footy final

full as a goog

full as a pommie complaint-box

full as a seaside shithouse on bank holiday

full as a state-school hat-rack

full as a tick

full as the family jerry/po/pot
1. very full.
2. drunk; intoxicated.
3. extremely well fed.

full blast/bore/out/tilt
with maximum effort; actively; quickly; at top speed; using all one's resources and energy: e.g. 1. They're working full blast tomorrow. 2. They drove full bore down the highway with the police in hot pursuit.
See also:
the full bore

full dress
formal attire.

full frontal
complete view of the naked body from the front.

full house
packed to capacity, such as a restaurant, theatre, show etc.

full of airs and graces
conceited; affected in manner; pompous.

full of beans
lively; energetic; frisky.

full of go
fast; energetic; anxious to work; animated.

full of holes
having many faults, flaws, loopholes, fallacies, errors: e.g. His argument is full of holes.

full of life
vivacious; energetic.

full of (oneself)
smug; conceited: e.g. He's so full of himself since he was promoted.

full of shit
(of a person) given to unwarranted boasting, lies.

full of wind
(of a person) 1. given to unwarranted boasting, lies. 2. given to excessively long, boring speeches.

full out/pelt
(see: full blast)

full points
1. (acknowledgement of) a minor victory or praiseworthy act:
e.g. Full points to him for standing up for himself!
2. (Australian Rules football) a goal.

full quid
mentally astute; in complete control of one's faculties: e.g. I don't think he's quite the full quid.

full steam ahead
at top speed; an expression indicating an energetic and enthusiastic start: e.g. Full steam ahead everybody!

full tilt
(see: full blast)

full up

full up to dolly's wax/pussy's bow
1. to have satisfied one's hunger; to have eaten sufficient.
2. totally full.

full-on
1. with complete, total, utter commitment; with maximum effort: e.g. We'll be working full-on this weekend.
2. totally; unrestrained; energetic; vital: e.g. 1. What a full-on fun weekend that was. 2. They had a full-on barney in front of everyone.

fully-fledged
mature; professional; qualified.

fuming
very angry, upset: e.g. He's fuming over the loss of his wallet.

fun
entertaining; spirited; lively: e.g. Sydney is a fun city for the night-life.
See also:
barrel of fun
for fun
like fun!
make fun of
poke fun at
time flies when you're having fun

fun and games
1. wasted time; useless activity.
2. difficulties; trouble; a problem: e.g. We're going to have fun and games trying to put this mess back together!
3. amorous play; sexual intercourse, activity: e.g. Jan and Mal had fun and games in the back seat of their Rolls.

fun-bags
woman's breasts.

fundament/fundamental orifice
the anus.

funeral
course of action that is detrimental; trouble; worry; concern: e.g. It's his funeral if he really wants to do something against my advice.

fungus-face
man with a beard.

funk
1. syncopated style of soul music.

2. non-conformist style of fashion and art, originating on the west coast of America.

funky
1. fashionable; excellent; trendy.
2. exciting.
3. in the style of funk music.
4. strong smelling.

funnies
cartoons, comic-strips, especially in the newspapers.

funny
1. strange; weird; queer; perplexing; odd: e.g. He's a bit funny.
2. mad; insane.
3. a joke: e.g. He told funnies at the party all night.
4. impertinent; cheeky; insolent: e.g. Don't get funny with me!
See also:
crack a funny
play funny-buggers
very funny!

funny business
1. amorous behaviour; sexual flirting and play: e.g. If he tries any funny business on the first date, slap his face!
2. underhanded, illegal activities; cheating; dishonest dealings.
3. foolish, naughty behaviour: e.g. Watch that the kids don't get up to any funny business while we're away.

funny-bone
1. elbow: e.g. I hit my funny-bone on the side of the table and it's still tingling.
2. pertaining to anything humorous, one's sense of humour: e.g. That joke tickled my funny-bone so much I couldn't stop laughing.

funny-farm
lunatic asylum; any hospital or establishment for psychiatric patients or the insane.

funny-money
counterfeit money.

fur
(see: make the fur fly)

fur-burger/pie
female pudendum; vulva; vagina (as seen by men as a sex object, such as in cunnilingus).

furphy
1. an early water-cart (made by Furphy, Victoria).
2. wild rumour; tall story; false report.

F.U.R.T.B.
full up ready to bust — very full (of food).

fussed
worried; concerned: e.g. I'm not fussed what we do tonight.

fusspot
1. worrier; complainer; malcontent.
2. an over-particular, fastidious person.

future shock
a neurotic state of mind brought about in people unable to cope with rapid technological development and resultant social change.

fuzz
1. police: e.g. The fuzz arrived at the scene of the accident.
2. hair (usually frizzy).
3. pubic hair.

fuzz-wagon
distinctively marked police-car.

fuzzy-headed
suffering from a hang-over, the after-effects of too much alcohol, or lack of sleep.

fuzzy wuzzy
1. unstable; vague; the state of being following a late or drunken night.
2. anything soft, fluffy to the touch.
3. native of Papua New Guinea.

G. and D.
(Australian Rules football) guts and determination.

gab
chatter; talk: e.g. The girls are having a gab in the kitchen.
See also:
gift of the gab

Gabba
the Queensland Cricket Assoc. ground at Woollongabba, Brisbane.

gabble-guts
talkative, loquacious person.

gabby
talkative; loquacious.

gabster
radio talk-host.

gad(s)!
mild oath; expression of surprise, wonder etc.

gadabout
person who leads an active social life.

gadzooks!
mild oath; expression of surprise, wonder etc.

gag
1. a joke: e.g. I heard this incredibly funny gag last night, and now I can't remember it.
2. any comic, humorous situation.

ga-ga
1. mad; insane; silly; foolish.
2. senile.
3. bewitched, besotted, enraptured by: e.g. He's completely ga-ga over her.
See also:
go ga-ga over

gal
1. girl.
2. galvanised iron.

galah
fool; ineffectual person: e.g. 1. He made a proper galah of himself. 2. That silly galah can't do anything right!
See also:
mad as a gumtree full of galahs
pack of galahs

galah session
special interval on the Flying Doctor radio service to allow people to gossip with their neighbours who may live hundreds of kilometres away.

gall
impudence: e.g. What gall you have to say that!

gallivant
to gad about; behave in a socially flirtatious manner: e.g. She goes gallivanting around the night-clubs often.

gallops
(the . . .) the horse-races.

galoot
stupid, awkward fool; clumsy dolt.

galumph
1. move, leap or prance clumsily, noisily.
2. leap for joy.

galvo
galvanised iron.

game
1. profession or business: e.g. 1. What game is he in? 2. What's his game?
2. daring; bravado: e.g. I'm not game enough to ride the corkscrew roller-coaster.
3. trickery; strategy; underhanded dealings: e.g. 1. I can see through his game. 2. He's always involved in some game or other.
See also:
easy game
fair game
give the game away
have/got the game by the throat
have/got the game sewn up
in the game
lift (one's) game
name of the game
off (one's) game
pack the game in
play games (with)
play the game
play the waiting game
two can play at that game

'Excessive penalty is no excuse, Son. We think you weren't having a go!'

No matter what the odds in life or sport, the Aussie is expected to have a go. If he isn't a battler, a doer, a goer or a trier he will be looked upon with contempt as a slack-arse, no-hoper or gutless wonder who couldn't run guts for a slow butcher, catch a cold or perform other acts of competence, such as dragging the skin off a rice-pudding.

game as a piss-ant
very daring, brave or willing (particularly when referring to someone small in stature).

game as Ned Kelly
very daring and devil-may-care.

game of cat and mouse
situation in which two parties constantly fight or struggle for an advantage: e.g. Their marriage is nothing but a game of cat and mouse.

game of ivories
the game of pool.

game of mis-spent youth
pool, snooker or related games.

game, set and match
a victory: e.g. It was game, set and match to Fred in the beer-drinking competition.

game's up
(the . . .) statement indicating the end of an activity, especially an illicit or illegal one in which someone is caught out or discovered.

gammy
crippled; lame: e.g. After that fall the horse had a gammy leg.

gander
a look: e.g. Have a gander at this!

gang up on
attack physically or verbally in a group so as to make the odds unfair: e.g. You and your friends always gang up on me.

gang bang/slash

gangie
an occasion of group sex, especially where several men have sexual intercourse with one woman; the woman who is the object of such an occasion.

gangster
a criminal.

gangway!
get out of the way!

ganja
marijuana; cannabis.

gaol-bait
a girl under the legal age of consent viewed as a sex object.

gaol-bird
habitual criminal.

garage sale
sale of private individual's unwanted miscellaneous goods, held at the home usually on a week-end.

garbage
1. nonsense; asininity; balderdash: e.g. What a lot of garbage that speech was!
2. anything unworthy of consideration: e.g. 1. That book is garbage. 2. She's garbage!
See also:
load of garbage

garbage-guts
greedy person; person who eats often, eats left-overs.

garbo
person who works as a garbage, waste collector.

garden
(see: lead someone up the garden path)

Garden of Eden
any beautiful, out-door place.

garlic muncher
1. European person; a Greek or Italian.
2. person whose breath smells of garlic.

garn!
(contraction of: go on) expression of disbelief.

gas
1. petrol.
2. empty, boastful talk; nonsense.
3. anything splendid or successful: e.g. That party was a gas.
4. to talk, gossip: e.g. What are they gassing about?
5. splendid; wonderful: e.g. What a gas idea!
See also:
cooking with gas
step on the gas

gas-bag
1. incessant talker; a gossip.
2. to talk at length, gossip.

gash
1. female pudendum; vagina.
2. woman as a sex object.

gasper
cigarette.

gasser
anything wonderful, splendid, successful.

gastro
stomach upset.

gat
revolver; firearm.

gate-crash
attend a social gathering, party etc. uninvited.

gate-crasher
person who attends a social gathering without an invitation.

gawk
1. a fool; stupid person.
2. stare openly: e.g. What are you gawking at?

gay
of or pertaining to homosexuality; a homosexual: e.g. All the gays go to that new gay bar in town.

gazodjule
a name for an object of which one cannot remember the name.

gazunder
(also: gezunder, gozunder) chamber-pot.

g'day
(contraction of: good day) a greeting.

gear
1. clothes: e.g. Change your gear in the bedroom.

2. equipment; implements; tools.
3. marijuana or other drugs: e.g. Got any gear?
See also:
get (one's) cogs into gear
get (oneself) into gear

geared up
ready; prepared: e.g. We were all geared up to go swimming when it started raining.

gee!/gee whiz!/gees!
exclamation of surprise, admiration, disappointment etc.

gee-gee
horse.
See also:
the gee-gees

geek
(also: geez, gig) a look: e.g. Have a geek at this.

gees/geez
(see: gee)

geese flying out of (one's) arse/backside
(to have . . .) to experience an orgasm.

geeser
(see: geezer)

geezer
1. eccentric person; oddball: e.g. Who's that geezer over there?
2. person; chap; fellow; bloke.
3. a look: e.g. Have a geezer at this!

gem
person or thing of great admiration.

gen
the necessary information: e.g. What's the gen on that new horse that's running today?

gender-bender
member or follower/ imitator of rock music band in which the members dress and apply make-up in a manner that makes it difficult to determine their sex.

genny
generator.

gents
public lavatory for men.

Geordie
a Scotsman.

geri
short for geriatric; used by the young to describe anybody over the age of 30 or 40.

germ
despicable person.

Germaine Greer
(rhyming slang) ear.

German band
(rhyming slang) hand.

geronimo!
exclamation of enthusiasm at the start of something, such as a race.

gerry
(see: jerry)

gerrymander
the arrangement of electoral boundaries to the advantage of a particular political party.

get
1. annoy; irritate: e.g. His mother will really get you!
2. attract; please; amuse: e.g. Those cute kittens got me!
3. affect emotionally: e.g.That sad movie will get you in the end.
4. seek revenge: e.g. I'll get him for that!
5. understand, comprehend: e.g. I don't get what he said.

get a bee in (one's) bonnet
to become obsessed with something.

get a big head
become vain; have an over-rated opinion of oneself.

get a bit
have sexual intercourse: e.g. Did you get a bit last night?

get a crush on (someone)
be infatuated, in love with (someone): e.g. She's got a crush on Paul Newman.

get a dose
contract venereal disease — gonorrhoea.

get a hammering
receive a sound beating; suffer a major defeat: e.g. Our team got a hammering in the finals.

get a hold of (oneself)
regain (one's) self-control or composure: e.g. Don't worry — get a hold of yourself! Everything will be fine!

get a kick out of
obtain a great amount of pleasure or satisfaction out of: e.g. Some people get a real kick out of flying — I hate it!

get a knock-back
receive a rebuttal, refusal or set-back.

get a leg in (the door)
make some progress: e.g. I've tried to reason with her but I can't seem to get a leg in the door!

get a length
(of women) receive sexual intercourse from a man.

get a lift under the ear
receive a beating or a punch in the ear, face.

get a line on
find information on: e.g. Try to get a line on that latest rumour that's been going around.

get a load
contract venereal disease: e.g. He got a load overseas.

get a load of
1. have a look: e.g. Get a load of the boobs on her!
2. have a listen: e.g. Get a load of what this guy is saying!

get a move on
hurry up.

get a swollen head
become vain; have an over-rated opinion of oneself.

get a word in edgeways
get a chance to speak: e.g. When she starts talking you can't get a word in edgeways.

get a wriggle on
hurry up.

get across (to someone)
make understood (to someone): e.g. We must get across to him how important this project is.

get ahead
be successful: e.g. He's going to get ahead in this business.

get along
1. cope; manage: e.g. Now that he's gone it'll be difficult, but we'll get along somehow.
2. go; depart: e.g. We have to get along as it's late.
3. get on well with someone: e.g. Those two really get along.

get an earful
1. listen to: e.g. Get an earful of this guy!
2. receive a long boring speech: e.g. He gave me an earful at the last meeting.
3. receive a severe scolding: e.g. Mum gave me an earful for coming home so late.

get an eyeball of
get a good look at.

get an invite
receive an invitation.

get any
have sexual intercourse: e.g. Did you get any last night?

get around to it
apply one's energies to (something) eventually; consider doing: e.g. I've asked him a thousand times to fix that leaking tap but he never seems to get around to it.

get at
1. hint at, or imply: e.g. What are you trying to get at?
2. tamper with: e.g. Watch the kids don't get at that video.
3. tamper with illicitly, fraudulently or so as to corrupt: e.g. He may try to get at the judge by offering a big bribe.

get away
1. take leave; go on a holiday: e.g. He needs to get away for a few weeks.
2. (as an exclamation) expression of disbelief or surprise.

get away from it all
to leave one's worries, anxieties, business and responsibilities and go on a holiday.

get away with (blue) murder
not have to suffer the consequences of one's actions: e.g. His mother lets him get away with blue murder!

get back at
take revenge upon someone: e.g. I'll get back at him one day for what he did to me.

get back on (one's) feet
recover after a major set-back.

get blood out of a stone
(see: can't . . .)

get booked
be charged by police for a minor offence: e.g. I got booked for speeding.

get buckled
1. be arrested.
2. be beaten up, defeated in a fight.

get bumped off
be killed.

get burned/burnt
receive a serious set-back; get into trouble as a result of one's actions: e.g. You'll get burnt if you have anything to do with that criminal.

get by
manage, cope in the face of difficulties: e.g. We'll get by.

get carried away
1. lose control of one's emotions.
2. have sexual intercourse after losing control in the heat and excitement of the moment.

get caught
(of women) to fall pregnant unexpectedly.

get cold feet
lose one's nerve, bravado, courage: e.g. Last week he said he'd do it but I think he's got cold feet now.

get conned
be tricked, deceived, cheated or duped.

get cracking
hurry up; begin vigorously.

get dark
become angry; lose one's temper: e.g. He gets dark every time I try to talk about that matter.

get done
1. be tricked, deceived, cheated or duped: e.g. You'll get done if you ask him to sell your car.
2. be defeated, beaten: e.g. Our team got done in the grand finals.

get done in
be killed.

get done over
be bashed, beaten, defeated in a fight.
See also:
done over

get down to brass/tin tacks
to deal seriously with the essential points of a matter

and to ignore irrelevant details.

get even
seek revenge.

get fobbed off
1. to put off: e.g. Each time I ask him for the money back he fobs me off with a new and better story about how he's going to get it.
2. be treated unceremoniously, rudely, in an off-handed manner: e.g. Every time I ask for a date with her I get fobbed off!

get fucked!
a rude rebuke, dismissal or indication of contempt; go away! get lost!

get gravel rash
behave in a sycophantic, obsequious manner: e.g. Every time he sees the boss he gets gravel rash!

get had
(see: get done, 1.)

get heavy
become too serious: e.g. I don't like going out with him because he always gets too heavy.

get hers/his/yours
1. receive a just reward, especially as the consequence of ill behaviour or dealings: e.g. That crook will get his one day!
2. be killed: e.g. He got his in a car accident.

get in a flap
become flustered, confused, worried, anxious.

get in for (one's) chop
seek (one's) share, cut, or part of the action: e.g. When Dad died, all the relatives from near and far tried to get in for their chop.

get in good with (someone)
ingratiate oneself with (someone): e.g. If you get in good with the boss he might give you a raise in salary.

get in on the act/action
be involved in; take part in.

get in on the ground floor
start from the beginning; grasp the earliest opportunity.

get in (someone's) hair
annoy, irritate (someone); get in (someone's) way; be a nuisance instead of a help to (someone).

get into
become seriously or enthusiastically involved or engrossed: e.g. I was just getting into a good book by the fire when visitors arrived.

get into a knot
become confused, upset, over-anxious.

get into a scrap
be involved in a fight.

get into deep/hot water
get into trouble or a difficult predicament: e.g. He really got himself into hot water by making that statement to the press.

get into (it)
attack, begin with gusto and enthusiasm.

get into (someone/ something)
(see: get stuck into someone/something)

get into (someone's) pants
have sexual intercourse with (someone). (also: get into someone)

get into strife
get into trouble.

get into the swing of things
become actively involved, familiar with.

get it
1. have sexual intercourse: e.g. He's in a bad mood because he didn't get it last night.
2. understand; comprehend: e.g. She didn't laugh at that joke because she didn't get it.
3. receive a severe scolding, reprimand.

get it all out in the open
reveal the truth or real facts publicly.

get it (all) together
achieve success or harmony mentally, or in any situation or matter: e.g. 1. He's successful now because he's got it together in his head.
2. Get it together you blokes, or we'll never finish this job!

get it down pat
execute perfectly, exactly.

get it in the neck
receive a severe scolding or punishment.

get it off (one's) chest
bring into the open, discuss a pressing worry.

get it off with (someone)
have sexual intercourse with (someone): e.g. I'd like to get it off with Gray but he's not that way inclined.

get it straight
understand correctly.

get it up
(of a man) achieve an erection of the penis.

get knotted/lost!
a rude rebuff, rebuke or dismissal.

get mileage out of
get good, successful use out of (something): e.g. 1. I got terrific mileage out of that old car. 2. He got a lot of mileage out of that old joke — had everyone in stitches for hours.

get mixed up in
become involved (often involuntarily): e.g. I got mixed up in their arguments and fights just because I lived there.

get nicked
1. (as an exclamation) rude rebuff, rebuke or dismissal.
2. get caught by the police or authorities in an illegal act.

get nowhere
achieve nothing; have no success or progress: e.g. We'll get nowhere if we argue all the time!

get off
1. exclamation of surprise, disbelief, scorn: e.g. Get off! You don't know what you're talking about!
2. escape or evade consequences: e.g. He was booked for speeding but got off with a good excuse.

get off at Redfern
(of a man) to withdraw the penis from the vagina just before ejaculation; coitus interruptus.

get off my back Scobie!
stop nagging, annoying, harassing me! (Scobie Breasley was considered one of the best jockeys in history)

get off on
1. receive pleasure or satisfaction from: e.g. He gets off on collecting stamps.
2. receive sexual gratification: e.g. She gets off on vibrators.

get off on the right/wrong foot
get off to a good/bad start; make a good/bad impression: e.g. I got off on the wrong foot with my new boss by coming late to work.

get off (one's) back
stop nagging, annoying, harassing: e.g. I wish Mum would get off my back about my long hair!

get off (one's) backside/butt
stop being idle and start work, do something.

get off (one's) bike
lose (one's) temper; lose control of (one's) emotions: e.g. Don't get off your bike!

get off (one's) case
stop annoying, harassing, pestering, nagging (one).

get off (one's) high horse
stop being arrogant, haughty: e.g. The council members should get off their high horses and do something about the complaints of the residents.

get off the grass!
exclamation of disbelief, scorn.

get off the ground
begin; be successful.

get off with (someone)
(see: get it off with)

get on
1. advance in age: e.g. Mum's getting on now.
2. agree, be on friendly terms with: e.g. I can't seem to get on with her.
3. prosper; do well: e.g. He's going to get on when he grows up.
4. (horse-racing) lay a bet in time: e.g. Did you get on?

get on her/him!
exclamation of scorn, disgust, contempt, amazement.

get on like a bushfire/house on fire
get on very well with (someone); agree: e.g. Those two get on like a house on fire.

get on (one's) goat/nerves/quince/wick
annoy, irritate, anger, upset (one): e.g. It really gets on my goat when he starts practising on that trombone late at night!

get on (one's) high horse
assume an arrogant and pompous air, attitude.

get on (someone's) back
annoy, harass, stand over (someone): e.g. It's time I got on the boss's back for a raise in salary.

get on the ball
be alert, knowledgeable of a situation and its implications.

get on the right side of (someone)
get in favour with (someone).

get on the wrong side of (someone)
incur (someone's) hostility; get out of favour with (someone): e.g. You really got on the wrong side of him when you told him his wife was a bag!

get on to
1. follow up; contact; pursue a matter: e.g. I must get on to her and have a talk about that.
2. discover; reveal: e.g. What did the police get on to when they questioned him?

get on with it/the job
pursue a specific task without being side-tracked: e.g. It's a pity the Government didn't just get on with the job instead of fighting and mud-slinging all the time!

get one
have sexual intercourse: e.g. Didn't you get one last night?

get (one's)
a threat of vengeance: e.g.
1. He'll get his one day!
2. You'll get yours!

get (one's) act together
regain, maintain or be in control of (one's) composure, stability, behaviour: e.g. You'd better get your act

together if you expect to keep this job!

get (one's) arse in a sling
get into trouble: e.g. You'll get your arse in a sling if you keep doing things that are illegal.

get (one's) arse into gear
get ready, prepared, organised to start work, activity.

get (one's) back up
become annoyed, angry, indignant: e.g. There's no need to get your back up just because I told the truth!

get (one's) cogs into gear
1. think clearly on a matter.
2. begin something, such as work, a task.

get (one's) dander up
become annoyed, angry, indignant: e.g. He really gets my dander up when he starts on the booze.

get (one's) ears lowered
have a haircut.

get (one's) end in
1. (of a man) have sexual intercourse.
2. have (one's) say; voice (one's) unwanted opinion.

get (one's) feet wet
obtain practical experience; start from the beginning and learn.

get (one's) fingers burnt
suffer the consequences of (one's) actions; suffer a set-back due to (one's) actions.

get (one's) hackles up
become angry, aggressive.

get (one's) hooks into
(of a woman) marry; tie a man down to a firm commitment in a relationship: e.g. She finally got her hooks into him.

get (one's) Irish up
become angry; lose (one's) temper.

get (one's) just deserts
to receive punishment, consequences deserving of (one's) crimes or actions.

get (one's) knickers in a knot/twist
become upset, confused, anxious or angry.
See also:
don't get your knickers in a knot/twist

get (one's) licence out of a cornflakes packet
to be unskilled or incompetent: e.g. With all the accidents he's been involved in, he must have got his driver's licence out of a cornflakes packet!

get (one's) lines crossed
to be confused, incorrect; to be misunderstood, misinterpreted.

get (one's) lumps
receive a severe beating, or deserved punishment.

get (one's) message across
make (one's) opinion, point of view known, understood — especially to an opponent.

get (one's) money's worth
to receive full value or satisfaction from: e.g. We really got our money's worth at that restaurant.

get (one's) oar in
have (one's) say; voice (one's) (often unwanted) opinion.

get (one's) own back
seek revenge: e.g. He's done a lot of terrible things to me but I'll get my own back one day!

get (one's) rocks off
1. to masturbate.
2. to have sexual intercourse.
3. have a good time; get (one's) thrills: e.g. He gets his rocks off by parachuting out of planes!

get (one's) second wind
feel rejuvenated; revive; recover after tiredness.

get (one's) shit together
regain, maintain or be in control of (one's) composure, mental stability, behaviour: e.g. No matter what the problem, Pam could always get her shit together.

get (one's) teeth into
begin, make a start with enthusiasm and energy: e.g. Merridy loves to get her teeth into a thick Steven King horror book.

get (one's) tits in a tangle
(see: don't get your . . .)

get (one's) two-bob's worth
receive full value or satisfaction from: e.g. You'll really get your two-bob's worth at that restaurant.

get (one's) water cut off
receive a severe set-back, rebuff, rebuke.

get (one's) wires crossed
to misunderstand; become confused.

get (oneself) into gear
prepare (oneself); get ready to start.

get (oneself) together
1. collect (one's) thoughts; think coherently: e.g. I need time to get myself together before I make a firm decision.
2. recover (one's) calm, composure, emotions: e.g. Get yourself together — there's no sense getting so upset!

get out
become public knowledge: e.g. I don't want a single thing that's been discussed tonight to get out.

get out and about
be socially active: e.g. You should get out and about more now that you're divorced.

get out from under
escape from a bad situation: e.g. I had no

choice in closing the business — things were going bad and I had to get out from under.

get out of the kitchen if you can't stand the heat
advice to withdraw from an argument or situation that one cannot cope with or deal with adequately.

get out on the wrong side of the bed
be bad-tempered, hostile, irritable.

get personal
talk about delicate, private or intimate matters.

get pinched
be arrested for a crime or minor offence: e.g. He got pinched for growing marijuana.

get ribbed
be teased, made fun of: e.g. He got ribbed by his mates all day because he got roaring drunk last night.

get rooted!
a term of abuse; rude rebuff, rebuke or dismissal.

get round
overcome, cope with, solve (a problem, difficulties): e.g. We'll get round it one way or another.

get round (someone)
ingratiate oneself with (someone): e.g. I know he's in a bad mood but I know how to get round him.

get round to (something)
(see: get around to it)

get saddled with
have something undesired foisted upon oneself: e.g. I got saddled with their cats while my parents went away for a holiday.

get screwed
1. have sexual intercourse (with): e.g. Did you get screwed last night?
2. be cheated, tricked, swindled, ripped off: e.g. You'll get screwed by that con-man.

get set
(horse-racing) place a bet in time: e.g. Did you get set in the fifth?

get shot
be in serious trouble: e.g. You'll get shot if you touch his things!

get shot of (someone/something)
get rid of; remove; be free of: e.g. I'd like to get shot of him as I don't think he's good for the business.

get side-tracked
be distracted from the relevant issue.

get some air
have a break or rest; take a stroll outside for some fresh air.

get (someone) down
depress, discourage (someone).

get (someone) wrong
misunderstand, misinterpret (someone).

get (someone's) back up
annoy, harass, arouse (someone's) anger, resentment.

get sprung
1. be arrested for a crime or offence: e.g. He got sprung for growing marijuana.
2. be caught out, surprised by someone: e.g. He got sprung letting down the tyres on my car!

get stuck into (someone/something)
1. begin something with enthusiasm and energy: e.g. It's time we got stuck into some gardening for spring.
2. severely scold, berate, criticise, abuse someone: e.g. Mum's going to get stuck into you when you get home!
3. assault; beat, bash someone.

get stuffed!
(see: get rooted)

get stung
1. become drunk, intoxicated.
2. be cheated, tricked, swindled, conned.

get sucked in
1. be cheated, tricked, swindled, conned, defrauded: e.g. I got sucked in by his lies and lost a lot of money.
2. be drawn into by artful pleading: e.g. I get sucked in by my friends to do free work for them all the time.
3. (Australian Rules football, of a team) drawn into fighting rather than playing, with the inference that it's a deliberate tactic on the part of the other side.

get technical
speak in technical terms, use jargon that is difficult to understand.

get the arse/axe/big A/boot/bullet/chop
be dismissed, fired, rebuffed, rejected unceremoniously or with contempt: e.g. He got the arse because he didn't work hard enough.

get the ball rolling
make a start; begin.

get the best of (someone)
defeat; beat; gain a substantial advantage over (someone).

get the better of (oneself)
to be overcome by emotion, feeling: e.g. The sad ending in that movie got the better of me.

get the boot
(see: get the arse)

get the bull by the horns
face a situation with courage.

get the bullet/chop
(see: get the arse)

get the digit out
stop wasting time and start work.

get the dirty end of the stick
receive an unfair, unjust, unpleasant ruling, task, deal or part to play in a situation.

get the drift
understand, comprehend: e.g. I didn't get the drift of what he was saying.

get the drop on (someone)
gain an advantage over (someone); get (someone) at a disadvantage.

get the dry-horrors
suffer from extreme thirst, a dry mouth, especially after drinking excessive amounts of alcohol.

get the edge on (someone)
gain an advantage over (someone).

get the evil eye
receive a disapproving, frowning look.

get the feel of
learn about something; become familiar with: e.g. You'll get the feel of it eventually.

get the full treatment
1. receive the best service: e.g. You really get the full treatment at that restaurant.
2. get a severe scolding, criticism or punishment: e.g. The newspapers gave him the full treatment after he was convicted for all those crimes.

get the good guts
receive reliable information: e.g. I got the good guts on which horse is going to win in race seven.

get the goods on
receive, find out information on, especially if it is incriminating: e.g. The police will eventually get enough goods on him to put him in prison for a long time.

get the gripes
become bad-tempered, ill-disposed, sulky.

get the hang of
(see: get the feel of)

get the hell out (of)
leave, depart quickly: e.g. I got the hell out before things got worse.

get the horrors
become frightened; feel repulsion.

get the hots for
feel sexually excited about someone: e.g. I think she's got the hots for Alf.

get the jack
1. reach the end of one's tolerance; become tired, weary of.
2. contract venereal disease, especially gonorrhoea.

get the jim-jams
feel fright, repulsion, anxiety, nervousness.

get the jump on (someone)
gain an advantage over (someone); take (someone) by surprise.

get the knack
become familiar with, learn about and do with ease: e.g. You'll get the knack after a few day's practice.

get the message
understand, comprehend.

get the miseries
become morose, miserable, depressed.

get the munchies
develop a craving for food, feel peckish, hungry — especially after smoking marijuana.

get the nod/okay
gain approval, permission or assent: e.g. That proposal to build a high-rise on the beach got the nod from the council.

get the picture
understand, comprehend the situation or circumstances.

get the pip
become annoyed, irritated, angry or petulant.

get the rough end of the pineapple
get the worst out of a situation; get an unfair, unsatisfactory or unpleasant deal or treatment.

get the run-around
be inconvenienced; receive evasive answers: e.g. Each time I ask for a direct answer from him on that matter I get the run-around.

get the shits
1. suffer from diarrhoea.
2. become angry, upset, annoyed, bad-tempered.
3. become miserable, depressed, petulant, sulky.

get (the) short shrift
be treated with lack of consideration, unceremoniously.

get the show on the road
start, begin.

get the shunt/spear
be fired, dismissed unceremoniously.

get the thumbs down
receive a refusal, lack of support.

get the trots
suffer from diarrhoea.

get the upper hand
gain an advantage over someone.

get the urge
1. feel a need (to do something).
2. need to urinate: e.g. It's typical for me to get the urge when there's no toilet in sight!

get the vapours
dissolve into tears; weep.

get the wind up
become frightened, alarmed, nervous, anxious, suspicious.

get the works
(see: get the full treatment, 1. and 2.)

get the worst of it
suffer defeat: e.g. The small dog got the worst of it in that dog- fight.

get the wrong end of the stick
(see: wrong end of the stick)

get this!
have a look at this! (in a disbelieving manner)

get through to (someone)
make (someone) understand, see reason: e.g. When he gets mad it's hard to get through to him.

get to first base
1. make a slight progress or start.
2. (didn't . . .) failed to establish a rapport with; failed to make any progress.

get to (one/someone)
1. annoy, irritate: e.g. Her nagging gets to me!
2. arouse deep feelings in (one/someone): e.g. Seeing those starving people in Africa on the telly really gets to me!

get under (one's) skin
1. annoy, irritate (one).
2. fascinate, attract (one).

get up
to win, especially in horse-racing: e.g. If that horse of Harry's gets up, he'll win a fortune.

get up on the wrong side of bed
(see: get out on the . . .)

get up (someone)
1. have sexual intercourse with (someone): e.g. I bet you'd like to get up her!
2. severely berate, scold, abuse (someone): e.g. I'm going to really get up him for saying those awful things about me!

get up (someone's) nose
annoy, irritate (someone) intensely.

get up to
do, especially mischief or act of misbehaviour: e.g. What did you get up to last night during my absence?

get uppity
become annoyed, angry, irritated or indignant.

get what for
to be punished severely: e.g. You're going to get what for when Dad finds out what you've done!

get what is coming (to one)
1. to receive what one deserves or is entitled to.
2. to be punished suitably.

get wind of
begin to suspect, know or find out about.

get wise
face or become aware of the true facts.

get wise with (someone)
be cheeky, impertinent to (someone).

get with it
1. become more fashionable, sophisticated.
2. become aware of the real facts.
3. concentrate; pay careful attention to.
4. join in; participate.

get with (someone)
have sexual intercourse with (someone): e.g. I'd love to get with him one night!

For other possible entries beginning with 'get' see entries listed under 'have/got'.

get-at-able
attainable; accessible.

getting a fair whack
being well paid.

getting any/it?
having any sexual intercourse? — a greeting between men that usually has a stock answer, such as 'Yeah, you bet! Have to put an extra man on'.

getting on (a bit)
becoming aged, old.

getting too close to the bone
1. becoming indecent, lewd, profane.
2. becoming embarrassingly truthful or indelicate.

getting warm
getting close to finding out something.

get-together
informal gathering or party; meeting.

get-up
1. an outfit of clothing; style of dress.
2. anything of notable or noticeable style, such as a piece of equipment: e.g. You should see the get-up he's driving around in now.

get-up-and-go
vigour; enthusiasm; energy: e.g. She's got a lot of get-up-and-go.

get-up-and-go got up and went
to be tired, worn-out, lacking in enthusiasm and energy: e.g. I was really keen to paint the house today but my get-up-and-go seems to have got up and went.

gezunder
(see: gazunder)

ghost of a chance
very small chance.

gibber
stone.

giblets
the penis and testicles.

gidday
(contraction of: good day) a greeting. (also: g'day)

giddy-up
command to go, go faster, especially to a horse.

gift
anything easily, cheaply obtained: e.g. That house was a gift at that price.
See also:
don't look a gift horse in the mouth

gift of the gab
the talent of being able to make people listen to, believe what one says; glib speech: e.g. Most successful salesmen have the gift of the gab.

gig
1. fool; stupid person; odd person.
2. a look: e.g. Have a gig at this!
3. musician's engagement to play: e.g. That band's got a gig at the local pub tonight.

giggle
an amusing situation, person or occasion: e.g. The meeting was a bit of a giggle.
See also:
hit-and-giggle

giggle bin/factory/house
mental or lunatic asylum.

giggling Gerty
woman given to giggling, behaving in a silly, giggling manner.

gild the lily
to spoil beauty or good taste with over-decoration and gaudiness.

gilt-edged
of the highest degree of reliability or quality: e.g. Buying shares in that company would be a gilt-edged investment.

gimme
contraction of: give me.

gimmick
1. an idea, style or act of eccentricity designed to attract publicity and attention.
2. tricky device or means; hidden trick or scheme: e.g. What's the gimmick? That deal sounds too good to be true.

gin
Aboriginal woman.

gin jockey
white man who has sexual intercourse with an Aboriginal woman.

ging
type of catapult made by boys to hurl stones; shanghai, sling.

ginger
bum; buttocks; anus: e.g. That dog needs a good kick up the ginger!

Ginger Meggs
(rhyming slang) legs.

ginger-beer
1. (rhyming slang) ear.
2. (rhyming slang) queer; homosexual.

ginger-up
to incite more liveliness, gaiety, energy into an occasion or activity.

gink
1. a look: e.g. Have a gink at this.
2. fool; silly person.

gi-normous
(combination of: giant and enormous) very big; huge.

gip
(see: gyp)

girl
1. a man's sweetheart: e.g. She's Fred's girl.
2. (of a man) effeminate; weak; lacking in strength: e.g. He's such a bloody girl!
See also:
old girl
working girl

girl Friday
secretary and assistant in an office.

girl/boy next-door
a wholesome, virtuous, chaste and unsophisticated person.

girlie magazine
men's magazine showing pictures of nude women.

girls
a woman's friends in general: e.g. She's having a night out with the girls.

girls' night out
an occasion on which a group of women go out for the evening together.

girls' week
time of menstruation.

gism
semen: e.g. There's gism all over the sheets.

gismo
(see: gizmo)

git
fool; idiot; dolt: e.g. You stupid git!

give
tell; offer by way of explanation: e.g. Don't give me that nonsense!
See also:
what gives?

give a bugger

give a continental

give a darn

give a fuck

give a hang/hoot

give a shit/stuff

give two hoots/stuffs
1. care; worry; be concerned about: e.g. After what he's done to you, do you really and truly give a shit if he leaves home?
2. (couldn't/doesn't/don't/wouldn't etc. . . .) to be utterly indifferent; not to care or worry at all: e.g. I don't give a stuff what he thinks about me!

give as good as (one) gets
to be able to successfully return, retaliate with witty remarks, sarcasm or deeds.

give birth to a politician
to defecate.

give ground
relent; yield to pressure.

give head
perform oral sex, especially fellatio.

give it a bash/burble/burl/fly
make an attempt; have a try: e.g. I'm afraid of roller-coasters but I might give it a bash if you go with me.

give it a go
1. (see: give it a bash)
2. a plea for fairness or moderation: e.g. Give it a go! He's too small to do that!

give it a miss
avoid; leave alone; refuse or elect not to participate: e.g. Everyone's going to the pub tonight but I think I'll give it a miss.

give it a nudge
1. attempt, try (it).
2. (of alcohol) drink (it) to excess: e.g. He likes to give it a nudge these days.

give it a whirl
attempt, try (it).

give it away
(see: give something away)

give it back to the Blacks
pertaining to any inhospitable, arid or useless part of Australia.

give it heaps/hell
1. make the utmost use of: e.g. You may as well give it heaps while you've got it.
2. have the utmost fun; have a mischievous time: e.g. We're all going out tonight and we're really going to give it heaps.
3. push, use or do to the limit: e.g. Give it heaps or else that old car won't make it to the top of the hill!
4. make things unpleasant by annoying, teasing, criticising, showing displeasure or dislike etc.

give it some/the herbs

give it the full bore
(especially of a car) accelerate; go faster.

give it to (someone) straight
relate the unvarnished truth or the main and relevant facts.

give me a break!
stop harassing, annoying (me).

give no quarter
be strict, ruthless, uncompromising.

give nothing away
keep (something) secret; refuse to reveal a fact.

give (one) the horrors
give (one) a feeling of revulsion, repugnance, fear.

give (one) the joes
give (one) a fit of depression, bad temper, ill-feeling.

give (one) the poops
annoy, vex, irritate (one): e.g. All this study gives me the poops!

give (one) the screaming irrits
annoy, vex, irritate (one).

give (one) the shivers/willies
(see: give one the horrors)

give (one's) all
give (one's) total devotion, attention to: e.g. She gives her all to raising money for charity.

give (one's) back teeth/eye-teeth for
to have great desire for: e.g. I'd give my back teeth to have his cushy job.

give (one's) right arm for
1. (see: give one's back teeth for)
2. pledge or offer (one's) total devotion or assistance: e.g. He'd give his right arm for his mate.

give (one's) tongue an outing
behave in an obsequious manner.

give (one's) word
assure, promise.

give (oneself) away
to accidentally reveal something about (oneself) or something that (one) has been hiding about (oneself).

give over!
1. expression of disbelief or disagreement.
2. plea for moderation, fairness, of action or speech.

give rise to
cause; induce.

give (someone) a bell
telephone (someone).

give (someone) a blast
severely berate, scold, admonish (someone).

give (someone) a break
show mercy; give (someone) a fair chance, opportunity.

give (someone) a bum steer
mislead, misinform, deceive or delude (someone).

give (someone) a buzz
1. telephone (someone).
2. give (someone) pleasure, amusement or a thrill.

give (someone) a doing-over
1. beat, bash, defeat, scold (someone) soundly.
2. have sexual intercourse with (someone) (in an aggressive domineering manner).

give (someone) a dressing-down
berate, scold, censure, reprimand, rebuke (someone).

give (someone) a facial
to bash (someone) in the face and disfigure.

give (someone) a fair go
give (someone) a fair chance or opportunity.

give (someone) a fat lip
beat, bash, hit (someone) in the mouth.

give (someone) a go
show mercy to (someone); give (someone) a fair chance or opportunity.

give (someone/something) a good wrap
praise, applaud, laud, flatter, extol, compliment (someone).

give (someone) a hand
help; offer assistance.

give (someone) a hard time
annoy, harass, irritate, inconvenience (someone).

give (someone) a hoy
1. telephone (someone).
2. call out to (someone) to gain attention.

give (someone) a peck
give (someone) a kiss.

give (someone) a piece of (one's) mind
(see: give someone a dressing-down)

give (someone) a ring
telephone (someone).

give (someone) a run for her/his money
give (someone) competitive pressure.

give (someone) a serve
(see: give someone a dressing-down)

give (someone) a taste of her/his own medicine
treat (someone) as unpleasantly as that person treated you or others.

give (someone) a thick ear
bash, hit, punch (someone) in the ear.

give (someone) a tingle
telephone (someone).

give (someone) a wide berth
avoid (someone).

give (someone) an earful
1. give (someone) unwanted and lengthy advice or gossip.
2. harangue, berate, scold (someone).

give (someone) an inch and she'll/he'll take a mile
pertaining to the belief that some people take advantage of others' generosity, hospitality etc.

give (someone) beans
scold, berate, criticise (someone).

give (someone) curry
1. abuse, berate, scold, reprimand, criticise (someone).
2. tease, annoy, taunt, harass (someone).

give (someone) enough rope to hang her/himself.
allow (someone) the opportunity to prove (her/his) unworthiness, guilt, stupidity or incompetence.

give (someone) full/top marks
acknowledge an act of excellence by (someone).

give (someone) head
perform oral sex, especially fellatio.

give (someone/something) heaps/hell
1. treat with firmness in order to get a desired response from (someone/ something).
2. annoy, tease, criticise, show displeasure or dislike etc.
3. (see: give it heaps)

give (someone) her/his due
acknowledge, attribute proper, earned credit to (someone).

give (someone) her/his head
allow greater freedom to (someone).

give (someone) Larry Dooley
harass, reprimand, scold, punish, annoy (someone).

give (someone) lip
answer back impertinently; be cheeky.

give (someone) one
1. have sexual intercourse with (someone).
2. give (someone) a punch, hit: e.g. I'll give him one next time I see him!

give (someone) points
acknowledge an act by (someone); give (someone) credit where it is due.

give (someone) shit
attempt to hoodwink, deceive or tell untruths to (someone).

give (someone/something) the arse/big A/boot/bullet/ chop
1. (of a person) dismiss or fire unceremoniously.
2. reject, rebuff, dismiss, spurn (someone/ something) with disdain or contempt.

give (someone) the bum's rush
give (someone) an abrupt dismissal, denial or rejection.

give (someone) the cold shoulder
deliberately treat (someone) in an unfriendly manner; ignore, spurn, shun (someone).

give (someone) the come-on
behave amorously with (someone); flirt with (someone); attempt to seduce (someone).

give (someone) the drum/ dinkum oil
give (someone) reliable information or advice.

give (someone) the evil eye
give (someone) a disapproving look or frown.

give (someone) the eye
give (someone) admiring looks.

give (someone) the finger
give (someone) a rude gesture of contempt, usually by thrusting an extended, upright fore or middle finger in the air.

give (someone) the gen
give (someone) reliable information or facts.

give (someone) the irrits
annoy, vex, irritate (someone).

give (someone) the message
do, act, say or hint in a manner that should make (someone) aware of one's thoughts.

give (someone) the nod
give (someone) permission.

give (someone) the pip
annoy, harass, anger, irritate (someone).

give (someone) the rounds of the kitchen
give (someone) a severe scolding.

give (someone) the run-around
inconvenience (someone) with untruths, evasion.

give (someone) the screaming irrits
(see: give someone the irrits)

give (someone) the shirt off (one's) back
be extremely generous; pledge (one's) loyalty, devotion to (someone).

give (someone) the shits
annoy, harass, anger, irritate (someone) very much.

give (someone) the slip
escape from (someone's) company; hide from, avoid (someone).

give (someone) the third degree
question (someone) severely.

give (someone) the willies
create fear, uneasiness, tension, worry in (someone).

give (someone) the wrong idea
misadvise, confuse (someone); misrepresent or pervert an idea or fact to (someone).

give (someone) three guesses
jocular remark to (someone) for knowing the obvious.

give (someone) what for
give (someone) a severe scolding, punishing.

give (something) away
1. reveal a confidence or secret accidentally.
2. give up, abandon, stop, cease operations: e.g. Did he really give his job away?

give (something) some lip-service
(see: pay lip-service to)

give (something) the nod/okay
approve, permit, agree to (something).

give (something) the sword
discard, reject (something) unceremoniously.

give the devil his due
reluctantly recognise, acknowledge that a disliked person is owed credit for a particular act, thought etc.

give the game/show away
1. reveal, disclose something inadvertently, unintentionally.
2. reject, abandon, stop, give up (something).

give two hoots/stuffs
(see: give a hoot)

give up on (someone/something)
to abandon.

give up the ghost
1. to despair, worry, suffer from anxiety, be negative.
2. to die.
3. fail; break down.

give way
1. yield; withdraw.
2. collapse; break down.

give-and-take
compromise; cooperation.

give-away
betrayal, disclosure, revelation, exposure that is usually not intentional. (also: dead give-away)

gizmo
a gadget; a word for a thing whose real name one cannot immediately remember.

glad/gladdie
gladiolus — plant like an iris with bright spikes of flowers.

glad rags
best clothes: e.g. Put your glad rags on for this party.

Gladwrap
thin plastic wrap for food. (Trademark)

glam
glamorous.

gland
penis.

glass can
a stubby — small squat glass bottle for beer.

glass jaw
weak — pertaining to easy injury of the jaw.

glass of amber
glass of beer.

gleam in (one's) eye
(have a . . .) to have a look of humour or mischief about (one).

glitch
malfunction; snag; hitch; irregularity: e.g. I can't find the glitch in this computer which is causing all the problems.

glob
rounded blob, lump, mass: e.g. I'll have a glob of ice-cream.

globe-trotter
person who travels widely through many foreign countries.

globe-trotting
travelling widely around the world through many foreign countries.

glory be!
expression of surprise, relief.

glory box
large chest in which a young woman collects necessary items in preparation for marriage (not so common today).

glory hole
place where one stores things haphazardly.

glowing
1. extremely pleased; exuding emotional warmth, enthusiasm, vigour.
2. excellent; first-rate: e.g. He got a glowing report this time.

glued to the box
watching television intently: e.g. Alf's glued to the box watching footy all day.

glue-sniffing
a highly lethal form of drug-taking adopted by teenagers in which not only glue, but other intoxicating vapours such as solvents, petrol, nail-varnish etc., are inhaled from a rag or plastic bag.

glug
a drink: e.g. May I have a glug of your beer?

gluggy
sticky, messy, gluey: e.g. The rice I cook always seems to go gluggy instead of fluffy.

glutton for punishment
person whose passion for work or tendency for creating troublesome situations for himself seems insatiable: e.g. He must be a glutton for punishment to stay with her as they never stop fighting.

gnat's cock
very small measure of something.

gnaw the nana
perform fellatio.

go
1. state of affairs; situation: e.g. What's the go?
2. energy; enthusiasm: e.g. He's got a lot of go in him.
3. definite arrangement: e.g. The party's a go for next Friday.
4. attack; fight: e.g. That dog looks savage enough to go anyone who steps through the gate.
See also:
all systems go
all the go
always on the go
fair go
from go to whoa
from the word go
full of go
give it a go
have a go
have a go at (someone)
let go
let (oneself) go
make a go of
no go
on the go
open go
that's the way it goes
there you go
touch-and-go

go a drink/feed etc.
desire a drink/meal etc. with relish, anticipation: e.g. I could really go a feed of juicy fat prawns right now!

go a long way
achieve success.

go a million
be ruined, done for, especially financially: e.g. You'll go a million if you invest in that crazy scheme!

go against the grain
provoke, revolt, annoy someone.

go ahead in leaps and bounds
perform extremely well, successfully, briskly; make great progress.

go all gooey
become sentimental; become overcome with shyness, emotion.

go all the way
1. agree totally; support wholeheartedly: e.g. I go all the way with what he says.
2. have sexual intercourse: e.g. Did you go all the way with him?

go all thing
change one's state of composure suddenly by becoming shy, angry, embarrassed etc.

go all-out
try one's utmost; use all one's possible resources and energy: e.g. Our team went all-out to win that grand final.

go along with
agree with.

go ape/ape-shit over
react with unrestrained emotion: e.g. He went ape over that present I bought him.

go around with
(see: go with)

go at it baldheaded
act impetuously, rashly.

go at it hammer and tongs
do something with energy and enthusiasm.

go back on (one's) word
renege, withdraw from a promise.

go backwards
deteriorate; fail to proceed successfully.

go bananas/batty
1. become crazy, mad, insane.

2. become angry; lose one's temper.

go between
a mediator.

go bonkers
(see: go bananas)

go bung
break down; fail; cease to operate: e.g. The telly's gone bung.

go bush
1. adopt a back-to-nature way of life away from the city; turn one's back on city life.
2. make oneself scarce; hide oneself from intrusion — especially in a remote place.

go bust
collapse; fail: e.g. His business went bust because of bad management.

go butchers (hook) at
become angry with: e.g. The boss went butchers at him for bungling that job.

go by the board
be discarded, neglected, forgotten: e.g. As usual, all those promises made at election time have gone by the board.

go by the book
to follow rules to the letter with no compromise: e.g. The police have to go by the book in order to be fair to everyone.

go cold on
retreat from a previous promise or agreement; renege.

go crackers
(see: go bananas)

go crook
become angry: e.g. Dad's going to go crook when he finds out what you've done!

go down
1. be received: e.g. How do you think this sexy dress will go down with all the frumpy wives?
2. be sentenced to a prison term: e.g. He'll go down for a long time for that crime.
3. be remembered: e.g. He'll go down as the biggest crook in politics.

go down bad/badly

go down like a lead balloon
be received with disdain, disapproval, displeasure: e.g. Those dirty stories about the groom went down badly at the wedding.

go down on (someone)
perform oral sex — fellatio or cunnilingus.

go down the drain/gurgler/plug/tube(s)
fail; lose a great deal of money in a business failure.

go down the wrong way
1. (of food) to enter the windpipe and cause choking.
2. (of an idea, statement, joke etc.) be received with hostility, or the reverse of what was intended.

go down well
be received with approval, pleasure: e.g. Farting at the table didn't go down too well at that dinner party.

go down without touching the sides
(of food or drink) be swallowed greedily, heartily; be insufficient to satisfy the hunger or thirst.

go downhill
deteriorate, fail, get worse.

go Dutch
an occasion where each person pays his own way: e.g. We all agreed to go Dutch at the restaurant.

go easy on
be lenient; treat carefully; use sparingly: e.g. Go easy on the booze for a while or you'll end up as pissed as a parrot.

go easy with
(see: go easy on)

go eyes out
exert oneself to the utmost; go, travel, do quickly.

go far
be successful.

go fly a kite!
a rude rebuff or dismissal.

go for a burn
speed in a car; test-drive a car.

go for a row (of shithouses)
be in serious trouble; be in a predicament from which there appears to be no escape: e.g. He's going to go for a row now that the Taxation Department has caught him.

go for a sixer
suffer a heavy and clumsy fall. (see: go for six)

go for a snake's (hiss)
(of a man) to urinate.

go for broke/bust
take a major risk; invest everything in an all-out effort.

go for it!
expression of encouragement, enticement to do or start something with energy and enthusiasm.

go for (one's) life/quoits
an encouragement to act, do in an unrestrained manner, with all possible resources and energy: e.g. You'd better go for your quoits if you want to catch that plane on time!

go for six
suffer a major set-back: e.g. He'll go for six if he acts on that poor advice.

go for the big spit
to vomit.

go for the doctor
(horse-racing) make an all-out effort; wager a large sum of money.

go for the growler
(of a man) to fondle, touch, reach for a woman's genitals; have sexual intercourse with a woman.

go for the jugular
attack someone's weakness: e.g. He really went for the jugular when he said all those things in court about her.

go for your life
an expression of encouragement; an encouragement to do, act in an unrestrained manner.

go from bad to worse
to deteriorate, worsen.

go ga-ga over (someone/something)
become infatuated with; show extreme desire or fondness for.

go, go, go!
intense activity: e.g. It's been go, go, go since we got back from the holidays.

go green around the gills
(see: green around the gills)

go halves
share, divide equally: e.g. We went halves in the cost of the meal.

go hell for leather
go very fast; use all one's resources and energy.

go hot and cold all over
suffer extreme anxiety, passion, anger etc.

go in for
like; take an interest in: e.g. I don't go in for drugs.

go in for the kill
seek to utterly defeat, destroy one's opponent.

go in off the red
(of a man) to have sexual intercourse with a woman who is menstruating.

go it alone
do something by oneself, without assistance.

go jump (in the lake)!
a rude rebuff, dismissal.

go like a bat out of hell
go very fast; use all one's resources and energy.

go like a bomb
1. go fast.
2. go well, successfully: e.g. The party went like a bomb.

go like a charm
go, perform, proceed well, successfully, satisfactorily: e.g. The car goes like a charm since I had it fixed.

go like a cut cat
to go, travel very fast.

go like a dream
go, perform, proceed well, successfully, satisfactorily.

go like a power of piss/shit

go like a shower of shit
go, travel, with speed, force.

go like a rocket
go extremely well, fast.

go like hot cakes
sell extremely well; be successful; received with pleasure and anticipation.

go like the clappers
go extremely well, fast.

go mad/nuts
(see: go bananas)

go off
1. become stale, rancid, spoiled, as of food.
2. become less popular, liked, trendy: e.g. That pub's gone off over the last few years.

go off at (someone)
reprimand, scold, abuse (someone) angrily.

go off half-cocked
1. act prematurely, without thought; burst into an angry tirade without thought.
2. (of a man) ejaculate prematurely.

go off (one's) brain

go off (one's) crumpet

go off (one's) head

go off (one's) nut

go off (one's) onion

go off (one's) rails

go off (one's) rocker

go off (one's) scone
(see: go bananas)

go off pop
suddenly become angry, lose one's temper.

go off the deep end
(see: go bananas)

go off the track
become side-tracked with irrelevant details.

go off with a bang
be highly successful, impressive: e.g. The surprise party went off with a bang.

go on
1. persist with an argument till trite, hackneyed: e.g. I wish you wouldn't go on — all that is in the past and finished with!
2. (as an exclamation) expression of disbelief.
3. behave, act: e.g. Don't go on like an idiot!

go on at (someone)
berate, scold, nag continually.

go one better
improve on someone else's performance: e.g. He always tries to go one better than the next bloke.

go out in a blaze of glory
to die or end a venture or career in a spectacular manner.

go out like a light
faint; collapse; lose consciousness; fall asleep suddenly.

go out of (one's) way
to make a special effort.

go out with
have a romantic relationship with

(someone): e.g. Who does she go out with now?

go over like a lead balloon
(see: go down like . . .)

go over (one's/someone's) head
1. fail to be understood by (one/someone): e.g. That joke went over her head.
2. go to a higher authority than (one/someone): e.g. He went over the supervisor's head to get special permission to do it.

go overboard
act, do, go to excess; over-do.

go places
be successful.

go spare
lose one's temper; to over-react.

go steady
be in a fixed, committed relationship with a lover.

go straight
live respectably and honestly after some form of dishonesty or prison term.

go take a running jump at yourself!
an expression of dismissal, contempt.

go the distance
to persevere; complete a set task.

go the grope
indulge in sexual intercourse or activity.

go the knuckle
to fight.

go the whole hog
commit oneself entirely.

go through fire and water for
suffer any hardship, do anything for.

go through on the padre's bike
go, travel swiftly, fast.

go through (someone)
(of a man) have sexual intercourse with: e.g. I'd love to go through her!

go through (someone/something) like a packet of salts

go through (someone/something) like shit through a goose
1. move quickly.
2. deal drastically with (someone/something); defeat (someone) soundly.

go through the mill
suffer hardship and problems in one's efforts.

go through the roof
1. become suddenly angry; lose one's temper.
2. (of prices) become exorbitant.

go to a turn
attend a party or social function.

go to any lengths
do anything necessary, even something bad or illegal.

go to bed with
to have sexual intercourse with.

go to billyo/blazes/buggery/hell!
rude rebuff, dismissal, refusal; get lost!

go to ground
retire from the public eye; disappear.

go to it
begin, do with gusto, enthusiasm, energy: e.g. You'd better go to it if you want to finish on time.

go to market
1. to lose one's temper.
2. do something without restraint (see: go to town).

go to (one's) head
1. (of alcohol) make (one) dizzy.
2. make (one) egotistical: e.g. Winning first prize has really gone to his head.

go to pieces
lose control of (one's) emotions, composure.

go to pot/rack and ruin/seed
deteriorate; get worse; become shabby.

go to see a star about a twinkle
(of a woman) urinate; express the need to urinate.

go to the bathroom
to urinate or defecate (especially of women).

go to the dogs/pack
to go to ruin; deteriorate; degenerate; cease to function; collapse; fail: e.g. The business has gone to the pack since he resigned.

go to the wall
go broke; fail in business.

go to town
1. do something with energy and enthusiasm.
2. celebrate; lose one's inhibitions.
3. over-indulge.

go to town on (someone)
severely berate, scold, reprimand, criticise (someone).

go to water
lose one's resolve, courage, determination.

go too far
act excessively; overstep the boundaries of good behaviour, decency.

go under
fail; collapse.

go under the hammer
sell at auction.

go underground
hide.

go up in smoke
lose, fail, collapse dismally.

go walkabout
1. go off; be missing, usually as a result of theft: e.g. My gold pen's gone walkabout.
2. to wander aimlessly; stroll casually.
3. (of the Aborigines) to

'We need all th' back up we can get! Send th' search and rescue squad out there now to round up my men. They were standing downwind when they burnt that acre of "grass" and th' entire force got stoned!'

For fear of reprisals from the law, people seldom use the word marijuana. They would rather use such innocuous-sounding terms as bhang, Buddha, dakka, dope, ganja, grass, hash, head, herb superb, hooch, J, joint, Maori's pyjamas, marry-you-later, Mary Jane, mull, pot, puff, reefer, shit, weed and hemp.

live a nomadic life.
4. (Australian Rules football) not minding (one's) opponent.

go walking
(see: go walkabout, 1.)

go west
1. to die.
2. to disappear.

go wild
respond with enthusiasm: e.g. The crowd at the concert went wild at that performance.

go with
have a romantic association, relationship with: e.g. Who does he go with?

go with the tide
follow the popular trend with no original thoughts of (one's) own.

go wrong
1. to cease virtuous behaviour.
2. behave in a manner that produces incorrect or undesired results, especially of parents with their children: e.g. I don't know where we went wrong!

For other possible entries beginning with 'go' see entries listed under 'goes', 'going', 'gone', 'went'.

goalie
goalkeeper.

goat
1. a fool: e.g. He's always making a goat of himself.
2. a licentious man.
See also:
act the goat
get on (one's) goat
run like a hairy goat
separate the sheep from the goats

goat country
1. steep, inaccessible terrain.
2. remote, sparsely populated country.

gob
1. a mass or lump: e.g. What's that gob of brown on your shoes?
2. the mouth: e.g. Shut your gob!

gobbledegook
pompous official jargon that is difficult to understand.

gobbler
1. a turkey.
2. performer of fellatio.

gobstopper
large, long-lasting sweet, lolly.

God!

God almighty!
expression of frustration, anger, surprise etc.
See also:
in God knows when
in the name of God
thank God!
there, but for the grace of God, go I
ungodly

God helps those who help themselves
self-motivated people are more likely to achieve success.

God only knows
no one knows: e.g. God only knows where he is — I'm worried.

God squad
any group of fanatical, over-enthusiastic religious people.

God-awful
terrible; second-rate.

God-damn!

God-damn-it!
(see: God!)

God's gift to women
(of a man) highly attractive to women. (see: thinks he's God's gift to women)

God's own country
one's own country, area, land etc. viewed as the best.

goer
1. anything that works, operates, functions: e.g. That antique gramophone is still a goer.
2. person or thing that moves fast: e.g. That old horse is a goer.
3. an enthusiastic worker: e.g. He's a real goer in the garden.
4. any event, happening, occasion or project that is a definite proposition, showing signs of success: e.g. The holiday we planned last year looks like being a goer this Christmas.

goes
says; said (especially in the telling of jokes or the recounting of other people's speech): e.g. Then this bloke goes, 'Get lost!'

goes in one ear and out the other
heard, but either not understood or ignored.

goes without saying
bears no contradictions; is obvious.

For other possible entries beginning with 'goes' see entries listed under 'go', 'going', 'went'.

goey
active; animated; busy; fast.

go-fer
(also: gofer, gopher)
1. lackey; yes-man; sycophant; toady.
2. person called upon to do unpleasant, or small tasks for others.

go-getter
pushy, enterprising person.

goggle-box
television set.

goggles
spectacles; eye-glasses.

go-in
a fight or brawl, especially among several.

going
(see: have/got a lot going for one)

going against the tide
1. struggling against all odds.
2. thinking, acting against the wishes of the majority.

going around like a fart in a colander wondering which hole to get out
running around in circles; confused; behaving in a confused, erratic manner.

going concern
successfully operating business, project.

going fifty to the dozen
acting with haste; going very fast.

going great guns
doing extremely well; successful: e.g. He's going great guns with that new business of his.

going places
achieving success: e.g. He's really going places now.

going strong
thriving; doing well; operating successfully: e.g. His business is still going strong.

going thing
popular, widespread, current fad, activity, gimmick, trend: e.g. The going thing at present is the game of Trivial Pursuit.

going-over
1. an overhaul; reconditioning; thorough examination: e.g. My car is due for a thorough going-over by a good mechanic.
2. a sound beating, thrashing: e.g. He got a real going-over in a pub brawl last night.

goings-on
1. odd, strange, bad, mischievous, or lewd behaviour: e.g. You should have seen the goings-on at the last staff party!
2. current events.

For other possible entries beginning with 'going' see entries listed under 'go', 'goes', 'gone', 'went'.

gold
(see: all that glitters is not gold; black gold; Dutch gold; good as gold; heart of gold; worth one's weight in gold)

gold-digger
woman who uses, exploits her physical attributes to wheedle money out of men.

golden doughnut
woman's pudendum, vulva, vagina.

golden duck
(cricket) out on the first ball.

golden girl/boy
1. outstanding, top athlete.
2. one who can't do wrong.

golden handshake
gratuity as compensation for compulsory retirement, resignation or dismissal.

golden mean
neither too much nor too little.

golden rule
the rule of good, honest conduct (do as you would be done by).

golden shower
(of a woman) to urinate during sexual intercourse, especially at the point of climax.

golden staph
(*Staphylococcus aureus*) virulent bacterium that has developed a resistance to most antibiotics and considered very prevalent in hospitals.

golden wedding
the fiftieth wedding anniversary.

goldmine
source of great wealth or information: e.g. That old man is a goldmine of information.

gold-tops
hallucinogenic mushrooms.

golly
1. mild exclamation of wonder, surprise.
2. gob of saliva or phlegm.
3. to spit.

gonads
testicles.

gone
1. drunk; intoxicated.
2. emotionally exhilarated.
3. in serious trouble: e.g. You're gone this time!
4. dead.
See also:
a bit gone
far gone
three parts gone

gone a million
ruined, defeated, especially financially; caught in an illegal act; in dire trouble.

gone by the wayside
neglected; bypassed; forgotten about: e.g. All those pre-election promises have gone by the wayside as usual.

gone on (someone)
infatuated, in love with (someone): e.g. He's really gone on her.

gone to billyo/buggery
1. disappeared; gone a very long way away.
2. gone to a remote, far-away place.

gone with the wind
lost; disappeared.

For other possible entries beginning with 'gone' see entries listed under 'go', 'going', 'went'.

goner
person or thing beyond help, doomed or dead: e.g. He's a goner if he keeps taking heroin.

gonna
(also: gunna) contraction of going to: e.g. Are you gonna go?

gonzo
crazy; mad; eccentric; insane.

goo
sticky, viscous substance.

goobie
hardened mucus from the nose.

good
(see: all for the good; as good as; as good as they come; come good; fat lot of good that is; for good and all; get in good with; get the good guts; have/got a good thing going; hold good; if you can't be good, be careful; in good form; in good with someone; make good; never had it so good; that's a good one!; too good to be true; too much of a good thing; up to no good)

good as gold
well behaved; in good working order.

good as (one's) word
reliable; dependable.

Good Book
the Bible.

good catch
person who is a highly satisfactory, desirable marriage prospect.

good few
many: e.g. There were a good few at the meeting.

good for
(of a person) predisposed, inclined to (especially to lend money): e.g. Dad's always good for a loan.

good for nothing
useless; worthless; of no value.

good for you!
expression of good-will, encouragement, approval.

good fuck
desirable, inventive partner for sexual intercourse.

good get
(tennis) athletic retrieval of the ball.

good grief!
mild oath; expression of surprise, annoyance etc.

good guts
reliable advice, knowledge or information: e.g. Did you get the good guts on the horse that's running in race seven?

good guys
the heroes in a movie, story or play (as opposed to the bad guys).

good hands
(sport) a good catcher.

good lady
wife; live-in lover: e.g. Where's the good lady tonight?

good life
(the . . .) pleasant living conditions filled with luxuries, material things, and good food: e.g. He's too used to the good life to enjoy going camping and roughing it in the bush.

good looker/looking
sexually attractive person.

good lord!
expression of amazement, surprise.

good loser
one who accepts defeat with good grace.

good luck
best wishes; good fortune.

good mixer
person who gets on well socially.

good monger
excellent food.

good oil
(see: good guts)

good on ya (you)
expression of approval, encouragement.

good one!
exclamation of approval, pleasure, agreement, delight.

good question
a difficult or demanding question or problem: e.g. That's a good question — I don't know where all this week's money has gone!

good run for (one's) money
full value.

good screw
1. profitable, rewarding career, occupation.
2. a pleasing sexual partner.

good set of boots
(of a car) tyres with plenty of tread.

good show
1. expression of approval, encouragement.
2. good chance: e.g. He's got a good show of winning the election.

good sort
1. sexually attractive person.
2. likeable, honest person.

good sport
1. easy-going, amicable person.
2. fair, just, honest, generous person.

good spread
1. an excellent meal, feast.
2. a glowing written report such as a feature in a newspaper.

good way
1. long distance: e.g. His house is a good way from here.
2. a considerable extent: e.g. He's gone a good way towards paying off his car.

good-for-nothing
person or thing that is worthless, bad, troublesome.

goodie/goody
1. a good, law-abiding person, especially a hero in a film.
2. expression of delight, pleasure: e.g. Oh goody! Dad's home.

goodies
desirable, attractive things, items, possessions or foods.

goodies and baddies
the good and the evil characters in a story, film etc.

goodness!

goodness gracious (me)!
exclamation of surprise.

good-oh
expression of approval, satisfaction.

goods
1. evidence, information, especially that which is incriminating: e.g. The police have enough goods on him to arrest him.
2. anything that has been promised or implied: e.g. 1. Many politicians make desirable promises before they are elected then don't deliver the goods after they are in power. 2. She may look sexy but she doesn't deliver the goods (have sexual intercourse).
See also:
come across with the goods
deliver (the goods)
get the goods on
have/got the goods
produce the goods

goodtime girl
woman of loose morals.

goody
(see: goodie)

goody gumdrops!
expression of pleasure.

goody-goody
excessively virtuous, honest, prudish.

gooey
sticky; unpleasant.
See also:
go all gooey

goof
1. a fool; stupid person.
2. make a mistake; blunder; bungle: e.g. Did he goof again!

goof around
behave like a fool, often for the entertainment of others.

goof balls
amphetamines — stimulant tablets, drugs.

goof off
to waste time; be idle, lazy.

goof up
(see: goof, 2.)

goofy
stupid; foolish; clumsy.

goog
1. an egg.
2. foolish, stupid person.
See also:
full as a goog

googy-egg
an egg.

goolies
1. stones, rocks.
2. testicles.
3. snot; phlegm from the nose.

goom
methylated spirits as a drink drunk by vagrants, homeless men.

goon
1. a fool; stupid person.
2. a thug hired to terrorise people.

goondie
an Aboriginal hut.

goony bird
the early Douglas Dakota C-47 Army cargo plane (also: bully-beef bomber).

goori
(derog.) a Maori.

goose
1. a fool; simpleton; stupid person.
2. an unexpected poke between the buttocks — generally in fun.
3. to poke someone between the buttocks — generally as a gesture of fun.
See also:
cook (someone's) goose
send (someone) on a wild-goose chase
wigwam for a goose's bridle
wild-goose chase
wouldn't say boo to a goose

goose is cooked
(someone's . . .) be in serious trouble, ruined or finished: e.g. His goose is cooked this time — the police arrested him with a suit-case full of heroin at the airport.

goose-egg
failure; fiasco.

goosies
goose-flesh/bumps/pimples; rough, pimply condition of the skin induced by cold or fear.

gopher
(see: go-fer)

gorbies
hardened mucus from the nose.

gorblimey!
mild oath, expression of surprise, amazement.

gorgeous
extremely pleasant: e.g. We had a gorgeous time on our holiday.

gormless
stupid; foolish; lacking in wit or intelligence.

gosh!
expression of surprise, wonder, amazement, annoyance.

go-slow
(see: work to rule)

got a big head
vain; conceited.

got into (someone)
causing (someone) to be bad-tempered, irritable, angry, petulant: e.g. What's got into you all of a sudden?

got me
reveal one's ignorance; I don't know: e.g. You've got me there — I don't know the answer to that one!

got religion
become (uncharacteristically) fanatically religious: e.g. After all these years behaving like a criminal, he's suddenly got religion.

For other possible entries beginning with 'got' see entries listed under 'have/got', 'get'.

gotcha!
contraction of got you.
1. exclamation over the capture of something.
2. exclamation indicating that one has understood, one agrees.

gotta
contraction of got to: e.g. You've gotta be joking!

gotta hand it to (someone)
(see: have/got to . . .)

gov
governor; sir; boss.

governor
the boss: e.g. Where's the governor of this operation?

govie
government: e.g. They sent a govie car around to pick him up.

gozunder
(see: gazunder)

G.P.O.
General Post Office.

grab
1. impress: e.g. How did that concert grab you?
2. (Australian Rules football) a mark.
See also:
up for grabs

grab a few zeds

grab forty winks
have a short nap.

grab (someone) by the balls
greatly impress (someone): e.g. This movie will really grab you by the balls!

gracious (me)!
exclamation of surprise.
See also:
goodness gracious

graft
1. to toil, work very hard: e.g. He's been grafting in the goldfields for years.
2. illicit gain, especially in business and politics, by bribery etc.

grampers/gramps
grandfather.

gran
grandmother.

grand
1. one thousand dollars.
2. splendid, wonderful: e.g. We had a grand time.

grand old lady
pertaining to something old, antique, worthwhile restoring for posterity, such as a house or boat.

grand slam
supreme win; major victory.

grandad
grandfather.

grandma
grandmother.

grandpa
grandfather.

grandstand
behave in a flamboyant, ostentatious, boastful manner in order to impress: e.g. Politicians are often accused of grandstanding for the press.

grannie/granny
1. grandmother.
2. (cap.) the *Sydney Morning Herald*.
3. a Granny Smith apple.

granny flat
self-contained flat or addition that is apart from the main house.

grape
(the . . .) wine: e.g. He's rather fond of the grape now instead of beer and spirits.
See also:
in the grip of the grape

grapes
haemorrhoids.

grape-vine
person-to-person system of communication (especially word-of-mouth communication) by which information, secrets and gossip are passed on: e.g. I heard on the grape-vine that Barry's about to get the sack.

grasp the nettle
approach an unpleasant or difficult task with courage and resolution.

grass
marijuana; Indian hemp; pot; dope.
See also:
can't grow grass on a busy street
can't see the grass for the trees
come off the grass!
exciting as watching grass grow
get off the grass!
let the grass grow under (one's) feet
put out to grass
snake in the grass

grass is always greener on the other side (of the fence)
pertaining to the mistaken belief that life must always be better somewhere else than where one is.

grassroots
1. pertaining to or arising from the thoughts of the common people.
2. essentials; basics: e.g. It's about time we started thinking about the grassroots of the matter.

grateful
(see: be grateful for small mercies)

gravel rash
(see: get . . .)

graveyard chompers
false teeth.

graveyard shift
late night or very early morning working hours.

gravy train
course of action or circumstance that results in benefits or perquisites: e.g. He's doing well since he jumped on the council gravy train.

grease (someone's) palm
offer a bribe.

grease-ball
(derog.) man of Greek or ethnic origin.

grease-monkey
person who works on engines; mechanic.

greaser
1. (derog.) man of Greek, Italian or ethnic origin.
2. obsequious person.

greasies
fish and chips, or other oily, take-away food.

greasy
1. a shearer of sheep.
2. a male cook for workers in the outback.

greasy spoon
cheap cafe.

great ape
a fool; stupid, clumsy person.

great Australian adjective
the word 'bloody' — notably Australia's greatest adjective because of its extensive use. (see: bloody)

great Australian salute
(also: Aussie salute) the action of the hand brushing away flies.

great balls of fire!

great galloping goannas!
expression of surprise, amazement.

great one for
enthusiastic about; exceptional at: e.g. He's a great one for telling jokes all night!

great Scott!
expression of surprise, amazement, wonder.

greatest thing since sliced bread
something exceptional, outstanding, noteworthy, first-class.

greedy guts
one who takes more than his share.

Greek
unintelligible; difficult to understand: e.g. The fine print in this contract is all Greek to me!

green
1. inexperienced: e.g. He's too green to hire for this job.
2. gullible; easily fooled.
3. pale; sickly; nauseated: e.g. He went green when I told him how much it cost him.
4. jealous: e.g. She's green about my new diamond ring.

green around the gills
1. inexperienced.
2. suffering from nausea.

green fingers
(see: green thumb)

green light
an affirmative answer; approval; permission: e.g. The council gave the developers the green light on that new high-rise building.

green thumb
skilled in gardening; knack for making anything grow successfully: e.g. My Dad has always had a green thumb.

green with envy
jealous.

greengrocer
type of large green cicada.

greenhorn
inexperienced newcomer.

greenies
conservationists: e.g. The greenies fought the Government hard to have that area saved as a sanctuary for wild life.

greens
green-coloured vegetables.

grey ghost
N.S.W. or Vic. parking police-officer.

grey matter
brains; intelligence; wit.

grey meanie
(see: grey ghost)

grey power
influence, especially political, exerted by old people and old age pensioners.

greyback
a one-hundred-dollar note.

grill
question severely.

Grim Reaper
death personified.

grin and bear it
tolerate, put up with, endure with good grace.

grin and chronic
gin and tonic.

grin like a Cheshire cat
smile, grin broadly, smugly.

grind
hard, laborious, monotonous work.
See also:
bump and grind
daily grind
nose to the grindstone

gripe
1. a complaint.
2. to complain.

grist to the mill
something that can be used profitably, to (one's) advantage.

grit
courage; endurance; pluck.

grit (one's) teeth
clench (one's) teeth in tolerance, endurance of something unpleasant.

gritty
1. down-to-earth.
2. courageous; plucky.

grizzle
complain; whinge; fret noisily.

grizzle-guts
person who complains, whinges constantly.

groan
a boring, tedious, monotonous person or thing.

grog
alcohol — beer, wine, spirits.
See also:
on the grog

grog on
drink to excess; indulge in alcohol.

groggy
1. unstable, staggering, as if from a blow, dizziness.
2. drunk; intoxicated.

grogin
a lump of faeces; turd.

grog-on
party where large amounts of alcohol are consumed.

grog-shop
a shop selling alcohol.

groovy
1. excellent; first-rate; wonderful.
2. trendy; fashionable.
See also:
in the groove

grope
1. sexual activity, intercourse: e.g. Now Denise is pregnant, poor old Gary won't be able to have a good grope for a while.
2. to sexually fondle, touch up in a clumsy, boorish manner.
See also:
go the grope

groper
person from Western Australia — sandgroper.

grot
1. dirty, slovenly, dishevelled person.
2. dirt; mess; filth.

grotty
1. dirty; filthy; untidy.
2. worthless; second-rate.

grouch
1. bad-tempered, sulky, irritable person.
2. complaint.
3. to complain.

grouchy
bad-tempered; irritable.

ground
(see: break new ground; common ground; cut the ground from under someone; down to the ground; get in on the ground floor; get off the ground; give ground; go to ground; have/got an ear to the ground; keep one's feet on the ground; lose ground; old stamping ground; on shaky ground; run someone to ground; shit one down to the ground; stand one's ground; thin on the ground; wear oneself down to the ground)

ground floor
the most advantageous position in a business deal or matter.

ground lice
sheep.

ground rules
conventions; customs; routine; dos and don'ts.

groundbreaking
innovative, inventive.

grounded
1. stranded; left without a means of transport.
2. forced to stay at home, to be not allowed to go out.

group grope/sex
an occasion of sexual activity with a group of people.

groupie
person — especially female — who moves around with rock or other music bands and offers herself sexually to them.

grouse
1. excellent; wonderful; terrific.
2. a complaint: e.g. What's his grouse?

grouter
(see: come in on the grouter)

grow hairs on (one's) palms
(of men) legendary affliction caused by masturbation.

grow legs on (one's) belly
to be obsequious, fawning.

grow on (one)
become likeable, attractive, to (one) after a time.

grow out of
to become too mature for.

growing pains
the difficulties, problems often associated with a new project, endeavour.

growl on
to eat: e.g. Growl on everybody — there's plenty of food!

growler
vagina; female pudendum.
See also:
go for the growler

grub
1. food.
2. dirty, slovenly, untidy person.

grubber
(cricket) ball that goes along the ground.

grubstake
something provided in an enterprise in return for a share in the profits.

gruesome
1. noteworthy, amazing.
2. horrible, harrowing.

gruff nuts
faeces; shit.

grump
1. bad-tempered, irritable person.
2. complain, whinge, nag, sulk.

grumpy-guts
(see: grizzle-guts)

grundies
undies; underwear.

grunter
1. a prostitute.
2. a pig.

G-string
narrow strip of cloth attached to strings tied around the waist — an erotic, minimal covering for the genitals.

G.T. stripes
coloured stripes — usually two — along the body of a car suggesting speed, class.

guard (something) with (one's) life
watch over, look after (something) carefully.

guck
dirt; filth; slime.

guesswork
uncertain; unknown.

guff
nonsense; rubbish; baloney.

guinea-pig
person used for an experiment or selfish exploitation.

gum up the works
spoil; interfere with; ruin.

gumboot
contraceptive sheath; condom.

gummies
gumboots.

gummy
toothless; old.

gumption
resourcefulness; enterprise.

gun
1. worker — especially a fruit-picker or shearer — who excels above everyone else.
2. to rev, accelerate an engine.
See also:
big gun
going great guns
jump the gun
spike (someone's) guns
stick to (one's) guns
the things you see when you haven't got a gun!
with guns blazing
you son of a gun!

gunna
(also: gonna) contraction of going to.

gunning for (someone)
looking, hunting for (someone) with the intention of severely reprimanding, beating or killing.

Gundabluey
heavy rainstorm.

gung-ho
(especially of men) bravado; macho behaviour; recklessness.

gunja
(also: ganja) marijuana; pot; dope.

gunk
1. over-sweet, unpleasant or junk food.
2. nonsense; rubbish; baloney.
3. medicine; ointment: e.g. I've got this great gunk that heals pimples and acne.

gunya
small, crude, rough bush hut or shelter.

gurgler
drain.
See also:
go down the gurgler

gush
speak or act effusively.

gut
stomach: e.g. He's got a huge gut!
See also:
bust a gut
have a gutful
rot-gut

gut response
instinctive feeling, attitude, response, reaction.

gutless (wonder)
1. (of a car, engine, machine) having poor performance; short of power, speed or strength.
2. (of a person) weak; cowardly.

guts
1. nerve; daring; bravado.
2. the stomach, belly.
3. a big eater; a greedy eater.
4. person who takes the biggest share.
5. reliable information.
6. power; performance; strength; speed; ability.
7. essential, main parts or components.
8. eat greedily; eat to excess.
See also:
come a gutser
come (one's) guts
couldn't run guts for a slow butcher
get the good guts
good guts
grizzle-guts
had a gutsful
hate (someone's) guts
have/got the guts
haven't got the guts
in the guts
mud-guts
rough as guts
spill (one's) guts
work (one's) guts out

guts (oneself)
over-indulge; eat to excess.

gutsy
1. daring; brave.
2. powerful; strong; full of life.

gutted rabbit
the female genitals, vulva.

guttersnipe
person given to spreading slanderous gossip.

guy
1. fellow; man; chap; person.
2. boyfriend; lover.
See also:
good guys

guzzle
1. a long, urgent drink.
2. to drink urgently, greedily.
3. to drink alcohol to excess.

guzzle-guts

guzzler
a heavy drinker of alcohol; an alcoholic.

gyno
gynaecologist.

gyp
1. a trick or swindle.
2. a cheat or trickster.
3. to cheat, swindle, defraud, con.

Gyppo
an Egyptian (also: Gippo, Gypo).

H
heroin.

hack
1. taxi cab.
2. pleasure horse for ordinary riding; tired, worn-out, old horse.
3. put up with; tolerate; endure: e.g. I can't hack those people.
4. (Australian Rules football; rugby) a kick.

hack the pace
keep up with; tolerate, endure a situation, strenuous pace or tedious activity.

hacking
1. driving a taxi.
2. (of a vehicle or horse) used for general, everyday purposes.

hackwork
tedious, boring or heavy work; the routine part of work that is considered boring or mundane.

hackworker
hired person doing the tedious jobs.

had
1. totally exasperated, annoyed, frustrated with: e.g. I've had those kids!
2. cheated, tricked: e.g. He's not easily had!
See also:
been had
get had

had a bellyful
1. eaten sufficient; satisfied one's appetite.
2. be totally exasperated, annoyed, frustrated, angry: e.g. I've had a bellyful of the Government and high taxes!

had a few (too many)
to have drunk too much alcohol: e.g. I wouldn't give him any more as he's already had a few too many.

had a good/long innings
to have had a successful life, career etc.

had a gutful/gutsful
(see: had a bellyful, 1. and 2.)

had a load of
(see: had a bellyful, 2.)

had a skinful
1. to have drunk too much alcohol; intoxicated, drunk.
2. (see: had a bellyful, 2.)

had an eyeful
(see: had a bellyful, 2.)

had it
1. to be totally annoyed, frustrated, exasperated (with): e.g. 1. I've had it! 2. I've had it with those noisy kids!
2. to be totally worn-out, exhausted, tired: e.g. After working so hard, he's finally had it!
3. broken-down; ruined; not functioning; wrecked: e.g. My old car has finally had it.
4. Had or indulged in sexual intercourse: e.g. He's in a bad mood because he hasn't had it for a week!
5. dead or close to death.

had it soft
to have had an easy life, career, job, time etc.

had it up to the eyeballs/neck
(see: had it, 1.)

had (one) in
to have (one) completely fooled, tricked, believing, duped: e.g. That crook really had me in for a while!

had (one's) chips
to have had and lost (one's) opportunity: e.g. He's had his chips as far as I'm concerned!

had (one's) fair share (of the shit)
to have had a fair share of the toils and troubles in life, career, a situation etc.

had (someone) dancing (to one's tune)

had (someone) running
to have had (someone) completely under one's control and doing exactly as one says; to have led

(someone) along and caused difficulty or trouble or enforced one's will: e.g. I had him dancing all day after telling him I'd fire him for laziness!

had the dick

had the gong

had the Richard

had the ridgy-didge/rigidij

had the sword
(see: had it, 1., 2., 3. and 5.)

had up for
convicted or accused of: e.g. He was had up by the federal police for bringing a suitcase of heroin into the country.

For other possible entries beginning with 'had' see entries listed under 'have'.

hair
a very small measure or degree: e.g. I lost the race by a hair.
See also:
didn't turn a hair
get in (someone's) hair
grow hairs on (one's) palms
have/got (someone) by the short hairs
hide nor hair
keep out of (someone's) hair
keep your hair on!
let (one's) hair down
make (one's) hair curl
make (one's) hair stand on end
put hairs on your chest
split hairs
tear (one's) hair out
within a hair's breadth

hair like a bush pig's arse
wild, untidy, frizzy, hard-to-manage hair.

hair of the dog (that bit you)
an alcoholic drink taken as relief from a hangover and usually taken first thing in the morning.

hair pie
1. cunnilingus.
2. female pudendum, genitals.

hair-do
a hairstyle.

hair-raiser
any situation or thing that frightens, terrifies, excites or thrills.

hair-raising
full of excitement or terror: e.g. The new roller-coaster at Dreamworld amusement park is hair-raising.

hairy
1. frightening, terrifying; exciting.
2. difficult; tricky: e.g. That's a hairy problem.

hairy goat
(racing) a horse that performs poorly.

half
(see: and a half; better half; by half; by halves; go halves; go off half-cocked; meet someone halfway; not half!; other half; that's not the half of it)

half a chance
any chance at all: e.g. If I had half a chance I'd go out with him.

half a d
half a dozen: e.g. Buy half a d of cold beer.

half a mo
just a moment: e.g. I'll be there in half a mo.

half a sheet to the wind
nearly drunk, intoxicated.

half dead
exhausted, tired: e.g. He's half dead after all that work.

half shot
nearly drunk, intoxicated.

half time
break in the middle of a team sport.

half your luck!
an expression of envy at someone else's good fortune.

half-baked
incomplete; immature.

half-baked state of mind
not fully coherent; half-witted; stupid.

half-hearted
lacking courage and enthusiasm.

half-mast
(of trousers) not long enough to reach the ankles.

half-measure
an inadequate, incomplete, unsatisfactory action, taken often as a compromise.

half-nelson
wrestling hold in which an arm is passed under the opponent's arm from behind and a hand applied to the neck.

half-pint
a person small in stature.

half-seas-over
half drunk.

half-wit
foolish or stupid person; simple-minded.

ham
actor who over-acts.

ham and eggs
(rhyming slang) legs.

ham it up
over-act; behave in an exaggerated, flamboyant manner.

ham-fisted
clumsy; heavy-handed.

hammer
1. bash, beat up, strike: e.g. If I ever see him around here again I'll hammer him!
2. drive a point or argument home persistently and aggressively: e.g. You'd

better hammer some sense into that young fool before he gets into any more trouble.
3. the back (rhyming slang: hammer and tack).
See also:
go under the hammer
on (one's) hammer
stay on (someone's) hammer

hammer and tack
1. heroin.
2. (rhyming slang) back.

hammer and tongs
with great energy and enthusiasm: e.g. He went at it hammer and tongs all day until it was finished.

hammering
1. a sound beating, bashing, hiding.
2. intense criticism, cross-examination, questioning.
See also:
get a hammering
take a hammering

hammy
pulled hamstring muscle.

hamstrung
disadvantaged; thwarted; at a loss.

hand
1. a helper, hired worker.
2. round of applause: e.g. Give him a hand everyone!
See also:
all hands on deck
backhanded
bite the hand that feeds (one)
change hands
clean hands
dead hand at
declare (one's) hand
eating out of (one's) hand
firm hand
first-hand
force (someone's) hand
free hand
get the upper hand
give (someone) a hand
have a hand in
have/got (one's) hands full
have/got to hand it to (someone)
heavy hand
heavy-handed
high-handed
hold (someone's) hand
holding the hand out
in good hands
in (one's) hands
in the palm of (one's) hand
keep (one's) hand in
keep (one's) hands clean
know it like the back of (one's) hand
lay a hand on (someone)
lay down (one's) hand
lay (one's) hands on
lend a hand
live from hand to mouth
master hand
member of the Wandering Hands Society
off (one's) hands
off-hand
off-handed
old hand at (something)
on (one's) hands
on the other hand
one in the bush is worth two in the hand
out of hand
out of (one's) hands
overplay (one's) hand
play into (someone's) hands
putty in (one's) hands
red-handed
right hand must never know what the left is doing
shake hands with the unemployed
shake hands with the wife's best friend
show (one's) hand
smack on the back of the hand
take a hand in
take (someone) in hand
throw (one's) hand in
time on (one's) hands
try (one's) hand at
turn (one's) hand to
upper hand
wait hand and foot on
wash (one's) hands of
wipe (one's) hands of
wring (one's) hands

hand in hand
in close association; conjointly: e.g. They worked hand in hand to get that business going.

hand in the pocket
(to have one's . . .) to be always spending money, especially to pay bills.

hand in the till
(to have one's . . .) to be stealing, embezzling money from one's employer.

hand is quicker than the eye
trickery and deception (of the hand) is not always easy to see.

hand over fist
with steady, rapid progress; easily: e.g. They were making money hand over fist with that scheme of theirs.

hand (someone) a line
tell a lie; fabricate a story; deceive.

hand (someone) in
turn (someone) over to the authorities; betray (someone).

hand the hat around
take up a collection of money: e.g. We're handing the hat around for the bereaved family.

handbag carriers
1. (caps) Geelong VFL football team.
2. (Australian Rules football) weak players.

handed to (someone) on a plate/silver platter
given freely (to someone) without work or effort (by someone): e.g. He expects everything to be handed to him on a silver platter.

handfed
getting more help than is required; getting so much help that individual effort is not required: e.g. Too

many kids are handfed these days and don't have the knowledge or the enthusiasm to make it on their own.

handful
a troublesome person, task or thing: e.g. My kids are a real handful during the holidays.

hand-in-glove
on intimate terms; in close collaboration: e.g. If the Government and the unions worked hand-in-glove, we'd all be a lot better off.

handle
1. a name for a person, business, organisation etc.
2. treat, deal with, satisfactorily; take care of; do with skill and responsibility: e.g. I know how to handle him.
See also:
can't handle (someone/something)
fly off the handle

handle with kid gloves
1. treat tactfully: e.g. He's so sensitive you have to handle him with kid gloves.
2. treat carefully, gently: e.g. Handle those explosives with kid gloves!

handles like a bag of shit tied in the middle with a piece of string
(of a car or vehicle) has poor performance, manoeuvrability.

hand-me-downs
items of clothing that belonged to one's elders; second-hand clothes or things.

hand-out
social benefits money; charity: e.g. Since her husband died, she's been living on hand-outs to support the children.

hand-picked
carefully chosen.

hands are tied
be in a situation where one can do nothing to change the status quo or help.

hands down
easily; without effort: e.g. He won the election hands down.
See also:
beat (someone) hands down

hands off!
don't touch or interfere!

hands off cocks, on socks
an order to get to work; stop wasting time and begin.

hand-to-mouth
having few or no resources: e.g. The poor live a hand-to-mouth existence.

handy
capable; clever; skilled; adept with the hands.

hang
(see: doesn't give a hang; get the hang of; give a hang; let it all hang out)

hang a lefty
(of the driver of a vehicle) turn left (quickly).

hang a lefty on (someone)
punch, hit, bash (someone), especially with the left fist.

hang a U-ie
(of the driver of a vehicle) make a U-turn; turn around and go back the other way.

hang about
1. loiter; linger.
2. (as an exclamation) wait!

hang around
1. wait; loiter; tarry; linger.
2. frequent, visit or go to regularly: e.g. Which pub does he hang around?
3. stay around, cling to a place where one is not welcome or wanted: e.g. I wish he'd go home instead of hanging around here all day!

hang around like a bad smell
(see: hang around, 3.)

hang around with
associate, mix with.

hang, draw and quarter
punish severely.

hang fire/five
delay action; stop awhile; wait before doing.

hang in (there)
persevere; keep trying against all odds.

hang it!
exclamation of scorn, dismissal, anger, irritation, frustration.

hang loose
1. relax and idly fill in time.
2. relax and don't worry or be anxious.

hang of a
1. very great; exceptional: e.g. That's a hang of a hill we have to climb!
2. awful; difficult; unpleasant: e.g. This hang of a damned thing doesn't work!

hang on
1. wait: e.g. Hang on — I'll be there in a minute.
2. persevere against all odds: e.g. We'll hang on as long as we can.

hang on a min/mo/tick
wait a minute, moment, short time.

hang on every word
listen intently.

hang on like grim death
hold on, stay put; act, behave tenaciously, firmly.

hang one on (someone)
punch, hit, bash (someone).

hang (one's) head
to suffer shame.

hang out (at)
frequent; visit regularly: e.g. 1. Where do they hang out? 2. Which pub do they hang out at?

hang out for
wait in adamant expectation; crave, want, desire, need: e.g. I'm really hanging out for a good feed.

hang ten
to ride the tip of a surf-board with all the toes hanging over the edge.

hang the expense!
the cost is not important!

hanger-on
a parasitic person who clings to someone, an organisation for whatever benefits he can extract without contributing; freeloader; sponger: e.g. Every political party has its fair share of hangers-on who don't do much to help.

hanging
(see: have/got something hanging over one)

hanging by a thread

hanging on by the skin of (one's) teeth
in a very precarious situation or position.

hanging out for a nosebag
craving for food, a good meal.

hangout
favourite place; frequently visited place.

hangover
the after-effects of over-indulgence in alcohol, intoxication.

hang-up
1. a difficulty, snag, obstacle, complication: e.g. What's the hang-up stopping work this time?
2. mental difficulty, obsession, problem, inhibition: e.g. He's got quite a few sex hang-ups.

hankie/hanky
handkerchief.

hanky-panky
1. trickery; cheating; deception; fraud.
2. misbehaviour; mischief; naughtiness.
3. sexual play — often illicit in the sense of cheating on one's partner.

happy
(used in combination: e.g. dope-happy, girl-happy) show an obsessive or excessive liking for, desire to use: e.g. He's so girl-happy he'd go out with any old bag!
See also:
trigger-happy

happy as a bastard on Father's Day
unhappy; miserable; sad.

happy as a dog with two tails

happy as a pig in shit

happy as Larry
very happy; elated.

happy hour
1. the cocktail hour; 5 p.m.
2. an allotted time at a pub, club, hotel during which drinks are sometimes free or sold at a reduced price.

happy hunting ground
1. a good place in which to pursue a hobby or activity.
2. a good place in which to find a sexual partner.

happy hunting ground in the sky
pertaining to death and the release of the spirit or soul: e.g. My cat went to the happy hunting ground in the sky.

happy-go-lucky
carefree; taking things cheerfully as they happen.

hard
1. (of a person) ruthless; relentless; unfeeling; merciless.
2. (of a woman) worldly in a cheap, sleazy way; tarty; knowing.
See also:
do it the hard way
put the hard word on (someone)

hard act to follow
excellence or outrageousness of performance, behaviour by someone else that would be difficult to better.

hard and fast
binding; strict: e.g. Hard and fast rules.

hard as nails
1. (of a person) stern; severe; tough; merciless; hardened by experience.
2. (of a woman — see: hard, 2.)

hard at it
completely involved, working diligently at a task.

hard case
1. an unyielding, stubborn person.
2. a tough, cynical person hardened by experience.
3. an alcoholic or drug addict.
4. a funny character; persistently funny, witty, amusing person: e.g. Mick's a hard case — he's always got a new joke to tell.

hard cash
money: e.g. He wants hard cash — not promises or bank cheques.

hard/stiff cheddar/cheese
(expression) bad luck! — conveying either sympathy or scorn, depending on tone of voice.

hard doer
joker, wag, comedian.

hard done by
to have experienced a great deal of bad luck, misfortune or troubled

times: e.g. That family is hard done by since the death of the father.

hard drugs
potent or addictive drugs; potentially dangerous drugs.

hard hit
1. severely affected by; disadvantaged: e.g. The farmers have been hard hit by the drought.
2. (rhyming slang) shit.

hard knocks
bad luck; unfortunate, difficult times.

hard luck
1. bad luck; misfortune: e.g. Losing all that money was hard luck.
2. (see: hard cheese)

hard luck story
misfortune; bad luck.

hard nut to crack
1. a difficult problem to solve.
2. a difficult person to work out, become familiar with or try to convince.

hard on (someone)
harsh, strict, unjust, cruel to (someone).

hard on (someone's) heels
following closely.

hard put
in difficulty; under pressure: e.g. He'll be hard put to finish on time.

hard sell
aggressive salesmanship.

hard slog
difficult, tedious work.

hard stuff
strong alcoholic liquor or dangerously addictive drugs.

hard to come by
difficult to obtain; rare.

hard to fathom
difficult to understand or work out.

hard to swallow
1. unbelievable.
2. difficult, unpleasant to accept.

hard yacker/yakka
difficult, tedious work.

hard-boiled
(of a person) tough; shrewd.

hard-core
extremely explicit pornography.

hard-fisted
miserly; mean; stingy.

hard-headed
practical; unsentimental; realistic; shrewd.

hard-hearted
unfeeling; merciless; callous; mean.

hard-hitting
aggressive; merciless; pulling no punches verbally.

hard-nosed
firm; unyielding; mean; stubborn; obstinate.

hard-on
erection of the penis.

hard-up
short of, especially money.

hare
(see: can't run with the hare and hunt with the hounds)

hare along
go fast: e.g. That car can really hare along.

hare-brained
stupid; foolish; irrational.

hark back to
remember back; revert back to a subject or matter.

harp on
speak persistently and at length on a subject or point; dwell tediously on.

harping
nagging: e.g. Will you quit harping!

has-been
someone or something that is no longer in fashion, popular or effective and now held in contempt.

For other possible entries beginning with 'has' see entries listed under 'have/got', 'get'.

hash
1. hashish — the resinous extract from marijuana.
2. confusion; jumble; chaos; mess.
See also:
make a hash of

hash it out
work out; solve, sort out by going over old facts, material: e.g. We'll hash it out one way or the other.

hash oil
hashish distilled to a viscous oil.

hasn't got a brain in (her/his) head

hasn't got enough brains to give (her/himself) a headache
hasn't got much intelligence, sense or wit.

For other possible entries beginning with 'hasn't' see entries listed under 'haven't'.

hassle
1. a quarrel, argument or disagreement: e.g. Those two are having a hassle over which way to run the business.
2. a struggle or difficult time: e.g. They're having a real hassle putting the tent up in the wind.
3. problem; difficulty: e.g. What's the hassle?
4. to quarrel, argue or disagree: e.g. Those two kids are always hassling.
5. annoy; irritate; worry; harass.

hassled
worried; anxious; irritated; annoyed: e.g. What's he so hassled about?

hassles
problems; worries; anxieties: e.g. He's got lots of hassles.

hat
pertaining to position or rank: e.g. He's wearing the boss's hat while the boss is away on holidays.
See also:
at the drop of a hat
hand the hat around
have/got (one's) hat in the ring
if the hat fits, wear it!
I'll eat my hat
keep it under (one's) hat
keep your hat on!
old hat
pass round the hat
take (one's) hat off to
talking through (one's) hat
throw (one's) hat in first
throw (one's) hat in the ring
wearing two (or more) hats

hatchet job
severe criticism or denunciation: e.g. The press did a hatchet job on his new book.

hatchet man
someone employed to do the nasty or unpleasant tasks, such as firing employees, reducing costs and spending etc.

hate (someone's) guts
dislike (someone) intensely.

hate to be in (someone's) shoes
hate, dislike to be in (someone's) predicament, position.

hate to be on the wrong side of (someone)
feel discomfort at the possibility of having (someone) as an enemy, opponent.

hate-session
discussion about someone or something intensely disliked : e.g. The wives are having a hate-session about the annoying things their husbands do.

hats off to (someone)
congratulations, honours, credits to (someone): e.g. Hats off to the council for refusing development along the beach-front.

hatter
silly, crazy person.
See also:
mad as a hatter

hat-trick
1. (cricket) three wickets taken by a bowler with three successive balls.
2. achievement of three identical wins, actions etc. in succession: e.g. If he wins the cup again this year it will be a hat-trick for him!

haul
amount gained or acquired, often relating to ill-gotten gains: e.g. The robbers got a big haul of jewellery.
See also:
bank haul

haul (someone) over the coals
scold, reprimand, berate severely.

hauled up
brought before an authority for a reprimanding: e.g. He was hauled up again for drink-driving.

haunt
1. favourite or frequently visited place.
2. close associate; friend: e.g. He's a good haunt of mine.

have
1. a trick, con, act of cheating or deception: e.g. That was a bit of a have if ever I saw one!
2. fight; defeat; take on and win: e.g. I'm going to have him!
See also:
let (someone) have it

have a ball
have a good time.

have a bang
have sexual intercourse.

have a barney
fight; argue; quarrel.

have a bash
1. have a go; attempt; try.
2. have a wild party: e.g. We're going to have a big bash this weekend.

have a bingle
have a minor accident in a car.

have a bit of a lie down
have a nap, short sleep, rest.

have a blue
have an argument, fight or quarrel.

have a bo-peep
have a look.

have a burl
have a go; attempt; try.

have a change of heart
to change one's mind, alter one's previous decision.

have a crack at (it)
have a go; attempt; try.

have a crap
defecate.

have a decko/dekko
have a look.

have a dig (at)
tease; taunt; hector.

have a do
have a party or social function.

have a domestic
have an argument with a family member — usually (but not always) at home.

have a drop
have a small drink of alcohol.

have a falling-out/fall-out
have a disagreement or argument with someone.

have a fling
unrestrainedly indulge in one's desires or pleasures by spending, partying, betting etc.

have a flutter
have a small gamble, wager, especially on a horse-race.

have a gander/geek/geezer/gig
have a look.

have a go
have a try; make an attempt.

have a go at (someone)
1. fight, bash, punch, hit (someone).
2. abuse, scold, berate, reprimand (someone).

have a gutful
reach the end of one's tolerance.

have a hand in
be involved; play a part: e.g. Did he have a hand in that robbery?

have a hard time
have a difficult time; be in a difficult or unpleasant situation.

have a heart
show mercy or be reasonable, compassionate.

have a lash
have a go; attempt; try.

have a leak
to urinate.

have a pasho
indulge in sexual play, kissing, petting.

have a perve
have a look.

have a prang
have an accident in a car.

have a session
(see: have a pasho)

have a shot
have a go; attempt; try.

have a shot at (someone)
ridicule, criticise, make fun of (someone).

have a smack at
have a go, try, attempt.

have a snort
have a drink of alcohol.

have a spell
have a short rest.

have a splash
spend some money, especially on a wager or gamble.

have a squat
(of a woman) urinate.

have a squint at
have a look at.

have a stab at
have a go at; attempt; try.

have a sticky-beak
have a look.

have a tiff
have an argument, disagreement.

have a tub
have a wash, bath.

have a turn
1. have a party.
2. have a bout of sudden illness.
3. have a momentary nervous shock or surprise.

have a word with
speak to bluntly, candidly: e.g. I'm going to have a word with him about his heavy drinking.

have an optic/optic-nerve
have a look.

have it both ways
(see: can't . . .)

have it off
indulge in sexual play, intercourse: e.g. Who's she having it off with at the moment?

have it out
argue, discuss frankly, candidly, bluntly: e.g. You had better have it out with him before you listen to any further gossip from others.

have kittens
1. receive a shock, surprise; be amazed, astounded: e.g. He nearly had kittens when he found out he'd won the lottery!
2. become angry; lose one's temper: e.g. Mum will have kittens when she finds out what you've done!

have learnt (one's) lesson
be penitent, apologetic for (one's) mistake or wrong action.

have one for the road
have a last drink (of alcohol) before departure.

have one too many
indulge in too much alcohol: e.g. I had one too many last night and woke up with a splitting headache this morning.

have (one's) cake and eat it
to have the enjoyment of two apparently opposing or contradictory pleasures etc.; to be free of disadvantages in a particular situation. (see: can't . . .)

have (one's) ears burn
suffer with embarrassment upon overhearing remarks about (oneself).

have (oneself) on
to delude (oneself) with the egotistical belief that (one's) worth is much greater than it really is: e.g. He's having himself on if he thinks that scheme of his will really work!

have relations
have sexual intercourse: e.g. Did you have relations with him at any time?

have second thoughts
to be doubtful about one's previous decisions, course of action: e.g. He's having second thoughts about buying that car since he found out it was involved in a bad accident.

have (someone) in stitches
amuse (someone) enormously; cause (someone) to laugh heartily.

'They say that liquor improves with age. I must say I agree. Th' older I get, th' better it tastes!'

Aussie men love their booze — especially beer, which is more often referred to as brew, favourite poison, grog, hops, liquid amber, piss, sherbet, slops, suds or a ten-ounce sandwich. Beer can come in a bottle, brownie, coldie, frostie, jug, middy, niner, pony, pot, schooner, stubbie, tinnie or tube.

have (someone) on
1. tease, taunt, hector (someone).
2. deceive, delude, fool, trick (someone).
3. fight, bash, hit, punch (someone).
4. accept (someone) as an opponent, adversary.

have (someone) up
charge; arrest; apprehend: e.g. The police had him up for theft.

have (someone's) balls/head
reprimand, punish, scold (someone) severely: e.g. I'm going to have his balls for telling all those lies about me!

have the last laugh
be ultimately victorious or successful in the face of adversity, disbelief, opposition or contempt.

have the last say
to have the final authority: e.g. The wife will have the last say over the colour of the carpet we choose.

have the time of (one's) life
have an extremely good, enjoyable experience.

have words with
1. to argue, speak angrily with.
2. to berate, reprimand, scold severely.

have/got a big head
vain; conceited.

have/got a big mouth
excessively talkative; apt to divulge secrets or confidences, either deliberately or accidentally.

have/got a bone to pick with (someone)
have a quarrel, disagreement that needs resolving with (someone).

have/got a card up (one's) sleeve
to have a plan, strategem or advantage.

have/got a crush on (someone)
be infatuated, in love with (someone).

have/got a death adder in (one's) pocket
exceptionally mean, parsimonious, stingy, miserly.

have/got a down on (someone)
have a feeling of hostility, dislike for, grudge or prejudice against (someone).

have/got a face as long as a fiddle/wet week

have/got a face like a chook's bum
morose; miserable; dismal; sour; of an unhappy disposition.

have/got a few marbles missing
not in full control of (one's) faculties; mad; silly; insane.

have/got a finger in every pie
have shares, or be involved in many activities, especially profitable ones.

have/got a finger in the pie
have a share or involvement in a matter or enterprise.

have/got a good head on (one's) shoulders
sensible; practical; enterprising.

have/got a good nose for money
enterprising in ways of making money, profits.

have/got a good step
(rugby) able to manoeuvre, jink well.

have/got a good thing going
have an extremely satisfactory arrangement, position, set of circumstances.

have/got a hold over (someone)
to have (someone) at a disadvantage, under one's power and influence.

have/got a job in front of (one)
have a very difficult task to do: e.g. He's got a job in front of him raising three young boys on his own.

have/got a lot going for (it/one)
have great potential, attributes for success; have many favourable assets or characteristics.

have/got a memory like a sieve
extremely forgetful.

have/got a memory like an elephant
have an extremely good memory, recall.

have/got a mouthful of teeth
have large, prominent teeth.

have/got a nerve
to have impudence; be shamelessly brazen: e.g. He's got a nerve speaking to me like that!

have/got a plum in (one's) mouth
to speak affectedly, pretentiously, artificially — especially in imitation of a high-class British accent.

have/got a quid
wealthy, rich: e.g. He may not look like it, but he's got a quid!

have/got a record as long as my arm
to have a long list of criminal convictions.

have/got a screw loose
mad; insane; silly; stupid, irrational.

have/got a sharp nose
1. to have a keen sense of smell.

2. be astute: e.g. He's got a sharp nose for making money.

have/got a skeleton in the closet
(see: skeleton . . .)

have/got a snout on
to sulk or bear ill-will towards someone.

have/got a swing on the back porch
to have a mincing style of walking.

have/got a swollen head
egotistical; vain; conceited.

have/got a thick skin
insensitive to criticism or verbal abuse.

have/got a thing about (someone/something)
have a strong emotional feeling or attitude (good or bad) about (someone/something): e.g. She won't put on a bikini because she's got a thing about being overweight.

have/got a trick up (one's) sleeve
(see: have/got an ace up one's sleeve)

have/got a voice like a foghorn
loudly spoken.

have/got a way with
have a special skill in dealing with people or things: e.g. Harry's got a way with horses.

have/got an ace up (one's) sleeve
have a hidden advantage on which to act: e.g. My solicitor's got an ace up his sleeve which will win this case.

have/got an ear to the ground
well-informed and up-to-date on the latest trends, news, gossip.

have/got an edge against (someone)
(see: have/got a down on someone)

have/got an eye for
be discerning; have an appreciation, admiration for: e.g. He's got an eye for pretty girls.

have/got an in with
to have influence, clout, favourable connections with (someone): e.g. Those illegal casinos must have an in with the local police because they never get closed down.

have/got ants in (one's) pants
restless; unable to sit still.

have/got bats in the belfry
mad; silly; crazy; full of irrational ideas; not in full control of (one's) faculties; lacking in intelligence.

have/got broad shoulders
able to handle responsibility.

have/got Buckley's
have no chance at all: e.g. The police have got Buckley's of ever wiping out big crime syndicates.

have/got counter-sunk shit
(of a man) homosexual.

have/got egg on (one's) face
suffer or be exposed in an embarrassing situation — usually as a result of (one's) own foolish actions.

have/got 'em bad
suffering from nervous anxiety or symptoms associated with the withdrawal from drugs, alcohol, tobacco.

have/got enough on (one's) plate
have a full schedule, timetable of work, responsibility etc. without being able to take on more: e.g. With six young children, she's got enough on her plate without getting pregnant again.

have/got eyes in the back of (one's) head
have the apparent ability to see all; be acutely aware.

have/got eyes only for
1. to desire nothing else but.
2. to look, seek for nothing else but.

have/got half a mind to
half decided: e.g. I've got half a mind to leave this job.

have/got hollow legs
have an ability to eat huge amounts of food.

have/got it all (one's) way
1. be totally independent, in control.
2. be totally selfish.

have/got it (all) together
be in control of one's emotions, situation, circumstances etc.

have/got it bad
1. (for someone) be infatuated, smitten, in love with (someone).
2. (see: have/got 'em bad)

have/got it by the throat
be in full control or command of a situation.

have/got it coming to (one)
deserve the consequences resulting from (one's) actions or an unpleasant fate: e.g. After all the terrible things he's done, he's got it coming to him.

have/got it easy
1. wealthy; comfortably well-off; prosperous.
2. in a comfortable and highly satisfactory position: e.g. He's got it easy in that new job.

have/got it in for (someone)
bear a grudge against (someone): e.g. The police have got it in for that drug-pusher — they'll catch him soon.

have/got it in (one)
have the ability, potential, skill, bravery: e.g. He hasn't got it in him to kill anyone.

have/got it made
1. be assured of success: e.g. I'll have it made when this book sells a million copies.
2. successful: e.g. After all that hard work, she's got it made.

have/got kangaroos in the top paddock
not in full control of (one's) faculties; mad; silly; eccentric.

have/got legs like matchsticks
to have thin, skinny legs.

have/got money to burn
to be extremely wealthy.

have/got more arse/hide than an elephant
have a greal deal of audacity.

have/got more arse than class
gutsy rather than genteel approach to life; extremely lucky; successful through chance rather than planning.

have/got no brains
dumb; stupid; foolish.

have/got no time for
unable to tolerate; dislike: e.g. I've got no time for people who complain all the time.

have/got one foot in the door
to have grasped an opportunity that gives the potential for further advancement.

have/got one foot in the grave
seriously ill; close to death; behaving in a manner injurious to health.

have/got one foot in the grave and the other on a banana-skin
in a serious predicament from which there seems to be little chance of escape.

have/got (one's) arse in (one's) hands
extremely angry.

have/got (one's) back to the wall
have no option or choice in a matter or situation.

have/got (one's) face against the pub wall
in disgrace.

have/got (one's) feet (planted firmly) on the ground
stable; sensible; level-headed.

have/got (one's) hand in the till
be guilty of embezzlement, stealing from the cash-register or funds where (one) is employed.

have/got (one's) hands full
be totally occupied; extremely busy; over-worked or taxed: e.g. Kate's got her hands full now that she's a wife and mother.

have/got (one's) hat in the ring
to be in the draw, game; be a contender, entrant.

have/got (one's) head in the clouds
be unrealistic.

have/got (one's) head screwed on right
practical; clear-thinking; sensible; enterprising.

have/got (one's) heart in (one's) boots
to be sad, morose, unhappy, dejected.

have/got (one's) heart in (one's) mouth
be frightened, anxious, nervous: e.g. I had my heart in my mouth when we had to search for that poisonous snake in the house.

have/got (one's) heart set on (something)
desire, want (something) urgently, desperately.

have/got (one's) lines crossed
confused; incorrect; to have misunderstood, misinterpreted.

have/got (one's) mind in the gutter
to think or say sordid, obscene, lurid things.

have/got (one's) sights set on
aim, scheme for, aspire to (something): e.g. He's got his sights set on being the boss of the company one day.

have/got (one's) wits about (one)
to be alert.

have/got (one's) work cut out
1. to have a difficult task ahead of (one).
2. to be extremely busy, pressed.

have/got (oneself) to thank
be responsible (oneself): e.g. You've got yourself to thank for all the trouble you're in!

have/got only one oar in the water

have/got rocks in (one's) head
(see: have/got bats in the belfry)

have/got several irons in the fire
1. have several options or choices.
2. be involved in several activities or projects at once.

have/got shit for brains
exceptionally stupid, irrational, foolish.

have/got short arms and long pockets
to be mean, parsimonious, miserly, stingy.

have/got some lights out upstairs
(see: have/got bats in the belfry)

have/got (someone) by the balls
1. (of a woman) have the total devotion of a man: e.g. Annette's got Ashley by the balls — they're getting married.
2. (see: have/got someone by the short and curlies)

have/got (someone) by the short and curlies

have/got (someone) by the short hairs

have/got (someone) over a barrel
have (someone) at one's mercy, under one's power, influence or authority, or at a grave disadvantage.

have/got (someone) pegged/tabbed
have (someone) identified, labelled, summed up: e.g. I had him pegged as a cheat.

have/got (someone) pegged out
to stake a claim on (someone).

have/got (something) hanging over (one)
be worried, anxious, intimidated, threatened by (something): e.g. I hate having late bills hanging over my head.

have/got (something) on the brain
to be obsessed with (something).

have/got the ball at (one's) feet
be in a position of advantage, gain.

have/got the ball in (one's) court
have the obligation or opportunity to act or react.

have/got the balls to
have the nerve, daring, courage, bravado to (do something): e.g. I didn't think he had the balls to do that!

have/got the britts
to be angry. (rhyming slang: Jimmy Britts — shits)

have/got the britts up
be alarmed, afraid. (rhyming slang: Jimmy Britts — shits)

have/got the drips
(of a woman) menstruating.

have/got the drop on (someone)
(Australian Rules football) to be in a perfect position to take a mark.

have/got the edge on (someone)
have the advantage over (someone).

have/got the face to
have the nerve, courage, boldness, impudence to (do something).

have/got the flags out
(of a woman) menstruating.

have/got the floor
have the total attention of all present.

have/got the game by the throat

have/got the game sewn up
in a position of advantage, full control.

have/got the goods
1. have reliable information, truthful facts.
2. (Australian Rules football) inside information on the opposing side which gives a team the advantage.

have/got the goods on (someone)
1. have information about (someone) — especially incriminating evidence.
2. (Australian Rules football) inside information on the opposing side which gives a team the advantage.

have/got the guts
1. brave, daring.
2. have reliable information, truthful facts.

have/got the heart to
have the courage or conviction: e.g. I didn't have the heart to go out shooting kangaroos with them.

have/got the hide
have the impudence, boldness, gall, audacity: e.g. He had the hide to tell me that I had bad breath!

have/got the hots for (someone)
to lust after (someone).

have/got the jimmies
(see: have/got the britts)

have/got the knack
1. have a natural ability, talent, aptitude.
2. become familiar with and do with ease.

have/got the pip
in a state of anger, irritation, annoyance.

have/got the shits/tom-tits
1. annoyed, angry, irritated, bad-tempered.
2. to have diarrhoea.

have/got the wood on (someone)
have an advantage over (someone): e.g. The Magpies have got the wood on the Swans in the Grand Final.

have/got the works
has everything; has all the attachments, optional extras: e.g. This car has got the works!

have/got the world at (one's) feet
to have every opportunity, good fortune available to (one).

have/got tickets on (oneself)
be conceited, vain; have an over-rated opinion of (oneself) that is not shared by others.

have/got to be in it to win it
taking a chance, having a go; participating is necessary in order to have a chance at success or winnings.

have/got to be kidding!
exclamation of disbelief, surprise.

have/got to hand it to (someone)
give, acknowledge credit where it is due: e.g. I've got to hand it to him — he's good.

have/got to walk backwards to a door to open it
pertaining to someone with very large feet.

have/got too much of what the cat licks itself with
to be too talkative.

have/got two chances/hopes — Buckley's and none
to have no chance/hope.

have/got what it takes
have the necessary abilities, skills, aptitude for success.

have/got whiskers on it
distasteful; unpleasant; old-fashioned; useless: e.g. Spending the weekend mowing lawns in the hot sun has got whiskers on it!

For other possible entries beginning with 'have' see entries listed under 'get', 'got', 'had'.

have-not
poor person.

haven't got a brass razoo
haven't got any money.

haven't got a clue
haven't got any knowledge of.

haven't got a cracker
haven't got any money.

haven't got a feather to fly with
1. haven't got any money.
2. haven't got a valid reason, excuse, alibi.

haven't got a hope in hell
haven't got any hope, chance at all.

haven't got a leg to stand on
haven't got a valid reason, excuse or alibi.

haven't got a penny to bless (oneself) with

haven't got a sausage
haven't got any money; broke; destitute.

haven't got a shit's show (in hell)

haven't got a show (in hell)
haven't got a chance or hope at all: e.g. He hasn't got a shit's show of moving that log by himself.

haven't got an earthly
1. haven't got any chance or hope at all.
2. haven't got any knowledge; have no idea or clue: e.g. Don't ask me where he is — I haven't got an earthly!

haven't got enough sense to come in out of the rain

haven't got much grey matter
to be stupid, lacking in intelligence.

haven't got the guts
haven't got the courage, bravado, daring, nerve: e.g. He hasn't got the guts to tell his boss what he thinks of him!

haven't got the head for (it)
haven't got the potential, ability, knowledge: e.g. I haven't got the head for chemistry and physics.

haven't got the heart/nerve to
haven't got the courage, conviction, strength or will-power to.

haven't got the stomach (for/to)
1. haven't got the tolerance; squeamish, sensitive, queasy: e.g. Wayne hasn't got the stomach to shoot a bunny.
2. (see: haven't got the heart to)

haven't got two bob to rub together
haven't got any money; destitute.

haven't had this much fun/laughed this much since Granny got her tits caught in the wringer
jocular expression of pleasure.

haven't lived yet
haven't enjoyed fully, experienced life to the fullest: e.g. If you haven't eaten at that restaurant, you haven't lived yet!

haves and have-nots
the rich and the poor: e.g. Life in India is an explicit example of the struggle between the haves and the have-nots.

having a bad trot
having an extreme run of bad luck, misfortune: e.g. He's having a bad trot with the business at the moment because of lack of finance.

having a good trot
having a run of good luck, fortune.

having a lend/loan of (someone)
teasing, taunting, deceiving gently: e.g. Are you having a lend of me or are you being honest?

having (oneself) on
(see: have oneself on)

Hawkers/Hawks
Hawthorn VFL football team.

hay
money.
See also:
hit the hay
make hay while the sun shines
roll in the hay

hayseed
rustic; yokel; country bumpkin.

haywire
gone wrong; chaotic; out of order; inoperative: e.g. Since he left the business has gone haywire.

haze
LSD — an hallucinogenic drug.

he
1. male person or animal: e.g. That cat's a he, not a she.
2. the person elected or caught to be the chaser in children's games of chasy or tiggy.
See also:
I'll go he

he himself
the master of the house; the boss.

he only thinks of his belly and what hangs on the end of it
derog. remark made by women about a man considered to think of little else but food and sex.

he who hesitates is lost
if one does not act upon an opportunity when presented, one may lose one's chance.

head
1. a drug-addict, especially one with a penchant for marijuana or hallucinatory drugs such as LSD.
2. the froth on top of a poured glass of beer.
3. a very important, intellectual person: e.g. All the heads are meeting at the office tonight.
4. the headmaster, principal of a school.
See also:
acid-head
all in the head
beating (one's) head against a brick wall
blockhead
bury (one's) head in the sand
come to a head
dead-head
dick-head
do it on (one's) head
do it standing on (one's) head
don't lose your head
drop on your head!
dunderhead
eyes fall out of (one's) head
eyes in the back of (one's) head
from head to foot
fucked in the head
get a swollen head
give head
give (someone) head
give (someone) his head
go off (one's) head
go to (one's) head
have (someone's) head
have/got a big head
have/got a good head on (one's) shoulders
have/got a swollen head
have/got (one's) head in the clouds
have/got (one's) head screwed on right
have/got rocks in (one's) head
haven't got the head for it
hide (one's) head in the sand
hit the nail on the head
hothead
I've seen better heads on a glass of beer
keep (one's) head
keep (one's) head above water
knock it on the head
light-headed
lose (one's) head
make head or tail of
need a head job
need it like a hole in the head
need (one's) head read
not right in the head
off (one's) head
off the top of (one's) head
on (one's) head
out of (one's) head
over (someone's) head
pull your head in!
put (one's) head in the sand
put (our/their) heads together
shithead
snap (someone's) head off
talk off the top of (one's) head
talk (one's) head off
turn (someone's) head
two heads are better than one
want (one's) head read

head and shoulders above
far superior: e.g. That one is head and shoulders above the other.

head down, arse up
diligent work, activity: e.g. She had her head down, arse up in the garden all day.

head in the clouds
(to have one's . . .) unrealistic; dreamy; day-dreaming.

head in the sand
(to have one's . . .) to ignore or refuse to see or understand the realities, relevant or salient points of a matter.

head like a Mini with the doors open
(to have a . . .) to have big, protruding ears.

head off
leave; depart: e.g. We're heading off now.

head on down
go: e.g. Let's head on down to that new night-club.

head over heels/tail/turkey
(see: head-over-heels)

head screwed on the right way
(to have one's . . .) sensible; clear-thinking; enterprising.

head start
an initial advantage.

headache
troublesome person or thing: e.g. That car has been nothing but a headache since I bought it.
See also:
not now, I've got a headache
not tonight darling, I have a headache

headfirst
rashly; impetuously; without thinking of the consequences: e.g. He went into that deal headfirst and lost a lot of money.

head-hunter
(sport) basher.

head-hunting
1. searching for personnel, employees, members.
2. elimination of opponents — especially political ones.
3. searching for a scapegoat.

heading 'em/them
playing the gambling game of two-up.

head-job
1. oral sex performed on the penis; fellatio: e.g. She gave him the best head-job he's ever had!
2. sarcasm, pertaining to (someone) being ugly, having an ugly face that could be fixed with surgery: e.g. Her legs are nice but she sure could do with a head-job!

head-over-heels/tails/turkey
1. to tumble, somersault as (one) falls: e.g. He went head-over-heels down the stairs.
2. completely, utterly, totally: e.g. He's head-over-heels in love with that new girl.

heads I win, tails you lose
(joc.) a wager, decision on the toss of a coin that makes it impossible for one's opponent to win; to give one's opponent no choice at all.

heads or tails?
(see: odds or evens?)

heads will roll
some people are due to face the unpleasant consequences of their actions.

headshrink/headshrinker
a psychiatrist.

headstrong
obstinate; self-willed; impetuous.

health kick
an obsession with one's health, food, life-style.

healthy
exceptionally good; powerful: e.g. Dad gave him a healthy smack on the bum for being naughty.

heap
a dilapidated, unroadworthy car or vehicle.

heap of rubbish
nonsense; worthless talk, gossip, literature, print etc.

heap of shit
1. dilapidated, unroadworthy car or vehicle.
2. (see: heap of rubbish)

heap shit on (someone)
disparage, condemn, criticise (someone).

heaps
1. a lot; very large number or amount: e.g. Heaps of people went to the concert even though it rained.
2. a lot of money: e.g. He's got heaps.
See also:
give it heaps
give (someone/something) heaps

heard every excuse in the book
to have heard many excuses, alibis, reasons.

heard it all before
to have heard the same things over and over until they have become hackneyed.

heard it on the grape-vine
to have found out or learnt something, gained information by word-of-mouth.

hearing things
imagining noises: e.g. There's nobody at the door — you must be hearing things.

heart
considered the very essence of emotion, feeling, soul, thought, affection, courage: e.g.
1. He's got real heart (all the mentioned attributes).
2. He hasn't got a heart (none of the mentioned attributes).
See also:
after (one's) own heart
all heart
at heart
break (someone's) heart
close to (one's) heart
cross (one's) heart (and hope to die)
cry (one's) heart out
Dead Heart
eat (one's) heart out
eat your heart out!
follow (one's) heart
from the bottom of (one's) heart
half-hearted
hard-hearted

have a change of heart
have a heart
have/got (one's) heart in (one's) boots/mouth
have/got (one's) heart set on
have/got the heart to
haven't got the heart to
heave (one's) heart out
home is where the heart is
in (one's) heart of hearts
join the lonely-hearts club
know it off by heart
light-hearted
lonely-heart
lonely-hearts' club
lose (one's) heart to
my heart bleeds!
nearly had heart-failure
off by heart
put (one's) heart into it
set (one's) heart at rest
set (one's) heart on
steal (someone's) heart
sweet-heart
take heart
take it to heart
to (one's) heart's content
tug at (one's) heart-strings
warm the cockles of (one's) heart
warm-hearted
wearing (one's) heart on (one's) sleeve
win a heart
with all (one's) heart

heart and soul
completely; utterly; with total devotion: e.g. He put his heart and soul into that project.

heart as big as a pumpkin/the oval/himself etc.
(Australian Rules football) courageous player.

heart in (one's) boots
(to have one's . . .) to be low in morale; be depressed in spirit.

heart is torn between
unable to make up one's mind; unable to choose between two things because one feels strongly for both: e.g. Her heart is torn between her family and her career.

heart isn't in it
not enthusiastic or interested: e.g. He failed the test because his heart wasn't in it.

heart missed a beat

heart nearly jumped out of my throat
to have received a sudden shock or surprise: e.g. When he jumped out from behind the bushes my heart missed a beat!

heart of gold
pertaining to a generous, kind, helpful, affectionate, thoughtful personality: e.g. He's got a heart of gold when it comes to helping people in trouble.

heart of stone
pertaining to a mean, unemotional, cold, merciless and unkind personality.

heart of the matter
the essence, core, most essential and relevant aspect: e.g. They'll never sort their marriage problems out until they discuss the heart of the matter with each other seriously.

heart went out to (someone/something)
to empathise with, feel for: e.g. When I saw all those starving people in Ethiopia my heart went out to them.

heart-breaker
person known to make others unhappy or cause grief in matters of love and relationships.

heart-broken
crushed by grief, distress and sorrow.

heart-sick
despondent; desperately unhappy; desolate.

heart-starter
strong drink such as alcohol or coffee, taken early in the morning before work or activity.

heart-stopper
a surprising, shocking, amazing, astonishing or terrifying thing.

heart-stricken
(see: heart-broken)

heart-throb
person as the object of one's infatuation, love or desire: e.g. Many women thought Elvis Presley was a heart-throb.

heart-to-heart
1. a frank, sincere, intimate talk, discussion: e.g. All parents should have a heart-to-heart talk with their adolescent children about sex.
2. frankly, sincerely, intimately: e.g. We talked about her marriage problems heart-to-heart for the first time.

heart-warming
emotionally moving in a pleasant manner.

heat
investigative pressure by any authority, especially the police: e.g. Most criminals lie low while the heat is on over a recent drug bust or bank job.
See also:
dead heat
on heat
put the heat on
turn on the heat
when the heat's on

heat in the meat
pertaining to a man's sexual arousal, hardening of the penis: e.g. She really puts the heat in my meat.

heave
(see: the old heave-ho)

heave it out
throw away; discard.

heave (one's) heart out
to vomit.

heaven
wonderful; extremely pleasant and satisfying: e.g. After that old mattress, our new water-bed is just heaven!
See also:
in heaven
in seventh heaven
move heaven and earth
stairway to heaven
stinks to high heaven

heaven dust
cocaine.

heaven knows
no one knows: e.g. I looked for it all day and couldn't find it — heaven knows where it is!

heavens (to Betsy)!
mild oath; exclamation of surprise, disbelief, wonder, annoyance, frustration etc.

heavies
1. body-guards; people employed for their strength; bouncers, strong-arm men; men with authority employed to keep the peace, such as police, or to use violence if necessary, such as a criminal's hench-men.
2. any talk that puts unwanted pressure on one: e.g. He really put the heavies on me last night to go to bed with him.
See also:
put the heavies on (someone)

heavy
1. threatening or coercive.
2. pertaining to anything serious, important, grave, meaningful, intellectual, depressing, trying, difficult etc.
3. an intimidating, rough, bullying, or coercive person.
4. a detective or investigator.
5. a man who tries to sexually intimidate a woman: e.g. He's a heavy — don't go out with him.
6. a villain or crook.
See also:
come on real/too heavy
get heavy
put the heavy word on (someone)

heavy hand
oppressive, strict, severe method or manner: e.g. Most dictators rule with a heavy hand.

heavy metal
the style of rock music using loud amplification and distortion of electronic music.

heavy petting
intimate sexual play, fondling without the actual act of intercourse.

heavy-handed
1. oppressive; over-bearing; domineering.
2. clumsy; insensitive; bungling.

heavyweight
person of considerable influence and power.

heck!
1. exclamation of annoyance, frustration or disappointment.
2. euphemism for hell, damn, blast: e.g. What the heck are you doing?
See also:
to heck with it!
what the heck

heck of a
1. awful; terrible; damned; stupid; annoying etc: e.g. That's a heck of a job.
2. an intensifier, meaning greater, wonderful, terrific, big etc.: e.g. 1. She's one heck of a woman in his eyes. 2. That's a heck of a car he's driving now.

he'd fuck a barber's floor if it had enough hair on it

he'd fuck a hole in the ground if it smiled at him

he'd fuck anything on two legs
derog. remark about a man's supposed lack of discrimination with regard to sexual partners.

heebie-jeebies
1. condition or feeling of nervousness, tension, worry: e.g. Driving with him gives me the heebie-jeebies.
2. feeling of revulsion, fright, horror, distaste: e.g. Spiders give Debbie the heebie-jeebies.
3. the D.T.'s; shaking and trembling due to an excessive intake of alcohol: e.g. Richard's got a bad case of the heebie-jeebies after last night's party.

heel
1. despicable person; scoundrel.
2. (of a dog) follow close behind the master's heels.
See also:
bring (someone) to heel
cool (one's) heels
dig (one's) heels in
down at heel
hot on the heels of
kick up (one's) heels
show a clean pair of heels
take to (one's) heels
well-heeled

Heinz 57
mongrel dog; anything of mixed constitution.

heist
robbery; burglary.

hell
1. mild oath or expression of frustration, annoyance, wonder, astonishment.
2. pertaining to anything troublesome, difficult, annoying, unpleasant: e.g. 1. Working in the hot sun is hell. 2. It's hell going shopping with the kids.

See also:
beat the hell out of
been to hell and back
blast hell out of (someone)
bloody hell!
come hell or high water
for the hell of it
get the hell out
give (someone/ something) hell
go like a bat out of hell
go to hell!
haven't got a hope/shit's show/show in hell
holy hell!
like hell!
merry hell
not a hope in hell
play hell with
raise hell
risk hell and high water
rot in hell
sure as hell
to hell with
what the hell!
when all hell breaks loose
when hell freezes over

hell for leather
very fast: e.g. The taxi drove hell for leather to get to the airport on time.
See also:
go hell for leather

hell hath no fury like a woman scorned
the vindictiveness, temper of a rejected woman is unsurpassed.

hell of a
(also: helluva)
1. excellent, very good.
2. terrible, awful, very bad.

hell of a lot of good (that is/that will do)
no good at all.

hell to pay
serious consequences to face; trouble to face: e.g. I'm going to have hell to pay for staying out so late.

hell-bent
determined: e.g. He's hell-bent on being a millionaire before he's thirty.

hellbound
heading for destruction, ruin, downfall.

hellcat
aggressive, bad-tempered woman.

hell-hole
any place that is extremely unpleasant, evil, dirty etc.

Hell's Angel
member of a motor-bike gang (of the same name) characterised by leather jackets, evil appearance and lawless behaviour.

hell's bells/teeth!
mild oath; expression of frustration, annoyance, amazement etc.

helluva
contraction of: hell of a (see: hell of a).

help (oneself)
take without permission; steal; pilfer: e.g. He broke into the mansion and helped himself to a colour telly and a video set.
See also:
beyond help
God helps those who help themselves
if you don't help yourself, no one else will
not if I can help it
so help me (God!)

hem and haw
(also: hum and ha) avoid coming to the point or giving a direct answer.

he-man
masterful, tough, virile, macho man.

hemmed in
confined, restricted, limited: e.g. She left home because she felt hemmed in by her parents.

hemp
marijuana.

hen
fussy woman (or man).
See also:
scarce as hen's teeth

henfruit
eggs.

henpecked
(of a man or husband) dominated by a wife or lover; subordinate to a wife or lover.

hen's night
1. (see: hen's party)
2. night out on the town for the women only.

hen's party
a party for women only, especially a party held in honour of a woman just prior to her marriage.

hep up
revitalise; inject enthusiasm and vigour into: e.g. We need more booze to hep this party up.

her indoors
(also: 'er indoors) a man's wife.

her ladyship
pretentious, affected and snobbish woman.

her thighs wouldn't chafe her ears

her thighs wouldn't stop a pig in a hall
bandy-legged; pertaining to a woman with a wide gap between her thighs.

herb
1. (the . . .) marijuana; pot; grass.
2. (of a car) go fast; speed: e.g. That car can really herb along.

herb over
pass; give: e.g. Herb over those boxes please.

herb superb
marijuana; Indian hemp; pot; grass.

herbs
(of a car) speed; performance; power: e.g. That car has lots of herbs.

See also:
give it some herbs

here
(see: out here)

here goes!
exclamation heralding a daring, exciting or unpleasant start.

here to stay
accepted as a permanent feature: e.g. Computers are here to stay.

here today, gone tomorrow
around for only a short time; not lasting or permanent: e.g. Many rock bands are here today, gone tomorrow.

here we go again!
exclamation of frustration, exasperation over something about to be repeated.

here's looking at you!

here's looking up your kilt!

here's mud in your eye!
a salute or proposal for a toast.

herk
to vomit.

herps
herpes — infection characterised by sores on the lips or genitals.

he's so far up himself he's on the way down again
he's conceited, egotistical; he thinks much more of himself than he is worth.

het-up
1. angry.
2. worried; anxious.

hey-day
prime of life; period of fullest vigour, success: e.g. He was the best race-horse in his hey-day.

hey-diddle-diddle
1. (rhyming slang) the middle.
2. (rhyming slang) piddle; urination.

hey-presto!
exclamation of success on completion of a trick, task etc.

hi
greeting; hello.

hick
1. an unsophisticated, rustic, country person.
2. a pimple.

hick town
backward, rustic, country town.

hickey
1. love bite; red mark on the skin given in sexual play by sucking the skin to draw a bruise to the surface.
2. a pimple.

hide
impudence; cheek; gall; effrontery: e.g. He's got a hide saying that to me!
See also:
nothing to hide
tan (someone's) hide
thick hide

hide nor hair
any sign of; any clue to: e.g. I can't find hide nor hair of him anywhere around town.

hide (one's) head (in the sand)
1. to be ashamed, disgraced, humiliated.
2. to refuse to acknowledge, recognise the facts or truth.

hide the sausage
sexual intercourse.

hideaway
secret place of refuge, concealment.

hide-out
secret place of refuge, especially from the law.

hi-diddle-diddle
(see: hey-diddle-diddle)

hiding
1. a beating; thrashing or belting.
2. a sound defeating: e.g. Our team got a hiding in the grand finals last week.

hidy-hole
a secret place or spot; a personal place of refuge.

hieroglyphics
writing that is difficult to read; untidy writing.

hi-fi
high fidelity record player or music system.

higgledy-piggledy
mixed up; jumbled; confused; in utter disorder: e.g. I'm sick of seeing his clothes lying higgledy-piggledy all over his bedroom.

high
1. happy; elated.
2. a feeling of euphoria induced by drugs: e.g. She is on a real high after trying that dope.
3. intoxicated by alcohol or drugs: e.g. Greg's high! What's he high on?
4. having an unpleasant smell: e.g. Those prawns are high.
5. expensive; costly: e.g. That's too high!
See also:
get off (one's) high horse
live high
live high on the hog
on a high
on (one's) high horse
riding high
stinks to high heaven

high and dry
helpless; abandoned: e.g. He ran off with another woman and left his family high and dry.

high and low
everywhere: e.g. I searched high and low and couldn't find it.

high and mighty
arrogant; conceited; pompous; snobbish.

high as a dingo's howl
having an unpleasant smell.

high as a kite
1. intoxicated, drunk.
2. under the influence of drugs.

high flying
doing extremely well; successful.

high hopes
high expectations: e.g. You've got high hopes if you think that is going to work.

high key about (something)
elated, excited, enthusiastic about (something).

high old time
good time; fun; enjoyable experience: e.g. We had a high old time at the zoo.

high on the nose
having an unpleasant smell.

high places
upper levels of society, government, business, organisations: e.g. He moves in high places.

high roller
gambler of large sums of money at a casino.

high sounding
pretentious; affected; unbelievable.

high time
1. about time; the last moment before it is too late: e.g. It's high time you had a bath!
2. a good time; fun: e.g. We had a high time at that party.

high up
holding a senior, important or influential position: e.g. He's pretty high up in the organisation.

high words
a heated argument.

highbrow
superior in intellect and artistic taste.

higher-than-thou
pertaining to a person who has pretensions of superiority: e.g. Him and his higher-than-thou attitudes make me sick! (see: holier-than-thou)

highfalutin
pretentious; pompous; snobbish; affectedly superior.

high-flier
enthusiast.

high-handed
authoritarian; over-bearing; arrogant.

highly strung
nervous; tense; on edge.

high-rise
tall building with many storeys.

high-stepping it
living a hectic, pleasurable life-style.

high-strung
(see: highly strung)

hightail it
go, leave, depart, especially quickly: e.g. We'd better hightail it before the police arrive.

highway robbery
unashamed swindling, cheating, robbery, charging of exorbitant prices: e.g. What she paid for that was highway robbery!

hike
(of prices, costs) to increase rapidly: e.g. There's going to be another hike in the cost of petrol.

hill
(see: old as the hills; over the hill; take to the hills)

hill climb
motor-car or cycle race held over a hilly course.

hillbilly
a rustic, unsophisticated country person.

hinges on
depends on: e.g. The success of the project hinges on getting a loan from the bank.

hip
1. stylish; with-it; fashionable; trendy.
2. aware; knowledgeable; in the know.
See also:
fire from the hip

hippie
(also: hippy) person who rejects socially accepted standards of dress and behaviour and is characterised by notions of and indulgence in free love, peace and drugs.

hippo
hippopotamus.

hip-pocket
pertaining to one's money, finances: e.g. The new tax will hit everyone in the hip-pocket.

hipsters
trousers worn at the hip rather than the waist.

his lordship
1. one's husband: e.g. His lordship is still in bed!
2. an overbearing, affected man.

his nibs
1. the boss.
2. (see: his lordship, 1. and 2.)

hiss and boo
express dislike, scorn, disapproval; jeer; mock; shout down: e.g. Each time he tried to speak the crowd hissed and booed at him.

history
1. ruined, broken, beyond repair: e.g. My lawnmower was history after he borrowed it!
2. ruined, as in a business or relationship; irrevocably damaged.
3. completely intoxicated, drunk or under the

influence of drugs: e.g. After drinking all day he's history!
4. in serious trouble and having little hope: e.g. He's history now that the police know about him.
5. dead.
See also:
ancient history

hit
1. a shot, dose of heroin (or other drug); a fix: e.g. Many robberies are committed by drug-addicts to pay for a hit.
2. a success; famous; popular: e.g. The play is a hit.
3. arrive at: e.g. When did you hit town?
4. have effect on; affect severely: e.g. The death of his wife hit him hard.
5. demand, ask for money: e.g. 1. I got hit with the bill for my rates. 2. I'll hit Dad for a loan.
6. a tackle.
See also:
couldn't hit a cow in the tit with a tin can
couldn't hit the side of a barn
didn't know what hit him
hard hit
in one hit
king hit
king-hit
make a hit with (someone)
never knew what hit him

hit a bad patch
strike difficulty or problems; experience misfortune, especially financial.

hit a sour note
1. strike difficulty or problems.
2. touch on, mention a point or matter that is controversial, delicate, embarrassing or better left unsaid.
3. make a bad impression on: e.g. I must have hit a sour note with him because he didn't give me the job.

hit below the belt
use unfair, underhanded tactics.

hit for six
utterly defeated, surprised or set back: e.g. He was really hit for six when he was told he was fired.

hit home
make a strong impression; have a severe or strong effect on: e.g. You finally hit home when you told him he'd be dead in six months if he didn't stop taking drugs.

hit it off
get on well with; make a good impression: e.g. We hit it off from the very start of our relationship.

hit man
1. hired assassin.
2. (Australian Rules football) tough footballer prone to clocking opponents.

hit me with
1. give, pass, hand over: e.g. Hit me with a beer!
2. tell, relate: e.g. Hit me with the bad news.

hit on it
guess correctly; get (information, facts) right; discover; arrive at: e.g. After all these years of research I've finally hit on the right answer.

hit parade
selection of the most popular songs played on the radio.

hit rock bottom
pertaining to the worst, lowest possible position to be in; finished, ruined, at the end: e.g. 1. My finances have really hit rock bottom. 2. Our marriage has hit rock bottom.

hit (someone) hard
affect (someone) strongly, severely, in a distressing manner: e.g. The death of his wife has hit him hard.

hit (someone) up for
bring pressure to bear on, ask (someone), especially for money.

hit (someone) where it hurts
affect (someone) severely; put (someone) at a disadvantage.

hit the anchors
(of a car) apply the brakes suddenly.

hit the big time
achieve success, fame and fortune: e.g. He's finally hit the big time after having a best-seller published.

hit the booze/bottle
drink alcohol to excess.

hit the bullseye
ascertain, guess (information) correctly; get the facts correct.

hit the ceiling
lose one's temper; become suddenly angry.

hit the cot
go to bed, sleep.

hit the deck
1. fall heavily to the ground.
2. get out of bed; arise: e.g. He usually hits the deck at six in the morning.

hit the frog and toad
(rhyming slang) hit the road — depart, leave, go.

hit the grog
(see: hit the booze)

hit the hay
1. go to bed; retire; go to sleep.
2. go to bed for the purpose of sex.

hit the headlines
achieve notoriety, publicity and fame: e.g. She hit the headlines over that terrible murder last year.

hit the jackpot
to be extremely successful and lucky — especially after a long wait.

hit the nail on the head

hit the right note
1. say or do the correct or obvious thing.
2. sum the situation up precisely; ascertain the facts.

hit the panic button
over-react under stress.

hit the road
go; depart; leave.

hit the roof
lose one's temper; become suddenly angry.

hit the sack
got to bed to sleep; retire.

hit the skids
1. go, depart, leave quickly.
2. (of a car) apply the brakes suddenly.
3. find oneself in a very poor state of affairs — broke, destitute, penniless, out of work, homeless etc.

hit the slops
(see: hit the booze)

hit the spot
completely satisfy: e.g. That dinner hit the spot.

hit the toe/trail
go, depart, leave.

hit the ton
reach one hundred, either in a score or in speed: e.g.
1. It looks like he's going to hit the ton in this innings of the game.
2. We hit the ton on that straight stretch of road.

hit up
inject drugs: e.g. He's hitting up on heroin now.

hit-and-giggle
social game of tennis, especially among women.

hit-and-miss
1. random; casual; haphazard; careless.
2. (rhyming slang) piss.

hit-and-run
car accident in which the negligent driver leaves the scene of the accident without offering assistance in order to escape prosecution.

hitch
1. an obstruction to progress: e.g. Why the hitch?
2. a cleverly disguised trick, deception or hidden trap: e.g. That deal sounds too good to be true — what's the hitch?
3. hitchhike.
4. obtain a ride in a car with somebody: e.g. You can hitch home with one of the boys later.

hitched
1. married: e.g. We got hitched last week.
2. obtained a ride with somebody (see: hitch, 4.)
3. hitchhiked.

hitchhike
travel by seeking rides in passing vehicles without payment.

hither and dither
(also: hither and thither) this way and that; everywhere; all over the place in a confused manner.

hitting gear
heroin.

hiya!
a greeting — hello!

hobbyhorse
favourite topic; obsession: e.g. Arguing about politics is his favourite hobbyhorse.

hobnob
to associate, drink, talk with on friendly, amicable terms: e.g. His hobnobbing with the racing fraternity gets him a lot of good tips for the races.

Hobson's choice
no choice at all; one takes either the thing offered or nothing.

hock
1. pawn, mortgage (something): e.g. Many old ladies hock their jewellery for extra money to spend on bingo and the pokies.
2. sell, especially illegally, illicitly.
See also:
in hock

hocus-pocus
1. nonsense; unbelievable talk.
2. trickery; deception; fraud.
3. extravagant elaboration designed to deceive or cover up for something essentially simple.

hodge-podge
jumble; muddle; conglomeration; miscellany.

hoe into
1. commence eating heartily.
2. start work energetically and vigorously.
3. verbally attack, abuse (someone): e.g. The opposition really hoed into the Prime Minister in Parliament today.

hoedown
rustic, country party or dance.

hoffman brick
(rhyming slang) dick; penis.

hog
1. selfish, greedy person.
2. Phencyclidine — a highly dangerous hallucinogenic drug.

3. to take more than one's fair share; appropriate greedily and selfishly: e.g. He hogged all the best ones.
See also:
go the whole hog
live high on the hog

hog the limelight
strive to be the centre of attention.

hogwash
nonsense; meaningless, insincere talk; anything worthless: e.g. What a lot of hogwash that meeting was!

ho-hum
boring; plain; lacking interest: e.g. The party was very ho-hum.

hoick
1. lift, jerk or hoist abruptly: e.g. The policeman hoicked him out of the car.
2. discard; throw away unceremoniously: e.g. He hoicked it out the window.
3. spit; expectorate: e.g. I hate men who hoick on the footpath!
4. (cricket) agricultural shot (swipe).

hoist
1. a housebreaking theft.
2. steal; pilfer; shoplift.

hoity-toity
snobbish; haughty; petulant; pretentious; arrogant; supercilious.

hokey-pokey
(see: hocus-pocus)

hold
(see: Christmas hold; don't hold your breath; get a hold of oneself; have/got a hold over; no holds barred)

hold down
maintain (a job or position): e.g. He can't seem to hold down a job for more than a few months.

hold good
to be true or valid; maintain credibility: e.g. His story just doesn't hold good as far as the jury is concerned.

hold it
stop; cease; wait.

hold it in
refuse to show one's emotions or feelings.

hold off
wait; refrain from starting or doing: e.g. We'll hold off until he gets here.

hold on
1. wait! stop!
2. persist against all odds: e.g. Instead of selling out, we've decided to hold on.

hold (one's) breath
wait in anticipation.

hold (one's) own
maintain (one's) position against many odds: e.g. He may be young and inexperienced in the business but he seems to be holding his own quite well.

hold (one's) tongue
1. be quiet!; remain silent; refrain from voicing (one's) opinions.
2. keep a secret or confidence.

hold out
1. refuse to submit; stand fast; endure; persist; maintain resistance.
2. wait until an expected fee is paid.

hold (someone) to it
see that (someone) fulfils his promise, boast, obligation.

hold (someone's) hand
provide moral support; lend courage to (someone).

hold the fort
maintain the existing state of affairs, position, circumstances.

hold the line
request the other party in a telephone conversation to wait (or wait oneself).

hold the purse-strings
have the power to allocate or spend available funds.

hold the reins
be in charge.

hold the stage
be the centre of attention.

hold together
remain true, valid, sound, believable, credible: e.g. As far as the jury was concerned, his story didn't hold together.

hold up
1. to commit a robbery by threat of violence.
2. obstruct; stop; impede; delay.
See also:
hold-up

hold water
bear examination; prove valid, sound or credible.

hold with
agree; approve of: e.g. I don't hold with anything he says or does.

hold your horses/water
wait; restrain your impulses or impetuosity.

holding
pertaining to having money: e.g. How are you holding?

holding the hand out
taking advantage of government welfare; living on the dole.

holds the key
has the answers, solution: e.g. That new witness holds the key to the whole court case.

hold-up
1. a robbery committed by force and threat of violence.
2. obstruction; stoppage; delay.

hole
1. an awful, wretched place or town: e.g. That town is a hole!
2. dilemma; predicament: e.g. He's in a hole.
3. fault; defect; flaw; fallacy: e.g. His alibi has too many holes in it.
4. vagina.
5. the mouth, anus or any other aperture of the body.
See also:
fill (someone) full of holes
fill the hole in (one's) stomach
full of holes
hell-hole
made a hole in it
need it like a hole in the head
pick holes in
score a hole-in-one
watering hole

hole up
to hide, especially from the police or authorities; find shelter, refuge, retreat; hibernate.

hole-in-one
(of sexual intercourse) a direct penetration of the vagina with one thrust of the penis.

holier-than-thou
smug; sanctimonious; pompous; vain; self-righteous.

hollies
holidays.

hollow
insincere; false; meaningless; without substance, value or worth: e.g. Politicians make many hollow promises at election time.

hollow legs
pertaining to a voracious appetite: e.g. He must have hollow legs with the amount he eats!

hols
holidays.

holus-bolus
1. completely; all of it: e.g. He ate it holus-bolus.
2. all at once: e.g. The crowd tried to push through the door holus-bolus.

holy Christ!

holy cow!

holy dooley!

holy hell!

holy Jesus!

holy mackerel!

holy Moses!

holy shit!

holy snapping duck shit!
1. an oath, curse.
2. an exclamation expressing surprise, amazement, bewilderment, anger, frustration, wonder etc.

home
1. an institution for the aged, sick, homeless; reform institution for uncontrollable young people.
2. (Australian Rules football) a goal scored.
See also:
a man's home is his castle
at home with
bring home the bacon
bring home to (someone)
broken home
do (one's) homework
drive it home
eat (someone) out of house and home
feel at home
hit home
keep the home fires burning
make (oneself) at home
nail it home
nothing to write home about
on the home straight/stretch
romp home
strike home
who's he when he's at home?

home and away
(Australian Rules football) pre-finals rounds of matches.

home and dried/hosed
pertaining to a task, project, carried out or completed successfully: e.g. After all those problems we're finally home and hosed.

home away from home
any place away from home having the comforts and feelings of home.

home brew
beer brewed in one's own home.

home free
(see: home and dried)

home is where the heart is
one's true home is wherever one's affections are engaged.

home on the pig's back
certain to succeed; an easy task.

home straight/stretch
the final stage in anything; coming to the end: e.g. They're into the home straight with that building project now.

home truth
a fact that is usually disagreeable, painful, delicate: e.g. He needs to be told some home truths about what his wife gets up to when he's away on his business trips.

homebake
a form of heroin that can be manufactured at home involving the heating of pain-killing medications.

homebody
person who prefers and enjoys staying at home.

home-breaker
person (husband, wife or other) behaving in a manner that causes problems possibly ending in divorce.

homely
1. plain; unattractive.
2. warm; cosy; snug; comfortable surroundings; domestic, cheerful and inviting.

home-maker
person who works hard at creating a warm, comfortable and enjoyable home environment.

homey
(see: homely, 2.)

homo
a homosexual man.

honcho
the boss, leader: e.g. Where's the head honcho around here?

honda-head
a bikie, biker, especially one interested in Honda motorcycles.

honest as the day is long
very honest, dependable.

honest to dinkum/God
1. genuine; real: e.g. This is an honest to God antique!
2. expression or plea to be believed, taken seriously: e.g. Honest to God — I didn't do it!

honey
1. someone or thing that inspires admiration; an excellent example of its kind: e.g. That new car is a honey!
2. term of endearment: e.g. Hello honey!
See also:
milk and honey

honeybun/honeybunch
term of endearment.

honeymoon
initial period of success or enthusiasm: e.g. Now that the honeymoon's over he doesn't want to work.

honeypot
1. woman's pudendum, genitals, vagina.
2. term of endearment.
3. a dive-bomb into a swimming pool.

honk/honker
the nose.

Honkers
Hong Kong.

honky
(mainly U.S.) derog. term for a white man.

honky-tonk
1. a sleazy, cheap night-club.
2. a style of rag-time, bar-room piano playing that originated in the United States.

hoo-boy!
exclamation of wonder or relief.

hooch
1. alcohol, liquor, especially of inferior quality.
2. marijuana, pot, grass, dope.

hood
1. hoodlum; petty criminal or gangster.
2. an unsavoury, rough, destructive, anti-social teenager (or other); ratbag.

hood around
move about socially; associate with: e.g. Who's he hooding around with now?

hoodwinked
misled; cheated; tricked.

hooer
term of abuse, especially among men: e.g. Why don't you get lost, you drunken hooer!

hooey
nonsense; rubbish; lies; worthless, insincere talk.

hoof
1. the foot.
2. a kick or to kick: e.g. He needs a hoof in the arse!
3. (Australian Rules football) a long kick (also: big hoof).
See also:
on the hoof

hoof it
1. to walk.
2. go; depart; leave.
3. hurry up! move fast!

hoof off
go; depart; leave.

hooha(h)
1. (see: hooey)
2. an argument or fuss; noisy row: e.g. What's all the hoohah about?

hoojar/hoojarpiviss
temporary name for something for which one cannot immediately remember the real name.

hook
1. pilfer; steal; take without permission: e.g. He hooked that pair of sunglasses from the chemist.
2. to attract or catch someone through artifice or trickery.
3. to marry: e.g. She finally hooked him.
See also:
by hook or by crook
fall for it, hook, line and sinker
let (someone) off the hook
off the hook

hook, line and sinker
completely; totally: e.g. He went for that story we told him, hook, line and sinker.

hooked
1. addicted to; captivated by; obssessed with: e.g. She's hooked on horror movies.
2. married: e.g. I got hooked years ago!
3. cheated; tricked: e.g. You've been well and truly hooked!

hooker
prostitute.

hooks
fingers: e.g. Keep your hooks off my husband!

'Good driving, Fred — I think you gave him the slip!'

Anyone trying to give a speed-cop the slip will incur his wrath and make him very cross. He is likely to throw the book at you and slap you with a bluey. It won't help to do your block because you'll not only do your licence — you'll have to fork over a lot of fiddly-dids after you've been fined.

See also:
get (one's) hooks into
put the hooks into

hooky
(see: play hooky)

hooley
a wild party.

hooligan
a hoodlum; rowdy, tough, rough, unsavoury youth; member of a street gang.

hoon
1. (see: hooligan)
2. foolish show-off; braggart.
3. one who lives off the earnings of prostitutes.

hoop
a horse-racing jockey.
See also:
jump through the hoops
put through the hoops

hoo-ray
1. expression of pleasure, joy, applause.
2. good-bye; see you later.

hoo-roo
good-bye.

hoot
money: e.g. He needs some hoot badly to pay for a hit of heroin.
See also:
don't care a hoot
don't care two hoots
give a hoot

hoot around
play around; fool about.

hooter
the nose.

Hoover
1. a vacuum-cleaner.
2. to clean the floor with a vacuum-cleaner: e.g. I Hoover the carpet once a week. (Trademark)

hop into
1. to begin something with energy and enthusiasm: e.g. Hop into the tucker — there's plenty there.
2. (of clothes) put on: e.g. I'm going to hop into something more comfortable.
3. attack (someone) physically or verbally.

hop into bed (with)
to have casual sex (with); have sexual intercourse (with): e.g. She'll hop into bed with anybody!

hop it!
go away! get lost!

hop on the bandwagon
follow, do, copy, benefit from a currently popular, successful trend.

hop, step and jump
only a short distance: e.g. He lives only a hop, step and jump away from me.

hop to it
act quickly; get moving; start the job immediately.

hop up and down
become agitated, angry, anxious, worried.

hope against hope
to continue to hope, have faith in the face of great odds.

hopping mad
very angry.

hops
beer.

horn
an erection; an erect penis.
See also:
lock horns with (someone)
take the bull by the horns

horn in
butt in aggressively; attempt to enter into a matter, usually against the wishes of others.

hornet's nest
a potentially troublesome, hostile situation.
See also:
mad as a hornet

horny
1. sexually aroused; feel sexually excited.
2. sexual; admirable; desirable: e.g. That's a horny car!

horror
naughty, unpleasant child or person.

horror of horrors
1. exclamation of dismay, disappointment.
2. a very naughty, unpleasant child.

horrors
1. a sensation or feeling of repugnance or fear: e.g. Spiders give me the horrors!
2. the D.T.'s (delirium tremens); state of trembling, shaking, usually induced by over-indulgence in alcohol or drugs: e.g. He's got a bad case of the horrors this morning.
See also:
get the dry-horrors

horse
heroin.
See also:
backing the wrong horse
change horses in mid-stream
dark horse
dead horse
don't spare the horses
drink the piss from a brewer's horse
eat a horse and chase the rider
eat like a horse
favourite hobby-horse
flogging a dead horse
get off (one's) high horse
hold your horses
iron horse
look a gift horse in the mouth
no use shutting the stable door after the horse has bolted
on (one's) high horse
one-horse town
put the cart before the horse
straight from the horse's mouth
water the horse
wild horses couldn't keep (one) away

willing horse
work off a dead horse
workhorse

horse and cart
(rhyming slang) fart.

horse around
play, behave, foolishly or roughly.

horse feathers!
nonsense; rubbish; lies; worthless, insincere talk.

horse of another colour
something different entirely.

horse sense
common sense.

horse shoe
a symbol of good luck.

horseplay
rough, boisterous behaviour.

horsepower
1. unit of measurement of power.
2. speed; strength; power: e.g. That engine has a tremendous amount of horsepower.

horses for courses
pertaining to the belief that no person should be expected or asked to perform beyond his capabilities or talents; a person or object should be suited to the task at hand.

horse's hoof
(rhyming slang) poof; homosexual.

horse-shit
nonsense; rubbish; meaningless talk.

horse-trading
shrewd bargaining and swapping of ideas.

hostie
air-hostess.

hot
1. stolen; procured illegally: e.g. That car's hot.
2. lustful; ardent; sexually aroused: e.g. He makes me feel hot.
3. fashionable; trendy; exciting; popular: e.g. He wears some hot clothes.
4. (of motor-cars and cycles) modified and tuned for speed and performance.
5. skilful; formidable: e.g. He's hot on the guitar.
6. excellent; admirable; having high prospects or potential: e.g. That new horse is really hot!
See also:
a bit hot
blow hot and cold
crash-hot
get the hots for (someone)
go hot and cold all over
go like hot cakes
in hot water
like a cat on a hot tin roof
make it hot for (someone)
not so hot
not too hot
running hot
sell like hot cakes
shit-hot
too hot to handle

hot air
boastful talk; nonsense; rubbish; insincere talk: e.g. His speech was a lot of hot air.

hot and bothered
flustered; upset.

hot cock
(see: hot air)

hot off the press
up-to-date news.

hot on (someone's) heels

hot on the heels of

hot on the trail
following or watching closely; in close pursuit.

hot potato
anything that is so controversial, delicate, as to need tact and care in handling; a burning, controversial issue.

hot property
person or thing of high commercial value.

hot seat
1. the electric chair.
2. an awkward, difficult or dangerous position.
3. a position of responsibility.

hot spot
1. a lively night-club or place of entertainment.
2. an awkward, difficult or dangerous position.

hot stuff
1. anything exciting, excellent or worthy of attention: e.g. That new play in town is really hot stuff.
2. sexually adept, exciting person: e.g. He's hot stuff in bed!
3. pornography.

hot to trot
eager to begin, go, make a start; enthusiastic.

hot under the collar
very angry.

hot up
1. to excite, stir up, inject life and vigour into: e.g. This party needs hotting up!
2. to modify and tune the engine of a motor-car for speed and performance: e.g. He's going to hot up his old Ford.

hot water
danger; disgrace; trouble; a difficult and precarious position: e.g. You're going to get yourself into hot water if you mix with those criminals.

hotbed
place, source, favouring the growth of illicit, illegal or underhanded activities.

hot-blooded
1. virile; sexually aggressive; having strong sexual desires.
2. impetuous.

hotch-potch
(see: hodge-podge)

hot-dog
1. a bun with a saveloy or sausage and tomato-sauce.
2. exclamation of pleasure, applause, surprise, wonder.

hot-foot it
go, depart, leave in haste.

hothead
impetuous person; person easily incited to anger.

hotline
direct telephone link.

hotpants
1. person of strong sexual desires.
2. very short shorts worn by women.

hot-rod
car (generally an old one) modified for speed.

hot-shot
a very proficient, adept, skilled person in a particular field (often used in a sarcastic sense): e.g. If that hot-shot thinks he can do better then let him!

hotted-up
(of a car) modified for speed and performance.

hot-tempered
easily incited to anger.

hottie
rubber hot-water bottle to warm the bed.

hound
chase; annoy; harass: e.g. He's been hounding me to fix his car on the cheap.
See also:
keep the hounds at bay

hour of darkness
a critical, unfortunate time.

house
(see: bring the house down; built like the side of a house; like a house on fire; little house; on the house; open house; put one's own house in order; run of the house; safe as houses; the house that Jack built)

house of ill fame/repute
a brothel.

house-broken
(of domestic animals) trained not to urinate or mess in the house.

household name
famous person; film-star, personality etc. well known to everybody: e.g. Elvis Presley is a household name.

household word
familiar name or saying.

house-trained
(see: house-broken)

house-warming
a party celebrating occupancy of a new house or dwelling.

housey-housey/housie-housie
bingo — a gambling game.

how
(see: and how!)

how about it?
a blunt request for sexual intercourse.

how about that!
exclamation of triumph, irony, surprise, amazement, sarcasm etc.

how are the bots biting?

how are you?

how are you keeping?
standard form of greeting; hello.

how come?
why?

how did you make out?
1. how did you succeed, do, progress?
2. did you have sexual intercourse?

how dumb can you get?!
scornful, mocking remark about someone's stupidity, foolishness.

how it is

how things stand
the current situation, facts, status quo, state of affairs.

how would ya (you) be!?
exclamation of amazement, horror, disbelief as one imagines oneself in a certain situation: e.g. That poor family lost everything in the fire — how would ya be!?

how ya goin' mate — orright?
a standard form of greeting; hello (how are you going mate — all right?).

how-de-do
1. a form of greeting — how do you do?
2. a problem; a messy or embarrassing situation; fuss or bother; confusion.

howdy
a greeting — hello.

howler
an embarrassing blunder or mistake.

howling
an intensifier meaning extreme, glaring: e.g. 1. that was a howling mistake. 2. He's a howling idiot!

howling success
a great success; extremely popular.

how's it going?
a standard form of greeting — hello.

how's them apples?!
how do you like that?!

how's things/tricks?
a form of greeting; hello.

how's-your-father
1. a temporary name for a thing for which one cannot immediately remember the real name: e.g. Pass me that how's-your-father over there.
2. euphemism for something obscene, lewd.

howzat!?
1. an appeal for approval, admiration (how's that!).
2. (cricket) an appeal for a dismissal (how's that?).

hoy!
exclamation or shout to attract attention.
See also:
give (someone) a hoy

H.P.
hire-purchase.

hubble-bubble
a noisy confusion; fuss or bother.

hubby
husband.

huddle
a secret discussion or meeting.

huff and puff
to bluster; complain; do noisily.
See also:
in a huff

huffy
angry; irritated; annoyed; petulant; offended; sulky.

Hughie
a jocular name for God, the divine powers above, particularly in reference to the weather: e.g. Of course the weather will be good for our fishing trip — I've had a word to Hughie about it.

huh
(depending on the inflection of the voice) expression of contempt, surprise, amazement, interrogation.

hullo!
1. a form of greeting.
2. an exclamation of surprise, astonishment or discovery: e.g. Hullo! Look what I've found!

hum and ha/haw
(see: hem and haw)

humbug
1. a hard, boiled, peppermint sweet or lolly with decorative stripes.
2. a cheat; deceitful, low person.
3. nonsense; rubbish; drivel; insincere and worthless talk.

humdinger
1. exceptionally good, excellent person or thing: e.g. That band's latest record is a humdinger.
2. night-cart; sanitary-cart; dunny-cart (it used to ding a bell and the blowies following it always hummed!).

humdrum
monotonous; dull, boring routine.

humming
in a state of busy activity, productiveness, excellent progress.

hump
1. (of a man) have sexual intercourse: e.g. Who's he been humping?
2. to carry, usually on the back of the shoulders.

hump (one's) bluey/drum/swag.
(obsolete) live the life of a tramp, hobo, swaggie.

humpy
any sub-standard dwelling.

Hun
a German.

hunch
premonition; intuitive feeling.

hundred per cent
complete(ly); absolute(ly); perfect(ly); total(ly).

hundred-to-one
very slim, remote, chance or possibility.

hung
(see: well-hung)

hung, drawn and quartered
severely punished.

hung-over
suffering from the after-effects of excessive indulgence in alcohol.

hungry
acutely interested, devoted to getting, making money: e.g. She's a hungry bitch — that's why she married a millionaire.

hungry as a black dog

hungry enough to eat a horse and chase the rider
be very hungry; have a good appetite.

hung-up
1. upset; worried; anxious.
2. full of emotional anxieties, difficulties, inhibitions that reflect in one's behaviour.

hunk
sexually attractive, handsome man.

hunky-dory
splendid; excellent; all right; going well.

hunt up
look for; procure.

hurk/hurl
to vomit.

hurly/hurly-burly
confusion; commotion; uproar.

hurry-scurry
disorderly haste.

husband-beater
1. rolling-pin.
2. long, narrow loaf of bread.

hush my mouth!
expression of amazement, disbelief, wonder.

hush up
suppress the facts; keep the truth from disclosure.

hush your mouth!
a request to cease bad language; be quiet!

hush-hush
secret; highly confidential.

hush-money
a bribe.

hush-up
suppression of the facts or truth; a cover-up of the truth.

husky
(of a man) vigorous, tall, tough, strong.

hustle
1. obtain money illegally, illicitly, questionably.
2. sell aggressively; aggressive salesmanship.

hustle and bustle
energetic activity.

hustler
1. one who uses aggressive salesmanship.
2. one who gains or profits in illegal, illicit or questionable dealings.
3. one who solicits for or as a prostitute.

Hydraulics
nickname for a compulsive thief: e.g. Everyone calls him Hydraulics — he'd lift anything!

hype
1. a stimulating experience.
2. over-done publicity.
3. a drug-addict who uses hypodermic needles.

hyped up
1. over-excited; wildly enthusiastic; hyperactive; stimulated.
2. (of a car or engine) modified to improve power, speed and performance.

hyper
1. (see: hyped up, 1.)
2. nervous; on edge; anxious.

hypo
hypodermic needle.

hysterical
1. extremely funny.
2. extremely ridiculous, ludicrous.

hysterics
fits of uncontrolled laughter: e.g. That comedian had everybody in hysterics all night.

I ask you!
expression of amazement, disbelief, surprise.

I bags
I want to be first, have the first choice: e.g. I bags the blue one.

I can't, for the life of me
under no circumstances; in no way. (see: for the life of me)

I kid you not
seriously.

I say!
exclamation of wonder, surprise.

I suppose
(rhyming slang) nose.

ice
diamonds: e.g. She's covered in ice.
See also:
break the ice
cut no ice with
keep it on ice
on ice
on thin ice

iceberg
1. a cold, unemotional and reserved person.
2. a woman who refuses to bestow sexual favours.
See also:
tip of the iceberg

ice-breaker
anything that breaks down the barriers of formality, reserve: e.g. That joke was a good ice-breaker.

icing on the cake
the best part; the finishing touches: e.g. How come he gets the icing on the cake while we do the hard work?

icky
1. repulsive, offensive, disagreeable.
2. risky or dangerous position or situation: e.g. I don't think I'll do it as it sounds a bit icky to me.

icy
cold; unemotional; reserved; aloof; without feeling or warmth.

icypole
an ice confection on a stick.

ID
(pronounced: eye-dee) identification: e.g. When you go for your driver's licence you must take some ID with you.

I'd like to have that nose full of gold-dust!
said of a person with a very big nose.

identity crisis
critical point in a person's life where he has self-doubts, and questions who he is in relation to society.

idiot-board
cue card for newsreaders, announcers etc.

idiot-box
the television set: e.g. Mike's eyes are always glued to the idiot-box when the footy is on.

idiot-lights
warning lights, such as in a car dashboard or console.

idiot-sheets
instruction sheets; cue cards; operation manuals.

idle rich
people who have a great deal of money (often inherited) and thus need not worry about having to work for a living.

if brains were dynamite he wouldn't have enough to blow his nose

if brains were dynamite he wouldn't have enough to part his hair

if brains were shit he wouldn't have enough to soil his collar
(an insult) he is not very intelligent.

if bullshit was music he'd be a big brass band on his own
(an insult) he talks too much nonsense.

if he had a shit his head would cave in
an insult to someone who is dumb, stupid, not intelligent.

if he laughed his face would crack
(an insult) he always looks morose, never smiles.

if it moves shoot it, if it doesn't chop it down
(derog.) the Australian national motto, creed of the authorities, as conservationists see it.

if it was raining palaces I'd get hit on the head by a dunny door

if it was raining pea soup I'd only have a fork
to be very unlucky.

if looks could kill — I'd be dead
referring to someone who is scowling or looking at you with disdain or anger.

if she turned side-on, she'd slip through a crack in the floorboards
said of a very thin person.

if that doesn't/don't take all!
expression of amazement, disbelief.

if the cap/hat/shoe fits, wear it
if an opinion, judgement or assessment applies — accept it.

if the worst comes to the worst
if the worst happens.

if walls could speak
1. expression of one's desire to know what has occurred inside certain rooms or places while one was not present; if one could only know what was said privately one would have access to the truth, startling information etc.
2. expression of one's fear that what has occurred or been said privately could become public knowledge.

if you ask me
in my opinion (whether asked for or not): e.g. If you ask me the whole deal stinks!

if you can't be good — be careful!
a form of farewell with sexual innuendo, intimating that if one can't refuse sexual advances, then one should protect oneself with contraceptives.

if you can't beat 'em, join 'em!
if you can't do anything to change matters, circumstances or people then you might as well accept things with grace and enjoy oneself.

if you don't help yourself, no one else will
no one can help you if you are not motivated and enthusiastic yourself.

if you had a brain it would be lonely
an insult to someone who is dumb, stupid, not very intelligent.

if you play your cards right (you can't miss)
if you do the correct or expected thing, or act wisely you will reap the benefits.

if you think . . . you've got another think coming!
a refusal to comply, agree, cooperate.

if you're still in one piece
if you have emerged from a situation unscathed physically or mentally: e.g. If you're still in one piece after asking the boss for a raise, we'll celebrate at the pub.

if you've got it, flaunt it!
(joc.) if you have certain talents or physical attributes (particularly sexual) make the most of them.

iffy
1. of a questionable, dubious, suspicious or odd nature: e.g. Don't sign a contract that looks a bit iffy.
2. not sure; unable to make up one's mind: e.g. We're still a bit iffy over whether we'll sign the contract or not.

ifs or buts
excuses: e.g. I don't want to hear any ifs or buts.

ikey/ikeymo
1. cunning; devious.
2. mean; parsimonious; stingy.
3. (cap.) a Jew.

I'll be!

I'll be a monkey's uncle!

I'll be a son of a gun!

I'll be blowed/buggered!

I'll be damned/darned!

I'll be fucked!

I'll be hanged!

I'll be jiggered!

I'll be stuffed!
exclamation of surprise over something one did not expect.

I'll drink to that!
to agree, acknowledge.

I'll eat my hat
an expression declaring one's total belief in the correctness of one's own thoughts; to wager that one is absolutely sure of being right: e.g. I'll eat my hat if he can jump that high!

I'll get shot
I'll get into serious trouble.

I'll go bail!
I warrant!; I'm sure, positive!: e.g. I'll go bail you'll never see him again!

I'll go he!
an assurance of one's absolute faith in what one says: e.g. If we can't do that in a day's work, I'll go he!

I'll knock your teeth so far down your throat you'll have to stick a toothbrush up your arse to clean them!
a threat of violence.

I'll pay that
an acknowledgement that one has been outwitted or bested in repartee.

I'll pin your ears back (if you're not careful)
a threat of violence.

I'll scratch your back if you'll scratch mine
I'll help you if you help me — an offer of assistance only if benefits for oneself are offered or promised.

I'll stand fucking
(see: I'll eat my hat)

I'll tell you what
1. an offering of (one's) opinion whether it is asked for or not.
2. to offer advice: e.g. I'll tell you what — you go that way and I'll go this way.

ill-gotten gains
anything acquired deviously, illegally or by using questionable means.

I'm all right Jack!
a sarcastic remark of selfish complacency.

I'm easy
a statement of one's casual indifference — it makes no difference to me.

immense
very good; great; wonderful; splendid: e.g. What an immense idea!

imp
naughty child.

impossible
outrageous; intolerable: e.g. He's impossible!

in
1. modern; fashionable; stylish; currently popular: e.g. This summer, the mini-skirt is in.
2. (of a player) having the right of turn to play.
3. placed at the end of a particular activity, 'in' denotes a communal participation: e.g. sleep-in; sit-in; eat-in.
See also:
all in
be in it
count (someone) in
do (oneself) in
dob in
dob (someone) in
don't go in much for
drop (someone) in
fill (someone) in
get sucked in
go in for
had (one) in
hand (someone) in
have/got an in with
have/got it in for (someone)
have/got it in (one)
keep in with (someone)
nothing in it
pull in
put (someone) in
well in with
well-in

in a bad/good light
in bad/good favour: e.g. That won't be viewed in a good light by the board of directors.

in a bad way
poor condition of health, prosperity etc.

in a big way
on a large scale; lavishly.

in a bind
in trouble, difficulties; in a predicament or dilemma.

in a brace of shakes
immediately.

in a dither
flustered; confused; in a state of panic.

in a fashion
in a mediocre, passable manner.

in a fix
in a difficult predicament, situation, circumstance, from which there appears to be little hope of escape.

in a flap
(see: in a dither)

in a hole/jam
(see: in a fix)

in a huff
angry; petulant; sulky; offended; resentful.

in a jiff/jiffy
quickly; in a very short time: e.g. I'll be there in a jiff.

in a knot
1. in a predicament, difficult situation; having problems.
2. confused, worried, anxious: e.g. Don't get yourself in such a knot — everything will work out okay.

in a manner of speaking
so-so; in a fashion.

in a mix
confused and having problems, worries, troubles.

in a nutshell
in brief; exactly; the meaning or crux in a minimum of words: e.g. you just said it in a nutshell!

in a pickle
(see: in a knot)

in a rut
in a fixed and unpleasant pattern of behaviour or living that is difficult to change: e.g. He's moving to another town and a new job because he's been in a rut all his life here.

in a shit
1. angry; upset; irritated; annoyed.
2. petulant; sulky; resentful.

in a spin
confused; agitated; excited.

in a spot of bother
in a difficult predicament or some form of trouble.

in a state
in an agitated or excited mental or emotional condition: e.g. Ever since his wife took ill yesterday he's been in a state.

in a tick
(see: in a jiff)

in a tight corner
in an awkward, embarrassing, difficult situation or predicament: e.g. She's been in a tight corner financially since she lost that contract.

in a tizz
(see: in a dither)

in a word
to summarise; briefly: e.g. In a word, you stink!

in a world of (one's) own
(see: in another world)

in and out like a fiddler's elbow
1. in an agitated, ineffective or useless manner.
2. pertaining to sexual intercourse and the movement of the penis.

in another world
out of touch with other people; insular; totally involved with (oneself) and what (one) is doing.

in bad with
out of favour with: e.g. He's in bad with the wife for coming home so late last night.

in big with
to be highly favoured (by someone): e.g. He's in big with the boss.

in black and white
in writing: e.g. Make sure you get him to sign in black and white.

in business
successfully operating, performing: e.g. We're in business now!

in calf
(of a cow) pregnant.

in charge of the purse-strings
to have the power to spend or allocate available funds.

in cloudland
in a dream-like state; not concentrating.

in clover
luxury; comfort; financially sound: e.g. Since he won all that money he's been in clover.

in cold blood
deliberately; without emotion: e.g. He was murdered in cold blood.

in deep

in deep water

in dire straits
in serious trouble; in a serious predicament, such as considerable debt.

in droves
in great numbers.

in fine feather
fit; healthy; full of vitality and spirit.

in fits
uncontrolled laughter; absolute merriment and hilarity: e.g. Joan and I spent hours in fits collecting sayings for this book.

in fits and starts
irregularly.

in for
about to be involved, about to undergo — especially something unpleasant: e.g. 1. He doesn't know what he's in for! 2. He's in for a few nasty surprises!

in for a penny, in for a pound
to go all the way; commit oneself entirely; be impetuous.

in for a rude awakening
about to be the recipient of an unpleasant truth or fact.

in for it
about to be punished or face some unpleasant consequences: e.g. You really are in for it this time!

in for (one's) chop
claim, or always ready to claim (one's) share: e.g. Since he died all the relatives have been in for their chop.

in for (one's) cut
participate with expectations of sharing in profits, gains.

in for the kill
act, move to completely defeat, overwhelm, embarrass one's opponent.

in full cry
1. in hot pursuit: e.g. There were five police-cars chasing him in full cry through the winding back streets.
2. (shouting, talking, espousing, lauding, bragging etc.) noisily, loudly, vehemently: e.g. Politicians in full cry are a wonder to behold!

in full feather
(see: in fine feather)

in full force
with everyone present: e.g. The club was there in full force.

in full swing
operating at peak efficiency; fully and energetically active: e.g. The party was in full swing by the time we arrived.

in God knows when
for a long time: e.g. I haven't been to church in God knows when!

in good form
1. operating at peak efficiency.
2. up to one's usual tricks, pranks, jocular behaviour, argumentative manner: e.g. My husband was in good form at the party as usual.

in good hands
in the care of someone reliable and trustworthy.

in good nick
1. in good condition: e.g. For an old car, it's still in good nick.
2. in good health: e.g. He's in good nick for his age.

in good time
1. eventually: e.g. The pain will stop in good time.
2. early: e.g. We arrived in good time.

in good with (someone)
in favour with (someone): e.g. He's trying to get in good with the boss so that he can ask for a raise.

in heaven
in an extremely pleasant, enjoyable state of well-being; totally happy: e.g. He's been in heaven since he met that girl.

in high places
in upper levels of society, government, business, organisations etc.: e.g. He'll be rubbing shoulders with people in high places now that he's been promoted.

in hock
1. pawned.
2. in debt.

in hot water
(see: in deep water)

in irons
imprisoned or to imprison: e.g. They'll put him in irons for what he's done.

in it
profitable; of advantage for: e.g. What's in it for me if I do what you ask?
See also:
be in it

in it for kicks
involved in an activity for fun, pleasure, stimulation rather than profit.

in it up to (one's) ears/ eyeballs/neck
totally embroiled, implicated, involved.

in kind
in goods or payment other than money: e.g. You can pay me back in kind.

in like a lion, out like a lamb
to be deflated, belittled or humbled after the failure of a daring or boastful act.

in like Flynn
quick to act, and usually successful (especially in sexual matters).

in luck
experience, be the recipient of an excellent opportunity, good luck or fortune: e.g. You're in luck — there's one seat left on the plane!

in mid-stream
at a critical stage; well after the start of something: e.g. You can't change your mind in mid-stream!

in milk
(of a cow) lactating.

in no time

in nothing flat
very quickly; immediately: e.g. He'll be here in no time.

in on
1. to be willing to undergo, participate in some activity: e.g. Are you in on the deal or not?
2. having or sharing a knowledge about something secret, clandestine, that not many others know about: e.g. The police are in on several drug-dealing gangs and are waiting for the right moment to make a bust.
See also:
let (someone) in on

in one ear and out the other
1. heard but not comprehended or understood.
2. passed unheeded; deliberately ignored.

in one fell swoop

in one hit
all at once: e.g. He ate the lot in one hit.

in (one's) blood
be an essential part of (one's) personality, make-up, desires: e.g. Car racing is in his blood.

in (one's) book
in (one's) opinion: e.g. In my book, he's the best footy player there ever was!

in (one's) element
in circumstances completely suiting (one): e.g. One isn't in one's element swimming in shark-infested waters.

in (one's) hands
in (one's) power; under (one's) responsibility: e.g. The business is in his hands now that his father is dead.

in (one's) heart of hearts
in (one's) innermost feelings, emotions, opinions.

in plain language
(see: plain English)

in pocket
1. having made a profit after some form of transaction, deal.

2. to have money, be financial: e.g. He's in pocket — he's just been paid.

in possession of (one's) faculties
sane, lucid.

in season
fertile; broody.

in seventh heaven
in an extremely elated, happy, joyful state of physical and mental well-being.

in short order
quickly; promptly.

in so many words
unequivocably; explicitly.

in (someone's) bad books/ black book
out of favour with (someone).

in (someone's) clutches
under (someone's) control, power.

in (someone's) good books
in favour with (someone).

in step
in harmony; conforming.

in stitches
in a state of uncontrollable laughter: e.g. The audience was kept in stitches all night by that comedian.

in strife
in trouble.

in the air
about, likely to happen; a coming event: e.g. Spring is in the air — I just saw a butterfly!

in the altogether
in the nude; naked: e.g. We went swimming in the altogether.

in the bad
in debt.

in the bad books
out of favour: e.g. I'm really in the bad books with the boss now!

in the bag
assured of success: e.g. The deal is definitely in the bag.

in the big league
important; influential; high-up; in the upper levels of society, business, government etc.

in the black
having no debts; solvent: e.g. After a bad year, the business is doing well and we're in the black again.

in the blink of an eye
very quickly; in no time at all; immediately.

in the bollocky/buff
nude; naked: e.g. We went swimming in the bollocky.

in the box seat
in the most favourable, successful, powerful position.

in the cactus
in trouble; in a difficult predicament.

in the can
1. in prison.
2. assured of success.
3. completed successfully.

in the chair
1. be next in turn to buy, shout a round of drinks.
2. be in a position of responsibility.
3. be in a difficult situation; be in a predicament, trouble.

in the chips
wealthy; rich; financial.

in the chute
(see: in the pipe-line)

in the clear
innocent; free of blame; law-abiding: e.g. The police questioned him but decided he was in the clear.

in the clink
in prison.

in the cold
neglected; uninformed: e.g. I'm always in the cold as far as his business is concerned — he never tells me anything.

in the cooler
in prison.

in the cot
1. in bed.
2. pertaining to sexual intercourse: e.g. Have you had her in the cot yet?

in the dark
uninformed.

in the dogbox/doghouse
in disgrace; out of favour; in trouble with someone: e.g. He's in the doghouse because he came home drunk.

in the doldrums
miserable; unhappy; sad; depressed; gloomy.

in the drink
in the water (such as the sea, a swimming pool etc): e.g. I was thrown in the drink with all my clothes on!

in the dumps
(see: in the doldrums)

in the eye of the storm
in the centre of a troublesome or bad situation.

in the eyes of
in the opinion, view of: e.g. In the eyes of the law he's a criminal.

in the family way
pregnant.

in the fast lane
at a hectic pace: e.g. Since being promoted, he's been living life in the fast lane.

in the firing-line
in the centre of a controversy: e.g. Politicians often find themselves in the firing-line.

in the flesh
in person: e.g. I met him in the flesh.

in the game
1. in the business of prostitution: e.g. She's been in the game for years.
2. (Australian Rules football) playing well.

in the good books
in favour: e.g. I'm in the good books again because I spent the day mowing lawns.

in the grip of the grape
an alcoholic addicted to wine; a wino.

in the groove
1. trendy; fashionable; chic.
2. in a state of euphoric happiness or satisfaction.

in the guts
in the middle, centre.

in the hot seat
(see: hot seat)

in the know
1. having inside information and knowledge; aware of a secret or a matter in question: e.g. Are your parents in the know about you smoking dope?
2. completely familiar with; having all the required information for proficiency and expertise: e.g. I need somebody in the know to help me restore an antique car.

in the land of the living
1. actually alive.
2. conscious and in full control of one's mind and body.

in the lap of luxury
living in luxurious, opulent conditions.

in the lap of the gods
in the hands of fate; unknown: e.g. Whether it rains or not is in the lap of the gods — it sure isn't in the hands of the weather bureau!

in the light of
because of; owing to.

in the limelight
at the centre of attention, public exposure and publicity.

in the long run
eventually; finally, after all else: e.g. Everything will work out fine in the long run.

in the main
mostly: e.g. In the main, he's not a bad bloke.

in the market for
wanting to purchase: e.g. He's in the market for antique cars.

in the middle of nowhere
in a very remote, sparsely populated area or place: e.g. He lives out in the middle of nowhere.

in the middle of things
actively engaged, employed, doing: e.g. I can't stop to answer the phone right when I'm in the middle of things!

in the miseries
1. sick; ill; not well.
2. in a wretched, depressed state of mind or circumstances.

in the money
wealthy; rich; financial.

in the muck
in trouble; in a difficult or embarrassing predicament or situation.

in the name of
under the authority and recognition of; in recognition of: e.g. All nations should put down their nuclear arms and work together in the name of peace.

in the name of God!
expression of complete exasperation, frustration: e.g. In the name of God — will you shut up!

in the neighbourhood of
approximately: e.g. That car costs in the neighbourhood of a hundred thousand dollars.

in the nellie/nelly/nick
nude; naked: e.g. He ran down the crowded street in the nelly!

in the nick of time
just in time before it is too late: e.g. He was pulled out of the shark-infested water in the nick of time.

in the nud/nuddy
nude; naked.

in the offing
likely to happen; probable.

in the palm of (one's) hand
under (one's) power or control: e.g. She's got him in the palm of her hand.

in the pen
in prison.

in the picture
understand; be aware of the facts of a matter; informed: e.g. You had better tell me what happened as I'm not in the picture yet.

in the piece
in the (pertinent) matter, situation: e.g. It's a bit late in the piece to complain now!
See also:
earlier
early in the piece

in the pink
becoming free of debt (but not entirely): e.g. Instead of being in the red like we were last month, we're in the pink this month.

in the pipe-line
in readiness; beginning; ready to start, go, happen.

in the poo
in trouble or difficulty, especially financial.

in the poor-house
destitute; broke; having no money.

in the public eye
well known; famous; well publicised.

in the pudding club
pregnant.

in the raw
nude; naked.

in the red
in debt or financial difficulties.

in the right
correct; innocent; having truth and justice on one's side: e.g. The other party has to pay for the damages to my car in the accident because I was in the right.

in the right place at the right time
to be in the position to seize and act upon an opportunity.

in the running
having a good chance of success: e.g. I think he's in the running for winning the election.

in the same boat
sharing a predicament: e.g. We're all in the same boat — we never seem to have enough money!

in the same league
as good as; as proficient, skilled, adept as; equal: e.g. That team won't win — they're not in the same league as the opposition!

in the same vein
similarly; like; alike.

in the shit/soup
in serious trouble: e.g. Ron's in the shit with Lyn because he came home as drunk as a skunk last night.

in the silk (department)
in an extremely advantageous, prosperous position.

in the slightest
at all: e.g. I'm not worried in the slightest.

in the spotlight
(see: in the limelight)

in the sticks
in remote, sparsely populated areas; in the bush.

in the swim
actively engaged, operating; doing successfully.

in the thick of
in the centre of a controversy, predicament, situation: e.g. Every time my parents have an argument I end up in the thick of it because I take Mum's side.

in the throes of
totally involved in; struggling with: e.g. Fleeb's in the throes of inventing some crazy new gadget.

in the twinkling of an eye
in an instant; quickly.

in the wars
involved in a series of minor injuries, misfortunes, arguments etc.: e.g. I've really been in the wars this month — first I broke my arm, then I did my back in, and yesterday the dog died!

in the wee small hours
very early in the morning.

in the wind
1. circulating as a rumour.
2. about, likely to happen; probable.

in the wings
waiting in readiness in the background.

in the world
1. anywhere: e.g. He's the best in the world.
2. ever: e.g. Where in the world did you get that dress?

in the wrong
to blame; responsible for a quarrel, offence or error; guilty.

in the year dot
a long time ago: e.g. He was elected president of the club in the year dot.

in touch with
sympathetic; in agreement with; having personal knowledge of: e.g. Some politicians are not in touch with the needs of the general public.

in tow
in attendance; following one around; under one's guidance: e.g. I've got my little brother in tow for the weekend.

in trouble
pregnant out of marriage: e.g. Her daughter is in trouble and the bloke has disappeared.

in two minds about (something)
undecided: e.g. I'm still in two minds about whether to go or not.

in two shakes (of a dog's tail)

in two ticks
in a very short time: e.g. I'll be there in two shakes.

in with
friendly with; on favourable terms with: e.g. He's in with some of the worst criminals in town!

in writing
in written form so as to be legal and binding.

in your boot!
1. an insult; expression of scorn, contempt, dismissal.
2. be quiet! shut up!

in-and-out
sexual intercourse.

inch
(see: by inches; every inch; every inch of the way; give someone an inch and she'll/he'll take a mile; within an inch of)

inch by inch
by small degrees.

incog
incognito; in disguise.

Indian file
single file (of people in a line).

Indian giver
one who later takes or demands back a gift he has given.

indulge
to drink alcohol, usually in excessive amounts.

inferiority complex
a feeling of inadequacy, incompetency, inferiority: e.g. She's got an inferiority complex about wearing bikinis.

infighting
conflicts and struggles for power within an organisation, among its members: e.g. The Labor Party loses a great deal of public support because of its infighting.

info
information: e.g. What's the latest info on that story?

infra dig
beneath one's dignity.

in-house
pertaining to something that is relevant only to members of a household, club, group of people etc. — such as a joke that is not understood by others.

in-joke
(see: in-house) understood only by a certain group of people, members etc.

Injun
an American Indian.

inked
drunk; intoxicated; inebriated.

in-laws
relatives by marriage.

innards
entrails; gizzards.

innings
opportunity or turn at doing something; career, position: e.g. He's had a good innings in politics and now feels it's time to retire.
See also:
had a good/long innings

innocent as a cat in a goldfish bowl
guilty; not innocent at all.

in-out-in-out
sexual intercourse.

ins and outs
workings of; intricacies of; details: e.g. He really knows the ins and outs of that business.
See also:
nosey enough to want to know the ins and outs of a chook's bum

insane
1. a wild confusion, imbroglio.
2. great; wonderful; splendid: e.g. That concert was insane!

insect
a contemptible, despicable person.

inside
in prison: e.g. He's been inside for five years.
See also:
on the inside

inside info/information
private knowledge about a situation; information not usually accessible to non-members: e.g. The police managed to get inside info on that gang's activities which led to some arrests.

inside job
a crime committed by a person who is employed by the organisation against which the crime was committed.

inside out
thoroughly; intimately: e.g. He knows his job inside out.

insider
a member or close associate of a group or organisation that is inaccessible to others.

insides
intestines; entrails; stomach.

intercom
intercommunication system.

interested in only one thing
usually said indignantly by a woman about a man who has sex as his prime objective.

in-thing
modern; fashionable; currently popular; trendy: e.g. This dress isn't exactly the in-thing, but I like it.

into
enthusiastic about; interested in; be absorbed in thought and action with something: e.g. She's really into health foods.

into thin air
lost; disappear; out of reach: e.g. Our savings seem to have gone into thin air.

intro
introduction: e.g. Will you give me an intro to that gorgeous friend of yours?

invertebrate
person of little strength of character; weak-willed; spineless.

inverted snob
person whose snobbery takes the form of an emphatically claimed allegiance with the poor and needy instead of the rich, wealthy and influential.

invest in
spend money: e.g. I need to invest in some new clothes.

invite
an invitation: e.g. Did you get an invite to the party?

I.O.U.
(I owe you) a written confirmation of a debt.

I.Q.
intelligence quotient; measure or level of intelligence, cleverness:

e.g. He hasn't got a very high I.Q. if he can't work that out!

Irish
(see: get one's Irish up; luck of the Irish)

Irish curtains
cobwebs that gather in the corners of windows.

Irish luck
ridiculously good luck or fortune that seems against all odds.

iron
unyielding; strong; adamant; tough; stern: e.g. He's got an iron will to succeed.
See also:
have/got several irons in the fire
in irons
rule with a rod of iron
strike while the iron's hot
talk the legs off an iron pot
too many irons in the fire

Iron Age
any period of degeneracy or evil.

Iron Curtain
a physical and political barrier dividing East Germany from West Germany.

iron hand
strict; ruthless: e.g. He rules that country with an iron hand.

iron horse
train; locomotive.

iron horses couldn't drag/ keep (one) away
for no reason will (one) fail to attend.

iron lung
an Esky — a portable ice-box used mainly to keep beer cold, also jocularly termed a 'survival kit'.
See also:
wouldn't work in an iron lung

iron maiden
a particularly difficult, strict, severe woman.

iron man
man of exceptional strength or athletic ability.

iron (oneself) out
get drunk, totally intoxicated.

iron out a few wrinkles
to resolve any difficulties, problems or misunderstandings.

iron (something/someone) out
1. bash, hit, fight and defeat (someone).
2. put matters straight; smooth out, resolve, misunderstandings or difficulties.

iron underpants
(of women) girdles; step-ins; figure-control underpants.

iron-clad
absolutely safe; unalterable; rigid: e.g. He's got an iron-clad alibi as to where he was that night.

iron-fisted
1. ruthless; cruel; merciless; severe.
2. parsimonious; miserly; mean; stingy.

iron-handed
(see: iron-fisted, 1.)

iron-pants
sexually unobtainable woman; woman who will not bestow sexual favours.

irons
(prison) chains.

irrits
(see: give one the screaming irrits)

is it a goer?
1. is it going to proceed, happen, as planned?: e.g. Is that party still a goer for tomorrow night?
2. does it work, operate, function?: e.g. Is that antique car a goer?

is it a he or a she?
is it a man or a woman?

Is the Pope a Catholic? Do bears shit in the woods?
stock reply to someone who asks a question to which the answer is obviously yes.

isn't it a small world!
an expression of surprise, pleasure at meeting someone, seeing something where one did not expect to.

isn't that the living end!
an expression of contempt, disgust, frustration.

it
1. sex appeal: e.g. She just hasn't got it.
2. sexual intercourse: e.g. Did you get it last night?
3. showing a lack of definite sexuality in terms of being either male or female; transvestite or trans-sexual: e.g. He's an it!
4. the perfect person or thing (sarcastically): e.g. He really thinks he's it!
5. chosen; selected: e.g. We need a good man for this job, and you're it!
See also:
all for it
asking for it
at it again
blew it
crack it
for it
get it
get it off with (someone)
get it together
have it off
have it out
have/got it coming to (one)
have/got it in for (someone)
have/got it in (one)
have/got it made
if you've got it, flaunt it
in for it
in it for (someone)

made it
make it
out of it
out to it
pack it
past it
take it
what about it?
with-it

it all boils down to
after all the facts have been considered, one fact is glaring or obvious.

it all hinges on
everything depends on.

it and a bit
perfect; exceptional (often in a sarcastic sense) : e.g. He thinks he's it and a bit!

it never rains but it pours
things seem to happen all at once.

it pays to advertise
(see: pays to advertise)

it takes one to know one
(see: takes one to know one)

it takes two to tango
(see: takes two to tango)

itch
sexual urge, desire.
See also:
seven-year itch

itchy feet
having a strong desire to travel.

itchy palm
having a desire for money; greed; avarice.

Itie
an Italian person or thing.

it's a crying shame
regrettable; disappointing.

it's a dog-eat-dog world
life is extremely competitive and only the strong and tough survive and prosper.

it's a goer
1. it is definitely going to proceed, happen.
2. it is in working order, operative, sound.

it's a man's world
(of the belief of women) a world, society in which the best opportunities are denied to women.

it's a small world
pertaining to the belief that no matter how far one travels one eventually meets people or sees things one knows.

it's a take
this situation is a fraud, con, deception, swindle.

it's all right for you!
petulant, sarcastic remark directed to someone in a better position than oneself.

it's all settled
everything has been decided, definitely arranged.

it's either a feast/flood or a famine
pertaining to the belief that either nothing happens or too much happens at once.

it's not the done thing
it is not the socially accepted thing to do.

it's not the end of the world
the situation is not as bad as you think.

it's on the cards
it is likely to happen, probable.

it's sweet
it is satisfactory, all right, okay, acceptable.

it's the done thing
it is the socially acceptable thing to do.

it's the thought that counts
a consoling statement to someone, when the outcome of an action has not been successful or as intended, to the effect that it's the intention behind the action which is important.

it's times like these you need Minties!
an expression of exasperation, frustration (from an advertising slogan for Minties sweets).

it's you
it is definitely reflective of your character, personality: e.g. I love that dress — it's you to a T!

it's your funeral
if anything goes wrong it's your fault and you must bear the unpleasant consequences.

it's your pigeon
it's your responsibility.

itsy-bitsy
very small; tiny; a tiny amount.

I.U.D.
intra-uterine device; a contraceptive device for women.

I've had it!
1. expression of complete frustration, exasperation, having reached the limit of one's tolerance.
2. I'm completely exhausted, tired, worn out.

I've seen better heads on a glass of beer
an insult about someone you consider to have an ugly face.

ivories
1. the teeth.
2. keyboard of a piano.
3. the game of pool, billiards or related games.
See also:
tickle the ivories.

ivory tower
seclusion, imaginary or otherwise, from the harsh and unpleasant realities of the world: e.g. Since the failure of that project, he's been sitting in his ivory tower refusing to see anyone.

J
marijuana.
See also:
Mary J

jab
an injection with a hypodermic needle.

jabber
idle talk, gossip, palaver.

jabberwocky
nonsense; rubbish; drivel; inconsequential talk.

jack
1. man, guy, fellow; general name used in greeting between men.
2. venereal disease: e.g. He's got the jack.
See also:
all work and no play makes Jack a dull boy
bugger you Jack, I'm all right!
I'm all right Jack!
the house that Jack built

jack of
fed up with; totally exasperated with; sick and tired of: e.g. I'm jack of this job!

jack off
(especially of a man) masturbate.

jack up
1. raise the price of suddenly and unexpectedly.
2. become indignant and refuse to cooperate; revolt (against): e.g. It's about time everyone jacked up about the spiralling cost of living.
3. refuse; resist: e.g. Next time he asks me to do heavy work like that I'll jack up!

jackass
1. fool; idiot; ineffective and incompetent person.
2. kookaburra.

jackeroo
apprentice worker on a sheep or cattle station.

jackie/jacky
1. kookaburra.
2. nickname for an Aborigine.
See also:
work like Jackie

Jackie/Jacky Howe
the standard navy-blue or black singlet worn by workers, labourers, farmers etc.

jack-in-the-box
person who can't seem to sit still.

jack-of-all-trades
person who can do many different things but specialises in none.

jackpot
1. large (especially accumulated) prize from a lottery, poker machine etc.
2. to accumulate by the amount of the unclaimed prize: e.g. As there were no winners in this week's lottery, the prize-money will jackpot by that amount for next week.
See also:
hit the jackpot

jackshay
tin pot used for brewing tea in the outback.

jade
a hussy, flirt, slut.

jag
1. (cap.) Jaguar car.
2. a spree (especially a drinking spree).

jail-bait
(see: gaol . . .)

jake
Okay; all right; satisfactory; acceptable: e.g. She'll be jake!

jalopy
dilapidated old car.

jam
difficult, awkward, embarrassing position, predicament or situation: e.g. I'm in a bit of a jam and need some help.
See also:
put on jam
toe jam

jam session
impromptu, spontaneous musical activity with whatever people, skills and instruments are at hand.

'It could be serious. This mob of galahs wouldn't be on a fun run — the pub must be out of beer!'

Without doubt, the fastest way to disperse a crowd at a pub, function or party is to announce that there is no beer or booze left. This is sure to make every man and his dog beat it, bugger off, buzz off, fuck off, hit the frog and toad, make a move, piss off, scarper, scram, shoot through, split, take a powder, take off like a larrikin's hat in the breeze, vamoose or vanish into thin air.

jam tart
(rhyming slang) heart; sweet-heart.

jam tart attack
(rhyming slang) heart attack.

jamies
(see: jarmies)

jam-jars
eye-glasses, prescription spectacles that are very thick and solid-looking; a nick-name for a person wearing them.

jammed in/jam-packed
over-crowded; filled to capacity: e.g. The theatre was jam-packed on opening-night.

jangle (one's) nerves
upset; irritate; annoy: e.g. Music played so loud that one can't speak jangles my nerves.

Jap
1. a Japanese person.
2. Japanese: e.g. Australia imports Jap cars.

Jap crap
Japanese manufactured items of dubious quality.

Japanese bladder
need to urinate frequently.

Japanese riding boots
thongs (particularly worn to horse riding).

Japanese safety shoes
thongs.

jargon
1. nonsense; rubbish; foolish and meaningless talk.
2. any writing or speech so full of technical terms as to be difficult to understand.

jarmies
(also: jamies) pyjamas; night dress.

jaw hit the floor
to be very surprised, astonished, wide-mouthed with wonder: e.g. My jaw hit the floor when she walked in with him!

jawboning
1. incessant, boring, tedious talk or lecturing.
2. gossiping at length.

jaw-breaker
1. a large, difficult sweet or lolly.
2. word that is difficult to pronounce.

Jay-cee
Jesus Christ.

Jay-dub
Jehovah's Witness.

jay-walking
careless and illegal manner of crossing a street against lights or traffic direction.

jazz
1. spirit; gaiety; energy; vivaciousness.
2. nonsense; rubbish; pretentious talk; drivel.
See also:
and all that jazz

jazz up
inject life, vigour, brightness, colour etc. into; enhance; improve: e.g. Now that we've got some extra money we're going to jazz up the house.

jazzy
1. excellent; first-class: e.g. That's a very jazzy restaurant.
2. swinging; lively; spirited; active: e.g. What a jazzy party that was.
3. loud; vividly coloured; showy; flashy; garish: e.g. What's that jazzy car he's driving now?

J.C.
Jesus Christ (often used in sarcasm): e.g. Who the hell does he think he is — J.C.?

jeepers/jeepers creepers!
exclamation of frustration, amazement, disbelief, surprise, disappointment etc. e.g. Jeepers! Did you see that?

jees!
(also: geez!; jeez! see: jeepers!)

jeezus!
(adulteration of: Jesus) (see: jeepers!)

Jekyll-and-Hyde
(of a person) having markedly good and bad personality traits.

jell
come together; take definite form: e.g. Once we get ourselves more organised, the whole project will finally jell.

jelly
gelignite — a form of explosive.
See also:
turn to jelly

jellyfish
coward; weakling; person lacking in courage or moral strength.

jerk
1. fool; idiot; dolt.
2. disliked person.

jerk off

jerkin' the gherkin
1. to masturbate (especially of men).
2. delude oneself; deceive oneself: e.g. He's jerking off if he thinks that idea will actually work.

jerk-off
a fool, idiot.

jerry
1. a German person; of German origin or make.
2. chamber-pot; piss-pot: e.g. I use a jerry because I don't like using the outside toilet at night.
3. shoddy; cheap; second-rate; unskilled: e.g. I wouldn't get that jerry builder to do my place.
See also:
full as the family jerry

jerry to
to be suddenly wise, alert to: e.g. It was some time before I jerried to who he was.

jerry-built
(of a house, building etc.) of shoddy, inferior, cheap and unsound construction.

Jesus (Christ)!
an exclamation of frustration, surprise, indignation, annoyance, amazement etc.
See also:
since Jesus Christ played fullback for Jerusalem

Jesus-freak
fanatically religious (often not of the established churches).

jet set
the wealthy and elite who have the means to travel by plane all over the world in pursuit of pleasure.

Jets
Newtown N.S.W. Rugby League football team.

jew
(derog.) person of miserly, mean, stingy manner: e.g. That bloody jew wouldn't shout if a shark bit him!
See also:
off like a Jew's foreskin

jiff/jiffy
a very short time; quickly; no time at all: e.g. We'll be there in a jiff.

jiffy bag
strong lightweight bag for sending items through the post.

jig is up
the game, activity, enterprise (especially illicit) is over, indicating that one has been caught out.

jig-a-jig
sexual intercourse.

jigger
1. name for something for which one cannot immediately remember the correct name: e.g. Pass me that jigger over there.
2. the penis.
3. break; ruin; destroy; spoil: e.g. Don't touch or you'll jigger it for good!

jiggered
1. broken; ruined; spoiled.
2. exhausted; tired; worn-out.
3. dead.

jigglers
1. tea-bags.
2. breasts.

jilleroo
female jackeroo (see: jackeroo).

jim-dandy
any person or thing that is first-rate, excellent, wonderful.

jiminy (cricket)!
a mild exclamation of surprise, wonder.

jimjams
extreme nervousness, tension, worry, fright.

jimmies/Jimmy Brit(t)s
(rhyming slang) shits; state of anger, anxiety: e.g. He's got the Jimmy Britts because he lost his money at the Casino.

Jimmy Dancer
(rhyming slang) cancer.

Jimmy Woodser
a lone drinker in a bar, or an alcoholic drink taken without company.

jingoes!
mild exclamation of surprise, wonder.

jink
(rugby) manoeuvre, change direction.

jinx
1. a person or thing believed to bring bad luck.
2. to bring bad luck, curse someone with misfortune.

jinxed
plagued by bad luck or misfortune.

jissum
(see: gism)

jitterbug
nervous, tense, anxious, worried person.

jitters
nerves; tension; anxiety; worry: e.g. Exams give most students the jitters.

jittery
nervous; tense; anxious; worried.

jive
1. nonsense; rubbish; insincere and worthless talk: e.g. Don't give me that jive!
2. to tease jokingly.

job
1. a difficult task: e.g. He's going to have a job finishing that on time!
2. a crime, such as a robbery.
3. hit, bash, punch (someone).
4. the act of defecating: e.g. He jobbed in his pants!
See also:
bag over the head job
blow-job
devil's own job
do a job on (someone)
get on with the job
have/got a job in front of (one)
head-job
just the job
make a good job of
on the job
paper-bag job

job (someone) one
hit, punch, bash (someone).

jock
1. a jockstrap — worn by sportsmen to support their genitals.
2. (cap.) nickname for a Scottish man.

jockeys/jocks
tight-fitting briefs for men (TM Jockey Int., Inc.)
See also:
jock

joe
1. ewe; female sheep.
2. man; bloke; fellow: e.g. He's not such a bad joe.
See also:
give (one) the joes
sloppy joe

Joe Blake
(rhyming slang) snake.

Joe Bloggs/Blow
1. the average citizen, man in the street.
2. fictitious person, used as an example.

Joe Hunt
(rhyming slang) cunt.

joes
1. shaking; trembling; the D.T.'s — usually from excessive amounts of alcohol.
2. depression; the blues: e.g. He's had a bad case of the joes since his wife died.

joey
baby kangaroo.

jog (someone's) memory
incite (someone) to remember.

john
1. a policeman.
2. the toilet.
See also:
dear John
long johns

John Citizen
the average man in the street.

John Hop/Hopper
(rhyming slang) cop; copper; policeman.

Johnny
nickname for any youth, man, fellow.
See also:
little Johnny

johnny-cake
damper, bread cakes the size of scones.

Johnny-come-lately
a recent arrival.

join the club!
ironic exclamation indicating that the recipient is only experiencing what the speaker has already experienced: e.g. So you've finally seen through Gary — join the club!

join the lonely-hearts' club
find oneself alone after the break-up of a marriage or relationship.

join the queue!
ironic, exasperated etc. expression to another indicating that you are both waiting for the same thing or both have the same purpose: e.g. So you're trying to get your money back from Nick, too — join the queue!

join up
enlist for military service.

joint
1. house; place of abode: e.g. He's got a nice joint.
2. sleazy, disreputable place, night-club, place of entertainment: e.g. I wouldn't be seen dead in that joint!
3. a marijuana cigarette.
See also:
double-jointed
nose out of joint

joke
a fiasco; ridiculous situation, thing or person; disappointing: e.g. The meeting was a joke — nothing was achieved.
See also:
beyond a joke
broad joke
can't take a joke
in-joke
stick that for a joke!
the joke's on (someone)
what a joke!

joke Joyce!
a consoling exclamation to someone who missed the intended humour in something you said.

joker
1. bloke; fellow; person.
2. funny, amusing person.

jollies
sexual excitement, gratification: e.g. He gets his jollies by watching porn movies.

Jolly Roger
a pirate's flag, symbolised by skull and crossbones.

jolly well
1. euphemism for damned well; a mild oath emphasising anger or annoyance: e.g. If you don't like it, you can jolly well do it yourself!
2. extremely well; very well.

jonah/jonas
a person believed to bring bad luck and misfortune; a jinx.

joshing
good-natured joking, teasing, kidding.

journo
journalist.

joy-ride
a pleasure ride, usually in a stolen car: e.g. My car was stolen and taken for a joy-ride, but the police found it undamaged.

joy-stick
1. control lever of aircraft, computer or electronic games.
2. the penis.

J.P.
Justice of the Peace.

judas
a traitor.

judas hole
a peephole in a door.

jug
1. prison.
2. a jug of beer, served in hotels.

juggle
1. an act of deception or trickery.
2. manipulate, often in an underhanded, illicit manner: e.g. He gets his accountant to juggle the books so that it appears that his business is running at a loss.

juggle the pennies
budget carefully.

jugs
breasts; boobs; tits.

juice
1. petrol.
2. electricity: e.g. That cable has enough juice running through it to knock you off your feet.

juicy
(of news, information) scandalous; sexual; interesting: e.g. That was a juicy bit of gossip I heard about her!

jumble sale
sale of miscellaneous second-hand items.

jumbo
1. an elephant.
2. anything oversized, huge, very large: e.g. We're having a jumbo sale this week-end.
3. a large, intercontinental jet plane carrying many passengers.

jumbuck
a sheep.

jump
(see: get the jump on someone; go jump!; one jump ahead; take a running jump at yourself!; when I say 'jump', I want you to ask 'how high?')

jump at it
take the chance, opportunity eagerly: e.g. I jumped at it when I was offered that job.

jump bail
to disappear, abscond, after obtaining freedom by paying bail money.

jump down (someone's) throat
lose one's temper and suddenly speak harshly to (someone).

jump in and out of bed
behave in a promiscuous manner.

jump in the lake!
expression of scorn, dismissal, derision — go away, get lost!

jump on (someone)
scold, severely berate, criticise, reprimand (someone).

jump on the bandwagon
(see: climb on the bandwagon)

jump on your head!
an expression of scornful dismissal — get lost!

jump out of (one's) skin
receive a sudden fright, shock.

jump (someone)
1. attack, assault (someone) by surprise.
2. (of a man) have sexual intercourse with a woman.

jump start
1. an initial advantage: e.g. He has a jump start in the election that may lead him to victory.
2. start a vehicle by using cables connected to another car's battery.

jump the gun
make a premature start; start too soon.

jump the queue
take unfair precedence; obtain unfairly before one's turn.

jump through hoops
obey without question: e.g. I'm sick of jumping through hoops for you!

jump to conclusions
reach hasty conclusions, think the worst before knowing all the facts.

jump to it
act quickly, promptly.

jump to the bait
(see: rise to the bait)

jump up and down
make a fuss; protest strongly: e.g. A lot of people are jumping up and down over the council's decision to increase rates.

jumped-up
conceited; highly self-opinionated.

jumper
(see: kick up the jumper; need a kick up the jumper; right up one's jumper; stick it up your jumper!; up your jumper!)

jumping
lively; boisterous; gay: e.g. That party was really jumping by midnight.

jumpy
nervous; tense.

jungle-bunny
(derog.) a dark-skinned person.

jungle-juice
any strong, inferior alcoholic drink.

junior
a child: e.g. Grandma's minding junior tonight.

junk
1. anything considered worthless, cheap, shoddy.
2. narcotic drugs, especially heroin.
3. discard as worthless; throw away: e.g. Junk all that stuff!

junk food
food, especially from take-away shops, considered to be of little nutritional value.

junk jewellery
cheap imitation jewellery containing no precious metals or stones.

junk mail
advertising pamphlets and material other than personal mail deposited in letter-boxes and considered a nuisance.

junk shop
a shop selling cheap second-hand articles.

junket
a trip made by politicians or government personnel, at the tax-payer's expense, ostensibly to collect information.

junkie
a drug-addict addicted to potentially lethal drugs, especially heroin.

junky
cheap; shoddy; of poor quality.

just a mo/sec/tick
just a moment/second; a very short time.

just around the corner
just down the street
not very far-away; close by: e.g. He lives just around the corner.

just my luck!
an expression of frustration indicating that (one's) luck is typically bad.

just not on
an emphatic denial, refusal or expression of distaste, displeasure: e.g. What he did is just not on!

just one of those things
an unavoidable, and usually undesirable, set of circumstances.

just quietly
between ourselves: e.g. Just quietly, I think she looks awful.

just say the magic word
say yes.

just so
in perfect order; precisely like this: e.g. I want that job done just so.

just the job/thing
(see: just what the doctor ordered)

just the same
nevertheless: e.g. He may be old enough to go alone, but I'd like you to go with him just the same.

just what the doctor ordered
exactly what is required; proper; necessary; suitable; the perfect solution: e.g. Painting the roof a lighter colour to cool the house down in summer is just what the doctor ordered.

k
kilometre: e.g. The next town is about fifty k's away.

kafuffle
commotion; row; argument; upset.

kamikaze
dangerous; wild and suicidal: e.g. His kamikaze driving makes me nervous.

Kanaka
a Pacific Islander.

kanakas
testicles (play on: knackers).

kanga
1. kangaroo.
2. (cap.) a jack-hammer. (Trademark)

kangaroo bar
a heavy metal bar across the front of a vehicle to prevent damage if it strikes a kangaroo or other beast on the road.

kangaroo court
court — authorised or not — conducted with a perversion of legal procedures; mock court where members of a group judge others who don't follow group procedures.

kangaroo-hop
(of a car) jerky movement of a car due to uneven release of the clutch (or other fault).

Kangaroos
North Melbourne VFL football team.

kapow!
onomatopoeic word suggesting a blow or any sudden explosive sound.

kaput
1. broken; ruined; not working; no good.
2. dead.

kark
(see: cark)

karsi
(see: kharsi)

kayo
(see: K.O.)

keel over
1. fall over; faint.
2. to die.

keelhaul
to reprimand, scold, berate severely.

keen as mustard
enthusiastic; eager.

keen on (someone)
sexually attracted to (someone).

keep
a threat, either jocular or serious, that the matter or person will be dealt with at a later date: e.g. I won't deal with him right now — he'll keep!
See also:
for keeps
how are you keeping?

keep a clear head
maintain calm, reserve, logic.

keep a close eye on
maintain a close vigil.

keep a low profile
remain inconspicuous; stay away from publicity.

keep a stiff upper lip
face a difficult time or misfortune with bravery and courage against all odds; maintain one's stand, resolution.

keep a straight face
refrain from smiling or showing emotion.

keep a tight rein on
maintain firm, strict control.

keep a weather eye open
be alert, on guard.

keep an ear to the ground
listen for, search out, more information on a matter.

keep an eye on things
maintain a close vigil; watch over; look after.

keep an eye out
watch out for; look for: e.g. I've been keeping an eye out for a new house to buy.

keep an open mind
remain unbiased; reserve one's opinions until more facts are known: e.g. I like

to keep an open mind about the supernatural.

keep at it
persist; persevere: e.g. Keep at it — you'll eventually get it right.

keep at (someone)
1. persist in one's efforts to encourage (someone): e.g. I always have to keep at him to fix things around the house.
2. badger, tease, bully: e.g. I wish you wouldn't keep at me all the time!

keep back
restrain; resist; desist; withhold.

keep hanging in (there)
persevere, persist against all odds: e.g. Their marriage is shaky but they manage to keep hanging in there.

keep in touch
communicate; maintain a friendship.

keep in with (someone)
maintain one's good standing, friendship with: e.g. I'd like to keep in with him because he gives me a good discount on everything in his shop.

keep it all in the family
maintain activities, discussions, confidentialities, secrets etc. among the members of a group to the exclusion of outsiders.

keep it on ice
keep something waiting in readiness for another time.

keep it to (oneself)

keep it under (one's) hat
refuse to reveal a confidence, secret or fact.

keep it up
1. persist, persevere against odds.
2. (of a man) maintain an erection.

keep nit
to act as a guard or sentinel for someone doing an illegal activity.

keep on
persist in an argument; nag; harass verbally: e.g. I wish you wouldn't keep on about it!

keep on keeping on
persevere; persist.

keep on the ball
maintain constant alertness.

keep (one) on (one's) toes
maintain (one's) alertness, energy.

keep (one's) bib out
refrain from interfering, prying.

keep (one's) chin up
maintain (one's) composure, courage, bravery, against all odds.

keep (one's) cool
maintain (one's) calm, reserve; refuse to become angry or hostile; remain sensible and practical.

keep (one's) distance
maintain a reserved aloofness.

keep (one's) ears open
listen, search for more information on a matter.

keep (one's) end up
maintain (one's) part, share of the work, in a project.

keep (one's) eye on the ball
remain alert, vigilant, aware.

keep (one's) eyes open/ peeled/skinned
watch out for; look out for: e.g. The police are keeping their eyes peeled for any sign of illegal activity at the casino.

keep (one's) feet
maintain balance or stability.

keep (one's) feet on the ground
1. admit to having a fear of flying or of heights.
2. remain sensible and practical.

keep (one's) finger on the pulse
maintain a constant watch over, knowledge of and familiarity with something.

keep (one's) fingers crossed
maintain fervent hope.

keep (one's) hand in
remain involved in; stay in practice.

keep (one's) hands clean
(see: keep one's nose clean)

keep (one's) head
(see: keep one's cool)

keep (one's) head above water
survive a difficult situation, especially financial problems.

keep (one's) mind above (one's) belt
refrain from saying or doing lurid, obscene, vulgar things.

keep (one's) mouth shut
1. refrain from speaking, commenting.
2. refrain from divulging a confidence or secret.

keep (one's) nose clean
stay out of trouble through honest and legal dealings; live by the rules, thus avoiding trouble or blame.

keep (one's) nose out
refrain from interfering or prying.

keep (one's) nose to the grindstone
maintain a high and intensive level of work.

keep (one's) peace
remain silent.

keep (one's) pecker up
remain cheerful — especially of a man.

keep (one's) wits about (one)
remain sensible, practical and alert.

keep (oneself) together
1. remain practical, sensible and alert.
2. refrain from losing (one's) composure, calm, temper.

keep out of (someone's) hair
stay out of (someone's) way; refrain from being a nuisance, annoyance to (someone).

keep (someone) guessing
to deliberately hide the truth, facts from (someone).

keep (someone) on a string
maintain emotional control of (someone) — often unfairly.

keep tabs on
check on or keep an account of; constant knowledge of; have under constant observation.

keep the ball rolling
maintain progress.

keep the home fires burning
maintain a warm, welcome home atmosphere.

keep the hounds at bay
avert unpleasant publicity, confrontation.

keep the party clean!
an expression of censure when obscenity or sexual innuendo enters into a conversation in mixed company.

keep the pot boiling
agitate; maintain activity, argument, hostility.

keep the wheels turning
maintain progress.

keep the wolf from the door
avert poverty, hunger.

keep to
adhere to (a promise or agreement).

keep to (oneself)
refrain from socialising; remain distant, aloof, reserved and unapproachable.

keep track of
(see: keep tabs on)

keep up
maintain equal rate of work, speed, activity etc.

keep up appearances
pretend that all is well.

keep up with the Jones's
pertaining to the competitive struggle between neighbours in the acquisition of material possessions as status symbols.

keep your hair/hat/shirt/wig on!

keep your wool!
don't lose your temper; stay calm.

keg
a barrel of beer — either 9 or 18 gallons (in the imperial system).

keg party
a beer-drinking party at which a keg of beer has been installed.

kelpie
an Australian sheep or cattle dog.

kempt
well groomed.

kept in stitches
caused, made to laugh for a considerable time.

kept in the dark
caused to remain ignorant due to a deliberate lack of disclosure of facts.

kept under wraps
remained secret, undisclosed, unavailable to the general public.

kept woman
1. woman supported as a mistress by a man.
2. (joc.) wife supported financially by her husband.

kerfuffle
(see: kafuffle)

kero
kerosene.

kerp
the penis.

kerplunk
onomatopoeic word suggesting splashing into water.

kettle
(see: arse over kettle; fine kettle of fish; now look who's calling the kettle black; pot calling the kettle black)

kettle of fish
matter; problem; difficult situation.
See also:
different kettle of fish
fine kettle of fish

key money
a sum of money paid by a prospective tenant for the interest or good will that a property has accumulated.

keyed up
stimulated; excited; anticipating: e.g. We're really keyed up about starting this new business.

kharsi
toilet; dunny.

khyber/Khyber Pass
(rhyming slang) arse; bum.
See also:
kick up the khyber
need a kick up the khyber

kibosh
(also: kybosh) nonsense; rubbish.
See also:
put the kybosh on

kick
1. thrill; temporary enthusiasm, excitement or pleasure: e.g. I got a real kick out of that roller-coaster ride!

2. the sharp, stimulating effect of alcohol or drugs: e.g. This dope will give you a good kick.
3. buying of a round of drinks (or other); shout: e.g. It must be his kick because I shouted the last round!
4. funds; petty savings: e.g. I put a few dollars in the kick every week for Christmas.
5. the trouser pocket: e.g. Put that money back in your kick — I'll pay for this round.
6. complaint or objection: e.g. What's his kick?
See also:
alive and kicking
could kick a bullock up the arse and walk away with the hide
drop-kick
get a kick out of
shit-kicker
still kicking

kick a goal
1. (football) score.
2. achieve sexual intercourse.

kick around
1. to mistreat, abuse, persecute (someone or something): e.g. The way he kicks her around, I'm surprised she's still with him!
2. drift aimlessly; rove, wander; loaf around.
3. discuss; talk over; debate: e.g. We'll kick those suggestions around at the next meeting.

kick around with
associate with; be in constant company with: e.g. He kicks around with some tough-looking characters.

kick him where his mother never kissed him
kick him in the bum or genitals.

kick in
contribute or donate money to a common cause: e.g. We're all kicking in a few dollars for a present for his retirement.

kick in the arse/pants
1. a severe scolding, reprimand.
2. a severe set-back, disappointment or failure.

kick in the teeth
severe set-back, disappointment or failure.

kick off
1. to die.
2. commence, begin: e.g. When does the party kick off?

kick on
to continue having a good time long after most people have left: e.g. We kicked on till dawn.

kick (oneself)
berate or reproach (oneself); feel angry and annoyed with (oneself): e.g. I could kick myself for not taking that opportunity when it was presented to me.

kick over
1. finish, complete: e.g. We should kick that job over in a day.
2. (of an engine) start: e.g. There must be something wrong with my car — it won't kick over sometimes.

kick (someone) in the teeth
betray (someone); let (someone) down badly.

kick (someone) out
sack, dismiss unceremoniously; get rid of (someone).

kick (someone's) head/teeth in
bash, beat, punch, assault (someone) violently.

kick the bucket
to die: e.g. My old dog finally kicked the bucket.

kick the cat/dog
(see: flog the cat)

kick the eye out of a needle
(of a horse) wild, unruly and given to kicking.

kick the habit
give up, abandon a habit, such as smoking or drug-taking.

kick the tin
1. pay for a round of drinks; shout: e.g. Whose turn is it to kick the tin?
2. donate, contribute money to a common cause.

kick up a fuss/stink
1. protest vigorously; complain vehemently.
2. create trouble, commotion.

kick up (one's) heels
enjoy (oneself); go out and have fun.

kick up the arse/bum/ jumper/khyber/pants/quoit
1. severe encouragement or incentive: e.g. He needs a kick up the arse every now and again or else he gets lazy.
2. severe discipline, scolding, reproach, beating, thrashing, punishment: e.g. He needs a good kick up the jumper over the way he's been treating that poor dog.

kick upstairs
to promote (someone) to a higher position which usually has less power.

kick-back
1. payment or favour in return for a favour — often in association with illegal or illicit dealings.
2. response.

kicked from pillar to post
treated poorly; mistreated so as to go from one predicament to another: e.g. Since his parents split up, that child has been kicked from pillar to post.

kick-in
(Australian Rules football) return of football to play after a point.

kicking around
active; present.

kick-over
an easy task: e.g. The exams were a kick-over.

kicks
excitement; thrills; pleasure: e.g. What do you do for kicks?
See also:
do it for kicks
in it for kicks

kid
1. young child.
2. term of address — either with affection or aggression.
3. joke; tease; hoax; deceive: e.g. Would I kid you?
See also:
handle with kid gloves

kid brother/sister
younger brother/sister.

kid show/stuff
an event, movie, show that is too unsophisticated for adult viewing or participation.

kiddie/kiddiewink
young child.

kidding
joking; deceiving; bluffing; teasing.
See also:
have/got to be kidding!
stop kidding (oneself)
you must be kidding!
you're kidding!

kiddo
familiar form of address.

kids
children.

kid-stakes
small; insignificant; trifling; unimportant.

kike
(derog.) a Jew.

kill
1. have an irresistible, stunning and overwhelming effect on: e.g. This new play is really going to kill you.
2. cause hilarity: e.g. I heard a new joke that'll kill you.
3. threaten with violence, but often in a jocular manner: e.g. I'll kill him if he's not here on time!
See also:
dressed to kill
go in for the kill
if looks could kill
laugh fit to kill

kill a brown dog
anything potent, deadly: e.g. Her cooking is bad enough to kill a brown dog!

kill a snake
(of a man) urinate.

kill (oneself) laughing
to laugh fitfully.

kill the fatted calf
to make elaborate preparations for a festive occasion, welcome, party etc.

kill the goose that lays the golden eggs
to ruin, put an end to a situation that reaped (one) great benefits, prosperity.

kill time
idly fill in time with inconsequential activity while waiting for something else.

kill two birds with one stone
achieve two goals with one action.

kill with kindness
to unwittingly have a detrimental effect on something or someone by over-doing one's kind, good intentions: e.g. I killed that plant with kindness by over-watering it.

killer
1. something very effective, stunning.
2. something extremely funny, amusing.
3. something that finally ruins, destroys, ends hopes or chances of success.

killer instinct
fierce competitiveness, determination to win.

killing
1. a great success, especially a financial one: e.g. We made a killing at the races last week.
2. a successful sexual encounter: e.g. Did you make a killing with her last night?

kill-joy
depressing person; spoil-sport.

kills me
amuses, delights me: e.g. His jokes just kill me!

kilter
(see: out of kilter)

kind
(see: pay in kind)

kind of
rather; somewhat: e.g. The thing we saw looked kind of like a flying saucer!

kinder/kindy
kindergarten.

king
1. (in combination) the largest: e.g. king-sized bed; king prawns; king tide; king sheets.
2. (in combination) extremely powerful, wealthy in one's field: e.g. cattle king; oil king; sheep king.
See also:
fit for a king
uncrowned king

King Dick
a person who has an excessively high opinion of himself, who sees himself as far above ordinary people: e.g. 1. Who do you think you are — King Dick? 2. He

must think he's King Dick to treat everyone like that!

king hit
1. a sudden and crushing misfortune.
2. a sudden blow that knocks one out: e.g. He was put into hospital by a lucky king hit.
3. (Australian Rules football) hit, usually behind play, when the receiver is not ready for it.

King Richard the Third
(rhyming slang) turd; shit.

kingdom-come
(figurative) the next world after death: e.g. He can go to kingdom-come for all I care!

king-hit
punch, bash, beat, assault — usually in the head or face.

king-pin
the leader; boss.

king's ransom
a large amount of money: e.g. The dealers want a king's ransom for a new car now!

king-size
1. the largest; larger than usual.
2. the largest size bed: e.g. We sleep in a king-size.

kink
1. a sexual pervert.
2. idiosyncracy; fetish; quirk; odd notion; deviation, especially sexual.
3. cramp, twinge or stitch, as in the muscles of the back or neck.
4. imperfection; defect; flaw: e.g. The plan may have a few kinks in it but we'll sort them out.

kinky
1. having bizarre, unusual or perverted tastes, especially sexual.
2. bizarre, yet appealing: e.g. He wears some kinky clothes.
3. mad, weird; eccentric; peculiar; queer.

kip
1. a sleep or nap: e.g. He's having an afternoon kip.
2. small piece of board used to toss the coins in the game of two-up.

kip down
sleep; to take a nap.

kipper
(derog.) an Englishman (a two-faced bastard with no guts).

kiss and make up
reconciliation after an argument.

kiss and tell
to reveal, be indiscreet about one's private amorous experiences with others.

kiss it good-bye
resign oneself to having lost something: e.g. Now that he's been declared bankrupt, everyone can kiss their money good-bye.

kiss my arse!
expression of scorn, dismissal, disdain, contempt: e.g. You can kiss my arse!

kiss the dust
(see: lick the dust)

kisser
1. the mouth: e.g. You'll get a smack in the kisser if you're not careful!
2. the face: e.g. He's got an ugly kisser!

kiss-of-life
mouth-to-mouth resuscitation — a form of artificial respiration carried out by breathing air into the mouth of the patient.

kitchen
(see: do the rounds of the kitchen; get out of the kitchen if you can't stand the heat; give someone the rounds of the kitchen; everything but the kitchen sink)

kitchen tea
pre-wedding party for women where the guests bring an item for the kitchen as a gift.

kite
1. a hang-glider.
2. forged or stolen cheque.
3. fabricated or fictitious set of circumstances, dealings or transaction designed to sustain or raise credit.
See also:
fly a kite
go fly a kite!
high as a kite

kite flying
1. fraudulent use of cheques and accounts.
2. the testing of public opinion by spreading rumours.

Kitekat
pet food for cats. (Trademark)

kitten
(see: have kittens; like stalking a lion and coming back with a kitten)

kitty
1. a cat.
2. a common fund usually of smaller amounts of money: e.g. All the tenants put some money into the kitty each week to buy food and groceries.

Kiwi
a New Zealander or pertaining to New Zealand.

Kleenex
any soft tissue serving as a substitute for a handkerchief. (Trademark)

klicks
kilometres.

klutz
a fool, dolt or stupid person.

klutzy
foolish; stupid: e.g. That was a klutzy thing to do.

knackered
1. tired; exhausted: e.g. He's knackered after all that work.
2. useless; worn-out; broken; ruined: e.g. This tape's knackered.
3. castrated: e.g. That cat has been knackered.

knackers
1. testicles.
2. a place where old and useless horses are taken for slaughter.

knee
(see: bring someone to his knees; melt at the knees; on one's knees; weak at the knees)

knee-deep
very busy or involved with: e.g. I'm knee-deep in work this weekend so I can't go out to the party.

knee-high to a grasshopper
small in stature; short.

kneel on (someone)
oppress, subjugate, harass, pressure (someone) into submission: e.g. We'll get the gang to kneel on him a bit — after that he'll pay up.

knee-trembler
1. something frightening, terrifying.
2. sexual intercourse in a standing position.

knee-trembling
frightening; terrifying; scary.

knickers
underpants for women.
See also:
get (one's) knickers in a knot/twist

knick-knacks
trinkets; bric-a-brac; small items.

knife
pertaining to betrayal, double-crossing: e.g. He'd knife his own mother if it meant making money, so don't trust him!
See also:
air was so thick you could cut it with a knife
put the knife in

knife in the back
betrayal; double-cross; malicious gossip or slander: e.g. You'll get a knife in the back from him one day — he simply can't be trusted.

knife-edge
a dangerous, risky situation or position.

knob
penis: e.g. He's got a throb in the knob for her.
See also:
be there with knobs on

k'n-oath!
euphemism for fucking oath!; emphatically, yes!; an expression of complete agreement.

knock
1. criticise; find fault with; condemn; disparage: e.g. He's always knocking me for one thing or another.
2. (of an engine) make a noise due to a fault.
3. have sexual intercourse: e.g. Who's he been knocking lately?
See also:
don't knock it till you've tried it
hard knocks

knock about/around with
associate with; keep company with.

knock back
1. refuse; say no to: e.g. I'm going to knock back his offer.
2. drink or eat something rapidly, with enthusiasm: e.g. He can knock back a beer quicker than anyone I know.

knock down
1. drink quickly: e.g. He can knock down ten beers in an hour!
2. sell by auction to the highest bidder: e.g. The house was knocked down for a good price.
3. reduce the price of: e.g. He might knock it down a bit for cash.

knock it off
1. (as an exclamation) stop!; be quiet!; shut up!; desist!
2. eat or drink everything (quickly).
3. steal it; take it without permission or authority.
4. make, do something, or finish a task rapidly and without effort: e.g. We'll knock it off in no time.

knock it on the head
put a stop to (it, something).

knock off
1. officially cease work: e.g. What time does he knock off?
2. deduct a sum; reduce by an amount: e.g. He'll knock off fifty bucks for cash.
3. steal: e.g. He'll knock off anything that's not nailed down!
4. (of police) to make a raid or arrest: e.g. The police are going to knock off all the illegal casinos in the area.
5. have sexual intercourse with (someone): e.g. He'd love to knock that sheila off.
6. kill.

knock on the head/scone
1. a reminder: e.g. He needs a knock on the head every now and again because he's so forgetful.
2. stop; put an end to: e.g. Lack of funds knocked that idea on the head.

knock on wood
saying used to ward off bad luck or the possibility of something happening:

e.g. I haven't been caught for speeding yet — knock on wood!

knock (one) around
tire, exhaust, cause considerable discomfort or hardship to (one): e.g. Sitting in a plane for twenty hours knocks one around a bit.

knock (one's) eye out

knock (one's) socks off
cause great admiration in (one): e.g. This new car will knock your eye out!

knock (oneself) out
exhaust, tire (oneself).

knock out
to earn money, a living: e.g. He knocks out about 600 dollars a week.

knock over
to steal, as in a robbery: e.g. Thieves knocked over the jewellery store last night.

knock (someone) bandy
completely overwhelm, flabbergast, defeat (someone).

knock (someone) off
1. (of men in particular) to have sexual intercourse with (someone): e.g. He'd love to knock her off.
2. kill (someone): e.g. She knocked her husband off with poison.

knock (someone) out
1. bash, hit, beat up (someone); render senseless.
2. exhaust, tire (someone): e.g. You'll knock him out if you keep him working at that pace.
3. evoke great admiration, wonder from (someone): e.g. This new dress will knock him out.

knock (someone) rotten/silly
1. strike, bash, hit (someone) forcefully.
2. cause (someone) to be overwhelmed: e.g. 1. That last drink of rum knocked him rotten. 2. You really knocked him rotten with what you said at the debate.

knock (someone's) block off
thrash; beat up; punch in the head.

knock (something) about/around
treat roughly; abuse; spoil by rough handling: e.g. He's knocked that car around too much for it to be worth anything.

knock spots off (someone)
get the better of, defeat (someone).

knock the bottom out of
refute; render invalid or worthless: e.g. Big increases in loan interest rates have knocked the bottom out of the real-estate market.

knock the stuffing out of (someone)
1. thrash; beat up; render senseless.
2. amaze, overwhelm, stupefy, humble (someone); set (someone) back: e.g. The latest bit of news is going to knock the stuffing out of him.

knock them dead
amaze, overwhelm, stun and excite: e.g. Our costumes knocked them dead at the fancy-dress ball.

knock together
make, construct or arrange in a hurried (and often shoddy) manner: e.g. We'll knock together some salads for the barbecue.

knock up
1. make, construct or arrange in a hurried manner: e.g. I'll knock up something to wear tonight.
2. (of a man) cause a woman to become pregnant: e.g. Did you knock up my wife?
3. exhaust; tire; wear out: e.g. I'm going to knock up this horse to teach him a lesson.

knock-about
1. casual, easy-going, informal person or item of clothing.
2. rough, boisterous, unruly and rowdy person.
3. car used for general purpose, rough handling or odd jobs.

knock-back
1. a set-back; rebuff; rejection; bad turn of events.
2. a refusal or rejection (particularly sexual): e.g. Did you get a knock-back last night?

knock-down
an introduction.

knocked off
1. killed.
2. stolen.

knocked up
1. pregnant: e.g. She looks knocked up to me.
2. exhausted; tired; worn out.
3. increased in price: e.g. That house has been knocked up by thousands.

knocker
person who consistently derides, criticises and condemns everybody and anything.
See also:
on the knocker

knockers
breasts; boobs; tits.

knock-off (time)
official end of working hours.

knock-out
1. outstanding person, thing, or event.
2. stunningly beautiful person.

knock-out bomb/drop/pill
sedative or sleeping tablet.

knock-over
1. easily accomplished task: e.g. These exams are going to be a knock-over.
2. person easily cheated, duped, convinced.

knocks like a Mack truck
(derogatory of women) sexually willing or promiscuous.

knock-shop
brothel.

knot
(see: don't get your toga in a knot; get into a knot; get knotted!; in a knot; tie the knot; tied up in knots)

know
(see: didn't know what hit him; didn't know which way to look; doesn't know whether it's Pitt Street or Christmas/Tuesday or Bourke Street; doesn't know whether one is Arthur or Martha; in the know; that's for me to know and you to find out; what do you know?; wouldn't know one's arse from a hole in the ground etc.)

know a thing or two
1. to be shrewd, knowledgeable, well-informed: e.g. He knows a thing or two about fixing cars.
2. to be worldly, especially in sexual knowledge: e.g. I bet she knows a thing or two!

know all the lurks (and perks)

know all the wrinkles
(see: know a thing or two, 1.)

know chalk from cheese
recognise differences.

know how many beans make five
to be well informed, aware of the facts.

know (it) backward

know (it) inside out

know (it) like the back of (one's) hand

know (it) off by heart

know (it) off pat
be completely familiar with; know everything about (it): e.g. He can tell you the words to that song — he knows it backwards.

know next to nothing
1. not well informed or familiar with: e.g. He knows next to nothing about horse-riding.
2. be stupid; be lacking in intelligence.

know no bounds
to go on endlessly, tirelessly, forever: e.g. His drinking knows no bounds.

know (one's) onions
be familiar with (one's) job, subject etc.; be skilled in (one's) field, profession, trade: e.g. He really knows his onions when it comes to computers.

know (one's) place
to be aware of (one's) lower social standing and behave accordingly: e.g. Many male chauvinists think women today no longer know their place as a result of the women's liberation movement.

know (one's) stuff
(see: know one's onions)

know sweet F.A./Fanny Adams/fuck-all
to know very little; be ill-informed; have little or no relevant knowledge about: e.g. He knows sweet F.A. about fixing cars!

know the ropes
be familiar and well acquainted with the details and workings of: e.g. Before you hire him make sure he knows the ropes.

know the score
be familiar with the details, facts, of a case; understand the implications, position, ramifications of a situation: e.g. He knows the score — if he comes here again I'll call the police.

know what it is to (be)
to sympathise, feel for, have intimate knowledge of: e.g. He may have a lot of money now but he knows what it is to be poor and hungry.

know what's what
have good judgement; know the facts, true position of the matter in hand and make sensible judgements or decisions.

know where to draw the line
know one's limitations; know how far one can go in a situation as well as when to stop.

know whether it's Pitt Street or Christmas

know whether it's Tuesday or Bourke Street

know whether (one) is Arthur or Martha
(see: doesn't know whether . . .)

know which side (one's) bread is buttered on
to know where (one's) advantage is.

know who's who
to know which are the people who have power, influence, importance, authority.

know-all
person who claims to know everything about any particular matter (but who usually doesn't, and is hence extremely irritating).

knuckle
(see: close to the knuckle; go the knuckle; rap over the knuckles)

knuckle down to
apply oneself earnestly to a task: e.g. I have to knuckle down to some study for the exams next week.

knuckle in on
move in on, intrude in a bullying manner.

knuckle sandwich
a punch, hit, bash in the mouth.

knuckle (someone)
punch, hit, bash, assault (someone).

knuckle under
give way; collapse; succumb; yield.

knuckle-duster
metal guard wrapped around the fist as a weapon in fighting.

knucklehead
fool; dolt; stupid person.

K.O.
(knock-out) render someone senseless with a punch; knock someone out.

Kombi
any small multi-purpose van-like vehicle. (Trademark)

konk
(also: conk) the nose.

kook
eccentric, weird, odd or crazy person.

kooky
1. eccentric; weird; odd; crazy.
2. kookaburra.

koori
an Aborigine.

kosher
genuine; correct; real; the done thing.

kowtow
act obsequiously; be servile and fawning.

kraut
a German person; pertaining to Germany.

kronk
(see: cronk)

kryptonite
fictitious metal that destroys the powers of the comic-strip character, Superman.

k's
1. kilometres: e.g. How many k's is it to Melbourne?
2. kilometres per hour: e.g. We were doing a hundred k's.

kuri
(derog.) Maori. (also: goori, goorie)

kwaka
a Kawasaki motorcycle.

KY
KY jelly — a lubricant widely used for sexual intercourse.

kybosh
nonsense; rubbish.
See also:
put the kybosh on

L plates
small sign marked L, attached to front and back of vehicle to denote a learner-driver.

lab
laboratory.

label
1. assign to a stereotyped category: e.g. She's been labelled a slut just because she's been to bed with a few blokes.
2. a trade name for records, cassettes, clothes etc.

lace into
scold, reprimand, attack, abuse verbally.

lacker band
elastic band; rubber band.

lackey
obsequious person; yes-man.

lad
1. familiar term for any male: e.g. Me and the lads are going fishing tomorrow.
2. daring, playful, devil-may-care, reckless man; womaniser.

ladder
1. hierarchical order; social or business rank: e.g. He's pretty high up the ladder.
2. fault, run in a stocking, hosiery.
See also:
climb up the ladder

la-di-da
(also: la-te-da)
1. affected manner; pretentious; snobby; posh.
2. (especially of women) the toilet.

ladies
women's toilet.

ladies' man
man noted for his attention and attraction to women.

ladle out
hand out or distribute in a lavish manner.

lady
1. the wife: e.g. Where's the little lady tonight?
2. cocaine.
See also:
little lady
old lady
that's no lady, that's my wife
white lady

Lady Muck
a woman who affects airs and graces, behaves pretentiously, in an affected, snobby manner.

lady-killer
any man considered dangerously attractive to women; womaniser, heart-breaker.

lag
a habitual criminal, convict.

lagerphone
a home-made musical instrument made of beer-bottle tops, loosely nailed to a stick, which rattle when hit or tapped.

lagger
police informer.

laid
to have had sexual intercourse: e.g. Did you get laid last night?

laid it on the line
came to the point; said truthfully and specifically: e.g. It's about time some of our politicians laid it on the line instead of being evasive about their policies.

laid up
incapacitated; sick; bed-ridden; immobilised: e.g. Since he broke his leg he's been laid up.

laid-back
nonchalant; relaxed; easy-going; casual.

For other possible entries beginning with 'laid' see entries listed under 'lay'.

lair
1. any person (especially a man) who is a flashy show-off, vulgar exhibitionist, public nuisance; show pony.
2. person's hiding place or retreat.

3. a favourite haunt or place to visit.
See also:
mug lair
two-bob lair

lair around

lairise
1. behave in a flamboyant, showy, vulgar, exhibitionistic manner: e.g. If he keeps lairising around in that car the way he does, the police will soon catch him for speeding and dangerous driving.
2. (Australian Rules football) to show off when in front in a game.

lairiser
vulgar exhibitionist.

lairy
vulgar; flashy; gaudy; exhibitionistic: e.g. He drives a lairy red car with noisy extractors.

lam into (someone)
beat; thrash; bash; hit hard.

lamb
innocent, weak person; dear person.
See also:
in like a lion, out like a lamb
may as well be caught for a sheep as for a lamb

lamb-brained
stupid; impractical: e.g. That's a lamb-brained idea!

lame dog/duck
any person or thing that is useless, inefficient, inadequate or ineffective: e.g. That investment deal we made last year has been a bit of a lame duck for the business.

lame excuse
poor, ineffective, inadequate excuse or reason.

lame-brain
inadequate, ineffective, stupid person.

lamington
a cake — generally a sponge that has been cut into blocks, rolled in chocolate icing and shredded coconut, and sometimes having a jam filling.

lampoon
scurrilous, abusive criticism or satire.

lamp-post
very tall, thin person.

land
obtain; gain; win; secure; catch; get: e.g. He landed an excellent job with that new company.
See also:
in the land of the living

land of milk and honey
a place of easily obtained wealth and good opportunity.

land of nod
the state of sleep: e.g. He's in the land of nod at present and can't come to the phone.

land of plenty
(see: land of milk and honey)

land on (one's) feet
1. to come through a bad set of circumstances relatively unscathed, successfully.
2. to experience good luck: e.g. You really landed on your feet with that big lottery win!

land on (someone's) doorstep
arrive unannounced and unexpectedly.

land shark
a land speculator who makes excessive profits buying and selling.

land up
end up; find oneself: e.g. He'll land up in prison sooner or later for his crimes.

land with (one's) bum in the butter
to experience good luck, fortune, especially after a series of bad circumstances.

landed with
forced to accept unwillingly: e.g. I've been landed with all the relatives at my house for Christmas.

land's sake!
expression of amazement, wonder, surprise.

landslide
an election in which one side wins by an overwhelming majority of votes.

lap
(see: in the lap of luxury; in the lap of the gods; under the lap)

lap dog
an obsequious, fawning, servile person.

lap it up
enjoy, delight in: e.g. She runs around after him all day and he just sits around and laps it up.

large as life
in person; the actual presence of: e.g. I saw him there — large as life.

large-hearted
generous.

larger than life
(of a person) extremely vital, charismatic, attractive.

lark
1. amusing incident; prank: e.g. What a lark that was!
2. joke, tease, play pranks: e.g. He was only larking.

'Righto, move to the back of the bus. Make room for the lady with a pram!'

Australians use many expressions that mean full to capacity. Not only is this bus full as a fairy's phone-book, footy final, pommy complaint box, seaside shithouse on bank holiday or state-school hat-rack, it is also bursting at the seams, chock-a-block, chockers, crammed, jam-packed, loaded or stuffed. Naturally enough, the same expressions apply to a bloke who is full to capacity with beer!

larrikin
hooligan; loutish youth; rough, rowdy, boisterous young man.
See also:
off like a larrikin's hat in the breeze

lash
(see: have a lash at)

lash out
1. spend money freely; not to worry about the expense: e.g. We lashed out and bought some new clothes.
2. denounce, castigate, criticise severely.

lashing
a severe scolding: e.g. The principal gave the boys a lashing.

lashings
plenty; lots of: e.g. I'll have lashings of cream on my peaches.

lashings of splosh
wealthy; a lot of money.

last day
the final day of work, school etc. prior to a vacation, resignation etc.

last laugh
the ultimate victory: e.g. He had the last laugh.

last of the big spenders
1. someone who spends extravagantly and conspicuously, splashes his money around.
2. miserly, parsimonious person: e.g. Isn't Paul the last of the big spenders — he went to the casino for a big night out and spent four dollars!

last one in is a rotten egg
a jocular exclamation enticing a group to race into a swimming pool etc.

last resort
the final option after all else has failed or been considered.

last straw
the final thing, incident, mishap etc. that leads to reaction or outburst of emotion: e.g. What he did was the last straw — he's going to get fired!

last word
1. the final authority or say in a matter.
2. perfection; the ultimate or best: e.g. This wine is the last word as far as reds go.
3. in vogue; fashionable; the newest rage: e.g. Fake diamonds are apparently the last word these days.

last-ditch effort
final and desperate effort using all one's remaining resources.

latch on (to)
1. to understand what is said or going on: e.g. Has he latched on that there's a surprise party for him yet?
2. to cling to somebody; become closely associated with or dependent on.

latchkey kid
child who has the key to the house in order to let himself in after school because the parents are away at work.

late
(of a woman) overdue for menstruation, indicating pregnancy.
See also:
better late than never

latest
1. news; gossip; most recent information: e.g. What's the latest?
2. most recent, current love relationship: e.g. Who's his latest?
See also:
the latest

lather
1. a state of agitation, anxiety: e.g. He's in a lather over his coming wedding.
2. to beat, bash someone.

laugh
1. a comical, amusing person or thing: e.g. He's such a laugh.
2. ridiculous, ludicrous situation or state of affairs: e.g. The whole idea is a laugh — it won't work!
3. scoff at; ridicule: e.g. Don't laugh — this thing actually works.
See also:
don't make me laugh!
have the last laugh
raise a laugh

laugh a minute
extremely amusing, funny person.

laugh all the way to the bank
to experience wealth, good fortune, especially when others did not expect you to.

laugh at
deride; ridicule; belittle; make fun of; disparage.

laugh at the lawn
to vomit.

laugh fit to kill
to laugh heartily; split one's sides laughing.

laugh it off
to dismiss or shrug off any embarrassing situation, criticism or matter by light ridicule, treatment or jest.

laugh on the other/wrong side of (one's) face
experience displeasure, humiliation, disappointment, embarrassment: e.g. He'll laugh on the other side of his face after I tell everyone what he really did!

laugh up (one's) sleeve
to secretly, inwardly scoff at, ridicule, laugh at.

laughable
ridiculous; ludicrous: e.g. This situation is laughable!

laughed out of court
dismissed with ridicule instead of being given a fair hearing: e.g. You'll get laughed out of court if you tell people you saw a flying saucer and little green men!

laughing
in an extremely satisfactory, fortunate or advantageous position: e.g. He's laughing since he won all that money.
See also:
no laughing matter

laughing gas
nitrous oxide — used as anaesthetic in dentistry and producing a feeling of euphoria.

laughing gear
the mouth: e.g. Wrap your laughing gear around this yummy cake.

laughing jackass
kookaburra.

laughing-stock
object of general derision, ridicule.

launch into
1. abuse loudly: e.g. Some members of the public angrily launched into the minister as he arrived for the press conference.
2. plunge into; get started on (something).

launder
(of money) to transfer illegally or ill-gotten funds in a manner that appears legitimate.

laundromat
coin-operated laundry. (Trademark)

lav/lavvy
lavatory; toilet; dunny.

law
(see: above the law; lay down the law; long arm of the law; Murphy's law; possession is nine points of the law; take the law into one's own hands; unwritten law)

law of averages
pertaining to the principle that there exists an equality in the number of times things will happen: e.g. Going by the law of averages, if I toss a coin a hundred times, I should get approximately the same number of heads and tails coming up.

law of the jungle
the principle or belief that the strongest, most clever, cunning, devious, or unscrupulous shall survive or be successful in business and life in general.

law unto oneself
to do whatever one desires without worry or thought to the normal restrictions of the rules of society.

lay
1. a person considered as a sex object: e.g. He looks like a good lay.
2. to have sexual intercourse: e.g. I'd like to lay her!
3. to wager, bet: e.g. I'm going to lay a fiver on the Melbourne Cup next week.
See also:
easy lay

lay a cable
to defecate.

lay a hand/lefty on (someone)
beat, bash, hit, assault: e.g. If he lays a hand on me again, I'll leave him!

lay an egg
1. create a flop, blunder or failure: e.g. I think we've laid an egg with this latest show.
2. to defecate.

lay bare
reveal, expose feelings, facts, secrets etc: e.g. We have a witness prepared to lay bare the entire truth of the matter to the court.

lay down (one's) hand
reveal (one's) advantages.

lay down the law
be the boss, authority; expect people to do what one says: e.g. I lay down the law around here, so what I say goes!

lay eyes on
catch sight of: e.g. Next time I lay eyes on him I'll bash him!

lay hold of
to find: e.g. I can't seem to lay hold of that document anywhere.

lay in the hay
have sexual intercourse.

lay in there
persist, persevere against all odds: e.g. Things have been difficult, but we're still laying in there!

lay into (someone)
1. beat, bash, hit, attack, assault: e.g. I'd like to lay into the rat who pinched my car!
2. abuse, berate, castigate severely: e.g. She really laid into him for coming home so late.

lay it at (someone's) door
attribute the blame to (someone): e.g. The disappearance of much of our heritage can be laid at the door of our greedy politicians.

lay it on (someone)
1. ask (someone) for a favour, loan of money etc.: e.g. It's about time you laid it on the boss for a raise.
2. to severely chastise, reprimand, scold, abuse, castigate (someone): e.g. Your mum's going to

really lay it on you when she finds out what you've done!

lay it on the line
1. risk (something); take a chance that exposes (something) to injury or loss: e.g. you're laying a fortune on the line with that venture.
2. tell the truth; state the case honestly.

lay it on (thick)
1. exaggerate; flatter to excess: e.g. When he tells a story he lays it on so thick I never know what to believe.
2. scold, abuse, chastise, castigate severely: e.g. The principal really laid it on after the two boys were caught stealing.

lay it out straight
(see: lay it on the line, 2.)

lay low
hide from social contact; remain hidden: e.g. The bank robbers will probably lay low for a while until the heat's off.

lay off
1. desist; stop; refrain from annoying, harassing: e.g. Will you lay off and shut up!
2. discharge from work or job owing to shortage of work: e.g. The factory is going to have to lay off some of its workers.

lay on
provide; supply: e.g. They're going to lay on all the food and booze at their party.

lay (one's) cards down/on the table
(see: lay down one's hand)

lay (one's) hands on
find; locate; obtain; acquire: e.g. Where did you lay your hands on all that money?

lay (one's) neck on the line
expose (oneself) to risk, danger: e.g. I'm not going to lay my neck on the line for him — I don't owe him any favours!

lay (oneself) open
to expose (oneself) to criticism, ridicule: e.g. Politicians always lay themselves open to public abuse when they fail to carry out their election promises.

lay out
spend money, often unwillingly: e.g. I had to lay out hundreds to fix my car after that accident.

lay (someone) out
beat up, punch, knock (someone) to the ground; knock unconscious.

lay them in the aisles
be extremely funny, amusing or popular with the audience: e.g. This new play will lay them in the aisles.

lay to rest
to bury (a dead body).

lay waste
to destroy, ruin.

lay you tens
wager with (someone): e.g. I'll lay you tens that he won't do it!

layabout
lazy, idle person; habitual loafer.

lay-down misère
a certainty: e.g. It's a lay-down misère that he'll win this election.

lazy Suzan
a revolving centre tray enabling condiments to be within easy reach of everyone.

lazybones
(see: layabout)

lead
1. (Australian Rules football) run by full-forward out to a position where a team-mate can pass the ball to him.
2. (see: put lead in your pencil; swinging lead; went down like a lead balloon)

lead a dog's life
live an unhappy, harassed life.

lead a double life
lead a life that appears honest on the surface but is secretly involved with illegal or immoral activities.

lead feet
1. a tendency to drive too fast: e.g. The way he drives, he must have lead feet (too heavy to lift off the accelerator).
2. tendency to move, walk, run etc. slowly.

lead (someone) a merry chase/dance
to cause (unnecessary) trouble, problems, difficulties for (someone); frustrate (someone).

lead (someone) by the nose
force (someone) into submission; completely control (someone) in thought and action; have (someone) under one's power.

lead (someone) on
1. tease, jest, joke by telling untruths or aggravating remarks.
2. entice, tempt, seduce (someone) into going further than was intended, often to that person's detriment.

lead (someone) up the garden path
advise (someone) incorrectly, falsely; mislead (someone); lie to (someone); cheat, con, swindle, hoodwink (someone).

lead-foot
a fast, reckless, dangerous driver.

lead-in
1. an opportunity, opening.
2. introduction to (something).

leading question
question framed in such a way as to extract a desired response.

leak
1. the act of urinating: e.g. I need a leak.
2. to urinate: e.g. Aren't men lucky to be able to leak standing!
3. disclose secret or confidential information: e.g. Somebody leaked everything to the press.

leak out
disclosure of secret or confidential information; become known.

lean on (someone)
1. depend, rely, count on (someone): e.g. He needs someone to lean on after all that tragedy.
2. intimidate, put pressure on (someone): e.g. The Mafia leans heavily on people who don't pay their debts.

lean over backwards
go to a great deal of trouble and effort; try very hard: e.g. He's so generous he'd lean over backwards to help anyone.

lean times/years
time of scarcity; depression; financially hard and difficult times: e.g. The way inflation keeps spiralling, there are some lean years ahead for the not-so-rich.

leap at
to grasp an opportunity with enthusiasm: e.g. I'd leap at the chance of working at that job if a vacancy came up.

See also:
look before you leap

leap forward
sudden progress: e.g. Getting promoted was a big leap forward for him and his family.

leap in the dark
an action taken with no knowledge of the outcome or possible consequences; a risky chance.

leaping lizards!
exclamation of surprise, amazement.

leaps and bounds
quickly; rapidly; in swift progression: e.g. That business is going ahead in leaps and bounds.

learn the hard way
refuse to listen to sound advice; choose a needlessly difficult method of doing something.

learner
person learning to drive a car prior to obtaining a licence.

leave it at that
say, do no more.

leave no stone unturned
try everything possible concerning a situation or matter: e.g. The police left no stone unturned in their investigations into that crime.

leave off!
cease; desist; stop annoying and harassing: e.g. Will you leave off!

leave (one) cold
1. make no worthwhile impression on (one); not particularly please, amuse or affect (one): e.g. That play had so much good publicity yet it left me cold.
2. make (one) feel displeasure, disapproval, anger etc.: e.g. Movies combining sex with violence leave me cold.

leave (someone) for dead
beat (someone) in a contest; out-class, do better than, out-do (someone): e.g. That candidate looks like leaving the others for dead in the coming election.

leave (someone) holding the baby/bag
desert, leave (someone) to face the unpleasant consequences of a problem for which he is not responsible.

leave (someone) to it
let (someone) alone to get on with a task: e.g. Now that you know what to do I'll leave you to it.

leave well enough alone
refrain from interfering or further aggravating a situation.

For other possible entries beginning with 'leave' see entries listed under 'left'.

Leb red
hashish.

lech
lecher; debauched, lustful person.

lecky
electric: e.g. It's cold enough tonight to switch the lecky blanket on.

led by the nose
completely controlled in thought and action by someone else.

For other possible entries beginning with 'led' see entries listed under 'lead'.

leech
person who extorts profit from others; sponger; hanger-on; a parasite on the fortunes of others.

leery
1. sly, cunning; knowing.
2. wary of; suspicious, cautious; distrustful.
3. looking debauched, intoxicated.

leeway
1. allowable deviation, margin, scope.
2. extra as in money, time: e.g. There's not a lot of leeway after we pay all the bills.

left
the more innovative, radical, socialist, liberal, or extremist section of any group, especially in politics.
See also:
two left feet.

left cold
be disappointed, unenthused, indifferent, uninspired: e.g. I was left cold by that performance.

left high and dry
deserted; abandoned in time of need: e.g. His family was left high and dry when he died suddenly.

left in the lurch
abandoned in time of need, especially by a friend or lover.

left on the shelf
1. deserted by friends in time of need; unwanted; not included.
2. (of a woman) with no prospects of marriage.

left (one's) mark on
to have had some lasting effect on something or someone: e.g. He's really left his mark on her — she's still broken-hearted after he's been gone for years.

left out in the cold
not informed; not told the facts or truth.

left, right and centre
everywhere: e.g. I had to search left, right and centre for that thing!

left to the wolves
abandoned, deserted in time of need and support.

For other possible entries beginning with 'left' see entries listed under 'leave'.

left-booter/footer
a Roman Catholic.

left-handed
1. awkward, clumsy.
2. ambiguous; insincere; indirect; sardonic; cynical: e.g. That was a left-handed compliment.

leftie
(see: lefty)

leftist
member of the left, or one sympathising with their views.

left-wing
(see: left)

lefty
1. a punch or hit with the left fist: e.g. He was floored by a lefty to the eye.
2. a left-handed turn in a vehicle: e.g. Chuck a lefty at the next street.
3. a leftist — one who supports the left-wing in politics.

leg
(see: crooked as a dog's hind leg; get a leg in; grow legs on one's belly; haven't got a leg to stand on; hollow legs; nice legs, shame about the face; on one's last legs; pull someone's leg; pull the other leg; shake a leg; show a leg; talk the legs off a wooden table/an iron pot)

leg man
a man who favours legs as the most desirable attribute of a woman.

leg room
freedom to do as one desires.

legal-eagle
lawyer; solicitor.

legend in (one's) own mind
an unmerited high opinion of (oneself).

leggy
long-legged.

legit
1. legitimate; lawful; legal; permitted: e.g. That deal doesn't sound legit to me.
2. authentic; genuine; reliable: e.g. I don't think those antiques are legit — they look like repros to me.

leg-opener
alcohol (or other enticement) given to a woman in the hope of having her agree to sexual intercourse.

leg-pull
a trick, hoax or act of deception.
See also:
pull (someone's) leg

legs like matchsticks
very thin legs.

legwork
busy work involving running around, doing errands or seeking information: e.g. The police had to do a lot of legwork before they found enough evidence to incriminate him.

lemon
1. something shoddy or faulty, such as a new car that constantly breaks down; a reject or failure: e.g. That brand new car is a bloody lemon — it's broken down six times in as many weeks!
2. a sour, humourless person.

lemon squash
(rhyming slang) wash.

lemon/orange time
(Australian Rules football) three-quarter time.

lend
(see: having a lend of someone)

lend a hand
help; assist.

lend an ear
listen attentively: e.g. The council never seems to lend an ear to the complaints of the residents any more.

length
the penis in reference to sexual intercourse: e.g. Did you slip her a length last night?
See also:
get a length
measure (one's) length

leopard can't change its spots
(of a person, especially a bad one) the principle or belief that a person is set in his ways and can't change his personality or make-up.

leprechaun
an Irishman.

lesbo/les-be-friends/leso
a lesbian.

lesser of two evils
an evil, bad or unpleasant person or thing that is not as bad as its alternative; the more agreeable of two unpleasant choices: e.g. I think that both of them are bastards, but I voted for him because he's the lesser of two evils.

lesso
a lesbian.

lesson
(Australian Rules football) a drubbing.
See also:
have learnt one's lesson
teach someone a lesson

let alone
not to mention; not even: e.g. I'm too tired to walk, let alone run!

let bygones be bygones
forget grievances and forgive, reconcile.

let 'er rip!
exclamation signalling an enthusiastic start.

let fly
burst out with a barrage of insults: e.g. She let fly at him in front of everyone!

let go
1. release one's pent-up emotions.
2. cease to restrain oneself: e.g. He'd like to let go and have fun but he's too shy.
3. expel wind from the anus; fart: e.g. Judging by the smell I'd say that someone just let go!

let it all hang out
1. behave in an uninhibited, free manner: e.g. When he's away from the office and at home, he lets it all hang out.
2. show emotions without fear or embarrassment: e.g. Women let it all hang out much easier than men, especially in crying.
3. speak one's mind freely: e.g. I'm going to let it all hang out at the next meeting.

let it rest/ride
refrain from saying, doing or interfering any more.

let it rip!
exclamation signalling an enthusiastic start.

let off
expel wind from the anus; fart.

let off steam
relieve pent-up energy through (usually) harmless activity; express harmless anger or frustration.

let on
1. reveal, tell a secret or confidence (especially indiscreetly): e.g. I didn't let on that I was married.
2. pretend: e.g. He let on all night that he was rich and she believed him.

let (one's) hair down
behave in an uninhibited and informal manner; do something daring that is not characteristic of (one's) personality.

let (oneself) go
1. act in an informal or uninhibited manner; do something daring: e.g. I got drunk at the party and really let myself go.
2. neglect (oneself); allow (oneself) to become untidy, slack, sloppy etc.: e.g. Since he went on the booze again he's really let himself go.

let (oneself) in for
become involved in: e.g. before you take that job on, make sure you know what you're letting yourself in for.

let rip
1. vent one's emotions, particularly anger, without restraint.
2. swear; use foul language without restraint: e.g. I wish he wouldn't let rip all the time in front of my parents.
3. expel wind from the anus; fart: e.g. Who let rip?

let sleeping dogs lie
leave well enough alone; refrain from further interference that might cause further trouble.

let slip
reveal a secret or confidence unintentionally: e.g. She let slip in front of a detective that she'd robbed a bank.

let (someone) down
disappoint, fail, betray (someone).

let (someone) have it
1. bash, attack violently.
2. abuse (someone) vehemently.

let (someone) in on
share a secret with, reveal a confidential matter: e.g. I think we should let him in on what's going on.

let (someone) off the hook
exempt (someone) from punishment or from doing something distasteful: e.g. The police let him off the hook this time.

let (someone) stew for a while
purposefully refrain from easing (someone's) worry or anguish.

let the cat out of the bag
reveal a secret or confidential matter (often unintentionally).

let the devil take the hindmost
a selfish statement that those following, everyone else, will have to look after themselves.

let the grass grow under (one's) feet
stagnate; become idle, lazy.

let the side/team down
fail to give support when most needed.

let things slide
1. neglect things; be negligent; allow deterioration.
2. allow matters to rest for a while.

let up
become less severe or harsh; ease off: e.g. The storm didn't let up for days.

let-down
disappointment; failure; disillusionment; anti-climax: e.g. The show was a let-down.

let's see what you're made of!
a menacing invitation among men to fight or to prove oneself.

lettuce
money (paper — not coin).

let-up
slackening in pace; a pause or slowing-down.

level
(see: on the level)

level-headed
sensible; composed; practical; having common sense.

leverage
power; influence; clout: e.g. The left-wing has a lot of leverage in politics.

lezzo/lezzy
a lesbian.

Lib
member of the Liberal Party.

libber
liberationist — especially of the women's liberation movement.

licence
(see: get one's licence out of a cornflakes pack)

licence to print money
a lucrative, profitable scheme.

lick
1. thrash; beat; bash: e.g. He's big enough to lick his father.
2. defeat: e.g. Our team licked them in the grand finals.
3. overcome a burden or problem: e.g. We're going to lick this thing together.
4. perform cunnilingus.

lick and a promise
superficial, perfunctory attempt: e.g. The housework will have to do with a lick and a promise until next week.

lick into shape
1. put into proper condition; rejuvenate; repair.
2. overcome a problem or burden.

lick (one's) chops/lips
anticipate eagerly, greedily.

lick (someone's) arse/boots
behave in an obsequious manner.

lick the dust
1. humble oneself; grovel in shame.
2. die or be seriously wounded.

licked
beaten; defeated.

lickety spit
a wash, especially a quick one.

lickety-spit/split
quickly; fast.

licking
1. a thrashing, beating, physical assault.
2. sound defeating.

licking (one's) chops
anticipating eagerly.

licking (one's) wounds
in retirement or seclusion recovering from a beating, defeating.

lid
a hat.
See also:
dip (one's) lid
flip (one's) lid
lift the lid on
put the lid on

lie
(see: couldn't lie straight in bed)

lie doggo
to hide, remain hidden, especially when something is expected of one, such as work.

lie in
sleep in; stay in bed later than usual.

lie low
hide; take cover; go underground; keep quiet and out of view, especially from the authorities or police.

lie straight-faced

lie through (one's) teeth
tell lies convincingly with a look of innocence.

lie with (someone)
have sexual intercourse with (someone).

lie-in
an extra length of time in bed in the morning.

life
the maximum prison sentence covering the remainder of the person's natural life: e.g. He's doing life for murder.
See also:
change of life
for the life of me
full of life
go for your life
good life
guard (something) with (one's) life
have the time of (one's) life
kiss-of-life
large as life
larger than life
look at life through rose-coloured glasses
low-life
matter of life and death
new lease of life
not on your life!
see (one's) life flash before (one's) eyes
such is life!
take (one's) life in (one's) hands
that's life!
this is the life!
walk of life
you can bet your life

life at the top
life, existence at the top levels of society, business, organisations etc.: e.g. It's about time Ken enjoyed life at the top after struggling all his life for recognition and money.

life begins at (40)
a jocular expression emphasising the positive side of getting older.

life in the raw
the barbaric, unsavoury and vulgar aspects of life.

life is a bed of roses
the condition or quality of life is excellent, easy, opulent: e.g. Life is a bed of roses since he won the lottery.

life is not a bed of roses
the condition or quality of life is difficult, fraught with problems: e.g. Life with him isn't exactly a bed of roses, but I still love him.

life of Riley
an easy, trouble-free, luxurious existence: e.g. He's living a life of Riley since he won a fortune on the Pools.

life of the party
person full of fun and sure to turn a dull party into a lively and interesting one.

life wasn't meant to be easy
catch-phrase popularised by a Liberal Prime Minister of Australia, Malcolm Fraser, and now used as a jocular scoff at anyone complaining of hard times.

life-blood
vitalising or animating influence.

life-line
sole means of communication.

lifer
person convicted and sentenced to a life term in prison.

life-saver
1. any person or thing that helps or benefits in a time of need.
2. a sweet, round lolly, confection with a hole in the middle.

lift
1. steal; pilfer; take without permission: e.g. He'd lift anything that wasn't nailed down!
2. free ride in a vehicle: e.g. I can give you a lift home.
3. feeling of euphoria, elation: e.g. This drink will really give you a lift.

lift a finger
help in any way: e.g. He never lifts a finger around the house!

lift doesn't go all the way to the top
(of a person) lacking in intelligence.

lift (one's) game
improve (one's) performance; try harder: e.g. He's going to have to lift his game or else the boss will sack him.

lift the lid on
expose, reveal (something): e.g. The police have enough evidence now to lift the lid on a suspected drug syndicate.

lifted
stole: e.g. Someone lifted my push-bike!

lift-out
a free supplement in a magazine, newspaper.

liger
the sterile offspring when a lion mates with a tiger.

light
(see: at first light; bring to light; come to light; green light; have/got some lights out upstairs; in a bad/good light; in the light of; make light of; out like a light; red light; see the light; shed some light on; strike a light!; throw new light on; trip the light fantastic)

light into (someone)
attack (someone) verbally or physically.

light of (one's) life
the most important thing, influence in (one's) life.

light (on)
in short supply: e.g. We're a bit light on with funds this week.

light out
depart, leave, go in haste.

light (someone's) fire
arouse (someone) sexually.

light the way
lead; direct.

light years
many, many years.

lighten the load
help make a problem less burdensome.

light-fingered
given to stealing.

light-footed
nimble; quick.

light-handed
understaffed; not having enough personnel.

light-headed
giddy; delirious; dizzy; confused: e.g. I feel light-headed after all that booze.

light-hearted
cheerful; happy; untroubled; carefree.

lights are on but there's nobody home
(of a person) lacking in intelligence.

light-weight
a person of little importance or power.

like a bandicoot on a burnt ridge
lonely; forlorn.

like a bat out of hell
fast; with great haste or speed.

like a bear with a sore head
bad-tempered; grumpy.

like a bird
extremely well, easily, fast: e.g. This car goes like a bird.

like a bitch on heat
sexually aroused; horny.

like a blue-arsed fly
in a frenzied manner; erratically.

like a broken-down record
repetitive.

like a bull at a gate
anxious to start; headstrong; impatient.

like a bull in a china shop
extremely clumsy or inept.

like a candle in the wind
unstable; unsure of which direction or allegiance to take.

like a cat on a hot stove/tin roof
agitated; extremely worried, nervous, jittery.

like a charm
successfully; perfectly; extremely well.

like a chook with its head cut off
in a dither; flustered.

like a cut snake
in an extremely active, busy manner.

like a dream
successfully; perfectly; extremely well.

like a fart in a bottle
agitated; unable to keep still.

like a fish out of water
uncomfortable and ill at ease in unfamiliar surroundings or circumstances.

like a greasy stick up a dead dog's arse
easily; with no effort.

like a house on fire
extremely well: e.g. They get on like a house on fire.

like a leaf in the breeze
easily swayed by others, ideas etc.; changing course with every new idea, influence etc.; unsure of which direction or allegiance to take.

like a lily on a dust-bin
lonely; neglected.

like a madwoman's breakfast
(see: all over the place like . . .)

like a mole/wombat — eats, roots, shoots and leaves
pertaining to the sexual nature of men considered from a single woman's point of view.

like a moll at a christening
out of place; confused.

like a mushroom — kept in the dark and fed on shit
pertaining to a person who is deliberately kept ignorant of the true facts.

like a new pin
tidy; clean; looking as good as new.

like a one-armed taxi-driver with crabs
(see: busy as a . . .)

like a one-legged man at an arse-kicker's party
out of place; uncomfortable in one's surroundings; ill-equipped.

like a petunia in an onion-patch
1. alone; forlorn; neglected.
2. out of place.

like a pick-pocket at a nudist camp
out of place; confused; not comfortable with one's surroundings.

like a pimple on a pumpkin
very obvious.

like a pork chop
in a silly, foolish manner: e.g. He always acts like a pork chop when he's got an audience.

like a rat up a drainpipe
very quickly.

like a red rag to a bull
anything that excites or induces anger.

like a scalded cat
very quickly.

like a shag on a rock
alone; forlorn.

like a shot
very quickly.

like a spare groom/prick at a wedding
out of place; confused; not comfortable with one's surroundings; not needed or necessary.

like a stunned mullet
1. bewildered; surprised; astonished.
2. inert.

like a thief in the night
unexpectedly; stealthily.

like a tin of worms
extremely active; unable to remain still.

like a ton of bricks
with great force, commitment, energy: e.g. The Tax Department is going to come down on him like a ton of bricks.

like a two-bob watch
unreliable; second-rate; of poor quality.

like an octopus
seeming to have many hands (particularly when referring to the sexuality of men).

like an old maid's pram
empty; having no substance.

like anything
greatly; with energy, force, speed etc.: e.g. That car goes like anything.

like billyo
with gusto, speed, enthusiasm: e.g. We laughed like billyo at that joke.

like buggery
1. greatly; with energy, force, speed etc.: That car goes like buggery when you put the foot down!
2. no way! definitely not!: e.g. Like buggery! I'm not going to do what I don't believe is right!
3. exclamation of scorn, derision, disbelief; bullshit!

like chalk and cheese
nothing alike; opposites.

like clockwork
with mechanical precision; regular.

like crazy
quickly; extremely well; with enthusiasm: e.g. This book should sell like crazy.

like death warmed up
pale and exhausted; ill-looking.

like fun!
1. no!; not at all!; definitely not!
2. exclamation of derision, scorn, disbelief; bullshit!

like greased lightning
extremely fast.

like grim death
tenaciously: e.g. He clung to the cliff edge like grim death.

like having a shower with a raincoat on
descriptive phrase used by men to describe the wearing of a contraceptive sheath.

like hell
1. (as an exclamation) no way!; definitely not!: e.g. Like hell you can!
2. very fast, quickly: e.g. We're going to have to work like hell to finish on time.
3. exclamation of derision, scorn, disbelief; bullshit!

like it or lump it!
an expression conveying that it's immaterial whether a person likes something or not, he will just have to put up with it. (also: if you don't like it, lump it!)

like it was going out of fashion
very much; fast; quickly; in large amounts; excessive indulgence in: e.g. He drinks beer like it was going out of fashion.

like mad

like nobody's business

like one thing
extremely energetically, enthusiastically or intensely: e.g. Chris worked like nobody's business on our house.

like pushing shit uphill with a pointed stick/rubber fork
an extremely difficult task.

like shitting in bed and kicking it out with your feet
a sticky, unpleasant, disagreeable task.

like shooting fish in a barrel
an extremely easy task.

like something else
1. in a big way; greatly; energetically; enthusiastically: e.g. He can swing an axe like something else!
2. terrific; wonderful; excellent: e.g. You'll look like something else in that bikini!

like squeezing blood out of a stone
an impossibility, extremely difficult task, especially in regard to obtaining money.

like stalking a lion and coming back with a kitten
to achieve much less than what was expected, especially after boasting.

like taking candy from a baby
an extremely easy task.

like talking to a brick wall
said of someone who doesn't listen, comprehend, understand or respond.

like the clappers
very fast: e.g. That car goes like the clappers.

like trying to get blood out of a stone
(see: like squeezing blood . . .)

like two ferrets fighting in a sack
said of a woman who has a large bum.

like two peas in a pod
very similar, alike.

like water
liberally; unlimitedly: e.g. He spends money like water.

like water off a duck's back
1. unnoticed; unheeded; ignored; not understood.
2. having no effect.

like wildfire
rapidly; quickly: e.g. The disease spread like wildfire.

For other possible entries beginning with 'like' see entries listed under 'looks like'.

likely story
fabrication; seeming like truth or fact, but not credible: e.g. His alibi sounded like a likely story to me.

li-lo
inflatable rubber bed.

lily
(see: gild the lily; like a lily on a dustbin)

lily-livered
cowardly; weak; not brave or daring.

lily-white
innocent; beyond reproach; pure; chaste.

limelight
attention; public exposure; publicity.
See also:
in the limelight
steal the limelight

limey
a British sailor, ship or person.

limmo/limo
limousine.

limp rag
person of no vitality, firmness, energy or spirit.

line
1. a story, spiel, especially of a man's approach to a woman for sex: e.g. He handed me the same old line!
2. a short note or letter: e.g. Drop me a line during your trip.
3. vocation; business; calling; occupation: e.g. What line is he in now?
4. a trick, swindle or act of deception.
5. a thin line of cocaine prepared for inhaling, snorting.
See also:
bring (someone) into line
do a line with
draw a fine line
draw the line
drop (someone) a line
fine line
get a line on
have/got (one's) lines crossed
know where to draw the line
lay it on the line
on the line
out of line
pay on the line
put it on the line
put (one's) neck on the line
read between the lines
string (someone) a line
toe the line
treading a fine line
walking a thin line

line of fire
centre of trouble, controversy: e.g. Many politicians find themselves in the line of fire over their mismanagement of public funds.
See also:
step into the line of fire

line (someone) up
procure, convince (someone) to do something: e.g. I think I might be able to line him up to do that job for us.

line (someone) up with (someone)
scheme, contrive to get one particular person to meet another with a view to forming a relationship, having sex etc.: e.g. Do you think you could line me up with a good sort for tonight?

line the pockets
to gain financially, often at the expense of others: e.g. There are many unscrupulous con-men who line their pockets at the expense of gullible people.

line up
1. set one's sights on a person with a view to forming a relationship, having sex etc.: e.g. Who have you lined up?
2. recruit, procure: e.g. We'll line up a good builder to do this job.

lines
a school punishment in the form of repetitive writing.

line-up
gathering, arrangement of people or things for view, inspection, entertainment: e.g. That concert had a good line-up of singers.

lingo
1. language: e.g. I can't speak his lingo.
2. jargon, idiom or language associated with any particular subject: e.g. I don't understand computer lingo.

lion
(see: enter the lion's den; in like a lion, out like a lamb; like stalking a lion and coming back with a kitten)

Lionel Rose
(rhyming slang) nose.

Lions
Fitzroy VFL football team.

lion's share
the biggest portion or part — often taken greedily or selfishly.

lip
cheek; impertinence; back-chat; impudence: e.g. Don't let any of those kids give you any lip!
See also:
bite (one's) lip
button your lip!
curl (one's) lip up
don't give me any of your lip!
give (someone) a fat lip
keep a stiff upper lip
lick (one's) lips
smack (one's) lips
tight-lipped

lippie/lippy
lipstick.

lips
the labia of the female genitals.

lip-service
insincere support given by word only.
See also:
pay lip-service to

liquid amber
beer.

liquid laugh
vomit: e.g. Who had a liquid laugh on the floor of the dunny!?

liquid lunch
beer as opposed to food at lunchtime.

lire
money: e.g. That must have cost him a lot of lire!

listen in
eavesdrop.

listen to who's talking!
an expression of scorn, ridicule, sarcasm.

listens but doesn't hear
pertaining to someone who appears to be listening but doesn't understand or chooses to remain unsympathetic.

lit up
drunk; intoxicated.

lit up like a Christmas tree
1. very brightly lit with many lights.
2. showed sudden joy, enthusiasm, pleasure: e.g. Her face lit up like a Christmas tree when she received her present.
3. drunk; intoxicated.

litterbug
person guilty of littering.

little
1. an adjective denoting approval, pleasure: e.g. little beaut; little bottler.
2. adjective denoting disapproval: e.g. little shit; little idiot.
See also:
make little of
think little of

little beaut
very good, excellent, first-class person or thing: e.g.
1. You're a little beaut!
2. This car's a little beaut.

little bird/birdie told me
stock, standard answer about a secret source of information: e.g. Never mind how I know — a little birdie told me!

little bottler
person or thing of excellence, worthy of admiration.

little boys
cocktail sausages.

little boys'
men's toilet.

little brother/sister
younger brother/sister.

little buggers
children.

little does he know
he is not aware of the present circumstances.

little girls' room
women's toilet.

little green men
imaginary creatures from outer space.

little hours
the very early hours of the morning after midnight.

little house
the toilet — especially an outside one.

little Johnny
a child: e.g. Whose little Johnny is that?

little lady
wife.

little lunch
a snack eaten at morning recess at school (Queensland).

little man
businessman operating on only a small scale.

little man in the boat
the clitoris.

little people
1. legendary or imaginary fairies.
2. people or businessmen operating on only a small scale; unimportant, ordinary people.

little pigs have big ears
a warning that what is being said may be overheard by unwanted eavesdroppers, especially children.

little ripper
(see: little beaut)

little up top
dumb; stupid; lacking in intelligence.

little Vegemite
jocular term for a person or fellow, but especially for a child.

little woman
wife.

littlie
a small child, tot.

live a charmed life
to be always lucky, fortunate, especially in the face of danger.

live and learn
acquire knowledge through (sometimes bad) experience.

live and let live
go about one's own life and interests without interfering and meddling in other people's lives.

live close to the knuckle
live poorly, with barely sufficient money to survive (see: live from hand to mouth).

live dangerously
take risks continually.

live from hand to mouth

live from one day to the next
live on the breadline with barely enough money to last from one week to the next for such immediate needs as food, clothing and shelter.

live high (on the hog)
to live in wealth and luxury.

live in a box
to dwell in extremely confined, second-rate quarters.

live in a fool's paradise
to fantasise, have unrealistic notions and ideas so that (one's) happiness is only an illusion.

live in a pigsty
live in squalid, dirty conditions.

live in each other's pockets
live in close association with others, to the extent of losing privacy and individuality.

live in sin
to live with one's lover in an unmarried state.

live in style
to live in luxury.

live in the lap of luxury
live in wealth and luxury.

live in the past
to be obsessed with reminiscence, refusing to accept modern advances in technology and progress.

live it down
maintain one's composure until people forget the bad mistake, scandal etc. in which one was involved: e.g. After all the preaching she's done about other people's kids, she's never going to be able to live it down having a son convicted of rape and murder.

live it up
indulge oneself in pleasure, a spending spree, a good time etc.: e.g. After winning all that money I'm going to chuck my job in and live it up for a while.

live like kings
live in wealth and luxury.

live like pigs
live in squalid and dirty conditions.

live off the fat of the land
to work and enjoy the profits and products of one's property, land, country.

live off the land
to survive from the produce of the land, soil, farm etc.

live on
extract great enjoyment and fulfilment out of (something): e.g. Many housewives live on daytime soap operas on the telly.

live on a pipe-dream
live with futile and fanciful hopes and dreams: e.g. He's living on a pipe-dream if he thinks that invention of his is going to make him a fortune.

live on a razor's edge
be in extreme danger; faced with imminent threats on all sides.

live on a shoestring
(see: live from hand to mouth)

live on the smell of an oily rag
to have the ability to survive on the most meagre of incomes.

live out of a suitcase
to have no permanent or fixed place of abode; to live constantly in hotels, motels etc.

live out the back of beyond
live in a remote, sparsely populated district.

live (someone's) life for her/him
be a crutch for, do everything for, be in a position of being emotionally depended on by (someone): e.g. Too many parents live their children's lives for them in the hope of achieving, through their children, things they may not have achieved themselves.

live together
to live together as lovers, usually unmarried.

live under the same roof
live in the same house, dwelling: e.g. He's such a grub that I couldn't live under the same roof with him.

live up to
1. maintain a certain standard or expectation: e.g. He couldn't live up to what was expected of the job so he was fired.
2. emulate, equal, aspire to: e.g. Fathers should be the type of people their sons can live up to.

live with (oneself)
retain (one's) self-respect; come to terms with (one's) conscience, feelings of guilt: e.g. He's going to find it difficult to live with himself after killing his friend in a car accident whilst under the influence of alcohol.

live with (something)
come to terms with (something) in one's conscience: e.g. It's been difficult for him to live with the fact that his

father is a convicted murderer.

lived
(see: haven't lived yet)

lived-in
well-worn; untidy, shabby, homely due to use: e.g. His room has that lived-in look.

lives, eats and breathes
to base one's entire life, enjoyment, thinking, on something in particular: e.g. He lives, eats and breathes motor-racing.

live-wire
energetic, vivacious and spirited person.

livid
very angry.

living
enjoying the best (usually luxuries) that life can offer: e.g. Since winning the million-dollar lotto, he's really been living.
See also:
in the land of the living

living daylights
(see: beat the, scare the living daylights . . .)

living death
a wretched existence: e.g. It must have been a living death for the prisoners-of-war in Hitler's concentration camps.

living end
insufferable; intolerable; the ultimate; the worst possible: e.g. That dress she wore to the ball was the living end!
See also:
isn't that the living end!

living high
(see: live high)

living skeleton
emaciated, thin person.

lizard
(see: done up like a pet lizard; drain the lizard; flat out like a lizard drinking; leaping lizards!; starve the lizards!; stiffen the lizards!)

L.O.
initials for: leg-opener — anything that is an enticement for a woman to consent to have sex, such as strong alcohol, money etc.

load
1. an infection of gonorrhoea or other venereal disease.
2. plenty: e.g. He's got a load of money.
3. the ejaculated semen: e.g. He shot his load all over the wall.
See also:
get a load of

load of bull(shit)

load of codswallop

load of garbage

load of old cobblers

load of rubbish

load of wank
nonsense; worthless, insincere, untruthful talk, literature etc.: e.g. That magazine article was a load of bull.

load the dice
to fraudulently alter a situation to one's advantage.

loaded
1. wealthy, rich: e.g. He's loaded!
2. drunk, intoxicated: e.g. He's allowed to get loaded tonight as it's his birthday!
3. under the influence of drugs; stoned.
4. fraudulently altered to someone's advantage: e.g. Those dice were loaded.
5. full to capacity.

loads
plenty of: e.g. There were loads of people at the party.

loaf
1. the head, pertaining to intelligence: e.g. If he used his loaf more often, he wouldn't get into so much strife!
2. an easy, secure, cushy job, position, career.

loan
(see: having a loan of someone)

loan shark
person who lends money at excessive rates of interest.

lob
1. arrive: e.g. When did he lob into town?
2. arrive unexpectedly and uninvited: e.g. All the relatives lobbed for the weekend.
3. (tennis) high, looping shot.

lob on over
come to; go to; arrive at: e.g. There's a party at his place tonight — are you going to lob on over?

lob on to
to discover, find by chance: e.g. I lobbed on to a terrific little second-hand shop where the prices are very cheap.

lobbies
lobsters; yabbies; crayfish.

lobster
a twenty-dollar note.

local
1. person who lives in the locality.
2. a preferred and often visited pub in the local vicinity: e.g. He's down at the local with a few friends.

local bike
1. (derog.) promiscuous girl, woman.
2. well-known prostitute working in a particular locality.

local rag
newspaper particular to an area.

local yokel
1. a well-known character or resident.
2. (see: local, 1.)

lock horns with (someone)
be in dispute, disagree with (someone).

lock (someone) up and throw away the key
(often joc.) put (someone) in prison or an asylum for life.

lock, stock and barrel
totally; completely; thoroughly; absolutely: e.g. He lost everything he owned in the fire — lock, stock and barrel.

lockup
prison: e.g. He's serving life in the lockup.

loco
silly; crazy; mad; insane.

lofty
nickname or form of address for a tall or (joc.) extremely short man.

log of wood
lazy, stupid, slow, inefficient person.

Logies
Australian annual festival of awards held for excellence in the television industry.

lollipop lady/man
person in charge of school crossings — so named for the bright round stop-sign carried.

lollop
flop about, move in an ungainly, bounding or lounging manner.

lolly
1. sweet confection.
2. money.
3. head or temper: e.g. Every time I buy a new dress my husband does his lolly!
4. a fool or stupid person.
See also:
do (one's) lolly

lolly-water
softdrink; lemonade.

London to a brick
(see: bet London to a brick)

lone wolf
person who prefers to be or act alone.

lonely-heart
lonely person who does not have a partner or relationship.

lonely-hearts' club
an imaginary (or real) club for lonely, single people: e.g. He's just joined the lonely-hearts' club — his wife left him.

long
measure of time: e.g. How long will you be?
See also:
in the long run
so long
so long as

long and the short of
the gist of the matter; the crux; the essential facts.

long arm of the law
far-reaching, influential effects of law: e.g. He won't escape the long arm of the law forever — they'll catch him eventually.

Long Bay
prison in Sydney.

long chance
slim chance; not likely; not a good prospect.

long drink
alcoholic drink served in a tall glass with softdrink mixer.

long drop
execution by hanging.

long face
dismal, miserable, forlorn expression.

long haul
tedious, long trip, journey or task.

long in the tooth
old; aged; elderly.

long johns
men's warm underwear with full-length legs.

long odds
very uneven or poor chances of success.

long paddock
the territory between the bitumen road and the boundary fence — a grassy no-man's land alongside the roads.

long shot
1. slim, uncertain chance that could reap benefits if successful.
2. a wild guess or venture.

long streak of pelican shit/ weasel piss
(joc.) tall, lanky and clumsy person. (see: built like a . . .)

long talk
a serious discussion, lecturing or scolding: e.g. I'm going to have to have a long talk to him about his bad school report.

long-distance call on the big white telephone
to vomit in the toilet bowl.

long-hair
1. (derog.) an intellectual, bookish person.
2. hippie-type man with long hair: e.g. You won't get a job there — they won't hire long-hairs!

longhand
ordinary writing where the words are written in full as opposed to shorthand.

long-standing
long-lasting; perpetual; continual.

long-time-no-see
form of greeting to one you haven't seen for some time.

long'uns
long trousers: e.g. Better wear some long'uns — it's going to be cold tonight.

long-winded
inclined to talk at length; boring; monotonous.

loo
lavatory; toilet.

look a gift horse in the mouth
criticise a gift; accept a gift ungraciously, ungratefully, suspiciously. (see: don't look . . .)

look a treat
have an appealing appearance.

look after number one
take care of one's own interests.

look after the cents and the dollars will look after themselves
being careful with every small amount of money, being of thrifty habit must automatically ensure that (one) will always have sufficient funds.

look ahead
plan for the future.

look alive
hurry up; speed up.

look at life through rose-coloured glasses
see only the good things in life and ignore or avoid the sadder, cruel or ugly aspects.

look before you leap
think before acting in haste.

look daggers at (someone)
scowl, show anger, hate by the expression on the face.

look down on (someone)

look down (one's) nose at (someone)
consider oneself superior to (someone); hold (someone) in contempt, disdain; regard with ill-concealed scorn: e.g. Just because he's wealthy he looks down on everybody else.

look high and low
search everywhere.

look into
investigate: e.g. The police are looking into the case.

look like a million dollars
look very good, excellent, stunning.

look like (one) has been chasing parked cars
to appear beaten up, bloodied — especially of the face.

For other possible entries beginning with 'look like' see entries listed under 'like'.

look on the bright side of things
regard a situation with cheerful optimism.

look on the worst side
be pessimistic.

look out
be careful, wary.

look out for (oneself)
to have (one's) own interests at heart: e.g. He's so selfish, he only looks out for himself.

look sharp!
be quick! hurry up!

look (someone) in the face
meet (someone) without embarrassment, fear or shame.

look the other way
ignore, over-look deliberately, especially in the sense of official corruption: e.g. Many police look the other way as far as illegal brothels and casinos are concerned.

look through rose-coloured glasses
(see: look at life through rose-coloured glasses)

look up to
respect, admire: e.g. Not many Aussies look up to politicians who fail to act on their pre-election promises.

look what the cat dragged in!
(often joc.) expression of scorn, contempt for someone who has just entered.

looked straight through (one/someone)
ignored or failed to recognise, acknowledge (one/someone): e.g. I waved at him but he looked straight through me!

looker
very attractive person, especially a woman: e.g. She's going to be quite a looker when she grows up.
See also:
good looker

look-in
chance of success: e.g. He was so good at tennis that I didn't even get a look-in when we played.

looking at
liable to pay: e.g. You're looking at about ten thousand dollars for that car.

looking chipper
1. looking happy, elated.
2. well-dressed.

looking for a bit of skirt
(of men) seeking sexual gratification with a woman.

looking up
improving; getting better: e.g. After a bad start in the business, things are finally looking up.

looks
appearance: e.g. I don't like the looks of him.

looks good from Footscray/ the Western Suburbs
expression of contempt, indicating that the only way someone could look good is from a long distance away, from the bottom of the pile.

looks like a Chinese brothel (on Sunday morning)
pertaining to a dirty, unkempt, untidy place, especially a person's bedroom.

looks like a drowned rat
pertaining to someone or thing looking bedraggled, wet and soiled.

looks like a madwoman's breakfast/knitting/washing
in total confusion; messed up; muddled; in disarray.

looks like a rat looking over a straw broom
pertaining to a man with a beard.

looks like it
seems, appears likely: e.g. The weather forecast said it wasn't going to rain but it sure looks like it to me!

looks like something the cat dragged in
pertaining to someone who is slovenly, bedraggled, dirty or untidily dressed.

looks like the cat that swallowed the canary/ cream/mouse
pertaining to someone who looks pleased with himself, smugly self-satisfied.

looks like the wild man from Borneo
(of a man) unkempt; having untidy, unruly hair and a generally untidy appearance.

looks like two ferrets fighting in a sack
pertaining to a fat woman with an opulent backside.

For other possible entries beginning with 'looks like' see entries listed under 'like'.

look-see
a good look: e.g. Come and have a look-see at this!

loon
idiot; fool; crazy person.

loony
1. lunatic.
2. idiot; fool; crazy person.
3. idiotic; stupid; ludicrous: e.g. That's a loony idea.

loony bin
lunatic asylum.

loop
1. type of intra-uterine contraceptive device.
2. a fool or stupid person.

loop-hole
means of evading a rule, the law etc. without actually breaking the law or doing anything illegal: e.g. He made his fortune by finding loop-holes in the tax laws.

loop-the-loop
1. a loop through the air as might be performed by an aeroplane.
2. (rhyming slang) soup.

loopy
crazy; mad; insane; eccentric; stupid.

loopy about (someone)
extremely fond of, in love with (someone).

loose
(see: at a loose end; hang loose; on the loose)

loose change
coins, usually the change from spending a note.

loose end
a matter that is incomplete, or unfinished: e.g. I still have to attend to a few loose ends and then I'm going on a long holiday.
See also:
at a loose end

loosen up
relax; become less nervous, anxious.

loot
money.

loppy-lugs
lop-eared; having ears that hang down, as on a rabbit.

lord it over (someone)
domineer, tyrannise (someone).

lord, love a duck!
an expression of surprise, astonishment, disbelief, scorn etc.

Lord Muck
man full of affectation, one who puts on airs and graces or who has an unjustifiably high opinion of himself.

lord of the manor
1. (joc.) the owner of a residence; the man of the house.
2. man (or boy) who constantly attempts to evade household chores.

lord of the roost
the man of the house, such as the father, husband.

lose a bundle/packet
lose a large amount of money, especially in a wager or gamble.

lose face
lose one's reputation, prestige or good name; be humiliated.

lose ground
1. become less accepted or favourable: e.g. The popularity of the Prime Minister is losing ground in the face of spiralling inflation and unemployment.
2. lose something gained that one has worked for: e.g. The company lost a lot of ground during the power strike.

lose (one's) cool
(see: lose one's head)

lose (one's) dibs
(see: lose one's marbles)

lose (one's) head
become angry; lose one's temper, self-control, calm, composure.
See also:
don't lose your head

lose (one's) head if it wasn't screwed on
to be forgetful, absent-minded.

lose (one's) heart to
become infatuated with someone or thing.

'Does this mean I'm fired?!'

A bloke who has just been fired has had his employment abruptly terminated. In other words, he has been given the arse, axe, big A, boot, bullet, chop, marching orders, order of the boot, push, sack, shunt, spear, ticket or walking papers.

lose (one's) marbles
become silly, crazy, insane.

lose (one's) nerve
become afraid to do something.

lose (one's) scalp
get into serious trouble; get a severe scolding.

lose (one's) shirt
to lose everything, especially on a wager.

lose (one's) tongue
become speechless due to shyness, bewilderment.

lose (one's) touch
to become less adept, confident, skilled than (one) used to be.

lose (one's) train of thought
become confused and entangled in irrelevancies.

lose (one's) wool
lose (one's) temper.

lose (oneself) in
become totally involved, engrossed with: e.g. I love to lose myself in a good suspense novel.

lose out
be defeated or bettered by: e.g. Our company lost out to a cheaper tender.

lose out on
fail to achieve a goal, purpose: e.g. I lost out on getting the bargain of the year because I was late for the auction.

lose sleep over
to worry about excessively: e.g. I won't lose any sleep over that ratbag going to prison!

lose track of
fail to stay in touch, communication with.

loser
incompetent, unsuccessful person.
See also:
bad loser
born loser
good loser

lost cause
any thing or person that has failed or is doomed to failure.

lost for words
speechless due to astonishment, amazement, surprise etc.

lost in thought
engrossed in thought.

lost me
1. caused me to lose respect, faith etc.: e.g. After what he did he's lost me!
2. caused me to lose interest in or maintain comprehension of what is being said: e.g. He lost me when he started talking about computers.

lost soul
an outsider, loner, often due to socially unacceptable behaviour.

lost weekend
1. a weekend spent away exploring sexual delights with one's lover.
2. a weekend wasted through inactivity, or excessive indulgence in alcohol.

lot
a type of person or group of people: e.g. 1. He's a bad lot, he is! 2. They're a good lot to party on with.
See also:
have/got a lot going for (it/one)
throw (one's) lot in with

lot of water has flowed under the bridge (since then)
much has happened (since then).

lots
many; a large number; plenty.

lotus eater
idle, lazy, forgetful person.

loud
vulgar in manner, style of dress or speech; garish; flashy.

loud and clear
able to be heard, understood.

loudmouth
1. a person who speaks in a coarse, vulgar, blatant manner.
2. to speak in a vulgar, blatant, self-assured manner.
3. to reveal confidences or embarrassing facts for all to hear.

louse
a contemptible, despicable person.

louse up
spoil; ruin; bungle; make a mess of; mismanage.

lousy
1. sick, unwell or depressed: e.g. I feel lousy today.
2. awful; disgusting; filthy; revolting.
3. contemptible; mean; hateful; dreadful: e.g. That was a lousy thing to do.
4. mean with money; parsimonious: e.g. He's too lousy to shout a round of drinks.
5. inferior; shabby; second-rate: e.g. I'd hate to live in that lousy flat.
6. trifling; paltry; mere: e.g. He donated a lousy dollar!

lousy act
a contemptible, despicable thing to do.

lousy as a bandicoot
miserly; parsimonious; stingy; mean.

lousy break
a stroke of bad luck or misfortune.

lousy fuck
sexual partner whose performance is regarded as unsatisfactory.

lousy sod
contemptible or stingy person.

lout
a rough-mannered youth or young man.

love
1. (of games) no score; nil.
2. affectionate term of address: e.g. How are you love?
See also:
all's fair in love and war
for the love of God/Mike
free love
make love

love at first sight
to fall in love with someone or something at first meeting: e.g. When he saw that new sports car it was love at first sight.

love bite
(see: hickey)

love child
an illegitimate child; one born out of wedlock.

love juice
sexual secretion from the vagina or penis.

love me, love my dog
a declaration that others must accept without reservation something that is dear to one (such as a dog, cat, foible etc.)

love to be a fly on the wall
to express a desire to know what is happening or being said in a room in which one is not present.

love you and leave you
an expression of farewell, good-bye, departure.

loved ones
relatives.

love-life
pertaining to a person's amorous relationships.

love-making
sexual intercourse.

lover's balls
(of a man) pain experienced in the testicles as a result of not having a highly aroused sexual desire satisfied.

lovey-dovey
openly affectionate: e.g. Those two are so lovey-dovey since they made up after that argument.

low
1. depressed; miserable; unhappy; dejected: e.g. He feels a bit low today.
2. inferior; shabby; second-rate: e.g. That's a low neighborhood he lives in.
3. despicable; mean; dishonourable; vulgar: e.g. That was a low thing to do to someone.
See also:
keep a low profile
lie low
so low (one) could parachute out of a snake's bum
so low (one) has to reach up to touch bottom

low as shark shit
despicable; contemptible.

low-brow
an uncultured or unintelligent person.

low-down
1. knowledge; information; true facts: e.g. I want the low-down on the entire deal before I sign the contract.
2. despicable; dishonourable; mean: e.g. He's nothing but a miserable low-down, two-timing bastard!

lower (one's) sights
to lower (one's) ambitions.

lower (oneself)
to lose (one's) dignity: e.g. I'm not going to lower myself by behaving the way he does.

lower than a snake

lower than a snake's belly in a wheel rut

lower than a snake's tail down a well

lower than shark shit

lowest of the low
(of a person) despicable; contemptible.

lowie
a despicable, contemptible person.

low-key
understated; moderate; controlled; unobtrusive.

low-life
a despicable, contemptible person.

low-minded
vulgar, coarse, obscene.

LSD
lysergic acid diethylamide, a powerful hallucinogenic drug.

lube
lubrication, especially of a vehicle or engine.

lubra
(often derog.) an Aboriginal woman.

lubra-lips
(derog.) having large, protruding lips.

luck
(see: as luck would have it; bad luck!; devil's own luck; don't push your luck; down on one's luck; half your luck; in luck; Irish luck; just my luck!; never know one's luck in the big city; no such luck; press/push/stretch one's luck; stroke of luck; worse luck!)

luck of the draw
result or outcome of chance rather than design.

luck of the Irish
ridiculously good luck or fortune that seems to go against all odds.

lucky break
chance or opportunity.

Lucky Country
pertaining to Australia — coined from a book of the same name by Donald Horne.

lucky dip
a chance or undertaking for which the outcome is uncertain.

lucky dog
lucky, fortunate person.

lucre
money.

Lucy looselegs
a promiscuous woman.

lug
1. the ear: e.g. You'll get a belt in the lug if you're not careful!
2. fool; idiot; dunce; incompetent person.

lukewarm
indifferent; half-hearted; apathetic; dispassionate.

lulu
person or thing of outstanding quality or excellence; first-rate; amazing: e.g. Wait till you meet our new friend — he's a lulu at telling jokes!

lumbered with
to have foisted or palmed off upon oneself something or someone unpleasant or distasteful: e.g. I got lumbered with all the relatives and their kids over the holidays.

lummox
stupid, clumsy, foolish or incompetent person.

lump
1. tolerate, endure or put up with ungraciously because one has no choice.
2. clumsy, ungainly, stupid person.
3. to carry something heavy in an ungainly manner: e.g. She had to lump those heavy sacks down to the shed by herself.
See also:
get (one's) lumps
like it or lump it

lump in the throat
a heart-rending, emotional feeling that is often close to tears.

lump sum
total amount of money: e.g. He got his retirement benefits in a lump sum.

lungs
woman's breasts: e.g. She's got a huge set of lungs!

lurch
(see: left in the lurch)

lurgi/lurgy
an illness such as a cold or the flu.

lurk
1. a good scheme, thing, strategy that offers a short-cut to success.
2. a job, vocation, profession.
3. an unethical or moderately underhanded scheme, strategy.

lurks and perks
pertaining to schemes (often unethical) and resulting benefits, profits etc.: e.g. He knows all the lurks and perks of the gambling industry.

lush
1. drunkard; alcoholic.
2. sexually attractive, promiscuous woman.
3. luxurious; expensive; extravagant; plush.

luv
term of endearment — love.

lying through (one's) teeth
telling gross lies.

ma
mother.

Mac(k)
term of address between men (often unfriendly): e.g. Listen here Mac — who do you think you are!

macaroni
nonsense; rubbish: e.g. What he said was a lot of macaroni!

mace
a chemical irritant or incapacitating gas used in warfare, crowd or riot control or interrogation.

machine
person who follows orders without thought; a yes-man; puppet.

mad
1. angry; annoyed; furious.
2. merry; gay: e.g. That was a mad party we had last night.
See also:
go mad
like mad
looks like a madwoman's breakfast/knitting/washing

mad about
infatuated with; in love with; obsessed with: e.g. He's mad about his new car.

mad as a cut snake
1. crazy; insane; stupid; foolish; demented; unbalanced.
2. very angry.

mad as a gumtree full of galahs

mad as a hatter/March hare
1. crazy; insane.
2. silly; foolish; eccentric; odd; queer.

mad as a hornet/maggot/meat-axe
extremely angry.

mad as a two-bob watch
crazy; eccentric; silly; foolish; unpredictable; unreliable.

mad if you don't!
expression of encouragement.

madam
1. a woman in charge of a brothel.
2. vain, affected, conceited woman.

Madam Muck
an affected woman who puts on airs and graces far above her social standing.

made
assured of success: e.g. After that successful tender, he's really made now.
See also:
have/got it made
let's see what you're made of!
self-made

made a hole in it
to have got work well under way, started: e.g. We tried to clear the land manually at first, but the bulldozer has really made a hole in it.

made it
1. achieved success, wealth, fame etc.
2. arrived; were able to come, attend: e.g. I'm so glad you made it — the party would have been dull without you!

made it big/to the big time
achieved success, fame, fortune etc.

made of money
wealthy; very rich: e.g. He's made of money.

made-up
1. wearing facial cosmetics.
2. fabricated; an unbelievable story: e.g. His entire alibi was made-up.

For other possible entries beginning with 'made' see entries listed under 'make'.

madhouse
confused uproar; bedlam; chaos: e.g. The meeting errupted into a madhouse after a few people started to argue.

mag
magazine.

mag wheels
magnesium alloy or alluminium wheels for a car.

maggies
magpies.

maggot
a despicable, despised person.
See also:
mad as a maggot

maggoty
very angry, furious.

magic
great; wonderful; excellent; first-class: e.g. That was a magic restaurant we went to last night.

magic mushie/mushroom
hallucinogenic mushroom, eaten for the feeling of euphoria or high that it produces; gold-top (mushroom).

magic word
1. any word pertinent to a particular subject: e.g. If he said the magic word (yes) I'd go running to him.
2. vulgar swear word, especially 'fuck': e.g. My mother wasn't too pleased when my boyfriend dropped the magic word.
See also:
just say the magic word
drop the magic word

magnetic
physically attractive; having charisma, charm; fascinating.

magnetism
personal charm, charisma, glamour.

magpie
1. woman who is a gossip, chatterbox, incessant talker.
2. a collector of miscellaneous objects; a bowerbird.
3. a person from South Australia.

Magpies
1. Collingwood VFL football team.
2. Western Suburbs N.S.W. Rugby League football team.

maidenhood
virginity.

mail
information; facts: e.g. I'll give you the mail — that new horse is a winner!

main drag
the principal street: e.g. The office is on the main drag.

mainland
(joc.) Tasmania, as referred to by Tasmanians; New Zealand as referred to by New Zealanders.

mainline
to inject a narcotic drug directly into the veins.

mainliner
a drug-addict who injects narcotic drugs directly into the veins.

maitre d
maitre d'hotel — the head waiter.

make
origin of manufacture; brand.
See also:
on the make

make a bee-line for
travel in a direct path for; head straight for: e.g. After work we're all making a bee-line for the pub.

make a big splash
have a striking effect on; an ostentatious display; create a sensation.

make a blue/blunder/boo-boo
make a glaring error or mistake.

make a botch of
mess up; ruin, spoil: e.g. I made a botch of cooking the dinner.

make a break
disassociate oneself from: e.g. It's time he made a break from work and had a long holiday.

make a clean breast of
to confess.

make a clean sweep
1. to make a fresh and new start.
2. to completely get rid of (something).

make a face
grimace at; show disapproval, disgust or ridicule by one's facial expression.

make a false step
make an error or blunder.

make a go of
try to succeed at: e.g. They're trying to make a go of their marriage for the second time.

make a goat of (oneself)
make a fool of (oneself).

make a good fist of
do something exceptionally well.

make a good job of
1. (something) to complete satisfactorily; do well.
2. (someone) bash, beat, physically assault.

make a hash of
ruin, spoil, bungle (something); mess up.

make a hit with
cause, create admiration, wonder among: e.g. The new casino is sure to make a hit with the fun-loving public.

make a killing
be assured of success.

make a liar of (someone)
prove (someone) wrong: e.g. I've been telling my visitors all year how sunny Queensland always is, but the cyclonic weather is making an awful liar of me at the moment!

make a mess of things
ruin, spoil, bungle (something).

make a million/mint
make a great deal of money; become wealthy.

make a monkey of (someone)
make a fool of, embarrass (someone).

make a mountain out of a molehill
to turn an insignificant situation into a seemingly difficult problem; to complain to a degree that is out of proportion to the problem.

make a move
1. go, depart, leave.
2. begin; start some action; make a start; take some action.

make a muck of
spoil, ruin, bungle, make a mess of (something).

make a pass at (someone)
make an amorous advance or gesture to (someone): e.g. He made a pass at me but I told him to get lost.

make a pig of (oneself)
over-indulge (oneself), especially of food.

make a play
(see: make a pass)

make a point
state a pertinent fact.

make a point of
emphasise; insist on.

make a practice of
make a habit of.

make a production of (something)
be over-fussy, extreme or exaggerated in one's method of doing something or handling of a situation.

make a proper galah of (oneself)
make a complete fool of (oneself).

make a quid
1. earn a living: e.g. What does he do to make a quid?
2. make a lot of money; become wealthy: e.g. That idea of his should make a quid.

make a rod for (one's) back
cause, create a difficulty, problem, burden for (oneself).

make a scene
create a commotion, stir, uproar, turmoil.

make a song and dance about (something)

make a thing of (something)
to turn a minor incident into a major issue.

make a splash
do something with style, extravagance; call attention to oneself.

make a welter of
create confusion, disorder in the process of doing something; over-indulge to excess.

make an arse of (oneself)
make a fool of (oneself).

make an honest woman of
(of a man) to marry his girlfriend, mistress, lover.

make as if
pretend: e.g. Whenever junior doesn't feel like going to school he makes as if he's sick.

make away with
1. steal; pilfer; pinch: e.g. I left my purse on the counter and within ten minutes some rotter had made away with it!
2. destroy; get rid of: e.g. We finally made away with all the rubbish around the yard.

make believe
pretend; pretence.

make custard out of (someone)
defeat, beat (someone) soundly, either physically or as in a contest.

make do
manage; cope; get by with the few resources one can muster; improvise: e.g. Times have been hard but we always manage to make do with what we've got.

make ends meet
keep one's finances or spending within one's means.

make every penny count/work
be thrifty, economical, astute.

make eyes at (someone)
flirt with by giving seductive glances.

make faces
(see: make a face)

make for
1. go, proceed towards: e.g. The boys made straight for the pub after work.
2. be conducive to; help to promote, achieve: e.g. Many hands make for light work around the garden.

make fun of
ridicule, tease.

make good
1. succeed: e.g. He works so hard that he'll eventually make good in his business.
2. compensate for; repair; fulfil or carry out a promise: e.g. He is a very trustworthy person and will definitely make good his promises.

make good money
earn a profitable living.

make good time
arrive or do something punctually, with time to spare.

make hay while the sun shines
make the most of good opportunities or situations while they last.

make head or tail of
understand; work out; comprehend; solve: e.g. I couldn't make head or tail of what he was talking about.

make heavy weather of
do something the hard way, find something unnecessarily fraught with problems and difficulty.

make it
1. have sexual intercourse: e.g. Did you make it with her?
2. achieve success in life, wealth, power etc.: e.g. After a lot of hard work he made it.
3. arrive at a destination: e.g. I'm glad you could make it to the meeting.

make it hot for (someone)
create trouble for (someone); make life difficult and unpleasant for (someone).

make it out
understand; comprehend; solve: e.g. I can see faint writing on this page but it's hard to make it out.

make it right with (someone)
1. make amends; repay a debt.
2. bribe (someone).

make it snappy
hurry up; be quick.

make it to the big time
achieve renowned success, wealth, power etc.

make it up
(see: make up)

make it with flying colours
be triumphantly successful.

make life unpleasant
cause trouble and unpleasantness.

make light of
treat as insignificant; assign no importance to: e.g. The law doesn't make light of drug offenders.

make like a boong's armpit

make like a tree (and leave)
depart; leave; go.

make like (someone/something)
pretend; imitate; behave like: e.g. He makes like a deaf mute when I ask him for a loan.

make little of
1. fail to understand: e.g. I could make little of what he said.
2. tone down; moderate: e.g. The police made little of allegations of corruption in the force.

make love
have sexual intercourse.

make love, not war
catch-phrase of anyone opposed to war, nuclear weapons etc.

make mince-meat out of (someone)
1. beat, bash, hit, physically assault (someone).
2. berate, verbally attack, criticise (someone) with success.

make music together
get on extremely well with someone.

make no bones about (something)
be absolutely frank, candid, honest, direct about (something): e.g. She made no bones about telling him what she thought of him!

make no odds
make no difference; be of no importance; not to matter: e.g. It makes no odds with me which way we go as long as we get there.

make noises like (someone)
sound like; behave in a manner like: e.g. He's starting to make noises like a jealous husband, so I think I'll stop dating him.

make off
depart in haste.

make off with
steal; pilfer: e.g. Someone made off with my push-bike!

make (one) or break (one)
be the success or the ruination of (one): e.g. This new venture that he's sunk thousands of dollars into is either going to make him or break him.

make (one) sick
disgust, annoy or irritate (one) intensely: e.g. He makes me sick!

make (one's) alley good
improve (one's) prospects of success, especially (of a man) with a woman; make the grade.

make (one's) blood boil
cause (one) to be intensely annoyed or angry.

make (one's) blood curdle/run cold
cause intense fear, fright or disgust.

make (one's) day
cause great merriment, joy, satisfaction; an event that would be the highlight of (one's) day: e.g. It would really make my day if hubby thought of giving me brekky in bed!

make (one's) flesh creep
repel, repulse, revolt, frighten (one).

make (one's) hair curl
astonish, amaze, shock (one).

make (one's) hair stand on end
frighten, terrify, shock (one).

make (one's) mark on
to have an influence on; become successful, well known or famous: e.g. She's really made a mark on the fashion industry with her outrageous designs.

make (one's) mouth water
cause to anticipate eagerly.

make (one's) peace
seek reconciliation: e.g. He's trying very hard to make his peace with his mother-in-law.

make (one's) way in the world
achieve success.

make (oneself) at home
feel comfortable and at ease in (one's) surroundings.

make (oneself) scarce
1. depart; go; leave.
2. to stay out of sight, hidden: e.g. He likes to make himself scarce whenever the relatives visit.

make or break (something)
be the success or the ruination of (something).

make out
1. have sexual intercourse: e.g. He'd love to make out with her.
2. understand; comprehend; decipher: e.g. I couldn't make out what he was trying to say.
3. give cause to believe: e.g. He tried to make out to the police that he didn't do it.
See also:
how did you make out?

make sheep's eyes at (someone)
give (someone) amorous, adoring looks, glances.

make short work of
to finish or deal with quickly: e.g. With the extra help, we made short work of that job.

make (someone) eat (his) words
cause (someone) to retract what he has said; prove (someone) wrong.

make (someone) open his eyes

make (someone) sit up and take notice
1. astonish, amaze, astound (someone).
2. force (someone) to accept, see, understand the truth or facts.

make (someone) see red
cause (someone) to be furious, very angry.

make (someone) squirm
cause (someone) to suffer extreme anxiety, embarrassment.

make something of (oneself)
be ultimately successful in (one's) career or choice of profession.

make the best of
to manage as well as possible against all odds or with a bad set of circumstances.

make the big time
to achieve success, wealth or power in high society or business.

make the feathers/fur fly
cause a commotion; create trouble.

make the grade
1. achieve success.
2. reach the standard set.

make the kindergarten left-overs
(see: couldn't . . .)

make time
1. to work quickly: e.g. We made good time on that job.
2. set aside the time to do something: e.g. I'm so busy I can't seem to make time to visit anybody.

make tracks
go; depart; leave.

make tracks for
go towards or in pursuit of: e.g. We're making tracks for the nearest pub.

make up
1. invent; fabricate; concoct a story: e.g. None of it's true — I made it all up.
2. to settle differences amicably after a quarrel: e.g. They finally made up after years of arguing.

make up for lost time
to attempt to do now the things one did not do in the past.

make up to
1. behave in an obsequious, fawning manner to (someone).
2. attempt to seduce or make amorous advances to (someone).

make waves
cause trouble, create disturbances within an existing set of circumstances.

make whoopee
engage in noisy merry-making, enjoyment, amorous play: e.g. We made whoopee all night on his birthday.

make with the
hand over; give; pass; prepare; offer: e.g.
1. Make with the munchies — I'm starving!
2. He'd better make with the money soon or I'll sell this car to someone else.

make-believe
1. pretended; imaginary; simulated: e.g. The make-believe space ride at that fun-park is terrific!
2. counterfeit; fake; phony: e.g. His house is full of genuine antiques, not make-believe ones.

makings
1. potential: e.g. He's got the makings of a good musician.

2. materials necessary for rolling one's own cigarettes, that is papers and tobacco.

malarky
nonsense; rubbish; foolish talk.

male chauvinist pig
man who is excessively loyal to other men and totally opposed and prejudiced against women, believing them to be inferior.

mallee
any remote, isolated and unpopulated scrub or bush land: e.g. He lives out in the mallee somewhere.
See also:
randy as a mallee bull
strong as a mallee bull

mallee root
(rhyming slang) prostitute.

malt
beer: e.g. He's very fond of a malt or two after work.

mammaries
woman's breasts.

man
1. term of familiar address between men: e.g. G'day man — where have you been all this time?
2. (as an exclamation) expression of surprise, wonder: e.g. Man — that was amazing!
3. (preceded by: the) the boss, leader, person in charge: e.g. Where's the man — I want to speak to him.
4. (Australian Rules football) cry from barrackers when an opponent grabs one of their players. (also: holding the man!)
See also:
a man's home is his castle
angry young man
another good man down the drain
are you a man or a mouse?
best man
clothes don't make the man
dirty old man
every man and his dog
every man for himself
every man has his price
front man
he-man
iron man
ladies' man
like a one-legged man at an arse-kicker's party
little man
looks like the wild man from Borneo
marked man
middleman
new man
no-man's land
odd man out
old man
one-man band
right-hand man
the way to a man's heart is through his belly and what hangs on the end of it
yes-man

man about town
man who frequents night-clubs, theatres, restaurants etc.

man enough
strong enough; courageous, brave, daring enough: e.g. He's not man enough to do what he says.

man in the rubber boat
the clitorus.

man in the street
the average person: e.g. The man in the street certainly doesn't want to see the proliferation of nuclear weapons.

man in white
the umpire.

man of God
clergyman; priest; believer and follower of God.

man of his word
man who is trustworthy and reliable.

man of iron
strong, wilful man.

man of straw
1. effigy; imaginary person set up as an opponent, surety etc.
2. one who is insignificant, a nonentity; morally frail.

man of the world
sophisticated, knowledgeable man.

man on man
(Australian Rules football) close, checking defence.

man on the land
pertaining to farmers, graziers, primary producers.

man outside Hoyts
so flamboyant in dress and manner as to be jokingly referred to as an authority on various subjects (the man outside Hoyts was the crier who stood outside Hoyts Theatre in Melbourne during the 1930s).

man the lifeboats
an order to get to work, start industrious activity.

man up
(see: man on man)

mandies
(Mandrax) barbiturates, as used by drug-addicts.

man-eater
woman who has little concern for the emotions of her lovers.

mangy
squalid; dirty; shabby.

man-hole
woman's vagina.

man-hole cover
menstrual pad.

manhood
pertaining to a man's genitals or sexual experience.

man-oh-man!
expression or exclamation of wonder, admiration, amazement, surprise etc.: e.g. Man-oh-man! What a party that was!

man's best friend
1. a dog.
2. the penis.

man's man
man who displays flamboyant masculinity, machismo, and who often shows little regard for women.

man's world
(see: it's a . . .)

man-to-man
pertaining to a discussion that is frank, open, honest and direct: e.g. I'm going to have to have a man-to-man talk to him about his boozing and dope-smoking!

manual
a car with a manual gear-shift as opposed to an automatic.

many a time
frequently.

many's the day
often; several, many times: e.g. Many's the day he's tried to give up smoking, but it hasn't worked yet!

Maori PT
(joc.) idleness; lying down or resting.

Maori's pyjamas
marijuana.

marbles missing
(have one's . . .) lacking in intelligence, sense; pertaining to being silly, crazy, mad, odd or eccentric.

march down the aisle
to marry.

marching orders
dismissal; be fired or sacked: e.g. His work was so bad that the boss gave him his marching orders today.

marg(e)
margarine.

margin of error
difference allowed for mischance or miscalculation.

mark
(see: easy mark; black mark; give someone full/top marks; left one's mark on; make one's mark on; off the mark; on your mark; overshoot/step the mark; quick off the mark; top marks; up to the mark; wide of the mark)

mark down
reduce the price, cost.

mark (one's) words
believe, take note of what (one) says or advises: e.g. Mark my words — if you do that again I'll have to fire you!

mark time
to be held up; wait.

mark up
increase the price of for profit: e.g. During the holiday season all the restaurants mark up their meals.

marked man
to be singled out, watched: e.g. After having several drug-related convictions, he's a marked man to the police.

market
(see: black market; buyer's market; go to market; in the market for; meat market; up-market)

marks
money.

mark-up
increased price for profit: e.g. The mark-up on most goods in retail stores is very high.

marriage material
suitable or desirable for marriage: e.g. The way he likes to play around, he's not very good marriage material.

marriage of convenience
to marry for profit rather than love and romance.

marriage on the rocks
pertaining to a marriage relationship that is breaking down and likely to end in separation or divorce.

marry-you-later
marijuana.

marties
tomatoes.

Mary J/Jane
marijuana.

Mary Pickford in three acts
a quick, perfunctory wash of the body — face, feet and genitals.

Mary's room
the toilet — especially for women.

mash
mashed potatoes.

massage parlour
an establishment that is generally believed to provide sexual gratification as the main business of massage.

masses
the bulk of the population; the ordinary people.

master hand
an expert, skilled, adept person: e.g. He's a master hand at wood-work.

mat
(see: on the mat; pull the mat out from under someone; put on the mat; sweep it under the mat)

mate
1. term of address among men (sometimes in aggression): e.g. Listen here mate! You'll get a poke in the nose if you don't shut up!
2. best friend; pal; buddy; chum.

material
(of a person)
demonstrating potential in something: e.g. He's good foreman material.
See also:
marriage material

mates' rates
reduced prices for goods, labour etc. for friends.

mates with
friendly with: e.g. I'm not mates with him any more.

matey
1. friendly with: e.g. Those two are very matey (with each other).
2. term of friendly address among men.

matey with
familiar or friendly with: e.g. He's being matey with the boss so that he can ask for a raise.

mateyness
friendship.

matilda
a swag, as carried by a tramp or swagman.

matter of life and death
something that is very important, critical.

maul
to fondle sexually in a boorish, clumsy manner.

maulers
hands: e.g. Take your maulers off my jewels!

mausoleum
a gloomy, dark and depressing building.

may as well be caught for a sheep as for a lamb
pertaining to the belief that if one is going to do something — especially something risky or illegal — one may as well commit oneself entirely, for the consequences are just the same; to behave impetuously.

may your chooks turn into emus and kick your dunny door down

may your ears turn into arseholes and shit all over your shoulders
an insult, popularised by Barry Humphries's character — Bazza McKenzie.

M.C.
Master of Ceremonies; em-cee.

M.C.G.
Melbourne Cricket Ground.

meadow cake
cow pat, dung.

meal ticket
any means of financial support: e.g. He's her meal ticket.

mealy-mouthed
insincere; hypocritical; afraid to speak plainly, truthfully.

mean
effective; powerful; energetic: e.g. That sure is a mean machine (car) he drives now.

mean as cat shit
nasty; unpleasant; unkind; selfish; miserly.

mean business
be serious about carrying out a threat or course of action: e.g. Perhaps the government means business this time over its threat to deregister the union if there's any more strife.

meanie
nasty, unpleasant, unkind, selfish or miserly person.
See also:
blue meanies
grey meanie

means doesn't justify the end
the method or way in which something is done to attain a goal is unfair, unjust or contemptible.

measly
petty; paltry; meagre; inferior; contemptible: e.g. He donated a measly dollar to the charity.

measure
(see: for good measure)

measure (one's) length
fall flat on the ground: e.g. He tripped and measured his length in a pile of cow shit.

measure up to
be suitable for; equal: e.g. He doesn't measure up to my expectations of a world champ.

meat
1. male or female genitals.
2. people as sex objects: e.g. That night-club is nothing but a meat market.
3. essence, gist, main substance of.
See also:
Australian as a meat pie
beat the meat
heat in the meat
mad as a meat-axe
make mince-meat of (someone)
run at (someone) with a meat-axe

meat in the sandwich
(see: filling in the sandwich)

meat market
any place where sex is easily obtained.

meatball
fool; idiot; incompetent person.

meaty
1. profound; deep; meaningful; significant: e.g. Some meaty points were discussed at the last meeting.
2. lurid; sensational; explicit; vulgar, bawdy or obscene: e.g. That movie sure had a lot of meaty bits in it!

mechanical mind
ability or skill at working with machinery.

medical
medical examination.

medicine
any experience, situation or action that is unpleasant or difficult to accept: e.g. If someone gave him a taste of his own medicine he wouldn't treat other people so badly.
See also:
take (one's) medicine

medic(o)
doctor.

meet (one's) Waterloo
1. to die.
2. to suffer a crushing defeat.

meet (someone) halfway
come to a compromise with (someone).

mega
1. a great amount.
2. wonderful; terrific; excellent; astounding: e.g. That concert was mega!

megabucks
a great amount of money.

Melbournian/Melburnian
pertaining to Melbourne; a person from Melbourne.

melon
1. stupid, ineffectual person.
2. the head.

melonhead
stupid, ineffectual person.

melt at the knees
to succumb to passion, love, infatuation over someone.

melt into thin air
to disappear without trace.

melting pot
any place or situation in which vigorous and diverse ideas, beliefs, customs or people come together and mix.

member
the penis.

member of the mushroom club (kept in the dark and fed on shit)
a person who has been deliberately kept ignorant of the facts.

member of the Wandering Hands Society
a man who is noted for his touching and fondling of women in a lewd manner.

memo
memorandum; reminder note.

memory like a sieve
forgetful.

memory like an elephant
(to have) a very good memory.

menace
an annoying person or thing.

mend (one's) ways
change (one's) attitude, actions for the better; reform.

mental
mad; insane; stupid.
See also:
chuck a mental
drive (someone) mental

mental block
a lapse in memory.

Merc
Mercedes (car).

merchant
person who is well known for a particular aspect of his behaviour or personality: e.g. panic merchant; stand-over merchant.

mercy killing
euthanasia.

mere shadow of (one's) former self
thin; emaciated; lacking (one's) former energy, sparkle etc.

merry
slightly tipsy, drunk, intoxicated.
See also:
drink and be merry
lead (someone) a merry dance

merry hell
trouble; upheaval; chaos; pain: e.g. All the beer he drinks plays merry hell with his ulcers.

merry old time
a difficult time: e.g. I had a merry old time trying to change the tyre on that old bomb!

merry-go-round
pertaining to a rapid course of events.

mesc/mescal/mescal buttons
peyote — hallucinogenic drug prepared from a Mexican cactus.

mess
1. a person whose life is in a depressing, muddled and confused state: e.g. He's such a mess since his wife died.
2. an unappetising meal.
3. an unpleasant situation, dilemma or predicament.
See also:
make a mess of things

mess around
1. waste time.
2. behave foolishly.
3. busy oneself with; potter, tinker with: e.g. He loves to mess around with antique cars.
4. engage in sexual activity.
5. philander, flirt with: e.g. Many married men still mess around.

mess around with
1. to associate with (someone) considered an undesirable: e.g. He's messing around with some bad people these days.
2. philander, flirt, have sexual relations with, usually of an illicit nature.

mess (someone) about/ around
cause inconvenience to (someone); fail to come to the point, or be honest with (someone).

mess up
ruin, spoil, bungle; fail.

mess with
associate with; have dealings with: e.g. I don't like to mess with the likes of him.

mess-up
a fouled, ruined, bungled, spoiled, chaotic situation.

messy
pertaining to a situation that is difficult to deal with; confused; troublesome: e.g. He's got himself into a messy state of affairs.

met (one's) match
came up against (one's) equal; someone or something that (one) cannot best.

met up with
1. met, found after a long time.
2. met with, introduced to.

meth
Methedrine.

metho
1. methylated spirits.
2. an habitual drinker of methylated spirits.
3. (cap.) a member of the Methodist church.

method in (one's) madness
reason or logic behind (one's) apparent foolishness, stupidity or disorganisation.

methuselah
a very large wine bottle holding up to eight times the amount of an ordinary one.

Mexican
a person from Victoria to a person from New South Wales (someone south of the border).

Mexican stand-off
a situation in which two opponents abuse and threaten each other loudly without taking any action.

michael/mick/mickey
female pudendum, genitals, vagina.
See also:
take the mickey out of (someone)

Mick
1. a Roman Catholic.
2. an Irishman.

Mickey Finn
(also: mickey) an alcoholic drink that has had something surreptitiously added to it, causing some discomfort or reaction from the drinker.
See also:
slip (someone) a mickey

Mickey Fritt
(rhyming slang) shit.

Mickey Mouse
1. (rhyming slang) grouse; wonderful; excellent.
2. childish; unsophisticated; shoddy; cheap.

mickey-muncher
(of a man) one who indulges in cunnilingus.

micky
(see: mickey)

micro oven
a panel van (does a chick in three minutes).

microdot
small amount of hallucinogenic drug such as LSD — users often impregnate blotting paper with it.

Midas touch
uncanny ability to make money easily.

middie
(see: middy)

middies
shoes with small heels for women.

middle
stomach; waist: e.g. She's got a huge middle.

middle-aged spread
noticeable weight gain, especially around the waist, as a person gets older.

middleman
any trader who acts as intermediary between the producer and the retailer, making a profit in the exchange and effectively causing the goods to be more expensive to the consumer.

middle-of-the-road
1. (of music) appealing to a wide range of people.
2. moderate; not extreme.
3. impartial; neutral; noncommittal.

middling
1. fairly well in health.
2. second-rate; so-so; mediocre.
See also:
fair to middling

middy
1. (of a dress) length being halfway between the knees and the floor.
2. a measure of beer: 10 ounces for N.S.W., 7 ounces for W.A. or 284 ml.

midge
1. a small person.
2. tiny, biting sandfly.

midsummer madness
foolishness; extreme folly.

miffed
annoyed; irritated; offended.

miffy
offended; sensitive; easily upset.

mighty
very; great in degree, extent: e.g. That was a mighty good effort.

mike
microphone.

mile
(see: country mile; from a mile off; miss is as good as a mile; missed by a mile)

mileage
usefulness; service; benefit; advantage; profit: e.g. We got a lot of mileage out of that record.

mile-high club
pertaining to the airline industry and hostesses — especially with reference to sex and having intercourse during flying in aeroplanes.

milestone
a significant point or stage in one's life.

milk
exploit; take advantage of; use, manipulate; extract money or information from: e.g. Those crooks have been milking the public for years with that scheme.
See also:
cry over spilt milk.

milk a car
extract or siphon petrol out of the tank of a car.

milk and honey
luxury; the best; opulence.

milk bar
corner shop where many general purpose items may be purchased, such as bread, milk, confectionery, newspapers etc.

milk the till
to steal, pilfer money from a cash register where one is employed.

milkie/milko
a milkman; person who sells or delivers milk.

milk-sop
1. effeminate man; coward; weakling.
2. spiritless, dull, boring person; fuddy-duddy.

mill
(see: been through the mill; go through the mill; grist to the mill; put through the mill; run-of-the-mill)

million
(see: go a million; look like a million; make a million; one in a million; thanks a million; two-bob millionaire)

million to one chance
very remote chance of success.

millstone around (one's) neck
a heavy burden or problem to cope with; hindrance or impediment.

mince pies
(rhyming slang) eyes.

mince words
speak politely, using euphemistic rather than direct language.

mince-meat
(see: make mince-meat out of)

mind
(see: blow one's mind; give someone a piece of one's mind; have/got half a mind to; in two minds about; keep an open mind; keep one's mind above one's belt; legend in one's own mind; one-track mind; out of one's mind; pissed out of one's mind; set one's mind to; speak one's mind; take a load off one's mind; the mind boggles; time out of mind; to one's mind; twisted mind)

mind bender
a puzzle.

mind keeps wandering
to experience difficulty in concentrating on the matter at hand; to think about irrelevant matters.

mind (one's) own beeswax/ business/chookhouse/ fowlhouse
not interfering, meddling in other people's affairs.

mind (one's) p's and q's/ tongue
make an effort to speak, behave well, properly; refrain from using vulgar language.

mind out
watch out; look out: e.g. Mind out for the traffic when you take the dog for a walk.

mind over matter
the force or power of clear thinking overcoming something unpleasant.

mind turning over
(to have one's . . .) to be thinking about all possible aspects.

mind went blank
suffer from momentary forgetfulness: e.g. My mind went blank when I tried to tell him my phone number.

mind your manners/p's and q's
a warning to behave better or to refrain from using vulgar language.

mind your own beeswax/ business/chookhouse/ fowlhouse!
stop interfering, meddling!

mind-bending/blowing
exciting, stimulating: e.g. That concert was mind-blowing.

mind-boggling
overwhelming: e.g. It's mind-boggling to try to imagine infinity in space.

minder
a bodyguard.

mind's eye
the imagination.

mingy
mean; stingy; miserly; parsimonious.

mini
anything small, such as a car, the length of a skirt etc.

mint
a great deal of money: e.g. That new car cost me a mint!

mint condition
as new.

minus
1. second-rate; inferior; poor; weak.
2. demerit; drawback; failure; defect.

minute man
man who ejaculates prematurely or after only a very short time during intercourse.

mischief
(see: do oneself a mischief)

miscue
slip-up; mistake; blunder; fault.

miserable
1. mean; stingy; parsimonious; miserly.
2. inferior; worthless; trashy; second-rate; shoddy.

miserable as a bandicoot
1. unhappy; sad; dejected.
2. mean; stingy; parsimonious; miserly.

miserable as a shag on a rock
dejected; lonely; forlorn.

miseries
1. wretched, unhappy state of mind or circumstances.
2. illness; sick.
See also:
bag of misery
get the miseries
in the miseries
put (someone) out of his misery

misery guts
1. wretchedly unhappy person.
2. constant complainer, whinger.

misfire
fail; fall through; abort; fizzle; be unsuccessful.

mish-mash
a mixture, jumble, confusion.

miss
(see: doesn't miss a trick; give it a miss; hit-and-miss; near miss; wouldn't miss it for the world)

Miss Goody Two-shoes
(of a woman, girl) affectedly prim, proper, chaste, good.

Miss House and Garden
(derog. of a woman) over-proud of the appearance of one's house and garden.

miss is as good as a mile
losing by a little is no better than losing by a lot — the result (failure, loss) is the same.

miss out
1. (of sexual intercourse) to fail to achieve having sexual intercourse with someone.
2. to fail to receive something one desires.
3. to fail to be present: e.g. I missed out on that party because I had to study that night.

Miss Right
compatible partner in romance: e.g. I was Pat's Miss Right until he left me for a gorgeous-looking model.

missed by a long shot/a mile
to have failed significantly.

missed out when the brains/good looks etc. were handed out
an excuse for some failing in one's intelligence, good looks or body.

missed the boat/bus
1. (of a person) inadequate in many respects; a failure.
2. to have failed to grasp at opportunities when they presented themselves.

missed the point
failed to understand, comprehend the essence, crux of a matter.

missing
(of an engine) not firing or turning over smoothly.

missing link
1. the hypothetical anthropoid linking the apes to man in the theory of evolution.
2. anything missing that would complete a sequence.

missionary position
sexual intercourse in the position of the man on top of the woman — often considered dull and uninventive if this is one's only way.

missus
1. (the . . .) one's wife: e.g. Where's the missus tonight?
2. term of address to a woman.

Missus Kafoops
(derog.) pseudonym for a disliked woman whether the real name is known or not, especially for a woman who affects airs and graces.

Missus Palmer and her five daughters
(of men) the hand, pertaining to masturbation: e.g. He's so ugly he has to sleep with Missus Palmer and her five daughters.

mistake
an unplanned or unwanted pregnancy or child.

Mister Big
the person in charge; person with the most authority, power; the boss, leader: e.g. Many small-time drug dealers have been brought to justice, but the police haven't nailed Mister Big yet.

Mister Right
compatible partner in romance: e.g. She's not married because she hasn't met Mister Right yet.

misunderstanding
an argument or disagreement.

mite
a child.

mitt
the hand.

mix
1. (see: mix-up, 2.)
2. associate with socially; socialise; mingle; get along: e.g. She doesn't seem to mix very well at parties.
See also:
get mixed up in
in a mix

mix business with pleasure
combine work with fun at the same time.

mix it
to fight with (someone): e.g. You wouldn't want to mix it with him — he's a champion boxer.

mix (one's) drinks
to drink various alcoholic drinks indiscriminately, usually resulting in a hang-over.

mix up
muddle; ruin; make a botch of; spoil.

mix with
associate with; be social, friendly with.

mixed bag
an assortment, medley, variety or jumble of people, things, ideas etc.: e.g. The market has a mixed bag of items for sale.

mixed blessing
an advantageous situation which also carries with it some hidden or unexpected disadvantages.

mixed marriage
a marriage between two people of different race, colour or religion.

mixed up in/with
involved: e.g. I don't want to get mixed up with any more of his hare-brained ideas!

mixed-up
emotionally confused or ill-adjusted; disturbed; confused; bewildered.

mixer
1. person who associates, mingles, gets along with others socially: e.g. She's a good mixer at parties.
2. softdrink used to mix with alcohol, spirits.

mix-up
1. a fight, argument or scrap.
2. a confused state of affairs; a muddle, botch-up.

mo
1. moment: e.g. Just a mo!
2. moustache.
See also:
curl the mo!
half a mo
just a mo

moan
1. a complaint: e.g. What's his moan?
2. complain; grumble; whinge; nag: e.g. She's always moaning about something or other.

moaning and groaning
complaining; whingeing; nagging.

mob
1. collective name for people with similar peculiarities or interests: e.g. 1. They're a weird mob! 2. That football team is a mob of galahs!
2. group of friends, acquaintances: e.g. Invite the whole mob to the party.
3. any large number of people, animals or things.
See also:
the Mob

mobs
lots of; plenty of: e.g. He's got mobs of money.

mobster
gangster; crook; criminal.

mockered up
well dressed.

mockers
(see: put the mock/mockers on someone)

mod cons
modern conveniences: e.g. That house has all the mod cons.

mog/moggy
one's domestic cat.

mohair stockings
(of women) hairy legs.

moke
donkey or poor horse.

mole
person who establishes himself in the ranks of the opposition in order to spy for his side when eventually required.

molecule mauler
a microwave oven.

moll
1. promiscuous woman; tart; prostitute.
2. girlfriend of a member of a bikie gang.
See also:
like a moll at a christening

molly the monk/mollo
(rhyming slang) drunk.

mollycoddle
pamper; fuss over; over-indulge, spoil (someone).

molly-dooker
person who is left-handed.

molotov cocktail
a home-made bomb, usually made from a bottle filled with an inflammable liquid and stopped with a wick which is lit prior to throwing.

mom
mother (also: mum).

moment of truth
any situation in which one's character is put to a test.

Mondayitis
general lack of desire to go to work, often experienced on Monday after the weekend break; a fictitious illness due to this.

money
(see: black/blood/conscience/danger/dirt/easy money; for my money; funny-money; get one's money's worth; give someone a good run for his money; have/got a good nose for money; have/got money to burn; hush-money; in the money; key money; licence to print money; made of money; pin money; put one's money where one's mouth is; time is money)

money behind (one)
(to have . . .) an assurance of wealth, assets and power: e.g. Big companies have enough money behind them to continue development and expansion.

money burns a hole in (one's) pocket
(one) is prone to spending money as soon as it is acquired.

money doesn't buy everything
money does not necessarily bring happiness, love, peace of mind.

money doesn't grow on trees
a statement to someone who treats money with little care or respect for how difficult it may have been to earn.

money spider
a tiny spider which, if seen, is considered to mean that one is due to come into a great deal of wealth.

money talks
pertaining to the belief that money, wealth means power and influence.

money to burn
to be very wealthy, rich.

moneybags
a very wealthy, rich person.

money-bin
a bank.

money-grubber
a mercenary person devoted entirely to acquiring money.

money-monger
person involved in making, earning money, often in a sordid or illicit manner.

money-spinner
lucrative undertaking; profitable enterprise or business: e.g. Selling second-hand junk at flea-markets has been a real good money-spinner for him.

mong
mongrel dog.

monger
1. food; tucker: e.g. This is delicious monger!
2. dealer, trader (often an illicit one): e.g. money-monger; scandal-monger.

mongrel
despicable, deplorable person or thing: e.g. I can never start that mongrel lawnmower of mine!

moniker
name; signature: e.g. Sign your moniker on the dotted line.

monkey
1. the sum of five hundred dollars.
2. a mischievous child.
3. a fool, dolt, simpleton.
4. female pudendum, genitals.

See also:
brass monkey weather
done up like an organ-grinder's monkey
freeze the balls off a brass monkey
grease-monkey
I'll be a monkey's uncle!
make a monkey of
mouth tastes like a monkey's armpit

monkey about with
tinker, play, meddle, trifle, tamper with.

monkey around
engage in mischief, idle play or pranks; fool around: e.g. Watch those kids don't monkey around too much while I'm gone.

monkey bars
playground or gym equipment designed for children to swing and climb on.

monkey business
1. trickery; deceit.
2. mischief-making; fooling around; playing pranks.
3. illicit sexual flirting or play.

monkey in it (for someone)
an offer of a five-hundred-dollar bribe: e.g. There's a monkey in it for you if you do what I ask.

monkey on (one's) back
an obsession, fad, that has become a burden.

monkey suit
dinner suit; suit and tie.

monkey with
trifle with; interfere, meddle, tamper, fiddle with.

monkey's nose is bleeding
expression stating that a woman is menstruating.

monsters
children: e.g. Grandma is looking after the monsters today.

monte
(see: monty)

'Goondiwindi, mate? It's about twenty stubbies straight ahead — or you can go back to the crossroads and turn left and it's about fifteen stubbies!'

The estimation of distance in Australia can be very confusing to the newcomer. The traveller needs to be well versed in Aussie units of measure. He could be told that Goondiwindi is so many k's, clicks, minutes, hours or stubbies away, a few country miles up the road or just around the corner.

montezumas
breasts; boobs; tits.

month in, month out
with regularity: e.g. She visits his grave month in, month out.

month of Sundays
a long time: e.g. I haven't seen him in a month of Sundays.
See also:
slow as a month of Sundays

monthlies
(of women) menstrual period.

monty
a certainty: e.g. That horse is a monty to win.

moo
silly, foolish woman: e.g. What's that silly old moo doing?

mooch
1. beg, cadge: e.g. He's always mooching off his father.
2. steal, pilfer: e.g. Watch that character, he's likely to mooch anything that isn't nailed down!

mooch around
1. loiter, sneak around.
2. saunter, slouch around.

moocher
person who begs, cadges or obtains something at someone else's expense.

moo-juice
milk.

moolah
money: e.g. I need to get my hands on a lot of moolah by tomorrow.

moon
(see: cry for the moon; once in a blue moon; want the moon)

moon about
1. gaze or wander about in a stupidly dreamy, dazed or listless frame of mind; idle time away.
2. think wistfully about something.

moon-face
person with a very round face.

moon-juice
whiskey, especially illicitly distilled.

moonlight flit
to run away, elope, especially in order to avoid an unpleasant situation or responsibility: e.g. He did a moonlight flit without paying the rent he owes.

moonlighter
person having two jobs, paid occupations, usually consisting of a main job and another part-time job at night.

moonlighting
1. having two paid occupations.
2. night activities — often illegal or illicit.

moonshine
1. nonsense; rubbish; idle, romantic and fanciful talk.
2. illicit making of liquor, alcohol; the liquor so produced.

moonstruck
1. lunatic; deranged in mind; insane.
2. dazed; in a foolishly romantic state of mind.

moony
dazed; dreamy; silly; stupid; romantic.

moosh
the face or mouth: e.g. He's got an ugly moosh.

mop
the hair.

mopoke
stupid, ineffectual person.

moral
a certainty to win — especially in horse-racing.

more arse than class
(see: have/got more arse than class)

more arse/hide than an elephant
(see: have/got more arse/hide than an elephant)

more front than Myers
1. excessive daring, cheek, effrontery, exaggeration.
2. (of women) having large breasts.

more off than on
relationship, project etc. with a history of only very sporadic enthusiasm, action etc. and more likely to peter out than to succeed.

more often than not
mostly; usually: e.g. More often than not, he remembers my birthday.

more than meets the eye
hidden facts or matters; more to a situation than appears at first.

more than (one) can poke a finger/stick at
ample; more than enough; a great deal, amount: e.g. He's got more money than you can poke a stick at!

more-ish
irresistible; tempting; so pleasant that one desires more: e.g. Nuts and olives are so more-ish.

morf
morphine, as used by drug-addicts.

morning glory
sexual intercourse first thing in the morning.

morning sickness
nausea in the early stages of pregnancy, usually experienced in the morning.

morning-after
pertaining to a hang-over, tiredness or feeling of illness after a particularly gay or active night of over-indulgence.

moron
stupid person; dunce; dimwit.

morph/morpho
morphine, as used by drug-addicts.

mosey
saunter, amble, go, depart: e.g. It's late and we have to mosey.

mossie
mosquito (also: mozzie).

moth-eaten
1. antiquated; old-fashioned; obsolete; out of date.
2. tatty; shabby; decayed; ragged; worn-out.

mother
1. something big, outstanding: e.g. That spider was a big mother!
2. (as an exclamation) exasperation, annoyance; amazement.
See also:
kick him where his mother never kissed him

mother/mother-fucker
despicable, contemptible, annoying person.

mother's boy
man who is effeminate, weak of character, lacking in courage or conviction.

mother's ruin
gin.

motor
1. a woman's body as an object of sex: e.g. She's got a really hot motor.
2. go; depart: e.g. We have to motor — it's getting late.
3. move, act, do, quickly or in haste: e.g. If we don't motor we'll never get finished in time to go to the pub.

motor-mouth
person who talks too much, gossips at length, gives secrets or confidences away, talks too fast.

motsa/motser/motza/motzer
1. a certainty — especially to win.
2. a large gambling win or sum of money.

mouldy
out of date; old-fashioned; antiquated.

mountain
(see: make a mountain out of a mole-hill)

mountain dew
whiskey, especially illicitly distilled.

mountain oysters
testicles of lambs as a delicacy.

mouse
an extremely shy or introverted person; weakling; coward.
See also:
are you a man or a mouse?
tight as a mouse's ear

mouser
pertaining to a cat's ability to hunt and catch mice: e.g. Our old moggy's an excellent mouser.

mousetrap
inferior cheese.

mousy
shy; introverted; dull and boring.

mouth
1. loud-mouthed, ranting, abusive or self-praising person.
2. person who is a gossip, known to divulge confidences or secrets.
See also:
all mouth
another mouth to feed
by word of mouth
big mouth (to have a)
big-mouth
down in the mouth
fire (one's) mouth off
hand-to-mouth
have/got a big mouth
have/got a plum in (one's) mouth
hush my mouth!
hush your mouth!
keep (one's) mouth shut
make (one's) mouth water
mealy-mouthed
motor-mouth
open (one's) mouth to change feet
put (one's) foot in (one's) mouth
put (one's) money where (one's) mouth is
put words into (someone's) mouth
run off at the mouth
shoot (one's) mouth off
shut mouth catches no flies
shut (one's) big mouth
shut your mouth!
straight from the horse's mouth
take the words out of (one's) mouth
wash (someone's) mouth out with soap
watch (one's) mouth
what doesn't fit in your mouth is a waste

mouth feels like a camel-driver's crutch

mouth feels like the bottom of a bird/cocky's cage

mouth feels like the lee side of a Lebanese loo
to experience an unpleasant after-taste and furriness of the tongue after a night of over-indulgence in alcohol.

mouth full of teeth
(to have a . . .) to have prominent, large or protruding teeth.

mouth like a torn pocket
(to have a . . .)
1. to have a large, unshapely and unattractive mouth.
2. to be guilty of divulging secrets.

mouth off
1. deride, scorn, scoff at, criticise loudly and with sarcasm; use loud and abusive language.
2. boast; exaggerate loudly.

mouth tastes like a monkey's armpit
(see: mouth feels like a camel-driver's crutch)

mouthful
a long or difficult to pronounce word or phrase.

mouthpiece
representative speaker; one who speaks for someone else.

mouth-to-mouth
1. a form of artificial respiration done by breathing air into the mouth of the patient; kiss-of-life.
2. information or gossip spread verbally: e.g. That restaurant is so good it doesn't need to advertise as most customers hear about it mouth-to-mouth.

mouth-watering
appetising; desirable.

move
go; depart; leave: e.g. It's getting late so we'd better move.
See also:
get a move on
if it moves shoot it, if it doesn't, chop it down
make a move
on the move

move heaven and earth
do, try everything possible.

move in on
impose on, interfere with, attempt to be part of or become involved through force, badgering or unwanted persistence: e.g. The police are expecting a criminal element to move in on the new casino.

move in the right/wrong circles
associate with the right/wrong types of people.

move it!
hurry up!

move like greased lightning/the wind
move very quickly.

move up in the world
improve one's social status, wealth or position.

move with the times
adapt to changes in society, such as changes of attitude, fashion etc.

movies
1. the cinema: e.g. We're going to the movies tonight.
2. cinema, television or video films.

mow down
kill or destroy indiscriminately and cold-heartedly.

mozzie
mosquito (also: mossie).

mozzle
luck, especially bad luck.
(see: put the mozz on)

Mr Big
(see: Mister Big)

Mrs
(see: Missus)

much
(see: a bit much; don't go in much for; too much!)

much of a muchness
very much the same; similar; little difference between: e.g. I don't mind which brand of beer you buy — they're all much of a muchness to me.

muck
rubbish; nonsense; worthless talk or literature; trash.
See also:
in the muck
make a muck of

muck around
fool around; waste time; idle, potter around.

muck around with
1. associate, cohabit with: e.g. He mucks around with some odd-looking people.
2. tamper, tinker, interfere with: e.g. Don't muck around with my things!

muck in with
share or join in, as with tasks, chores, living quarters.

muck things up
spoil; ruin; make a mess of; botch; bungle.

muck-raker
trouble-maker; one who is a particularly nasty or vicious gossip; disseminator of prejudicial information against an enemy etc.

muck-raking
slander, defamation, character assassination (by either true or false accusation); seeking out and publication of scandals: e.g. Most politicians are guilty of muck-raking at one time or another.

muck-up
a ruined situation; muddle; mess; fiasco.

mud
1. slander; defamatory gossip.
2. mortar, cement.
See also:
clear as mud
drag (someone's) name through the mud
name is mud
sling mud at (someone)
stick-in-the-mud
throw mud at (someone)
up to mud

mud in your eye!
(here's . . .) a salute or toast; expression uttered just prior to people drinking their drinks.

mud map
sketch drawn on the ground to give directions.

mud-bath
a messy, muddy, wet, slushy situation: e.g. Because of the rain the footy match was a mud-bath.

muddie
Queensland mud crab.

mud-guts
fat, obese person.

mudhook
an anchor for a boat.

mudlark
a horse that performs well on a wet track.

mud-slinging
(see: muck-raking)

mud-slinging match
a situation between two parties that has degenerated to reckless name-calling, slander, abuse and scandalous remarks.

muff
1. the female pudendum, genitals.
2. to fail, ruin, bungle, spoil or mismanage: e.g. I tried that cake-recipe three times and muffed it each time!

muff-diver/muncher
one who performs cunnilingus.

muff-up
mistake; bungling error; ruined, spoiled situation.

mug
1. person who is easily tricked, duped, deceived, cheated.
2. the face: e.g. He's got an ugly mug.
3. term for someone held in contempt.
4. physically assault, bash, beat up and rob.

mug lair
an obnoxious exhibitionist, public nuisance.

mug shot
photograph taken of the face for police records.

mugged
physically assaulted, attacked, beaten up and robbed, especially in a public place.

muggins
1. person who allows himself to be outwitted, talked into doing something unpleasant (often used by the speaker to refer to himself): e.g. And who do you think had to do all the dishes and cleaning up? Muggins here, that's who!
2. fool; simpleton; person with no mind of his own.

muggy
humid, clammy, hot and oppressive weather conditions.

mug's game
any job, activity, enterprise that is unpleasant, unrewarding or held in contempt.

Muldoon
a fool; stupid person.

mule
stubborn, obstinate or stupidly dumb person.

mulesing
the removing of wrinkled folds of skin around a sheep's anal area to prevent fly and maggot infestation.

mulga
the bush; any remote back country: e.g. He lives out in the mulga somewhere.

mulga wire
person-to-person system of communication by which information and gossip are passed on; word-of-mouth spreading of news etc.; grape-vine: e.g. You'll never guess what I heard over the mulga wire!

mull
marijuana, dried and prepared for smoking.

mullamatic
machine for grinding marijuana leaves.

mulligatawny
curried soup.

mullocker
clumsy, ineffectual person.

mullygrubber
(cricket) a bowled ball that hits the ground and rolls without bouncing.

mum
1. mother.
2. silent secrecy: e.g. Stay mum about what I've told you.

mumbo-jumbo
1. gibberish, jargon, unintelligible speech; double-talk; nonsense; obscure language designed to be impressive or difficult to understand.
2. superstition; witchcraft.

mummy
mother.

mummy's boy
(see: mother's boy)

mum's the word
refrain from revealing what one knows or has heard; remain silent about a matter; keep a secret.

munchies
1. light snacks between meals.
2. a craving for food: e.g. I've got a bad case of the munchies.
See also:
get the munchies

munga/munger
food.

murder
1. (joc.) scold, berate, threaten with violent disapproval: e.g. I'll murder him if he comes home late for dinner!
2. spoil, ruin, through poor performance: e.g. The poor acoustics of the hall murdered the concert.
3. an exceptionally difficult or unpleasant task: e.g. Painting the roof on a hot day is murder!
See also:
get away with (blue) murder
scream blue murder

murphy
a potato.

Murphy's Law
a supposed law that states that if anything can

possibly go wrong or cause trouble, it will.

muscle
1. ruthless political, financial strength, power, clout or influence; influential authority: e.g. Some unions have a great deal of muscle.
2. to elbow, shove, push, shoulder.

muscle in on
to force, either through violence or deception, one's way in on something even in the face of hostility: e.g. Criminals have been known to muscle in on the operations of a casino.

muscle-bound behind the ears
stupid; lacking in intelligence.

museum piece
person or thing that is old-fashioned or out-dated.

mush
1. food that is pulpy, soft and unappetising.
2. feeble sentimentality: e.g. That movie was so full of mush that we all cried.
3. get going! hurry up!

mushie
mushroom.
See also:
magic mushie

mushroom
(see: like a mushroom; member of the mushroom club)

mushy
1. soppy, feebly sentimental.
2. mushroom.

music
(see: face the music; make music together)

music to (one's) ears
anything that (one) is pleased to hear.

muso
musician.

muss up
mess up; disarrange; spoil; ruin.

must
something that should not be missed or over-looked: e.g. We're electing a new president, so tonight's meeting is a must.

must have hollow legs
pertaining to a person who eats a great deal but never seems to put on weight.

mutt
1. any dog, but especially a mongrel.
2. stupid person.

mutton
the penis.
See also:
underground mutton

mutton dressed as lamb
(derog.) an older woman dressed in clothing much too young in style and hence looking ridiculous.

mutton-bird
someone from Tasmania.

mutton-chops
type of beard, whiskers, where the chin is shaved in front and beneath.

mutton-dagger/gun
the penis.

mutton-head
stupid, foolish person.

Muzak
soft, nondescript recorded background music, of the type played in motels, restaurants and public places and designed to create a feeling of calm or to increase work efficiency. (Trademark)

my!/my-oh-my!
exclamation of surprise.

my bloody oath/colonial/colonial oath!
expression of total agreement; emphatically yes!

my foot!
exclamation of disbelief, scorn, ridicule.

my heart bleeds!
sarcastic expression of sympathy.

my heart was in my mouth
expression of fearful, nervous, anxious anticipation: e.g. That movie was so scary that my heart was in my mouth all the time.

my! my!
exclamation of surprise — often in a smug or sarcastic manner.

my oath!
expression of total agreement; emphatically yes!

my stomach thinks my throat's cut
expression indicating that one is hungry.

my word!
1. expression of mild annoyance, surprise.
2. expression of agreement.

mystery bags
(rhyming slang) snags; sausages.

myxo
myxomatosis — a viral disease of rabbits introduced to reduce the rabbit population.

nab
1. arrest, capture, apprehend or catch, as in a police matter: e.g. They got nabbed for stealing cars.
2. grab, seize or catch suddenly.

nabraska
toilet; lavatory.

naff
laughable; ridiculous; useless.

naff off!
piss off! go away!

nag
1. a horse, especially an old or inferior one.
2. persistently complaining or badgering person, especially a woman.

nail
1. to catch a person doing a wrong: e.g. The police will eventually nail the people involved in that crime.
2. to secure something or someone's promise or word by prompt and direct action: e.g. I'll try to nail him to do that job for us when I see him tonight.
See also:
hard as nails
hit the nail on the head
on the nail

nail it home
to push a point, fact before someone's notice; force to understand: e.g. You've got to nail it home to him how important this matter is.

nail (someone)
shoot (and kill) someone.

nail (someone) to the wall

nail (someone's) hide to the dunny door
1. reprimand, scold, berate (someone) severely.
2. thrash or beat (someone) soundly.

nail-biting
full of suspense.

namby-pamby
person or thing that is insipid, weak, overly sentimental, simpering or wishy-washy.

name
1. a famous or well-known person: e.g. He's quite a name around here.
2. reputation: e.g. He's got a bad name.
See also:
in the name of
to (one's) name
what's-'is-name

name is mud
of a person in disgrace, out of favour, unpopular, disliked or held in contempt: e.g. His name is mud around here.

name of the game
the crux, essential aim in life: e.g. In his mind, making money is the name of the game.

name your poison
designate your preferred alcoholic drink, cigarette brand, drug etc.

name-calling
abusive and derogatory remarks directed at a person.

name-dropper
person guilty of name-dropping.

name-dropping
the practice of casually referring to famous people, places or things as though they are personal friends or completely familiar to one in order to impress.

names
derogatory and abusive things to call people: e.g. He can call me as many names as he likes — it doesn't concern me in the least!

nana
(also: narna)
1. short for: banana.
2. person who is easily fooled, tricked, duped, cheated.
See also:
do (one's) nana
gnaw the nana
off (one's) nana

nanna/nanny
grandmother.

nanny-goat
(rhyming slang) tote; TAB.

nap
a tip that a horse in a race will be a certain winner: e.g. He's a nap to win.
See also:
don't go nap on (something)

napping
unawares; idle and off one's guard; not working as hard as one should: e.g. If I catch you napping again, you're fired!

nark
1. person who continually complains, nags and irritates.
2. a spy or informer, especially for the police or authorities.
3. federal policeman or investigator, especially in the field of narcotics.
4. to annoy, infuriate, irritate: e.g. I wish he didn't nark me so much.

narked
irritated; annoyed; angry; upset: e.g. He's really narked over not getting that job.

narks
police; narcotic agents, investigators.

narna
(see: nana)

narrow
(see: narrow-minded)
See also:
on the straight and narrow

narrow between the ears
(of a person) stupid; dumb; witless; lacking in intelligence.

narrow escape/squeak
to barely escape from trouble, or to just miss out on doing something unpleasant, distasteful.

narrow the field down
narrow the margin
limit, restrict in scope, range or numbers.

narrow-minded
prejudiced; biased; small-minded; petty; bigoted.

nasho
national service; compulsory military duty.

nastie
(rhyming slang) pastie.

nasty
1. the penis; male or female genitals: e.g. He gets his kicks by flashing his nasty in public places.
2. sexual intercourse.

nasty piece of work
nasty-pastie
a despicable, bad-tempered or mean person.

natch
naturally; of course.

national game
(Australia's . . .) the gambling game of two-up.

Nats
members of the National Party.

natter
talk; chat; gossip.

natural
a person (or thing) innately adept at or suited to a particular task: e.g. David is a natural at painting.

nature strip
the narrow tract of land between the front boundary of a property and the road, often used to plant grass, trees or shrubs.

naughty
1. sexual intercourse: e.g. Did you get a naughty last night?
2. obscene, improper; sexually suggestive: e.g. He likes his women to wear naughty knickers.

naughty but nice
perverse, wicked, improper yet attractive.

N.B.
nota bene (Latin); note well, take note.

N.B.G.
no bloody good.

near at hand
close by.

near miss
1. a close shave or narrow escape.
2. something which just fails to achieve a desired aim.

near thing
a narrow escape, close call.

near to the bone/knuckle
indecent; improper; lewd.

nearly died
received an unpleasant shock: e.g. I nearly died when he dropped that priceless antique vase.

nearly died laughing
collapsed into uncontrollable fits of laughter.

nearly fell flat on (one's) face
nearly made a disastrous error, mistake, blunder.

nearly fell for it (hook, line and sinker)
nearly accepted, believed or was hoodwinked by deceit, trickery or dishonesty.

nearly fell over backwards
received a surprise, shock: e.g. I nearly fell over backwards when I was told I had won the lottery.

nearly had a fit
received a shock unpleasant enough to make one angry; came close to losing emotional control, by becoming furious or hysterical.

nearly had a heart-attack
received an unpleasant surprise or shock.

nearly had a pink fit
(see: nearly had a fit)

nearly had heart failure
(see: nearly had a heart-attack)

nearly had pink kittens
(see: nearly had a fit)

nearly jumped out of (one's) skin

nearly pissed (oneself)
received a sudden fright, shock.

nearly pissed (oneself) laughing
collapsed into uncontrollable laughter.

nearly scared the pants off (one)

nearly shit/wet (oneself)
received an unpleasant surprise, shock or fright.

neat
excellent; wonderful; very good; okay: e.g. That party was neat.

neat as a pin
very tidy; orderly.

nebbie
Nembutal sleeping pill.

nebraska
the toilet. (also: brasco)

necessary/necessary necessity
money: e.g. I haven't got enough of the necessaries to buy that flash car.
See also:
shy on the necessary

neck
exchange amorous caresses; pet, kiss and cuddle: e.g. Many teenagers go to the drive-in and spend their time necking in the back-seat.
See also:
albatross around (one's) neck
break (one's) neck
breathe down (someone's) neck
chain around (one's) neck
dead from the neck up
fed up to the neck
get it in the neck
had it up to the neck
in it up to (one's) neck
lay (one's) neck on the line
pain in the neck
pull your neck in
put (one's) neck on the line
redneck
risk (one's) neck
rubberneck
stick (one's) neck out
stiff-necked
talking through the back of (one's) neck
up to (one's) neck
wring (someone's) neck

neck of the woods
neighbourhood; area: e.g. What are you doing in this neck of the woods?

neck on the line
(put one's, have one's . . .) to put oneself at risk; be in danger.

neck (someone)
1. reprimand (someone) severely.
2. wound superficially, as with a bullet.

neck to neck
evenly matched; equal.

neckful
enough to try one's patience: e.g. I've had a neckful of her complaining and noisy children!

necktie
hangman's noose.

neck-to-knees
old-fashioned bathing costume that covered the body from the neck to the knees.

ned 'em
to throw two heads in the game of two-up.

neddies
horses, especially in reference to racing: e.g. I like to have a flutter on the neddies sometimes.

need a crutch to lean on
to need something or someone to depend, rely on.

need a head job
(of a person) ugly; unattractive, especially in facial features.

need a kick up the arse/bum/jumper/khyber/pants/quoit
1. to need admonishing, reprimanding, scolding.
2. to need stimulating, encouraging.

need a push in the right direction
to need stimulating and encouragement.

need a shoulder to cry on
need a sympathetic person to tell one's troubles or worries to.

need it like a hole in the head
1. to not need, want, desire it at all.
2. to be extremely inconvenienced or upset by (it).

need (one's) head read
to be insane, silly, stupid, foolish, unrealistic: e.g. He needs his head read if he thinks that stupid idea will work!

need (something) like a dog needs a flogging
need, want, desire (something) urgently, very much.

needle
1. an injection with a hypodermic needle.
2. annoy; tease; heckle; provoke; harass: e.g. Those two are always needling each other!

needle in a haystack
something difficult to locate, see or find; something totally obscured by its surroundings.

neg driving
negligent driving: e.g. He got booked for neg driving.

neither here nor there
doesn't matter; makes no difference; not one or the other: e.g. It's neither here nor there whether we go today or tomorrow.

nellie
(also: nelly) cheap red wine.
See also:
in the nelly
not on your nellie

Nellie Bligh
(rhyming slang) fly or eye.

nerd
(also: nurd) fool; idiot; stupid, ignorant person.

nerve
1. courage; bravery; daring: e.g. I would never have enough nerve to parachute from a plane.
2. impudence; audacity; impertinence: e.g. He had the nerve to tell me I was fat!
See also:
get on (one's) nerves
have/got a nerve
haven't got the nerve
lose (one's) nerve

nerve-racking
trying; irritating; harassing; anxiety provoking; worrying; vexing.

nerves of steel
unyielding; determined; brave; not easily frightened.

nervous as a long-tailed cat in a room of rocking chairs
very nervous, anxious.

nest
1. cosy, warm hide-away or retreat; bed.
2. any place where bad or evil proliferates: e.g. That night-club is a nest of drug-dealers and criminals.
See also:
feather (one's) own nest
shit in (one's) own nest

nest-egg
money or assets saved as a reserve: e.g. That investment account is a nice little nest-egg for the future.

neurotic
obsessively anxious: e.g. He's so neurotic about losing his hair, he's going to have a transplant.

never
(see: better late than never; now or never)

never had it so good
one's opportunities have never been better.

never knew what hit him
1. was taken completely unawares, causing confusion and dismay.
2. was killed instantly.

never know (one's) luck in the big city
expression of encouragement stressing the possibility of success and fortune in some enterprise, especially in the city.

never look a gift horse in the mouth
1. don't accept a gift with poor grace.
2. don't question the origins of a gift or a surprising stroke of good luck or fortune.

never looked back since
has gone ahead, progressed ever since a particular event etc.: e.g. She's never looked back in her career since she went in that soapie.

never say die
refuse to give up, concede defeat.

never see eye to eye
to never agree or find a happy compromise: e.g. Those two never see eye to eye about anything and always argue.

never the twain shall meet
no way in which two people can ever meet because their worlds are so different; can never be a meeting of minds between two people because their ideas are so different.

never too old
jocular expression of encouragement to the effect that one is never too old to take part in a particular activity, especially sex.

never-never
1. any remote, sparsely populated place: e.g. He grew tired of city life and now lives out in the middle of never-never somewhere.
2. imaginary: e.g. never-never land.

new
(see: nothing new; what else's new?)

New Australian
migrant to Australia; migrant to Australia whose native language is not English.

new blood
new, fresh ideas or people: e.g. What this club needs is some new blood to get it motivated again.

new broom sweeps clean
new people, employees, bosses etc. revitalise and inject enthusiasm into a project etc., rid an organisation of corruption.

new chum
1. newly arrived British immigrant.
2. novice; beginner.

new ground
any new or unpreviously experienced situation, knowledge, ideas or development: e.g. It's about time we tried some new ground instead of

doing the same thing every week.
See also:
break new ground
cover new ground
treading on new ground

new kid
child who is new to a school, or who has just arrived at a club, street etc.

new lease of life
renewed vigour, zest, interest and enthusiasm: e.g. By renovating this old house we've given it a new lease of life.

new look
a completely changed or renovated appearance; radical new style in fashion.

new man
physically or morally improved person: e.g. Since going to that clinic to kick his drug habit, he's a new man.

new one on me
any fact, joke, matter about which one does not know: e.g. That's a new one on me!

new wave
a trend or movement that breaks away from traditional concepts, ideas, beliefs or fashion.

New York city
(rhyming slang) tittie; breast; boob.

new-fangled
modern, as opposed to old-fashioned; gimmicky; novel: e.g. Many old people refuse to use any of the new-fangled electronic gadgets for the kitchen and house.

newie
new, fresh idea, person or thing.

news
(bad news; latest news; no news is good news)

news-hawk
a keen reporter or journalist.

next on the cards
next in line; likely to happen.

next port of call
next place to visit or stop at.

next to nothing
1. (of expense, money) cheap; very little: e.g. This dress cost next to nothing at the market.
2. very little: e.g. That bludger did next to nothing all day!

next-door
the premises, property or building next to you; your immediate neighbours abutting either side of your property.
See also:
girl (boy) next-door

Niagara Falls/niagaras
(rhyming slang) balls; testicles.

nibbles
tentative inquiries about something you have for sale: e.g. I've only had the house on the market for a week and we've already had quite a few nibbles.

nibblies
snacks, munchies, small tit-bits of food to nibble on between meals.

nibs
(see: his nibs)

nice
used in a sarcastic manner, meaning not nice at all, unsatisfactory, displeasing: e.g. That's nice that is! Now look at the mess you've made!
See also:
pick a nice time to

nice drop
1. pleasant-tasting alcohol.
2. sexually attractive girl, woman.

nice legs, shame about the face
derogatory remark about a woman who has attractive legs but an ugly face.

nice little drop
(see: nice drop, 1. and 2.)

nice piece of work
1. sexually attractive girl or woman.
2. anything pleasing or well done.

nick
1. prison: e.g. He's been in the nick for five years now.
2. condition; state: e.g. He keeps in good nick at the gym.
3. steal; pilfer: e.g. People often nick things from shops for the excitement.
4. capture; arrest: e.g. He'll get nicked by the cops sooner or later.
See also:
in good nick
in the nick
in the nick of time

nick off
1. depart; go; leave: e.g. We have to nick off — it's getting late.
2. (in anger) get lost! go away! piss off!

nick out
to go somewhere for just a short time: e.g. I have to nick out to the shop for a loaf of bread.

Nick System
glorified work-avoidance scheme where two men are rostered to do one job and take it in turns to 'nick off' while on full pay.

nicked
1. stole; pilfered.
2. caught; captured; arrested.
See also:
get nicked!

nickers
(see: knickers)

nickname
familiar name given to a person, animal or thing in place of the real name, and used jokingly, in friendship or to ridicule.

nickywoop!
go away! piss off! get lost!

nicotine stains
(see: skid-marks)

niffy
having an offensive odour.

nifty
excellent; smart; stylish; pleasing.

nigger
offensive term for a dark-skinned, negroid person.

nigger in the woodpile
an unexpected or hidden problem or snag.

niggly
irritable; annoyed; angry; bad-tempered.

night cart
sanitary cart employed to empty toilet cans in areas without sewerage.

night is young/but a pup
it is still early; it is not too late in the evening.

night on the town
an entertaining evening out.

night out
an evening of entertainment in a club, restaurant, theatre etc. breaking the usual habit of staying at home: e.g. It's about time we all had a night out together.

nightcap
a drink, usually alcoholic, taken before going to bed.

night-club
a place of entertainment, usually open until the early hours of the morning.

nightie
(also: nighty) woman's night dress.
See also:
off like a bride's nightie
up and down like a honeymoon nightie
wouldn't that rip the crutch/fork out of your nightie!

nightie-night
expression for: good night, farewell.

night-life
the various activities, entertainments, clubs etc. that operate at night: e.g. The night-life in Sydney is very good.

nightmare
terrifying, awful ordeal or experience: e.g. Meeting his mother was a nightmare!

night-owl
person who enjoys staying up late.

night-spot
(see: night-club)

nig-nog
1. (derog.) dark-skinned, negroid person.
2. fool; dunce; simpleton; idiot.

nincompoop
fool; moron; idiot; simpleton.

nine
(see: done up to the nines; on cloud nine; stitch in time saves nine)

nine till five
pertaining to the everyday monotony of regular working hours, usually construed as being from nine o'clock in the morning to five o'clock at night.

nine-day wonder
any person or event that arouses only short-lived popularity.

niner
a keg of beer, formerly 9 gallons, but now 40.5 litres.

nineteen and six in the pound/bob in the quid
(to be . . .) to be stupid, lacking in intelligence, not in full control of one's faculties.

nineteen to the dozen
very quickly; in great haste: e.g. He's so tall that my legs have to go nineteen to the dozen to keep up with him.

nineteenth hole
the bar in a golf clubhouse.

nineteenth man
(Australian Rules football) replacement player.

ning-nong/ninny
fool; idiot; simpleton; dunce.

nip
1. steal; pilfer.
2. (cap.) Japanese person or thing: e.g. The Nips make excellent cars these days.
3. go somewhere for just a short while: e.g. Nip down to the pub and buy some beer and wine.
See also:
put the nips into (someone)

nip and tuck
1. cosmetic surgery, such as a face-lift.
2. (Australian Rules football) close game all day.

nip it in the bud
stop it at the beginning before it starts progressing.

nip over
go, visit somewhere for just a short time: e.g. Since moving to Queensland I really miss nipping over to Ruth's for a cuppa.

nipper
young child.

nippy
1. nimble; agile; quick; fast: e.g. That's a really nippy car!

2. cold, chilly, biting weather, the term often being used in the presence of a woman whose distended nipples are obvious beneath her clothing.

nit
fool; idiot; simpleton; dolt.
See also:
keep nit

nit-keeper
one who acts as guard for someone doing something illegal.

nit-picker
1. person who is always over-fussy and concerned with petty details; pettifogger.
2. person who is always critical, quibbling, finding fault.

nit-picking
to behave in the manner described for: nit-picker.

nitro
nitroglycerine — a highly explosive oil.

nitty-gritty
the basic facts, crux, core, fundamentals, essence of a matter.

nit-wit
fool; idiot; simpleton; dunce.

nix
1. nothing; zero.
2. forbid; prohibit; deny; reject: e.g. The council nixed that development proposal because of public objection.

no
(see: no-no; not take no for an answer)

no angel
not free from corruption, wrong-doing, guilt: e.g. He's no angel!

no ball
1. no; absolutely not.
2. (cricket) illegal delivery.

no bloody fear!
absolutely not! emphatically no!

no brain, no pain
jocular statement of consolation to someone who has injured or hurt himself, especially on the head.

no brains
lacking in intelligence; stupid; foolish.

no buts about it
no objections, complaints or compromise, will be countenanced.

no deal/dice
absolutely not; no; a refusal: e.g. As far as I'm concerned, it's no deal!

no end
very much; a great amount: e.g. He's no end of trouble!

no fear!
emphatically no!

no flies on (someone)
(someone) is smart, clever, shrewd, alert, informed.

no go
emphatically no; not successful; a refusal, denial; cancelled: e.g. The planned barbecue was no go because of the rain.

no great shakes
nothing outstanding or noteworthy: e.g. After all that publicity hype, that concert was no great shakes!

no holds barred
without restrictions.

no laughing matter
a serious matter: e.g. Getting into trouble at school is no laughing matter!

no more monkey business
a warning that the end of one's tolerance has been reached regarding a particular type of behaviour.

no news is good news
no communication or word from someone carries the consolation that probably nothing bad has happened.

no object
no problem or obstacle; not of importance: e.g. Money is no object in this case — he wants the best there is.

no oil painting
not endowed with beauty; ugly: e.g. I may not be a nubile beauty but you're no oil painting either!

no picnic
no easy task; difficult; unpleasant: e.g. Looking after ten young children for the week-end would be no picnic!

no probs!
no problems!

no punches pulled
no skirting of the truth with irrelevancies, but complete frankness: e.g. There were no punches pulled at the last meeting!

no raving beauty
(see: no oil painting)

no rest for the wicked
jocular consolation to someone who leads an extremely active life.

no risk!
exclamation of assurance: e.g. We can do that — no risk!

no room to swing a cat
pertaining to extremely cramped quarters: e.g. I'd hate to live in that house — there's no room to swing a cat!

no shit
1. an emphatic exclamation of sincerity: e.g. No shit — the fish that got away was bigger than me!

2. (as a question indicating one's surprise) is that so, true, correct?
3. no lies, but the absolute truth; no tactics designed to inconvenience, but candid honesty: e.g. He's a very shrewd business-man and he'll take no shit from anybody.

no shortage of oscar
to have plenty of money.

no show
no chance of success: e.g. He's got no show of getting that job.

no skin off (one's) nose
not to matter to (one); of little concern: e.g. He's so wealthy that it's no skin off his nose to lose a grand at the races.

no sooner said than done
(of a task) only had to be mentioned to be undertaken immediately; promptly.

no stranger to
familiar with: e.g. He's no stranger to boats — his father was a fisherman on a trawler.

no strings attached
no limitations, impositions, restrictions or obligations: e.g. She likes a relationship with a man that has no strings attached.

no such luck!
unfortunately not!

no sweat!
an expression of assurance; no problem!: e.g. I can do that for you — no sweat!

no ties
(see: no strings attached)

no troubs!
an expression of assurance; no trouble! no problem!

no two ways about it
no choice: e.g. There's no two ways about it — to be absolutely sure we have to count the whole lot again!

no use shutting the stable door after the horse has bolted
it is too late to do, after an error or mishap has occurred, what one should have done in the first place to prevent the mishap from occurring.

no way!

no way in the world!
emphatically no! under no circumstances.

no worries!
an expression of assurance; no problem!: e.g. You can borrow the car — no worries!

no wuckers/wucking furries!
(euphemism for: no fucking worries!) an expression of assurance: e.g. Sue Mudguts can stay with us for a holiday — no wuckers!

Noah/Noah's ark
(rhyming slang) shark.

nob
1. the head.
2. person of wealth, importance or high social standing.
3. the penis.
See also:
big nob
top-nob

nobble
1. to tamper illegally with a race-horse, such as by drugging.
2. to obtain dishonestly; swindle; cheat.
3. to capture; seize; grab; arrest.
4. to delegate a task to someone unwilling to do it: e.g. I got nobbled with the late shift on New Year's Eve.

nobby
first-class; elegant; plush.

nobody
person of little importance, social standing or influence.
See also:
like nobody's business

nod
(see: get the nod; give someone the nod; land of nod; on the nod)

nod is as good as a wink to a blind man
in the circumstances the difference does not matter.

nod off
go to, fall asleep.

noddy
fool; dunce; stupid, silly person.

no-frills
pertaining to basics, necessities without superfluous, added extras or unnecessary elaboration.

nog/noggy
(see: nig-nog)

noggin
1. the head.
2. a drink.

no-good
worthless; useless; contemptible: e.g. They're a no-good bunch of bludgers.

no-hoper
1. incompetent person or animal.
2. social outcast; person who does not meet socially acceptable standards of dress and behaviour, is unable to hold a job etc.
See also:
pack of no-hopers

noise
(see: big noise; make noises like)

noise off
speak loudly, brashly.

no-man's land
1. any place of wilderness considered dangerous.

2. any place, thing or situation that is neutral, not possessed, uncharted or unfamiliar.
3. disorder; chaos; jumble; mess.
4. bewildering, confused state of mind.

non compos
1. unconscious or completely incapable due to alcohol or drugs.
2. mentally incapable.
3. in a dazed and confused state of mind.

none the wiser
not any more informed or knowledgeable; still ignorant: e.g. If you take his car and bring it back before he gets home from work, he'll be none the wiser.

none the worse for
not harmed by: e.g. After all he's been through, he's none the worse for it.

non-event
a failure, fiasco.

nong
fool; idiot; simpleton; silly person.

no-no
1. something that is strictly not allowed: e.g. Alcohol on these premises is a no-no.
2. total failure: e.g. The last fund-raising do was a real no-no.

no-nonsense
1. practical; sensible.
2. strict; conventional.
3. unpretentious; candid; ethical.

noodle
1. the head: e.g. Use your noodle, you dill!
2. fool; dunce; simpleton.
3. the penis, especially a limp one.

nookie/nooky
sexual intercourse: e.g. Did you get a nooky last night?

nope
emphatically no.

norks
breasts; boobs; tits.

Norm
favourite Aussie fictional character made popular by the 'Life Be In It' advertising campaign — an opinionated slob who sits around watching telly and drinking booze.

North
North Melbourne VFL football team.

north-and-south
(rhyming slang) mouth.

nose
an ability to seek out, detect or succeed in: e.g. He's got a good nose for making money.
See also:
brown-nose
by a nose
can't see past (one's) own nose
cut off (one's) nose to spite (one's) face
don't pick your nose or your head will cave in
follow (one's) nose
get up (someone's) nose
hard-nosed
have/got a good nose for money
have/got a sharp nose
I'd like to have that nose full of gold dust
keep (one's) nose clean
keep (one's) nose out
keep (one's) nose to the grindstone
lead (someone) by the nose
look down (one's) nose at
no skin off (one's) nose
on the nose
parson's nose
pay through the nose
plain as the nose on your face
poke in the nose
poke (one's) nose in
powder (one's) nose
put (someone's) nose out of joint
stick (one's) nose in
sticky-nose
take a nosedive
thumb (one's) nose at
toffee-nosed
turn (one's) nose up
under (one's) nose
up your nose!

nose around
pry; meddle; eavesdrop; snoop: e.g. What are the police nosing around here for?

nose candy
cocaine.

nose down, bum up
extremely busy; hard at work.

nose for money
a keen sense or faculty for profitable ventures that make money.

nose in the air
snobby; pompous; assuming an air of being much better or more important than others.

nose out of joint
out-of-sorts; upset; to have one's ego deflated: e.g. Losing that beauty contest put her nose out of joint!

nose to the grindstone
intensive and persistent level of work with little time for rest: e.g. With the exams so close, he's going to have his nose to the grindstone for the next few weeks.

nosebag
a meal, feed: e.g. It's about time we had a nosebag isn't it — I'm starving!

nose-rag
handkerchief.

nosey enough to want to know the ins and outs of a chook's bum
(also: nosy) inquisitive; prying; snoopy.

nosey parker
person who pries, is over-inquisitive, meddlesome and snoopy.

nosh
1. a snack; food, especially taken between main meals.
2. to eat.

nosh-up
a large meal; an excellent feed: e.g. After getting home from the movies we raided the fridge for a nosh-up.

not a bad drop
1. a pleasing alcoholic drink: e.g. That's not a bad drop!
2. an attractive young woman.

not a bad old stick

not a bad sort
a good person; a pleasing sort of person.

not a hope in hell
no hope at all; no chance of success: e.g. With only five minutes to go to closing-time, there's not a hope in hell that you'll make it to the bank in time.

not a patch on
not nearly as good as; not equal to; inferior to: e.g. This brand of beer's not a patch on the other.

not a show
no chance of success; no hope; no.

not a stitch on
naked; nude: e.g. She came out of the pool with not a stitch on.

not a wink
no sleep or rest at all: e.g. I couldn't sleep last night — not a wink.

not able to take a trick
to have little or no success; to be habitually unlucky.

not again!
expression of exasperation at a recurring incident.

not all (one's) dogs are barking

not all there
(one) is not in full control of (one's) faculties; (one) is slightly silly, mad, crazy, eccentric or queer.

not an earthly
no chance at all.

not backward in coming forward
not shy or hesitating; brash; forward; outspoken.

not bad
1. very good; satisfactory; excellent: e.g. That movie's not bad.
2. mediocre; ordinary; passable.

not badly off
wealthy; prosperous.

not by a long shot/sight
not at all; not by any stretch of the imagination; not close to or approaching something: e.g. He's not good enough to win — not by a long shot.

not by any stretch of the imagination
under no circumstances; not at all.

not come at
refuse to do, attempt, take part in, accept: e.g. The boss is not going to come at those demands by the workers.

not cricket
not fair; unjust; not the accepted thing to do: e.g. Pinching a man's last beer is not cricket!

not doing (one's) whack
not doing (one's) fair share of the work; not pulling (one's) weight.

not for all the tea in China

not for quids
under no circumstances or inducement; no way; never: e.g. He wouldn't do that — not for quids!

not fussed
not concerned or worried; not caring about what alternative is chosen: e.g. I'm not fussed where we go tonight.

not get a look-in
not get, have, a chance, opportunity, luck or success: e.g. There were so many applicants for the job that he didn't even get a look-in.

not get a thing out of
1. to obtain no benefit or pleasure from: e.g. I didn't get a thing out of that concert.
2. fail to obtain a desired response, information from: e.g. I couldn't get a thing out of him about his latest project.

not get past first base
not make good progress; fail to make a good start.

not give a bugger/continental/damn/darn/fuck/hang/hoot/shit
not to care or worry at all: e.g. I don't give a shit what he says about me.

not give anything away
to remain silent; refuse to provide any facts or information.

not half!
1. very, very much!
2. an expression of sarcastic disbelief.

not have a bar of
have nothing to do with; refuse to associate oneself with.

For other possible entries beginning with 'not get', 'not give', 'not have' etc. see entries listed under 'couldn't', 'haven't', 'wouldn't' etc. or look up a key word in the phrase.

not if I can help it
veiled threat expressing one's disapproval and lack of support.

not in the race/running
having no chance of success.

not in the same street
not to be classed, compared with; not comparable to.

not just a pretty face
(joc.) one's worth, value, goes much deeper than just being physically attractive.

not know (someone) from Adam/a bar of soap

not know (someone) if I fell over him/her
(see: wouldn't know . . .)

not know whether it's Pitt Street or Christmas

not know whether it's Tuesday or Bourke Street

not know whether (one) is Arthur or Martha
(see: doesn't know . . .)

not likely!
no way! emphatically no!

not miss a trick
(see: doesn't . . .)

not much chop/cop
not good; not up to standard or as expected; not worthwhile: e.g. That latest movie's not much chop!

not my cup of tea
not what one finds interesting or agreeable; not to one's taste: e.g. Parties where everyone gets pissed out of their brains are not my cup of tea.

not now, I'm too tired/I've got a headache
standard and classic excuse from a wife or (woman) lover who is not in the mood for sex.

not on
not acceptable; unsatisfactory: e.g. Resorting to physical abuse during a domestic argument is just not on!

not on your life/nellie!
under no circumstances! no way! never! absolutely not!

not (one's) bag/scene/thing
(see: not my cup of tea)

not out of the woods yet
not out of trouble yet; still in difficulties.

not playing with the full deck
crazy; mad; insane; not in full control of one's faculties.

not pull (one's) weight
(see: pull . . .)

not put a foot wrong
to be successful.

not right in the head/skull
silly; stupid; insane; crazy; foolish.

not see past (one's) nose
(see: can't see . . .)

not short of a bob/dollar or two
wealthy; having plenty of money: e.g. He's not short of a bob.

not so hot
1. not feeling well; ill: e.g. I'm not so hot today — I think I'll stay in bed.
2. disappointing; not as good or pleasing as one would have hoped: e.g. That concert wasn't so hot.

not take no for an answer
to persist in the face of rejection.

not the clean potato
not free of guilt; of ill repute; having a bad reputation.

not the done thing
not socially acceptable: e.g. Farting at the dinner table is not the done thing.

not the end of the world
the problem is not as bad as it looks — there is still hope.

not the full packet of bickies

not the full quid/quid's worth

not the full two bob/two-bob's worth
not in full control of one's faculties; mad, crazy or insane; silly, eccentric, queer or odd; lacking in intelligence.

not the only fish in the sea/pebble on the beach
not the only choice available — there are many other suitably attractive people to meet.

not think twice about (something)
1. to consider only briefly before doing (something).
2. to forget about (something).

not to be sneezed/sniffed at
definitely worthy of consideration.

not to worry!
expression of assurance, consolation.

not tonight darling/Josephine, I have a headache
(see: not now, I've got a headache)

not too hot
(see: not so hot)

not up to scratch
not of a satisfactory standard; second-rate; of poor quality.

not what it's cracked up to be
(something that is) not of the expected quality or standard.

not with (someone)
to fail to understand, comprehend (someone): e.g. I'm not with you — could you explain that again.

not within cooee
1. not in hearing range.
2. not anywhere near the ultimate goal, end: e.g. He's not within cooee of finishing that job yet.

not worth a brass razoo/bumper/button

not worth a cracker/crumpet

not worth a cunt full of cold water

not worth a damn/deener/drum

not worth a pinch of goat-shit

not worth a rat's arse

not worth a row of beans

not worth a shit

not worth a tuppenny damn

not worth a zac

not worth tuppence/two bob
of little or no value; worthless; insignificant.

not worth feeding
(of a person) despicable, despised.

not worth (one's) salt
incapable; incompetent; not able.

not worth the paper it's written on
(of a document) worthless; not legally binding.

not worth thinking about
not worthy of consideration.

notch up
score; gain; attain.

nothing
person, thing or event of no importance or significance: e.g. He's a nothing.
See also:
double or nothing
for nothing
in nothing flat
know next to nothing
next to nothing
thanks for nothing

nothing between the ears
(of a person) stupid; foolish; dumb; slow-witted.

nothing doing!
absolutely not! no way! under no circumstances!

nothing for it
no other course of action: e.g. There was nothing for it but to run.

nothing in between
(see: nothing between the ears)

nothing in it
of little significance or importance.

nothing new
news, facts or information that is already known: e.g. That's nothing new — I was told that a year ago!

nothing on top
(of a man) bald.

nothing out of the box/way
not extraordinary or uncommon; ordinary.

nothing succeeds like success
one success generates further successes.

nothing to hide
innocent; having no guilt.

nothing to it
(of a task) easy.

nothing to rave/write home about
disappointing; ordinary; not as exceptional as expected; not very remarkable; uninteresting.

nothing up top
1. (to have . . .) dumb; slow-witted; lacking in intelligence.
2. (of a woman) having small breasts.

nous
common sense: e.g. He's got lots of nous as far as making money is concerned.

nouveau riche
pertaining to newly acquired wealth (often derog.).

now
trendy; fashionable; popular; current: e.g. Her fashion designs are very now at present.

now and again/then
occasionally.

now is the hour
1. (rhyming slang) shower.
2. (see: now or never).

now I've seen it all!
expression of amazement, wonder, astonishment or exasperation.

now look who's calling the kettle black
statement of reproach to someone who has just proved by his actions etc. the hypocrisy and sanctimonious insincerity of his professed beliefs.

now, now!
expression used to propitiate, appease or reprove.

now or never
the time to act is now, or the opportunity may never arise again.

now you see it, now you don't
1. pertaining to any trickery, sleight of hand or deception.
2. pertaining to any short-lived, unstable situation; not permanent.

now you've done it!
1. now you're really in trouble, in a fix, usually as a direct consequence of something you've just done.
2. now you've ruined, bungled, spoiled it!

nowhere man
person who achieves little.

nowt
nothing.

nozzle
the nose.

N.R.C.
film rating — Not Recommended for Children.

nth
(see: for the nth time)

nth degree
the utmost extent.

'Actually my customers find th' pokies a stimulating mental challenge — they haven't stopped racking their brains for new ways to diddle them!'

In actual fact, the ones who get diddled, brassed, conned, done, dudded, fleeced, foxed, fucked, got at, gypped, had, hoodwinked, put up, ripped off, set up, screwed, short-changed, stung, sucked in, taken or touched are the turkeys who play the pokies!

nub
the point or gist of anything: e.g. Let's get to the real nub of this meeting.

nubbies/nubs
breasts; boobs; tits.

nud/nuddy
nude; naked: e.g. We went swimming in the nud.

nudge
(see: give it a nudge)

nudge nudge, wink wink
an expression, often ribald, lewd or sly in meaning, drawing attention to something meant to be private, secret or discreet.

nudge on the funny-bone
funny; hilarious; amusing: e.g. That joke was a real nudge on the funny-bone.

nudge the bottle/turps
to drink alcohol to excess: e.g. I wish he wouldn't nudge the bottle so much!

nuggetty
stocky; short; thick-set.

nuke
1. nuclear; pertaining to nuclear weapons.
2. to cook food in a microwave oven: e.g. He won't eat nuked food!

null and void
not valid; having no legality.

nulla-nulla
an Aboriginal weapon.

number
1. stunning, extraordinary, especially of an article of clothing: e.g. That's a gorgeous number she's wearing.
2. sexually attractive woman: e.g. She's a nice-looking number.
3. marijuana cigarette or joint.
4. a song.
See also:
there's safety in numbers

number one
1. yourself; oneself: e.g. I'm looking after number one from now on.
2. the boss; chief; first in rank or authority.
3. foremost; the most important: e.g. This is the number one newspaper for classified ads.
4. urination: e.g. I need to do number one but I can't find the loo!

number two
1. second in rank or importance.
2. defecation.

number's up
1. one is in serious trouble: e.g. His number's up — the police are on to him.
2. one is about to die.

numb-skull
fool; idiot; dolt; simpleton.

numero uno
(number one)
1. yourself; oneself.
2. the boss; chief; leader; first in rank or authority.

nummy
delicious; tasty.

num-nums
tasty, delicious food; snacks.

nungers
breasts; boobs; tits.

nurd
(see: nerd)

nut
1. eccentric, silly, foolish person; a character.
2. mad, insane, crazy person.
3. the head.
4. an enthusiast; a buff; an expert: e.g. He's a real nut for vintage cars.
5. a testicle.
6. to castrate: e.g. We're going to nut our tom cat.
See also:
do (one's) nut
do (one's) nuts over
go off (one's) nut
hard nut to crack
off (one's) nut
sweet as a nut

nut case
1. foolish, eccentric, odd person.
2. insane, mad, crazy person.

nut out
solve; figure out.

nut-chokers
briefs, underwear for men.

nut-house
1. asylum for the insane.
2. any disorderly, messy or noisy place.

nuts
1. crazy; insane; mad.
2. foolish; stupid; eccentric; irrational.
3. the testicles.
4. (as an exclamation) nonsense! rubbish!
See also:
do (one's) nuts over
go nuts

nuts about/over
in love with; infatuated with; smitten with: e.g. He's nuts about that new car of his.

nutshell
(see: in a nutshell)

nutted
castrated.

nutter
(see: nut, 1., 2. and 4.)

nutty as a fruitcake
1. mad; insane; crazy.
2. foolish; stupid; eccentric; silly; irrational.

nutty over
(see: nuts about)

nympho
nymphomaniac: a woman of uncontrolled sexual desires.

oar
(see: get one's oar in; have/got only one oar in the water; put one's oar in; rest on one's oars)

oats
(see: feel one's oats; sow one's wild oats)

obs
objections.

ocean-going
pertaining to any vessel capable of travelling in the open sea.

ocker
anything typically Australian, but especially referring to the uncultivated Australian male, displaying qualities such as excessive boozing, chauvinism, uncouthness, footy worship and so on.

ockerism
pertaining to the ocker character.

octopus
pertaining to a man who appears to have many hands everywhere, especially when sexually motivated.

OD
1. overdose, especially of narcotic drugs.
2. consume to excess: e.g. I OD'd on chocolates last week and now my face is covered with zits!

odd bod
(see: oddball)

odd jobs
casual, isolated items of work.

odd man out
1. social misfit.
2. person who has not been paired up, who has been left over after everyone else has been arranged in pairs or groups.

oddball
eccentric, strange, peculiar or weird person.

odd-job man
person who does odd jobs, such as gardening, cleaning, minor repairs etc.

odds and ends
stray, miscellaneous articles, remnants, scraps.

odds and sods
1. miscellaneous or random collection of people or things.
2. (see: odds and ends)

odds are (stacked) against it
chances of success are slim: e.g. The odds are against our team winning because our best player is injured.

odds or evens?
an invitation to choose on the outcome of the toss of two coins — odds being a head and a tail, and evens being two heads or two tails. (see also: heads or tails?)

odds-on
a situation where success is more likely than failure; a situation where one thing is more likely to happen than another.

of the blackest/deepest dye
of the worst kind: e.g. He's a criminal of the deepest dye.

of the first water
of the first or best quality; excellent.

of the old school
old-fashioned; staunchly traditionalist or conservative.

of the order of
approximately; about.

of the world
sophisticated: e.g. She's a woman of the world.

off
1. (of food) tainted; rotting; bad: e.g. These prawns are off.
2. in bad taste; vulgar: e.g. That joke was a bit off.
3. unwell; sick; ill: e.g. He feels a bit off today.
4. leaving; departing: e.g. We're off now.
5. awful; terrible: e.g. I had an off day at work.
6. not up to standard: e.g. He's off his game today.

7. to refrain, stop from doing: e.g. He's off cigarettes now.
See also:
back off
bring it off
bring (someone) off
browned off
bug off!
cool off
drop off
drop (someone) off
eye off
fly off the handle
fuck off!
get it off with (someone)
get off
get off on
get off with (someone)
have it off
hit it off
jack off
jerk off
kick off
knock it off
knock off
knock (someone) off
laugh it off
lay off
leave off
let off
let off steam
make off with
more off than on
mouth off
nick off!
nod off
on and off
piss off
piss (someone) off
pissed off
pull it off
pull (someone) off
push off
put off
put-off
rack off!
rack off hairy-legs!
rack off noddy!
rip off
rip-off
rub off
run off with
send-off
set (someone) off
shat off
shove off
spout off
suck off
switch off
take off
take off with
take-off
throw off at
throw (someone) off (the track)
tick off
turn off
way off
way off the beaten track
well off

off and on
occasionally; sometimes: e.g. We visit them off and on.

off by heart
to know from memory: e.g. He knows that poem off by heart.

off like a bride's nightie
1. remove an item of clothing in haste.
2. depart in haste; act promptly, quickly.

off like a bucket of prawns/ lubra's loincloth
extremely smelly.

off like a Jew's foreskin

off like a larrikin's hat in a breeze
1. removed quickly.
2. depart hastily.

off like a robber's dog
to depart in great haste.

off like a rocket
1. be very successful: e.g. The party went off like a rocket.
2. depart in haste: e.g. She was off like a rocket to the store's sale.

off like a whore's drawers
1. removed quickly.
2. depart hastily.

off on a tangent
concerned with irrelevant details.

off on another tack/track
concerned with irrelevant details or a different subject altogether.

off (one's) block/cruet/ crumpet
1. insane; crazy; mad; eccentric; foolish; stupid; irrational.
2. extremely angry.

off (one's) face
1. insane; crazy; mad; eccentric; foolish; stupid; irrational.
2. under the influence of alcohol or drugs; drunk; stoned.

off (one's) game
not performing at (one's) best; out of form.

off (one's) hands
no longer under, in, (one's) responsibility: e.g. I'm glad I've got that problem off my hands!

off (one's) head/nana/nut/ onion
1. insane; crazy; mad; eccentric; foolish; stupid; irrational.
2. over-excited.
3. very angry, upset.

off (one's) own bat
independently: e.g. He did it entirely off his own bat.

off (one's) pannikin/rails/ rocker/scone/trolley
1. insane; crazy; mad; eccentric; foolish; stupid; irrational.
2. very angry, upset.

off (one's) tucker
having lost (one's) appetite for food: e.g. He was off his tucker while he was sick and lost a lot of weight.

off pat
perfectly; by memory, or heart: e.g. He can recite that poem off pat.

off the air
1. no longer being broadcast: e.g. That programme has been put off the air.
2. angry; furious: e.g. He's been off the air ever since he lost all that money.
3. crazy; insane; mad.

off the beam
crazy; unsound; insane; mad.

off the beaten track
1. secluded; out of the way: e.g. We know a nice camping spot that's off the beaten track.
2. remote; unfamiliar.

off the cuff
perfectly, by memory or heart; impromptu.

off the deep end
1. weird; odd; eccentric: e.g. That movie was a bit off the deep end!
2. (go . . .) become angry, enraged; lose one's temper: e.g. Your parents will go off the deep end when they find out what you've done!

off the hook
1. out of trouble; no longer facing a difficult predicament or unpleasant consequences: e.g. The police let him off the hook this time with a severe warning.
2. (of a telephone) not having the receiver engaged: e.g. We like to leave the phone off the hook around tea-time so that we don't get disturbed.

off the mark
not relevant to the situation at hand: e.g. His testimony was way off the mark.

off the peg/rack
pertaining to ready-made clothes.

off the planet
1. very angry; furious.
2. drunk; intoxicated; under the influence of drugs.
3. in a confused state.
4. excellent; wonderful; worthy of admiration: e.g. That concert was really off the planet!

off the point
(see: off the mark)

off the rails
1. mentally unbalanced; crazy; insane.
2. unbalanced; chaotic; out of control.

off the record
unofficial; not for publication.

off the top of (one's) head
impromptu; unrehearsed; ad-lib; an educated guess.

off the track
irelevant; departing from the subject.

off the wall
crazy; unsound; insane; mad; eccentric; weird.

off with the fairies
not concentrating; absent-minded; in a dazed, dreamy state of mind.

off-beam
1. incorrect; irrelevant.
2. out of touch; foolish, crazy or unrealistic.

off-beat
irregular; different; unconventional.

off-centre
crazy; insane.

off-chance
remote possibility: e.g. There's an off-chance that you might find him at the races.
See also:
do it on the off-chance

off-colour
1. sick; unwell; ill.
2. tasteless; coarse; vulgar; crude: e.g. That joke he told was a bit off-colour for mixed company.

offhand
1. without preparation; casual; unrehearsed; impromptu.
2. curt; rude; impolite: e.g. He has such an offhand manner over the phone!
3. an educated guess or estimation: e.g. Offhand, I'd say the car's worth about ten thousand.

off-handed
curt; rude; brusque; impolite.

office-hours
regular working hours as opposed to leisure or after-hours.

offish
aloof; distant; haughty; pompous.

off-load
1. get rid of, often in a devious or underhanded manner: e.g. After bogging up all the dents, he off-loaded his car on some gullible fool who paid far too much for it.
2. (Australian Rules football) tackle, get rid of an opponent.

off-peak
operating at a period of less activity than normal: e.g. off-peak electricity.

off-putting
disconcerting; rude; impolite; discouraging: e.g. His manner was very off-putting.

off-sider
friend; partner; helper; assistant.

oh boy!
exclamation indicating either dismay, disappointment, or delight, wonder.

oh my God!

oh no!
exclamation of dismay, disappointment.

oh yeah!
exclamation of mocking, scornful disbelief.

oh-oh!
exclamation of surprised dismay, disappointment. (also: uh-oh!)

oil
reliable advice or information: e.g. I was given the oil on

corruption in the racing industry by an insider.
See also:
burn the midnight oil
dinkum oil
good oil
no oil painting
pour oil on troubled waters
the good oil
well-oiled

oil slick
(derog.) a Greek person.

oil (someone) up
1. advise, give (someone) reliable information: e.g. Don't worry — I'll oil him up on what has to be done.
2. flatter (someone) in order to get (him) to do something.

oil (someone's) palm
offer (someone) a bribe.

oily rag
(see: run on/live on the smell of an oily rag)

oinker
1. a pig.
2. a policeman.

O.K./okay/okey dokey
1. good; satisfactory.
2. affirmative; yes.
3. approval of; acceptance: e.g. We finally got the okay from the council to start building.

old
1. out-dated; no longer in fashion.
2. adjective used to express the extension of time, usually enjoyable, of a particular activity: e.g. We had a good old time.
See also:
never too old
the old one-two

old as the hills
1. very old.
2. out-dated; no longer fashionable.

old bag
(derog.) term for a disliked woman.

old bag of bones
term for an old, weary, decrepit person or animal.

old bat
1. (derog.) old woman.
2. (derog.) term for a disliked woman.

old biddy
old woman.

old bitch
(derog.) term for a disliked woman.

old boiler
an older woman, as opposed to a young, nubile one.

old bomb
dilapidated car.

old boy
1. the penis.
2. affectionate term of address for a male person or animal.
3. husband or father.
4. an old man.

old bus
the family (or personal) car — usually a dilapidated one.

old cheese
1. one's mother: e.g. My old cheese won't let me go out tonight.
2. any older person.

old chook
(derog.) term for a disliked woman.

old codger
old man — often strange, eccentric or odd.

old country
(see: the old country)

old cow/crow
(derog.) term for a disliked woman.

Old Dart
(the . . .) England: e.g. Some poms still identify themselves with the Old Dart even though they've lived here for twenty years.

old dear
one's mother: e.g. The old dear doesn't approve of everything I do, but we still get on very well.

old dears
parents: e.g. I have to visit the old dears this weekend.

old dog at
skilled at; well versed in or familiar with due to a long association with: e.g. He's an old dog at the racing game.

old eagle eyes
jocular term for a person who notices everything, or is difficult to hide things from: e.g. Whenever I try to hide his birthday present, old eagle eyes manages to find it!

old enough to be (one's) father/mother
term (generally of contempt) for someone who is much older than (one).

old enough to know better
having the advantage of age and its supposed accumulation of wisdom and experience (but often not drawing on that wisdom and, hence, acting foolishly).

old fella/feller/fellow
(see: old boy, 1., 2., 3. and 4.)

old flame
a lover from one's past.

old fogey
boringly conservative, old-fashioned person.

old geeser/geezer
1. old man.
2. chap, person, fellow: e.g. He's not such a bad old geeser.

old girl
1. an elderly woman.
2. affectionate term of address for a female friend or animal.
3. mother.
4. wife.
5. pet name for one's car, especially if it is a

dilapidated one: e.g. The old girl still gets me there and back.

old grouch
bad-tempered, ill-disposed or constantly complaining person.

old hand at (something)
experienced, well-practised, skilled at (something): e.g. He's an old hand at training horses.

old hat
boring; tediously familiar; old-fashioned: e.g. The Beatles are old hat as far as today's teenagers are concerned.

old Hughie
(see: Hughie)

old lady
1. mother, mum.
2. wife; girlfriend.

old man
1. father.
2. husband.
3. employer; boss.

old school/school-tie
pertaining to staunch traditionalism or conservative people.

old stamping ground
the familiar and favourite places and haunts from one's youth: e.g. That disco used to be my old stamping ground.

old thing
familiar term of address: e.g. G'day old thing, how are you?

old timer
old person, especially a man.

old wives' tale
a belief, folk remedy or superstition that is usually false.

old woman
1. mother, mum.
2. wife.
3. effeminate, timid or over-fussy person, especially a man.
See also:
the old woman

older than Adam's father
very old person or thing.

oldies/olds
1. parents: e.g. He's forty and still lives with his oldies.
2. elderly people.

on
1. happening; occurring; event is taking place: e.g. 1. What's on next week? 2. The party for next weekend is definitely on.
2. liability for expense: e.g. The drinks are on me!
3. excessive indulgence: e.g. He's on the bottle again!
4. accept as a wager, bet, gamble: e.g. You're on! I bet you can't do it!
See also:
bring (someone) on
crap on
crash on
get on her/him!
get on to
getting on (a bit)
go on
go on at (someone)
hard-on
have (oneself) on
have (someone) on
hit on it
keep on
keep on keeping on
let on
light on
not on
push on
put it on (someone)
put on
right on!
take on
take (someone) on
turn (one) on
turn-on
you're on!

on a bad trot
experiencing bad luck or misfortune.

on a bender
drinking alcohol to excess; intoxicated: e.g. The boys have been on a bender all night celebrating their team's victory.

on a downer
experiencing misfortune or depression.

on a good cop
to have a profitable job or position: e.g. He's on a good cop with that new job of his.

on a good lurk
1. to have a successful and profitable job or position.
2. to be involved in a successful and profitable venture, enterprise or activity.

on a good screw
1. to have a profitable job or position.
2. to be involved with a sexually satisfying partner.

on a good thing
1. to be involved in a successful or profitable job, enterprise or activity.
2. (of a man) believing in the possibility of being successfully intimate with a woman; optimistic about a sexual pursuit.

on a good trot
experiencing good luck, fortune or success.

on a good wicket
(see: on a good lurk, 1. and 2.)

on a high
1. in a state of euphoria induced by drugs.
2. in a state of happiness, joy.

on a plate/platter
pertaining to something that was easily obtained, without much work or effort: e.g. Nothing was given to me on a platter — I had to work hard for everything I've got!

on a promise
(usually of a man) assured of a sexual partner: e.g. He's all smiles because he's on a promise tonight.

on a razor's edge
in an extremely difficult, dangerous position, predicament, situation.

on a shoestring
having little money; poor; destitute: e.g. The spiralling cost of living is forcing many people to live on a shoestring.

on a sticky wicket
in trouble; experiencing difficulty, problems.

on a sure thing
1. optimistic about the success of an enterprise or venture.
2. (of a man) optimistic about a sexual pursuit.

on a winning streak
experiencing good luck or fortune.

on about
excessive and persistent nagging, talking or concern about a particular subject: e.g. 1. I wish you'd stop going on about it! 2.What are you on about now?

on all fours
down on one's hands and knees.

on an even keel
steady; safe; balanced; secure; calm and untroubled: e.g. Their marriage always seems to be on an even keel.

on an upper
in an extremely happy frame of mind; elated.

on and off
occasionally; sometimes.

on and on
persistently; at great length.

on another planet
in a dream-like state of mind; not concentrating.

on appro
on approval; without obligation to purchase.

on at (someone)
berating; scolding; nagging: e.g. You're always on at me for one thing or another!

on bended knee
meekly; submissively.

on borrowed time
pertaining to time that is very short, likely to end at any time: e.g. He's living on borrowed time since learning he has cancer.

on both sides of the fence
having no loyalties to one side or the other; undecided as to where one's loyalties lie.

on cloud nine
elated; in a euphoric state of mind: e.g. She's been on cloud nine since she met that new bloke.

on deck
1. present: e.g. Is everyone on deck yet?
2. awake and out of bed.
3. alive: e.g. Is that old man still on deck?

on earth
ever — used as an intensive: e.g. 1. Not on earth! (not ever). 2. What on earth have you got there? 3. Where on earth are you going dressed like that?

on easy street
comfortably well-off financially; wealthy; prosperous: e.g. Since winning that million in the lottery he's been on easy street.

on edge
1. irritable; nervous; anxious.
2. acutely sensitive and easily offended.

on for young and old
an outbreak of disorder; commotion; absence of restraint: e.g. Someone threw a punch at the pub and then it was on for young and old as everyone started fighting.

on heat
sexually aroused.

on ice
ready; waiting; in readiness.

on it
drinking heavily: e.g. He's been on it all night!

on (one's) ace
alone; on (one's) own.

on (one's) back
1. ill in bed.
2. lazy; idle; doing nothing constructive.
3. (of a woman) pertaining to or ready for sexual intercourse: e.g. That tart spends most of her time on her back!
4. annoying; harassing; badgering; watching closely: e.g. The boss is always on my back!

on (one's) beam-ends
in a state of poverty, trouble, misfortune or distress.

on (one's) brain
obsessed, preoccupied with; unable to rid (one's) thoughts of: e.g. 1. He's always got sex on his brain! 2. That song has been on my brain all day!

on (one's) ear
1. in trouble or difficulties.
2. out of favour; in disgrace.

on (one's) feet
successful, especially after a difficult time: e.g. After all that hard work he's finally on his feet.

on (one's) hammer
on (one's) back; badgering, watching (one) closely: e.g. If I don't stay on his hammer he doesn't do any work.

on (one's) hands
responsibility; be responsible for: e.g. She's

got enough on her hands as it is with six kids and now she's pregnant again.

on (one's) head
1. easily; without effort: e.g. He's so good he can do it on his head!
2. as (one's) responsibility; be responsible for: e.g. I don't want my son's death on my head so I won't let him have a motorcycle.

on (one's) high horse
assuming an arrogant and pompous air, attitude: e.g. What's he on his high horse about?

on (one's) knees
1. begging; pleading.
2. reduced to a state of poverty, rejection or ruin.

on (one's) last legs
exhausted; on the verge of collapse, ruin.

on (one's) pat/Pat Malone
(rhyming slang) alone; on (one's) own.

on (one's) plate
pending; waiting to be dealt with, handled: e.g. I've got enough on my plate now without taking any more jobs on.

on (one's) toes
alert; prepared for action.

on paper
1. in writing; confirmed legally: e.g. You should get all business dealings down on paper.
2. in theory rather than in practice: e.g. It looks okay on paper, but have you tested it yet to see if it works?

on pins and needles
anxious; fretting; in a worried or agitated state.

on record
publicly, legally acknowledged or recorded: e.g. He's on record for saying those things — I saw it during an interview on T.V.

on shaky ground
unstable; doomed to failure.

on skid row
destitute; in a state of poverty and ruin.

on spec
on speculation; as a gamble.

on special
at a reduced price.

on strike
(cricket) of the batsman who is facing the bowler.

on tenterhooks
in a state of suspense or anxiety: e.g. We were on tenterhooks for days waiting to hear what the verdict was to be.

on the . . . side
tending to be like the thing mentioned: e.g. 1. He's a bit on the fat side since he stopped smoking. 2. That's a bit on the expensive side.

on the air
being broadcast on television or radio.

on the ball
alert; keenly aware; ready for action; prepared.

on the beam
aware; alert; in touch with a situation.

on the blink
malfunctioning; out of order: e.g. My telly's on the blink again.

on the blower
on the telephone: e.g. 1. He's on the blower talking business. 2. Are you on the blower? (Do you have a telephone?)

on the bludge
living off the expenses or hospitality of others; cadging, borrowing, with no intention of paying back.

on the bones of (one's) bum
destitute; ruined — especially financially.

on the booze
(see: on the bottle)

on the bot
cadging; borrowing, usually with no intention of paying back.

on the bottle
excessive indulgence in alcohol; an alcoholic: e.g. He's been on the bottle for years.

on the breadline
in a state of poverty; having little money for necessities.

on the bugle
1. (see: on the blower)
2. having a highly offensive smell.

on the cards
probable; likely to happen.

on the carpet
(see: on the mat)

on the cheap
obtained very cheaply, or at no cost: e.g. We get a lot of things on the cheap because the manager is a close friend.

on the con
1. predisposed to cheating, swindling, fraud, deceit.
2. intent on personal gain.
3. intent on making a sexual conquest.

on the conk
having a highly offensive smell.

on the crest of the wave
prospering; at the height of good fortune, luck.

on the cuff
on credit.

on the dole
receiving social security benefits, payments for being unable to find employment.

on the dot
1. immediately: e.g. Come here on the dot!

2. on time; punctually: e.g. We were at the meeting on the dot.

on the double
immediately: e.g. I want it done on the double!

on the edge of (one's) chair
in a state of fear, excitement, anticipation.

on the face of it
judging by the appearance of; superficially.

on the fiddle
involved in illicit money-making activities, especially in tampering with records or documents.

on the fritz
broken down; malfunctioning.

on the go
1. busy; active: e.g. She's always on the go.
2. making good progress: e.g. That new shop is really on the go.

on the grog
excessive indulgence in alcohol.

on the home straight/ stretch
at the last stages of finishing, completing something.

on the hoof
(of animals) alive: e.g. They're taking so long to cook my steak that it still must be on the hoof!

on the hop
1. unprepared; by surprise: e.g. Inspectors of any kind usually try to catch people on the hop.
2. busy; active; on the move: e.g. I've been on the hop all day.

on the house
free of charge, especially from the management.

on the improve
getting better, especially after an illness or misfortune: e.g. He's on the improve since his operation.

on the inside
1. in prison.
2. in close association; part of a group inaccessible to outsiders: e.g. The only way our opposition could have got that classified information was by having a secret agent on the inside.

on the job
1. busy; actively getting on with a specific task.
2. (joc.) performing sexually: e.g. She looks frustrated — I don't think hubby's been on the job!

on the knocker
on time; punctually: e.g. Be there on the knocker.

on the level
truthful; honest; candid; sincere: e.g. Are you on the level?

on the line
in a state of risk or danger: e.g. He'd put his very life on the line for her.

on the loose
1. on a spree; having a good time.
2. unattached; independent; single; not restrained by a partner, spouse or lover.

on the make
(see: on the con, 1., 2. and 3.)

on the mat
1. in trouble; in a difficult or embarrassing predicament: e.g. Those reporters really put him on the mat with their pertinent questions.
2. in a position of ridicule or chastisement.

on the mend
1. recovering after an illness.
2. improving; getting better: e.g. Our business is on the mend.

on the move
1. actively engaged in some activity.
2. not static; moving from place to place.

on the Murray cod
(rhyming slang) on the nod — on credit.

on the nail
right on target or on the spot; relevant and to the point.

on the nod
on credit: e.g. Most of what he's got is on the nod.

on the nose
1. having a highly offensive smell.
2. anything viewed with contempt.

on the other hand
as a contrast to what is already being discussed: e.g. On the other hand, it might be better to do it the other way.

on the other side of the fence
having one's loyalties with the opposition.

on the outer
not included in a particular group or activity; a social misfit.

on the pill
taking oral contraceptive tablets.

on the piss
excessive indulgence in alcohol, especially beer.

on the point of
close or about to: e.g. I was on the point of choking on that fish-bone, when he slapped me on the back and I swallowed it.

on the prowl
1. actively moving around and watching; on the alert: e.g. The police are on the prowl for disorderly behaviour.

2. intent on sexual gain: e.g. Whenever his wife is away, he goes on the prowl.

on the quiet
1. secretly; without anybody else's knowledge.
2. in an underhanded manner; illicitly.

on the rags
(of women) menstruating.

on the rampage
1. involved in riotous merry-making.
2. extremely angry: e.g. The headmaster's on the rampage because someone painted obscenities on his car.

on the ran-tan
drinking heavily; on the booze.

on the rebound
a period of reaction after an unhappy break-up of a relationship, when a person may cling to, or desire to become closely involved with, the first person that comes along.

on the receiving end
to be the recipient of unpleasant actions or consequences: e.g. I hate being on the receiving end of his bad temper.

on the right foot
doing commendably; in favour.
See also:
get off on the right foot

on the right side of (someone)
in favour with (someone): e.g. He can't seem to get on the right side of the boss who blames him for everything.

on the rocks
in a state of ruin, decay, danger; in danger of failing: e.g. Their marriage is on the rocks after only one year.

on the ropes
in danger of failing: e.g. His business is on the ropes.

on the run
1. quickly, due to being busy or lack of time: e.g. He always has lunch on the run.
2. evading the police, law, authorities etc.

on the same wavelength
in agreement, or harmony of thought.

on the scrap-heap
useless; failed; broken down.

on the shady side
1. disreputable; of doubtful or dubious honesty, integrity.
2. beyond, past the age: e.g. He's on the shady side of forty.

on the shelf
neglected, dejected, especially of an unmarried woman.

on the shicker
excessive indulgence in alcohol.

on the side
something extra, especially of sex in a secret or illicit manner: e.g. Many married men don't think twice about getting a bit on the side as long as the wife doesn't know about it.

on the skids
any person, venture or situation that is in a precarious position, breaking down, destitute, in danger of failing.

on the slate
on credit.

on the slops
excessive indulgence in alcohol, especially beer.

on the sly
in a sly manner; secretly; illicitly.

on the spot
1. immediately; without delay: e.g. I want it done on the spot.
2. at the scene, place: e.g. I was on the spot when it happened, so I saw everything.
3. embarrassed; placed in an embarrassing situation: e.g. He was really on the spot when the reporter asked him that question.
4. to be in a difficult situation in which one is compelled to take action: e.g. I was really on the spot when they all arrived at once, so I had to send some of them away.
See also:
on-the-spot fine

on the spur of the moment
impulsive or sudden behaviour: e.g. I did it on the spur of the moment without really thinking of the consequences.

on the square
1. abstaining from alcohol or illegal activity.
2. fair; fairly; just: e.g. I think the court's decision was on the square.

on the straight and narrow
leading a law-abiding existence, especially after a life of crime.

on the strap
broke; penniless.

on the streets
1. out of work with nowhere to live or call home.
2. living as a prostitute: e.g. She's been on the streets since she was thirteen.

on the surface
superficially.

on the take
intent on gain using underhanded or illegal means; receiving illicit profits, bribes.

on the tear/tiles/town
out on a wild spree, enjoying oneself to the fullest: e.g. We're going out on the tear tonight.

on the tip of (one's) tongue
to know the answer but to be unable to recall it immediately due to a lapse in memory.

on the turps
excessive indulgence in alcohol.

on the up and up
1. improving; achieving success: e.g. His whole life is on the up and up since getting that new job.
2. honest; credible.

on the vinegar stroke
at the point of climax, especially with regard to sexual intercourse: e.g. He was on the vinegar stroke when the phone rang!

on the wallaby (track)
obsolete term referring to the swagman looking for work.

on the warpath
hostile; very angry.

on the (water) wagon
abstaining from alcoholic drinks.

on the way out
1. becoming unfashionable, obsolete, out of date: e.g. Baggy jeans are on the way out and tight ones are in.
2. broken; out of order: e.g. My telly's on the way out!

on the whole
generally.

on the wrong side of (someone)
out of favour with (someone): e.g. I'd hate to be on the wrong side of her!

on the wrong tack/track
misguided, irrelevant thinking; not concerned with the relevant issues.

on thin ice
in a risky, dangerous, precarious position or situation.

on tick
on credit: e.g. I don't have anything on tick at present.

on to
aware of the true facts, nature, meaning of; to have discovered or learnt about: e.g. It's only a matter of time before he's arrested because the police are on to his illegal schemes.

on to a good lurk
(see: on a good lurk)

on to a good thing
(see: on a good thing)

on to something
on the verge of discovery: e.g. The police must be on to something because they've stepped up their investigations.

on top
successful; in a superior position.

on top of
1. in addition to: e.g. On top of all his other hassles, his mother died last week.
2. fully in control, command: e.g. There's no need to worry — we're on top of the problem now.

on top of the world
in a state of complete happiness, satisfaction, euphoria.

on with
involved with sexually, especially of an illicit nature: e.g. Everyone except his wife knows that he's on with his secretary.

on ya!
an expression of encouragement; contraction of: good on you!

on your mark(s)
get ready to start immediately.

once and for all
1. finally and decisively: e.g. I want this problem cleared up once and for all.
2. for the last time: e.g. I've told you once and for all — no!

once bitten, twice shy
after having experienced something unpleasant as a consequence of one's actions, one is wary of trying again.

once in a blue moon

once in a month of Sundays
very rarely; not often: e.g. Once in a blue moon he gives me flowers.

once in a while
sometimes, but not often.

once upon a time
a long time ago: e.g. Once upon a time, he used to bring me flowers!

once-over
1. a severe beating or physical assault.
2. a quick, preliminary inspection of a person (especially as a sex object) or a thing: e.g. Most men give an attractive girl the once-over as soon as she enters a room.

oncer
something that happens only once or very rarely.

one
1. a person, usually of an unusual, eccentric, amusing or bad character: e.g. 1. He's a bad one. 2. He's a one!
2. sexual intercourse: e.g. Did you get one last night?
See also:
all one to (one)
drop one
fast one
get one
give (someone) one
go one better

great one for
hang one on (someone)
it takes one to know one
look after number one
number one
put one over/past (someone)
raise one
takes one to know one
the old one-two
thousand and one
try another one!
try one on (someone)

one and all
everybody.

one and only
unique.

one bad apple doesn't spoil the rest
one bad, disreputable person or thing does not mean the rest are bad or disreputable.

one foot in the door
(see: have/got one foot in the door)

one foot in the grave
to be very ill, old or close to death: e.g. He's got one foot in the grave now, so he shouldn't smoke!

one for the pot
(of the beverage tea) an extra spoonful of tea leaves.

one for the road
a last drink of alcohol before departing.

one in a million
1. something or someone that is extraordinary.
2. (of a chance or possibility) very remote: e.g. What do I think your chances are? One in a million!

one in the bush is worth two in the hand
(said by men) a pun on the original saying 'a bird in the hand is worth two in the bush', meaning that sexual intercourse is preferable to any amount of masturbation.

one jump ahead
1. to have the advantage.
2. to be completely prepared and ready for anything.

one of a kind
special; unique; unusual; eccentric.

one of the boys
member of a select group of mates, men, friends.

one of these days
sometime in the future: e.g. I'll get around to fixing the lawnmower one of these days.

one out of the box
an outstanding person or thing.

one thing after another
a succession or continuum of events.

one too many
(of alcohol) having had more than enough; intoxicated: e.g. Don't give him any more — he's already had one too many!

one up on (someone)
to have the advantage over (someone): e.g. I can't ever seem to win an argument with him — he's always one up on me.

one-armed bandit
poker machine of the type found in licensed clubs and casinos.

one-eyed
partial; biased: e.g. Staunch footy supporters are very one-eyed about their teams.

one-eyed trouser snake
the penis.

one-horse town
an insignificant, small town that is lacking in amenities.

one-man band
person who takes on all the tasks of a situation without help, often in a selfish or egotistical manner.

one-man show
a situation that is dominated by one person.

one-night stand
1. a sexual encounter not meant to be taken seriously or any further than the one occasion.
2. person with whom one has had such an encounter.

one-off
anything made or done only once; not to be repeated or made again; a once-only occurrence.

one-sided
prejudiced; partial; biased; unfair in judgement.

one-tonner
a small truck or utility vehicle.

one-track mind
fixed persistence on one idea, line of action, or thought; single-minded, especially in regard to sex.

one-up
to outwit or do better than someone, especially in conversation.

one-upmanship
the practice of always trying to out-do or show superiority over others.

one-way ticket
a course of action that allows no return: e.g. His despicable behaviour deserves a one-way ticket to hell!

onion
1. the head: e.g. Use your onion, you fool!
2. a girl who has sexual intercourse with more than one man during the same occasion.
See also:
do (one's) onion
know (one's) onions
off (one's) onion

onka/onkaparinga
(rhyming slang) finger.

onkus
out of order; not functioning properly.

only as strong as the weakest link
something is only as strong as its weakest point because that is where failure under pressure will first occur.

only drove it to church on a Sunday
(joc.) (of a car) having had only one owner — usually a little old lady — and very little use.

only eighteen bob in the pound
(of a person) crazy; mad; slightly insane; dim-witted.

only the tip of the iceberg
just the smallest amount of knowledge, information, on a subject or certain matter.

only way to fly
the best way, method, means etc.: e.g. Being rich is the only way to fly.

on-the-spot fine
a fine for a minor traffic offence issued immediately.

oobidat
term for something for which one cannot think of the real name; thingummyjig; gadget.

oodles
large quantities: e.g. He's got oodles of money.

oodles of boodle
large amounts of money; wealth.

oomph
1. vitality; enthusiasm: e.g. What this party needs is a bit of oomph!
2. sex appeal: e.g. She's got lots of oomph!

oops!
expression of mild surprise, shock, apology.

oopsidaisy!
1. (see: oops!)
2. an expression used to encourage or mollify someone who is about to jump, alight from something etc.

oozidatsit
(see: oobidat)

oozing money
displaying great wealth, prosperity, luxury.

open
1. honest; truthful; candid: e.g. He's very open about discussing his marriage problems.
2. (in combination) honest, friendly, warm: e.g. open-hearted, open-handed, open-faced.
See also:
get it all out in the open
lay (oneself) open
with open arms

open a can of worms
create trouble, tension, problems.

open book
person whose thoughts and emotions are easily readable or recognised.

open doors
offer opportunities: e.g. Gaining sufficient training and experience will open doors to a varied range of well-paid positions.

open go
unrestricted opportunity: e.g. This race is open go to anybody.

open house
1. hospitable, friendly, welcoming house where the occupants are willing to entertain visitors at any time: e.g. We always keep an open house during Christmas.
2. pertaining to an occasion when an invitation is extended to anybody and everybody to drop in.

open mind
state of mind that is unprejudiced, unbiased, receptive: e.g. I like to keep an open mind about the possibility of intelligent life on other planets.

open (one's) heart to
be sympathetic, generous to.

open (one's) mouth to change feet
to make an already embarrassing or tactless slip of the tongue worse by saying something just as bad again.

open (one's) trap
1. speak; talk; utter.
2. tell, divulge a secret or confidence: e.g. If you open your trap about this to anybody, I'll bash you!

open season
unrestrained and concerted verbal attack: e.g. It's open season between those two — they never stop abusing each other.

open sesame
a jesting incantation uttered just before one tries to open something, such as a door.

open slather
1. unrestrained activity, opportunity: e.g. Myer is having a once-only clearing sale and it's going to be open slather for everybody.
2. an occasion where authority turns a blind eye to infringements of regulations and allows complete freedom.

open up
1. reveal one's thoughts or feelings in a truthful and candid manner: e.g. It's so hard to get her to open up about her problems.
2. (of guns or firearms) start firing.

open your eyes!
a remark of contempt to someone who does not see or perceive the obvious.

open-and-shut case
obvious; unmistakable; unquestionable: e.g. That was an open-and-shut case of premeditated murder.

openers
1. a start or initiation: e.g. For openers, the band will play 'Waltzing Matilda'.
2. (cricket) first two players on a side to bat.

open-eyed
1. having eyes wide open with wonder.
2. alert; watchful.

open-faced
honest; frank; candid.

open-handed
generous.

open-hearted
1. kind, generous, sympathetic.
2. frank; sincere; straightforward; honest.

open-minded
receptive; unbiased; unprejudiced; broad-minded.

operator
shrewd, often unscrupulous person: e.g. He's a smooth operator.

opposite ends of the pole
contrary in position or opinion.

O.P.'s
(other people's) cigarettes — the type one smokes when one does not buy one's own.

op-shop
opportunity shop — selling second-hand goods for charity.

opt out
1. to decide to take no part in the accepted norms of society: e.g. Many young and disillusioned people opt out for a life on the dole.
2. to decide not to participate in an activity: e.g. I'll have to opt out of next week's game as I have to stay home and study.

optic
a look: e.g. Come and have an optic at this!

optic nerve
(rhyming slang) perve.
1. a pervert; person who looks at (someone, something) slyly.
2. a very good look at.

or else!
a veiled threat: e.g. Come here, or else!

or so
approximately; thereabouts; give or take a few: e.g. He's not drunk — he only had half a dozen beers or so.

orchestra stalls
(rhyming slang) balls; testicles.

order
(see: in short order; of the order of; tall order)

order of the boot
dismissal; the sack.

order of the day
the agenda or plans for the day's activities.

order (someone) about/around
bully, domineer (someone).

organ
the penis.
See also:
play the organ

orgasm
drink made with Cointreau and Bailey's Irish Cream on ice.

original
insane; mad; crazy: e.g. Grandma is a bit original these days.

ornery
mean; surly; unco-operative; ill-tempered.

ort
anus: e.g. Stick it in your ort sport! (term of contempt)

O.S.
overseas.

oscar
(should get an . . .) (Australian Rules football) a free kick; an academy award.
See also:
no shortage of oscar

other fish to fry
other matters to settle or deal with: e.g. Don't bother me with petty matters — I've got other fish to fry!

other half
1. wife, husband or spouse.
2. the rest of society apart from the social class you fall into — the division usually being between rich and poor: e.g. Seeing how the other half live must be distressing to the very poor.

other side of the coin
the other side of an argument or situation; opposite point of view.

other world
life after death.

otherie/othery
other: e.g. Pass me the otherie.

ouch!
expression of sudden pain.

ounce of sense
measure of one's (usually poor) intelligence: e.g. He hasn't got an ounce of sense!

out
1. no longer in style; out of fashion: e.g. Long hair is out.
2. incorrect: e.g. He's out by a mile in his estimation.
3. strike by workers: e.g. The union has been out for three weeks.

4. any means of escaping retribution, consequences or responsibility: e.g. I can't see an out to this problem.
5. (sport) dismissed from play by being caught, run out etc.
6. (sport) beyond the boundary lines.
See also:
do (someone) out of
draw out
draw (someone) out
fall out with
far out
far-out
feel (someone) out
full out
get out
get out and about
get out from under
go all out
on the outer
on the way out
put (oneself) out
put out
way-out

out at sea
in difficulties; experiencing problems: e.g. Many women are out at sea trying to change a flat tyre on a car.

out at the elbow
poor; impoverished; destitute; ragged: e.g. It's good to see a big lottery win go to a family that has been out at the elbow all their lives.

out cold
unconscious: e.g. He drank a whole bottle of rum and now he's out cold.

out for blood
intent on revenge.

out for the count
exhausted; tired; worn out.

out here
in Australia: e.g. How long have you been out here?

out in the backblocks/ backwaters

out in the middle of nowhere

out in the mulga

out in the never-never

out in the sticks
in remote or sparsely populated, unsophisticated areas: e.g. They sold up everything and now live out in the sticks somewhere.

out like a light
1. deeply asleep.
2. unconscious.
3. incapacitated due to intoxication; inebriated.

out of character
not behaving normally or as expected.

out of circulation
socially inactive.

out of depth
in a situation beyond one's capabilities to control: e.g. Most people are out of depth when it comes to understanding computers.

out of hand
out of control; chaotic; disorderly: e.g. This situation is getting out of hand.

out of it
drugged; drunk; intoxicated.

out of kilter
1. out of condition, working order.
2. crooked; not straight.

out of line
1. non-conforming; against popular agreement.
2. overstepping the boundaries of one's usual behaviour or status.

out of luck
to be frustrated in one's desires, wants: e.g. You're out of luck — they've all been sold!

out of mid-air
unexpectedly; from somewhere unknown.

out of (one's) cotton-picking mind
1. insane; mad; crazy.
2. delirious; anxious; worried: e.g. I've been out of my head with worry!
3. impetuously foolish; unrealistic or impractical in ideas, notions: e.g. He's out of his mind if he thinks that crazy idea will work!

out of (one's) hands
out of (one's) control, responsibility: e.g. It's out of my hands now — you'll have to see the boss about it.

out of (one's) head/mind/ tree
(see: out of one's cotton-picking mind)

out of (one's) way
1. far removed from where one was going: e.g. I'll drive you home as it's not far out of my way.
2. to try very hard; exert oneself (see: go out of one's way).

out of (one's) wits
1. frightened; terrified.
2. anxious; worried.

out of order
1. broken; not functioning.
2. acting in an unconventional, uncharacteristic or troublesome manner: e.g. The meeting was out of order.

out of place
out of harmony; incongruous.

out of plumb
not aligned; crooked; not straight: e.g. That beam looks out of plumb.

out of pocket
1. having no money.
2. having lost money after some transaction, deal, gamble etc.

out of practice
no longer having former skill, adeptness.

out of reach
1. unattainable: e.g. Jobs like that are out of reach for untrained people.
2. unattainable due to being too expensive: e.g. A Mercedes is out of reach on our income.

out of sight
wonderful; remarkable; excellent: e.g. That concert was out of sight!

out of sight, out of mind
if something is not in one's view or is out of sight, one does not think about it.

out of sorts
1. ill; unwell; feeling poorly.
2. upset; unhappy; dissatisfied: e.g. He's been out of sorts about something all day.

out of step
not in harmony: e.g. The jewellery is out of step with the rest of the costume.

out of the blue
unexpectedly; from somewhere unknown; seemingly from nowhere.

out of the box
exceptional; extraordinary: e.g. 1. This show is really something out of the box. 2. That's nothing out of the box!

out of the fat/frying-pan and into the fire
from one bad situation into something worse.

out of the ordinary
1. unexpected; unusual.
2. remarkable.

out of the question
absolutely not; not practical or possible.

out of the race
1. having no chance of victory or success: e.g. The other candidate is so popular that it looks like our bloke is out of the race.
2. dismissed; no longer participating; not a contender.

out of the red
out of debt.

out of the way
1. remote; inaccessible: e.g. That area of the forest is very out of the way.
2. unusual; uncommon: e.g. Your idea is a bit out of the way, but we'll try it.
3. disposed of; dealt with: e.g. The Mafia wants him out of the way.

out of the wood
out of trouble; safe.

out of thin air
unexpected; from somewhere unknown.

out of this world
1. remarkable; unusual; outrageous.
2. excellent; first-rate; wonderful.

out of touch
1. having no realistic or practical contact; no longer familiar with: e.g. He's out of touch with workers and their problems.
2. having lost one's skills, familiarity, adeptness: e.g. Because he hasn't practised he's a bit out of touch.

out of whack
1. disorderly; chaotic; out of routine: e.g. Since we moved, everything has been out of whack.
2. crooked; not aligned or straight; out of balance: e.g. That house beam looks out of whack.

out on a limb
1. in a difficult, precarious or dangerous position, situation.
2. isolated; alone.

out on (one's) ear
dismissed in disgrace: e.g. He's out on his ear if he makes one more mistake!

out on (one's) own like a country dunny
alone; forlorn.

out on the tear
enjoying oneself to the fullest; having a wild spree; boisterous merry-making out on the town.

out on the town
in carefree pursuit of urban pleasures; having a good time out: e.g. We're going out on the town for our anniversary.

out the back
1. in the back yard, garden: e.g. Hubby's out the back mowing the lawn.
2. in the back rooms: e.g. The dunny's out the back.

out to it/the world
1. asleep.
2. unconscious.
3. incapacitated due to intoxication; drunk; drugged.

out with it
tell; reveal; make known.

out-and-out
thorough; utter; complete; absolute: e.g. He's an out-an-out ratbag!

outback
remote inland districts of Australia.

outed
rejected; dismissed.

Outer Mongolia
any remote, sparsely populated area.

outfit
equipment — such as syringe, needles — used by addicts to inject drugs.

out-fox
be more smart, clever than; out-wit.

outhouse
an outside toilet.

out-of-doors
outside; in the open air: e.g. He loves an out-of-doors life.

out-of-the-way
remote; secluded; isolated; private: e.g. I know a nice little out-of-the-way restaurant that serves the best French food you've ever had.

outside (of)
with the exception of: e.g. Outside of five, the whole class failed the exam!
See also:
at the outside

outsider
1. one not belonging to a particular group: e.g. Outsiders aren't allowed into that club — you have to be a member.
2. a racehorse that is not among the favourites to win: e.g. An outsider won the last Melbourne Cup.

outsmart
be too clever for; out-fox.

over
(cricket) six deliveries by a bowler.
See also:
all over
all over someone like a rash
all over the place like a madwoman's breakfast
bowl someone over
do someone over
get done over
once-over
work someone over

over a barrel
at a disadvantage: e.g. I've got him over a barrel.

over and above
in addition to: e.g. Anything over and above fifty dollars, you have to pay.

over and over
repeatedly.

over my dead body!
a veiled threat; never! absolutely not!

over (someone's) head
1. beyond (someone's) comprehension, understanding: e.g. That joke went way over her head.
2. to a higher authority: e.g. I'm going to have to go over his head if I want anything to be done about this matter.

over the edge
1. insane; crazy; mad; demented.
2. (see: over the fence)

over the fence
unreasonable; vulgar; lewd; not socially acceptable: e.g. That joke was a bit over the fence for mixed company.

over the hill
(joc.) getting old; past one's prime.

over the odds
1. too much, great.
2. unreasonable; not socially acceptable.

over the top
ridiculously excessive, exaggerated, unreasonable.

overboard
in excess; carry a situation too far: e.g. Children need discipline, but you don't have to go overboard and beat them senseless!

overdo
to continue behaving in a manner that is unpopular; carry an action too far; excessive behaviour.

overkill
the use of more resources than is necessary for the job.

overlander
stockman, drover on horseback who drives stock long distances across the country.

overnight success (story)
sudden and unexpected success.

overplay (one's) hand

overshoot the mark
to make a mistake in judgement; overestimate; exaggerate.

over-shoulder-boulder-holder
brassiere — woman's undergarment for breast support.

overstep the mark
to break the rules or act over and beyond an accepted standard.

ow!
expression of sudden pain.

own
(see: come into one's own; get one's own back; hold one's own)

own up
confess: e.g. If the person who stole the money doesn't own up, the entire class will be punished!

Oxford scholar
(rhyming slang) dollar.

oy!
call to gain attention.

oyster
1. taciturn person.
2. place or thing from which one derives advantage, gain, profit: e.g. The world is your oyster.

Oz
1. Australia: e.g. Land of Oz.
2. Australian: e.g. The best beer is Oz beer!

'It's only my first offence, officer. Couldn't you overlook it?'

The competence of women drivers is always in question. An uncouth bloke might say that women 'couldn't drive a greasy stick up a dead dog's . . .' (the rest of the expression you'll have to look up for yourself). Most women are accused of having got their licences out of a cornflakes packet, and the most popular thing to call them is 'bloody women drivers'!

pa
father.

P.A.
public-address system.

pack
1. set or group of people or things: e.g. 1. What he told you was a pack of lies. 2. They're a pack of bludgers!
2. select, so as to ensure a biased decision in one's favour: e.g. pack a jury.
3. (Australian Rules football) group of contesting players.
See also:
go to the pack
send (someone) packing

pack a punch
1. to have great influence; to have a great effect upon someone; have a lot of flair: e.g. We need someone who can really pack a punch as our next club president.
2. to hit, punch with considerable force.

pack a shitty
lose one's temper.

pack a wallop
1. hit, punch with considerable force.
2. have a forceful effect.

pack death/it
to be afraid: e.g. We were all packing it when that robber burst into the bank with a gun.

pack it in
1. give up; retire from; stop: e.g. I'm sick of all this work — I think I'll pack it in and go to the pub.
2. break down; fail; malfunction: e.g. My car's packed it in again!

pack of bludgers/derros/galahs/no-hopers
a group of lazy, idle, non-working people held in contempt; any group of people held in contempt.

pack shit
(see: pack death)

pack the game in
give up; retire from; stop doing a particular activity.

pack up
break down; fail; cease to work or operate: e.g. My new car packed up after the first week!

package deal
transaction agreed to as a whole and not in part: e.g. Many travel agencies offer a package deal that includes air-fares, accommodation, food and sight-seeing trips that are all-inclusive.

packapoo ticket
(parcel of shit) pertaining to anything that looks chaotic, stupid or incomprehensible; disorganised and messy situation; contract you shouldn't buy into or a situation you shouldn't get involved with. (also: pakapoo)

packed out
filled to capacity; crowded: e.g. The hall was packed out.

packet
a large sum of money: e.g. That car must have cost him a packet.

pad
1. home; abode; place of living; a bedroom.
2. (cricket) protective legging.

pad out
exaggerate: e.g. He pads out his stories so much that it's hard to know what to believe.

paddle
spank; punish with a beating.

paddle (one's) own canoe
act independently: e.g. It's time he learnt to paddle his own canoe without the help of his parents.

paddling up shit creek in a barbed wire canoe (without a paddle)
on a hopeless mission or involved in a hopeless enterprise that is doomed to failure.

paddy
1. (cap.) nickname for an Irishman.
2. an angry rage or fit of temper.

Paddy's lantern
the moon.

paddy-wagon
police van for carrying prisoners; black maria.

paddywhack
a spanking.

paid back in kind
paid back in means other than money.

paid off
1. successful; yielded good, rewarding results: e.g. Investing in that land ten years ago has really paid off now.
2. bribed; bought off: e.g. That witness was paid off by the gang not to give evidence.

paid the price
to have suffered or endured the consequences: e.g. He's paid the price for his crimes by losing his freedom for the last thirty years in prison.

For other possible entries beginning with 'paid' see entries listed under 'pay'.

pain in the arse/bum/butt/guts/neck
boring, tedious or annoying person or thing; a nuisance: e.g. He's such a pain!

pain in the pinny
a pain in the stomach.

painful
boring or tedious experience or person: e.g. His long speech was so painful!

paint
make-up; cosmetics for the face.
See also:
war-paint

paint a black picture of (something)

paint (something) black
describe (something) morbidly, in a bad, depressing or scathing manner.

paint the town red
have a celebration, good time, spree, out in town somewhere.

painted lady
woman of low morals; a prostitute.

pair
breasts; boobs; tits: e.g. She's got a nice pair.

pair of spectacles
(cricket) two ducks in two innings.

pakapoo ticket
(see: packapoo ticket)

Pakis
people from Pakistan; Pakistanis.

pal
1. friend; mate.
2. (cap.) canned dog food. (Trademark)
See also:
be a pal!

pal up with
make friends with; associate with.

pally
friendly; on friendly terms with.

palm
(see: grease/oil someone's palm)

palm off
attempt to pass, sell to someone else something in a fraudulent or devious manner.

palsy-walsy
1. close friends; intimating homosexuality.
2. in cahoots with; conspiratory.

pan
criticise; condemn; berate: e.g. The critics panned his latest movie.
See also:
flash in the pan

pan out
result; turn out: e.g. We'll see how this venture pans out before we do anything else.

Pandora's box
anything that causes troubles and problems after initially being believed to be a blessing.

panhandle
to beg.

panic button
an imaginary device which, when set off, creates panic, increasing fear or action.
See also:
hit the panic button

panic merchant
person well known to worry excessively over anything.

panic stations
(see: at panic stations)

pansy
homosexual or effeminate man.

pansy up
over-decorate.

Panthers
Penrith N.S.W. Rugby League football team.

panties
women's underpants.

pants
trousers; underpants.
See also:
ants in (one's) pants
arse out of (one's) pants
bore the pants off (someone)
caught with (one's) pants down
charm the pants off (someone)
get into (someone's) pants
kick up the pants
need a kick up the pants
poop (one's) pants
scare the pants off (someone)
shit (one's) pants
smartie-pants
the ant's pants

wear the pants in the family

paper
(see: couldn't fight one's way out of a wet paper bag; not worth the paper it's written on; on paper; walking papers)

paper boy
youth employed part-time to deliver newspapers or sell them on the streets.

paper money
existing on paper or in documents only, and not in reality or as actual, spendable money.

paper over
attempt to conceal or hide the truth from.

paper tiger
one who seems aggressive and strong, but who is actually weak and ineffective.

paper yabber
a letter.

paper-bag job
a woman considered to be ugly by men, but still viewed as a sex object.

par for the course
acceptable; usual; in accordance with what is normal or required.

para/paralytic
very drunk; incapacitated due to intoxication.

paranoid
emotionally over-sensitive; suspicious; distrustful: e.g. He's paranoid about someone pinching his beer so he's sitting on his Esky.

pard/pardner
partner; friend.

pardon my/the French
please excuse my bad/vulgar language — an apology offered after one has inadvertently used an offensive word, or just before one is about to use one: e.g. Pardon my French, but I think he's a dead-shit.

park
put; place; leave: e.g. Just park those things over on that table please.

park her/his shoes under my bed
jocular statement of one's desire for another: e.g. Paul Newman can park his shoes under my bed any time!

park (one's) tiger
to vomit.

park (oneself)
be seated: e.g. Park yourself on a comfortable chair.

parson's nose
the tail piece of a cooked chicken.

part and parcel
essential or necessary part of: e.g. Vulgar words are often part and parcel of telling jokes.

part up
pay, especially unwillingly: e.g. If he doesn't part up with what he owes, we'll take him to court.

part with
surrender; give up; relinquish: e.g. He's going to hate parting with his dog when he goes overseas.

parting of ways
dissolution of friendship, partnership, relationship, marriage etc.: e.g. Mum and Dad had a parting of ways last year.

partner in crime
(joc.) one's working partner or business associate.

parts
the genitals (also: private parts).

party
(see: come to the party)

party on
continue a party, merry occasion: e.g. We partied on until four in the morning.

party pooper
spoil-sport; one who spoils the fun or who refuses to take part.

party's over
the event, occasion, situation is over, finished: e.g. They were making a fortune with their illicit dealings, but the party's over now that the police know about them.

pash
a kiss and cuddle; amorous play: e.g. I saw them having a pash in the back seat of the car.

pash on
to cuddle and kiss; indulge in intimate behaviour: e.g. Most teenagers go to the drive-in theatres just to pash on.

pasho session
intimate behaviour: e.g. Mum caught them having a pasho session when she came home earlier than expected.

pass
forego one's opportunity; elect not to take part.
See also:
make a pass at

pass away
to die.

pass for
be accepted as: e.g. Many young teenage girls pass for being much older because of the make-up they wear.

pass in (one's) marble
1. to die.
2. to give up.

pass off
dispose of deceptively: e.g. He tried to pass that chair off as an antique, but I know it's a repro.

pass (oneself) off
falsify (one's) identity: e.g. He was arrested for trying to pass himself off as a police officer. .

pass out
1. faint; lose consciousness: e.g. She passes out at the sight of blood.
2. go to sleep: e.g. I think I'll pass out for an hour or two.

pass round the hat
take up a collection, donation of money for some cause: e.g. We're passing round the hat for a going-away present for the boss.

pass the buck
avoid responsibility by delegating it to another; avoid consequences by blaming others: e.g. Whenever there's a scandal, those responsible will inevitably try to pass the buck.

pass the pinch test
show that one is not overweight by not being able to pinch a large amount of flesh between the thumb and forefinger at the waist.

pass the time of day with (someone)
have a conversation with (someone).

pass up
1. refuse; reject.
2. fail to act on an opportunity.

pass wind
fart; belch; burp.

pass with a push
be accepted grudgingly.

pass with flying colours
be extremely successful.

passion pit
drive-in theatre or cinema.

past it
too old, especially for sexual activity: e.g. He may be over sixty, but he's not past it yet!

paste
scold, berate, beat or defeat soundly.

pasting
severe criticism, scolding, beating or defeat.

pat/Pat Malone
(rhyming slang) alone: e.g. He always drinks on his Pat Malone because he's too stingy to shout a round.
See also:
get it down pat
off pat
on (one's) pat
sit pat

pat on the back
encouragement, praise or congratulation: e.g. He deserves a pat on the back for that effort!

patch
(see: hit a bad patch; not a patch on)

patch (it) up
1. settle a quarrel; make amends: e.g. He tried to patch it up with his wife by bringing home some flowers but she threw him out again.
2. repair hastily: e.g. This car looks like it's been patched up for a quick sale.

pathetic
contemptuously inadequate, inviting scorn and derision: e.g. That was a pathetic effort!

patsy
scapegoat; person easily fooled, tricked or duped.

pav
pavlova — a large soft-centred meringue filled with whipped cream and fruit.

paw
1. the hand.
2. to handle, maul.
3. to caress, stroke, fondle in a lewd or rough manner.

pawn
unimportant person subservient to the wishes of others.

pay
1. to acknowledge that one has been outwitted: e.g. I'll pay that!
2. to suffer a punishment: e.g. I'll make him pay for that!
See also:
hell to pay
strike paydirt.

pay a visit
go to the toilet.

pay in kind
to pay in means other than money.

pay its way
financially self-supporting; yield a profit: e.g. The house pays its way in rent.

pay lip-service to
1. talk about; discuss.
2. talk about but not take necessary action; give insincere support by word only.

pay off
yield good, rewarding results; be financially profitable: e.g. Buying land for investment usually pays off in the long run.

pay on the line
pay promptly without delay.

pay (one's) own way
to succeed without financial support from others; be self-supporting; pay the cost for (one's) own expenses.

pay out on (someone)
1. give cheek, be impudent to (someone).
2. severely scold, abuse, berate (someone).

pay (someone) a visit
visit (someone), often with ill-intent: e.g. If he does

one more thing to annoy me I'll have to pay him a visit!

pay (someone) back
to exact revenge: e.g. I'll pay him back one day for the awful things he did!

pay (someone) in his own coin
treat (someone) likewise, the same as (he) treated you.

pay (someone) off
bribe (someone).

pay the price
suffer the consequences: e.g. He'll pay the price for his life of crime in prison.

pay through the nose
to pay a lot of money; pay far in excess of true value: e.g. There were no tickets left for the concert so I had to pay through the nose for one from a scalper.

pay up
to pay money on demand, especially under threat.

pay-off
1. settlement of a debt, bet, bribe etc.
2. climax, ending, often unexpected.

pays to advertise
the belief that advertising or public exposure of one's wares or what one has will provide the desired results (often construed in a sexual manner).

pea soup
thick fog.

pea-brain
stupid, dim-witted person lacking in common sense or intelligence.

peace-offering
anything offered that restores peace and forgiveness.

peach
attractive young woman, person or thing.

peaches-and-cream
pertaining to a clear and healthy complexion.

peachy
delightful; wonderful; excellent.

peak-hour
the hour during which traffic is at its heaviest.

peanut
insignificant, unimportant or small person or thing.

peanut factory
mental asylum.

peanut gallery
term for any public gallery, audience etc. believed to be full of noisy, interjecting fools and trouble-makers.
See also:
quiet in the peanut gallery!

peanuts
small, insignificant amount of money: e.g. He earns peanuts compared to his brother.

pearl/pearler
excellent, wonderful, delightful person or thing.

pearl necklace
droplets of semen on the neck, face or body, especially after orgasm induced by fellatio.

pearlies
the teeth.

pearls of wisdom
wise words or advice (often sarcastic or ironical).

pearly gates
1. the teeth.
2. (caps) the (imaginary) gateway to heaven.

pears
avocados (Queensland).

peasant
person who doesn't appreciate culture or sophistication.

peck
hasty kiss: e.g. All I got was a peck on the cheek!

peck at (one's) food
to eat very little.

pecker
the penis.
See also:
keep (one's) pecker up

pecking order
social hierarchy.

peckish
hungry; having an inclination for a snack.

pedalling uphill
having a difficult or trying time.

peddle (one's) wares
hawk, sell whatever (one) has to offer; solicit.

pee
1. urine: e.g. Is that pee running down his legs?
2. to urinate: e.g. I want to pee.

pee in (someone's) pocket
(see: piss in . . .)

peel off
undress.

peepers
the eyes.

peeping Tom
snooper, voyeur, often for sexual gratification.

peep-show
any spectacle arousing furtive, sly curiosity, especially with regard to sex.

peeved
irritated; annoyed.

peg
to throw: e.g. He pegged it in the bin with his eyes closed!
See also:
bring (someone) down a peg or two
clothes horse/peg
have/got (someone) pegged
have/got (someone) pegged out
off the peg
square peg in a round hole
take (someone) down a peg or two

peg above the rest
better than the others.

peg away at
work persistently at.

peg it on (someone)
blame (someone).

peg out
to die.

peg to hang it on
a reason, justification.

pegs
1. legs.
2. teeth.

pen
penitentiary; prison.

penis envy
(of women) the supposed envy of men for having a penis; the wish to have a penis.

penny
an unspecified amount of money: e.g. 1. He hasn't got a penny. 2. That must have cost a pretty penny.
See also:
bad penny
cost a pretty penny
haven't got a penny to bless (oneself) with
in for a penny, in for a pound
make every penny count/work
pretty penny
spend a penny

penny dreadful
any cheap and sensational piece of literature.

penny finally dropped
sudden comprehension, realisation, understanding.

penny for your thoughts
request to someone who is in a pensive, melancholy mood.

penny-bunger
a fire-cracker, generally banned from sale due to risk of injury to the user.

penny-pincher
miser; mingy, mean person; parsimonious person.

penny-wise and pound-foolish
wise in saving small sums of money only.

pen-pusher
one whose work entails much writing and considered a drudge.

pep
energy; drive; enthusiasm; spirit.

pep pill
stimulant tablet or drug.

pep talk
enthusiastic talk designed to encourage.

pep up
to inject with energy, spirit; invigorate; animate: e.g. We need some good music to pep up this party.

peppercorn (rental)
nominal rent (originally one peppercorn per year paid to the Crown).

peppy
energetic; spirited; fast.

percy
the penis.
See also:
point percy at the porcelain

performance
public display of bad temper or emotion.

period
the time of menstruation.

perish the thought!
expression said in the hope that whatever is being discussed will not happen.

perished
extremely hungry, thirsty or cold.

perisher
1. a mischievous child; annoying person.
2. a very cold day.

perk
1. perquisite; privilege: e.g. His job has quite a few good perks.
2. to vomit.
3. (of coffee) to percolate.

perk up
1. to vomit.
2. brighten one's outlook; cheer up; revive.

perks
perquisites; privileges; extras; benefits; profits.
See also:
lurks and perks

perky
lively; gay; spirited.

perm
permanent wave of the hair.

perv/perve
1. a pervert.
2. to stare at, especially lustfully.
See also:
have a perve at

perve on
to stare at, especially lustfully: e.g. He's always perving on the young girls.

pesky
annoying; irritating.

pester
1. annoy; harass; irritate.
2. harass sexually.

pet
1. warm, kind, lovable, affectionate person.
2. favourite: e.g. He loves to argue about anything, but his pet subject is politics.
3. to fondle erotically.

pet hate/peeve
a favourite complaint; thing hated or disliked the most: e.g. My pet hate would have to be religious bigots.

pet subject
favourite subject or topic.

peter
1. till; money-box; cash register.
2. the penis.
See also:
tickle the peter

peter out
come to an end; diminish.

petticoat
any attractive woman or girl.

petty cash
cash kept for small items of expenditure.

pew
a chair, seat or place to sit down.

phew!
expression of relief.

phone was running hot
pertaining to many incoming telephone calls.

phoney/phony
false; counterfeit; fraudulent person or thing: e.g. That antique table is a phoney.

phooey
1. nonsense; rubbish; worthless, insincere talk: e.g. His entire speech was a lot of phooey!
2. exclamation of contempt, disbelief.

photographic memory
the ability to remember, recall anything one sees.

phut!
exclamation of annoyance over something gone wrong.

physical jerks
exercises designed to keep fit.

physio
physiotherapy.

pic
picture.

piccadilly
(rhyming slang) chilly; cold.

pick
1. find fault with; criticise: e.g. She's never happy — she always finds one reason or another to pick.
2. eat without enthusiasm.

pick a fight
initiate a fight, argument.

pick a fine/nice time (to)
choose the wrong time (to): e.g. You picked a fine time to go on holidays — we're understaffed and can't afford to let you go!

pick and choose
be fussy in selecting.

pick at
1. nag, find fault with; criticise: e.g. I wish he wouldn't pick at me all the time!
2. (food) eat without enthusiasm.

pick holes in
find fault with; criticise: e.g. Political parties always pick holes in each other's policies and arguments.

pick of the bunch/crop
the best, ultimate.

pick off
single out and shoot: e.g. Any animal blinded by a spotlight is easy to pick off.

pick on
1. nag at; find fault with; tease; harass; blame.
2. select or single out someone for a task that is usually unpleasant.

pick on someone your own size
a request or warning to someone who is harassing a smaller person.

pick (someone) up
make (someone's) acquaintance at a pub, dance, party etc. for the purpose of having sex.

pick (someone's) brains
to find out, learn, gain information from (someone's) knowledge.

pick the eyes out of
select the best, choicest out of what is offered.

pick to pieces
to find fault with, criticise, especially in a petty way.

pick up
1. recover in health; improve; get better.
2. become more lively; accelerate.
3. acquire casually: e.g. I picked it up at a garage sale.
4. arrest; apprehend.

pick up on
come to understand, comprehend.

pick up the pieces/threads (and start again)
begin anew after misfortune or disaster.

pick up the tab
pay the bill, expenses.

picked
specially selected.
See also:
hand-picked

pickie
1. photograph.
2. movie, cinema film.

pickle
predicament; trouble; plight.
See also:
face like a festered pickle

pickled
drunk; intoxicated.

pick-me-up
any stimulus, such as a drink (especially alcoholic) that is refreshing.

pick-pocket
person who steals from others in public places.
See also:
like a pick-pocket at a nudist camp.

pick-up
casual acquaintance for the purpose of sex.

picky
1. over-fussy; obsessed with petty details.
2. finding fault; harassing; nagging; complaining.

picnic
1. an easy task: e.g. This job is going to be a picnic!
2. any difficult, awkward task or situation: e.g. We

had quite a picnic trying to keep all the children together in the crowd!
See also:
blackfellow's picnic
no picnic

picture
(see: get the picture; in the picture; paint a black picture of; put someone in the picture)

picture of health
healthy; vital; looking good.

pictures
the cinema: e.g. We're going to the pictures tonight.

piddle
1. urine: e.g. Whose piddle is that on the floor?
2. to urinate: e.g. I need to piddle.
3. do in an ineffective, trifling manner: e.g. Stop piddling about and get on with the job properly!

piddling
small; trifling; paltry: e.g. All he donated to our charity was a piddling dollar!

pie on
good, adept at or keen on: e.g. He's pretty pie on the piano.

piece
1. a woman: e.g. She's a sexy little piece.
2. a type of person: e.g. He's a nasty piece.
3. a hand-gun, pistol.
See also:
earlier in the piece
early in the piece
fall to pieces
go to pieces
if you're still in one piece
in the piece
nasty piece of work
pick up the pieces (and start again)
pull to pieces
ring-piece
say (one's) piece
take a piece out of (someone)
take/tear (someone) to pieces

piece of cake
an easy task: e.g. That job will be a piece of cake.

piece of (one's) mind
scathing and direct criticism from (one): e.g. I'll give him a piece of my mind next time I see him for what he did.

piece of piss
(see: piece of cake)

piece of the action
profitable involvement in an event, circumstance or enterprise: e.g. The casino shares were snapped up so quickly that many people missed out on a piece of the action by applying too late.

piece of work
person of a specified type: e.g. He's a nasty piece of work.

pie-eater
an Australian.

pie-eyed
drunk; intoxicated.

pie-in-the-sky
pertaining to false, illusory or pretentious beliefs about one's prospects: e.g. His pie-in-the-sky ideas for making money won't work because he's a lazy bludger and can't apply himself.

piffle
1. nonsense; rubbish; worthless and insincere talk.
2. (as an exclamation) disbelief; scorn.

piffling
trivial; paltry.

pig
1. person of foul habits; slob; glutton.
2. (derog.) policeman.
3. expression of scorn, derision, irritation: e.g. This pig of a thing doesn't work properly!
See also:
hair like a bush pig's arse
her thighs wouldn't stop a pig in a hall
home on the pig's back
little pigs have big ears
make a pig of (oneself)
riding on the pig's back

pig in a poke
something bought without being inspected; a bad deal or transaction.
See also:
wouldn't stop a pig in a poke

Pig Islands
New Zealand.

pig Latin
made-up language.

pig out
to eat greedily or to excess: e.g. I pigged out on chocolate cake and now I feel crook!

pigeon
one who is easily fooled, tricked or deceived.
See also:
it's your pigeon
stool pigeon

pigeon pair
1. a son and a daughter.
2. any matching pair of things.

pigeon-hole
1. categorise; order; put into compartments.
2. to put aside for later consideration, only to neglect and forget about.

pigging-it
living in squalor; living in primitive conditions.

piggy bank
a small money-box (often in the shape of a pig) for petty savings.

piggyback
carry on the shoulders or back; the act of such carrying: e.g. He gave me

a piggyback across the creek.

pig-headed
obstinate.

pigs!

pig's arse/bum/ring-hole!

pigs can/might fly!
exclamation of contempt, disbelief, denial, scorn.

pigsty
any dirty or untidy living quarters.

pike on (someone)
to let (someone) down.

pike out (on)
to back out of an arrangement, usually to the disappointment of others: e.g. He piked out at the last minute.

piker
person who lets others down by opting out of an arrangement or agreement.

pile
1. a large amount of money: e.g. That car must have cost a pile.
2. a large quantity of anything.

pile in/out
get in/out in a haphazard manner.

pile it on
to exaggerate to extremes; behave, speak in an over-bearingly affected manner.

pile up
to crash or wreck a car, vehicle.

piles
large amounts of money: e.g. He's got piles!

pile-up
1. multiple car crash: e.g. There was a big pile-up on the highway just out of town.
2. accumulation; back-log.

pill
1. an annoying, boring, tedious person.
2. (the . . .) oral contraceptive tablet.
See also:
bitter pill to swallow
on the pill
sugar the pill

pillow-biter
a homosexual man.

pill-popper
person addicted to pills or drugs taken orally.

pills
testicles; balls.

pimp
1. a person who solicits clients for prostitutes.
2. informant; tell-tale: e.g. Who was the pimp who told on me and got me into trouble?
3. to inform, tell tales on: e.g. Don't you dare pimp on me!

pimple on a pumpkin
anything grossly ridiculous or obvious, such as a silly hat, a small head.

pin
(see: like a new pin; neat as a pin; pull the pin on)

pin a medal on (someone)
congratulate (someone); acknowledge (someone).

pin it down
finally understand, comprehend (it).

pin it on (someone)
blame (someone): e.g. The police won't be able to pin that crime on him because he has a good alibi.

pin money
wife's allowance from her husband; any small amount for minor expenses.

pin number
acronym for Personal Identification Number — a private number used in conjunction with plastic credit cards.

pin (one's) hopes on
set (one's) expectations on; depend on.

pin (someone) down
bind (someone) to a promise or agreement.

pin (someone's) ears back
severely reprimand, scold, berate (someone).

pinch
1. to steal, pilfer.
2. (of police or authorities) to arrest, apprehend.
See also:
at a pinch
feel the pinch
get pinched
not worth a pinch of goat-shit
pass the pinch test
penny-pinching
take it with a pinch of salt
walks as though (one) is pinching sixpence

pinch the eye out of your cock if it wasn't stuck on
(he'd . . .) pertaining to a person who is a compulsive thief.

pines
pineapples (Queensland).

pinhead
fool; simpleton.

pink elephant
an hallucination.

pink fit/kittens
a highly emotional state of mind such as anger, outrage, hysteria: e.g. Mum nearly had a pink fit when she saw what colour I had dyed my hair!
See also:
nearly had a pink fit
wouldn't in a pink fit

pink oboe
the penis.

pinkie
1. little finger or toe.
2. person who leans towards communism.

pinko
1. a communist, or one whose politics lean towards communism.
2. drunk; intoxicated: e.g. Dad got a bit pinko last night.

pinny
1. pinafore.
2. (see: pain in the pinny)

pins
legs: e.g. She's got a nice set of pins.

pins and needles
tingling sensation in the limbs after a period of numbness.
See also:
on pins and needles

pint
pint of beer.
See also:
half-pint

pint-sized
small in stature or importance.

pin-up
picture to hang on the wall, usually of a famous person or attractive (naked) women; the person who is the subject of such a picture.

pip
(the . . .) a fit of bad temper, annoyance, irritation: e.g. There's no need to get the pip!
See also:
give (someone) the pip

pipe down!
be quiet; shut up!

pipe up
1. speak louder.
2. begin speaking one's mind suddenly and unexpectedly: e.g. We weren't going to say anything about it until you piped up!

piped music
recorded background music played continuously over a P.A. system in a restaurant, theatre etc.

pipe-dream
extravagant, impossible dream or hope.

pipe-line
channel of communication, information or supply: e.g. You'll never guess what I heard through the pipe-line!
See also:
in the pipe-line

piping hot
(especially of food or water) extremely hot.

pipped at the post
narrowly beaten, defeated: e.g. He was just pipped at the post in the election by another candidate.

pippy
annoyed; irritated: e.g. What's he pippy about?

pipsqueak
1. small in stature or importance.
2. young person or child.

pirate
pertaining to the reproduction, without copyright permission, of literary works, music, film etc. for one's own profit.

pish!
exclamation of contemptuous disbelief.

piss
1. urine.
2. beer: e.g. He's been on the piss all day!
3. to urinate.
4. an intensifier meaning very: e.g. That film was piss-awful!
See also:
all piss and wind
built like a streak of weasel piss
eyes like two piss-holes in the snow
go like a power of piss
long streak of weasel piss
piece of piss
stand around like a stale bottle of piss
take the piss out of (someone)
weak as piss
wouldn't piss down (someone's) throat if his guts were on fire

piss all over (someone)
to defeat or better (someone) soundly.

piss around
fool around; waste time with foolish or ineffectual behaviour.

piss down
to rain hard.

piss in it or get off the pot
do something constructive instead of complaining; don't be so indecisive.

piss in (someone's) pocket
to behave in an obsequious manner towards (someone) in the hope of personal gain.

piss into the wind
attempt something futile.

piss off
1. depart; leave: e.g. We have to piss off.
2. (offensive) go away! get lost!

piss off hairy legs!
(offensive) go away! get lost!

piss on
to drink excessively, especially beer: e.g. We pissed on till daylight on his birthday.

piss on (someone) from a great height
(I'd like to . . .) expression of one's utter contempt for (someone).

piss (oneself)
receive a shock or sudden fright.

piss (oneself) laughing
to laugh uncontrollably.

piss (someone) off
1. to annoy, irritate (someone) greatly: e.g. He really pisses me off the way he carries on!
2. to dismiss, tell (someone) to leave, usually in a manner indicating one's contempt.

piss-ant
person small in stature (but often big in bravado, courage).
See also:
game as a piss-ant

pissed

pissed as a cricket/fart/newt/parrot
drunk; intoxicated.

pissed off
1. annoyed; irritated; angry: e.g. I'm pissed off about not getting that job!
2. departed; went; left: e.g. They pissed off two hours ago.

pissed out of (one's) brain/head/mind

pissed to the eyeballs
completely intoxicated, drunk.

pisser
1. the pub: e.g. He's down the pisser with a few of his cronies.
2. (men's) urinal.

piss-fart
1. an insignificant or annoying person.
2. to mess around, fool about; waste time: e.g. I wish he'd stop piss-farting and get on with the job!

piss-flaps like Gene Autrey's saddle-bags
(joc.) large vulva, the labia, a woman's external genitals.

piss-head
drunkard.

pissing down
raining heavily.

pissing in the wind
attempting to do something with little or no chance of success.

pissing razor-blades
urinating painfully.

piss-poor
unsatisfactory; second-rate; worthless.

piss-pot
1. a drunkard, alcoholic or heavy drinker.
2. the toilet; a chamber-pot.

piss-up
party or occasion during which a great amount of beer is consumed.

piss-weak
1. unsatisfactory; disappointing; not up to expectations.
2. (of character) cowardly; irresolute.

pissy/pissy-eyed
drunk; intoxicated.

pitch
1. (baseball etc.) throw.
2. (cricket) area between the wickets.
See also:
queer someone's pitch

pitch a line
say something in an attempt to impress in order to gain sexual favours.

pitch in
1. help; participate.
2. donate money towards a common fund or purpose: e.g. The whole office pitched in to buy him a present.
3. begin, do, start, with energy and enthusiasm.

pitch into
1. attack, assault someone physically or verbally.
2. begin, do, start, with energy and enthusiasm.

pits
(the . . .) any unpleasant, obnoxious, awful place or situation: e.g. That night-club is the pits!

Pitt Street farmer
(N.S.W.) business-man living in the city with farming interests, usually for the purpose of avoiding tax.

Pittsville
1. any squalid living conditions or extremely poor situation.
2. bottom of despair.

pivot
(Australian Rules football) centre position.

pivot on
think about; consider.

pizzazz
1. drive; energy; vigour; enthusiasm.
2. class; prestige; quality: e.g. This particular restaurant has a lot of pizzazz.

pizzle
the penis.

PJ's
pyjamas.

place
1. social rank, position: e.g. He likes a woman who knows her place — the kitchen and the bedroom!
2. confirm or remember the identity of: e.g. I know the face but I can't quite place him.
See also:
go places
high places
in the right place at the right time
know (one's) place
out of place
put in (one's) place
put (someone) in his place

place where the big nobs hang out
men's toilet, urinal.

placky
1. plastic.
2. anything artificial, insincere, synthetic, spurious.

plain as a pikestaff
not remarkable or beautiful.

plain as the nose on your face
clearly understood; obvious.

plain English/language
language that is free from ambiguity and jargon, and easily understood: e.g. Legal documents should be written in plain English instead of being full of gobbledegook that no one can understand.

plain Jane
an unattractive and unsophisticated woman.

plain sailing
easy going; calmly and without problems.

plan of attack
procedure; agenda.

plant
1. something placed secretly as a means of incriminating the innocent.
2. a spy: e.g. If information is leaking out, the opposition must have a plant in our organisation.
3. to conceal, often illegally or illicitly.
4. to strike, hit: e.g. He planted a lefty on him and gave him a black eye.

plant it
(of the driver of a car) go faster: e.g. It frightens me the way he plants it around those corners!

plant one on (someone)
strike, hit, bash (someone).

plant the foot/herbs
(see: plant it)

plant the idea in (someone's) brain
instigate, initiate a thought in (someone's) mind.

plaster
hit, strike, bash severely: e.g. Next time I see that creep I'm going to plaster him!

plastered
1. drunk; intoxicated: e.g. He got really plastered at that party.
2. beaten, defeated soundly: e.g. Our team got plastered last week in the finals.

plastic
anything artificial, insincere, synthetic, spurious: e.g. Those ritzy, snobbish people are so plastic!

plate
(plate of) food brought to a party or function: e.g. Bring a plate to the party next week.
See also:
handed to (someone) on a plate
have/got enough on (one's) plate
on a plate
on (one's) plate
too much on (one's) plate

plates of meat
(rhyming slang) feet.

play
(see: make a play)

play a part
take part in something, often deceitful, wrong or illegal: e.g. The authorities have caught most of the crooks who played a part in that big robbery.

play along
cooperate; agree.

play around
to philander, flirt, often by or with a married person: e.g. Every time he goes away on a business trip without his wife, he plays around.

play at
take part in something deceitful, secret, clandestine: e.g. I'm not sure what he's playing at, but I'll find out.

play ball
1. begin; start.
2. cooperate: e.g. If the unions and the government played ball with each other more often, there wouldn't be as many industrial problems as there are now.

play both sides of the street
be traitorous, treacherous, unfaithful.

play by the rules
behave fairly, justly.

play cat and mouse
(see: game of cat and mouse)

play chicken
perform a daring deed that may be dangerous, such as standing in the path of an oncoming car and forcing it to swerve.

play dead
pretend to be dead, defeated, rendered inactive or inoperative.

play doctors and nurses
sexual exploration, intercourse, from the practice of young children who inspect each other's bodies.

play fair
behave, act, fairly or justly.

play footsies with (someone)
secret and flirtatious touching of feet, knees, ankles, thighs etc., usually under a table so that no one else sees.

play for dibs/keeps
1. play, gamble, with the intention of keeping the winnings.
2. do in total seriousness, earnest.

play for time
to manoeuvre, act slowly to gain extra time for one's own purposes.

play four quarters
(Australian Rules football) play consistently well throughout a match.

play funny-buggers
1. behave in a foolish, stupid, silly manner.
2. behave in a deceitful, cheating manner.

play games (with)
behave (towards people) in a disquieting, uncomfortable manner, designed to deceive, humiliate, get a desired response, create jealousy etc.

play hard to get
to pretend indifference to someone's amorous advances with the intention of making that person try harder.

play hell with
create havoc; cause harm, injury, damage etc.: e.g. This cold weather plays hell with his arthritis.

play hooky
(of children usually) indulge in wilful absenteeism from school, a job etc.; to wag: e.g. He missed so many lessons playing hooky that he failed his tests.

play hospitals
(see: play doctors and nurses)

play into (someone's) hands
fall into an unsuspecting trap or scheme that will benefit the opponent.

play it by ear
1. (of a tune) play on a musical instrument without using written music.
2. take a situation as it comes, without preparation or planning: e.g. No one knows how many people are coming to the meeting so we'll have to play it by ear.

play it cool
act cautiously; behave in a calm, easy manner; act without antagonism or suspicion; be indifferent.

play it down
soften, disguise, minimise a potentially explosive, controversial situation: e.g. Most governments try to play it down when a scandal within their ranks is discovered.

play it low key
keep a low profile; behave without attracting publicity or attention.

play on words
a pun.

play (one's) cards close to (one's) chest
be secretive.

play (one's) cards right
behave in a manner, plan and carry out a strategy, that is advantageous, beneficial to (one): e.g. If he plays his cards right he'll get a promotion this year.

play pocket billiards
(see: pocket billiards)

play possum
pretend to be dead, defeated, rendered inactive or inoperative.

play safe
behave cautiously: e.g. It looks like rain, so you'd better play safe and take the umbrella.

play second fiddle to
take a minor part; be less prestigious than; be less important than: e.g. His wife didn't like playing second fiddle to his domineering mother, so she finally left him.

play silly-buggers
behave in a foolish, stupid, silly manner.

play (someone) for a fool
deceive, cheat (someone).

play (someone) on the brake
lead (someone) on; tease, entice, deceive (someone).

play the field
1. to be unattached romantically and to go from one sexual pursuit to another: e.g. Since his divorce he's been playing the field.
2. to pursue a wide range of possibilities.

play the fool
indulge in nonsense, buffoonery, silly behaviour.

play the game
behave according to the rules: e.g. If he won't play the game my way then I don't want him in the business.

play the neddies
indulge in gambling on horse-racing: e.g. He likes to play the neddies occasionally.

play the organ
(of a man) to masturbate.

play the very devil with
create havoc; cause harm, injury, damage, ruin: e.g. This cold weather plays the very devil with Dad's arthritis.

play the waiting game
(see: waiting game)

play tootsies with
(see: play footsies with)

play up
1. philander, flirt; behave in a promiscuous manner, especially with a married person or without one's own partner's knowledge.
2. behave in a mischievous, naughty manner.
3. fail to work, operate properly; break down; malfunction: e.g. My car is playing up again!

play up to (someone)
behave in an obsequious manner, flirt with or flatter (someone) in the hope of personal gain.

play with dynamite/fire/matches
flirt with danger; tamper with, behave in a manner that is potentially risky or dangerous to oneself.

play with (oneself)
to masturbate, fondle (one's) genitals.

play-act
to pretend, make-believe.

playboy
man who is devoted to pleasure and women.

played-out
exhausted; tired.

play-lunch
a snack to be eaten at school recess before lunch.

playmate
sexual partner.

plaything
person who is used by another for personal gratification without thought to feelings or emotions.

plead dumb
pretend not to know about; deny liability or guilt.

please yourself!
do as you please, but do not expect approval.

pleased as Punch
extremely pleased.

pleb
plebeian, common, distasteful, vulgar person.

plenty tucked away
have great wealth: e.g. He must have plenty tucked away by now.

plodder
slow but effective worker.

plonk
1. wine, especially cheap and common.
2. fall; flop; plop; put down; place: e.g. Just plonk that stuff over there on the table.

plonko
person addicted to wine; wine alcoholic; a wino.

plooty
posh; extravagant; upper-class: e.g. That's a very plooty restaurant.

plop
faeces; shit.

plough into
begin energetically.

pluck
plunder; rob; cheat; swindle.

pluck (someone's) cherry
take (someone's) virginity; be the first to have sexual intercourse with (someone).

pluck up the courage
summon the bravado to do something.

plug
1. a worn-out, tired old horse.
2. a sanitary tampon worn during menstruation.
3. the type of hard-sell advertising promotion that makes use of frequent repetition to make a product known and popular: e.g. The art show has been getting a good plug over the radio and the telly.
4. to punch, strike, hit, bash.
5. to shoot: e.g. Make sure you plug it right between the eyes.
See also:
go down the plug
pull the plug on (someone)

plug on
persevere with a task.

plugger
(Australian Rules football) steady player.

plugging
(see: plug, 3.) advertising in such a manner.

plum
the best, such as a job, position, part in a play or film etc.: e.g. He got a plum role in that new television series.
See also:
walks as though (one) has a plum up (one's) bum

plum in the mouth
affected manner of speech, imitative of a high-class British accent: e.g. Since living in England, he's been talking with a plum in his mouth!

plumb crazy
utterly, downright, absolutely foolish.

plumb tuckered out
absolutely tired and worn-out; exhausted.

plunge
illicitly rigged race in which, for example, a good horse runs under another name and heavy bets are placed on it.
See also:
take the plunge

plunge into
act recklessly, impetuously.

plus
asset; advantage; bonus: e.g. The only plus with this job is the extra holidays.

plush
luxurious; opulent.

po
chamber pot; potty.

P.O.A.
price on application.

pocket
1. to steal, pilfer: e.g. I saw him pocket that watch.
2. (Australian Rules football) full-forward and full-back positions on the field.
See also:
have/got a death adder in (one's) pocket
have/got short arms and long pockets
in pocket
line the pockets
live in each other's pockets

money burns a hole in (one's) pocket
mouth like a torn pocket
out of pocket
piss in (someone's) pocket
put (one's) hand in (one's) pocket

pocket billiards
(of men) pertaining to the habit of keeping the hands in the pockets, and thus appearing to fondle the genitals.

pocket-money
small weekly allowance such as that given by parents to their children.

poddy-calf
handfed calf.

poddy-dodger
person who steals, poaches unbranded calves.

poetic justice
a just meting out of rewards and punishments (as often occurs in literature).

poet's day
(abbreviation of: Piss Off Early, Tomorrow's Saturday) Friday, the day when workers often leave a little early from work.

point
(see: at the point of; from point A to point B; give someone points; make a point; on the point of; sore point; stretch a point; win on points)

point percy at the porcelain
(of men) to urinate.

point (someone) at the door

point (someone) in the direction of home
to hint directly that it is time for (someone) to go home: e.g. By three in the morning I was so tired that I finally had to point them at the door.

point the bone at (someone)
accuse, curse, jinx (someone); wish (someone) wrong.

point the finger at (someone)
accuse, inform on (someone); identify a wrong-doer.

point-blank
1. (of a gun) fired at close range.
2. explicit(ly); blunt(ly): e.g. I told him point-blank that I didn't like him.

poison letter/poison-pen letter
an anonymous letter sent with malicious intent.

poison (someone's) mind
influence (someone's) thoughts with malicious intent against someone or something.

poke
sexual intercourse.
See also:
better than a poke in the eye with a burnt/pointed/sharp stick
more than (one) can poke a stick at
pig in a poke
slow-poke
take a poke at (someone)

poke around
1. eavesdrop; snoop; spy: e.g. What are the cops poking around here for?
2. indulge in idle or aimless activity: e.g. I had three hours before the meeting so I poked around the shops.

poke borack/borax/fun at
tease, make fun of, ridicule, especially covertly.

poke in the nose
a punch or blow in the face or nose.

poke in the ribs
a reminder: e.g. The boss needs a poke in the ribs about his promise to give everyone a raise.

poke mullock at
ridicule; make fun of.

poke (one's) nose in
interfere.

poke the finger at
accuse; inform on.

poker-faced
expressionless; showing no emotion.

pokies
gambling poker machines used in clubs and casinos.

Polack
person of Polish origin.

pole
(see: up the pole; wouldn't touch it with a barge-pole; wouldn't touch it with a forty-foot pole/ten-foot pole)

poles apart
having completely different views, ideas, opinions.
See also:
at opposite ends of the poles

pole-vault
1. to leap with the aid of a pole held in the hands.
2. (joc.) describing the way a man would move with an erection of the penis: e.g. That movie was so horny he had to pole-vault all the way home!

poley
1. dehorned animal.
2. saddle without kneepads.

polish off
1. to finish quickly: e.g. We'll polish this work off in no time with all the extra help.
2. to dispose of quickly, such as of food, opponents or an enemy.

polish up on
to improve, practise: e.g. I'm going to have to polish up on my guitar-playing for the concert next week.

pollies
politicians.

pom/pommy/pommy bastard
an Englishman; someone from England.
See also:
dry as a pommy's towel
full as a pommy complaint-box

Pommyland
England.

ponce
1. effeminate man; having homosexual qualities.
2. one who lives off the earnings of prostitution; a pimp.
See also:
all ponced up

ponce about
1. behave in an effeminate manner.
2. behave in an idle, ineffective, useless manner.

poncy
affected; effeminate.

pong
unpleasant smell, odour, stink; to smell as such.

pong ping
table tennis Down Under.

pongy
having an unpleasant smell, odour.

pony
1. (horse-racing) the sum of 25 dollars.
2. small glass of beer — 140 ml.

poo
1. faeces; shit.
2. to defecate.
See also:
in the poo

poo to you too!
remark of scorn, rebuke, contempt.

poo-bum-bugger-shit!
exclamation of frustration, anger.

pooch
dog.

poof/poofter
1. homosexual man.
2. weak, ineffectual, effeminate or cowardly man.

poofter-bashing
malicious behaviour towards homosexuals (or men reputed to be).

poofy
effeminate; weak; ineffectual.

pooh!
exclamation of ridicule, contempt, disbelief, anger, annoyance.

Pooh-Bah
a pompous, opinionated person.

poohey
unpleasant; smelly.

pooh-pooh
express contempt for; belittle; deride; dismiss: e.g. He pooh-poohs everything I suggest.

pool our resources
enter into an agreement to share resources for the common good of the participants.

pools
lottery-type game of chance, usually based on the outcome of football scores.

poon
1. stupid, foolish, weird or eccentric person.
2. a man who likes to sniff girls' bicycle seats.

poonce
1. a homosexual man.
2. weak or effeminate man.

pooncy
weakly effeminate.

pooned up
dressed to impress, especially sexually.

poop
1. faeces; shit.
2. to defecate.

poop (one's) pants
to receive a fright or shock; to become angry.

poop-catchers
trousers that are loose around the body but fit tightly at the knees or ankles.

pooped
exhausted; tired.

poor as a bandicoot/church-mouse
having no money; destitute.

poor bastard/cow
an unfortunate person deserving of sympathy, compassion, support.

poor excuse for a (something)
inadequate, inferior, pathetic example of (something): e.g. The awful way he treats her, he's a poor excuse for a husband.

pop
1. father; grandfather.
2. each: e.g. I paid five dollars a pop for those chickens.
3. an attempt, go, try: e.g. I'll have a pop at it.

pop in
come, enter, go, suddenly or unexpectedly: e.g. I need to pop in to the supermarket for a few things.

pop music
popular music, such as rock and roll, played over the radio.

pop off
1. to die suddenly.
2. to shoot.
3. go, depart suddenly, quickly.

pop (one's) cork
to display sudden anger or temper.

pop the question
propose marriage.

pop up
appear suddenly.

pop-eyed
with bulging or wide-open eyes.

poppet
affectionate term for a small child or person.

poppycock
nonsense; rubbish; worthless talk.

popsie/popsy
young girl; term of endearment for a young girl.

popular as a dag at a sheepshow
not popular at all.

P.O.Q.
piss off quick; go away; get lost.

P.O.Q. before you get a B.S.A.
piss off quick before you get a bloody sore arse; get lost!

pork sword
the penis; pertaining to sexual intercourse (of a man): e.g. I'd like to give her the pork sword!

porky
fat; overweight.

porn
1. pornography: e.g. He loves porn.
2. pornographic: e.g. He loves porn movies.

porno
1. pornography.
2. pornographic.
3. one who enjoys pornography.

port
(Queensland) suitcase; school bag.

poser
one who behaves in an affected, insincere manner.

posh
elegant; smart; sophisticated; luxurious.

positive
downright; absolute: e.g. He's a positive idiot!

possession is nine points of the law
actual possession of something gives one effective ownership, one's claims a certain force.

possie
position; place: e.g. We know a nice secluded possie at the beach.

possum
affectionate, cute term for someone.
See also:
play possum
stir the possum

postie
postman.

pot
1. marijuana.
2. medium-sized glass of beer (285 ml).
3. large sum of money won as a prize.
4. to shoot: e.g. He can pot a rabbit from a hundred metres away.
5. large, distended stomach associated with excessive drinking of beer.
See also:
beer pot
go to pot
keep the pot boiling
one for the pot
piss-pot
tin-pot
tosspot
watched pot never boils

pot calling the kettle black
bringing attention to someone else's failings when one is guilty of the same weaknesses.

potato
(see: clean potato; hot potato; not the clean potato; small potatoes; strain the potatoes)

pot-belly
large protruding stomach associated with excessive beer-drinking.

pot-hole
hole, depression in the road surface.

pot-luck
random choice or selection; whatever is offered or left.
See also:
take pot-luck

pot-shot
random shot from a gun: e.g. Someone took a pot-shot at us from that street.

potty
1. chamber pot (also: pottie).
2. silly; eccentric; crazy.

pouffe
a homosexual man.

pound
(see: only eighteen bob in the pound)

pound of flesh
something owing and insisted on mercilessly, ruthlessly.

pound the mound
(of men) to perform sexual intercourse.

pour oil on troubled waters
attempt to pacify, calm a troubled situation.

powder
(see: take a powder)

powder (one's) nose
(of women) to go to the toilet.

powder puff
weak, ineffectual, effeminate man.

powder room
women's toilet.

power
1. a great amount: e.g. 1. He's going to take a power of convincing. 2. That sleep did me the power of good.
2. to use rapidly: e.g. We powered through the food and beer.
3. to go, do quickly: e.g. We powered through all that work.

power of the pussy
(. . . — it'd drag you where dynamite wouldn't blow you) pertaining to

'Now that I've been booked we'll certainly be travellin' slower. After all, the fire we were going flat strap to get to wuz only *your cop shop!'*

Most of you as drivers will have the opportunity to meet one of our fine members of the constabulary, at some time or other. When this happens, you will find it's more prudent to call him constable or sarge than beak, bomber, bluebottle, cop, demon, dick, fuzz, grey ghost, grey meanie, John Hop, pig, speed-cop, trap or walloper.

the strong sexual attraction women have for men.

power-drunk
the conceited, haughty and over-bearing indulgence in one's (especially newly acquired) power, authority.

powerful
great amount; very: e.g. 1. He's got a powerful lot of money. 2. That's a powerful big problem.

powerhouse
a person of great drive and energy.

power-point
(derog.) an Oriental person.

powers that be
those in authority; those making the rules, laws: e.g. The powers that be have decided in their wisdom to raise taxes again.

pow-wow
a meeting or conference.

pox
venereal disease.
See also:
a pox on (someone)

pox-doctor
venereal-disease specialist.
See also:
done up like a pox-doctor's clerk

poxed
jinxed; cursed with bad luck or misfortune.

pozzie
(see: possie)

P.R.
Public Relations: e.g. He's our best P.R. man.

prac
practice: e.g. We've got a prac class in pottery today.

practice makes perfect
the repeated performance of something improves one's skill, ability.

prang
1. a crash or accident in a car.
2. to crash and damage, especially a car.

prat
bum, backside.

prawn
a weak, foolish, insignificant or ineffectual person.
See also:
come the raw prawn with
off like a bucket of prawns

prawn night
social occasion at which prawns and beer are served.

precious
1. (generally of a man) effeminate; foppish; exhibiting homosexual tendencies; affectedly refined.
2. very; extremely: e.g. We have precious little time left together.

prefab
prefabricated building, common for schools.

preggers/preggie/preggo
pregnant.

pre-loved
second-hand.

prem/premmie
child born prematurely.

prep
1. preparatory.
2. pertaining to preparatory school; a child at preparatory school.

presence of mind
alert state of mind whereby one can think calmly and clearly.

press (one's) luck
(see: push one's luck)

pressie
present; gift.

pretty
an intensive, such as considerable, very, quite, fairly: e.g. pretty good, pretty awful, pretty fast.
See also:
sitting pretty

pretty boy
(derog.) extremely attractive man.

pretty penny
a considerable sum of money: e.g. That diamond ring must have cost him a pretty penny.

pretty-pretty
too attractive in an effeminate, frilly or tizzy way.

prey on (someone)
manipulate, cheat, exploit (someone).

prezzie
present; gift.

price
the ultimate sum of money, terms or other to be given in order to achieve something or gain a person's support or favour.
See also:
at a price
at any price
pay the price

priceless
amusingly eccentric; extraordinary: e.g. He's priceless the way he tells jokes.

prices have skyrocketed
costs have risen excessively.

pricey
expensive.

prick
1. the penis.
2. a despicable person.
See also:
like a spare prick at a wedding
she's had more pricks than a pin-cushion

prick (one's) ears up
eavesdrop; listen with unexpected interest.

prick (someone's) conscience
cause remorse, sorrow, guilt in (someone).

prickly (as a porcupine)
sensitive; easily upset or angered; irritable.

prick-teaser
(see: cock-teaser)

pride of place
the most important position.

prim and proper
chaste; prudish; virtuous.

prima donna
temperamental, petulant woman who expects to get her way.

prime time
peak viewing hours on television.

primed
drunk; intoxicated.

Prince Alberts/Alfreds
the toe-rags of the swagman, worn to protect the feet.

Prince of Darkness
the devil; Satan.

prissy
prudish; affected.

private eye
private detective, investigator.

privates/private parts
the genitals.

privy
a toilet — especially an outside one.

prize (fool, idiot, moron etc.)
utter; complete; total; absolute.

pro
1. professional; expert.
2. prostitute.

prod (someone)
goad; stimulate; encourage.

Proddy dog
a Protestant.

produce the goods
1. have sexual intercourse, especially of women: e.g. She didn't produce the goods so I didn't ask her out again.
2. deliver, supply anything that has been promised or implied.

prof
professor.

professional ratbag
one who makes money out of doing weird, crazy, useless or unproductive things, schemes.

promise
(see: lick and a promise; on a promise)

promise the earth
make a promise that is usually too excessive to fulfil: e.g. At election time, most politicians promise the earth.

promo
promotion; advertisement.

prong
the penis.

pronto
quickly; immediately.

proof of the pudding is in the eating
testing, trial or actual evidence will establish the truth.

prop
1. propeller.
2. anything that is depended upon or serves as a support: e.g. Many insecure people need someone for a prop.
3. stay; sit; remain: e.g. I think we'll prop here for a while.

proper
absolute; thorough; complete: e.g. He made a proper galah of himself in front of everybody when he tripped and fell.

proposition
1. a proposal, suggestion, request for sexual intercourse.
2. to propose, suggest, request sexual intercourse.

props
the legs.

pros and cons
reasons for and against.

prossie
prostitute.

protection
contraceptive precaution: e.g. Withdrawal before ejaculation is not a safe method of protection.

proud as a peacock

proud as Punch
very proud.
See also:
do (someone) proud

prowl-car
police patrol-car.

p's and q's
manners; language: e.g. Mind your p's and q's when you meet my parents.

psych (oneself) up
persuade, convince (oneself): e.g. I have to psych myself up before I go to the dentist.

psyched out
1. demoralised; unbalanced; upset; disturbed: e.g. We were really psyched out after seeing that movie.
2. under the influence of marijuana or other drugs.

psyched up
aroused; persuaded; convinced; ready for action.

psycho
1. an insane person.
2. insane; mad.

P.T.
Physical Training.

pub
public house; hotel, especially the bar.

pub crawl
the practice of drinking at a series of hotels, especially in one evening.

pubes
lower part of the abdomen covered with pubic hair; pubic hair.

public enemy number one
a particularly despicable, criminal person.

pucker-up
prepare for a kiss.

pud/pudding
1. fat person.
2. stupid person.
See also:
proof of the pudding is in the eating

pudding club
pertaining to pregnancy: e.g. She's joined the pudding club.
See also:
in the pudding club

pudgy
fat; plump; obese.

puff
marijuana; marijuana cigarette: e.g. Have you got any puff for sale?
See also:
run out of puff

puffed
exhausted; out of breath.

puffed-up
1. filled with self-importance; arrogant; conceited.
2. exaggerated.

pug
a boxer.

puke
vomit; to vomit.

puku
stomach — especially a large or distended one.

pull
1. influence; power; authority: e.g. He's got a lot of pull in politics.
2. attempt; try to do (often with ill, malicious or devious intent): e.g. What trick is he trying to pull now?

pull a bird/chick
(of men) attempt to make the acquaintance of a woman with a view to seduction.

pull a fast one/fastie/fasty/shifty/swifty
try to trick, deceive or cheat; attempt to gain an unfair advantage over: e.g. He tried to pull a swifty by selling me a crook car.

pull a gun/knife
take out with intent to use.

pull apart
to criticise and analyse in detail, often with malicious intent.

pull faces
grimace; make distorted facial expressions as a means of being rude, impudent or contemptuous.

pull in
1. earn as a salary: e.g. How much does he pull in now?
2. arrest, apprehend: e.g. He was pulled in for drug-pushing.

pull it off
manage to do successfully; make a go of; succeed: e.g. He'll never pull it off without getting caught.

pull off a hat-trick
have three successes in a row.

pull (one's) belt in
reduce (one's) spending; budget more carefully.

pull (one's) finger out
1. hurry up.
2. do something; become active.

pull (one's) socks up
improve; make a greater effort; do better after a poor effort.

pull (one's) weight
do (one's) fair share of work.

pull (oneself)

pull (oneself) off
1. to masturbate.
2. to delude, deceive (oneself): e.g. He's pulling himself off if he thinks he can do that.

pull (oneself) together
recover (one's) self-control, composure, calm.

pull out
1. depart; leave.
2. withdraw; back out of an agreement.

pull out all the stops
1. use extreme effort, all one's resources.
2. speak emotionally, frankly.

pull punches
to not give full force to an argument: e.g. I didn't pull any punches when I told him the truth.

pull rank on
act on one's higher position, status or authority: e.g. When he wouldn't cooperate willingly, I had to pull rank on him.

pull round
recover safely, such as after an illness.

pull (someone) in
(of the police or authorities) arrest, apprehend (someone).

pull (someone) off
to masturbate (someone).

pull (someone's) leg
tease, make fun of (someone); deceive (someone) in fun.

pull something out of the bag
to come forward at a crucial moment with a surprise tactic or advantage.

pull strings
exert influence, either directly or indirectly: e.g. She only got the job because her father was able to pull some strings.

pull the coat
not make a genuine or concerted effort.

pull the digit out
(see: pull one's finger out)

pull the dirty
(see: pull a fast one)

pull the mat out from under (someone)
disconcert, ruin (someone); gain an advantage over (someone) by placing (him) in a disadvantageous position.

pull the other leg

pull the other one, it jingles

pull the other one, it's got bells on
a statement of derision, scorn, disbelief, at what is being said.

pull the pin/plug on (someone)
disconcert, ruin (someone); prevent, stop (someone's) activities by some strong means.

pull the rug out from under (someone's) feet
(see: pull the mat out from under someone)

pull the wool over (someone's) eyes
deceive, trick, dupe, fool, hoodwink (someone).

pull through
survive; recover; endure.

pull to pieces
(see: pull apart)

pull up
1. to stop, apprehend: e.g. The police pulled us up for speeding.
2. reprimand; rebuke; correct.

pull up a pew
find a chair and sit down.

pull up stakes
quit and move away.

pull wires
(see: pull strings)

pull your head/neck in!
mind your own business!

pulled in
arrested; apprehended.

pulled into it
coerced, intimidated, pressed into (doing something).

pulling my leg
deceiving, tricking, teasing me.

pulling (one's) pud

pulling (oneself)
1. (of a man) masturbating.
2. deceiving, deluding (oneself).

pulverise
defeat soundly.

pump (someone)
ellicit information from (someone) by persistent and clever questions.

pumpkin-head
someone who has a big head or is obese, fat.

punch
effect, force: e.g. His speech had a lot of punch.
See also:
beat to the punch
doesn't pull any punches
no punches pulled
pack a punch
pleased as Punch
proud as Punch
roll with the punches
telegraph (one's) punches

punch line
the last line upon which the humour of a joke depends.

punch out a nougat/steamer
to defecate.

punch shit out of (someone)

punch (someone's) head in
bash, assault violently.

punch-drunk
1. stupefied by repeated punches, as a boxer might be.
2. dull-witted; dopey; stupid.
3. aggressive.

punching the bundy
working set hours and operating a time-clock that records one's arrival and departure.

punch-up
a violent fight.

punish
to make excessive, heavy demands on a supply, stock or item: e.g. This holiday has really punished my bank-account.

punk
1. a worthless, detestable lout.
2. a criminal.
3. pertaining to an aggressive and rebellious style of dress, rock music, and anti-social behaviour.

punk rock
rock music styled on aggressiveness, rebelliousness and shock-tactics.

punt
attempt; try: e.g. I'll have a punt at it.

punter
a gambler — especially horse-racing.

pup
a conceited, unsophisticated young man.
See also:
be sold a pup
night is but a pup

puppet on a string
person who is dominated by someone else, bends to his will and does anything asked.

puppy fat
temporary fatness of adolescence.

puppy love
infatuation of young girls and boys for each other.

pure as the driven snow
innocent; morally and sexually wholesome.

purler
1. a heavy fall.
2. anything outstanding, excellent.

purple hearts
amphetamines (see: speed).

purse strings
the power to allocate or spend available funds: e.g. Mum controls the purse strings in our family.
See also:
hold the purse strings

push
1. influence; power: e.g. He's got a lot of push in politics.
2. enterprise; determination: e.g. He's got enough push to go a long way in politics.
3. dismissal; the sack: e.g. After that scandal, he was given the push.
4. promote; advertise; recommend; press for: e.g. That product is really being pushed with heavy advertising on prime time.
See also:
at a push
pass with a push

push in the right direction
strong encouragement to act in the correct manner, follow the most productive, beneficial avenue.

push it
1. exert (oneself), work harder to meet a deadline: e.g. We're going to be pushing it to get this finished on time.
2. demand persistently: e.g. If I don't keep pushing it he might forget about it and change his mind.
3. (see: push one's luck)

push off
go; depart; leave: e.g. It's time we pushed off.

push on
1. go; depart; leave.
2. continue, sometimes against strong odds.

push (one's) luck (too far)
try to stretch (one's) good chances or fortune, often to the point where the consequences are bad or dangerous.

push (one's) own barrow
further (one's) own interests; act for the betterment of (one's) own fortunes or opportunities — often in a selfish and uncaring manner towards others.

push (someone) over the edge
1. bring pressure to bear in such a manner as to cause an unwanted or undesirable result or reaction from (someone).
2. cause (someone) to become mentally unbalanced or insane.

push the button/panic button
1. cause, start, detonate a major nuclear war.
2. (see: panic button)

push up zeds
have a sleep, nap: e.g. He's pushing up zeds after a hard day's work.

pushed for (something)
lacking (something); having a difficult time providing or supplying (something): e.g. 1. We're a bit pushed for time so we can't stop and talk right now. 2. He was pushed for money last week so he asked me for a loan.

pusher
supplier, seller, of illegal drugs.

pushing
(of age) having nearly reached (a specified age): e.g. He's pushing forty so I don't think he'll make the footy team this year.

pushing shit uphill (with a pointed stick/rubber fork)
attempting an impossible task; trying to do something that cannot succeed, is doomed to failure.

pushing up daisies
to be dead: e.g. If you keep smoking that heavily, you'll be pushing up daisies in a few years.

pushover
1. an extremely easy task.
2. a person easily overcome, swayed, defeated, cheated.

pushy
1. annoyingly overbearing.
2. determined; aggressively enterprising.

puss
1. woman; girl.
2. the face, mouth: e.g. He needs a smack in the puss!

Pussies
Geelong VFL football team.

pussy
1. a cat.
2. the vagina; female pudendum.

pussy-foot around
be cautious and unwilling to commit oneself to a course of action.

put a cork/sock in it!
shut up! be quiet!

put a damper on
discourage; put a stop to; thwart; spoil: e.g. The rain put a damper on the outdoor concert.

put a spanner in the works
to upset, ruin, spoil; cause trouble.

put a spoke in (someone's) wheel
to hinder, spoil, ruin (someone's) plans or chances.

put across
communicate effectively: e.g. Many people find it difficult to put across their true feelings.

put all (one's) eggs in the same basket
risk all, everything one has on one enterprise.

put away
1. imprisoned: e.g. He was put away for his crimes.
2. save money: e.g. I try to put away a little every week.
3. (of food or drink) consume, usually to excess: e.g. He can put away a carton of beer in one night!

put down
1. kill, destroy an animal, especially for reasons of illness or old age.
2. criticise; humiliate; degrade: e.g. 1. He's always putting me down these days. 2. I'm always being put down by him!

put hairs on your chest
(of food or drink) a jocular expression of encouragement to drink or eat something that is strong, purportedly good for you, has a strong effect etc.: e.g. Drink this — it'll put hairs on your chest!

put heads together
scheme, plan, discuss, work out, together.

put in
1. betrayed to the authorities: e.g. He was put in by his best friend.
2. did: e.g. We put in a good day's work.
3. contribute money: e.g. We're all putting in for a present for him when he retires.

put in a good word for
to recommend favourably.

put in for
apply for: e.g. Are you going to put in for that new job?

put in (one's) place
(of an arrogant person) belittled; humbled; embarrassed.

put in the boot
1. attack physically or verbally.
2. take unfair advantage of (someone) less fortunate: e.g. The landlords really put in the boot when they raised the rents.

put it across (someone)
outwit, deceive, trick, fool (someone): e.g. He's too smart for anyone to put it across him again!

put it mildly
speak without exaggeration.

put it on
1. pretend, exaggerate one's emotions: e.g. He's not hurt — he's just putting it on!
2. to gain weight: e.g. I've really put it on this year!

put it on (someone)
1. confront (someone) directly about a matter: e.g. You've got to put it on him if you expect the boss to give you a raise.
2. blame (someone): e.g. Don't try to put it on me — I had nothing to do with it!

put it on the line
1. be direct, frank, candid.
2. take a calculated risk.

put it on the map
to make a town or place famous, well known, popular: e.g. The casino on the Gold Coast will really put Queensland on the map for international tourists.

put it on the slate
record as a debt, or as being on credit: e.g. I didn't have enough money to pay for the groceries, so I had to put it on the slate.

put it past (someone)
think it unlikely for (someone): e.g. I wouldn't put it past him to steal from his own mother!

put it to (someone)
ask (someone); tell (someone); provide (someone) with certain information, facts, requests etc. for consideration: e.g. I'll put it to him but I can't guarantee what his response will be.

put lead in your pencil
(of men) increase sexual performance: e.g. This drink will put lead in your pencil!

put off
1. disconcerted; discouraged; disgusted: e.g. I was going to rent that flat but I was put off by all the cockroaches.
2. delay; postpone; defer: e.g. We have to put the barbecue off because it's going to rain.

put on
assumed; false; pretence; pretended: e.g. Her sorrow for his death was put on for the sake of the insurance investigators.

put on a bold front
(see: put on a good face)

put on a dingo act
behave in a cowardly or treacherous manner.

put on a good face
pretended, false, outward appearance to hide one's true feelings, anger, hostility etc.

put on a real performance
display extreme bad temper; have a tantrum, emotional outburst; create a scene.

put on a turn
1. become angry; create a scene: e.g. He's going to put on a turn when he finds out what happened to his car!

2. have a party, social function: e.g. We're going to put on a turn for his birthday next week.

put on airs (and graces)
behave in an affected, haughty, conceited, pompous manner.

put on an act
(also: bung on an act)
1. indulge in fraudulent behaviour in order to impress.
2. indulge in a tantrum, display of bad temper or overstatement of emotion: e.g. If my kids put on an act for not getting their own way, they get a good spanking.

put on jam/side
to behave in an affected, haughty, conceited, pompous manner.

put on the mat
be severely reprimanded, scolded, berated, criticised: e.g. I was really put on the mat for coming late to work!

put on the ritz
do something in a luxurious, sumptuous, elegant or opulent manner.

put on the spot
1. severely embarrassed.
2. put into a difficult or embarrassing situation in which one is compelled to act.

put one across/over/past (someone)
deceive, trick, fool, cheat, outwit (someone): e.g. I've never been able to put one past my mother — she always knows if I'm telling lies.

put (one's) back into (something)
exert (oneself); expend great energy doing (something).

put (one's) best foot forward
1. make a good impression.
2. do (one's) best; try (one's) hardest.

put (one's) bib in
offer (one's) opinion, whether asked for or not.

put (one's) cards on the table
declare (one's) intentions; be frank, candid, blunt.

put (one's) face on
(of a woman) apply make-up, cosmetics.

put (one's) feet on the mantelpiece and make (oneself) at home
make (oneself) feel comfortable, relaxed.

put (one's) feet up
relax.

put (one's) finger on (it)
1. remember (it).
2. indicate exactly; find; locate: e.g. I know it's around here somewhere, but I can't put my finger on it.

put (one's) foot down
be severe, strong, determined, in the carrying out of (one's) decision, usually to put a stop to something: e.g. He started to drink too much so I put my foot down and told him if he didn't stop, then I'd leave!

put (one's) foot in it
1. make a mistake, blunder, mess of (it); spoil, ruin (it).
2. say the wrong thing by mistake and cause embarrassment.

put (one's) foot in (one's) mouth
make an embarrassing remark or statement.

put (one's) hand in (one's) pocket
spend money (often in the sense of being unwilling): e.g. I always seem to be putting my hand in my pocket to pay for his bills!

put (one's) head in the sand
ignore a problem or an issue that needs attention.

put (one's) heart into
try (one's) utmost, best.

put (one's) money where (one's) mouth is
an expression inviting (one) to support (one's) boasting, bragging, voluble speech about a matter with actual money in the form of a wager, donation etc.

put (one's) neck on the line
put (oneself) in a vulnerable or dangerous position or situation; take a risk.

put (one's) oar in
contribute, voice one's (often unwanted) opinions.

put (one's) own house in order first
clean up, organise, sort the muddle out in (one's) own life and affairs before criticising other people.

put (one's) shoulder to the wheel
exert (oneself).

put (one's) spoke in
have (one's) uninvited opinions aired.

put (one's) thinking cap on
think, consider carefully; puzzle something out.

put (one's) two-bob's worth in
have (one's) uninvited opinions aired.

put (oneself) out
try hard; devote great energy to, make a special effort, often at the cost of (one's) own time, money, resources etc.: e.g. He's so mean he won't put himself out for anybody!

put (our/their) heads together
scheme, plan, discuss, work things out, together.

put out
1. disconcerted; annoyed; frustrated; irritated: e.g. He was very put out when he was told there were no more seats in the restaurant.
2. inconvenienced: e.g. I wasn't put out at all when they stayed with us for a few weeks.

put out to grass
retired: e.g. He's too old for politics and it's about time he was put out to grass!

put over a fast one/fastie
try to cheat, trick, deceive, hoodwink; try to gain an unfair advantage over.

put paid to
thwart; put an end to; stop: e.g. The police put paid to his criminal activities.

put shit on (someone)
criticise, deceive, mock, deride, tease, often with malicious intent.

put (someone) down
criticise, find fault with, humiliate, degrade (someone).

put (someone) in
inform on, betray (someone) to the police, authorities.

put (someone) in his box/ place
humble, humiliate, embarrass, belittle an arrogant person.

put (someone) in the picture
explain the details to; disclose information to; make understood to (someone).

put (someone) off
dissuade; disconcert; discourage; render (someone) unenthusiastic; disgust (someone).

put (someone) out
inconvenience (someone).

put (someone) out of his misery
1. to kill or render unconscious so as to end pain or suffering.
2. to make better a circumstance that is distressing (someone).

put (someone) straight
(see: set someone straight)

put (someone) to shame
disgrace (someone), show (someone) up, especially by comparison with one's own superior qualities.

put (someone) up
accommodate (someone), usually for just a short time: e.g. We can put them up until they find a house to rent.

put (someone) up to it
instigate (someone) to do something; persuade (someone) to do something.

put (someone's) nose out of joint
upset (someone) by besting, outdoing, thwarting; deflate (someone's) ego; humiliate (someone).

put (someone's) weights up
embarrass (someone) by a disclosure; inform on (someone).

put that in your pipe and smoke it!
an insult to someone you have just humiliated, bested, outdone.

put the acid on (someone)
ask, pressure (someone), especially for a loan.

put the bite on (someone)
request, pressure for a loan, favour; cadge.

put the boots in
(see: put in the boot)

put the brakes on
put a stop to (something): e.g. If I don't put the brakes on his drinking, he'll turn into an alcoholic.

put the breeze up (someone)
frighten, disconcert (someone).

put the cart before the horse
change the usual order of things; confuse matters.

put the damper on
(see: put a damper on)

put the fangs in
1. have someone under one's power, control: e.g. She's really put the fangs into him!
2. (see: put the bite on someone)

put the hard word on (someone)
1. ask (someone) to have sexual intercourse (especially of a man asking a woman).
2. ask, pressure (someone) for a favour, especially a loan.

put the heat on
1. apply verbal pressure in order to attain a desired response.
2. ask, pressure for, a favour.

put the heavies/heavy word on (someone)
(see: put the hard word on, 1. and 2; put the heat on, 1. and 2.)

put the hooks into (someone)
1. ask, pressure (someone) for a loan.
2. (of a woman) seduce into marriage.

put the knife into (someone)
to betray, double-cross or destroy (someone's) reputation in an underhanded, malicious manner — usually in the person's absence.

put the kybosh on
(also: kibosh) put an end to, stop, thwart.

put the lid on
put a stop to; clamp down on: e.g. The police finally put the lid on the criminal activities of those crooks.

put the mock/mockers/ mozz on (someone)
prejudice the chances of; jinx; bring ill fortune and bad luck to bear on (someone).

put the nips into (someone)
(see: put the bite on someone)

put the pressure on
harass, compel, urge someone in the hope of achieving a desired response: e.g. The greenies are putting the pressure on the government for stricter controls over logging in rainforests.

put the screws on (someone)
1. borrow, cadge from (someone); ask, pressure (someone) for a loan.
2. intimidate (someone); apply pressure; coerce, force, compel (someone) to do something.

put the shits up (someone)
1. cause (someone) to become angry.
2. disconcert, frustrate, worry (someone).

put the skids under (someone)
ensure (someone's) downfall, ruin, destruction.

put the squeeze on (someone)
1. apply pressure to compel, coerce (someone) to do something.
2. blackmail, harass, extort.

put the wind up (someone)
1. frighten, intimidate, disconcert (someone).
2. alert, warn (someone).

put the wood in the hole
shut the door.

put through (one's) paces
placed in a situation where (one) has to show (one's) ability, skill etc.

put through the hoops
subjected to a series of tests, trials, questions etc. that are often unnecessary, unreasonable and unwarranted.

put through the mangle/ mill
emotionally or physically exhausted; to have gone through a gruelling or difficult experience.

put two and two together
draw conclusions from the available evidence.

put up
1. supply money: e.g. Each of us had to put up a thousand dollars.
2. persuaded to: e.g. He was put up to it by his friends.

put up or shut up
be prepared to support one's views or be quiet.

put up with
tolerate; endure.

put up your dooks!
an invitation to fight.

put upon
unfairly burdened; deceived.

put words into (someone's) mouth
allege that (someone) said something that he did not; tell (someone) what to say.

put-down
a rejection, insult, humiliation.

put-off
something disconcerting, discouraging, disgusting etc.

put-on
deception; hoax; trick; insincerity; fraudulent behaviour.

putter around with
fiddle, play, work with in an aimless, idle manner.

putting me on
deceiving, tricking, teasing me.

putt-putt
any small engine or vehicle.

putty
(see: up to putty)

putty in (one's) hands
easily controlled, swayed, convinced; under (one's) power.

put-up
deceptive scheme, trick, fraudulent act.

pyjama-python
the penis.

pyramid selling
a business practice in which those at the top sell agencies, not goods, to others who do the same in turn, so that only the people at the bottom of the structure actually sell goods.

qango
(see: quango)

Q-car
an unmarked police car.

QFRTB
quite full, ready to bust — said after one has had ample to eat.

quack
1. a doctor (not necessarily a fraudulent one).
2. a cheat or fraudulent operator.

quad
quadrangle.

quads
quadruplets — four infants born to a mother at the one time.

quaint-arse
QANTAS — Queensland and Northern Territory Aerial Service.

Quaky Isles
New Zealand.

quandong
disreputable person living off others.

quango
acronym for quasi-autonomous-non-governmental-organisation; an organisation held in contempt by the public because of its use of large amounts of government funding for services of dubious use.

queen
homosexual man.
See also:
closet queen
drag queen

queen it (up)
1. behave in a regal, queenly manner.
2. (of men) dress effeminately; behave like a homosexual.

Queen Street bushie
(Queensland) businessman living in the city (Brisbane) with farming interests, usually as a means of avoiding tax.

queer
1. a homosexual man.
2. mentally unbalanced.
3. of suspicious or dubious nature: e.g. That deal sounds a bit queer to me.

queer bird/card
eccentric, peculiar, odd person.

queer (someone's) pitch
upset (someone's) plans.

question
(see: ask me no questions and I'll tell you no lies; good question; pop the question; sixty-four-thousand-dollar question)

question mark
any person or thing that is open to dispute, doubtful, uncertain.

quick
(see: cut to the quick)

quick and the dead
pertaining to the living, being alive, in the sense that if you are not quick to act, react, think, then you minimise your chances of survival.

quick as a flash/wink

quick as greased lightning
very quick.

quick march!
hurry up!

quick off the mark

quick on the uptake
prompt action or response.

quick quid
money earned easily and often illegally: e.g. He's always involved in something that earns a quick quid.

quick smart
promptly; at once: e.g. I want those things here quick smart.

quickie
1. a short sexual encounter; sexual intercourse either in a hurried manner or at an unusual time or place.
2. anything done in a hurried manner.

quid
the sum of one pound before decimal currency.

See also:
earn a quid
full quid
have/got a quid
make a quid
nineteen bob in the quid
not for quids
not the full quid
quick quid
turn an honest quid

quids
a lot of money: e.g. That must have cost quids!

quiet
(see: just quietly; on the quiet)

quiet as a church mouse
very quiet; not having much to say.

quiet in the peanut gallery!
an irritated request for silence.

quiet the worms
have something to eat; appease one's hunger: e.g. I'll just have a pie to quiet the worms for the time being.

quim
the female pudendum, genitals, vagina.

quince
(see: get on one's quince)

quins
quintuplets — five infants born to a mother at the one time.

quit harping
stop nagging, harassing, haranguing.

quit it!
be quiet! stop it; cease behaving in such a manner.

quit the bullshit
cease talking nonsense, lies, insincerities and be genuine, frank, candid, honest.

quite a few
many; a considerable number.

quits
(see: call it quits)

quitter
a person who gives up easily.

quod
prison.

quoit
(also: coit) bum, anus.
See also:
go for (one's) quoits
kick up the quoit

R and R
rest and recreation.

rabbit
fool; silly person.
See also:
gutted rabbit

rabbit food
lettuce and other green vegetables.

rabbit-chop/killer
sharp blow to the back of the neck with the side of the hand.

rabbit-oh
hawker of rabbits as food.

Rabbitos
South Sydney N.S.W. Rugby League football team.

rabble
the lowest class of people and held in contempt: e.g. The champagne opening of the new centre isn't for the rabble — only the rich and influential have been given an invitation.

race
(see: not in/out of the race)

race against time
work in haste due to lack of time.

race off with
steal; pilfer: e.g. Someone raced off with my bike!

race (someone) off
seduce (someone): e.g. Many women would have liked the opportunity to race Paul Newman off.

racehorse
a very thinly hand-rolled cigarette.

rack and ruin
destruction; neglect; dilapidation; disrepair: e.g. The house has gone to rack and ruin because it's been empty for years.

rack off
1. go; depart; leave.
2. an insulting dismissal — piss off! go away!

rack off hairy-legs/Noddy!
an insulting dismissal — piss off! go away!

rack (one's) brains
make a great mental effort.

racket
1. loud noise, commotion.
2. occupation; line of business: e.g. What racket is he in now?
3. method of making money by devious, illegal means such as extortion, fraud; dishonest scheme.

racy
1. lively; vigorous; interesting.
2. suggestive; lewd; immodest; indecent.

radar (trap)
an instrument that measures the speed of motorists.

Rafferty's rules
no rules at all.

rag
1. any local newspaper.
2. handkerchief.
3. flag.
4. sanitary menstruation napkin.
5. to tease, torment: e.g. I enjoy ragging him every now and then.
See also:
chew the rag
like a red rag to a bull
limp rag
live on the smell of an oily rag
run on the smell of an oily rag
snot-rag

rag trade
the clothing manufacturing industry.

rag-and-bone-man
second-hand dealer.

ragbag
untidy, unkempt, slovenly person (especially a woman).

rage
1. a lively, entertaining party or social occasion: e.g. We went to a real rage on New Year's Eve.
2. vogue; fashion mania; style: e.g. The latest rage is baggy pants.
3. to enjoy with wild abandon: e.g. We're going to rage tonight.
See also:
all the rage

raggedy-Anne
person (usually a woman) of unkempt appearance; wearing dirty, tatty clothes.

raggle-taggle
unkempt; slovenly.

rags
1. clothes.
2. sanitary napkins worn during menstruation.
See also:
glad rags
on the rags

rags to riches
from poverty to wealth: e.g. Hers is a true rags to riches story.

raid the fridge
indulge one's hunger by eating anything available in the refrigerator — usually late at night.

raid the piggy-bank
to draw on one's savings — especially petty-cash kept somewhere in the house.

Raiders
Canberra N.S.W. Rugby League football team.

railroad
1. push, force, hurry, expediate.
2. to compel or force unfairly: e.g. He was railroaded into marrying her because she got pregnant.

rain
(see: haven't got enough sense to come in out of the rain; it never rains but it pours; right as rain; sure as rain)

rain dance
superstitious ceremony jocularly believed to cause it to rain.

raincheck
1. a postponement, such as of an invitation: e.g. I'll have to take a raincheck on that invitation as I can't make it this weekend.
2. the issue of a docket to guarantee supply of a sale-priced item that is unavailable at the time of sale.

raincoat
condom, contraceptive sheath for the penis.

raining cats and dogs
raining very heavily.

rainy day
time of need, especially in the future: e.g. I'm saving that money for a rainy day.

raise
establish communication with: e.g. I can't seem to raise anybody on the phone today.
See also:
couldn't raise a gallop

raise a bite
to tease until a reaction is obtained.

raise a laugh
create laughter in others: e.g. That joke always raises a laugh.

raise hell
cause trouble; make a big fuss.

raise one
(of a man) have an erection.

raise (one's) elbow
to indulge in the drinking of alcohol — especially beer.

raise (one's) eyebrows
look shocked, supercilious.

raise (one's) hopes
become more hopeful.

raise (one's) sights
to aim higher in (one's) ambitions.

raise the devil
make a loud noise, commotion.

raise the roof
create excitement; make a loud noise: e.g. That rock band raised the roof at last night's concert.

rake
a comb for the hair.
See also:
bug-rake

rake in
(of money) collect in large amounts.

rake (someone) over the coals
reprimand, scold, berate (someone) severely.

rake up
1. collect with difficulty: e.g. I need to rake up a thousand dollars by tomorrow.
2. reveal, particularly by incriminating information, scurrilous gossip, slander: e.g. Politicians are always trying to rake up scandal against their opposition.

rake-off
a share in (often illicit) profits.

Ralph
(see: cry Ralph!)

ram it down (someone's) throat

ram it home
force (someone) to accept information, advice.

ram it up (one's) bum
expression of scorn, derision, dismissal: e.g. He can ram it up his bum for all I care!

rambunctious
unruly; boisterous.

ramrod
a stiffly formal person.

randy

randy as a bitch on heat

randy as a drover's dog

randy as a mallee bull
sexually aroused; lustful.

rank
1. utter; total; unmistakable: e.g. He's a rank beginner.
2. offensive; despicable: e.g. What he did was rank!
See also:
pull rank on

rank and file
the ordinary people.

rankle
continue to cause bitterness, irritation or pain.

rant and rage
to behave in a very angry and hostile manner.

rap
1. a conversation: e.g. I had a rap with him the other day about that matter.
2. a criminal charge: e.g. He's in prison on a murder rap.
3. praise; recommendation: e.g. His new book got a good rap from the critics.
4. talk; discuss; chat: e.g. What are they rapping about?
See also:
take the rap

rap over the knuckles
a reprimand; scolding; censure; admonishment (often in the sense of not being severe enough for the crime).

rap session
talk; palaver; gossip.

rap-dancing/rapping
(see: breakdancing)

rapt
(also: wrapped) overjoyed; very enthusiastic about; totally infatuated: e.g. 1. He's rapt in her. 2. I'm rapt in that dress.

rap-up
extravagant praise.

rare as hen's teeth/rocking-horse shit
very rare, uncommon.

raring to go
eager to proceed, begin.

rasp
the act of sexual intercourse.

raspberry
noise made between the tongue and the lips expressing derision, scorn: e.g. If that creep keeps staring at me I'll give him a raspberry!

raspberry dip
sexual intercourse during menstruation.

raspberry tart
(rhyming slang) heart; fart.

rat
1. despicable, untrustworthy person.
2. person who goes back on his word.
3. to steal, pilfer: e.g. Watch those kids don't rat anything!
See also:
cunning as a shithouse rat
doesn't give a rat's arse
like a rat up a drain-pipe
looks like a drowned rat
looks like a rat looking over a straw broom
not worth a rat's arse
smell a rat
spunk-rat
suave as a rat with a gold tooth

rat on (someone)
1. betray, inform on (someone).
2. desert (someone) in a time of need.

rat through (something)
search, look for in a haphazard, untidy manner: e.g. He's been ratting through the cupboards all day looking for it.

ratbag
1. despicable, dishonest, untrustworthy person.
2. person whose behaviour is unconventional, disreputable; eccentric.

rat-fink
despicable, dishonest, untrustworthy person.

rat-race
the fierce competitiveness, unscrupulousness and frantic pace of city life, business, finance etc.: e.g. I'd like to leave the rat-race behind and go and live in the country.

rats!
exclamation of annoyance, frustration, disappointment, anger.

rats on stilts
greyhounds.

rat-shit
(also: R.S.)
1. broken; ruined; worthless; not operating.
2. second-rate; unsatisfactory; awful; no good.
3. depressed; dejected; ill; out-of-sorts; unwell.
4. dead.

ratter
1. deserter; betrayer.
2. (of a cat) ability to catch and kill rats: e.g. That cat's a terrific ratter.

rattle
disconcert; confuse; worry; agitate: e.g. This question will really rattle him.

rattle your dags!
get moving! hurry up!

rattled
disconcerted; confused; worried; agitated: e.g. Those reporters have got him so rattled he can't answer their questions properly.

rattle-trap
1. the mouth.
2. a rickety, dilapidated vehicle.

ratty
1. run-down; shabby; tatty; in a state of disrepair.
2. irritable; annoyed; bad-tempered.

raunchy
1. sexually appealing, provocative.
2. lewd; obscene; bawdy; coarse.

rave
1. a lively, animated party.
2. extravagant praise;

enthusiastic review, report: e.g. The critics gave it a rave.
3. animated conversation.
See also:
nothing to rave about

rave on
talk endlessly, tediously, at length: e.g. I wish she wouldn't rave on about it all the time.

raving idiot
1. mentally unbalanced person.
2. person who talks endless nonsense, or whose ideas are not considered worthy of serious consideration.

raw
1. inexperienced; unskilled; immature.
2. crude; lewd; indecent.
3. extremely frank, candid: e.g. That movie has raw sex in it.
See also:
come the raw prawn
in the raw

raw deal
unfair treatment: e.g. That was a raw deal he got from the court for that minor offence.

raw nerves
touchiness; irritability; sensitivity.

ray of hope
hint of hope, especially in times of trouble.

ray of sunshine
joyous, endearing person, especially a baby or small child.

Raygun
nickname for President Reagan of the U.S.A.

razoo
(see: haven't got a brass razoo)

razor gang
a group assigned to reduce expenditure, especially in politics.

razor-edge
1. sharp line of division.
2. critical, dangerous situation: e.g. His relationship with her is on a razor-edge at the moment.

razz
1. criticism.
2. tease; criticise; make fun of.

razzamatazz
1. showy, flashy, gaudy, extravagant display: e.g. There was a great deal of razzamatazz at the opening of the casino.
2. extravagant appeal: e.g. That new model car has a lot of razzamatazz.

razzing
criticism: e.g. I've had all the razzing I can take from him!

razzle-dazzle
1. exciting, showy display or activity.
2. excitement, animation.

RBT
Random Breath Test — roadside testing of the breath of drivers for alcohol content.

reach for the sky/stars
to aim high in ambition.

read
(see: you wouldn't read about it!)

read between the lines
to comprehend the truth hidden or implied behind outward appearances.

read (someone) like a book
understand the motives etc. of someone completely.

read (someone's) mind
to understand a person's thoughts in an intuitive manner.

readies/ready money
actual and available cash.

ready
a trick, scheme, act of deception.
See also:
work a ready

ready, steady, go!
a call to attention and the start of a race or some activity that is usually competitive.

ready, willing and able
willing, enthusiastic, especially with regard to sex.

real
very; total; utter: e.g.
1. He's a real idiot.
2. That's real good.
See also:
for real
the real McCoy/thing

really?
is that so, true?

really!
expression of surprise, censure, annoyance.

reams
lots of; plenty; a great number.

reap what (one) sows
to get back what (one) puts in; to receive as a consequence of (one's) actions; (ironically) to be treated as (one) treats others.

reaper and binder
cheese.

rear
buttocks; bum.
See also:
bring up the rear

rearrange (someone's) face
beat, punch (someone) in the face.

recap
tyre that has been retreaded.

reckon
conclude; think; suppose: e.g. 1. What do you reckon? 2. I reckon that's pretty good.
See also:
day of reckoning

record
history of one's criminal convictions: e.g. He's got a record as long as my arm.
See also:
like a broken-down record
off the record
on record

red
1. red wine: e.g. He only drinks red.
2. a communist.
3. pertaining to communism, socialism.
See also:
go in off the red
in the red
Leb red
like a red rag to a bull
make (someone) see red
out of the red
paint the town red
see red

red as a beetroot/lobster
1. very embarrassed: e.g. He went red as a beetroot when I took my top off.
2. sunburnt.

red carpet
highly favourable or preferential treatment: e.g. 1. The Queen gets the red carpet treatment wherever she goes. 2. The council rolled out the red carpet for her visit to the city.

red flag
1. a symbol of danger, warning.
2. pertaining to menstruation: e.g. She's flying the red flag this week.

red herring
irrelevant diversion designed to draw attention away.

red light
1. signal to stop, cease.
2. symbol for a brothel.

red ned
cheap red wine.

red peril
fear of invasion or expansion of communism, especially from the U.S.S.R.

red raw
1. red in the face with embarrassment.
2. very red, as of the skin after sunburn.

red sails in the sunset
pertaining to menstruation.

Red Socks
Melbourne VFL football team.

red steer
fire, either intentionally lit to burn off or bushfire: e.g. That raging bushfire was caused by some stupid farmer putting the red steer through his paddocks and it got out of control.

red tape
excessive adherence to formalities and rules, particularly in business and government.

red-blooded
virile; sexually aroused, aware.

red-faced
blushing with embarrassment or anger.

red-handed
in the act of committing a crime: e.g. The police caught him red-handed.

red-hot
1. (rhyming slang) pot (of beer).
2. current; the latest: e.g. Red-hot news.
3. angry; furious; violent: e.g. He's got a red-hot temper.

red-hot favourite
a sure winner, especially in horse-racing.

red-hots
(rhyming slang)
1. trots (diarrhoea): e.g. I've had a bad case of the red-hots since eating that stuff!
2. the trots, harness-racing: e.g. I won a lot of money at the red-hots last night.

Redlegs
Melbourne VFL football team.

red-light camera
photographic device recording drivers who fail to stop at a red light.

red-light district
an area where brothels abound.

redneck
prejudiced, biased, unsophisticated, uneducated person.

reds
1. communists.
2. amphetamines used by drug-addicts.

redskin
American Indian.

reef off
1. steal, pilfer.
2. take clothing off forcefully.

reef out
remove, pull out forcefully.

reefer
marijuana cigarette.

reel off
say, repeat, remember with ease.

ref
referee.

refadex
a street directory (Queensland).

refuse point blank
refuse absolutely, outright.

reg grundies

reginalds
(rhyming slang) undies; underpants.

register
make an impression: e.g. The fact that his wife and kids were killed last night hasn't registered with him yet.

rego
registration — especially for a car, vehicle.

regular
a regular customer: e.g. That pub survives on its regulars.

relations
(see: have relations)

relatives
(see: you can choose your friends but you can't choose your relatives)

relatives have arrived
(of a woman) menstruation has begun.

relieve oneself
to urinate or defecate.

rellies
relatives: e.g. I have to visit the rellies this week.

remember (oneself)
use caution with (one's) speech; speak politely; not swear or use vulgar language: e.g. Remember yourself when you meet my parents tonight.

remind (one) of
look like: e.g. You remind me of Elvis Presley.

rep
1. representative for some organisation.
2. travelling salesman for an organisation.

repeat
belch; experience an after-taste: e.g. Onions always repeat on me.

report card
student's assessment sent to parents.

repro
reproduction: e.g. That's not a genuine antique — it's a repro.

re-run
the showing again of a movie, television programme.

reserve (price)
the lowest (undisclosed) price a vendor will accept: e.g. The house sold for just over the reserve.

rest
short term of imprisonment.
See also:
at rest
day of rest
lay to rest
let it rest
no rest for the wicked.

rest home
place for old people who can no longer care for themselves.

rest on it
think about it.

rest on (one's) laurels
to be content with (one's) past achievements without trying or doing any more.

rest on (one's) oars
relax; cease work for a while.

rest room
lavatory facilities.

resting place
burial place.

return to the fold
to come back to the accepted way of thinking of a group; return to (one's) original loyalties.

returned soldier
soldier who has served overseas.

rev up
1. revitalise; inject with vigour, life; stimulate: e.g. This party needs some revving up.
2. (of a motor) speed up, accelerate.

reverse the charges
make a telephone call whereby the recipient pays the cost.

revs
revolutions.

revved up
full of life, vigour and enthusiasm; stimulated.

Rhodes scholar
(rhyming slang) dollar.

rhubarb
1. noisy argument, commotion: e.g. You should have heard the rhubarb going on next door last night!
2. rubbish; nonsense; worthless talk.

rhyme or reason
explanation for; logic: e.g. There's no rhyme or reason for the way he does things.

rhythm method
method of contraception that avoids intercourse during the times of ovulation in a woman.

rib
tease; make fun of: e.g. He's always getting ribbed by the others.
See also:
poke in the ribs
stick to (one's) ribs

rib-tickler
something funny, amusing.

rich
1. ridiculous; preposterous; exaggerated.
2. lewd; coarse; indecent; vulgar: e.g. That joke was a bit rich!
3. excessive; extreme.

Richard Cranium
dick-head — a stupid, disliked, contemptible person.

RID (Scheme)
(Queensland) Reduce Impaired Driving — a scheme similar in some respects to the Random Breath Test.

riddled with
abounding with; filled with: e.g. That dog is riddled with fleas.

ride (someone)
1. torment; tease; irritate: e.g. If he rides me any further I'll pack my bags and leave!
2. perform sexual intercourse with (someone).

'Frankly, I'm worried about your pa, Son. I've got this funny feeling that caring for 20,000 chooks is having an effect on him!'

Caring for 20,000 chooks has clearly caused Pa to become any number of the following: bananas, barmy, batty, bent, berko, bonkers, cracked, cuckoo, funny, ga-ga, gonzo, loco, loony, loopy, mental, nutty as a fruitcake, off the planet, out of his tree, potty, screwy, soft in the crumpet, troppo, unhinged, yarra. (For a more comprehensive list of synonyms for mad, see 'Foolishness and lunacy' in 'Word lists' at the end of the dictionary.)

See also:
let it ride
take (someone) for a ride
taken for a ride

ride roughshod over (someone)
to treat (someone) harshly and inconsiderately.

ridge/ridgy-didge
genuine; the truth; an unequivocal assurance: e.g. What I've just told you is the ridgy-didge (truth). (also: ridji-didge; rigidij; rijidij)
See also:
had the ridgy-didge

riding a wave of success
experiencing success, achievement.

riding for a fall
doing, behaving in a manner that is heading for trouble, failure.

riding high
elated; experiencing success, good fortune, happiness.

riding on
depending on: e.g. The whole project is riding on whether or not we get a bank loan.

riding on the pig's back
experiencing a period of success; extreme good fortune.

riding on the sheep's back
pertaining to the success of the Australian economy because of the sheep industry: e.g. Australia has been riding on the sheep's back for decades.

rifle-range
(rhyming slang) coinage; change (money).

rig
1. any horse-drawn or other vehicle equipped for something special.
2. semi-trailer; truck.
3. style of dress: e.g. Check the rig on that guy!
4. manipulate; pre-arrange, especially fraudulently: e.g. He's going to rig that race.

rig up
hastily make, arrange, erect, assemble.

rigged
fraudulently arranged or organised: e.g. That race was rigged.

rigged out
dressed up, especially conspicuously.

right
very; absolute; total: e.g. He's a right idiot!
See also:
dead right
do the right thing by
in the right
she'll be right!
she's right!
too right!

right as rain
okay; safe; satisfactory; as planned or expected.

right behind (someone)
supporting, backing, in total agreement with (someone): e.g. I'm right behind him on that matter.

right hand must never know what the left is doing
pertaining to total secrecy, confidentiality.

right on!
1. expression of approval, agreement.
2. indication that someone has guessed, understood, correctly.

right on target
1. punctual; as expected; true to form.
2. correct; true.

right slap-bang in the hey-diddle-diddle
in the exact centre; on target.

right under (one's) nose
in front of (one); obvious.

right up (one's) alley
in a field that one is familiar with, skilled, adept at: e.g. That new job is right up his alley.

right up (one's) jumper
following extremely closely behind (one) — especially of a vehicle: e.g. That police-car was right up my jumper all the way.

right up there
successful; amongst the elite of any enterprise.

right wing
group, political or otherwise, holding conservative views.

right-hand man
an indispensable helper.

righto
all right; okay; yes.

righto you lot!
interjection indicating that one has had enough of the activity, talk etc. going on; plea for the cessation of a particular activity, discussion, noise etc.

righty-o
(see: righto)

rigid digit
an erect penis.

rigidij/rijidij
(see: ridgy-didge)

rile
to anger, annoy, irritate, aggravate.

riled-up
very angry, annoyed.

ring
1. a telephone call or the act of telephoning.
2. bum; anus: e.g. He needs a kick up the ring!
See also:
dead ring
run rings around
throw (one's) hat in the ring

ring a bell
jog the memory: e.g. That name rings a bell.

ring of confidence
fresh breath and clean teeth — phrase coined by Colgate for a toothpaste advertisement.

ring true
appear sincere, truthful, honest, genuine: e.g. His alibi doesn't ring true to me.

ring up (someone)
make a telephone call to (someone).

ringer
1. a stockman, drover; station hand.
2. the fastest shearer of sheep.
3. identical with; twin: e.g. He's a ringer for his brother.
See also:
dead ringer for (someone)

ringie
person in charge of a two-up game.

ring-in
a substitute, especially a fraudulent one at the last moment in horse-racing.

ring-leader
chief trouble-maker, instigator.

ring-piece
rectum; anus; bum.

rinky-dink
(see: ridgy-didge)

riot
person or situation causing much hilarity or amusement: e.g. He's such a riot when he starts telling jokes.

rip
dangerous under-current in the sea.
See also:
let it rip
let rip
wouldn't it rip you?!

rip along
to drive, go, at great speed.

rip into it
attack, do with energy and enthusiasm.

rip into (someone)
abuse, berate, criticise, assail (someone) scathingly.

rip off
1. steal; pilfer: e.g. I'm sure he's the one who ripped my tools off out of my truck.
2. cheat; swindle; exploit; trick: e.g. 1. You've been ripped off. 2. Watch that crook doesn't rip you off.
3. over-charge; charge exorbitant prices for.

rip the crutch out of your nightie
(see: wouldn't that . . .)

ripe
1. drunk; intoxicated.
2. lewd; obscene; vulgar: e.g. That joke was a bit ripe!

ripe old age
advanced in years: e.g. That dog lived to a ripe old age.

rip-off
1. fraud; swindle; dishonesty; exploitation; act of cheating.
2. theft.
3. exorbitant price charged for something.

rip-off merchant
con-man; swindler; cheat.

ripped
intoxicated; drunk; under the influence of drugs; stoned.

ripper
excellent; splendid, admirable person or thing: e.g. 1. His new car is a ripper. 2. He's a ripper bloke!
See also:
you little ripper!

ripper-tune (Boris)!
exclamation of pleasure, excitement, admiration.

rip-roaring
boisterously wild and gay: e.g. What a rip-roaring party that was.

rip-snorter
(see: ripper)

rise
(see: give rise to; take a rise out of someone)

rise and shine
wake up and get out of bed and get going smartly.

rise to the bait
react to provocation, teasing, an enticement.

rise to the occasion
1. do something that is expected of you.
2. (of a man) have an erection when necessary.

rising star on the horizon
person whose ability, skill, talents etc. are becoming publicly renowned: e.g. He's a rising star on the political horizon.

risk hell and high water

risk (one's) neck
take grave personal risks, chances; place oneself in a position of danger; risk dire consequences.

rissole
R.S.L. — Returned Servicemen's League club.

ritzy
luxurious; sumptuous; elegant; opulent: e.g. He lives in a ritzy apartment in town.
See also:
put on the ritz

roach
the butt end of a nearly smoked marijuana cigarette.

roach clip
specially designed tweezers used to hold a marijuana cigarette when it gets too small to hold with the fingers.

road
(see: down the road; get the show on the road; hit the road; one for the road; rough road; take to the road)

road sense
knowledge about how to behave safely on the roads.

road-hog
motorist who drives without consideration for others.

roadie
manager of a travelling pop-group, musical band.

roadworthy
legally fit to be used on the roads; a certificate testifying to this.

roam around like a lost sheep
toil, wander, behave aimlessly, without direction or purpose.

roar off
depart; go in great haste.

roar shit out of (someone)

roar (someone) up
reprimand, scold, rebuke (someone) severely.

roaring success
highly successful; brisk: e.g. His business is a roaring success.

roast
1. a severe bout of criticism: e.g. That was a real roast they gave him.
2. criticise; deride; tease.
3. reprimand; scold: e.g. I'll roast him when he gets home!

roasting
a severe criticism, reprimanding, scolding.

rob Peter to pay Paul
to benefit one by depriving the other, especially in the matter of payment of money.

rob (someone) blind
cheat (someone) out of a great deal without much effort, easily.

rock
1. a large jewel, especially a diamond.
2. popular rock and roll music.
3. (plural) the testicles.
See also:
between a rock and a hard place
get (one's) rocks off
have/got rocks in (one's) head
like a shag on a rock
miserable as a shag on a rock
on the rocks
solid as a rock
the Rock

rock and roll
(see: rock-'n'-roll)

rock bottom
1. the lowest level: e.g. Prices have hit rock bottom.
2. the lowest level of fortune or luck.
See also:
hit rock bottom

rock college
prison.

rock on down
go to, especially with enthusiasm: e.g. We're rocking on down to the pub this afternoon.

rock the boat
to create, cause a disturbance, problem; upset or threaten the status quo.

rock-ape
1. oaf; idiot.
2. (derog.) dark-skinned person.

rock-bottom
the lowest level (of money, luck, fortune): e.g. These are rock-bottom prices.

rocker
a person whose style of dress and behaviour and taste in music are characteristic of those of the 1950s and 1960s.
See also:
go off (one's) rocker
off (one's) rocker

rocket
(of prices) increase dramatically: e.g. The cost of power will rocket in the next few years.
See also:
go like a rocket
off like a rocket
sky-rocket

rock-'n'-roll
style of pop-music, originating in the 1950s, with a simple and heavy beat.

rocky
1. unsteady; precarious: e.g. Their relationship is rocky at present.
2. (cap.) Rockhampton.

rod
an erect penis.
See also:
make a rod for (one's) back
rule with a rod of iron

rod-walloper
man who indulges in self-masturbation.

roger
the penis — especially an erect one.

roger!/roger dodger!
an expression indicating that one has understood, approves, or is in agreement with.

rogue's gallery
collection of police photographs of criminals.

roll
1. a wad of paper money: e.g. Did you see the size of the roll he had?
2. the act of sexual intercourse: e.g. I'd like to roll her.
3. to rob a person, often with violence: e.g. I got rolled in the park.
See also:
heads will roll

roll a joint
hand roll a marijuana cigarette.

roll in
1. arrive: e.g. Look who just rolled in!
2. retire; go to bed: e.g. It's time for me to roll in.

roll in the hay
have sexual intercourse: e.g. We had a roll in the hay last night.

roll over
resign, retire gracefully: e.g. It's time he rolled over and let a younger man take his place in the business.

roll over in (one's) grave
(of the dead) be offended: e.g. Dad would roll over in his grave if he could see what you've turned out like.

roll up
arrive: e.g. What time are your friends rolling up?

roll up (one's) sleeves
prepare for action, effort, a challenge.

roll with the punches
endure, tolerate, suffer, bear the bad with the good.

Roller
Rolls Royce car.
See also:
high roller

rollie
a hand-made cigarette.

rolling
1. very drunk.
2. very wealthy.

rolling in clover/dough/it/money
very wealthy, prosperous.

rolling in the aisles
extremely amused, overcome with laughter, especially of an audience: e.g. This comedian had us all rolling in the aisles.

rolling in the gutter
1. degenerate; depraved; decadent; debauched.
2. at the lowest possible level of poverty, ill-fortune.

rolling stone
aimless person; wanderer.

rolling stone gathers no moss
1. person who constantly moves around, changes jobs etc. will not gain possessions, riches.
2. an active, busy person will not stagnate or decline.

roll-ons
tight contour undergarment for women which also provides fastenings for stockings.

Rolls
Rolls Royce car.

Rolls Canardly
(of a car) dilapidated, powerless (rolls down one side of the hill and can hardly (canardly) get up the other).

Rolls Royce
the best of anything, when used as a comparison: e.g. This particular one is the Rolls Royce of them all.

roll-up
the attendance numbers at a meeting or occasion.

roll-your-own
a hand-made cigarette.

roly-poly
fat; obese; plump.

Roman hands and Russian fingers
(of a man) given to fondling, touching women in a lewd manner.

Roman nose
nose with a prominent, high bridge.

Rome wasn't built in a day
things of quality don't happen quickly — they take time.

Romeo
romantic man; womaniser.

romp home
do or win with ease: e.g. Our team romped home in the grand finals this year.

romp in the hay
have sexual intercourse.

romp it in
(see: romp home)

Ron
contraction of later on: e.g. I'll have one cigarette now and put another behind my ear for Ron.

roo
kangaroo.

roo bar
strong safety bar attached to the front of a vehicle to minimise the possibility of damage to the vehicle if an animal is hit.

roof
(see: go through the roof; hit the roof; live under the same roof; raise the roof; under one's roof)

roof over (one's) head
home; shelter; place to live.

roof party
drinks to celebrate the roof being finished in the building of a home.

rook
1. swindler; cheat.
2. an act of cheating; a swindle.
3. to swindle or cheat.

rookie
immature, inexperienced beginner.

room
(see: elbow-room; no room to swing a cat)

room to breathe/move
opportunity; scope; freedom: e.g. He left because there was no room to move in that business.

Roos
North Melbourne VFL football team.

rooster one day and a feather duster the next
(to be a . . .) pertaining to the uncertainty of success, especially in politics.

Roosters
Eastern Suburbs N.S.W. Rugby League football team.

root
1. sexual intercourse: e.g. Did you get a root last night?
2. partner in sexual intercourse: e.g. He's a good root.
3. to indulge in sexual intercourse: e.g. Did you root last night?
4. ruin; break; damage; destroy: e.g. He'll root the whole surprise party if he comes home too early.
See also:
wouldn't it root you?!

root for
barrack for; support; promote; applaud: e.g. We'll all be rooting for you when you go on stage tonight.

root out
seek out and destroy: e.g. The police will eventually root those criminals out.

rooted
1. tired; exhausted: e.g. I'm rooted after all that work!
2. broken; ruined; destroyed: e.g. This gadget is rooted!
3. thwarted; frustrated: e.g. He's rooted now that the taxation department knows about him.
4. dead.
5. indulged in sexual intercourse: e.g. He rooted my wife!
See also:
get rooted

roots like a rattlesnake
is extremely active and inventive during sexual intercourse.

rope
(see: at the end of one's rope/tether; give someone enough rope to hang himself; know the ropes; on the ropes; show someone the ropes; walk a tight-rope)

rope (someone) in
1. persuade, entice (someone) to take part.
2. cheat, trick or deceive (someone).

ropeable
(also: ropable) bad-tempered; angry; irritable.

rort
1. a boisterous, wild and energetic party or occasion.
2. an illicit scheme or racket.

rose
(see: bed of roses; look at life through rose-coloured glasses; smell like a rose)

rose among thorns
something good amid something bad.

rose buds
breasts; boobs.

rosiner
strong alcoholic drink; pick-me-up.

rosy
favourable; promising; cheerful: e.g. Things are looking rosy at last!

rot
1. nonsense; rubbish; worthless talk.
2. (as an exclamation) expression of scorn, dissent, contempt.

rot in hell
be damned, cursed forever; expression of contempt: e.g. He can rot in hell for all I care!

rot is setting in
failure, disaster etc. is taking hold; undesirable or corrupt influences are insidiously infiltrating.

rot your socks
expression of disgust, disappointment: e.g. Wouldn't it rot your socks the way prices keep going up!

rot-gut
strong, inferior liquor or unhealthy food.

rotten
1. drunk; intoxicated: e.g. He's rotten!
2. awful; unpleasant; disagreeable; despicable: e.g. He's a rotten crook!
3. unwell: e.g. I feel rotten today.
4. corrupt.

rotten apple
despicable, corrupt, unpleasant person.

rotten as a chop
very drunk; intoxicated.

rotten egg/sod

rotter
despicable, corrupt, unpleasant person.

rotten to the core
totally corrupt, despicable.

rough
1. unpleasant; awful; terrible: e.g. We had a rough time while we were lost in the bush.
2. worse luck, treatment, than one deserves: e.g. Losing his job over something that wasn't his fault was rough.
See also:
a bit rough
be rough on (someone)
cut up rough
ride roughshod over (someone)
take the rough with the smooth

rough around the edges
pertaining to a person or thing lacking refinement, sophistication.

rough as bags/guts/hessian drawers
1. uncultured; unsophisticated; uncouth; coarse.
2. rough; shoddy; not smooth.

rough as sandpaper
(see: rough as bags, 2.)

rough diamond
person lacking in sophistication, but nevertheless likeable.

rough end of the pineapple
unfair treatment.

rough guess
quick estimate made without prior consideration.

rough it
make do without ordinary comforts or conveniences: e.g. When we go camping we like to rough it.

rough on
1. unfortunate, unfair for: e.g. Losing his parents in that accident was rough on him.
2. treat severely; abuse; treat without consideration: e.g. 1. That headmaster is too rough on his students. 2. He's very rough on his cars.

rough road
a passage of time or a chain of events fraught with difficulty and problems.

rough (someone) up
abuse, beat, bash, assault (someone).

rough stuff
violence.

rough trot
(see: rough road)

rough-and-ready
suitable, satisfactory, in a crude and unsophisticated way.

rough-and-tumble
disorderly; haphazard.

rough-head
rustic, unsophisticated person.

roughie
a bawdy lout; one inclined towards violence and trouble.

roughly
approximately: e.g. He'll be here in roughly an hour.

rough-neck/nut
(see: rough-head; roughie)

rough-up
a brawl or noisy fight.

round
a drink for everybody in the group: e.g. I'll buy this round.
See also:
bring (someone) round
come round
do the rounds
do the rounds of the kitchen
get round (someone)
get round to (something)
give (someone) the rounds of the kitchen

round figures
to the nearest ten.

round file
the waste-paper basket, considered to be the best place to put or 'file' unwanted written material.

round it off
complete, finish off.

round robin
1. a petition signed by many, especially one in which signatures are arranged in a circle to disguise the order of signing.
2. sporting fixture designed so that each competitor or team plays against every other.

round the bend/twist
insane; mad; crazy.

round the corner
not far-away: e.g. He just lives round the corner.

round the traps
(been . . .) to have been here and there; knowledgeable about the gossip, news and happenings of a particular milieu.

round-the-clock
twenty-four hours continuously; all day and night.

rouse/roust on (someone)
scold, reprove, reprimand (someone).

row
(see: go for a row)

row
argument; commotion; dispute.

Roy
the sophisticated, status-conscious Australian — as opposed to 'Alf'.

Royal Alfred
(obsolete) large swag, as carried by a swagman.

Roys
Fitzroy VFL football team.

roziner
(see: rosiner)

R.S.
(short for: ratshit)
1. broken; damaged; ruined; not operating.
2. exhausted; tired; worn-out.
3. unsatisfactory; terrible; awful; no good.

RSPCA
Royal Society for the Prevention of Cruelty to Animals.

R.S.V.P.
répondez s'il vous plaît — please reply (French).

rub elbows with
come into social contact with: e.g. We rubbed elbows with the rich and famous at that ball.

rub it in
remind, tease someone continually about a mistake or shortcoming.

rub off
pass on to due to close contact: e.g. Some of his luck might rub off on to me if I keep seeing him.

rub salt into the wound
1. by word or action make someone who is already in a miserable situation feel worse.

2. make matters worse; exacerbate, aggravate, worsen the humiliation etc.

rub shoulders with
(see: rub elbows with)

rub (someone) out
kill, get rid of (someone).

rub (someone) up the wrong way
irritate, annoy (someone).

rub (someone's) face in it
remind (someone) in no uncertain terms of a mistake, error or shortcoming.

rub the shit in
(see: rub salt into the wound)

rub-a-dub-dub
1. pub; hotel; bar.
2. tub; a bath, wash.

rubber
1. condom; contraceptive sheath for the penis.
2. an eraser.
See also:
burn rubber to get there

rubber cheque
dishonoured cheque — such as one that 'bounces'.

rubber duckie
inflatable rubber boat.

rubber gumboot
(see: rubber, 1.)

rubberneck
1. over-curious person; sticky-beak.
2. tourist who is keen to see everything.
3. to look at with excessive curiosity.

rubber-stamp
to approve, give approval without due consideration: e.g. The council rubber-stamped that development along the beach-front against the wishes of the public.

rubbidy/rubbidy-dub/ rubbity/rubby
the pub.

rubbish
1. nonsense; worthless talk.
2. to criticise scathingly: e.g. He always rubbishes everybody.

ruby-dazzler
an outstanding, excellent person or thing.

ruckus
commotion.

ruddy
euphemism for bloody; damned: e.g. He's a ruddy idiot!

rude
unfair; excessive; inconsiderate: e.g. The price of that dinner was a bit rude!

ruffle (someone's) feathers
irritate, annoy, provoke, aggravate (someone).

ruffled
agitated; perturbed; worried.

rug up
put on clothing to keep warm.

rugged
1. difficult; demanding; uncomfortable; hard to tolerate: e.g. That was a rugged camping trip in the outback.
2. unsophisticated but strong, able-bodied.
See also:
a bit rugged

rugger
rugby football.

rugger bugger
rough, tough footballer.

rug-rats
young children, babies.

ruin with kindness
spoil, destroy good character by being too kind or doing too much for.

rule of thumb
procedure or method based on experience.

rule out
discard; abandon; eliminate.

rule the roost
be in charge, the boss, dominant.

rule with a rod of iron
to be severely strict, domineering.

Rules
Australian Rules football.

rum deal/go
unfair treatment.

rum sort of a do
an occasion or something that is odd, strange, unsatisfactory.

rumble
a fight, violent argument.

rummage sale
jumble sale; sale of second-hand items.

rummy
1. drunkard; alcoholic.
2. strange; queer; odd.

rumour has it
general talk, hearsay, of sometimes doubtful accuracy or validity: e.g. Rumour has it that she's pregnant again.

rump
bum; backside.

rumpus
commotion; noise; uproar.

rumpus room
informal room for recreation.

run
1. function; perform; operate: e.g. Does that motor run well?
2. manage; control: e.g. Who runs this business?
3. depart, go quickly: e.g. We have to run or we'll be late.
4. smuggle: e.g. He's running guns to the terrorists.
5. (sport) point scored.
See also:
cut and run
do a runner

had (someone) running
in the long run
in the running
not in the running
on the run

run a drum
(horse-racing) to perform, win, as tipped, forecast, expected.

run a tight ship
manage, control strictly.

run across (someone)
meet (someone) unexpectedly: e.g. I ran across him in the shopping centre.

run aground
ruined; foiled; in difficulties: e.g. His business operations have run aground due to lack of finance.

run all over (someone)
defeat, out-do, better (someone).

run around
behave promiscuously: e.g. I'd hate my daughter to run around like yours does.
See also:
get the run-around
give (someone) the run-around

run around in circles
act, do, behave in a haphazard, disorganised manner and consequently achieve little.

run around like a blue-arsed fly

run around like a chook with its head cut off
act, do, with great haste and activity, often in a haphazard and disorganised manner.

run around under the shower to catch the drops
(has to . . .) said of a person who is very thin.

run around with
keep company with; mix with, associate with: e.g. Who is she running around with now?

run at (someone) with a meat-axe
threaten with violence (often jocular or without real intent).

run away
1. elope; escape; flee.
2. an exclamation of dismissal: e.g. Run away! Can't you see I'm busy!

run away with
1. to steal, pilfer: e.g. Someone's run away with my beer!
2. to win easily: e.g. Our team ran away with the grand final.
3. believe, accept, especially wrongly: e.g. He's run away with the idea that he'll make a fortune from that crazy scheme!

run dead
(horse-racing) deliberately lose.

run dry
cease to flow or be provided: e.g. Our supplies of grog have run dry.

run for
stand as a candidate for election: e.g. He's running for president this year.

run for cover
flee, escape to safety.

run hot
1. perform extremely well, successfully.
2. be busy, active, used (of the telephone): e.g. After placing that advertisement in the newspaper, our phone has been running hot all day!

run in
arrested: e.g. He was run in for pushing heroin.

run into
1. amount to: e.g. That building ran into thousands of dollars over the original quote.
2. meet unexpectedly: e.g. I never expected to run into him on my holidays overseas.
3. expose oneself to: e.g. He ran into debt over that venture.

run it to earth
find (it) after a long search.

run like a hairy goat
1. run very fast.
2. run very slowly — especially in horse-racing.

run like stink
run, go, very fast.

run of bad/good luck
continuous course of bad/good fortune: e.g. He had a run of bad luck last year but things are improving now.

run of outs
(sport) losing streak.

run of the house
freedom to use, occupy, make oneself feel welcome in, a house.

run off at the mouth
to talk too much; say foolish things.

run off (one's) feet
exhausted, tired, due to excessive, busy activity.

run off with
1. steal: e.g. Someone's run off with my bag!
2. elope: e.g. She ran off with her boyfriend.

run on (something)
a time of public demand: e.g. There was a run on candles during the last power strike.

run on the smell of an oily rag
(of a car or motor) operate very efficiently, with a minimum of fuel.

run (one's) eye over
glance, look at briefly, quickly.

run out
1. to be completely depleted of stock, supplies: e.g. I've run out of beer.

2. drive out; expel: e.g. He was run out of town by the police for his criminal activities.

run out of puff/steam
wane; become less enthusiastic.

run out on (someone)
desert, abandon (someone) in a time of need.

run rings around/round (someone)
easily do better than (someone).

run short of (something)
not have enough of (something).

run (someone) down
slander, criticise, denigrate, discredit (someone) maliciously, scathingly.

run (someone) in
(of police or authorities) arrest (someone).

run (someone/something) to ground
track down and find eventually.

run the gauntlet/risk
expose oneself to chance or danger.

run the show
be in complete control.

run through
do, rehearse, review: e.g. We'll run through the rules one more time to make sure.

run up
1. erect, do, make hastily: e.g. 1. We ran up a fence to keep the cow from escaping. 2. Mum can run up a dress in a day.
2. accumulate quickly: e.g. He ran up a huge gambling debt at the races.

run up against
meet with difficulty: e.g. We ran up against a lot of problems at first, but things are better now.

run wild
behave in an unruly, unrestrained manner: e.g. Many parents let their children run wild.

runabout
small boat used for pleasure, fishing.

run-around
(see: get the run-around; give someone the run-around)

runaway
fugitive.

run-down
1. information; outline; summary: e.g. I want a run-down of the business by tomorrow.
2. tired; enfeebled; exhausted: e.g. I feel run-down and need a holiday.
3. dilapidated; derelict; in a state of disrepair: e.g. That house is run-down.

run-in
an argument, dispute, row, disagreement: e.g. I had a run-in with my boss and got fired.

runner
(sport) coach's messenger.

runners
sandshoes; tennis-shoes; sneakers.

runner-up
competitor taking second place.

running battle
1. a fight or commotion.
2. a continuing problem or set of difficulties: e.g. I've had a running battle trying to teach those kids some manners!

running hot
1. successful; performing extremely well.
2. extremely busy, active, used (of the telephone): e.g. The phone's been running hot all day.

running scared
in a state of panic, fear.

runny nose
nose that has mucus, snot leaking from it.

run-of-the-mill
ordinary; commonplace; average.

runs
(the . . .) diarrhoea; the shits.

runs in the family
inherent: e.g. Being overweight runs in the family.

runt
a small person.

rush
amyl nitrate — used as a stimulant drug by addicts.

rush in where angels fear to tread
act impetuously or dangerously.

rush (one's) fences
act without thinking.

rush-hour
busiest time; peak-hour.

Ruskies
people of Russian origin.

Russian roulette
a dangerous, life-threatening gamble.

rust-bucket
a dilapidated, rusty car.

rustle up
produce when needed: e.g. If you bring some snags for the barbie, I'll rustle up a salad.

rusty
unprepared; out of practice; unpolished: e.g. My guitar playing is rusty because I haven't played for years.

rut
a fixed pattern of behaviour or living that is difficult to change: e.g. I can't seem to get out of the rut I'm in.
See also:
in a rut
stuck in a rut

Ruth
(see: cry Ruth!)

sack
1. (the . . .) dismissal; termination of employment: e.g. He got the sack for coming late to work all the time.
2. to fire, dismiss from employment: e.g. I sacked him because he was too lazy.
3. a bed: e.g. Think I'll lie down in the sack for a rest.
See also:
fart sack
hit the sack
like two ferrets fighting in a sack
sad sack

sacred cow
delicate matter, revered topic or idea that is held to be immune from criticism.

sad sack
1. habitually morose, miserable person.
2. hopelessly ineffectual person.

saddle (someone) with
impose an unwanted responsibility or burden on (someone): e.g. I got saddled with the kids this weekend.

safe
(see: be on the safe side; play safe; there's safety in numbers)

safe as houses
not involving any danger or risk.

sail
(see: red sails in the sunset; take the wind out of someone's sails; trim one's sails)

sail close to the wind
to get close to the limits of decency or honesty.

sail in
act boldly.

sail under false colours
deceive by behaving abnormally.

sailing on unchartered waters
going into the unknown; doing something without experience or knowledge of what lies ahead.

Saint Louis blues
(rhyming slang) shoes.

Saints
1. St Kilda VFL football team.
2. St George N.S.W. Rugby League football team.

sale
(see: for sale)

salesman's dream
person who is easily convinced of the need to buy something.

salt
an experienced seaman.
See also:
go through (someone) like a packet of salts
rub salt into the wound
take it with a grain of salt
worth (one's) salt

salt away
store; accumulate; conserve.

salt of the earth
the finest of people: e.g. The Salvos, who do so much to help others in need, are the salt of the earth.

salt-mine
any place of drudgery and hard work.

Salvos
members of the Salvation Army.

sambo
(derog.) a negroid person.

sammie
sandwich.

sand
(see: head in the sand)

sandgroper
person from Western Australia.

sandie/sandy
Queensland sand-crab.

sandwich short of a picnic
(to be . . .) to be lacking in intelligence.

Sandy McNab
(rhyming slang) cab; taxi.

sanger
sandwich.

sap
foolish, weak person.

sappy
silly; weak; foolish.

sarge
sergeant; police officer.

sarnies
sandwiches.

sashay
strut; flounce; parade in an exaggerated manner.

sassy
impudent; brazen; impertinent.

sat
(see entries under 'sit')

sauce
impudence; cheek.
See also:
fair suck of the sauce bottle!

sauced
drunk; intoxicated.

saucy
impertinent; cheeky.

sausage
1. the penis.
2. a goal in Australian Rules football (from rhyming slang: sausage-roll).
See also:
haven't got a sausage
hide the sausage
silly sausage
sink the sausage
turn the lights out and play hide the sausage

sausage dog
dachshund breed of dog.

sav
saveloy.
See also:
fair suck of the sav!
sink the sav

save face
preserve one's reputation, prestige, ego, or good name.

save (one's) bacon
save, rescue (oneself) in a selfish manner.

save (one's) breath (to cool one's porridge)
1. don't bother speaking as it is not required, nor will it be listened to.
2. reserve (one's) energy for a more worthwhile, profitable cause.

save (one's) skin
escape from harm, danger.

save (someone's) bacon
rescue (someone) from an awkward situation or predicament.

save the day
rescue an occasion, situation, from ruin or failure.

saved by the bell
rescued from a bad situation at the last moment.

saving grace
a redeeming virtue that compensates for other faults.

savvy
1. intelligence; know-how; knowledge.
2. understand; comprehend: e.g. Do you savvy?

saw red
became infuriated, very angry.

saw stars
to have experienced the lights that flash in one's mind after a severe blow to the head.

For other possible entries beginning with 'saw' see entries listed under 'see'.

saw-bones
surgeon.

sawn-off
shotgun that has had the barrel sawn off to make it shorter.

sawn-off runt
contemptible small person.

sax
saxophone.

say
the right to speak one's views: e.g. Everyone will have their say at the next meeting.
See also:
have the last say
I say!
you don't say!

say a mouthful
to speak (one's) thoughts forcefully.

say (one's) piece
speak (one's) thoughts or opinions openly.

say the magic word
1. yes: e.g. He'd marry you tomorrow if you said the magic word.
2. fuck: e.g. He said the magic word in front of my parents and they kicked him out of the house.
3. say any word that is pertinent at the time.

say the wrong thing
say something that is inappropriate, unsuitable, embarrassing or improper.

say when
to indicate when to stop — especially in the pouring of a measure of alcohol.

say-so
1. ultimate authority, power of decision: e.g. The president has the final say-so.
2. command: e.g. On whose say-so did you do that?
3. gossip; mere assertion.

scab
1. a non-union worker; pertaining to non-union labour.
2. contemptible, mean person.

scabby
contemptible; mean; shabby; awful.

scads
large quantities of: e.g. He's got scads of money.

scale
to travel on public transport without paying: e.g. Kids often scale trams.
See also:
tip the scales

scallops
potato-cakes in Queensland — sea scallops in other states.

scallywag
rascal; naughty child.

scalper
person who buys tickets for a concert etc. and sells them later for a large profit.

scaly
crocodile.

scam
illegal, illicit business dealing; deceptive trick.

scandal
gossip; talk in general: e.g. What's the latest scandal around town?

scandalmonger
one who partakes in sordid gossip.

scarce
(see: make oneself scarce)

scarce as hen's teeth/ rocking-horse shit
very rare, scarce.

scare the dickens/living daylights out of (someone)

scare the pants off (someone)

scare the shit out of (someone)
frighten, alarm (someone) suddenly.

scarecrow
very shabbily dressed, unattractive person.

scared of (one's) own shadow
to be easily frightened, nervous.

scared shitless/stiff
very frightened.
See also:
running scared

scaredy-cat
(in children's language) a coward.

scarlet woman
woman of loose morals; prostitute.

scarper
to leave in a hurry.

scat
1. go away! get lost!
2. go away in a hurry.

scatterbrain
thoughtless, foolish, erratic person.

scatty
thoughtless; frivolous; silly; foolish.

scene
area of interest; subject of activity or involvement: e.g. Cooking and housework isn't his scene.
See also:
bad/good scene
behind the scenes
make a scene
not (one's) scene

schizo
schizophrenic person.

schlong
the penis.

schmaltz
1. rubbish! nonsense!
2. sickly sentimentality.

schmuck/schnook
fool; idiot; dill; contemptible person.

schnoz/schnozzle
the nose.

school
party of drinkers or gamblers.
See also:
of the old school
old school
old school-tie
tell tales out of school

school of thought
opinion; point of view.

schoolie
1. school teacher.
2. school prawn.

schoolies' week
boisterous end-of-year fun for school leavers.

school-kid
child of school age.

schoolmarm
1. female school teacher.
2. any old-fashioned, prim woman.

schooner
large glass of beer.

sci-fi
science-fiction: e.g. He's a real sci-fi fan.

Scobie
(see: get off my back Scobie!)

scoff
eat greedily: e.g. Mum baked a pie and he scoffed the lot!

scoff-out
a delicious and abundant meal.

sconce
the head.

scone
1. the head.
2. to hit on the head: e.g. I'll scone him if he does it again!
See also:
do (one's) scone
off (one's) scone

scone-gropers
young children.

scoob
a marijuana cigarette.

scoop
exclusive newspaper coverage of sensational value.

scoot
1. motorcycle.
2. to go along at high speed.
2. hasten off; depart quickly.

scorch
go, ride, travel at high speed: e.g. They were scorching down the highway with the fuzz in hot pursuit.

scorcher
very hot day.

score
1. a purchase of, or to purchase, a quantity of marijuana or other drug: e.g. He scored a good cheap score of dope from someone at the pub.
2. successfully attain one's goal of sexual intercourse: e.g. Did you score with that chick last night?
See also:
know the score
settle a score
what's the score?

score a hole-in-one
(of a man) obtain sex with a woman on a first date.

Scotchman's drawback
to sit in the path of and inhale smoke from another's cigarette.

Scotchman's Hill
over the road from Flemington Racecourse.

scot-free
unpunished; unharmed: e.g. He got off scot-free because of circumstantial evidence.

Scottie
a Scottish person or terrier. (also: Scotty)

scotty
vexed; angry; irritable.

scout
affectionate term for a man, fellow: e.g. He's not a bad scout.

scout around
to search, look for: e.g. I'll scout around for some firewood while you prepare the camp-site.

scrag
beat up, especially by wringing the neck of.

scrag-ends
the worst parts; left-overs.

Scraggers
Footscray VFL football team.

scram
1. to depart quickly.
2. go away! get lost!

scrambled
beaten, defeated soundly: e.g. Our team got scrambled by the opposition last week.

scrap
1. brawl; dispute; fight; quarrel: e.g. 1. What are they scrapping about now? 2. We had a scrap last night.
2. discard; reject; do away with: e.g. We scrapped that plan.

scrape
1. a shave.
2. a curette, abortion.
3. sexual intercourse; to copulate.
4. a noisy fight or brawl.
See also:
bow and scrape

scrape and scrounge
gain with effort or parsimony.

scrape the bottom of the barrel
1. call on, use, reserves (of money etc.) that are very low: e.g. I had to scrape the bottom of the barrel to pay for the rent this week.
2. call up scurrilous and slanderous criticism.

scrape through
get along under difficult conditions, especially financial.

scrape up
gain with effort or parsimony.

scrapper
argumentative person; fighter; trouble-maker.

scrappy
1. argumentative.
2. fragmentary, made up of odds and ends.

scratch
(see: from scratch; not up to scratch; unable to scratch oneself)

scratch my back and I'll scratch yours
do something for me and I'll do something for you — usually with reference to profitable gains.

scratched the surface
to have only just begun to realise the potential.

scratches
matches.

scratching
struggling for a living: e.g. That family is scratching for a crust since he died.

scratchy
1. irritable; ill-tempered.
2. out of practice; not very skilled or good at: e.g. He's a bit scratchy on the piano since he broke his arm.

Scrays
Footscray VFL football team.

scream
a funny, hilarious, amusing person or situation: e.g. He's a scream when he starts telling jokes.

scream blue murder
protest, complain loudly; cause a loud, vociferous commotion.

screamer
(Australian Rules football) a spectacular mark.
See also:
two-pot screamer

screaming for
in great need of: e.g. That car is screaming for a tune-up.

screaming heebies/irrits/meemies/willies
anything that causes intense irritation, annoyance, frustration: e.g. My lawn-mower gives me the screaming irrits — I can never seem to start it.

screw
1. sexual intercourse: e.g. Did you get a screw last night?
2. person as a sex object: e.g. He's a good screw.
3. a prison warder.
4. salary; wages; monetary arrangement: e.g. He's on a good screw with that new job.
5. a miser; niggard.
6. to have sexual intercourse: e.g. Did you screw him?
7. cheat; betray; defraud: e.g. Watch out that he doesn't screw you over that deal.
See also:
get screwed
good screw
have/got a screw loose
on a good screw
put the screws on (someone)

screw around
behave promiscuously; have many sexual partners.

screw (someone) to the wall
1. threaten (someone) with violence.
2. do wrong by, cheat, defraud (someone).

screw (something) up
ruin; mismanage; bungle; break; frustrate.

screw the arse off (someone)
indulge in vigorous sexual intercourse with (someone).

screw you!
term of contempt, dismissal.

screwball
eccentric or crazy person.

screwed
drunk; intoxicated.

screwed up
1. ruined; bungled; disorganised; chaotic; mismanaged; broken.
2. (of a person) mentally or emotionally disturbed or unbalanced; neurotic.

screwy
eccentric; weird; strange; odd; crazy; peculiar.

scrimp and save
save hard under difficult financial times.

scrimpy
meagre; paltry.

scrooge
miser; niggard.

scrounge
1. pilfer; steal.
2. borrow; cadge; sponge.
3. gain with effort or parsimony.

scrounge around
obtain by searching for, seeking out: e.g. He had to do a lot of scrounging around for the parts for that vintage car.

scrounger
1. cadger; sponger; free-loader.
2. person who acquires things without payment.

scrub
1. the country as opposed to the city: e.g. He sold up his business and lives in the scrub somewhere now.
2. a remote place.
3. cancel; do away with; discard: e.g. That idea didn't work so we scrubbed it.

scrub up all right
(of a person) look surprisingly good in fine clothes.

scrubber
1. domestic stock-animal that has escaped and taken to the wild.
2. immoral woman; slut.

scruff
1. shabby, untidy, slovenly person.
2. to pluck the feathers from a fowl.

scruff-nut
1. shabby, untidy, slovenly, unsophisticated person.
2. person with untidy, unkempt hair.

scruffy
untidy; shabby; slovenly; squalid; dirty.

scrumptious
delicious; tasty; delectable.

scuba
acronym for: Self-Contained Underwater Breathing Apparatus.

scum/scumbag
the lowest, most detestable type of person.

scunge
1. dirty, slovenly person.
2. mess; dirt; rubbish; filth.

scungy
messy; dirty; untidy; unpleasant.

scupper
to sink a boat on purpose.

sea
(see: all at sea; half-seas-over; not the only fish in the sea; out at sea)

Sea Eagles
Manly Warringah N.S.W. Rugby League football team.

seal (someone's) fate
irrevocably decide (someone's) fate.

search high and low
to search everywhere with determination.

search me
a statement meaning that one does not know.

sec
second; a short time: e.g. I'll be there in a sec.

secko
sexual pervert.

second
manufactured article that is below the required standard but still saleable at a reduced price.

See also:
come off second best
play second fiddle to

second childhood
senility.

second nature
acquired tendency, trait, habit that is now instinctive.

second sight
the faculty for seeing into the future; clairvoyance.

second string to (one's) bow
something kept in reserve; an alternative in case (one's) initial plan fails; two resources.

second thoughts
reconsideration.

second to none
the best.

second wind
(see: get one's second wind)

second-class/rate
inferior.
See also:
feel like a second-rate citizen

second-rate citizen
inferior person.

seconds
a second helping at meal-time.

security blanket
anything that provides the owner with a sense of security, confidence, safety, peace of mind.

security risk
person of doubtful loyalty.

see
1. deliberate; consider; think about: e.g. We'll have to see about that request, young man!
2. associate with, especially romantically: e.g. Does she see him any more?
3. make sure: e.g. I'll see that he does the job properly.
See also:
can't see for looking

see a man about a dog
1. euphemism for urination; to use the lavatory (especially of men).
2. to depart, leave, without telling.

see a star about a twinkle
euphemism for urination; to use the lavatory (especially of women).

see daylight through (someone's) ears
said of a person who is stupid, lacking in intelligence.

see eye to eye
agree; hold the same views, opinions: e.g. Those two never see eye to eye about anything.

see how the wind blows
to test public or other's opinion; to wait for some clues as to how things are going to turn out before taking decisive action.

see it out/through
continue, not abandon before completion.

see (one's) life flash before (one's) eyes
to experience vivid memories of (one's) lifetime at the moment of (one's) impending death.

see red
become suddenly enraged, angry: e.g. He saw red when he found out his car was stolen.

see (someone) for what he/she is
not be deceived by (someone); to perceive the true nature of (someone).

see (someone) out
to outlive (someone).

see (someone) through
to stand by, not abandon (someone) in a time of need.

see stars
to be dazed, experience the lights that appear to flash in the mind after a severe blow to the head.

see straight through (someone)
not be deceived by (someone).

see the back of (someone)
be rid of (someone).

see the light
1. understand fully; accept the truth of a matter.
2. be converted to Christianity.

see the light at the end of the tunnel
expression of hope, optimism at the near completion of a matter.

see the light of day
accept the truth; understand fully.

see the writing on the wall
perceive that some ominous event is about to take place.

see to it
make sure of; attend to.

see with half an eye
realise immediately; perceive the obvious.

see you

see you in the soup

see you later (alligator)
a form of farewell; good-bye.

seedy
1. shabbily disreputable: e.g. That's a seedy night-club.
2. feeling ill or out of sorts, especially after a hard night or a drinking session.
See also:
go to seed

seeing that
because; since; considering that: e.g. Seeing that you're going, I think I'll go too.

seeing things
hallucinating; imagining things.

seen
(see: now I've seen it all!)

seen better days
been in better condition: e.g. That old run-down house has seen better days.

seen better heads on a glass of beer
said of a person who has an unattractive or ugly face.

seen better legs on a billiard table
said of a person who has unattractive legs.

seen worse
a begrudging acceptance of what one is looking at.

self-made
successful; wealthy; powerful by one's own efforts: e.g. He's a self-made millionaire.

sell
(see: could sell boomerangs to the Blacks etc.; hard sell)

sell a dummy
(Australian Rules football) act of feinting at the ball, dummying: e.g. He really sold an outrageous dummy to his opponent.

sell like hot-cakes
be popular and sought after enough to sell quickly.

sell (one's) soul for
to go to any lengths for: e.g. He'd sell his soul to get that boat.

sell (oneself) short
under-rate, disparage (oneself); underestimate or belittle (one's) own worth or abilities.

sell (someone) down the river

sell (someone) out
to betray (someone).

Sellotape
sticky tape; adhesive tape. (Trademark)

sell-out
an act of betrayal.

semi
1. semi-trailer — a large transport truck.
2. semi-final sporting event.

send (one)
inspire, excite, enthusiastically enthrall (one): e.g. This music really sends me.

send shivers up (one's) spine
1. cause (one) to be afraid, full of fear.
2. excite (one).

send (someone) a line
write a letter to (someone).

send (someone) around the bend/twist
cause (someone) to become crazy, insane, mad, angry, very annoyed.

send (someone) on a wild-goose chase
inconvenience (someone) with a pointless, fruitless pursuit.

send (someone) packing
dismiss (someone) summarily.

send (someone) up
1. ridicule, mock, mimic, satirise (someone).
2. imprison (someone): e.g. The judge sent him up for ten years.

send-off
a going-away party for someone.

send-up
an act of sarcasm, mockery, satire, parody.

sensation
an event, person, that is wonderful, excellent, awe-inspiring, exciting: e.g. This new band is a sensation.

sent down
sentenced to a term of imprisonment: e.g. He was sent down for ten years.

sent up
1. (see: sent down).
2. mocked; satirised: e.g. The Prime Minister is often sent up in newspaper cartoons.

separate the men from the boys
separate, isolate the brave and the daring from the weak, irresolute.

separate the sheep from the goats
to separate the good, worthy, from the bad and unworthy.

seppo/septic/septic tank
(rhyming slang) Yank; an American person.

serious as a whore at a christening
not very serious at all.

serve
a severe rebuke, reprimand, scolding: e.g. He got a real serve from Mum for what he did.
See also:
give (someone) a serve

serves (someone) right
(someone's) punishment, misfortune, is deserved: e.g. Serves you right for being a cheat!

session
1. a steady drinking bout.
2. the opening hours of a pub, especially on a Sunday during restricted trading.
3. concentrated occasion of love-making or petting: e.g. Those two had a session in the back seat all the way through the movie.

set
breasts, tits: e.g. She's got a good set!
See also:
dead-set

set eyes on
catch sight of; see: e.g. I never want to set eyes on him again!

set foot in
enter; go in: e.g. If he ever sets foot in here again I'll call the police.

set for life
comfortably financial, wealthy: e.g. He's set for life since he won the lottery.

set in (one's) ways
unadaptable to change or others' points of view.

set of wheels
a car, vehicle: e.g. He just bought a new set of wheels.

set off
complement; improve, especially by contrast: e.g. That dress really sets off her complexion.

set on
determined: e.g. He's set on getting that job.

set on a bum steer
put on the wrong track or course of action through false suggestion; mislead into a fruitless course of action.

set on (someone)
attack (someone).

set (one's) heart at rest
stop worrying; ease (one's) anxieties.

set (one's) heart on
to desire a particular thing greatly.

set (one's) mind to
follow a determined course of action.

set (one's) sights on
determine, decide; be determined about something: e.g. He's set his sights on being the president of the company.

set (one's) teeth on edge
cause fear, discomfort, anxiety in (one).

set (someone/something) back
1. impede the progress of; interfere; cause problems, difficulties: e.g. His meddling and incompetence has really set the business back.
2. cost (someone) a specified or large amount of money: e.g. That car set me back a fortune.

set (someone) off
cause (someone) to start laughing uncontrollably.

set (someone) on (his/her) feet
1. make (someone) financially independent: e.g. That successful business has set him on his feet for the rest of his life.
2. help (someone) towards independence, especially after difficult or trying times.

set (someone) straight
tell (someone) the correct facts; point out an error to (someone).

set (someone) up
falsely incriminate (someone).

set the cat among the pigeons
create trouble, turmoil, chaos, activity.

set the pace
create a standard or speed for an activity for others to emulate.

set the wheels in motion
initiate, instigate, begin.

set the world on fire
achieve fame, success, public attention.

set up
falsely incriminated; framed: e.g. He's been set up — I know he didn't do it!

set up shop
to start a business or undertaking: e.g. He's going to set up shop in the main street.

set-back
disappointment; draw-back; arrest of progress: e.g. Losing him as manager was a set-back to the business.

settle a score
avenge a wrong; fulfil an obligation.

settle down
become established in a place, domesticity, a way of life etc., often with reference to marriage.

settle for
accept: e.g. He won't settle for that.

settle up
pay debts owing.

settler's clock
a kookaburra.

set-to
fight; argument.

set-up
1. a swindle, fraud.
2. a trap.
3. arrangement, manner of doing things: e.g. We'll explain the set-up before you start the job.

seven
(see: throw a seven)
See also:
at sixes and sevens

seven seas
the sailable oceans of the world.

seven-day wonder
anything that is short-lived, of no significance or importance.

seventh heaven
(see: in seventh heaven)

seven-year itch
boredom with married life or one's partner, said to happen after seven years and typified by a sexual desire for other partners.

sewn up
1. concluded; completed satisfactorily.

'We've landed in a way-out, remote place all right, Fred. But I've got a funny feeling we're not on the moon!'

The Ettamogah Pub is situated somewhere this side of the Black Stump, in the middle of nowhere. Any of the following would also describe its location: back o' Bourke, back of beyond, backblocks, backwaters, backwoods, billyo, brigalow, buggery, Bullamakanka, cactus, donga, goat country, mallee, mulga, never-never, outback, Outer Mongolia, scrub, sticks, Timbuktu, Woop Woop, wop-wops.

2. finished, out of business; ruined: e.g. He's sewn up now that the police are on to him.

sex
sexual intercourse: e.g. Did you have sex with her?

sex, Bex and Fourex

sex, drugs and rock-'n-'roll
catchphrase of anyone or pertaining to anyone whose main interest in life revolves around the three mentioned subjects.

sex kitten
a provocative woman.

sex shop
shop that sells pornography and other items for sexual gratification.

sexpot
a blatantly provocative woman.

S.F.A.
(Sweet Fanny Adams; Sweet Fuck-All) nothing at all or very little: e.g. He got S.F.A. from his parent's will.

shack up with
live with (usually intimately).

shades
sunglasses.

shadow
(see: mere shadow of one's former self)

shady
of doubtful honesty or character; disreputable; suspect.
See also:
on the shady side

shaft
1. malign; slander; abuse; criticise.
2. (of a man) perform sexual intercourse: e.g. Who has he been shafting lately?

shag
1. sexual intercourse: e.g. You're not getting a shag tonight.
2. person as a sex object: e.g. She's a good shag.
3. have sexual intercourse: e.g. He'd like to shag her.
See also:
like a shag on a rock

shagged
tired; exhausted: e.g. I'm shagged after all that work in the sun.

shagger's back
(joc.) tiredness of muscles after a particularly energetic occasion of sexual intercourse.

shaggin' wagon
a panel-van type of vehicle popularised by the young surfie generation and typically carpeted or converted into a sleep-out.

shaggle-baggle
friendly nick-name among friends.

shake a leg
hurry up.

shake hands with the unemployed

shake hands with the wife's best friend
(of a man) to urinate.

shake it up!
hurry up!

shake off
rid oneself of: e.g. He can't seem to shake off his cold.

shake (someone) down
search, frisk (someone).

shake (someone) off
elude, escape from, get rid of, evade (someone).

shake (someone) up
1. motivate (someone); arouse from lethargy.
2. un-nerve, worry, frighten (someone).

shake-down merchant
con-man; trickster; swindler; thief; criminal.

shakes
a state of nervous trembling induced by drugs, alcohol, a fright or shock etc.
See also:
in a brace of shakes
in two shakes (of a dog's tail)
no great shakes

shake-up
thorough revamping, change, renovation: e.g. This business needs a shake-up to get it going again.

shaking in (one's) shoes
trembling with fear, worry, anxiety.

Shaky Isles
New Zealand.

shame
a regrettable or unlucky occurrence: e.g. What a shame he didn't get that job.
See also:
put (someone) to shame

shanghai
1, child's catapult, slingshot.
2. involve someone in an activity without his knowledge or against his wishes.
3. steal.

shanks
the legs.

shank's pony
to walk, on foot, as opposed to travelling by any other means: e.g. How did he get there? On shank's pony!

shape up
1. develop; progress: e.g. How are things shaping up in the shop?
2. perform better; try harder; get better: e.g. He'd better shape up or else the boss is going to fire him.

shape up or ship out
do what is required or leave; improve one's performance or leave.

shaping up a beaut
developing, progressing well.

share and share alike
(often satirical) divide or distribute evenly goods, problems, possessions etc.

share-pusher
con-man; swindler; glib salesman.

shark
1. moneylender (usually at high interest rates).
2. extortioner; swindler; trickster.
See also:
compassionate as a starving shark
land shark
lower than shark shit
wouldn't shout if a shark bit him

sharkbait
swimmer at the beach taking risks outside safety areas.
See also:
wouldn't use (someone) for sharkbait

Sharks
Cronulla–Sutherland N.S.W. Rugby League football team.

sharp
1. a swindler, cheat.
2. shrewd, often dishonest; unscrupulous.
3. clever; intelligent; perceptive.
See also:
look sharp!
so sharp you must sleep in the knife-drawer!
so sharp you'll cut yourself one day!

sharp as a bowling ball
dumb; stupid; lacking in intelligence or wit.

sharp as a tack
mentally acute; quick-witted.

sharp-eyed
1. having keen eyesight.
2. perceptive; acute mental intelligence; quick-witted.

sharpie
member of a youth gang characterised by aggressive behaviour and very short hair.

sharp-shooter
1. skilled shooter.
2. person skilled in sorting out trouble and problems.

sharp-tongued
sarcastic; acrimonious; bitter.

shat
past tense of: shit.

shat off
extremely annoyed, frustrated, angry.

shatter (one's) dream
upset, destroy (one's) hopes.

shaver
fellow; young man; youngster.

shebang
affair; business; thing: e.g. This whole shebang smells fishy to me!
See also:
whole shebang

sheckles
(see: shekels)

she'd fuck anything wearing trousers
derog. remark about a woman's promiscuity or choice of men.

shed some light on
make clear; explain; make understood.

sheep
shy, submissive, stupid, brainless people.
See also:
black sheep of the family
make sheep's eyes at (someone)
may as well be caught for a sheep as a lamb
separate the sheep from the goats
wolf in sheep's clothing

sheep dip
cheap, inferior liquor, alcohol.

sheepish
shy; meek; submissive.

sheep's eyes
amorous glances.

sheet anchor
last resource; something depended on as one's last hope.

sheila(h)
1. young woman; girl; girlfriend.
2. a man who is weak, effeminate, lacking in bravado.

sheister
(also: shyster) trickster; swindler; cheat.

shekels
money.

shelf line
item sold in a shop.

she'll be apples/jake/right/sweet!
expression of reassurance, approval; all is well.

shell of a man
man weak in character.

shell out
pay, hand over money or goods, usually unwillingly: e.g. I had to shell out for the rent this month, so I'm broke.

shellacking
a sound thrashing, defeating, beating.

shelve
postpone; put away for later consideration.

shemozzle
a state of confusion, disturbance; muddle; uproar; mess.

shenanigan
1. nonsense; mischief; prank.
2. deceit; trickery.

shepherd's clock
a kookaburra.

sherbet
beer: e.g. We're all going to the pub to sink a few sherbets.

she's apples
(see: she'll be apples)

she's got balls
said of a woman with masculine characteristics, daring, bravado.

she's had more pricks than a dart-board/pin-cushion
said of a woman who is promiscuous.

she's on!
exclamation of one's acceptance of a wager, gamble, bet.

she's right/sweet!
exclamation of approval, indicating everything is fine.

shicer
a swindler, con-man, trickster.

shicker/shicky
drunk; slightly intoxicated.
See also:
on the shicker

shift house
move to another residence.

shift your butt/carcass!
move yourself!

shifty
deceitful; evasive; unscrupulous; devious; dishonest; sly.
See also:
pull a shifty

shilling short
(see: shingle short)

shilly-shally
procrastinate; refrain, shy from taking a positive course of action.

shimmy
1. a chemise.
2. wobbling of unbalanced wheels of a car.
3. a dance characterised by shaking hips, shoulders and arms.

Shinboners
North Melbourne VFL football team.

shindig/shindy
1. festive gathering; party, especially a noisy one.
2. quarrel; argument; noisy row.

shine at
excel at: e.g. He's not good at English but he shines at Maths.
See also:
take a shine to
take the shine out of

shiner
a black eye.

shingle short
(to be a . . .) to be mentally disturbed, stupid or lacking in intelligence.

shinny
to climb using the shins.

shiny-arse/bum
1. lazy, idle person; one who sits around a lot; a bludger.
2. an office worker; public servant.

ship (something) out
get rid of (something).
See also:
shape up or ship out

shipshape
neat; tidy; organised.

shiralee
(obsolete) a swag carried by a swagman.

shirt
(see: boiled shirt; give someone the shirt off one's back; keep your shirt on!; lose one's shirt; stuffed shirt)

shirt-lifter
a male homosexual.

shirty
angry; bad-tempered; annoyed; irritated.

shit
1. excrement; faeces.
2. a contemptible, despicable, ill-disposed person: e.g. He's a real shit!
3. nonsense; lies; worthless talk: e.g. That's a lot of shit!
4. marijuana; hashish; dope; heroin: e.g. This is real good shit.
5. to defecate: e.g. I need to shit.
6. (as an exclamation) annoyance; frustration; disappointment; disbelief.
See also:
a real shit
always in the shit — it's just the depth that varies
as much chance as pushing shit uphill with a pointed stick
blow shit out of (someone)
bored shitless
built like a brick shithouse
bullshit
came out like a shower of shit
chickenshit
could use her shit for toothpaste
couldn't give a shit
cunning as a shithouse rat
dead-shit
do bears shit in the woods?
easy as pushing shit uphill with a pointed stick
enough to give (one) the shits
frogshit
full of shit
get (one's) shit together
get the shits
give a shit
give (someone) shit
give (someone) the shits
go for a row of shithouses
go like a power of shit
handles like a bag of shit
happy as a pig in shit
have/got shit for brains
haven't got a shit's show
heap of shit
heap shit on (someone)

holy shit!
horse-shit
if bullshit was music, he'd be a big brass band on his own
if he had a shit his head would cave in
in a shit
in the shit
like pushing shit uphill with a pointed stick/ rubber fork
long streak of pelican shit
low as shark shit
no shit
not worth a pinch of goat-shit
not worth a shit
pack shit
paddling up shit creek in a barbed wire canoe
punch shit out of (someone)
put shit on (someone)
put the shits up (someone)
rat-shit
roar shit out of (someone)
rub the shit in
scarce as rocking-horse shit
scare the shit out of (someone)
scared shitless
shovel shit
so tight he wouldn't give you the steam off his shit
stick like shit to a blanket
stiff shit!
take the shitter out of (someone)
the shits
thinks his shit doesn't stink but his farts give him away!
treat (someone) like shit
up shit creek (without a paddle)
up the shit
up to (one's) neck in shit
weak as shit
weak shit
when the crow shits
when the shit hits the fan
wouldn't give you the steam off his shit
wouldn't say shit for a shilling

shit a brick!
expression of annoyance, frustration, irritation, wonder, disbelief, disappointment.

shit all over (someone)
1. defeat (someone) soundly; humiliate, better (someone).
2. betray, swindle, cheat (someone).

shit bricks
become angry, enraged: e.g. He's going to shit bricks when he finds out that his car was stolen.

shit for brains
(to have . . .) to be lacking in intelligence; to be foolish, stupid.

shit in (one's) own nest
to spoil, ruin (one's) own circumstances; disadvantage (oneself) through (one's) own actions.

shit it in (carrying a brick)
1. win, defeat, beat easily: e.g. We're going to shit this race in without a worry!
2. do a task with ease: e.g. We'll shit this job in by the end of the day.

shit of a thing
awful, unpleasant, despicable, annoying (person, thing, situation etc.).

shit on the liver
(to have . . .) to be bad-tempered, irritable, ill-disposed.

shit (one's) pants

shit (oneself)
1. be afraid, full of fear.
2. receive a sudden and unexpected shock (that is usually unpleasant): e.g. He'll shit his pants when he finds out his car has been stolen.
3. become very angry.

shit (someone) off
annoy, disgust, anger (someone): e.g. He will really shit me off if he doesn't arrive on time.

shit tacks
be afraid, full of fear: e.g. I shit tacks every time I go near that spooky old house.

shit through the eye of a needle at forty paces
to be suffering from diarrhoea or to have taken a purgative.

shite
euphemism for: shit.

shit-features
despicable, unpleasant person.

shithead
1. despicable, mean, unpleasant person.
2. regular smoker of marijuana.

shit-heap
dilapidated, worn-out, rusty car or vehicle.

shit-hot
excellent; first-rate; very good; admirable.

shithouse
1. the toilet, lavatory.
2. awful; despicable; unpleasant: e.g. That meal was shithouse.
See also:
built like a brick shithouse

shit-kicker
1. worthless, insignificant person.
2. one who does manual labour or menial tasks: e.g. He's just a shit-kicker in the business.

shit'ouse
(see: shithouse)

shit-puncher
a male homosexual.

shits
(see: the shits)

shits (one)
annoys, angers, disgusts (one): e.g. He shits me the way he behaves.

shit's show (in hell)
chance (usually in the negative): e.g. He hasn't got a shit's show of getting that job.

shit-scared
very scared, afraid.

shit-stabber
a male homosexual.

shit-stirrer
1. trouble-maker; activist.
2. practical joker; teaser; one who enjoys upsetting people.

shitty
1. bad-tempered; sulking; angry: e.g. What's he shitty about?
2. not satisfactory or up to standard; awful; disappointing: e.g. That was a shitty restaurant.
See also:
crack a shitty
pack a shitty

shitty-livered
bad-tempered; ill-disposed; angry; sulky.

shit-wit
stupid person; lacking in intelligence; a fool.

shiver me timbers!
exclamation of surprise, amazement, disbelief.

shivers!
exclamation of surprise, amazement, disbelief, annoyance, frustration, disappointment.
See also:
give (one) the shivers

shivoo
a rowdy party, social occasion.

shmo
foolish, stupid person.

shock tactics
sudden, sometimes violent action designed to cause a reaction.

shocker
1. something lewd, sensational, scandalous.
2. an unpleasant person or thing.
3. very bad or disappointing: e.g. That film was a shocker.

shocking
very bad; disappointing.

shocking pink
extremely bright, luminous pink.

shoe
(see: be in someone's shoes; hate to be in someone's shoes; if the shoe fits wear it; step into someone's shoes)

shoe's on the other foot
the situation, position is reversed, completely changed.

shoestring budget
meagre financial reserves; inadequate amount of money.
See also:
on a shoestring

shonk
underhanded, illegal or illicit transaction, business deal.

shonky
1. underhanded; illegal; illicit; crooked.
2. unreliable: e.g. Many new cars are shonky.

shoo!
go away!

shook on (someone/something)
infatuated with; wildly enthusiastic about.

shook up
emotionally upset; worried; anxious.

shoosh
be quiet; stop the talking, noise.

shoot
1. ask; speak (your question, request).
2. ejaculate, especially prematurely.
3. inject illicitly an intravenous drug: e.g. He's been shooting heroin for years.
4. (sport) kick, throw for goal.
See also:
if it moves shoot it, if it doesn't, chop it down

shoot a fairy
to fart.

shoot off
go, depart in haste.

shoot (one's) bolt/load
(of a man) ejaculate — especially prematurely.

shoot (one's) mouth off
1. to talk too much, especially indiscreetly.
2. exaggerate; boast.
3. use sudden, abusive and scathing language.

shoot (someone) down (in flames)
defeat (someone) soundly in an argument, debate; destroy (someone's) aspirations, hopes.

shoot through
go, depart, especially without proper formality: e.g. They shot through without paying the rent.

shoot through like a Bondi tram
1. (see: shoot through)
2. go, depart in haste.

shoot up
1. inject illicitly with an intravenous drug.
2. grow quickly: e.g. Those kids have really shot up since I last saw them.

shooter
(cricket) ball that goes along the ground; a grubber.

shoot-out
exchange of gunfire.

Shop
(the . . .) University of Melbourne as distinct from 'the Farm' (Monash University).
See also:
set up shop
shut up shop
talk shop

shop around
1. to look for the best bargain to purchase.
2. to look for a suitable (sexual) partner: e.g. He's shopping around for a wife.
3. make extensive inquiries.

shoplift
to steal from shops.

shoptalk
conversation centred around one's business instead of general conversation, and often considered as bad manners.

shopworn
over-used; soiled; stale; over-worked; sordid.

short
lacking in money; broke: e.g. I'm a bit short this week.
See also:
caught short
cut (someone) short
fall short of
make short work of
sell (oneself) short

short and curlies
pubic hairs.
See also:
got (someone) by the short and curlies

short and sweet
brief: e.g. Keep the speech short and sweet.

short list
final list of favourable candidates for a position.

short motor
a car motor, usually without the electricals and cylinder head.

short of a sheet of bark/shilling/shingle

short of change

short of/on grey matter
to be lacking in intelligence; foolish; stupid; crazy.

short shrift
(see: get the short shrift)

short wick
(to have a . . .) quick to lose one's temper; easily angered: e.g. He's got a short wick so be careful what you say to him.

short-arse
person small in stature; short person.

short-change
1. give less than the correct change of money.
2. cheat, swindle, fraudulently deceive someone.

short-circuit
1. shorten procedures; take a short-cut.
2. foil, ruin, spoil something or someone's plans.

shortie
a short person.

short-lived
lasting a short time only; of no significance or importance.

short-sighted
lacking foresight, imagination.

short-tempered
easily angered; quick to lose one's temper.

shorty
(also: shortie) a short person.

shot
1. an injection of drugs.
2. a measure of alcohol: e.g. I wouldn't mind a shot of brandy.
3. drunk; intoxicated: e.g. You won't get any sense out of him now — he's shot!
4. try; attempt: e.g. I'll have a shot at it.
5. photograph: e.g. That's a good shot of you.
6. reply; remark: e.g. Her parting shot was very sarcastic.
See also:
big shot
call the shots
get shot
get shot of (someone)
half shot
have a shot
have a shot at (someone)
hot-shot
I'll get shot
like a shot
long shot
not by a long shot
take a long shot
that's the shot!

shot in the arm
injection of vigour; boost; renewed confidence: e.g. Winning the finals was a shot in the arm for a team whose morale was low.

shot in the dark
random guess; wild speculation.

shot (one's) bolt
1. to have reached (one's) limits, the end of (one's) endurance.
2. (of a man) to have ejaculated — especially prematurely.

shot through (like a Bondi tram)
(see: shoot through; shoot through like a Bondi tram)

shot to the eyeballs
very drunk, intoxicated.

shotgun wedding
a forced or hurried wedding due to the pregnancy of the bride.

should have your shin-pads on you're grovelling so much
a remark to someone who is behaving in an obsequious manner.

shoulder
to assume responsibility for; answer for: e.g. The company will shoulder the cost of transport for its employees.
See also:
chip on (one's) shoulder
cold shoulder
give (someone) the cold shoulder
have/got broad shoulders
head and shoulders above
need a shoulder to cry on
over-shoulder-boulder-holder
rub shoulders with
square (one's) shoulders
straight from the shoulder
take a load off (one's) shoulders

shoulder to shoulder
1. crowded.
2. united in activity, support, action.

sh'ouse/shouse
abbreviation of: shithouse.

shout
1. a round of drinks (or something else) paid for by someone; someone's turn to buy: e.g. 1. This is my shout. 2. Whose shout is it?
2. to pay for or provide at one's own expense, particularly alcoholic drinks: e.g. I'll shout this round.
See also:
wouldn't shout if a shark bit him

shout (someone) down
to reduce (someone) to silence or drown out (someone's) voice by shouting, talking louder.

shove it (up one's arse)!
exclamation of contempt, dismissal, refusal.

shove off
1. exclamation of dismissal; go away!
2. to leave, go, depart.

shovel shit
to work at menial-labour-type jobs: e.g. I don't want to shovel shit for the rest of my life.

show
1. a theatrical performance for entertainment: e.g. That was a good show.
2. a party, social occasion: e.g. That was a terrific show at your place last night.
3. chance: e.g. He doesn't stand a show of winning.
4. organisation; business; undertaking: e.g. That company is quite a big show now.
5. ostentation; spectacle; mere display: e.g. He puts on a real show every time I take him to the dentist.
6. appear; arrive: e.g. What time is he due to show?
See also:
all show
for show
get the show on the road
give the show away
good show
haven't got a shit's show (in hell)
haven't got a show (in hell)
no show
peepshow
run the show
stand a show
steal the show
who's running this show!

show a clean pair of heels
escape; flee; bolt.

show a leg
put in an appearance; attend; go to: e.g. Are you going to show a leg at this year's ball?

show biz
show business — the business of public performance, entertainment, theatre etc.

show of hands
a method of voting — the raising of hands to be counted.

show off
to flaunt, boast, exhibit for attention: e.g. She always shows off in front of him.

show (one's) face
make an appearance; attend publicly: e.g. He's too ashamed to show his face after making such a fool of himself.

show (one's) hand
declare (one's) intentions.

show (one's) true colours
make (one's) true character, personality, known, especially where it had been previously hidden by deceit and false declarations.

show pony
1. one whose appearance is better than his actual performance.
2. (Australian Rules football) lairising footballer.

show pony or a work horse
false or genuine; mere appearance or actual performance: e.g. We'll find out whether she's just a show pony or a work horse after she's worked in this business for a month.

show (someone) a thing or two
1. a threat of violence towards (someone): e.g. I'll show him a thing or two next time I see him!
2. show, reveal something to (someone) that will undoubtedly surprise, astound, amaze, awe.

show (someone) one's etchings
joc. form of sexual innuendo, invitation.

show (someone) the door
turn (someone) out in anger, disgust.

show (someone) the ropes
teach, instruct, advise (someone) in the necessary skills, facts, methods.

show (someone) up
humiliate, embarrass (someone); better (someone).

show the way
set an example for others to follow.

show up
1. arrive; put in an appearance: e.g. When did he show up?
2. stand out by contrast; make obvious: e.g. His argument really showed up her ignorance.

showdown
confrontation; an open trial of strength.

show-off
braggart; ostentatious exhibitionist.

shrapnel
coinage; small change; coins as opposed to paper money.

shrewdie
1. shrewd, astute person.
2. con-man; trickster.

shrimp
small, insignificant person.

shrink
psychiatrist.

shrinking violet
shy, timid person; sissy; weakling.

shrug off
disregard; pay no attention to: e.g. He shrugged off their sarcastic comments.

shucks!
exclamation of annoyance, frustration, regret etc.

shunt
(see: get the shunt)

shush!
be quiet! hush!

shut down on
put a stop to: e.g. The police are going to shut down on illegal gambling halls.

shut mouth catches no flies
a warning not to disclose any confidences, secrets.

shut (one's) big mouth
1. cease talking.
2. cease disclosing confidences, telling secrets.

shut (one's) eyes to
to ignore on purpose; refuse to see, acknowledge the true facts.

shut up
1. be quiet! stop talking!
2. confine, imprison: e.g. The courts will shut him up for life for what he's done.

shut up shop
1. close, finish, end a business, enterprise: e.g. They went broke and had to shut up shop.
2. finish, end an activity for the day: e.g. It's time to shut up shop and go to the pub for a drink.

shut your face/mouth/trap!
1. be quiet!
2. cease revealing confidences, telling secrets.

shut-eye
sleep: e.g. I don't think I'll go out tonight — I need some shut-eye.

shutterbug
a camera, photographic enthusiast.

shy of chips

shy on the necessary
to be lacking money, broke.

shyster
cunning, deceitful person of questionable honesty; an unscrupulous dealer.

sic
to incite a dog to attack: e.g. I'll sic my dog on to you if you come back here again.

sick
morbid; in bad taste: e.g. That joke was sick!
See also:
make (one) sick

sick and tired of
weary of; had enough of; reached the limit of one's tolerance of; annoyed and disgusted with: e.g. I'm sick and tired of the way she always complains.

sick as a dog
ill; not feeling well.

sick of

sick to death of
(see: sick and tired of)

sickening
1. disgusting; annoying.
2. overly sentimental.

sickie
1. a day off work on the pretext of being sick: e.g. I took a sickie yesterday and went to the beach.
2. industrial absenteeism, a day's sick-leave whether one is sick or not.

sickle
motorcycle.

side
(see: bit on the side; get on the wrong side of; on the . . . side; put on side; take sides; whose side are you on?)

side effect
any effects produced in addition to those intended, such as the secondary (often unpleasant or dangerous) effects of a drug.

side with the devil
act, behave with evil intent.

sidekick
close associate, friend, assistant.

sideline
work or activity carried out in addition to one's main activity or job.

side-splitting
extremely amusing, funny.

side-tracked
diverted; distracted from the main issue or course.

sight
1. person or thing of odd, ridiculous, silly appearance: e.g. She was such a sight in that tight dress!
2. much; more: e.g. It could have been a sight worse!
See also:
have/got (one's) sights set on
lower (one's) sights
not by a long sight
out of sight
raise (one's) sights
set (one's) sights on

sight for sore eyes
a pleasant sight; a sight that gives relief: e.g. You're a sight for sore eyes! I've been looking for you all day!

sight unseen
without previous inspection: e.g. He bought the house sight unseen.

sign language
use of gestures to communicate with deaf people.

sign of the times
anything new, controversial (sometimes unpleasant) that is typical of the rapid (and often unwanted) change in society: e.g. The increase in crimes of violence is a sign of the times.

sign off
cease broadcasting, working etc.

sign on
hire or employ by contract: e.g. I just signed on a new manager.

sign on the dotted line
sign one's name to a contract; conclude, confirm or settle an agreement or contract: e.g. Make sure you know all the facts before you sign on the dotted line.

sign (one's) life away
(often joc.) to sign a binding contract, such as hire-purchase: e.g. I just signed my life away to buy that car!

sign up
to enlist in the armed forces: e.g. He signed up for the Army.

silent but deadly
expulsion of wind from the anus, fart that is not heard but smells very offensive.

silent cop
a traffic bump or dome designed to direct traffic in a specific way or direction.

silent partner
partner in business who takes no active part but is nevertheless necessary for some reason.

silk
(see: in the silk)

silly
pertaining to a state of surprise, stunned bewilderment: e.g. I was knocked silly by a flying tin can!

silly as a cut snake

silly as a square wheel

silly as a tin of worms

silly as a two-bob watch

silly as a wet hen

silly as a wheel
crazy; foolish; erratic; stupid; unreliable; unpredictable.

silly sausage
silly, foolish person.

silly season
the festive time of Christmas.

silly-billy
silly, foolish person.

silver
coins; small change excluding paper money and copper coins.
See also:
every cloud has a silver lining
handed to (someone) on a silver platter

silver wedding
the 25th anniversary of a marriage.

silvertail
rich, wealthy, upper-class person.

silver-tongued
persuasive; eloquent.

simmer down
become calmer, less agitated or angry.

simmering
seething with anger, excitement.

simple
unsophisticated; feeble-minded: e.g. He's a bit simple.

sin-bin
1. a panel-van (see: shaggin' wagon).
2. (rugby, ice-hockey) area off-field where player is sent for a certain time for a penalty.

since Adam was a boy/pup

since cocky was an egg

since I was in three-corner pants

since Jesus played full-back for the Apostles/Jerusalem
for a very long time: e.g. I haven't seen one of those things since Adam was a pup!

sing
inform; turn betrayer: e.g. The Mafia will put a contract out on him if he sings to the feds.

sing a different tune
to change one's allegiance or original ideas; modify or alter one's attitude to a more humble one: e.g. He's singing a different tune now that he knows he'll get fired if he talks like he did.

sing for joy
be extremely happy, elated.

sing out
call out loudly.

sing (someone's) praises
to boast enthusiastically about (someone): e.g. The newspapers have been singing his praises since he made such a success of himself overseas.

single
1. an unmarried person: e.g. This club is for singles only.
2. a room in a hotel etc. for one person.
3. a record played at 45 revolutions per minute.

single mother
unmarried mother.

singles
unmarried people or people without partners.

singsong
an informal gathering at which everyone joins in the singing of songs.

sink
invest money, especially in an unpredictable or unprofitable venture: e.g. He sunk thousands into that business that went broke.
See also:
enough to sink a battleship

sink a few
to drink beer, especially to excess: e.g. The blokes are going to sink a few tonight to celebrate their win.

sink in
be finally understood; to comprehend at last: e.g. When will it sink in that I don't want to see you any more!

sink like a brick
1. sink quickly without chance of floating.
2. (of a business venture etc.) to fail, collapse.

sink (one's) teeth into
become totally involved, engrossed, interested in: e.g. I like a good thick book that I can sink my teeth into.

sink or swim
to make a last desperate attempt or else fail.

sink the boot/slipper
1. (of the driver of a vehicle) to go faster.
2. (see: sink the boot in)
3. (Australian Rules football) kick the ball, a long one.

sink the boot in
1. criticise scathingly.
2. to kick someone viciously, especially when that person has fallen to the ground.

sink the sausage/sav
(of a man) have sexual intercourse.

sinker
a pie; heavy, filling food.

sinking
degenerating; declining; deteriorating: e.g. The business is sinking due to lack of funds.

sinking feeling
feeling of apprehension, foreboding, menace, threat.

siphon the python
(of a man) to urinate.

sis
1. sister.
2. (see: sissy, 1. and 2.)

sissy
1. effeminate man; pansy; homosexual.
2. coward; weakling.

sit back
to take no action.

sit in for
temporarily take someone's place: e.g. I'm sitting in for him because he's away sick.

sit in on
participate; attend; observe; visit.

sit on
delay action about; repress: e.g. He's sitting on his discovery until he's offered more money.

sit on it!
exclamation of scorn, contempt.

sit on my face
request (from a man) to perform cunnilingus for a woman.

sit on (one's) arse
be lazy, idle; not work hard; bludge.

sit on the fence
remain neutral.

sit on the throne
to sit on the lavatory.

sit out
1. take no part in: e.g. I think I'll sit this game out.
2. remain till the end: e.g. Not everyone sat it out till the end.

sit pat
to stand by one's decision, views, opinion.

sit (someone) on his arse
defeat (someone) in a fight, argument or war of words.

sit tight
1. refuse to yield; bide one's time: e.g. The strikers are going to sit tight until their demands are met.
2. stay where one is: e.g. Sit tight — I'll be back soon.

sit up
1. stay awake; not go to sleep.
2. to suddenly become interested in and alert to what is going on: e.g. What he has to say at the meeting will make everybody sit up for once.

sit with it
endure; remain faithful, loyal to the end.

sitcom
situation comedy television programme.

sit-down
a strike in which members refuse to leave their place of employment and do not allow anyone else to work until the dispute is settled.

sit-down money
unemployment benefits; the dole.

sit-in
a passive, organised protest meeting in which the demonstrators sit and refuse to move.

sitting duck
person who is an easy target or victim.

sitting on a goldmine
1. (of a woman) (joc.) pertaining to the money-making capacity of her body for prostitution.
2. have a resource that can be exploited.

sitting on an ant's nest
in a very awkward predicament that is likely to get worse.

sitting pretty
comfortably positioned in life, having opportunities, an established career etc.

six
(see: at sixes and sevens; go for six; hit for six)

six (two, three etc.) axe-handles across the acre
pertaining to a person with a very large backside, or one who is fat, obese.

six (two, three etc.) axe-handles between the eyes
pertaining to someone dumb, stupid, lacking in intelligence.

six foot under
dead and buried.

six of one, half a dozen of the other
a statement meaning that either this or the other will do; (something) makes no difference.

six to one, half a dozen to the other
equal chances to both options; either this or that will do.

sixer
1. (cricket) hit over the fence, six runs; (Australian Rules football) goal.
2. (see: go/went for a sixer)

six-footer
person or thing that is 6 feet (1.8 metres) tall or long.

sixth sense
intuition or perception beyond the five senses.

sixty-four thousand dollar question
the most difficult or crucial question (the term originated from a quiz programme).

sixty-nine/niner
an oral-sex position in which two people lie head to feet with each other in order to simultaneously stimulate each other's genitals orally.

size
(see: that's about the size of it)

size up
evaluate; form a judgement or opinion of: e.g. I sized him up for a crook as soon as I spoke to him.

sizzle
to be very hot.

sizzler
1. very hot day.
2. lewd, pornographic movie, book etc.

skag
heroin.

skedaddle
retreat, go quickly; hasten away: e.g. You had better skedaddle before the cops arrive.

skeeter
mosquito.

skeg/skeghead
a surfie — one who rides a surf-board.

skeleton in the closet/cupboard
some sordid fact or scandal kept a secret because it may cause shame or embarrassment.

skerrick
a very small amount: e.g. I haven't even got a skerrick left.

skew-whiff
haywire; muddled; askew; in disarray: e.g. All our plans have gone skew-whiff.

skid
(see: hit the skids; on skid row; on the skids; put the skids under someone)

skid row
slum; disreputable part of town.

skiddle
to run over, as with a car: e.g. That idiot nearly skiddled me!

skid-lid
protective crash-helmet.

skid-marks
any brown or faecal stains on one's underwear.

skim the cream off
to take the best part of anything.

skin
cheat; defraud; swindle; fleece, strip of money or belongings.
See also:
by the skin of (one's) teeth
couldn't drag/knock the skin off a rice-pudding
get under (one's) skin
had a skinful
have/got a thick skin
jump out of (one's) skin
keep (one's) eyes skinned
no skin off (one's) nose
save (one's) skin
thick-skinned

skin and bone
emaciated; thin.

skin (someone) alive
berate, scold (someone) severely; threaten (someone) with violence: e.g. I'll skin him alive if he doesn't get here on time.

skin-deep
superficial: e.g. Beauty is only skin-deep.

skin-flick
a pornographic movie, film.

skin-flint
niggard; miser.

skinful
1. as much alcohol as one can tolerate: e.g. He's already had a skinful today.
2. as much as one can tolerate, endure: e.g. I've had a skinful of those naughty kids of yours!

skin-head
member of a teenage cult identified by shaven heads and aggressive dress and behaviour.

skinner
1. (horse-racing) an unbacked horse that wins, making large profits for the bookmakers.
2. any gambling or betting coup.

skinny as a match/rake/ yard of pump-water
very thin.

skinny-dipping
swimming in the nude, naked.

skins
drums — in the speech of musicians.

skins game
(golf) form of betting with money for each hole going to the winner of that hole.

skint
having no money; broke.

skip
1. derogatory term for an Australian — used by non-Australians and taken from the television programme 'Skippy'.
2. a missing debtor; a defaulter on credit.
3. to leave in haste: e.g. They skipped town before the police could do anything.
4. absent oneself from; miss out on purpose: e.g. I think I'll skip the next class and go to the beach.

skip it
forget it; don't mention it.

skip over
take no notice; ignore; pass over.

skip the country
flee; leave in haste; get away.

skippy
children's game using a skipping rope.

skirt
girl or woman, especially as a sex-object.

skirt-happy
(of a man) interested in women as sex objects.

skite
1. braggart; boaster.
2. to brag, boast.

skittle
to knock over; run down, as by a car.

skol
to drink (alcohol) in one gulp; bottoms up!

skull
the head, considered as the source of intelligence: e.g. If you'd only use your skull you'd get things right!

skull and crossbones
warning symbol of death, such as for poisons.

skunk
fink; ratbag; undesirable, contemptible, unpleasant person.

sky-high
out of proportion; very high: e.g. Prices of fruit went sky-high after the storm ruined most of the crops.

sky-jack
hijack an aircraft.

sky-larking
high-spirited playing, pranking.

sky-pilot
clergyman.

sky-rocket
1. soar, go up suddenly, as of prices, fame etc.
2. (rhyming slang) pocket.

sky's the limit
there is no obstacle, limit: e.g. In this business with its capacity for making money, the sky's the limit.

skyscraper
very tall, multistorey building.

slack
lazy; inefficient; negligent; guilty of shirking one's duty or responsibilities: e.g. She's a slack housekeeper.

slack moll
1. promiscuous woman.
2. slovenly, untidy woman.

slack-arse/slacker
shirker; idler; lazy, inefficient, negligent person.

slag
1. spittle; saliva.
2. to spit.

slam
criticise severely: e.g. The critics slammed his new book.
See also:
grand slam

slam the anchors on
to brake, stop, violently: e.g. If I hadn't slammed the anchors on, that kid on the bike would have been skiddled!

slam the door in (someone's) face
to dismiss, reject (someone) perfunctorily, rudely.

slam-bang
(see: slap-bang)

slammer
prison.

slanging match
exchange of abuse, criticism; noisy and abusive quarrel.

slanter
a trick; an act of cheating or deception.

slant-eyes/slanty-eyed bastards
(derog.) Oriental people.

slap
1. give, issue, do forcibly, smartly: e.g. The police slapped a bluey on me for speeding (issued me with a ticket).
2. precisely; exactly: e.g. He hit the target slap in the middle.

slap a bluey on (someone)
(of police) issue with a ticket, fine, for a misdemeanour, minor offence.

slap in the face
sarcastic rebuke; rebuff or disappointment: e.g. Not getting that job after all that effort was a real slap in the face for him.

slap on the back
congratulations: e.g. He deserves a slap on the back for what he did.
See also:
back-slapping

slap up
do, make, hastily and carelessly: e.g. We managed to slap up some extra salads for the new arrivals at the barbecue.

slap-and-tickle
sexual play, activity.

slap-bang
1. suddenly.
2. exactly; precisely: e.g. He was hit slap-bang between the eyes.
See also:
right slap-bang in the hey-diddle-diddle

slap-dash
careless; hasty.

slap-happy
carefree; casual; cheerful.

slapped with
given smartly, forcibly, as of a fine: e.g. I was slapped with a bluey for speeding.

slap-stick
boisterous comedy.

slap-up
1. hastily or carelessly done.
2. first-rate, excellent.

slash
1. the vagina.
2. reduce prices dramatically: e.g. The price of petrol has been slashed during the latest price-war.
3. to urinate or the act of urination — especially of women.

slashing line
very attractive woman viewed as a sex object.

slate
reprimand, criticise severely: e.g. The critics like to slate everything he writes.
See also:
clean slate
on the slate
put it on the slate
wipe the slate clean

slather
use in large, copious quantities: e.g. He loves to slather his toast with Vegemite.
See also:
open slather

slaughter
defeat soundly: e.g. Our team slaughtered the opposition.

slave over a hot stove all day
(of a housewife) the drudgery of house-work: e.g. It's about time you took me out for dinner — I'm sick of slaving over a hot stove all day!

slave-driver
a hard boss, overseer, foreman; someone who makes others work very hard.

slave-labour
any work that is grossly underpaid; exploitation of labour.

slavery
difficult work; toil; drudgery: e.g. It's slavery working for that company.

slay them
amuse (them) greatly: e.g. This new book is going to slay them.

sleaze
despicable person of low character.

sleep around
be sexually promiscuous; have many sexual partners.

sleep in the dog-house
be in disgrace.

sleep it off
recover from the effects of alcohol, drugs etc. by sleeping.

sleep like a log/top
to sleep very soundly.

sleep on it
postpone a decision till the morning or some other time; think about it for a while.

sleep under the house
be in disgrace.

sleep with (someone)
have sexual intercourse with (someone).

sleeping on the job
not alert; ineffective; idle; lazy.

sleeping partner
person who puts money into a business but takes no active part in running it.

sleepyhead
lazy, idle or tired person.

sleeve
(see: have/got an ace up one's sleeve; laugh up one's sleeve; roll up one's sleeves; up one's sleeve; wearing one's heart on one's sleeve; wouldn't give you the sleeves out of his vest)

sleight of hand
clever and skilful deception using the hands.

slewed
drunk; intoxicated.

slice of the cake
share of the profits or benefits.

slick
1. adroit; cunning; sly; shrewd: e.g. That salesman is full of slick talk.
2. smart; fashionable: e.g. That new outfit looks slick.

slick operator
1. adroit, clever, efficient worker.
2. swindler; con-man; cunning or shrewd person in business matters.

slick trick
cleverly devised swindle, trick, act of deception or fraud.

slicker
slick person.
See also:
city slicker

slim excuse
poor, insufficient excuse.

slime
a repulsively obsequious person.

slimy
1. despicable; revolting.
2. servile; repulsively obsequious.

sling
1. offer money as a bribe: e.g. We'll sling him a few bob to keep his mouth shut.
2. tip: e.g. How much should we sling the waitress?
See also:
get (one's) arse in a sling

sling in
contribute, donate money: e.g. We'll all sling in to pay for the damage done to the car.

sling it in
leave, resign one's job.

sling mud/off at
make defamatory remarks about, speak ill of, usually when the person in question is not present; abuse; ridicule; deride.

slinging-match
abusive argument; noisy exchange of abuse.

sling-shot
brassiere; bra.

slip
1. error; mistake; blunder; accidental mistake.
2. petticoat.
3. decline: e.g. The real-estate market has slipped in the last year.
4. put quietly, secretly: e.g. He slipped a note into my hand.
See also:
give (someone) the slip
let slip

slip away
go quickly, quietly or secretly.

slip of a (person)
slim or young: e.g. She's only a slip of a girl.

slip of the tongue
an accidental mistake in speech which is often ironical.

slip one (in) to her

slip (someone) a length
(of a man) have sexual intercourse with (her).

slip, slop, slap
an advertising slogan — slip on protective clothing, slop on some sun-screen lotion and slap on a hat.

slip (someone) a mickey
1. offer (someone) a bribe.
2. secretly lace, contaminate (someone's) drink.

slip up
make a mistake, blunder; spoil; mismanage.

slipped (one's) mind
to have been forgotten: e.g. It completely slipped my mind that I had to be there yesterday.

slipped through (one's) fingers
eluded (one); to have missed the chance or opportunity.

slippery
elusive; unreliable; shifty; deceitful; cunning.

slippery as a butcher's penis

slippery as an eel
1. very slippery; hard to hold.
2. elusive; unreliable; shifty; deceitful; cunning.

slipping
losing one's acuteness, cleverness, dexterity: e.g. His playing is slipping because he doesn't practise enough.

slip-up
a mistake, blunder, error.

slit
the vagina.

slit (someone's) throat
(often jocular) threaten (someone) with violence.

slob
slovenly, untidy, lazy, stupid, ill-mannered or clumsy person.

slobber over
show excessive sentiment, desire for.

slobber-chops
1. affectionate term of address to someone, especially one's lover: e.g. Give us a kiss, slobber-chops!
2. greedy, gluttonous eater.
3. person or animal (dog) given to excessive salivation.

slog
1. spell of hard work: e.g. That was a hard slog!
2. to work hard: e.g. I'm going to have to slog all weekend to pass this exam.

slog it out
toil, work very hard.

slope
(derog.) an Asian person.

slope off
slink away, especially to evade work.

slopehead/slopey
(derog.) an Asian person.

sloppy
1. weakly or foolishly sentimental; over-sentimental.
2. untidy; careless; second-rate.

sloppy joe
large, loose jumper or sweater.

slops
1. beer: e.g. Old Norm loves getting into the slops.
2. unappetising, watery food.
See also:
on the slops

sloshed
very drunk; intoxicated.

slot
1. prison cell.
2. the vagina.

slouch
slovenly, lazy person; ineffective worker: e.g. He's no slouch when it comes to hard work!

slouch hat
the venerated, soft, Australian Army hat — symbol of courage and nationalism.

slow as a month of Sundays

slow as a wet hen/week
1. very slow; inefficient; tedious; boring; dull.
2. dull, stupid, inefficient person.

slow off the mark
(of a person) dull-witted; slow to act or react.

slow on the draw/uptake
(of a person) slow to comprehend.

slow-coach/poke
lazy, slow, inefficient, dull or stupid person.

slug
1. a bullet.
2. a serving of alcohol; a drink, gulp: e.g. I need a slug of brandy to calm my nerves!
3. a lazy, slothful person.
4. a heavy, high, sometimes unfair, payment or charging of money or tax: e.g. The recent slug in beer prices is going to upset a lot of blokes.
5. to hit hard, especially with the fist.
6. to charge an exorbitant price: e.g. I was slugged a hundred bucks just to get that tiny thing fixed!

slum it
to live below standard, or in squalid conditions.

slurp
1. a taste of a drink: e.g. Have a slurp of this.
2. eat or drink noisily: e.g. Stop slurping!

slush-fund
money used illicitly by organisations to bribe, or for use in campaign propaganda etc.; insurance against trouble for an organisation.

slushy
kitchen or cook's assistant.

sly
(see: on the sly)

sly grog shop
place where alcohol is sold illegally.

smack
1. heroin.
2. directly: e.g. He got hit smack in the middle.
See also:
have a smack at

smack in the eye/face
a disappointing set-back, rebuff.

smack on the back of the hand
perfunctory punishment or disciplinary action that is not severe enough to suit the crime: e.g. All he got was a smack on the back of the hand from the judge.

smack (one's) lips
anticipate with pleasure.

smacker
1. one dollar: e.g. That cost me ten smackers.
2. a loud kiss.
3. the mouth or lips.

smack-freak
person addicted to heroin.

smacks of (something)
indicates, smells of, tastes of, suggests: e.g. His behaviour smacks of corruption.

small
embarrassed; ashamed; humbled: e.g. I felt so small when I was caught stealing.

small change
coins of low value.

small fry
unimportant, insignificant people; children.

small hours
the time of night after midnight; early hours of the morning.

small mind
mean; petty; bigoted; unsophisticated; biased.

small potatoes
unimportant, insignificant people or matters.

small print
the limitations in a contract, printed in small writing designed to go unnoticed: e.g. Make sure you read the small print before you sign anything.

small screen
television.

small talk
idle chatter; gossip.

small wonder
hardly surprising.

small-time
unimportant; insignificant; petty: e.g. He's just a small-time criminal.

smarmy
ingratiating; full of false charm, affection and flattery.

smart alec(k)
person who skites and brags about his skills, abilities and knowledge although basically lacking in many of these qualities; a conceited know-all.

smart cookie
clever, shrewd person.

smart-arse
(see: smart alec)

smarten up
improve one's performance: e.g. He'd better smarten up or else he's fired!

smartie/smartie-pants
person who seems to smugly know all; one who tries to be too smart.

smash-and-grab
swift robbery, such as by smashing a store window and escaping with the goods.

smashed
1. drunk; intoxicated; drugged; under the influence of drugs.
2. utterly defeated: e.g. Our team was smashed in the finals.

smashed to the eyeballs
(see: smashed, 1.)

smasher
attractive, excellent person or thing.

smash-hit
person, book, movie etc. that is an instant success.

smashing
great; wonderful; excellent.

smash-up
a severe collision, as between two vehicles.

smear (someone's) name in the mud
discredit, speak in a defamatory manner about (someone).

smell
1. suggestion: e.g. His new book has the sweet smell of success about it.
2. anticipate; suspect: e.g. I can smell a trick!
See also:
hang around like a bad smell
live on the smell of an oily rag

smell a rat
to be suspicious; suspect that all is not what it seems.

smell fishy
appear suspicious, dubious: e.g. That deal smells fishy to me.

smell like a brewery horse's blurt
to have an extremely offensive odour.

smell like a rose
1. smell pleasantly.
2. to be innocent: e.g. She'll come out smelling like a rose after the new evidence is heard in court.

smell out
find; search out: e.g. A good reporter can smell out stories that sell newspapers.

smells like something crawled up your arse and died
pertaining to an offensively smelling fart.

smells like trouble
appears suspicious, wrong, troublesome.

smelly
a fart.

smidge/smidgen
a very small amount.

smile upon
approve; look at with favour: e.g. The boss isn't going to smile upon that sort of behaviour.

smiling from one ear to the other

smiling like a Cheshire cat
extremely pleased with oneself.

smithereens
tiny fragments; small bits and pieces: e.g. The antique vase smashed into smithereens when it hit the floor.

smoke
cigarette.
See also:
big smoke
end up in smoke
go/went up in smoke
where there's smoke, there's fire

smoke like a chimney
to smoke cigarettes heavily.

smoke (someone) out
discover, reveal something about (someone) through investigation.

smoke-oh/smoko
rest or short break from work, such as a tea-break.

smoky
race-horse or professional runner kept hidden in the bush, so no one will know how good he is; a dark horse.

smooch
1. person given to kissing and cuddling: e.g. He's a real smooch.
2. to kiss and cuddle.

smoocher/smoodge/smoodger
1. ingratiating, obsequious person; sycophant.
2. affectionate person who likes to kiss and cuddle.

smooth as a baby's bum
very smooth; not rough.

smooth operator
efficient, polished, diplomatic, suave but usually insincere person — a con-man.

smooth over
gloss over; cover up or hide the truth: e.g. The government tried to smooth over its latest tax increases.

smooth (someone) out
1. set (someone) straight as to the correct facts.
2. placate, calm (someone).

smooth talker/smoothie
flattering, unctuous, polished, polite but insincere speaker.

smorgasbord
a good variety, especially of available men or women from a sexual point of view.

smouch
a kiss.

snack
1. an easy task.
2. something to eat, small repast between meals.

snaffle
1. grab, take quickly.
2. steal or appropriate.

snafu
acronym for: situation normal, all fucked up.

snag
1. a sausage: e.g. We're cooking some snags for lunch.
2. an obstacle, hidden problem: e.g. There's been a snag in our plans so we'll have to stop until we sort it out.

snagger
poor quality shearer of sheep.

snake
treacherous person.
See also:
like a cut snake
lower than a snake
lower than a snake's belly in a wheel rut
lower than a snake's tail down a well
mad as a cut snake
one-eyed trouser snake
silly as a cut snake
so low (one) could parachute out of a snake's bum
trouser snake

Snake Gully
any remote, unsophisticated, rustic place or area.

snake in the grass
treacherous person, especially one who is not obvious.

snake juice
very strong alcoholic drink.

snakes alive!
exclamation of surprise, wonder.

snake's hiss
(rhyming slang) piss: e.g. He's gone for a snake's hiss.

snaky
spiteful; annoyed; treacherous; bad-tempered.

snap
1. anything easily done: e.g. That job's going to be a snap.
2. a photograph.
3. a short spell of weather: e.g. We're in for a cold snap.
4. to speak harshly, curtly: e.g. There's no need to snap!
5. give way; collapse: e.g. after all his problems, his mind finally snapped.

snap decision
hasty decision.

snap (one's) fingers (and someone comes running)
pertaining to the control or power (one) has over someone else: e.g. All she ever has to do is snap her fingers and he comes running.

snap (one's) fingers at
show scorn, contempt for.

snap (one's) twig
1. to die.
2. become suddenly angry; lose (one's) temper.
3. become crazy, mad, insane, erratically foolish.

snap out of it
to make an effort to recover quickly from a mood of depression, shock, anger, fear etc.

snap (someone's) head off
to speak harshly or very rudely to (someone).

snap to it!
hurry up! be quick!

snap up
to purchase hastily, as of a bargain: e.g. She's gone to the annual sale to snap up all the bargains.

snappy
1. brisk; lively; energetic: e.g. She works at a snappy pace.
2. smart; chic; fashionable: e.g. That's a snappy uniform.
See also:
make it snappy

'I only drink to forget my problem — my problem is I drink too much!'

A man who drinks too much likes to be in the grip of the grape, bend the elbow, down a few, drink like it's going out of fashion, give it a nudge, guzzle, hit the slops, indulge, piss on or sink a few. As a consequence of being on the bottle, grog, piss, shicker, slops or turps, he may be described as an alkie, barfly, booze artist, lush, piss-head, piss-pot, plonko, soak, souse, sponge, wino or write-off.

snark
1. an informer, especially for the police.
2. man who sniffs girls' bicycle seats.

snarler
a sausage.

snarl-up
confusion; mix-up.

snatch
1. female pudendum; vagina.
2. woman as a sex object.

snatch it

snatch (one's) time
to demand (one's) due wages and leave a job.

snatch-and-grab
quick robbery, theft.

snatches
small fragments: e.g. I can only remember snatches of that song.

snaz
(see: snazzy)

snazzed up
1. elegantly or stylishly dressed.
2. renovated; improved; fixed up: e.g. They snazzed up the house before they sold it and made a good profit.

snazzy
smart; stylish; elegant; excellent.

sneak
1. deceitful, contemptible person.
2. an informer, traitor.
3. to steal, pilfer: e.g. He got caught sneaking things from the shop.

sneak in/into
enter secretly without payment or invitation: e.g. We used to sneak into the picture-theatre when we were young.

sneak in by the back door
to enter into politics or some organisation in an illicit or underhanded manner.

sneak peek
a secret look at; private viewing or preview.

sneakers
soft-soled shoes styled on tennis shoes.

sneaking suspicion
persistent feeling of distrust: e.g. I have a sneaking suspicion that he's stealing money from the till.

sneeze at
show contempt, scorn for.
See also:
not to be sneezed at

snide
derogatory; malicious; sarcastic: e.g. He's always full of snide remarks about what I do.

sniff and giggle
the game of Rugby League football.

sniff around
search for information; investigate: e.g. The police have been sniffing around his place for clues to the crime.

sniff at
show contempt for: e.g. The management sniffed at her modern ideas.
See also:
not to be sniffed at

sniff (glue)
indulge in the often fatal habit of sniffing brands of glue for the intoxicating effect — especially of young children and teenagers.
See also:
glue-sniffing

sniffer dog
police dog trained to smell and seek out drugs.

sniffles
1. a cold or the flu: e.g. He's got a bad case of the sniffles.
2. emotional tears: e.g. Sad movies give me the sniffles.

snifter
1. small alcoholic drink.
2. balloon glass for brandy.
3. excellent.

snip
1. anything easily done.
2. a bargain.

snip of a thing
small insignificant person.

snitch
1. informant; one who tells tales or betrays: e.g. He's a snitch.
2. tell tales; inform on; betray: e.g. Did you snitch on me?
3. steal; pilfer: e.g. The store manager caught him snitching things from the shop.

snitchy
bad-tempered.

snobby
affected; having a high social opinion of oneself; believing oneself to be socially superior.

snook
gesture of contempt made with thumb to nose and outstretched fingers: e.g. He cocked a snook at the camera-man.

snookered
hindered; thwarted; defeated; unable to act.

snooks/snookums
term of endearment, especially for a young child or pet.

snoop
1. eavesdropper; one who pries.
2. to pry into the affairs of others.
3. search for information; investigate: e.g. The police have been snooping around his house again.

snoopy
prying; meddlesome; interfering.

snoot
1. affected snob.
2. the nose.

snooty
snobbish; supercilious; haughty.

snooze
nap; short sleep, especially in the daytime.

snorker
a sausage: e.g. Chuck some more snorkers on the barbie!

snort
1. alcoholic drink: e.g. Let's stop by the pub for a snort.
2. a sniff of cocaine.
3. to sniff cocaine: e.g. He snorts regularly.

snot
1. nasal mucus.
2. contemptible, ill-tempered, sulky person.
3. snobbish, haughty, arrogant person.
See also:
stick like snot to a cinder

snot (someone) one
to hit, bash, strike (someone).

snot-box
the nose.

snot-log
vanilla-slice — a custard-slice cake.

snot-nose
(see: snot, 2. and 3.)

snot-rag
handkerchief.

snotty
1. pertaining to mucus running from the nose, especially of small, grubby children.
2. ill-tempered; sulky.
3. conceited; arrogant.

snout
a large nose.
See also:
have/got a snout on

snow
1. heroin; cocaine.
2. bad television reception.

snow job
1. deliberate cover-up of the true facts.
2. false flattery; the fooling of someone by false flattery or information.

snowdropper
person who steals laundry, especially women's underwear, off clotheslines.

snowed under
overwhelmed with work.

snowing down south
warning that one's underwear, especially a woman's petticoat, is showing.

snow-white
pure; chaste; clean; innocent.

snoz/snozzle
the nose.

snuck
sneaked: e.g. He snuck out the back door.

snuff it
to die.

snuffler
disagreeably ingratiating person; crawler; obsequious person.

snuffles
influenza; a cold: e.g. He's got a bad case of the snuffles.

snuff-movie
a highly illegal, explicitly pornographic movie in which an unknowing victim is actually killed during the sexual act for the dubious gratification of the viewer.

snug as a bug in a rug
cosy; comfortable.

so!
exclamation of indignation, proof that one is right: e.g. So! You've been lying to me again!
See also:
and so on
just so
or so
say-so

so bare you could flog a flea across it
pertaining to land and vegetation devastated by drought.

so crooked (one) couldn't lie straight in bed
(of a person) deceitful; criminal; without ethics or scruples.

so far as
to the extent to which: e.g. So far as I know, he hasn't had a drink of beer for weeks.

so far gone
(see: far gone)

so far so good
there have been no problems up to the present time.

so hard a dog wouldn't sink a tooth in it
pertaining to an erection of the penis.

so help me Bob/God!
assurance of one's absolute intention: e.g. I'll make sure he doesn't get a penny in my will, so help me God!

so long
good-bye.

so long as
under the condition that: e.g. I'll go, so long as he doesn't.

so low (one) could parachute out of a snake's bum

so low (one) has to reach up to touch bottom
(of a person) despicable in character; having no scruples or ethics.

so much for
a contemptuous dismissal; that's the end of (something): e.g. So much for your high hopes of making a fortune!

so sharp you must sleep in the knife-drawer!

so sharp you'll cut yourself one day!
a sarcastic reproof to someone who is being over-clever or smart.

so smart he's/she's got more degrees than a protractor
(of a person) well educated; extremely intelligent.

so thin he/she has to run around under the shower to catch the drops
(of a person) extremely thin.

so tight he wouldn't sell you the steam off his shit

so tight you couldn't drive a pin up his arse with a sledgehammer
(of a person) parsimonious; stingy; miserly; mean.

so to speak
to express as a manner of speech: e.g. He doesn't want to be an ordinary employee forever — he'd like to be the 'top nob', so to speak.

so what!
what does it matter!

soak
drunkard; alcoholic.

so-and-so
1. contemptible, despicable person: e.g. He's a bloody so-and-so!
2. person or thing not definitely named: e.g. What's so-and-so doing today?

soap
(see: soft soap; wash someone's mouth out with soap and water; wouldn't know someone from a bar of soap)

soap-box
any temporary stand or platform (real or imagined) from which someone may address an audience, give voice to opinions etc.: e.g. She's on her soap-box about women's lib again!

soapie
a soap opera — a very sentimental radio or television serial largely depicting domestic scenes.

S.O.B.
son-of-a-bitch, despicable person.

sober as a judge
not intoxicated or under the influence of alcohol.

sob-story
an excuse or story meant to evoke sympathy or pity.

so-called
falsely, incorrectly named or styled as: e.g. All his so-called friends deserted him in his time of need.

social climber
person who tries to achieve social success by associating with people in higher social classes than himself.

social disease
venereal disease.

social finger
(of a man) the finger, usually the forefinger, used in sexual play, such as insertion into the vagina or anus.

sock
a hard or violent blow, punch: e.g. He needs a good sock in the mouth.
See also:
knock (one's) socks off
pull (one's) socks up
put a sock in it
rot your socks
stick a sock in it!
work (one's) socks off
wouldn't that rot your socks!

sock it to (someone)!
an encouragement to address (someone) with vigour and energy.

sock (someone) one
hit, punch (someone) hard.

sock (something) away
1. (of money) to save, accumulate, especially secretly.
2. (of food or drink) consume large amounts of.

sod
a disagreeable, unpleasant person.

soda
any easy task.

sod-buster
a farmer; one who tills the land.

soddy
saturated; wet.

soft
1. (of a person) easily influenced emotionally; foolish; weak; irresolute.
2. (of a person) generous; kind-hearted; sympathetic.
3. (of a job) easy: e.g. 1. His father got him a soft job in his business. 2. He's had it soft in that job.
4. (of drugs) non-addicitive.
5. (of pornography) not sexually explicit.

soft in the crumpet/head
silly; foolish; irresolute; weak.

soft on (someone)
1. to like, love (someone): e.g. He's soft on her.
2. to be less severe on (someone) than expected: e.g. The judge was too soft on that criminal.

soft soap
flattery, especially for gain.

soft spot for (someone)
to like, have sentimental affection for (someone, something): e.g. I've always had a soft spot for that boy even though he's always getting into trouble.

soft touch
a person easily duped or parted from his money.

soft-core
pornography that is not sexually explicit.

soften (someone) up
convince, bring (someone) round to one's way of thinking through flattery or tactful persuasion.

soften the blow
make less severe or emotionally distressing.

soft-hearted
sympathetic; compassionate.

softie
(see: softy)

soft-pedal
to tone down, lessen the impact of; put little emphasis on.

soft-soap
to flatter, especially for gain.

softy
(also: softie)
1. person who is easily duped or parted from his money.
2. generous, kind-hearted, sympathetic person: e.g. June is such a softy for animals that she'll take in any old stray.
3. weak person, lacking in bravery, courage or resolution.

soixante-neuf
(see: sixty-nine)

S.O.L.
ill-temper (shit on the liver): e.g. He's got a bad case of S.O.L.

sold
(see: be sold a pup)

sold on
enthusiastic about; in full agreement with: e.g. He's sold on the idea of investing money in that project.

sold out
1. completely sold: e.g. Tickets for that concert sold out in the first week.
2. betrayed: e.g. I've been sold out by my best friend.

sold out from under (one)
to have had something sold without (one's) knowledge or consent.

For other possible entries beginning with 'sold' see entries listed under 'sell'.

soldier of fortune
1. entrepreneur; opportunist.
2. mercenary.

soldiers bold
(rhyming slang) cold.

solid
unfair, unreasonable, severe treatment: e.g. I got fined a hundred bucks for speeding — a bit solid wasn't it!

solid as a rock
1. very stable, solid, strong.
2. (of a person) resolute; of strong character; reliable; responsible; unyielding.

solid smile
vomit: e.g. He had a solid smile all over the back seat of my car.

some
impressive; remarkable: e.g. That was some fish he caught!

some day or other
one day in the future: e.g. We'll take a much needed holiday some day or other.

some hope!
no hope — an expression of derision, scorn, disbelief.

somebody
an important or influential person: e.g. He's working hard to be a somebody in that organisation.

something/something else
impressive; an excellent example, specimen of: e.g. That show was really something!
See also:
make something of oneself

something else again
another topic, subject, matter altogether (usually bad, worse, poorer): e.g. Fred's a good player, but Alf's something else again!

something out of the bag/box
outstanding; excellent; exceptional: e.g. This new wine is really something out of the bag.

something to fall back on
resources; reserves — especially financial.

something to get (one's) teeth into
something of absorbing interest, challenging, that (one) can become totally involved with.

something's brewing/up
something's happening, imminent, about to take place (often trouble).

son of a bitch
1. despicable person.
2. anything that has extremely annoyed and frustrated one: e.g. This car won't start — the son of a bitch!

son of a gun
someone worthy of admiration, approval.
See also:
I'll be a son of a gun!
you son of a gun!

song
(see: bought for a song)

song and dance
excessive fuss: e.g. You don't have to make a song and dance about something so petty.

sook/sooky
1. a cry-baby; person prone to tears.
2. cowardly, frightened, timid person.

sool
to incite, encourage a dog to attack: e.g. I'll sool my dog on to you if you don't leave.

sooner or later
at some time or other.

sop
coward; weakling.

soppy
foolishly sentimental.

sore
angry; annoyed; upset; vexed: e.g. There's no need to get sore!
See also:
done up like a sore finger/toe
stand/stick out like a sore finger

sore loser
person who loses with little grace.

sore point/spot
a matter of vexation, irritation: e.g. That subject is a sore point with him.

sore spot for (someone)
sympathetic feeling for (someone).

sorf!
piss off! — a contemptuous dismissal.

sorf or I'll son ya!
piss off or I'll piss on you! — a contemptuous dismissal.

sort
1. an attractive person: e.g. He's a real sort!
2. type of person: e.g. He's not such a bad sort.
See also:
good sort
not a bad sort
out of sorts

sort of
to some extent: e.g. It's sort of round, but not quite.

sort (someone) out
1. set (someone) straight as to the true facts.
2. deal with, punish (someone).

SOS
urgent appeal for help.

so-so
mediocre; common-place; ordinary; average: e.g. After all the hype, the concert was only so-so.

sou
very small amount of money: e.g. I haven't got a sou on me.

soul
(see: sell one's soul for)

soul-destroying
monotonous; boring; demoralising: e.g. Working on a factory production-line day after day can be very soul-destroying.

soul-mate
person ideally suited in temperament, likes and dislikes to another person; perfect companion.

sound
1. implication: e.g. I don't like the sound of today's news.
2. give a certain impression; imply: e.g. His story sounds odd to me.

sound as a bell
in perfect condition, health.

sound off
1. express one's views angrily, loudly, dogmatically.
2. indulge in a verbal tirade of abusive language.
3. exaggerate; boast excessively.

sound (someone) out
investigate, observe (someone) cautiously before taking action; try to discover (someone's) views by means of indirect questioning.

sound the alarm
give due warning.

sounds like a bit of all right
a good idea.

sounding-board
1. person on whom new ideas are tested.
2. person who propagates, spreads ideas.

soup
(see: in the soup; see you in the soup)

soup up
increase the power of an engine through modification.

souped-up
(of an engine) greatly increased in power by modification: e.g. The police drive souped-up sedans.

soup-strainer
a moustache.

sour (as a lemon)
irritable; ill-tempered.

sour grapes
the act of criticising or pretending to despise something which one cannot have for oneself; malicious gossip because of a personal grudge: e.g. He's peddling sour grapes because he didn't win the competition himself!

sour-puss
ill-tempered person.

souse
alcoholic; drunkard.

soused
drunk; intoxicated.

South
originally the South Melbourne VFL football team — the Sydney Swans have now taken over the South Melbourne team.
See also:
north-and-south
snowing down south

southerly buster
(south-eastern Aust.) sudden change in weather

bringing windy conditions and a drop in temperature.

south-paw
left-handed person.

souvenir
steal; purloin; pilfer: e.g. I'm going to souvenir the ashtray from this restaurant.

sow
(see: as ye sow, so shall ye reap)

sow (one's) wild oats
indulge in the unrestrained excesses of youth, particularly in sex and promiscuity.

sow the seeds of discontent/doubt
introduce, spread, instigate ideas of discontent/doubt.

sozzled
very drunk, intoxicated.

S.P. bookie
(horse-racing) an unlicensed, off-course book-maker.

space base
combination of crack (derivative of cocaine) and angel dust (P.C.P.) — a highly addictive and potentially lethal drug.

spaced out
under the euphoric influence of drugs, alcohol or the like.

spade
(derog.) any dark-skinned person.
See also:
call a spade a spade/ fucking shovel

spag
1. spaghetti.
2. (derog.) an Italian person.
3. pertaining to anything Italian.

spaghett

spaghetti bender/muncher
an Italian person.

spaghetti western
Italian film in the style of the American western.

Spanish fly
aphrodisiac made from beetle of the same name.

spanking
very fine, excellent; striking.
See also:
brand-spanking

spanner in the works
a hindrance; anything that is an upset, trouble, or a spoiling influence; something that disrupts, confuses or obstructs.

spare
any spare part to replace a faulty part, such as a car tyre.
See also:
go spare

spare tyre
roll of fat around the waist, indicating obesity.

spark
liveliness; enthusiasm: e.g. He didn't show much spark at the party last night.
See also:
bright spark

spark off
initiate; stir into activity; start: e.g. His comments sparked off a riot.

sparkie
an electrician.

sparkler
1. diamond.
2. firework item that can be held in the hand when lit, sending out a shower of bright sparks.

sparks fly
pertaining to tension, anger, argument: e.g. The whole street can hear those two when the sparks fly!

sparring partner
person with whom one enjoys arguing.

sparrow fart
dawn; at first light: e.g. He always wakes up at sparrow fart.

sparrows/doves/geese flying out of (one's) arse
pertaining to the sensation of (one's) orgasm.

spas
1. (derog.) spastic; a spastic person.
2. fool; idiot; stupid person.
See also:
chuck a spas

spastic
1. fool; idiot; stupid person.
2. drunk; intoxicated.
3. extremely angry, furious.

spat
a minor argument or quarrel.

speak a different language
not sharing similar ideas, views or opinions due to different beliefs, attitudes, background or up-bringing: e.g. The greenies and the Government each speak a different language.

speak double-dutch
speak unintelligibly; use jargon that is difficult to comprehend.

speak for
recommend: e.g. I can speak for him — he's completely trustworthy.

speak for itself
is obvious.

speak for yourself!
an expression of disagreement with what someone has said.

speak of
worthy of mention or attention: e.g. He's nothing to speak of!

speak of the devil
an expression said when the very person being talked about enters: e.g.

Speak of the devil — look who just walked in!

speak (one's) mind

speak out
express one's opinions freely, boldly.

speak (someone's) language

speak the same language
share similar views, ideas and opinions as (someone).

speak with forked tongue
to tell lies, pervert the truth.

spear
(see: get the spear)

spear the bearded clam
(of a man) have sexual intercourse with a woman.

spec
speculation, as a risk or gamble: e.g. He's in the business of building spec homes for profit.
See also:
on spec

spec-built
a house built as a speculative investment by a builder rather than under contract.

special
something bought at a reduced price: e.g. There's a lot of good specials at the supermarket this week.

specs
spectacles; eye-glasses.

spectacular as a fart in a bathtub
not spectacular or noteworthy at all.

speed
amphetamines — stimulants of the nervous system — taken illegally for the 'high' feeling of well-being and alertness.

speedball
mixture of heroin and cocaine taken by drug-addicts.

speed-cop
motorcycle policeman who enforces the laws of the roads and speed-limits.

speed-merchant
one who drives too fast.

speedo
speedometer — indicator of speed in a vehicle.

speedster
one who drives fast.

speed-trap
any of various devices, such as radar, used by police to verify the speed of motor vehicles.

Speewa
legendary station or place used as the setting for tall tales of the outback.

spell
short period of rest.
See also:
under (someone's) spell

spell out
explain clearly; make understood: e.g. I'm going to spell out the rules now so you all know what to do.

spellbinder
anything that enthralls or captures one's complete attention, such as an exciting book or movie.

spend a penny
(of women usually) go to the toilet.

spend it like water

spend up big
(of money) spend extravagantly.

spending money
money for minor personal expenses; pocket-money: e.g. After all the bills are paid I never have any spending money left.

spending spree
a wild extravagant time purchasing items one usually doesn't buy, without regard to cost.

spew
1. vomit.
2. to vomit.
3. to become very angry, furious.

spew it out
to speak freely of one's feelings, anxieties, such as to a friend.

spew (one's) guts out
to vomit.

spewy
1. awful; vile; despicable.
2. very angry, furious.

spic
(derog.) a Spaniard or a person of Spanish or Latin descent.

spice
anything that adds zest, excitement, scandal, mystery etc.: e.g. Those two need a bit of spice in their marriage to pep it up again.

spick-and-span
neat and tidy.

spicy
scandalous; improper; risque; indecent: e.g. That book was a bit spicy.

spider
a drink made with soft-drink and ice-cream.

spiel
persuasive, glib talk, designed to sell, deceive: e.g. After listening to that salesman's spiel, anybody would believe his vacuum-cleaners were the best in the world.

spieler
con-man; fast-talker; persuasive, glib salesman.

spiffed
drunk; intoxicated.

spiffed up
dressed up in formal attire; dressed in one's best.

spiffing
excellent; very good: e.g. What a spiffing idea!

spiffs
incentives given to salespeople.

spiflicated
drunk; intoxicated.

spike
1. to add alcohol to a person's drink without that person's knowledge.
2. to add hard drugs to less dangerous ones.

spike (someone's) guns
to hinder, thwart (someone's) progress or success.

spill
tell; divulge: e.g. Who spilt the information to the newspapers?

spill it out
tell, divulge, such as one's emotions to a close friend.

spill (one's) guts
1. (see: spill it out)
2. betray; tell, divulge a secret; inform on.

spill the beans
tell, divulge a secret or confidence, usually inadvertently or treacherously.

spin
1. the sum of five dollars.
2. short, often fast, drive of a motor vehicle: e.g. We took his Rolls for a spin around the block.
3. time; experience: e.g. That flight home was a rough spin.
4. prison sentence of five years.
See also:
in a spin

spin a yarn
1. tell a good story, joke, tall tale.
2. fabricate; fib; falsify; exaggerate.

spin out
1. to skid out of control in a motor vehicle: e.g. He spun out on the second corner and crashed.
2. to prolong a discussion etc.: e.g. Try to spin the introduction out a bit until our guest speaker arrives.

spin the bottle
an adolescent party game whereby a bottle is spun in the middle of a circle of people, and whoever the ends of the bottle point to must kiss.

spine-basher
loafer; lazy, idle person.

spine-bashing
loafing; sleeping; lying down.

spine-chilling
causing fearful apprehension, terror.

spineless (as a jellyfish)
weak-willed; irresolute; cowardly.

spinner
(see: come in spinner)

spinning sensation
dizzy feeling as when affected by alcohol.

spin-off
incidental benefit; kickback: e.g. Pocket calculators are a spin-off from space research.

spit
1. exact counterpart of; mirror image of; exact likeness of: e.g. He's the very spit of Elvis Presley.
2. indicate one's hostility, anger, contempt: e.g. I spit on him and his violent ways!
See also:
go for the big spit

spit and polish
1. attention to detail in cleaning: e.g. That will come up looking like new with a bit of spit and polish.
2. ceremony and formality.

spit it out
speak one's mind, often vehemently.

spit the dummy
display sudden anger, hostility, petulance; lose one's temper: e.g. Steph really spat the dummy when her pet cockatoo chewed up her best leather shoes!

spitfire
person easily provoked to bad temper.

spitting chips
extremely angry, annoyed: e.g. Dad's spitting chips because you put a dent in his car.

spitting distance
a very short distance: e.g. He moved into a house within spitting distance of the pub.

spitting image
exact counterpart of; mirror image of; exact likeness of: e.g. He's the spitting image of his father.

spiv
black-market dealer or petty criminal, especially one who dresses in a vulgar or flashy manner and does no regular work.

spivved up
dressed in formal attire; dressed in one's best; dressed in a gaudy or flashy manner.

splash
1. display conspicuously, especially in print: e.g. That story was splashed all over the front pages of the papers.
2. spend freely: e.g. I haven't got any cash to splash this week after paying all my bills.
See also:
have a splash
make a big splash

splash (one's) boots
(of a man) to urinate.

splash out
spend money lavishly.

splendiferous
wonderful; splendid; excellent.

split
1. share: e.g. Here's your split of the loot from that robbery.
2. dessert made from sliced fruit and ice-cream covered with nuts.
3. drink of alcohol mixed with soft-drink; the soft-drink used as a mixer.
4. go; depart, especially quickly: e.g. We'd better split before the cops arrive.
5. give up; quit: e.g. It's time to split as things haven't worked out as well as hoped.

split hairs
make unnecessary, often ridiculous distinctions.

split on (someone)
betray, inform on (someone): e.g. The criminal finally split on his mates.

split (one's) sides
to laugh heartily.

split second
a very short time: e.g. A bomb will destroy in a split second what took years to build.

split the difference
take the average of two differing estimates etc.: e.g. He wanted a thousand dollars for the car, but I told him it wasn't worth any more than eight hundred, so we split the difference and I paid nine hundred.

split up
to end a relationship, marriage etc.; go separate ways.

split-beaver show
explicit pornography of women.

splits
action of dancers and gymnasts in which they leap, sink to the floor etc. with their bodies held vertically but their legs horizontally, one extended in front of them, the other behind.

split-second
performed with great precision: e.g. It took split-second timing to perform that trick without having a major accident.

splitting apart at the seams
deteriorating, collapsing, getting worse, especially of mental and physical stability and well-being: e.g. He's splitting apart at the seams since his divorce.

splitting head-ache
severe pain in the head.

splitting image
(see: spitting image)

splosh
money.

splurge
to spend lavishly, extravagantly: e.g. We had a splurge at the casino last night.

spoil
to harm or damage the character of (someone) by excessive indulgence or pampering: e.g. My parents used to spoil me when I was little.

spoiling for
desiring; eager for: e.g. Those guys at the pub were spoiling for a fight.

spoils
profits or advantages from enterprise, business or position: e.g. The spoils of public office, which have been at the great expense of the tax-payer, are finally being scrutinised.

spoil-sport
person who ruins the enjoyment of others.

spoilt rotten
indulged, given way to, to the detriment of (one's) character: e.g. Those kids have been spoilt rotten by their over-indulgent parents and now they're completely selfish.

spoken for
reserved; taken; accounted for: e.g. You can't have that chair — it's spoken for.

spondulicks
money.

sponge
1. a drunkard.
2. person who lives at the expense of others; free-loader; one who cadges all the time.
See also:
throw in the sponge

sponge off/on (someone)
to live at (someone) else's expense; be a parasite on (someone); take advantage of (someone): e.g. He's been sponging off his parents since he left school ten years ago.

sponger
free-loader; cadger; one who lives at the expense of others.

spoof
1. semen; excretions from the genitals produced during sexual arousal: e.g. He got into trouble because his mother found spoof all over the sheets on his bed.
2. parody; travesty; satire; caricature: e.g. That programme was a spoof on politicians.

spook
1. ghost; phantom.
2. ill-kept, odd, eccentric person.
3. secret informant; spy.

spooky
frightening; scary; creepy: e.g. That was a spooky movie.

spoon-fed
over-indulged; helped without any effort or thought on (one's) part being required: e.g. No wonder he can't look after himself — he's been spoon-fed all his life by his parents.

sport
1. familiar form of address among men, and often indicating hostility: e.g. Listen here sport — what do you think you're doing!
2. display ostentatiously: e.g. He was sporting a bright red scarf around his neck.
See also:
be a sport
good sport

sporting chance
reasonable possibility of success.

sporty
1. loud; flashy; showy; jazzy: e.g. He's driving a very sporty car these days.
2. interested in sport: e.g. I've never been sporty.

spot
1. small quantity of food or alcohol: e.g. Just a spot of rum in my coffee please.
2. the sum of one hundred dollars: e.g. I'm putting a spot on horse number seven in the next race.
3. place: e.g. This looks like a good spot to do some fishing.
4. predicament: e.g. I'm in a rather difficult spot at the moment and need some help.
5. a spotlight: e.g. We need a spot over the barbie at night.
6. recognise; catch sight of; find or discover: e.g. You'll never spot him in this crowd.
See also:
change (one's) spots
hit the spot
in a spot of bother
in the spotlight
knock spots off (someone)
leopard can't change its spots
on the spot
put on the spot
soft spot for (someone)
sore spot
tight spot
weak spot

spot check
unannounced and random examination: e.g. The police are doing spot checks on car regos this week.

spot fine
an immediate fine for a traffic offence: e.g. I was given a spot fine of twenty bucks for going through a red light.

spot-on
1. correct; absolutely right.
2. excellent; very good.
3. exactly on target.

spotter's fee
sum of money paid as a reward to a person who reports something, such as an accident to a tow-truck company or news to a newspaper reporter.

spout
(see: up the spout)

spout off
1. utter angrily; declaim; vociferate: e.g. She's spouting off again about the inequalities of women.
2. talk at length: e.g. He'll spout off for hours about the merits of his footy team if you get him going.
3. exaggerate; boast to excess: e.g. He's spouting off about how good in bed he is again.

sprat for a mackerel
the offer of something inconsequential in return for something profitable, valuable.

spray it again Sam
expression of disapproval to someone who sprays saliva with every sibilant sound (you'd be very good if you didn't with that sentence!).

spray the bowl/porcelain
1. to suffer from diarrhoea.
2. to urinate.

spread
1. a property, especially a large one: e.g. He lives on his spread in the outback.
2. a feast: e.g. That dinner was a real spread.
3. intensive, extensive publicity in a paper: e.g. That new shop got a good spread in the local rag.

spread it on thick
to boast, exaggerate, say or do to excess.

spread like wildfire
to spread, radiate extremely quickly.

spread (oneself) too thin
to over-burden, over-extend (oneself) so that (one) becomes inefficient or over-taxed.

spread-eagle
1. with the arms and legs stretched out.
2. to knock a person down flat: e.g. I'll spread-eagle him if he comes here again!

spring
1. to catch someone unexpectedly, especially doing something wrong or clandestine: e.g. They got sprung by the cops in the middle of robbing the joint.
2. to arrange an escape for someone from prison: e.g. He got sprung by the Mob and is still at large.

spring chicken
young person; inexperienced person.

spring fever
feeling of listlessness or restless desire, often experienced at the beginning of spring.

spring is sprung! The grass is riz!
exclamation acknowledging the beginning of spring, especially after noticing increased activity in nature, such as birds mating or the first appearance of a blowfly.

spring one on (someone)
surprise (someone).

spring-head
person with very curly hair.

sprout
person small in stature.

spruced up
tidied; cleaned; well dressed.

spruiker
someone employed to loudly advertise and solicit custom for a business.

sprung
caught unexpectedly: e.g. Mum sprung us smoking in the shed when we were nine years old.
See also:
get sprung

spud
1. potato.
2. an Irishman.
See also:
went down like a bag of spuds

spun out
1. under the influence of marijuana or other drugs: e.g. He's really spun out.
2. to have experienced a highly euphoric, frightening, excellent or bad state using marijuana, LSD or other drug: e.g. We really spun out on that stuff!
3. to have lost control of a vehicle, especially under high speed: e.g. We spun out on that corner in the rain and wrote the car off.

spunk
1. semen: e.g. There's spunk all over the sheets!
2. an extremely sexually attractive person: e.g. He's a spunk!
3. vitality; courage: e.g. He's got a lot of spunk for his size.

spunk-rat
an extremely sexually attractive person.

spunky
1. sexually attractive: e.g. He's really spunky!
2. full of vitality.

square
1. dull, old-fashioned, conservative person: e.g. He's such a square!
2. honest; straightforward; just; fair: e.g. 1. That deal sounds square enough to me. 2. I want a square answer!
3. directly; exactly: e.g. He got hit square in the middle.
4. settled; finalised: e.g. Our accounts are square now.
5. even: e.g. The players finished with their scores square.
6. agree with: e.g. His alibi doesn't square with yours.
7. settle; pay: e.g. You must square your debts before you go.
8. avenge; take revenge: e.g. I'll get square with him one day for all the rotten things he did.
See also:
back to square one
break square
fair and square
on the square
silly as a square wheel

square deal
fair and honest transaction.

square meal
good, substantial meal: e.g. That's the first square meal I've had all week!

square off with (someone)
1. make recompense; mollify (someone): e.g. That company is going to go broke squaring off with everybody who sues for damages.
2. get revenge: e.g. I'll square off with him one day for all the rotten things he did.

square (one's) shoulders
carry (oneself) erect, especially in the face of obstacles, problems or misfortune.

square peg in a round hole
(of a person) a misfit; outcast.

square the circle
attempt the impossible.

square up
settle an account, bill etc.; pay back: e.g. If you can lend me ten bucks now, I'll square up next payday.

square up to
face with courage: e.g. She must square up to the consequences.

square-eyes
1. person who must wear spectacles.
2. what one is supposed to get if one watches too much television.

squash
1. large number of people crowded into a relatively small area: e.g. That protest meeting at the council was a real squash.
2. to silence, suppress, put down: e.g. The rebellion was squashed by government troops.

squat
1. the entry and taking over of vacant land or buildings without legal right.

2. to enter an unoccupied building and live there without paying rent.
3. to sit: e.g. I'll squat on the floor.
4. (of women) to urinate; the act of urinating: e.g. We had to squat behind a tree because we couldn't wait.

squatter
1. (formerly) a person who settled on Crown land to run stock — usually sheep — without legal title.
2. wealthy pastoralist.
3. homeless person who takes over a vacant building without paying rent.

squawk
protest vehemently: e.g. Everyone's squawking about the price increases for beer and petrol.

squeaky-clean
1. fastidiously clean.
2. moralistic; chaste.
3. not guilty; beyond reproach.

squeal
1. betray; turn informer; divulge a secret or confidence: e.g. The traitor has squealed to the police.
2. complain bitterly.

squealer
traitor; informant; tell-tale.

squeeze
exert pressure; harass; extort; blackmail: e.g. The bank is squeezing us to repay the loan.
See also:
put the squeeze on (someone)
tight squeeze

squeeze a lemon
(of a woman) urinate.

squelch
suppress; subdue: e.g. His reply squelched the opposition.

squib
1. mean, parsimonious person.
2. coward; despicable person.

squib on
desert in a time of need or crisis: e.g. All his so-called friends squibbed on him when he needed them the most.

squiffed/squiffy
drunk; intoxicated.

squillions
a great amount, especially of money: e.g. He's got squillions!

squint
a look: e.g. Have a squint at this!

squirm
suffer extreme embarrassment: e.g. The students squirmed under the headmaster's scrutiny.
See also:
make (someone) squirm

squirrel
hoard; collect; save: e.g. She managed to squirrel away enough money for a holiday overseas.

squirt
person small in stature or importance, especially if impudent.

squish
squash; squeeze.

squitters
diarrhoea.

squiz
quick, close look: e.g. Did you get a squiz at that?

stab
attempt; try: e.g. At least have a stab at the answer.

stab in the back
treacherous, malicious assault on someone's character; betrayal.
See also:
back-stabbing

stab in the dark
an unprepared attempt; uninformed try; guess: e.g. I took a stab in the dark with the answer to that quizz and ended up winning the major prize!

stab (someone) in the back
betray (someone); be treacherous to (someone).

stack
1. large amount: e.g. I've got a stack of work to do today.
2. arrange unfairly or fraudulently so as to give oneself the advantage: e.g. He stacked the rally with his own supporters.
See also:
blow (one's) stack

stack it on
to exaggerate one's emotions, story, alibi, excuse: e.g. He really stacked it on in front of his parents so that they would feel sympathy and not punish him.

stack on
do lavishly: e.g. They stacked on a fabulous party for his birthday.

stack on a blue/turn
become extremely angry, emotional: e.g. Dad really stacked on a turn when he found out I had been arrested.

stack on an act
(see: put on an act)

stack the car
badly damage a car in some form of accident.

stacked
1. (of a woman) having large breasts.
2. arranged fraudulently so as to give oneself the advantage: e.g. He plays with a stacked deck of cards.

stack-up
an accident involving several vehicles.

stag night
party held by the male friends of a bridegroom on the eve of his wedding and which is often ribald and accompanied by pornography, wild pranks and excessive drinking.

stage is set
the atmosphere, scene, circumstances are suitable for a specific event: e.g. The stage is set for war in that strife-torn country.

stagger
amaze; overwhelm; astonish: e.g. We were staggered by the brilliant results of the enterprise.

stairway to heaven
a run or ladder in a woman's stocking, hosiery.

stake
(see: pull up stakes)

stake (one's) claim
make (one's) demands, desires known; to assert ownership: e.g. He's staked his claim on her.

stale
hackneyed; boring: e.g. That's a stale old joke!

stalemate
deadlock; impasse; standstill.

stalk
1. the penis.
2. to walk stiffly, angrily, emotionally: e.g. He stalked off in a huff after not getting his own way.

stamp of approval
acceptance; agreement; approval: e.g. That plan has the board's stamp of approval.

stamp out
wipe out; destroy; do away with; eliminate: e.g. The dictator is stamping out his opposition by killing them.

stamping-ground
habitual, favourite, most popular place, resort, haunt: e.g. That club used to be our stamping-ground when we were teenagers.

stand
1. tolerate; put up with: e.g. I can't stand him!
2. pay for: e.g. He stood us a meal at the restaurant.
See also:
take a stand

stand a show
have a good chance of success: e.g. He doesn't stand a show against that sort of opposition.

stand alone
1. have no equal: e.g. As a dancer, she stands alone.
2. have no supporters: e.g. He stands alone in that decision.

stand around like a stale bottle of piss
to be forlorn, at a loss, neglected, idle.

stand by
1. (someone) uphold, support (someone): e.g. She stood by me when I was in trouble.
2. (something) stick to; adhere to: e.g. You have to stand by your decision.

stand for
1. tolerate; endure; allow: e.g. I won't stand for any of your nonsense!
2. serve to designate or express: e.g. What does that symbol stand for?

stand in
be a substitute: e.g. We need someone to stand in for him while he's away.

stand in the way
impede the progress of: e.g. If he wants to do that I won't stand in his way.

stand it
tolerate; endure; put up with: e.g. I can't stand it any more!

stand on (one's) digs
be resolute in the face of opposition; to remain firm: e.g. I'm standing on my digs in this matter because I know I'm right.

stand on (one's) own two feet
be independent, self-sufficient, needing no outside help.

stand (one) in good stead
be of use to (one): e.g. This will stand me in good stead until I get the other repaired.

stand (one's) ground
to be resolute in the face of opposition.

stand out (a mile)
be prominent, conspicuous, noticeably different: e.g. That bright red one really stands out.

stand out like a bottle of milk/country dunny
figurative expression of loneliness and isolation.

stand out like a sore finger/toe

stand out like dogs' balls/like tits on a bull
be prominent, conspicuous, noticeably different.

stand over (someone)
intimidate (someone): e.g. I refuse to let them stand over me like that so I'm reporting them to the police.

stand (someone) down
terminate (someone's) employment.

stand (someone) on (his/her) ear
1. to fight, bash, assault, defeat (someone).
2. (of an alcoholic drink) extremely strong, potent: e.g. This home brew will stand you on your ear.

stand (someone) up
to fail to keep an appointment (often deliberately) with someone — usually a member of the opposite sex.

stand the test (of time)
prove worthy, true.

stand to reason
be obvious, clear, to reasoning, intelligent people: e.g. If he's broken his leg as badly as the doctor says, it stands to reason that he'll never race again.

stand up for (oneself)
support, defend (oneself).

stand up to
1. show courageous resistance to: e.g. He stood up to his boss because he knew he was in the right.
2. remain in good condition during: e.g. That furniture won't stand up to rough treatment.

stand-by
something kept for an emergency: e.g. The generator's just a stand-by in case we lose power.

stand-off
deadlock; stalemate.
See also:
Mexican stand-off

standoffish
cold in manner; aloof; remote; unsociable.

stand-over merchant
person who gains his wishes through intimidation, extortion etc.

starchy
stiff and formal in manner.

star-crossed
doomed; ill-fated; unlucky.

stare daggers
stare fixedly with an attitude of hate, contempt: e.g. She stared daggers at me all night across the table.

stare (someone) down/out
stare fixedly at (someone) until that person looks away in embarrassment.

stared straight through me
stared at me without recognising, acknowledging me.

staring (one) right in the face
1. obvious: e.g. The answer is staring him right in the face.
2. right in front of (one): e.g. The book you're looking for is staring you right in the face.
3. imminent; requiring attention: e.g. We have a lot of problems staring us in the face.

starkers
1. completely naked, nude.
2. crazy, mad, insane: e.g. He's starkers if he thinks that is going to work.

starry eyed
romantically enthusiastic, impractical.

Stars and Stripes
pertaining to the American flag and nationalism.

star-studded
having the presence of many notable and famous celebrities: e.g. The opening of the casino was a star-studded evening.

start from scratch
start at the beginning; start from the bottom.

start off on the right/wrong foot
make a good/bad impression, beginning.

start the ball rolling
begin: e.g. Start the ball rolling by bringing on the first act of the show.

starters
the first course of a meal: e.g. I'd like oysters for starters.
See also:
for starters

starting to get to (one)
beginning to annoy, irritate (one): e.g. His drinking is starting to get to me.

starting to see daylight
beginning to see the end or completion of a tedious or bad situation: e.g. After years of research and hard work, we're finally starting to see daylight.

starve (someone) out
force (someone) into the open or into action by denying something needed.

starve the bardies/crows/lizards!
exclamation of disgust, annoyance, surprise etc. (more common in lists of Australian colloquialisms than in actual speech).

starved
(joc.) hungry: e.g. What's for dinner — I'm starved!

stash
1. something hidden, especially a store of an illicit drug, such as marijuana, heroin.
2. conceal, hide, store: e.g. Where can we stash all this dope?

stat dec
statutory declaration — a legal document.

state
(see: in a state)

state of play
current position or situation: e.g. What's the state of play with that deal you were trying to organise?

state-of-the-art
embodying the very latest developments: e.g. Most people would need comprehensive training on how to operate a state-of-the-art computer.

status symbol
possession considered to show a person's high social status, wealth, position.

stay cool
remain calm, composed.

stay on an even keel
remain calm, composed; remain firm, balanced in the face of difficulties.

stay on (someone's) hammer
(rhyming slang: hammer and tack — back) keep a close watch over (someone); badger (someone): e.g. If I don't stay on his hammer he doesn't work.

stay one step ahead of
maintain the advantage.

stay put
remain in the same position, place; don't move: e.g. Stay put — I'll go and get help.

stay-at-home
person who rarely goes out and would rather stay at home.

stayer
person or animal of great stamina, endurance.

staying power
stamina: e.g. That horse has a lot of staying power in the rain.

steady
1. a regular, permanent partner in a love-relationship: e.g. Who's her steady?
2. (go steady) to go out regularly with one boy/girlfriend: e.g. Who's she going steady with?
See also:
ready, steady, go!

steady on/up!
wait! take care! be more cautious! slow down!

steak and kidney
(rhyming slang) Sydney.

steal
1. something gained at very little cost; a bargain: e.g. That car was a steal!
2. an extremely easy task: e.g. This new job is a steal.
3. (basketball) take ball away from opponent without fouling.

steal a march on (someone)
attempt to deceive, hoodwink, cheat, gain an unfair advantage over (someone).

steal (someone's) heart
win (someone's) affections.

steal (someone's) thunder
to use, appropriate (someone else's) idea; to lessen (someone's) impact by doing, saying what he was going to.

steal the limelight
take the centre of attention from someone.

steal the show
attract the most attention; do better; achieve fame and success: e.g. This new invention is going to steal the show at the awards.

steam
(see: let off steam; run out of steam; under one's own steam; wouldn't give you the steam off his shit)

steamed up
in an emotionally excited or angry condition: e.g. What's he all steamed up about?

steel (oneself)
prepare (oneself) with determination: e.g. You'd better steel yourself for some bad news.

Steelers
Illawarra N.S.W. Rugby League football team.

steep
(of prices) exorbitant; excessive; unreasonable: e.g. The price is too steep.

steep fine
heavy, costly, unreasonable fine: e.g. I got a steep fine just for speeding ten k's over the limit.

steer clear of
avoid: e.g. He might smoke a bit of dope but he steers clear of the heavy stuff like heroin.

stem the tide
hold back; moderate; stop.

step
(see: false step; in step; stay one step ahead; take steps; watch one's step)

step by step
by degrees; slowly; in sequence: e.g. We went through all the rules, step by step.

step down
resign; quit: e.g. After the scandal, the mayor decided to step down.

step in
intervene; become involved: e.g. It's time the government stepped in to prevent militant unions from holding the public to ransom.

step in the right direction
course of action that is correct, in the best interests, favourable.

step into (someone's) shoes
take over (someone's) role, position, situation.

step into the line of fire
become involved in a controversial, explosive, argumentative matter and become a/the centre of attention or attack.

step it up

step on it!
accelerate; hurry up.

step on (someone's) toes
antagonise, annoy, irritate, upset (someone).

step on the gas
hurry up; go faster; accelerate.

step out of line
get into trouble; be disobedient; indulge in insubordination: e.g. If those kids step out of line,

you have my permission to smack them.

step outside
a menacing invitation to fight, settle a score (between men).

step to it!
hurry up!

step up in the world
raise one's social, career status; become more famous, wealthy: e.g. Getting that job was a real step up in the world for him.

step-ins
women's elasticised undergarment, designed to flatten belly and buttocks and make the wearer appear slimmer.

stepping-stone
means of progress; opportunity: e.g. That job is just a stepping-stone to something much higher.

stew
1. a state of agitation or uneasiness: e.g. He's in a real stew waiting for his exam results.
2. to fret, worry, brood: e.g. I think I'll just let him stew for a while.
See also:
let (someone) stew for a while

stew in (one's) own juice
suffer the consequences of (one's) own actions.

stew over
1. worry; fret; brood.
2. think, consider at length.

stewed (to the gills)
drunk; intoxicated.

stick
1. a person: e.g. He's not such a bad stick.
2. (piece of) furniture: e.g. He doesn't own a stick of furniture.
3. to put or place in a particular position: e.g. 1. He stuck his hands in his pocket. 2. Stick the kettle on the stove.
See also:
better than a poke in the eye with a burnt stick
cop some stick
couldn't pull a greasy stick out of a dead dog's arse
flat stick
get the dirty end of the stick
like a greasy stick up a dead dog's arse
more than (one) can poke a stick at
wrong end of the stick

stick a sock in it!
be quiet! shut up!

stick around
stay; remain.

stick at
persevere; continue: e.g. We're going to stick at it for a few more hours.

stick by
support; defend; remain loyal to: e.g. His friends stuck by him.

stick in (one's) craw
(see: stick in one's throat)

stick in (one's) mind
stay, be remembered: e.g. The thought of their suffering really stuck in my mind.

stick in (one's) throat
difficult to accept: e.g. Knowing he's guilty and not being able to do anything about it because of lack of evidence really sticks in my throat!

stick it!

stick it in your gob!

stick it up your arse/ginger/jumper!
expression of dismissal, scorn, contempt, rejection.

stick it out
persevere; continue; endure: e.g. When a cyclone hits, you have to stick it out as best you can.

stick like shit to a blanket/snot to a cinder
1. adhere, stick firmly.
2. remain loyal, faithful, true.

stick movie
explicit pornographic film.

stick (one's) bib in
pry; interfere; intervene; meddle.

stick (one's) neck out
place (oneself) in a vulnerable or dangerous position, situation; take a risk.

stick (one's) nose in
pry; interfere; intervene; meddle.

stick out for
continue to demand: e.g. The union is going to stick out for better working conditions and more pay.

stick out like a sore thumb/toe

stick out like dogs' balls/tits on a bull
be very obvious, conspicuous.

stick that for a joke!
an expression of one's refusal to accept a suggestion.

stick that in your pipe and smoke it!
expression of scorn, contempt, dismissal; a smug assertion that one is right, correct.

stick the boots in
to criticise scathingly.

stick to
remain firm, faithful, adamant, persistent; persevere; continue: e.g. He stuck to his promise despite the difficulties.

stick to (one's) guns
remain faithful to (one's) decisions, opinions, resolutions.

stick to (one's) ribs
(of food) satisfying: e.g. After eating junk food all week, you need something that's really going to stick to your ribs — like one of Mum's roast dinners.

stick together
remain loyal, faithful.

stick up
to rob, especially at gunpoint: e.g. He's been sticking up corner stores to pay for his drug-addiction.

stick up for
defend; support; uphold; speak or act in defence of: e.g. He had a lot of people stick up for him at the time of that murder.

stick up to
resist boldly: e.g. It's difficult for small children to stick up to older bullies.

stick with
remain loyal, faithful; persevere: e.g. 1. You'll end up in prison if you stick with the likes of him! 2. Even though times are hard at present, he's going to stick with the business.

For other possible entries beginning with 'stick' see entries listed under 'stuck'.

stick-in-the-mud
an unadventurous person who is opposed to new ideas, novelty etc.

stickler
1. person who insists, perseveres without yielding: e.g. He's such a stickler for accuracy and perfection.
2. a difficult problem or situation.

sticks
(see: in the sticks; the sticks)

sticks and stones may break my bones, but names will never hurt me
retort to anyone giving malicious abuse.

stick-up
robbery at gunpoint.

sticky
1. (of a problem or situation) embarrassing; awkward; complicated; disconcerting; difficult: e.g. We'll have to engage some accountants and lawyers to sort this sticky mess out.
2. a look: e.g. Come and have a sticky at this!

sticky end
an unhappy, unpleasant ending, usually violent: e.g. He's going to come to a sticky end with his life of crime.

sticky wicket
delicate, difficult, embarrassing situation or problem; a disadvantage: e.g. He's on a bit of a sticky wicket at the moment.

stickybeak
1. person who pries, meddles or interferes.
2. a look: e.g. Have a stickybeak at this!

sticky-fingers
a thief.

sticky-nose
(see: stickybeak, 1. and 2.)

stiff
1. corpse; dead body: e.g. The police found a stiff in the river.
2. an erect penis.
3. formal; haughty; constrained: e.g. His manner is so stiff.
4. (of alcohol) strong: e.g. I need a stiff drink!
5. unlucky; bad luck (often in a sarcastic, mocking sense): e.g. So he lost — stiff! He deserved to!
6. harsh; heavy; severe; steep; demanding: e.g. 1. The teacher set a stiff exam and most students failed. 2. The judge gave him a stiff sentence.
See also:
bored stiff
scared stiff

stiff as a board
very stiff; not easily bent or changed in shape.

stiff cheddar/cheese/shit!
1. bad luck!; unlucky!
2. an off-hand, unsympathetic expression; rebuff to an appeal for sympathy or help.

stiff upper lip
(see: keep a stiff upper lip)

stiffen the crows/lizards!
a mild oath. (see: starve the lizards!)

stiff-necked
stubborn; obstinate; unyielding.

stiffy
an erect penis.

still kicking
1. alive: e.g. Is your grandfather still kicking?
2. barely alive: e.g. The dog was still kicking after being run over by a car.

still the worms
appease one's hunger: e.g. I'm getting a hamburger to still the worms.

still waters run deep
pertaining to the belief that quiet, silent people harbour deep, unknown thoughts and attitudes.

sting
1. a clever trick, act of deception.
2. to charge heavily in price: e.g. He wants to sting me a hundred bucks for that small job!
3. cheat, swindle; be cheated, swindled: e.g. 1. You wouldn't sting a good mate would you? 2. He got stung for a fortune by that con-man.

'Actually, Bert got injured watching the box. He had a telly installed in his ute so he wouldn't miss his favourite programme. He was drivin' home the other night when an ad came on. He forgot where he was and got up to go to the bathroom!'

In fact, most men *don't* go to the bathroom — the bathroom is mainly for women. Men go to drain the dragon, have a leak, have a snake's hiss, kill a snake, point percy at the porcelain, see a man about a dog, shake hands with the unemployed, splash their boots, spray the bowl, strain the potatoes, syphon the python, take their dog for a walk, train terrence at the terracotta or water the horse.

4. to cadge; borrow money: e.g. He stung me for ten dollars.
5. cause to suffer embarrassment or hurt: e.g. That cruel remark really stung.

stingy
1. parsimonious; mean; miserly.
2. scanty or meagre: e.g. We got such a stingy meal for the price we paid.

stink
loud complaint, noise, fuss, commotion; scandal: e.g. The latest news is going to cause a real stink.
See also:
kick up a stink

stink a dog off a gut-wagon
of something that has a highly offensive smell.

stinkbomb
an offensive fart, expulsion of wind from the anus.

stinker
1. unpleasant, annoying, despicable person.
2. difficult or unpleasant problem or situation.
3. an unpleasantly hot day or period of weather.

stinking
obnoxious; unpleasant; disagreeable: e.g. I can't get this stinking thing to work!

stinking hot
unpleasantly hot and humid weather conditions.

stinking rich
extremely wealthy.

stinko
drunk; intoxicated.

stinkpot
person or thing with a strong offensive smell.

stinks
anything that is extremely bad, disreputable, inferior, terrible, unpleasant: e.g. The whole situation stinks!

stinks of
1. has large amounts of: e.g. He stinks of money.
2. highly indicative, suggestive of: e.g. That government stinks of corruption.

stinks to high heaven
1. has a strong, offensive smell.
2. is extremely bad, disreputable, inferior, corrupt etc.: e.g. The entire plan stinks to high heaven!

stir
1. commotion; noise; trouble: e.g. What's all the stir about?
2. prison.
3. a wild party.
4. to incite, cause trouble; be provocative: e.g. Don't listen to him — he's only stirring.
See also:
cause a stir

stir along
to go, travel fast — especially in a vehicle.

stir the possum

stir up a hornet's nest
incite, cause trouble, dissent.

stirrer
trouble-maker; person who incites trouble and dissent.

stitch
1. piece of clothing: e.g. She went swimming without a stitch on.
2. pain in the side from exercise.
See also:
have (someone) in stitches
in stitches

stitch in time saves nine
initial action, careful planning and attention to detail at the beginning prevent a lot of trouble and wasted time later.

stock-in-trade
resources, talents, skills, ability, knowledge etc. of a person, company.

stoked
1. intoxicated; drunk; under the influence of drugs.
2. excited about; thrilled; extremely pleased: e.g. They're stoked about winning first prize.

stomach
endure; tolerate; like; accept: e.g. I can't stomach all that violence in movies.
See also:
eyes bigger than (one's) stomach
haven't got the stomach
my stomach thinks my throat's cut
turn (one's) stomach

stone
(see: can't get blood out of a stone; cast the first stone; heart of stone; leave no stone unturned; rolling stone)

stone the crows!
expression of surprise, amazement, wonder.

stone-broke
having no money at all.

stone-cold
dead.

stone-cold sober
not drunk or intoxicated.

stoned
1. drunk; intoxicated.
2. under the influence of a drug, such as marijuana.
3. persecuted: e.g. The Jews have been stoned for centuries.

stoned out of (one's) head
(see: stoned, 1. and 2.)

stone-motherless-broke
having no money at all.

stone's throw
very short distance: e.g. He lives a stone's throw from the pub.

stonkered
1. drunk; intoxicated.
2. bewildered; confounded: e.g. This problem has me stonkered.
3. exhausted; tired; defeated: e.g. After all that work, I'm stonkered.

stony broke
having no money at all.

stood up
failed to be met by a person for an appointment, especially a romantic one: e.g. She was stood up by him.

For other possible entries beginning with 'stood' see entries listed under 'stand'.

stooge
1. puppet, pawn, person who acts subordinately for another.
2. spy; informant: e.g. He's a police stooge.

stooge around
behave aimlessly; fool, play around: e.g. Stop stooging around and get to work!

stook
illicit hiding place, stash — especially in prison slang.

stool pigeon
informant or decoy, especially for the police.

stoop to conquer
to swallow indignities in order to gain one's ends.

stop
stay, remain: e.g. I think I'll stop home tonight.
See also:
pull out all the stops
wouldn't stop a pig in a poke

stop dead (in one's tracks)
to stop abruptly.

stop kidding/pulling (oneself)
to stop deluding (oneself), believing in impossibilities.

stop short
to stop abruptly.

stopgap
a temporary measure or substitute.

stop-out
person who stays out late at places such as night-clubs.

stop-work meeting
meeting of employees during working hours to discuss conditions, pay, strikes etc.

storm
(see: cook up a storm; take by storm)

storm in a tea-cup
a big fuss over an insignificant matter.

story
1. fabrication; lie: e.g. All that stuff about Santa Claus is a story.
2. excuse; alibi: e.g. And what's your story?
See also:
likely story
to cut a long story short
what's the story?

story about the one that got away
exaggerated, boastful fabrication of the facts — especially about fishing.

story of (one's) life
what has just been discussed or mentioned is characteristic of (one's) own life: e.g. You reckon he's got problems! That's the story of my life!

story-teller
liar.

stoush
1. a commotion, fight or brawl.
2. to punch, hit, bash, assault.

stove-pipes
trousers with tight-fitting, straight legs.

Straddie
Stradbroke Island (Queensland).

strafe
punish; attack; reprimand; berate.

straight
1. heterosexual: e.g. Is she straight?
2. respectable; not corrupted; honest: e.g. His business dealings are very straight.
3. orthodox; conservative: e.g. Her ideas on sex are very straight.
4. (of a drink) undiluted; neat: e.g. I like my rum straight.
5. correct: e.g. You must get your facts straight before you complain.
6. candid; honest; direct; open; truthful: e.g. I want a straight answer.
See also:
dead straight
give it to (someone) straight
go straight
keep a straight face
on the straight and narrow
put/set (someone) straight

straight answer
candid, truthful, honest answer.

straight as a die
(of a person) honest; candid; truthful; respectable; ethical.

straight as a dog's hind leg
1. crooked.
2. (of a person) dishonest; immoral; unorthodox.

straight as a yard of pump-water
(see: straight as a die)

straight down the line
honestly; directly; truthfully.

straight face
serious, unemotional expression of the face: e.g. He was so amusing I found it very difficult to keep a straight face.

straight from the horse's mouth
information obtained from a reliable, authentic source.

straight from the shoulder
blunt; honest; truthful.

straight off (the mark)
immediately: e.g. He wanted it done straight off.

straight out
candidly; frankly; truthfully: e.g. I told him straight out what I thought of him.

straighten (oneself) out
regain (one's) self-control; sort (one's) problems out; live a more respectable, honest life: e.g. It's about time he straightened himself out and got a job.

straighten out
put right; rectify; put into order: e.g. We'd better try to straighten out the mess this business is in.

straighten (someone) out
1. threaten (someone) with violence.
2. inform (someone) of the true facts of a matter.

straight-out
absolute; thorough; uncompromising: e.g. He's a straight-out Collingwood footy supporter.

straight-shooter/talker
honest, respectable, ethical person.

strain
(see: don't strain yourself!)

strain the potatoes
to urinate.

strait-laced
prudish; formal; conventional; moralistic.

stranded
(of a person) left helpless, deserted, in difficulties: e.g. He left me stranded without any money to get home.

strange
slightly odd or queer; mentally unbalanced: e.g. He's a bit strange since his wife died.

stranger than fiction
a situation that is odd, queer, suspicious, dubious.

strangle a darkie
to defecate.

stranglehold
tight control over: e.g. He's got a stranglehold on that business.

strap
(see: on the strap)

strapped for cash
to be short of money.

straw
(see: clutch at straws; draw straws; draw the short straw; final straw; last straw; man of straw)

straw company
business company established for the purpose of tax benefits.

straw in the wind
an omen, portent, hint of things to come.

straw that broke the camel's back
the final thing, incident, mishap etc. that leads to a reaction, outburst of emotion, break-down etc.

straw vote
unofficial ballot to test public opinion.

strawbs
strawberries.

streak
1. tall person.
2. run, spell of (luck): e.g. I had a winning streak at the casino last night.
3. to run naked in a public place: e.g. The game was interrupted when two men streaked across the grounds.
See also:
long streak of pelican shit/weasel piss
on a winning streak

streak of misery
unhappy, morose person — usually a tall person.

streaker
person who runs naked through a public place for effect.

street
(see: man in the street; not in the same street; on easy street; on the streets; play both sides of the street; up one's street; walk the streets)

streets ahead
better than; far superior to; in front: e.g. Our business is streets ahead of the competition.

streetwalker
a prostitute who seeks her customers in the street.

street-wise
having an acute awareness, knowledge of life, particularly of its more sordid aspects.

strength of it
the bare, essential facts, information about: e.g. That's about the strength of it!

stretch
1. a term of imprisonment: e.g. He's doing a stretch for murder.
2. a nickname for a tall person.
3. a period of time at some unpleasant task.
See also:
not by any stretch of the imagination

stretch a point
concede, agree to something not usual or allowed.

stretch (one's) legs
exercise; go for a walk; move about after a period of cramped inactivity.

stretch (one's) luck
take a risk after continued success.

stretch the dollar
be extremely careful with one's money in order to budget successfully: e.g. We really have to stretch the dollar these days just to cover living expenses.

stretch the friendship
to strain a friendship; go beyond the usual limits of, and thereby jeopardise a friendship: e.g. He's really stretching the friendship by always asking for money.

stretch the truth
exaggerate, distort the truth.

strewth!
(also: struth) mild oath, expression of surprise, amazement, indignation.

strictly for the birds
1. trivial; uninteresting: e.g. He thinks going to church every Sunday is strictly for the birds.
2. so risky as to be considered not worth doing: e.g. As far as I'm concerned, hang-gliding is strictly for the birds.

strides
trousers; pants.

strike!
mild oath, expression of surprise, amazement, frustration, indignation.

strike a chord
arouse a feeling, emotion: e.g. That sad movie will strike a chord on anybody's heartstrings and make them cry!

strike a light!
expression of surprise, amazement, indignation, frustration.

strike a snag
come across a problem, impediment, hindrance.

strike bowler
(cricket) fast bowler, taking early wickets.

strike home
deal an effective blow; get a message, the truth etc. across: e.g. Going to prison will really strike home that crime doesn't pay.

strike it rich
achieve, gain wealth and prosperity, especially suddenly: e.g. He struck it rich at the casino last night.

strike me dead/lucky/pink/roan!
expression of surprise, amazement, indignation, frustration.

strike (one)
impress: e.g. Does he strike you as an honest bloke?

strike (one's) fancy
impress (one): e.g. That new car strikes my fancy.

strike paydirt
achieve success, wealth, prosperity: e.g. He's finally struck paydirt with that new best-seller that he's written.

strike while the iron's hot
act, take advantage while the opportunity is available.

Strine
(supposed) Australian English: in Strine 'Strine' is the pronunciation of 'Australian'.

string
(see: keep someone on a string; no strings attached; pull strings; puppet on a string; tie up some loose strings)

string along
cooperate; go along with; join in: e.g. I'll string along with you blokes as long as there's no danger involved.

string it out
prolong: e.g. He strung the introduction out because the guest speaker was late.

string (someone) a line
deceive (someone) with a tall tale, yarn.

string (someone) along
deceive, cheat, hoodwink (someone); lead (someone) on: e.g. He never intended to marry you — he's just been stringing you along.

string (someone) up
kill by hanging.

strip
1. to undress, especially provocatively.
2. to take apart, dismantle a car, especially illegally for the purpose of selling the parts.
See also:
tear strips off (someone)

strip joint
night-club where strip-tease is performed.

strip poker
card game of poker, where the stakes are the players' clothing.

strip (someone) apart
severely reprimand, rebuke, beat, bash (someone).

stripe me pink!
expression of surprise, amazement, wonder.

stripper
strip-tease dancer.

strip-tease
form of dance entertainment performed to music, in which a person gradually and provocatively undresses.

stroke of genius
a sudden and brilliant act, decision, idea: e.g. Solving the problem in that

strange manner was a stroke of genius!

stroke of luck
piece, instance of good luck: e.g. Winning all that money was a stroke of luck for that poor family.

strong
1. very smelly, offensive: e.g. Those prawns are a bit strong!
2. unpleasant; offensive; disagreeable: e.g. That joke was a bit strong for mixed company!
See also:
come on a bit strong
going strong

strong as a mallee bull
physically very strong.

strong language
forceful, bad, abusive language; swearing.

strong of it
(see: strength of it)

strong point
one's particular talent, skill or ability: e.g. Singing isn't his strong point, but playing the piano is.

strong-arm
coerce; use force or violence: e.g. I won't be strong-armed into signing anything by those crooks!

strong-headed
having a vigorous, determined will or mind.

stroppy
1. (of a person) cantankerous; bad-tempered; complaining; angry; difficult to deal with.
2. (of a car) fast; high-performing.

struck on (someone/something)
infatuated with: e.g. He's really struck on that new girl.

struggle for existence
the (often difficult) pursuit of everyday living.

strung up
suffering from anxiety, worry, nervous tension: e.g. He's so strung up about the coming exams.

strut (one's) stuff
1. behave in an exhibitionistic manner.
2. show off, display (one's) best abilities, qualities.

struth!
(see: strewth!)

stub/stubbie
1. (also: stubby) small, squat bottle of beer.
2. (joc.) a measure of distance: e.g. Yackandandah is about six stubbies down the road.

stubbie-cooler
polystyrene insulation cover for a stubbie beer bottle.

stubbies
1. small, squat bottles of beer, made notable by the brand XXXX (Fourex).
2. strong, denim work-shorts for men.

stuck
(see: get stuck into someone)

stuck for words
at a loss for words; not able to think of the words to use: e.g. I get stuck for words when I have to speak in front of an audience.

stuck in a rut
in an unpleasant pattern of life that is difficult to break away from or to change.

stuck on
1. partial to; infatuated with: e.g. He's really stuck on that new girl he met.
2. kept in a certain position because of an impediment, puzzle etc.: e.g. I'm really stuck on number thirteen down in this crossword puzzle.

stuck out on a limb
isolated; stranded; exposed; in a difficult, dangerous situation.

stuck with
unable to get rid of; unable to get out of (a situation): e.g. I wanted this job in the first place, and now I'm stuck with it!

stuck-up
conceited; pompous; snobbish.

stud
man of vigorous sexual prowess.

stuff
1. personal property, belongings: e.g. Where can I put all my stuff?
2. paraphernalia; things; objects: e.g. Take all the stuff out of that room and put it in the shed.
3. work, especially in artistic, literary, musical fields: e.g. All the songs on that record are their own stuff.
4. (of a man) have sexual intercourse: e.g. He'd like to stuff her, given half the chance.
5. spoil; ruin; bungle; destroy; mess up: e.g. If he stuffs my plans up again, he's fired!
6. (see: stuff and nonsense)
See also:
beat the stuffing out of (someone)
do (one's) stuff
give a stuff
give two stuffs
knock the stuffing out of (someone)
know (one's) stuff
rough stuff
strut (one's) stuff
that's the stuff!

stuff a duck!
expression of surprise, amazement, astonishment.

stuff and nonsense
rubbish; foolish talk or actions: e.g. You should have heard the stuff and nonsense they were going on about!

stuff around
behave in a foolish, aimless manner: e.g. If he'd work for a living instead of stuffing around all day, he and his family would be a lot better off.

stuff dreams are made of
anything exciting extreme pleasure, satisfaction.

stuff it!
exclamation of anger, frustration, contemptuous dismissal, rejection.

stuff (one's) face

stuff (oneself)
eat greedily, and usually to excess: e.g. She stuffed herself at the party and ended up feeling sick.

stuff (something) up
ruin, spoil, bungle (something): e.g. Every time I try to bake bread I stuff it up.

stuffed
1. tired; exhausted; worn out: e.g. I was stuffed after that race.
2. broken; ruined; not functioning properly: e.g. The radiator in my car is stuffed.
3. completely full, satisfied, after having eaten enough (or too much): e.g. I can't eat another thing thanks — I'm stuffed!
4. dead.
See also:
get stuffed!

stuffed shirt
pompous, pretentious person.

stuffed up
1. ruined; broken; not functioning properly: e.g. The radiator on your car is well and truly stuffed up.
2. having one's nasal passages blocked as from a cold: e.g. I'm all stuffed up — I think I'm getting the flu.
3. made a mess of, ruined, bungled, spoiled (something, a situation): e.g. You really stuffed up this time didn't you!

stuff-up
a ruined, spoiled, bungled situation: e.g. Because of the rain, the barbecue was a stuff-up.

stuffy
pompous; formal; old-fashioned: e.g. Her parents are so stuffy.

stukered
exhausted; worn out; tired; broken down.

stumblebum
a clumsy, inefficient person.

stumered
broke; having no money.

stump
perplex; bewilder; confound; confuse: e.g. The next question in the quiz will really stump him.
See also:
Black Stump
this side of the Black Stump

stumps
1. end of the day's play in cricket.
2. the legs.

stung
1. drunk; intoxicated: e.g. He's really stung!
2. cheated; deceived; tricked; ripped off: e.g. I think I've been stung for a few hundred dollars by that crook!
3. emotionally hurt; aggrieved: e.g. That comment really stung.

stunk to high heaven
(see: stinks to high heaven)

stunned mullet
(see: like a stunned mullet)

stunner
strikingly attractive person or thing.

stunning
excellent; striking; beautiful.

suave as a rat with a gold tooth
(of a person) vulgar in a flashy way; poor taste in manner and dress.

sub
1. submarine.
2. substitute.

subbie
sub-contractor — a person who agrees to do part of a job for the main contractor.

suburban
conventional or narrow-minded.

suburbia
(derog.) the suburbs and its narrow-minded inhabitants.

such and such
particular but unspecified: e.g. It happened at such and such a time.

such is life!
an exclamation of resignation, tolerance, forced acceptance (Ned Kelly's last words before hanging).

suck in
deceive; cheat; swindle: e.g. Don't be sucked in by his innocent smile — he's a hardened criminal.
See also:
get sucked in

suck off
bring to orgasm through oral stimulation of the genitals: e.g. 1. Have you ever been sucked off?
2. I'd like to suck him off.

suck up to (someone)
behave ingratiatingly towards (someone); flatter (someone) in a fawning manner: e.g. He's been sucking up to the boss all week in the hope of getting a raise.

suck-arse
ingratiating, obsequious, fawning, servile person.

sucked in
(see: get sucked in)

sucker
person who is easily tricked, fooled, duped, deceived; person who is gullible.

sucker for punishment
person who seems to enjoy or accept without complaint hard work, unpleasant tasks and problems: e.g. Just look at him out there, mowing lawns in the hot sun — he's a real sucker for punishment!

suck'ole (suck-hole)
1. ingratiating, obsequious, fawning, servile person.
2. to behave in an ingratiating manner: e.g. I'm going to have to suck'ole the boss for a raise.

sucks
said of anything that is held in contempt, disliked, rotten, awful or despicable: e.g. That idea sucks!

suds
1. beer: e.g. G'day mate — want a glass of suds?
2. the frothy head on a glass of beer.

Sufferer's Parasite
pseudonym for: Surfer's Paradise (Queensland).

sugar
1. (as an exclamation) euphemism for shit; mild oath of anger, frustration, surprise.
2. term of endearment for someone.

sugar the pill
to try to make an unpleasant experience more bearable, tolerable.

sugar-daddy
elderly man who lavishes gifts or money on younger women.

sugary
sentimental; deceitful; cloying.

suggestive
indecent; lewd; provocative; immodest: e.g. That dress is very suggestive.

suicide
any action detrimental to one's best interests; dangerously foolish: e.g. It's suicide to invest all your money in one company.

suit (one) down to the ground
completely acceptable, appropriate or adequate to (one): e.g. This house suits us down to the ground.

suit (oneself)
to do as (one) pleases: e.g. He suits himself about what clothes he wears.

sum (someone) up
form an opinion, make an assessment of (someone): e.g. I summed him up as a fool as soon as I met him.

Sunday best
one's best clothes: e.g. Everyone arrived in their Sunday best.

Sunday driver
an annoyingly slow driver of a car.

sundowner
(obsolete) swagman who arrived at a place at sunset so that he could ask for food and shelter without having to work in exchange.

sunnies
sunglasses.

sunny side up
(of eggs) fried on one side only.

Sunshine State
Queensland.

super
1. excellent; first-class; extremely pleasing.
2. high octane petrol.
3. superannuation.
4. superphosphate fertiliser.
5. supervisor; superintendent.

supercool
1. sophisticated; in vogue; trendy.
2. calm; in control of (one's) emotions.

super-duper
excellent; fine; pleasing: e.g. We had a super-duper time!

super-duper-pooper-scooper
gumleaf used in lieu of toilet-paper.

superiority complex
an exaggerated idea of one's own worth.

superpower
extremely influential, powerful nation: e.g. The United States is a superpower.

superstar
extremely famous person; celebrity; famous actor, musician.

Supreme Being
God.

supreme sacrifice
one's life; the giving of one's life for another's safety.

sure!
interjection of disbelief.
See also:
better to be sure than sorry

sure as eggs/hell/rain
undoubtedly; certainly; absolutely; without fail: e.g. Every time I hang my washing out on the line, it rains — sure as eggs!

sure cop
a certainty: e.g. This horse is a sure cop to win.

sure enough
as expected: e.g. I knew he'd lose it — and, sure enough, he did!

sure of (oneself)
extremely confident.

sure thing
a certainty; certain to succeed: e.g. This investment is a sure thing.

sure-fire
certain to succeed: e.g. This horse is a sure-fire winner.

surface
1. to finally get up out of bed: e.g. After a heavy night on the booze, he didn't surface till late in the afternoon.
2. to finally appear somewhere.
See also:
on the surface

surfer/surfie
person who rides the surf or waves on a surfboard — generally seen as young, blonde, tanned and out of work.

survive
not affected, harmed to any great degree: e.g. It's only a small cut — don't worry, I'll survive!

suss
1. suspicious; distrustful: e.g. I'm a bit suss about him and his actions.
2. deceitful; underhanded; clandestine: e.g. What he's doing sounds suss to me.

suss out
investigate: e.g. I want to suss the whole thing out before I make a decision.

swag
1. pack carried by travellers, hikers etc.
2. stolen goods; thief's plunder.
3. a large number: e.g. He's got a swag of money in his pocket.

swaggie
swagman — drifter, tramp who wanders about from place to place on foot, living on gratuity or occasional jobs.

S.W.A.L.K.
Sealed With A Loving Kiss — printed on the back seal of an envelope, letter.

swallow
believe; accept without question: e.g. You don't expect your parents to swallow that fib do you?

swallow (one's) pride
humble (oneself): e.g. It's about time you both swallowed your pride and kissed and made up.

swallowed it whole
accepted, believed without question: e.g. He made up a ridiculous story to explain why he was arrested and his parents swallowed it whole.

swan song
last performance, work or creation of an artist: e.g. This tour will be the swan song of his career as a live performer.

swank/swanky
ostentatious style, as in appearance, dress, furnishings etc.; fancy; luxurious: e.g. We went to a very swanky restaurant in the heart of London.

Swans
the Sydney Swans VFL football team.

swear black and blue
guarantee; promise; profess great belief in; declare solemnly.

swear by
rely on; believe in; have complete confidence in: e.g. She swears by that folk-remedy.

swear like a (bloody) trooper
use abusive, profane and offensive language.

swear off
promise to give up, abstain from: e.g. He's sworn off cigarettes for life after the doctor told him he'd cark it with lung-cancer.

swear on the Bible/a stack of Bibles
to affirm with solemn earnestness: e.g. He swears on the Bible that what he saw was the truth.

swear to (something)
say that one is absolutely certain of (something): e.g. I didn't do it — I swear to it!

sweat
1. a state of extreme anxiety, worry or strain: e.g. What's he in such a sweat about?
2. to work extremely hard: e.g. He had to really sweat to pass his exams.
3. to worry, suffer anxiety: e.g. He made me sweat for weeks before he told me the job was mine.
See also:
no sweat!

sweat blood (and tears)
1. be extremely anxious, worried, nervous or apprehensive: e.g. I had to sweat blood and tears for a week before finding out the results of my exams.
2. to work very hard: e.g. He sweat blood to build this home for his family.

sweat, blood and tears
extreme effort; hard work: e.g. That job took a lot of sweat, blood and tears before it was finished.

sweat it out
1. wait with nervousness, anxiety, strain, apprehension: e.g. I had to sweat it out for a week before knowing the results of my medical examination.
2. endure until the end, completion: e.g. There isn't much one can do during a cyclone except sweat it out.

sweat on
wait anxiously for: e.g. I had to sweat on the results of my medical tests for two weeks!

sweep
sweepstake — a form of gambling on horse-races in which the money staked by all the entrants goes to those who draw the names of the winning and placed horses.
See also:
make a clean sweep
new broom sweeps clean

sweep it under the carpet/mat
to conceal or cover up a problem or incident; conveniently to remove troublesome problems or issues from consideration.

sweep (someone) off (one's) feet
impress, overwhelm (someone) with enthusiasm: e.g. My husband swept me off my feet when we first met.

sweep the board
(gambling, especially cards) to win everything.

sweeping victory
decisive, overwhelming victory.

sweet (as a nut)
1. satisfactory; okay; all right; in order: e.g. Don't worry — everything's sweet!
2. anything that is easy to perform.
See also:
cop it sweet

sweet cop
an easy job, career or task.

sweet F.A./Fanny Adams/fuck-all
nothing at all or very little: e.g. 1. He got sweet F.A. for all his time and effort! 2. That car's worth sweet fuck-all in the condition it's in.

sweet Jesus!
exclamation of surprise, indignation.

sweet on (someone)
infatuated with, fond of, in love with (someone): e.g. I think he's sweet on her.

sweet smell of success
sure knowledge of success.

sweet tooth
having a taste or desire for sweet foods.

sweetener
a bribe.

sweet-heart/sweetie
1. one's lover.
2. affectionate term of address.

sweet-talk
to flatter, talk ingratiatingly for personal gain: e.g. They tried to sweet-talk me into accepting the new proposals.

swell
excellent; very good; wonderful: e.g. What a swell idea!

swelled head
conceited; vain; an excessively high opinion of oneself: e.g. He's developed a swelled head since he got promoted.

swept off (one's) feet
(see: sweep . . .)

swiftie/swifty
a deceitful act; trick: e.g. He tried to pull a swifty on me but I got wise to him.

swig
a deep drink, especially of alcohol: e.g. He took a swig straight from the bottle.

swill
inferior liquor or liquid food.

swim
(see: in the swim)

swim like a brick
to sink, be unable to swim.

swim like a fish
to swim very well.

swim or sink
succeed or fail: e.g. Whether this business swims or sinks depends on what the bank does about our loan application.

swim with the tide
follow the majority, or fashionable trend; agree with the majority.

swimmers
bathing suit; swimming costume.

swimming against the tide
1. following a course of action against the wishes of the majority.
2. working, struggling against many odds: e.g. With rising bank interest-rates, we're swimming against the tide trying to keep up the payments on our house.

swine
contemptible person or thing.

swing
1. to die by hanging.
2. organise; manipulate; complete successfully: e.g. He's trying to swing a big deal with the government.

3. be full of action and excitement: e.g. 1. This night-club doesn't swing until late at night. 2. I want to go to a disco that really swings.
4. to exchange sexual partners on a casual basis.
See also:
get into the swing of things
have/got a swing on the back porch
in full swing
what you lose on the swings, you make up on the roundabouts

swing it
(see: swing, 2.)

swinger
1. lively, modern, sophisticated, socially active person.
2. person who freely exchanges sexual partners on a casual basis.

swinging
lively; with-it; modern; sophisticated; exciting: e.g. That's a real swinging disco.

swinging lead
not pulling one's weight; not doing one's fair share of work; malingering.

swipe
to steal, pilfer: e.g. Who swiped my last beer?

swish/swisho/swishy
glamorous; sophisticated; fashionable; luxurious: e.g. He took me to a very swish restaurant.

switch off
1. lose interest in: e.g. Whenever the conversation turns towards cars and footy, I switch off.
2. ignore on purpose: e.g. Some mothers can manage to switch off when the children start nagging and complaining.
3. lose sexual arousal: e.g. A big hairy spider on the ceiling would make most people switch off.

switch on
1. become interested in, enthusiastic about.
2. become sexually aroused.

switched on
(of a person) aware; sophisticated; alert; knowledgeable.

switcheroo
a turnabout, change of events.

swiz/swizzle
1. a deception, fraud.
2. to swindle, deceive.

swizzle stick
small rod for stirring alcoholic drinks.

swollen-headed
conceited; vain; having an excessively high opinion of oneself.

swoop
(see: in one fell swoop)

sword
(see: cross swords; give someone the sword; had the sword; pork sword)

sword-play
lively arguing or repartee: e.g. There was a lot of sword-play between opposing factions at the last meeting.

sworn enemies
irreconcilable enemies, opponents.

swot up on
1. study, learn hurriedly: e.g. I have to swot up on my maths for the test tomorrow.
2. re-inform oneself on a matter.

swy
the game of two-up (Greek: zwei — two).

Sydney or the bush
all or nothing; complete success or total failure.

Sydneyite
person who lives in Sydney.

sync
synchronisation; synchronised: e.g. Make sure all your watches are in sync.

synchro
(of motor vehicles and gears) synchromesh.

syphon the python
(of a man) to urinate.

syrupy
excessive sweetness of manner or sentiment.

System
(the . . .) the network of established institutions which controls a country, regarded as suppressing any attempt to change it: e.g. It's almost impossible for the average citizen to try to buck the System.

ta
thank you.

tab
a bill, such as in a restaurant: e.g. I'll pick up the tab for this meal.
See also:
have/got (someone) tabbed
keep tabs on

TAB
Totalisator Agency Board — government-operated betting agency for horse-racing.

tabby
silly old woman.

tables are turned
a reversal of the state of affairs or situation.

tacho
tachometer — instrument in a car measuring speed in terms of the rate at which the engine is turning.

tack
(see: flat as a tack; on the wrong tack; shit tacks)

tack on
add; supplement: e.g. I tacked on a few dollars extra pay for the good work.

tackle (something)
attempt; try to do, solve, deal with.

tacky
of an inferior taste or style; shoddy in quality: e.g. They live in a tacky house in that new estate.

taddie
a tadpole.

tag
1. to follow closely.
2. a word applied as characteristic of a person: e.g. She doesn't like the tag of being the 'town bike'.
3. to apply a word as characteristic of a person: e.g. He's been tagged as the town drunk.

tag along
to go along, join in with: e.g. I tagged along just to see what would happen.

tah-dah!
(joc.) a fanfare announcing someone or something, a joke, a surprise etc.

tail
1. the buttocks.
2. a woman seen as a sex object: e.g. She's a nice-looking bit of tail.
3. a spy; someone employed to follow someone else: e.g. The police have put a tail on the suspect.
4. (see tails)
5. to follow inconspicuously and watch someone: e.g. I think I'm being tailed.
See also:
chasing (one's) own tail
turn tail
with (one's) tail between (one's) legs

tailgate
to drive too closely to the vehicle in front.

tailor-made
1. appropriate; suitable for a special purpose.
2. a commercially produced cigarette.

tails
1. evening-dress with tailcoat for men.
2. the reverse side of a coin, that is the side that does not bear the image of a head.

tailspin
a state of panic: e.g. He's in a tailspin over his financial affairs.

take
1. a swindle, hoax, rip-off, act of cheating: e.g. Convincing those old ladies to part with their life-savings was a take.
2. profits: e.g. The take at the casino today was very good.
3. a scene filmed without stopping the camera: e.g.

That stunt took many takes before it was filmed successfully.
4. regard, consider, often mistakenly: e.g. Don't take him for a fool as he's smarter than he looks.
5. to swindle, cheat, rip off someone: e.g. When they split up, she took him for everything he had.
See also:
double take
have/got what it takes
if that doesn't take all!
on the take

take a back seat
retire into the background or into a subordinate position.

take a bit of doing
require considerable effort: e.g. This big job is going to take a bit of doing.

take a break
have a short rest from work.

take a deep breath
1. pause briefly to collect oneself before plunging into a task etc.
2. be relieved.

take a dim view of
disapprove of.

take a dive
1. take a sharp downturn.
2. come to ruin; collapse, fail: e.g. His business took a dive after the bank refused to extend his loan.

take a fancy to
be enchanted, drawn, infatuated by.

take a fit
become very angry; lose one's temper.

take a hammering
1. receive a sound beating, defeat.
2. receive heavy criticism, ridicule or questioning.

take a hand in
play a part in; be involved in doing: e.g. He didn't take a hand in any of their criminal activities.

take a leaf out of (someone's) book
to follow (someone's) example.

take a load off (one's) feet
to sit and rest.

take a load off (one's) mind
cease worrying or being anxious.

take a load off (one's) shoulders
ease (one's) work load, worries or anxieties.

take a long shot
take a risk.

take a long walk off a short pier!
scornful remark of dismissal, contempt, rejection to someone, telling him to go away, shut up, or that his opinion is not wanted or agreed with.

take a nose-dive
(see: take a dive).

take a piece out of (someone)
to reprimand (someone) severely: e.g. Mum took a piece out of me for coming home so late.

take a poke at (someone)
aim a punch at (someone).

take a powder
disappear, depart, go, especially quickly.

take a punt at
have a go; try; attempt.

take a rise out of (someone)
provoke, annoy, irritate (someone).

take a running jump at yourself!
a rude rebuffal or dismissal telling someone to go away, shut up, or that his opinion is not wanted or agreed with.

take a shine to
develop a liking for.

take a sickie
to take a day off from work, whether one is sick or not.

take a slow boat to China
1. a scornful dismissal (see: take a long walk off a short pier).
2. to opt out; express the desire to have nothing to do with a situation: e.g. The way the business is going at the moment, I think I'll take a slow boat to China!

take a squiz
have a look.

take a stab at
1. attempt to guess (the answer etc.).
2. have a go, try, attempt.

take a stand
1. to remain firm in one's convictions, beliefs.
2. to decide to oppose, confront: e.g. It's time someone took a stand against those bullies.

take a thumping
suffer a sound thrashing, defeat, especially in sport.

take a tumble
1. to fall: e.g. His horse took a tumble on the last fence.
2. to fail; suffer defeat, ruin, collapse: e.g. His business took a tumble during the credit squeeze.

take a walk
1. to urinate: e.g. I have to take a walk.
2. rude dismissal, rebuff: e.g. Why don't you go and take a walk! (see: take a long walk off a short pier).

take a while to sink in
take time to be fully understood; take time for the full implications to be comprehended: e.g. It took a while for the news of the death of his family to sink in.

take after
resemble, especially family members: e.g. He takes after his father.

take by storm
overwhelm; captivate the attention of: e.g. This news is going to take the world by storm.

take care of
1. attend to; deal with: e.g. I'll take care of it tomorrow.
2. to threaten with violence or actually kill, destroy, ruin (someone).

take cover
seek safety, shelter; to hide.

take down
1. write down: e.g. Did you take down everything he said at the lecture?
2. (of a person) bring to ruin; destroy; cheat; swindle: e.g. I'm going to take him down one day for what he did.

take five
have a short rest, break from work.

take for granted
1. assume, accept without question: e.g. 1. Don't take everything he says for granted. 2. I took it for granted that he was married.
2. fail to give credit, merit to: e.g. I'm sick and tired of being taken for granted!

take forty winks
have a short sleep.

take heart
approach a matter with renewed spirit, hope.

take it
1. assume: e.g. You're coming too, I take it?
2. accept; endure; tolerate: e.g. I can't take it any more, so I'm leaving.

take it and shove it!
a rude rebuff, dismissal, rejection, denial.

take it for a spin
(of a car) take for a test drive.

take it in (one's) stride
find no serious impediment, problem, worry in (it); to cope or deal with effectively.

take it lying down
accept or submit without protest: e.g. I'm not going to take this lying down — I'm going to sue him!

take it on the chin
accept consequences or a task bravely and without complaint.

take it or leave it
accept it or reject it; show indifference: e.g. As far as booze is concerned — I can take it or leave it.

take it out of (one)
exhaust, tire (one): e.g. All those late nights are really taking it out of me!

take it out on (someone)
to vent one's anger, frustration etc. on (someone): e.g. Whenever he has a bad day at work, he takes it out on me when he gets home!

take it to heart
1. be offended or hurt by something said or done in jest.
2. be deeply affected or grieved by.

take it with a grain/pinch of salt
be wary, sceptical of the truth of a matter.

take leave of (one's) senses
behave, act foolishly, rashly, stupidly.

take off
1. to imitate a person in a jesting, mocking, satirical or ironical manner: e.g. He takes off the Prime Minister better than anyone I've ever seen.
2. get started; begin: e.g. When's the next meeting going to take off?
3. become famous, popular: e.g. This new book is really going to take off.
4. leave, go, depart: e.g. We have to take off by midnight.
5. (of prices) to increase, escalate: e.g. The cost of living has really taken off over the last few years.

take off like a rocket
1. go, depart, leave in great haste, speed.
2. become famous, popular, wildly successful: e.g. That new band took off like a rocket!

take off with
1. steal: e.g. Someone took off with my handbag!
2. run away with; steal away: e.g. She took off with her husband's best friend.

take on
1. hire (someone): e.g. We need to take on another two workers over the busy holiday time.
2. fight (someone): e.g. It's not wise to take on someone who is twice your size.
3. accept (a task, job, activity): e.g. I can't take on any more work as I'm too busy.
4. accept a wager, gamble, bet: e.g. I'll take you on!
5. (in sport) play the opposing team: e.g. We take on the highest ranking team in the finals next week.

take (one) at (one's) word
to believe literally, without question, what (one) has said.

take (one's) breath away
astonish, amaze (one); cause great wonder, admiration in (one): e.g. The beauty of the scenery will take your breath away.

take (one's) dog for a walk
to urinate.

take (one's) hat off to
to congratulate, acknowledge (someone/something).

take (one's) life in (one's) hands
take great risks; risk death or grave injury.

take (one's) medicine
suffer the consequences of (one's) actions: e.g. Now that the police are on to him he has to take his medicine.

take (one's) time
do something slowly, in a leisurely manner.

take out
to win, defeat, especially at sport: e.g. 1. We took out first prize in the competition. 2. We took out the best team in the finals.

take part
participate: e.g. Did you take part in that prank?

take pot-luck
take whatever is to be had.

take sides
support one party against the other in a dispute; show favouritism, bias.

take some doing
require considerable effort: e.g. It's going to take some doing to finish this job on time.

take some pickies
take some photographs.

take (someone) apart
1. abuse, scold, berate, criticise (someone).
2. assault, beat, bash (someone).

take (someone) down
(see: take down)

take (someone) down a peg or two
to humble, embarrass, humiliate (someone).

take (someone) for a ride
1. deceive, trick, swindle, cheat (someone).
2. kill (someone): e.g. The Mafia took him for a ride.

take (someone) in hand
severely discipline, reprimand (someone); pull (someone) into line after a misdemeanour.

take (someone) on
1. fight (someone).
2. accept a bet, wager, debate, contest with (someone).

take (someone) out
1. treat (someone) to a night of entertainment on the town.
2. defeat (someone) in a battle, fight, contest.

take (someone) to pieces
1. fight, beat up (someone).
2. reprimand, criticise (someone) severely.

take (someone) to task
accuse, reprimand, scold, berate, censure (someone).

take (someone) to the cleaners
strip (someone) of as much money and assets as possible: e.g. Those crooks took a lot of people to the cleaners before the police stepped in.

take (someone/something) with a grain/pinch of salt
be sceptical about the truth, honesty or integrity of (someone/something).

take (someone's) part
defend, sympathise with (someone).

take (someone's) word for it
accept without question the truth of what (someone) has said.

take steps
take, initiate action: e.g. I'm going to take steps to see that it never happens again.

take the bait
1. to be fooled, tricked, conned, enticed.
2. to be provoked.

take the bit between (one's) teeth
1. tackle a task or problem promptly and energetically.
2. act impetuously, without restraint or control.

take the bull by the horns
act promptly and without procrastination, especially in the face of difficult circumstances.

take the cake
beat, better every other option, opponent, circumstance: e.g. Boy! That last remark of his really takes the cake!

take the covers off
reveal, disclose: e.g. The reporters have taken the covers off one of the biggest political scandals of the century.

take the flak
accept, be the victim of severe criticism, repercussions: e.g. I'm not going to take the flak for something I didn't do.

take the floor
accept the responsibility of speaker; assume the centre of attention: e.g. Everyone's sick of listening to you — it's about time someone else took the floor for a while!

take the hot seat
accept, assume, the responsibility, leadership, highest position or centre of attention, especially under hostile or difficult circumstances.

take the law into (one's) own hands
to seek justice or revenge personally, disregarding the usual legal procedures.

take the mickey out of (someone)
make a fool of, tease (someone); act disrespectfully to (someone) in the hope of causing grave embarrassment; humble, degrade, belittle (someone).

take the piss out of (someone)
1. (see: take the mickey out of)
2. humble, degrade, belittle (someone) by getting the better of him.

take the plunge
decide on a course of action (that may be distasteful) and then act immediately; take a reckless gamble, risk.

take the rap
accept blame, especially when one is innocent of the crime: e.g. She took the rap for the murder he committed.

take the rough with the smooth
endure, tolerate the bad with the good.

take the shine out of
1. spoil the fun and pleasure of: e.g. The rain took the shine out of the weekend camping trip.
2. humiliate; humble: e.g. His cutting remarks took the shine out of her.

take the shirt off (someone's) back
to take, steal, extort the last remaining asset from (someone).

take the shitter out of (someone)
(see: take the piss out of someone, 1. and 2.)

take the sting out of
lessen, ease the hurt, emotional impact of.

take the veil
to become a nun.

take the wind out of (someone's) sails
to deflate (someone's) ego, prestige, by doing better; to humiliate, humble (someone).

take the words out of (one's/someone's) mouth
say, express exactly what (one/someone) was going to say.

take time out
make an effort to do something: e.g. I must take some time out to go fishing with the kids this week.

take to (one's) heels
escape; run away: e.g. As soon as he saw the police, he took to his heels.

take to (someone)
1. attack; beat up; assault physically or verbally: e.g. She took to him with a barrage of insults.
2. like: e.g. I took to him as soon as I saw him.

take to (something) like a duck to water
adapt well, especially to new circumstances.

take to the bottle
drink excessive amounts of alcohol: e.g. He takes to the bottle every time he gets depressed.

take to the bush
1. to run away and hide.
2. to abandon a life in the city for one in the country.
3. to go, disappear.

take to the hills
run away and hide: e.g. As soon as the gang realised that the police were after them they took to the hills.

take to the road
1. to depart on a journey by road.
2. to abandon conventional life's values and become a tramp, wanderer.

take turns
to alternate: e.g. We took turns at driving.

take two bites at the cherry
1. to have two chances or opportunities to do something.
2. (Australian Rules football) mark a ball after two attempts.

take under (one's) wing
take in and protect, care for, treat as (one's) ward, responsibility: e.g. From my earliest years away from home, Bloss took me under her wing and treated me as one of the family.

take up with
associate with; be on familiar, friendly terms with: e.g. I don't want my son to take up with the members of that bikie gang.

take what (someone) says with a grain/pinch of salt
be wary, sceptical, of the truth of what (someone) says.

take your pick
choose whichever you desire.

take-away
food bought and taken out of the shop to be eaten elsewhere; fast food.

take-down
a trick, swindle or act of deception.

taken
cheated; swindled; tricked; deceived; ripped off: e.g. I think I've been taken by that crook!

taken by storm
overwhelmed; captivated; enthralled.

taken for a ride
1. cheated; swindled; tricked; deceived.
2. killed; murdered.

taken in
cheated; tricked; deceived: e.g. I was taken in by his innocent appearance.

take-off
act of mimicking someone or something; spoof; caricature; imitation: e.g. He does a very funny take-off of the Prime Minister.

taker
1. person who selfishly takes but never gives friendship, gifts, hospitality etc.
2. potential buyer for something.

takes one to know one
an insinuation that it is not possible to have given an opinion (usually bad or derogatory) about a person without having some of his (bad) qualities oneself.

takes two to tango
pertaining to the belief that the total fault or blame (such as in a relationship gone bad) cannot lie entirely with one person — both must share the blame.

tale
a lie, fib, fabrication.
See also:
tell tales out of school

talent
unattached men or women viewed as possible sex partners: e.g. There's usually a lot of talent at the disco on Saturday night.

talk
1. gossip; rumour; hearsay: e.g. That's nothing but a whole lot of talk!
2. nonsense; worthless talk: e.g. Nothing will be done — it's all a lot of empty talk!
3. betray someone; inform on: e.g. Did you talk when the police interviewed you?
4. criticise: e.g. You can't talk — you're just as bad!
5. berate, scold, censure: e.g. I'll have to talk to him about his rudeness.
See also:
big talk
couldn't talk if (one) lost (one's) arms
double-talk
long talk
money talks
sweet-talk

talk a lot of crap/shit
indulge in meaningless, empty or insincere talk.

talk about . . .!
used to add emphasis: e.g. Talk about dumb! He's the most stupid person I've met!

talk as if (one) has a plum in (one's) mouth
(see: plum in the mouth)

talk back
answer impertinently: e.g. Don't you talk back to your father like that!

talk behind (someone's) back
utter unkind, scurrilous, scandalous, derogatory remarks about (someone) in that person's absence.

talk big
talk boastfully or with exaggeration.

talk double-dutch
speak gibberish or language which is difficult to understand.

talk down to
speak patronisingly or condescendingly to.

talk nineteen to the dozen
talk fast and in an excited manner that is difficult to understand or decipher.

talk of the devil
(see: speak . . .)

talk of the town
subject of gossip, rumour (good or bad): e.g. She's the talk of the town after what she did.

talk off the top of (one's) head
1. speak nonsense; proffer worthless, ill-considered information, opinions etc.
2. speak fluently on a matter without prior preparation: e.g. He got up in front of the audience and gave a talk about computers off the top of his head.

talk (one's) head off
speak at length in an animated manner: e.g. She talked her head off about her divorce and other problems.

talk shop
to discuss one's business, profession, job etc. to the detriment of other topics of conversation: e.g. Teachers always talk shop when they get together for social functions.

talk show
an interview programme on television or radio.

talk (someone) blind
to talk at length and bore (someone).

talk (someone) down
1. speak patronisingly, condescendingly to (someone).
2. to speak more loudly than someone else so that he is unable to be heard.

talk (someone) into
convince, persuade (someone): e.g. She talked him into doing it even though he didn't want to.

talk (someone) round
persuade (someone) to change a view or opinion: e.g. I know he doesn't want to do it, but don't worry — I'll talk him round.

talk (someone's) ears off
talk at length, often boring (someone).

talk (something) out
resolve arguments or differences through discussion: e.g. We're going to talk this thing out before it goes any further.

talk the legs off a wooden table/an iron pot
1. to talk and prattle on at great length, often boring the listener.
2. to be very persuasive: e.g. Larissa can convince anyone to part with his money — she could talk the legs off an iron pot!

talk through (one's) bum
(see: talking through one's arsehole)

talk till the cows come home
1. to talk and prattle on at great length.
2. to talk to no avail, in vain.

talk turkey
talk, discuss the facts or business seriously.

talkie
an old word for a movie with a soundtrack: e.g. Charlie Chaplin's career took a turn for the worse after the introduction of talkies.

talking
beginning to talk sense, seriously: e.g. Now you're talking!

talking point
subject for discussion, controversy, dispute.

talking through (one's) arsehole/hat

talking through the back of (one's) neck
speaking ill-informed nonsense; talking meaninglessly or insincerely: e.g. He's talking through his hat if he thinks that idea will seriously work.

talking to a brick wall
speaking but not being heard, listened to: e.g. Asking him to do anything is like talking to a brick wall.

talking-to
a severe reprimand, scolding: e.g. He needs a good talking-to before he gets into serious trouble.

tall
extravagant; unbelievable: e.g. That story he told about his experiences sounds a bit tall to me.

tall order
a difficult requirement or thing asked of one to perform: e.g. That's a very tall order but I'll do my best.

tall poppy
very important person; influential person; person with status — often held in contempt by others, who try to bring about this person's downfall or ruin.

tall story
story or thing said that is far-fetched or difficult to believe.

tall streak of misery
person who is always morose or miserable.

tally-ho!
good-bye!

tan (someone's) hide
give (someone) a hiding, beating.

tangle with
come into conflict with; argue with: e.g. I'd hate to tangle with that huge bloke!

tangle-foot
one who is clumsy on his feet.

tank
a large, gaudy, pretentious car (especially an American one).

tank loaf
round, cylinder-shaped bread with corrugated pattern.

tank top
garment resembling a singlet.

tank up
to fill a vehicle with fuel, petrol.

tanked
intoxicated; drunk.

tanner
(formerly) sixpence; a sixpenny coin.

tanning
a beating or defeat.

tap (someone's) brain
exploit (someone's) knowledge; profit from (someone's) knowledge.

taped
(see: got someone taped)

tar
sailor; seaman.
See also:
touch of the tar-brush

tar and feather (someone)
to severely punish (someone) (taken from the practice of covering a person with tar and feathers: an old form of punishment or humiliation).

tarnation!
mild oath — damnation!

tarp
tarpaulin.

tarred with the same brush
having similar faults: e.g. Those two boys have been tarred with the same brush — they're always getting into trouble together!

tart
immoral woman; prostitute.

tart up
embellish, decorate, make up in a garish, cheap manner: e.g. 1. That

'One thing about Bert, he always leaves the rubbidy-dub the same as he went in — under the weather!'

You can find Bert, like lots of other average Aussie ockers, leaving his favourite boozer in any one of the following conditions: blasted, blind, blithered, blotto, bombed, cock-eyed, corked, drunk as a skunk, full as a boot/bull's bum/goog/tick/the family po, high, history, inked, lit up, loaded, mollo, pissed as a cricket, plastered, primed, para, ripped, rotten, sauced, sloshed, smashed, soused, sozzled, spiflicated, stinko, tanked, tight, wasted, well oiled, whacked or zonked. (For a more comprehensive list of synonyms for drunk see 'Alcohol, drinking and inebriation' in 'Word lists' at the end of the dictionary.)

young girl looks awful tarted up like that! 2. They tarted up the house for a quick sale.

Tas
Tasmania.

tassel
penis: e.g. He's got a tassel the size of a peanut!

Tassie
Tasmania.

taste of (one's) own medicine
to experience the (unpleasant) treatment (one) usually metes out to others.

tat
tattoo: e.g. He's got tats all over his back.

ta-ta
good-bye.

tater/tatie
potato.

tattle-tale
one who discloses confidences or secrets; one who informs on or betrays others.

tatty
shabby; ragged; inferior.

tax dodge/lurk
a scheme of tax avoidance.

tax dodger
one who is involved in schemes to avoid paying tax.

tax haven
any place or country in which little or no tax is paid by the residents.

tax lurk
a scheme of tax avoidance.

tax (one's) mind
make one think very hard; make demands on (one's) mental resources and knowledge.

tax (someone)
borrow, cadge from (someone) with no real intention of paying back: e.g. Can I tax you for a cigarette?

taxi doors
pertaining to unattractive, large ears: e.g. He's got ears like taxi doors!

TB
tuberculosis.

tea
the evening meal and usually the main meal of the day: e.g. I'm cooking a roast for tea.
See also:
kitchen tea
not for all the tea in China
not my cup of tea
storm in a tea-cup
tea-leaf

tea-break
short rest from work to have tea, coffee etc., usually taken mid morning and afternoon.

teach
teacher (used impertinently by students): e.g. G'day teach!

teach one's grandmother to suck eggs
presume to teach or explain something to one more experienced than oneself.

teach (someone) a lesson
1. cause (someone) to learn by an unpleasant experience: e.g. Going through the unpleasant experience of being caught for stealing has really taught him a lesson. 2. threaten (someone) with violence, vengeance: e.g. Next time I see him, I'm going to teach him a lesson!

teach (someone) a thing or two
1. an assertion of one's superior knowledge and experience: e.g. He could teach you a thing or two! 2. threaten (someone) with violence, vengeance: e.g. I'm going to teach him a thing or two next time I see him!

teacher's pet
child who is favoured by the teacher.

tea-leaf
(rhyming slang) thief.

team up with
collaborate with; associate with.

tear
move with force, speed, violence: e.g. They were tearing down the highway at a hundred and sixty kilometres an hour!
See also:
on the tear
out on the tear

tear into
1. attack physically or verbally: e.g. You didn't have to tear into me with all those insults in public! 2. begin with gusto, enthusiasm: e.g. They were so hungry they tore into their dinner without further ado.

tear off
leave, depart, go in haste: e.g. We're going to have to tear off or we'll be late for the meeting.

tear (one's) hair out
an expression of extreme frustration, anxiety, anger: e.g. I've been tearing my hair out wondering where you've been all night!

tear (oneself) away
leave unwillingly: e.g. 1. That meeting was so interesting that I had to tear myself away. 2. That meeting was so interesting that I couldn't tear myself away before midnight.

tear (someone) to pieces
1. fight, assault, beat (someone) up severely. 2. reprimand, criticise (someone) severely: e.g. The newspaper reports tore him to pieces.

tear strips off (someone)

tear the arse out of (someone)
scold, reprove, reprimand (someone) severely.

tear-arse
1. a wild, reckless, impulsive or delinquent person.
2. a fast driver.

tearaway
uncontrollable, boisterous person; rascal.

tear-jerker
anything that is extremely sad, emotional, causing one to be reduced to tears: e.g. That movie is a real tear-jerker.

tease/teaser
(of a woman) behaving enticingly and flirting but not actually giving sexual favours: e.g. She's nothing but a tease.
See also:
cock-teaser

tech
technical; technical college.

technical
(get . . .) to speak in technical terms, jargon that is difficult to understand.

technicolour yawn
vomit; the act of vomiting: e.g. He did a technicolour yawn all over my garden!

teddy (bear)
1. extravagantly dressed man.
2. show-off.

tee up
organise; arrange: e.g. I'll tee up a meeting with him for you by next week.

tee-hee
giggle; ha-ha.

teeny
tiny; small; minute.

teeny-bopper
young teenager who is wildly enthusiastic about pop music.

teeny-weeny
(also: teensy-weensy) tiny; small; minute.

teeth
(see: armed to the teeth; by the skin of one's teeth; cut one's teeth on; enough to set one's teeth on edge; fed up to the back teeth; get one's teeth into; give one's back teeth for; grit one's teeth; kick in the teeth; lie through one's teeth; sink one's teeth into; take the bit between one's teeth; thrilled to the back teeth)

teeth like a row of condemned houses
(to have . . .) to have bad, decaying, crooked or protruding teeth.

teething problems
the initial problems, difficulties in a venture, enterprise: e.g. We've got a few teething problems to sort out, but otherwise the business is doing very well.

Teledex
device for alphabetical listing of telephone numbers which can be opened automatically at the letter selected. (Trademark)

telegraph (one's) punches
give prior warning of (one's) intentions, especially to an opponent.

telethon
television programme to raise money for charity whereby viewers telephone the programme to pledge donations.

tell me about it!
expression of emphatic agreement, empathy with someone else's problems.

tell on (someone)
betray, inform, tattle on (someone).

tell (someone) a thing or two
1. to admonish, reprimand, scold (someone).
2. to be able to provide much information from one's vast experience: e.g. That old man can tell you a thing or two about the war and what went on.

tell (someone) off/what for
scold, reprimand (someone): e.g. Mum's going to tell you what for when you get home!

tell tales out of school
to discuss one's friend's or associate's confidences, secrets, misdemeanours etc. indiscriminately, needlessly or maliciously with someone else.

tell that to the Marines!

tell us anotherie!
expression of scornful disbelief.

tell-tale
1. informant; one who betrays, reveals other people's secrets or confidences; a dobber.
2. something that is unconsciously revealing: e.g. He's got the tell-tale signs of a man heading for a nervous break-down.

telly
television.

temperature
body heat above normal, indicating a fever, illness: e.g. I kept him home from school because he's got a temperature.

ten
first-rate; excellent; the best when rated on a scale from 1 to 10: e.g. She's so gorgeous, she's a ten!
See also:
lay you tens

ten cents short of the dollar
(to be . . .) to be dumb, slow-witted, lacking in

intelligence, mentally retarded.

tenderfoot
inexperienced person; beginner; novice.

ten-four
(also: 10–4) exclamation of acceptance, understanding, agreement, especially in the dialogue of CB radio users.

tenner
a ten-dollar note; the sum of ten dollars.

ten-ounce sandwich
(joc.) a glass of beer for lunch.

ten-ton tessie
a very large, fat, obese woman.

terrible
1. very great; extreme: e.g. That cost a terrible lot of money.
2. bad; awful; unsatisfactory; second-rate: e.g. My finances are in a terrible state.

terrible twos
the stage of an infant's life — two years old — reputed to be the most tiresome and wearing on the parents.

terribly
very; extremely: e.g. He was terribly nice.

terrif/terrific
1. very good; excellent: e.g. That film was terrific.
2. very great: e.g. She drove at a terrific speed.

terror
person of great nuisance value, especially a child; troublesome, annoying person or thing.

test-drive
sample, try, especially of a car prior to purchase.

test-tube baby
baby resulting from in-vitro fertilisation; baby who is conceived outside the mother's body and then implanted in the mother's womb.

thank
(see: have/got oneself to thank)

thank God
expression of relief: e.g. Thank God the fire department arrived so quickly to save our house from total destruction.

thank (one's) lucky stars
be relieved, elated at (one's) good fortune.

thanks a bunch/million
1. thank you very much; an expression of gratitude.
2. sarcastic remark or reply to something unwanted: e.g. Thanks a million! Now look what you've done!

thanks for nothing!
sarcastic remark in response to receiving little help or no benefit.

that
an intensifier meaning so, very much: e.g. He was that rude!
See also:
and all that
at that

that did it!
1. that was the end of (one's) patience, tolerance!
2. that was just what was required!

that does it!
exclamation indicating the limit of one's patience, tolerance: e.g. That does it! If you're late for work again, you're fired!

that figures!
that was to be expected!

that was a bit rich
that (joke, language, act, behaviour etc.) was in bad taste, not socially acceptable, too strong, excessive.

that way inclined
homosexual: e.g. I didn't know he was that way inclined!

that wraps it up
that finishes, settles a matter.

that'll be the day!
a cynical expression of disbelief.

that's a good one!
expression of disbelief.

that's a no-no
that is not acceptable socially, morally, ethically, according to the rules etc.

that's about the size of it
that is the way it is, the true condition, the actual circumstances.

that's for me to know and you to find out
an expression of refusal to answer a question about one's age, where one got something from, how one achieved something etc.

that's got whiskers on it!
an expression of one's dislike of, displeasure with (something).

that's it!
an expression indicating the end, limit of one's tolerance, endurance, patience.

that's life!
an exclamation of resignation, tolerance, forced acceptance of things about life that one cannot change.

that's no lady — that's my wife!
(joc.) a man's stock reply to another who asks him about a lady he has been seen with.

that's not the half of it
that's not the most significant aspect.

that's that!
exclamation of dismissal signalling the end of the matter.

that's the breaks!
an exclamation of resignation, tolerance, forced acceptance of unfortunate incidents over which one has no control.

that's the shot/stuff/trick!
exclamation of approval of something that is exactly what is required; that's the right thing to do; that's the desired result or action.

that's the way it goes!

that's the way the ball bounces/cookie crumbles!
(see: that's the breaks!)

that's torn it!
that (action, occurrence etc.) has ruined, spoiled, messed up (something).

the ant's pants
the best, ultimate; first-class: e.g. He thinks he's the ant's pants!

the axe
1. dismissal from a job, position etc.: e.g. 1. He got the axe for always coming late to work. 2. That television programme is getting the axe.
2. drastic reduction of something such as expenses.

the bee's knees
the best, ultimate; first-class. (see: the ant's pants)

the bends
symptoms of caisson disease — the formation of nitrogen bubbles in the blood when external pressure changes too quickly, as when a diver ascends to the surface too quickly.

the big A
the arse, the axe, dismissal from a job, position etc.: e.g. If he does the wrong thing again, the boss is going to give him the big A.

the big C
cancer.

the big spit
vomit: e.g. He went for the big spit all over the back seat of the car!

the big sticks
(Australian Rules football) the goals.

the box
television; a television receiver: e.g. What's on the box tonight?

the boys
term of friendship among men; a man's mates, allies, cohorts, buddies, companions: e.g. He's having a drink at the pub with the boys tonight.

the cat's whiskers
the best, ultimate; first-class; excellent: e.g. This new model car is just the cat's whiskers!

the chop
(see: the big A)

the creeps
(see: the horrors)

the Cross
1. King's Cross — a lively, sophisticated and entertaining area of Sydney.
2. the Southern Cross star formation.
3. the cross Jesus was crucified on.

the curse
(of women) menstruation.

the dinkum oil
true and correct advice or information.

the Don
Sir Donald Bradman — best all-round cricket player.

the done thing
the socially accepted, correct thing to do: e.g. Sneezing all over the dinner table is not the done thing.

the end of the world
emotional disaster; anything that is very distressing: e.g. He thinks it's the end of the world because he failed his exams.
See also:
it's not the end of the world

the few
the minority: e.g. The few who cause trouble have given the whole club a bad name.

the fuck
an intensive, akin in meaning to on earth, in heaven's name: e.g.
1. Who the fuck are you?
2. What the fuck are you doing?

the full bore
the maximum, especially of power: e.g. We gave it the full bore when we took it for a test-drive and the car performed very well.

the full treatment
1. severe criticism, punishment: e.g. He got the full treatment from his wife when he arrived home very late and very drunk.
2. the best service available: e.g. We got the full treatment at that hotel.

the full two bob
1. genuine; real; sincere: e.g. That deal doesn't sound like the full two bob to me.
2. of sound mind; mentally sound: e.g. He's not the full two bob.

the gallops/gee-gees
the horse-races.

the Good Book
the Bible.

the good oil
true and correct advice or information: e.g. He gets the good oil on the best

investments from someone who works at the stock exchange.

the horrors
intense feeling of displeasure, dislike, disgust, fear: e.g. He gives me the horrors!
See also:
get the dry-horrors

the house that Jack built
venereal disease clinic (the jack: venereal disease).

the in-thing
anything that is modern, fashionable, stylish, currently popular.

the joke's on (someone)
statement made to or about (someone) who is the object of ridicule, especially after a blunder or mistake.

the last straw
the final thing, incident, mishap etc. that leads to a reaction, outburst of emotion or break-down: e.g. That's the last straw — you're fired!

the last word
1. the closing statement or remark; the final say: e.g. After an argument, she always likes to have the last word.
2. the latest, most modern, up-to-date: e.g. This particular machine is the last word in computer technology.

the latest
the most up-to-date fashion, trend, news, gossip etc.: e.g. 1. Have you heard the latest about her? 2. This hairstyle is the latest for this summer.

the little woman
wife.

the look(s) of
the appearance of: e.g. By the looks of him I'd say he's had a very bad time.

the magic word
1. any word pertinent to a particular subject or matter, especially 'yes': e.g. If she'd only say the magic word, I'd marry her tomorrow!
2. a vulgar or profane swear-word, especially the word 'fuck': e.g. When he dropped the magic word in front of my parents, I nearly died with embarrassment.
See also:
drop the magic word
say the magic word

the mind boggles
one is astounded, amazed at: e.g. The mind boggles at the thought of infinity and endless space in the universe.

the missus
(of men) wife: e.g. I left the missus at home.

the Mob
an organised crime syndicate such as the Mafia.

the old cheese
one's mother: e.g. The old cheese won't let me go to the concert.

the old country
one's place of birth, origin apart from the country in which one is now living: e.g. Grandpa always had dreams of going back to the old country.

the old dear
one's mother.

the old dears
one's parents: e.g. I have to visit the old dears this weekend.

the old heave-ho
dismissal from one's job, position; the sack: e.g. He was given the old heave-ho because he was incompetent.

the old lady
1. one's mother.
2. (of a man) the wife.

the old man
1. one's father.
2. (of a woman) the husband.
3. employer; boss.

the old one-two
1. a beating or severe censure: e.g. Mum really gave him the old one-two for what he did!
2. sexual intercourse: e.g. I'd love to give her the old one-two!

the old woman
1. one's mother.
2. (of a man) the wife.

the other day/night
one or two days/nights ago: e.g. I saw him the other day.

the penny finally dropped
understanding, comprehension suddenly came.

the pill
oral contraceptive in tablet form.

the push
dismissal, sacking, firing from one's job, position: e.g. I was given the push for something I didn't do.

the real McCoy/thing
genuine; sincere; true: e.g. This antique is the real McCoy.

the Rock
Ayers Rock.

the shits
1. diarrhoea: e.g. I've got the shits after eating all that curry and spice.
2. feelings of anger, annoyance, frustration, bad temper, irritation : e.g. He's got the shits with me because I didn't do what he asked.
3. feelings of petulance, sulkiness, misery: e.g. He's got the shits because his dog died.
See also:
get the shits
give someone the shits
put the shits up someone

the sticks
the country as opposed to the city; unsophisticated backwoods as opposed to urban life: e.g. 1. He lives out in the sticks. 2. He originally comes from the sticks.

the things you see when you haven't got a gun!
expression of amazement, wonder.

the treatment
(see: the full treatment)

the trots
diarrhoea.

the usual
one's usual requirement, especially a favourite alcoholic drink: e.g. What'll you have — the usual?

the way to a man's heart is through his belly and what hangs on the end of it
pertaining to the belief (held by women) that the best way to please a man is with good food and sex.

the Wet
the rainy season in tropical climates.

the works
1. (see: the full treatment, 1. and 2.)
2. everything available; the lot: e.g. 1. When she left her husband she took the works and left him with nothing. 2. I want the works on my hamburger.

the worse for wear
1. damaged by use.
2. not looking its/one's best.

them's the breaks!
(see: that's the breaks!)

then and there
immediately and on the spot: e.g. He wanted his money then and there but I couldn't give it to him.

there
(see: all there; not all there)

there are more fish in the sea/pebbles on the beach
expression of condolence, sympathy, consolation (to someone) for having lost something, especially a potential sexual relationship.

there are more ways of killing a cat than by drowning it

there are more ways than one to skin a cat
there are always other ways of doing things if the first attempt or method failed.

there are no flies on (someone)!
(someone) is smart, alert, clever, not to be underestimated.

there are two sides to a coin
there are always two points of view in an argument or dispute.

there are ways and there are ways
there are many options open for doing the same thing, achieving the same goal.

there, but for the grace of God, go I
an expression of relief that one is not in the same unpleasant circumstances as the person one is looking at.

there, there!
exclamation of sympathy: e.g. There, there! Everything will be fine!

there you are/go!
expression asking for agreement with, recognition of one's views: e.g. There you are! I told you it was broken, didn't I?

there'll be hell to pay
there is going to be a lot of trouble; there will be severe repercussions or consequences: e.g. There'll be hell to pay when he finds out what you've done!

there's often a rainbow after the storm
expression of condolence, sympathy, consolation; the present unpleasant situation will get better.

there's safety in numbers
1. the safest course of action is to go, agree with the majority.
2. it is wise to have many friends or supporters in a risky confrontation.

thick
1. dull; stupid; slow-witted; lacking in intelligence: e.g. He's so thick he wouldn't know what you meant.
2. very close; intimate; friendly: e.g. Those two are really thick.
See also:
a bit thick
in the thick of
lay it on thick
spread it on thick
through thick and thin

thick as a brick/log of wood
dull; stupid; slow-witted; lacking in intelligence.

thick as thieves
very close; intimate; friendly.

thick as two short planks

thick between the ears
(see: thick as a brick)

thick ear
a beating, hiding, physical assault: e.g. I'm going to give him a thick ear next time I see him!

thick hide
insensitivity to any criticism or verbal abuse: e.g. He's got such a thick hide that nothing you say will offend him.

thick with
abounding with: e.g. The place is thick with police, so be careful.

thick-headed
stupid, dull-witted person; fool.

thick-skinned
insensitive to criticism or verbal abuse.

thick-skulled/witted
stupid; dull-witted; lacking in intelligence.

thieve the eye out of a needle and come back for the thread
pertaining to someone who is a compulsive thief.

thin
(see: spread oneself too thin; wearing thin)

thin edge of the wedge
small beginning or situation that may lead to something greater, more significant; only a small part of the total.

thin on the ground
rare; uncommon: e.g. Honest, ethical people are very thin on the ground.

thin up top
balding.

thing
1. the penis: e.g. He got his thing stuck in the zipper of his pants.
2. person: e.g. You poor thing!
3. special attitude or feeling: e.g. He's developed a thing about motor-bikes since his brother was killed on one.
4. one's special interest, hobby, vocation etc.: e.g. His thing is model boats.
5. term of address when one has temporarily forgotten a name: e.g. What time is thing arriving?
See also:
a good thing
close thing
do (one's) thing
do the right thing by
done thing
enough of a good thing
go all thing
going thing
have/got a good thing going
have/got a thing about (someone)
interested in only one thing
in-thing
just the thing
know a thing or two
like one thing
make a thing of
near thing
not get a thing out of
not (one's) thing
not the done thing
old thing
on a good thing
on a sure thing
seeing things
show (someone) a thing or two
sure thing
teach (someone) a thing or two
tell (someone) a thing or two
the done thing
the real thing
too much of a good thing

thingamabob/ thingummy(bob)

thingamajig/thingummyjig
term for something whose name one has temporarily forgotten; gadget; object; article.

thingie/thingo
1. thing; object; name for something (or someone) that can't be immediately remembered.
2. over-sensitive; anxious: e.g. There's no need to get all thingie about it!

things
1. personal belongings: e.g. Put your things on the table.
2. general state of affairs: e.g. How are things with you two?
See also:
don't let things get to you
how's things?
just one of those things
let things slide
the things you see when you haven't got a gun!

things are crook (at Tallarook)
expression for any bad, unpleasant, unsuccessful situation.

things are looking up
the situation is getting better, improving.

think
(see: if you think . . . you've got another think coming)

think all (one's) birthdays/ Christmases have come at once
(see: thought . . .)

think better of
decide against an original intention.

think big
have great ambitions, ideals, aspirations.

think little of
have a low, poor opinion of.

think nothing of
1. have a low opinion of.
2. disregard.

think over
to consider carefully: e.g. I have to think it over before I decide what to do.

think the world of
have the highest regard for: e.g. He thinks the world of you.

think twice
avoid hasty action with careful thought; consider again before taking rash action: e.g. You'd better think twice before you commit yourself to that course of action.
See also:
not think twice about (something)

thinking aloud
uttering one's thoughts as one has them.

thinks he's God's gift to women
(of a man) to have an egotistically high opinion of (himself) and to believe vainly that he is sexually appealing to all women.

thinks (he's/she's) Christmas

thinks (he's/she's) the ant's pants

thinks (he's/she's) the bee's knees

thinks (he's/she's) the cat's whiskers

thinks his shit doesn't stink, but his farts give him away

thinks the sun shines out of his/her arse
to have an egotistically high opinion of him/herself that is not shared by others.

thinks only of his belly and what hangs on the end of it
said by a woman of a man who is chauvinistic, thoughtless, and whose mind is always on food and sex.

thinks with his dick
(of a man) to constantly think of sex.

think-tank
a conference, group, organisation etc. of experts brought together to solve national, commercial etc. problems and to generate creative ideas.

thin-skinned
sensitive to criticism and verbal abuse; easily offended, hurt.

third degree
intense and often unpleasant interrogation: e.g. He was given the third degree by the police, who suspect he was involved in the crime.

third time lucky!
expression of encouragement after having twice failed.

Third World
non-industrialised, under-developed, poor nations or parts of the world such as Africa, South America, South-East Asia.

third-rate
very low in standard or quality; inferior.

thirsty work
work that generates a desire for a drink — especially beer.

this arvo
this afternoon: e.g. We're going fishing this arvo.

this is it!
exclamation indicating some profound, meaningful event is about to occur.

this is the life!
exclamation indicating extreme pleasure, satisfaction with one's life or present situation.

this is where it's at
this is the best, ultimate, most pleasant or sophisticated place to be or situation to be in.

this minute
immediately.

this side of the Black Stump
an imaginary point of reference: e.g. That's the best pub this side of the Black Stump.

this-an'-that
(rhyming slang) hat.

thorn in (one's) side
source of continued annoyance, irritation: e.g. He's nothing but a thorn in her side now, and she wants a divorce.

those are the breaks!
(see: that's the breaks!)

those were the (good old) days!
expression of wistful reminiscence about days gone by.

thou
1. thousand (dollars, items etc.): e.g. That car cost me twenty thou!
2. thousandth (of a centimetre, second etc.).

thought
(see: have second thoughts; it's the thought that counts)

thought all (one's) birthdays/Christmases had come at once
1. to believe falsely that (one) has had an extraordinary stroke of good fortune: e.g. We thought all our Christmases had come at once when we found that huge nugget, but it turned out to be worthless fool's gold.
2. to feel extremely elated over some extraordinary good fortune: e.g. Wayne thought all his birthdays had come at once when he found an old Ford on an abandoned farm.
3. to have received a severe fright or close call in which (one) faced grave, life-threatening danger: e.g. When he pulled a gun on me I thought all my birthdays had come at once!

thousand and one
many; myriad; numberless: e.g. There are a thousand and one ways to make a fortune if you're enterprising enough.

thrash
defeat soundly, easily: e.g. Our team thrashed the opposition.

thrash out
ponder, think, debate, discuss all details of a matter or problem.

threads
clothes: e.g. I had to buy some new threads for the wedding.
See also:
hanging by a thread
pick up the threads

three parts gone/pissed
intoxicated; drunk.

three R's
the three main disciplines of education in a school — Reading, wRiting and aRithmetic — and pronounced in a jocular manner as: reading, riting and rithmetic.

three sheets to the wind
intoxicated; drunk.

three-D
(also: 3-D) pertaining to three dimensions or three dimensional; having or appearing to have the dimension of depth: e.g. One has to wear special spectacles to see the effects of a three-D movie.

three-on-the-tree
a car having three forward gears on a column shift (as opposed to four-on-the-floor).

three-ring circus
1. spectacular, exhibitionist performance.
2. a confusion, commotion, disorganised shambles: e.g. That meeting was like a three-ring circus — nobody could agree about anything.

threw (one/someone)
disconcerted, confused, puzzled, caught (one/someone) off guard: e.g. That last question really threw me — I didn't know what to say in reply.

For other possible entries beginning with 'threw' see entries listed under 'throw'.

thrilled to bits/the back teeth
extremely pleased, happily excited, elated: e.g. I was thrilled to bits when I found out about my big win in the lotto.

throat
(see: at each other's throats; cut one's own throat; have/got it by the throat; jump down someone's throat; my stomach thinks my throat's cut; ram it down someone's throat; stick in one's throat)

throb in the knob
(of a man) sexual excitement, arousal; an erection of the penis.

throne
the toilet.

through and through
thoroughly; absolutely; completely; totally: e.g. He's a Labor supporter through and through.

through thick and thin
1. under all circumstances in spite of trouble or difficulties: e.g. Their business and marriage have survived through thick and thin.
2. through many difficult and trying times: e.g. Our relationship has been through thick and thin and we still love each other.

through with
finished with; not wanting to have any more to do with: e.g. She's through with him.

throw
1. deliberately lose a contest, usually for a bribe: e.g. He's been offered a lot of money to throw the fight.
2. astonish; disconcert; confuse; puzzle; catch (someone) off guard: e.g. This next question I have will really throw him because he doesn't think I know about it.
3. put (often in a hasty manner): e.g. Throw all your stuff in the spare room.
4. (Australian Rules football) exclamation: not a handball!
See also:
a throw
don't let it throw you
wouldn't trust (someone) as far as I could throw him

throw a fit
become suddenly angry, violent, furious: e.g. Dad's going to throw a fit when he finds out that I've put a dent in the car.

throw a party
have, stage, be the host of a party: e.g. We're going to throw a surprise party for his birthday.

throw a seven
1. die.
2. faint, collapse.
3. vomit.
4. become angry; lose one's temper.

throw a spanner in the cogs/works
confuse, hinder, obstruct, spoil a situation or something; create a difficulty or problem; disrupt.

throw a turn
1. (see: throw a party)
2. become suddenly angry, furious, violent.

throw a willy/wobbly
(see: throw a fit)

throw away
1. discard; dispose of: e.g. I'm going to throw away all the clothes in my wardrobe which I never wear any more.

2. squander; waste: e.g. He's always throwing money away on stupid, useless things.

throw away the key
to imprison someone for a long time: e.g. They should lock murderers up and throw away the key!

throw caution to the wind
behave recklessly, impetuously.

throw cold water on
to spoil the enthusiasm of; discourage.

throw in
1. give up; abandon: e.g. Why did you throw in your job?
2. include free of charge: e.g. If I buy the house now, the vendors will throw in all the furniture.

throw in (one's) hand

throw in the sponge/towel
concede, accept defeat; give up.

throw it in
1. accept, concede defeat; give up: e.g. He's so old it's about time he threw it in and let a younger man take over.
2. stop, cease work: e.g. It's time to throw it in for the day.
3. give (it) up; abandon: e.g. This job's so bad that I'm going to throw it in as soon as I find another.

throw mud at
(see: sling mud at)

throw new light on
bring new, relevant information forward that will aid understanding, or change the perspective of a matter.

throw off at
criticise; ridicule; deride: e.g. He's always throwing off at any suggestion I try to make.

throw (one's) hand in
concede, accept defeat; give up.

throw (one's) hat in first
to test public opinion, reception.

throw (one's) hat in the ring
take part in, join, enter the competition or contest.

throw (one's) lot in with
to support entirely: e.g. He's thrown his lot in with the Liberal Party.

throw (one's) voice
to vomit: e.g. You didn't have to throw your voice all over the back seat of my car!

throw (one's) weight around
to bully, domineer, coerce, intimidate using (one's) superior strength, power or authority.

throw (oneself) at (someone)
to attempt to seduce, or attract the attention or admiration of (someone): e.g. It's awful the way she always throws herself at the husbands of her supposed friends.

throw (oneself) into
to attack a task energetically and enthusiastically: e.g. He really throws himself into the club's fund-raising activities.

throw out the anchors
to suddenly apply the brakes of a car.

throw over
abandon; jilt; suddenly terminate (a relationship): e.g. He threw her over for her best friend.

throw some light on
make clear, understood; explain: e.g. The police have new evidence that should throw some light on the matter.

throw (someone) off
1. contrive to get rid of or free oneself of (someone): e.g. He's been trying all week to throw her off.
2. to escape from, elude (someone): e.g. I'll try to throw the police off while you sneak out the back door.
3. disconcert, confuse (someone): e.g. The astute questions of the reporters really threw him off his well-organised propaganda speech.

throw (someone) off the track
1. attempt to confuse, get rid of (someone) with irrelevant or false information: e.g. They tried to throw the investigators off the track by telling lies.
2. confuse, disconcert, astonish, bamboozle, fluster (someone): e.g. Constant interjections from the audience threw him off the track.

throw (someone) to the wolves
abandon (someone) in a time of need; pledge no support for (someone).

throw the baby out with the bath water
to give up more than one intended by an impetuous or thoughtless action.

throw the book at (someone)
punish (someone) to the maximum: e.g. The police threw the book at him even though his crime was a minor one.

throw together
1. cause to associate, be with: e.g. We were thrown together through a strange set of circumstances.
2. erect, build, assemble in a hasty, slipshod, unsystematic manner: e.g. That house was thrown together by a bodgy builder.

throw up
1. to vomit.
2. erect, build in a hasty manner: e.g. The concert organisers threw up a temporary stage for the performers.

thumb (it)
solicit for a free ride in a car; hitch-hike: e.g. We thumbed all the way around Australia.

thumb (one's) nose at
scoff at; show scorn, disregard and lack of respect for: e.g. He's always thumbed his nose at the Royal Family.

thumbs down
a denial, refusal: e.g. His proposal was given the thumbs down by the committee.

thumbs up
1. gesture of approval, success (given by holding out a clenched fist with thumb raised).
2. gesture of contempt (given by upward thrusting movements of a clenched fist with thumb raised).

thumping
severe beating or sound defeat: e.g. He got a thumping for giving cheek to a bloke twice his size!
See also:
take a thumping

thumping big/great
remarkable; huge: e.g. We had to hire a thumping great truck to move all our junk!

thump-wit
stupid person; fool; dolt; idiot.

thunder
(see: steal someone's thunder)

thunder-box
the toilet.

thundering
big; very great; extraordinary: e.g. Someone dumped a thundering great rock in the middle of our driveway!

thunder-struck
astonished; amazed; confounded.

tich
1. (cap.) nickname for a small person.
2. a very small amount of anything.

tick
moment; a very short time: e.g. I'll be there in a tick.
See also:
any tick of the clock
on tick
what makes (one) tick

tick off
reprimand; scold; berate: e.g. I was ticked off for coming late.

tick over
1. (of a car engine) idle; to run slowly in neutral.
2. (of a person's mind) operate, work: e.g. After he realised how much all the junk in his yard was worth to an antique dealer, you could see his mind ticking over.

ticker
1. the heart.
2. a wrist-watch.

ticket
1. a notification of a traffic offence: e.g. I was given a ticket for speeding.
2. blotting-paper impregnated with the hallucinogenic drug, LSD.
3. desirable or correct thing to do: e.g. That's the ticket!
See also:
have/got tickets on (oneself)
meal ticket
one-way ticket
packapoo ticket
walking ticket

tickle (one's) fancy
1. please (one); appeal to (one).
2. sexual innuendo — to have intercourse.

tickle the ivories
to play the piano.

tickle the peter/till
to misappropriate funds; to rob, pilfer, steal from a till or cash-register: e.g. He was accused of tickling the peter.

tickled (one's) tonsils
highly amused (one): e.g. That joke really tickled my tonsils!

tickled pink

tickled to bits/death
highly pleased or amused; delighted: e.g. He was tickled pink when he won first prize for his painting.

ticklish
sensitive, risky, delicate; requiring careful, tactful handling: e.g. That's a very ticklish matter to discuss openly.

ticky-tacky
shoddy; plastic; inferior; second-rate; superficially attractive.

tiddler
1. something very small, especially a fish.
2. a child.

tiddly
slightly drunk, intoxicated.

tide has turned
the circumstances of a situation have been reversed or changed: e.g. The public was against the proposal at first, but now the tide has turned.

tide (one) over
enable (one) to cope, especially under difficult circumstances: e.g. I need to borrow a few dollars to tide me over till next payday.

tide-mark
the ring of dirt around a bath-tub.

tide's out
a remark indicating that one's glass (of beer, tea etc.) is empty and needs refilling.

tidy
considerable: e.g. He inherited a tidy fortune from a distant old aunt he didn't even remember!

tie
hindrance; obligation: e.g. He doesn't want a permanent relationship with any ties.
See also:
no ties

tie in with
connect or agree with: e.g. His evidence doesn't tie in with that given by his accomplice.

tie (someone) down
restrict, hinder, impose limits or obligations on (someone): e.g. The responsibilities of having babies and raising a family will tie you down.

tie the knot
marry, wed.

tie up some loose ends
attend to the details that will complete a matter.

tied down
1. restricted; obligated: e.g. Since his father died, he's been tied down looking after his invalid mother.
2. occupied in a task completely: e.g. He's been tied down all week building a model boat.

tied to (someone's) apron strings
emotionally dependent upon: e.g. He's thirty years old and he's still tied to his mother's apron strings!

tied up
1. occupied; busy: e.g. I can't go out as I'm tied up every night this week.
2. connected with: e.g. He was tied up with that scandal, so the boss fired him.
3. hindered: e.g. The strike by the wharfies tied up shipping for weeks.
4. (of money) not available immediately: e.g. He's got a fortune tied up in land, but it may take some time before he can raise some ready cash.
5. concluded; settled; finalised: e.g. We tied up the deal last night.

tied up in knots
1. having troubles, problems; in an extremely awkward situation: e.g. I'm tied up in knots trying to work out this knitting pattern.
2. experiencing emotional anxiety: e.g. I've been tied up in knots worrying about you all night.

tiff
(see: have a tiff)

tiger
(joc.) extremely energetic person.
See also:
paper tiger
park (one's) tiger

tiger for punishment
extremely energetic, hard worker; one who persists with something, even though the consequences may be unpleasant.

Tigers/Tiges
1. Richmond VFL football team.
2. Balmain N.S.W. Rugby League football team.

tiggy
children's game of chasing and catching (tigging) others.

tight
1. drunk; intoxicated.
2. not easily obtainable; in short supply: e.g. Money from finance companies is very tight at present.
3. miserly; mean; parsimonious.
See also:
sit tight
so tight he wouldn't sell you the steam off his shit
so tight you couldn't drive a pin up his arse with a sledgehammer
walk a tight-rope

tight as a fish's arse/nun's nasty/Scotchman's purse
miserly; mean; parsimonious.

tight as a mouse's ear
1. parsimonious.
2. (of a woman as a sex object) having a small, tight vagina making penetration, if not more difficult, more pleasant for a man.

tight corner
a predicament or difficulty.

tight spot
1. a predicament or difficulty.
2. short of money; broke: e.g. I'm in a bit of a tight spot this week.

tight squeeze
a predicament or difficulty: e.g. The business is going through a tight squeeze, but things will improve.

tight-arse
parsimonious, mean, miserly person.

tighten the belt
restrict one's spending; budget carefully: e.g. The government has had to tighten the belt on public spending because funds are in short supply.

tight-fisted
miserly; mean; parsimonious.

tight-knit
1. well organised: e.g. The profits are good because it's a very tight-knit organisation.
2. closely integrated; loyal; impervious to outside influences: e.g. We have a very tight-knit family.

tight-lipped
taciturn; saying little or nothing.

tight-wad
miser; parsimonious, mean, mingy person; skinflint.

tile
(see: night on the tiles; on the tiles)

till (one) goes blue in the face
for a long time to no avail: e.g. You can talk till you go blue in the face — it won't change my mind!

till the cows come home
1. (see: till one goes blue in the face)
2. at length; for a long time: e.g. She'll talk till the cows come home if you let her.

tilt
(see: full tilt)

tilt in his kilt
(of a man) an erection of the penis.

timber!
a warning that something is about to fall.

Timbuktu
any remote place, real or imaginary: e.g. You can go to Timbuktu for all I care!

time
1. a prison sentence or term: e.g. He's doing time for armed robbery.
2. the moment of death: e.g. His time has come.
3. the end of a woman's pregnancy; the time for giving birth: e.g. She was in an aeroplane when her time came.
See also:
about time!
ahead of (one's) time
at one time
at the same time
behind the times
big time
do time
for the umpteenth time!
from time to time
give (someone) a hard time
have a hard time
have/got no time for
high old time
high time
in good time
in no time
kill time
make good time
make time
make up for lost time
many a time
move with the times
on borrowed time
pass the time of day with
play for time
race against time
sign of the times
take (one's) time
take time out
wrong time of the month

time and time again
time after time
repeatedly.

time bomb
potentially disastrous situation.

time flies when you're having fun
an expression of surprise at how quickly the time seems to have passed.

time heals all wounds
grief (or injury, misfortune) is lessened with the passage of time.

time is money
waste of time is loss of profit.

time of (one's) life
an extremely enjoyable time: e.g. We had the time of our life at that amusement park.

time on (one's) hands
to have spare time with no particular commitments: e.g. I'll fix the leaking tap next time I have some time on my hands.

time out
a short rest or break from work or commitments.

time out of mind
extending beyond memory or recorded history: e.g. That's been a family tradition since time out of mind.

time to bail/bale out
time to give up, opt out, leave, abandon.

time to pack it in
1. time to give up, opt out, leave, abandon.
2. time to finish work, a job, an activity etc.

time will tell
the future will provide the answer: e.g. Time will tell whether he's cured himself of his drug habit.

time-honoured
revered and respected: e.g. That's been a time-honoured tradition for centuries.

tin
(see: belting a tin; kick the tin)

tin lizzie
an old, dilapidated or antique car.

tin tacks
(see: down to tin tacks)

tin-arse/bum
a person who always seems to get amazingly good luck or fortune: e.g. Kristin's such a tin-arse — she just won a small fortune at the casino while the rest of us did our dough.

ting-a-ling
tingle
a telephone call: e.g. Give me a tingle some time.

tin-horn
(see: tin-pot)

tinker with
repair or alter in an amateurish way: e.g. He's always tinkering with the car.

tinned dog
canned meat.

tinnie
(also: tinny) a can of beer.

tinny
1. extremely lucky or fortunate: e.g. He's so tinny! He always wins the raffles.
2. not durable; cheap; shoddy; inferior: e.g. Modern cars are so tinny compared to older ones.
3. a can of beer.
4. small alluminium boat, often fitted with an outboard motor.

tin-pan alley
the world of pop-music, composers, publishers, retailers, recording companies etc.

tin-pot
inferior; shoddy; second-class; cheap; worthless.

tinsel town
1. (caps) Sydney.
2. sophisticated city, all glitter rather than substance.

tinselly
gaudy; cheap; showy; flashy but second-class; pretentious.

tip
1. a rubbish dump.
2. informal information, advice, a hint or clue: e.g. I got a good tip from a reliable source on which horse to back in the Cup.
See also:
on the tip of (one's) tongue

tip of the iceberg
only a very small part of the whole: e.g. What the newspapers reported was only the tip of the ice-berg as far as that scandal was concerned.

tip (someone) off
warn, alarm, inform (someone) in advance: e.g. Someone tipped him off before the police arrived and he escaped.

tip (someone) the wink
give important information, advice to (someone).

tip the bucket on (someone)
criticise (someone) scathingly; make scandalous revelations about (someone).

tip the scales
to influence in favour of.

tip-off
a warning, hint in advance: e.g. The police were given a tip-off by an anonymous caller and were able to catch the gang in the act of robbery.

tipper
a truck with a tray that may be raised and lowered automatically.

tippler
a heavy drinker of alcohol.

tipsy
slightly intoxicated, drunk.

tip-top
excellent; first-rate.

tired of
bored with; had enough of: e.g. I'm tired of this car — I think I'll buy another.

tit
breast; boob.

tit for tat
repayment, especially retaliation; revenge; reprisal.

titch
1. a tiny amount.
2. a small person.

titfer
(rhyming slang: tit for tat) hat.

tits/titties
breasts; boobs.
See also:
don't get your tits in a tangle
tough titties!

tittle-tattle
1. idle gossip, especially the revealing of confidential or private matters.
2. person who informs on, betrays others.
3. to inform on, betray someone.

tizz
1. state of flustered confusion: e.g. She's in such a tizz about what to wear for her new date tonight.
2. gaudy; tawdry; showy and pretentious: e.g. Her clothes are so tizz!

tizz up
attempt to improve the appearance of — often in a tawdry manner.

tizzy
gaudy; tawdry; showy and pretentious.

TLC
Tender Loving Care — sympathetic attention, repairs: e.g. That old house is basically very sound — all it needs is some TLC and it will look like new.

T.M.
tailor-made — a commercially produced cigarette as opposed to a hand-rolled one.

to a T/turn
perfectly; just right; exactly: e.g. 1. The meal was cooked to a turn. 2. That new suit fits to a T.

to and fro
backwards and forwards.

to and from
(rhyming slang) pom — an Englishman.

to boot
(an intensifier) as well; also: e.g. He not only caught the most fish, but the biggest to boot!

to cut a long story short
to be brief.

to heck/hell with it!
1. an expression of annoyance, frustration, scornful dismissal, rejection: e.g. To heck with it — I don't want it any more!
2. an expression of carefree bravado: e.g. To heck with it — I might as well do it!

to (one's) heart's content
as much as (one) pleases or desires: e.g. I ate and drank to my heart's content and didn't have to pay for a thing!

to (one's) mind
in (one's) opinion: e.g. To my mind, he's not the right person for the job.

to (one's) name
in (one's) possession; belonging to (one); to (one's) credit: e.g. He hasn't got a cent to his name.

to the ends of the earth
to any lengths anywhere: e.g. I'd go to the ends of the earth to save his skin!

to the hilt
as far as possible; to the utmost; completely; fully: e.g. 1. He was armed to the hilt. 2. He's borrowed money to the hilt and can't get any more.

to the letter
exactly; precisely; in full: e.g. You must obey these instructions to the letter.

to the manor born
of the wealthy upper class.

to the nth degree
to the utmost or greatest extent..

to the point
relevant; pertinent; apt: e.g. 1. What he said was very much to the point, whether you agree or not. 2. I wish he'd get to the point instead of waffling on.

to the tune of
to the value of; in the vicinity of; amounting to or costing: e.g. He lost assets to the tune of half a million dollars when that company went bankrupt.

toad
repulsive, obnoxious person.

toady
sycophantic, obsequious person.

toast of the town
celebrated person.

toddler
small child learning to walk.

to-do
noise; commotion; fuss: e.g. What's all that to-do in the next room about?

toe
(sport) speed: e.g. He's got a bit of toe.
See also:
done up like a sore toe
from top to toe
hit the toe
on one's toes
step on someone's toes
stick out like a sore toe
turn up one's toes

toe jam
tinea; any dirt, filth or dry skin from the feet.

toe the line
conform; obey, especially under pressure: e.g. Army recruits are expected to toe the line or face severe disciplinary measures.

toey
1. keen; anxious to go, start, do something; excitable: e.g. He's been toey ever since we said we'd take him shooting with us.
2. bad-tempered; touchy; irritable: e.g. What's he so toey about?
3. (of a car, horse etc.) fast; excellent in speed and performance.

toey as a Roman sandal
bad-tempered; touchy; irritable.

toff
person of the well-dressed, wealthy upper class.

toffee-nosed
pretentious; snobbish; haughty.

toffy
of the wealthy; plush; posh; upper class.

together
self-possessed; collected; sane; calm and composed; free from confusion: e.g. He's a really together sort of person after giving up his drug habit.
See also:
get it (all) together
get (oneself) together
have/got it (all) together
hold together
keep (oneself) together

togs
1. bathing suit.
2. clothes.

toke
a draw on a cigarette, especially a marijuana joint.

tom
a male cat.

Tom, Dick and Harry
anybody or everybody in general: e.g. I don't want you inviting every Tom, Dick and Harry to this party!

tombstone teeth
protruding teeth; buckteeth.

tom-catting
(of a man) behaving in a very promiscuous manner; having sexual intercourse with many partners.

tomfoolery
1. foolish, mischievous behaviour.
2. sexually promiscuous behaviour.

tommyrot
nonsense; worthless talk.

tom-tits
(rhyming slang) shits.

ton
1. any heavy weight: e.g. This case weighs a ton!
2. a great amount; much; many: e.g. I've got a ton of work to do tonight.
3. the speed of 100 miles per hour, or 160 kilometres per hour: e.g. That car does over the ton easily.
See also:
hit the ton

ton up
(cricket) 100 runs.

tone down
moderate; soften; make less severe, harsh: e.g. Tone down your language — Mum doesn't like to hear swearing!

tongue
(see: bite one's tongue; cat got your tongue?; find one's tongue; give one's tongue an outing; hold one's tongue; lose one's tongue; mind one's tongue; on the tip of one's tongue; slip of the tongue; speak with forked tongue; with one's tongue in one's cheek)

tongue like a viper
the ability to speak extremely harshly, cruelly, sarcastically.

tongue sandwich
cunnilingus.

tongue-in-cheek
facetious; satirical; teasing: e.g. His speech may have sounded serious, but it was very tongue-in-cheek.

tongue-lashing
a severe scolding, berating.

tongue-tied
speechless; too shy or embarrassed to speak; at a loss for words; suddenly unable to pronounce words correctly; stuttering.

tongue-twister
any word or sequence that is difficult to pronounce correctly without error: e.g. 'Round the rugged rock the ragged rascal ran' is a good tongue-twister.

tonk
1. the penis.
2. an effeminate man.
3. (cricket) hit ball high in the air.

tons
many; much; a great amount: e.g. We had tons of food left over after the party.

too big for (one's) boots/britches
vain; conceited.

too big to handle
too important or difficult to cope with; beyond one's capabilities.

too close for comfort
very precarious, dangerous or risky.

too far gone
beyond help.

too good to be true
suspiciously good.

too hot to handle
(see: too big to handle)

too many chiefs and not enough Indians

too many cooks
too many people supposedly in charge and not enough helpers or workers.

too many cooks spoil the broth
too many people in charge or issuing orders can ruin, spoil, mess up a situation.

too many fingers in the pie
1. too much interference from too many people.
2. (to have . . .) (see: too many irons in the fire)

too many irons in the fire
(to have . . .) to have too many things, enterprises, activities, interests going on at once, with the result that it is difficult to manage any of them efficiently.

too much!
an expression of surprise, wonder, admiration: e.g. Too much! Is that Mercedes really a present for me?

too much of a good thing
spoiled by over-indulgence.

too much on (one's) plate
to have too much work etc. to be able to cope with it efficiently: e.g. I can't take another appointment today — I've got too much on my plate already!

too right!
emphatically yes!

toodle-oo!/pip!
good-bye!

too-hard basket
an imaginary place to file matters that are too difficult to deal or cope with at present: e.g. I think the Council has put that matter in the too-hard basket — they don't know what to do about it yet.

took the words out of my mouth
1. said or expressed exactly what I was going to say before I had a chance to speak.
2. presumed to know what I was going to say;

expressed my thoughts incorrectly: e.g. That's not what I meant — you took the words out of my mouth!

For other possible entries beginning with 'took' see entries listed under 'take'.

tool
1. the penis: e.g. He's got the biggest tool I've ever seen!
2. (of a man) to have sexual intercourse: e.g. Who's he tooling now?

tool around
1. (of a man) have casual sex with many partners.
2. drive around in a leisurely, casual manner: e.g. He's been tooling around town all day showing off his new car.

toot
1. the toilet: e.g. Where's the toot?
2. cocaine.

toot for
barrack for; support.

toot-paper
toilet-tissue.

tooth
(see: long in the tooth; sweet tooth)

tooth and nail
with all one's strength and resources; fiercely: e.g. All the relatives have been fighting tooth and nail to get their hands on the dead man's estate.

tooth fairy
mythical fairy in children's stories who leaves money in return for an extracted or deciduous tooth left in a glass overnight.

tootle
drive: e.g. We were tootling down the highway when we were pulled up by the police.

tootle along
drive, go fast: e.g. That car of his can really tootle along!

tootle off
go; depart; leave: e.g. We'd better tootle off as it's getting late.

toots
an affectionate nickname for someone, especially by a man for a woman.

tootsies
toes: e.g. Don't step on my tootsies!
See also:
play tootsies with (someone)

top
1. an item of clothing, such as a T-shirt.
2. the highest position of success: e.g. After years of hard work in that organisation, he's finally reached the top.
3. the highest forward-driving gear of a vehicle: e.g. This car won't get up a steep hill in top.
4. first-rate; excellent: e.g. That was a top book to read.
5. surpass; out-do; do better than: e.g. If I train hard, I'm sure I'll be able to top the world record.
See also:
big top
blow (one's) top
from the top
life at the top
little up top
nothing up top
off the top of (one's) head
on top
on top of
on top of the world
over the top
sleep like a top
tip-top

top brass
the bosses; those with the highest rank or authority.

top dog
the leader; the person with the highest rank or authority: e.g. Who's the top dog around here — I want a word with the boss.

Top End
the northern part of the Northern Territory.

top forty
a constantly revised list of the forty most popular songs played on the radio: e.g. Our band's song is doing well in the top forty.

top marks
full approval or recognition for excellence: e.g. He deserves top marks for setting up that disco for the local kids.

top off
complete satisfactorily; finish: e.g. To top off an excellent meal, we had a cheese platter.

top-drawer
excellent; first-class: e.g. This bottle of wine is very expensive, top-drawer stuff!

top-ender
person living in the most northern parts of the Northern Territory.

top-heavy
1. overweight at the top.
2. (of a woman) having very large breasts.

topless
(of women) having exposed breasts.

top-nob
the boss, leader; the person with the highest rank or authority.

top-notch
excellent; first-class: e.g. I know a top-notch little restaurant we can all go to.

tops
1. excellent; outstanding: e.g. That free concert in the park was tops.

'Knock it off, fellers. Th' match finished an hour ago!'

The footy: a beaut excuse for players and spectators alike to have a good barney, blue, bust-up, ding-dong, donnybrook, dust-up, go-in, hoohah, punch-up, rough-up, round of fisticuffs, row, rumble, run-in, scrap, set-to, spat, stoush or yike, or just generally to let off steam by giving some mug a good belt in the lug, clip in the ear, doing-over, fat lip, fist full of fives, knuckle sandwich, lathering, licking, plastering, poke in the nose, roughing up, thick ear or towelling.

2. surpasses; out-does; beats all; is better than: e.g. That joke tops them all!

top-secret
highly confidential.

top-shelf
excellent; first-class.

top-up
a refill of a partly filled container, glass: e.g. Does anyone need a top-up before we propose a toast to the bride and groom?

torn
(see: that's torn it!)

torn between
unable to choose between: e.g. He's torn between his job and his family at the moment.

tosh!
rubbish! nonsense!

toss
(Australian Rules football, cricket) decide which way a team will kick, or which side will bat first.
See also:
argue the toss

toss in (one's) alley
to die.

toss off
(of a man) to masturbate or ejaculate.

toss (someone) for it
decide a choice with (someone) by throwing a coin and gambling on which side lands up: e.g. If we can't agree on who is going to wash the dishes, then I'll toss you for it.

tossle
the penis.

tosspot
an alcoholic or heavy drinker.

toss-up
doubtful either way; an even chance or odds: e.g. Both horses are good, so it's going to be a toss-up over which one wins.

tot
small child; infant.

tot up
add up: e.g. If you tot up the empty bottles lying around, it's obvious a lot of drinking goes on around here!

totalled
completely ruined, wrecked, demolished: e.g. Although the other car was only slightly damaged in the accident, my car was totalled.

tote
1. totalisator; (cap.) government-run betting agency (Totalisator Agency Board): e.g. He likes to have a dollar each way on the Tote every week.
2. carry: e.g. I had to tote that heavy bag by myself!

touch
1. a person one can easily obtain money from, either honestly or through deception: e.g. He's such an easy touch.
2. artistic style or skill: e.g. Sindelar's got an excellent touch with water-colours.
3. obtain, get money from someone; cadge; the money thus obtained: e.g. Can I touch you for a loan until next payday?
4. have anything to do with: e.g. He never touches alcohol or drugs.
5. compare with: e.g. Nobody can touch him when it comes to drinking beer.
6. (rugby) over the boundary line.
See also:
easy touch
in touch with
keep in touch
lose (one's) touch
out of touch
soft touch
wouldn't touch it with a ten-foot pole

touch of the tar-brush
having dark skin colouring indicating Aboriginal, African etc. as well as Anglo-Saxon ancestry.

touch of the trots
diarrhoea: e.g. I must have eaten something funny — I seem to have a touch of the trots.

touch on
mention only briefly: e.g. She only touched on the subject in her talk.

touch (someone) up
1. obtain, get, borrow money from (someone), either honestly or through deception and trickery.
2. to fondle, caress (someone) sexually — especially of a woman by a man in an indecent or indiscreet manner.

touch the sides
(didn't, won't . . .) insufficient to quench the thirst or desire, such as of a drink.

touch up
correct; add finishing improvements: e.g. We'll touch up the paint work and then sell the car.

touch wood!
superstitious interjection or action to ward off bad luck after expressing a hope or fact: e.g. I've never broken a bone yet — touch wood!

touch-and-go
uncertain; risky: e.g. The situation was very touch-and-go for a while, but it all worked out satisfactorily in the end.

touched
1. slightly insane or mad: e.g. He must be touched the way he talks to himself all the time.
2. cheated, deceived, hoodwinked — especially out of some money.

touchy
sensitive; temperamental; easily provoked.

tough
1. ruffian; bully; hardened, merciless person: e.g. Those toughs work with the Mafia.
2. (as an interjection) bad luck! (often in a sarcastic, unsympathetic manner).
3. unyielding; resolute: e.g. He's pretty tough — I don't think you'll be able to change his mind.
4. strict; stern; severe: e.g. 1. That was a very tough sentence the judge gave him for such a minor offence. 2. There was no need to be so tough on him as his crime was a very minor one.

tough as bull's hide
1. very strong; not easily cut, broken or worn out.
2. unyielding; resolute; hardened; strict.

tough cookie
a strong, aggressive, incorrigible character; one who is not easily influenced.

tough shit/titties!
sarcastic, mocking or jocular interjection — bad luck!

toughie/toughy
ruffian; bully; villain.

towel
(see: throw in the towel)

towelling
a sound thrashing or defeating.

tower of strength
person who gives reliable, strong support.

town
(see: go to town; hick town; night on the town; out on the town; paint the town red; talk of the town; toast of the town)

town bike
well-known, promiscuous woman; slut.

townie
a person from the city as opposed to a country person.

T.P.I.
pertaining to returned injured servicemen — Totally and Permanently Incapacitated.

track
(cricket) the pitch.
See also:
born on the wrong side of the tracks
cover one's tracks
go off the track
keep track of
lose track of
make tracks
off the beaten track
on the wrong track
one-track mind
stop dead in one's tracks
throw someone off the track

track down
discover; unearth; expose; search for and find.

track meet
athletics or sporting meeting.

track record
history of past performance: e.g. His track record for holding on to a job hasn't been very good.

track with
associate with; mix with: e.g. He's tracking with a gang of bikies at present.

tracks
scars left by users of hypodermic injections — especially of drug-addicts.

trade with the devil
to be unscrupulous, involved in criminal activities.

traffic cop
traffic officer who enforces road regulations.

trailblazer
innovator; leader.

train (someone) well
(joc.) to teach (someone) to do, perform duties or acts of service, especially of a husband or wife: e.g. I've trained my husband well — he does the dishes every night!

train Terrence at the terracotta
(of men) to urinate.

traipse
to go, gad about aimlessly; do errands or trudge wearily: e.g. I've been traipsing around the whole town looking for you!

tramp
1. promiscuous woman; slut; woman of low morals.
2. vagabond; vagrant; homeless person.

trams and trains
(rhyming slang) brains; drains.

trannie
1. small transistor radio.
2. a trans-sexual; one who has had a sex-change operation — usually male into female.

trap
the mouth: e.g. Shut your trap!
See also:
open (one's) trap

trap for young players
anything that is hazardous, risky or dangerous for the inexperienced.

trapped between the devil and the deep blue sea
(see: caught between . . .)

traps
1. luggage; personal belongings.
2. policemen or law enforcement officers.

See also:
been around the traps
round the traps

trash
reject, criticise scornfully: e.g. The critics trashed his book.

trashie
garbage collector.

travel
1. move with speed: e.g. That car of his can really travel!
2. (basketball) run with the ball without dribbling, bouncing.

tray bit
a threepenny coin (before decimal currency was introduced in 1966).

tread all over (someone)
domineer; treat (someone) harshly or unfairly.

tread lightly/tread on eggs
be extremely cautious or careful: e.g. Tread lightly as far as any dealings with him are concerned as he's a crook.

tread on (someone's) corns/toes
offend (someone); hurt (someone's) feelings.

tread the boards
live the life of an actor on the stage.

treading a fine line
coming close to the limits of propriety, safety.

treading on air
elated; extremely pleased or happy: e.g. He's been treading on air since he found out he won the lottery.

treading on eggs
in a dangerous, risky or precarious situation or position.

treading on new ground
entering into unfamiliar circumstances.

treasure
a highly valued, important or indispensable person.

treat
1. anything that provides pleasure, joy, happiness: e.g. This new car is a real treat after our old bomb.
2. turn to bear the expense, pay for: e.g. Keep your money — this meal is my treat.
3. pay the expense of; shout: e.g. He treated us to a meal in that restaurant.
See also:
look a treat

treat (someone) like dirt/shit
to behave very badly, rudely, unfairly towards (someone).

treat (someone) with kid gloves
to treat, handle (someone) with tact, care, gentleness.

treatment
(see: get the full treatment; the full treatment; the treatment)

treat's on me
the entertainment is provided at my expense.

tree
(see: anyone would think it grew on trees; barking up the wrong tree; can't see the trees for the forest; make like a tree — and leave; money doesn't grow on trees; out of one's tree; three-on-the-tree)

tremendous
remarkable; excellent; considerable; noteworthy: e.g. That was a tremendous concert!

trendy
1. a person who embraces the latest fashions in life-style and thinking (and is often held in contempt for being false and pretentious).
2. fashionable; current; popular; modern; up-to-date: e.g. That's the most trendy restaurant in town.

trial and error
the process of investigation, experiment etc., in which various theories and methods are tried until a successful solution is found.

trial handicap
(horse-racing) race restricted to horses classified as in the trial class.

triangle
an illicit love affair in which three people are involved — usually husband, wife and a third person.

tribe
family; circle of friends: e.g. Invite the whole tribe to the party.

Tribunal
(Australian Rules football) body before which a footballer who has been reported for infringements of rules or violence in a match has to appear.

trick
prostitute's client, customer or act.
See also:
bag of tricks
can't teach an old dog new tricks
dirty trick
do the trick
doesn't miss a trick
have/got a trick up (one's) sleeve
how's tricks?
not able to take a trick
slick trick
that's the trick!
use every trick in the book

trick out
dress up in one's best and finest clothes: e.g. She was tricked out in a stunning new gown for the ball.

tried-and-true
reliable; proven; successful.

trier
one who tries hard despite failure, hardship or disappointment.

trigger-happy
1. having an overwhelming desire to discharge a gun: e.g. I don't like taking him duck-shooting because he's too trigger-happy.
2. reckless in relation to matters that could lead to war: e.g. World peace will never be attained as long as some national leaders continue to be trigger-happy.

trim
haircut that neatens the style of the hair: e.g. You need a trim.

trim (one's) sails
change (one's) tactics, policy, to suit changing occasions or circumstances: e.g. Most politicians are prepared to trim their sails in order to win votes.

trimmings
extras; accompaniments; additions.

trim, taut and terrific
in vibrant good health and spirits.

trip
1. hallucinatory experience under the influence of a drug, such as LSD or marijuana: e.g. He only wanted to try the stuff, but ended up having a really bad and frightening trip.
2. method of doing something; fad; obsession: e.g. Drugs aren't my trip.
3. to hallucinate under the influence of a drug: e.g. He really enjoys tripping on marijuana.

trip out
to hallucinate, especially badly or frighteningly under the influence of a drug such as LSD or marijuana: e.g. I never want to touch that stuff again — it really made us trip out!

trip (someone) up
cause (someone) to fail, make a blunder, error or mistake.

trip the light fantastic
(joc.) to go dancing: e.g. Where's the best disco to trip the light fantastic?

tripe
nonsense, rubbish; worthless talk or writing.
See also:
beat the tripe out of

troglodyte
1. prehistoric cave-dweller.
2. stupid, moronic person.

troop
go or walk off, away.

troppo
crazy; mad; insane: e.g. He's a bit troppo.

trot
(see: having a bad/good trot)

trot out
produce or bring out: e.g. As long as you keep trotting out the beer, he'll stay and drink.

trots
1. diarrhoea: e.g. He had the trots all week after eating that spicy food.
2. harness horse-racing; trotting-horse race meeting.

trouble
(see: in trouble)

trouble-and-strife
(rhyming slang) wife.

troubled waters
state of unrest or confusion: e.g. The entire union movement is in troubled waters at present.

trouble-shooter
an expert in solving problems, disputes etc.

trouser snake
the penis.

trousers are at half mast
one's trousers are too short.

trout
an ugly or disagreeable person.

truck
(see: fell off the back of a truck)

truck on down
go: e.g. Everybody's going to truck on down to the rock concert tonight.

truckie
a truck-driver.

true dickens/dinks
(used either as a questioning exclamation or an affirmative one) true?; true!; really?; really!; is that so?; that is so!; fair dinkum.

true to (one's) word
honest; reliable.

true-blue
1. faithful; sincere; unwavering; loyal: e.g. He's a true-blue Liberal supporter.
2. genuine; real: e.g. This is a true-blue example of Australian colonial furniture.

trump card
a decisive factor or advantage: e.g. He's got a trump card up his sleeve that will decide the outcome of this particular situation.
See also:
come/turn up trumps

try another one!
expression of disbelief.

try another tack
try a different approach, method.

try before you buy
before you purchase or make a commitment, sample, test or try out (something) to see if it suits your requirements

(especially with reference to sexual matters when making a commitment to a relationship).

try it/one on (someone)
attempt to deceive, hoodwink, cheat or test the temper or patience of (someone): e.g. That con-man tried to try one on me.

try (one's) hand at
attempt something for the first time: e.g. I'm going to try my hand at putting the wallpaper on instead of paying a tradesman.

try (one's) patience
annoy, anger, irritate, exasperate (one): e.g. Those ratty kids of hers really try my patience!

try (someone) out
test, strain the patience of (someone).

try to put one over (someone)
attempt to deceive, hoodwink, cheat (someone): e.g. Don't try to put one over me — I know all the facts!

tub
1. a dilapidated, slow old boat.
2. wash, bath: e.g. After working in the dirt I need a good tub.

tub of lard
fat, obese person.

tubby
fat; obese; plump.

tube
1. the television: e.g. He's always glued to the tube when the football season starts.
2. a can or bottle of beer: e.g. Pass me another tube.
3. underground electric railway: e.g. The tube is the fastest way through the city now.
See also:
down the tube(s)

tuck away/in/into
eat heartily, greedily: e.g. 1. He can tuck away a huge steak and six eggs for breakfast! 2. Tuck in everyone — the food's on the table! 3. I can't wait to tuck into the prawns!

tuck into the tucker
eat heartily, greedily.

tucked away
1. hidden, concealed: e.g. I've got it tucked away where you'll never find it.
2. saved (as of money): e.g. He's tucked away a tidy fortune.

tucker
food: e.g. The tucker at the barbie was beaut!
See also:
bib and tucker

tucker-bag
any bag for carrying food.

tucker-box
a refrigerator, or any container for food.

tuckered out
tired; exhausted: e.g.
1. That hike really made me feel tuckered out.
2. That hike tuckered everybody out.

tuckshop
shop selling food and drinks, especially at a school.

tug at (one's) heartstrings
affect (one) at the deepest level of emotional feelings, such as pity, sympathy, love, compassion.

tug of war
trial of strength, power between two opposing sides or forces: e.g. Their divorce case turned into a nasty tug of war to see who could get the most.

tumble
(see: take a tumble)

tumble in the hay
sexual intercourse.

tumble to
suddenly comprehend or grasp the true meaning of: e.g. She finally tumbled to what he was insinuating.

tummy
stomach.

tune
(see: call the tune; change one's tune; dance to someone's tune; sing a different tune; to the tune of)

tune in on
listen intently.

tune up on
revise, update one's knowledge: e.g. I'll have to tune up on my facts before I give a speech at next week's meeting.

tuned in
1. listening: e.g. He speaks so well that he can get everybody tuned in.
2. aware of the facts; alert; knowledgeable: e.g. He's really tuned in to politics.

tune-up
a check and adjustment of a vehicle's engine to obtain maximum power and efficiency: e.g. My car needs a tune-up badly.

tunnel vision
the inability to be flexible about ideas; obsession, fixation with one idea or method to the detriment of the success of a venture.

tuppence
1. prior to decimal currency, the sum of two pence.
2. a very small amount; a bit; anything at all: e.g. 1. She doesn't care tuppence about him! 2. I wouldn't give you tuppence for that old thing!
See also:
not worth a tuppenny damn
not worth tuppence

Tupperware party
form of incentive selling whereby a woman elects to have her acquaintances and friends come to her home for the purpose of viewing and purchasing plastic Tupperware containers and goods (the gatherings often being ridiculed for their banality).

turd
1. faeces; excrement; shit.
2. a contemptible, despicable person: e.g. He's a turd!

turd-bandit/burglar/puncher
a homosexual man.

turd-strangler
a plumber.

turf out
1. throw out; discard.
2. fire; sack; dismiss: e.g. He was turfed out of that job after being caught for stealing.

turkey
1. flop, dud, especially theatrical.
2. person who is easily duped, tricked, cheated or deceived.
See also:
arse over turkey
cold turkey
head-over-turkey
talk turkey

turn
1. a party or social occasion: e.g. That was a terrific turn we went to last night.
2. a bout of sudden illness: e.g. He had a bad turn and had to be taken to hospital.
3. momentary nervous shock or surprise: e.g. The bad news gave me quite a turn.
4. (of food) go bad: e.g. That milk will turn if you don't put it in the fridge.
5. (of the head) experience a dizzy spinning sensation: e.g. My head's turning after that roller-coaster ride.
See also:
at every turn
bad turn
do (someone) a good turn
done to a turn
have a turn
put on a turn
stack on a turn
take turns
throw a turn
to a turn
whatever turns you on

turn a blind eye
ignore deliberately; refuse to see or recognise: e.g. The police in that town turn a blind eye to prostitution.

turn a deaf ear
refuse to listen, help or cooperate.

turn a new leaf
begin a better manner of behaviour; start again afresh: e.g. He's turned a new leaf since getting out of prison.

turn an honest quid
earn one's living honestly, ethically.

turn dingo/dog
become an informant; betray; become a coward; turn treacherous.

turn down
refuse; reject: e.g. She turned down his offer.

turn in
1. retire; go to bed.
2. surrender: e.g. The escapee finally turned himself in.

turn in (one's) grave
(of a dead person) be offended: e.g. Dad would turn in his grave if he knew what you were doing with your life!

turn it up!
a plea for moderation: be reasonable!; shut up!; stop it!

turn off
close one's mind to something; become bored, tired, displeased, disgusted or repulsed; lose interest: e.g. 1. Men who pick their noses and spit in public really turn me off! 2. When the men at a party start talking about footy, I turn off.

turn on
1. become excited, stimulated, attracted by; become sexually aroused: e.g. 1. Do porno movies make you turn on? 2. He really turns me on!
2. take a hallucinatory drug; experience the euphoric effect after taking a drug, such as marijuana, coke, LSD: e.g. This dope will really make you turn on!

turn on (someone)
behave in a suddenly hostile manner towards (someone); to attack (someone), either physically or verbally.

turn on the heat
apply coercive pressure; be extremely and forcefully persuasive.

turn on the waterworks
to cry profusely, often for the devious purpose of gaining one's way or sympathy.

turn (one) on
excite, stimulate, arouse (one) — especially sexually: e.g. Men with big fat beer guts don't turn me on!

turn (one's) back on
disregard; ignore; refuse to help or have anything to do with.

turn (one's) bowels to water
cause extreme fear, anxiety in (one).

turn (one's) hand to
direct (one's) energies and efforts to.

turn (one's) nose up at
show ill-concealed scorn, disdain at; be contemptuously ungrateful: e.g. She turns her nose up at any gift that costs under a hundred dollars!

turn (one's) stomach
sicken, revolt, repulse (one).

turn out
develop; result; end up: e.g. How did the surprise party turn out?

turn over
(basketball) loss of possession without scoring.

turn over a dollar
make; earn money.

turn over a new leaf
(see: turn a new leaf)

turn over every stone
try, attempt everything; try every possibility: e.g. We've turned over every stone and still can't find the solution.

turn (someone) in
inform on (someone); report (someone) to the authorities.

turn (someone) out (of house and home)
evict (someone); throw (someone) out.

turn (someone's) head
make (someone) conceited; unsettle (someone); add to (someone's) vanity: e.g. Too much praise will turn his head.

turn tail
run away; flee: e.g. The louts turned tail when the old man came back out with a rifle.

turn the lights out and play hide the sausage
jocular expression for amorous, lascivious play, sexual intercourse.

turn the other cheek
ignore deliberately; refuse to be intimidated or drawn into conflict: e.g. When my neighbour starts abusing me, I just turn the other cheek.

turn the tables on
reverse the state of affairs to one's own advantage.

turn to jelly
1. to weaken with fear, horror: e.g. I turn to jelly whenever I see a big hairy spider.
2. to feel overcome with love, infatuation: e.g. He's so handsome that I turn to jelly when he speaks to me.

turn turtle
1. to capsize, turn over: e.g. Many boats turned turtle in that wild storm.
2. to change one's opinion, point of view, original stand.

turn up
1. vomit: e.g. He turned up his whole dinner.
2. arrive; appear: e.g. What time is he going to turn up?
3. unearth; discover; expose; bring to light: e.g. Many new and interesting facts were turned up at the investigation.
4. be found, recovered: e.g. Have those lost documents turned up?

turn up (one's) toes
to die.

turn up trumps
work out, turn out successfully.

turn yellow
become cowardly, afraid.

turncoat
traitor; defector; betrayer.

turned off
not interested, excited or aroused; repulsed or revolted by.

turned on
excited; highly interested; sexually aroused.

turning point
decisive point at which change will occur: e.g. Finding out that my husband was gay was the turning point in our marriage.

turn-off
anything that is distasteful, revolting, repulsive, boring, lacking in interest.

turn-on
anything that is highly interesting, exciting, arousing.

turnout
1. party, festive gathering, entertainment.
2. the number of people who have come to, turned up at a gathering, occasion, event etc.

turn-over
the total amount of money received from the sale of goods in a certain time; the rate at which goods, money, employees etc. are replaced.

turn-up
1. attendance: e.g. The turn-up to the meeting was much better than expected.
2. fight; row; commotion; disturbance.
3. an unexpected surprise or reversal of fortune or luck.

turn-up for the books
1. an unexpected surprise or reversal of fortune or luck.
2. (horse-racing) lucky result for a bookmaker.

turps
1. mineral turpentine.
2. strong alcohol; booze:

e.g. He's been on the turps for years.
See also:
on the turps

tush
1. bum, backside.
2. woman viewed as a sex object.

tute
tutorial teaching session.

tut-tut!
interjection of disapproval, rebuke.

tux
tuxedo; a dinner jacket for men.

twaddle
nonsense; rubbish; idle talk.

twang
opium.

twanging the wire
masturbating.

twat
1. female pudendum, genitals, vagina.
2. silly, foolish woman.

tweeds
trousers; pants.

twelfth man
(cricket) replacement player.

twenty to the dozen
fast; quickly; in haste.

twenty-two
(also: ·22) twenty-two calibre rifle.
See also:
catch 22

twerp
silly, insignificant, stupid person.

twiddle (one's) thumbs
1. gesture of turning (one's) thumbs around each other, indicating boredom, idleness.
2. to be idle; to do nothing: e.g. He seems to think I sit around and twiddle my thumbs all day!

twig
perceive; understand; notice; finally, suddenly grasp the meaning of: e.g. He hasn't twigged to the surprise party we have planned for him.
See also:
snap (one's) twig

twinkle
to urinate, or the act of urinating, especially of women: e.g. We were so desperate that we had to squat behind a tree for a twinkle.
See also:
in the twinkle/twinkling of an eye

twinkle-palace
(especially of women) the toilet.

twinkle-toes
one who is very nimble on the feet, such as a good dancer.

twin-set
matching cardigan and jumper worn by women.

twin-set and pearls
(derog.) of conservative, naive, prim and chaste women.

twist
1. unexpected development or turn of events: e.g. That movie has a very surprising twist at the end.
2. vigorous type of dance popularised in the 1960s and performed by twisting to and fro.
See also:
around/round the twist

twist (someone) around (one's) little finger
have the ability to dominate, influence or have (someone) completely under (one's) power.

twist (someone's) arm
persuade, coerce (someone): e.g. Nobody had to twist your arm — you did it entirely of your own free will!

twist (someone's) words
pervert the true meaning of what (someone) has said.

twisted mind
queer, odd, sinister, evil or peculiar tendency of the mind, thinking or belief.

twit
silly, foolish, stupid person.

two
(see: add/put two and two together; takes two to tango; terrible twos; the old one-two)

two and a half sheets to the wind
drunk; intoxicated.

two bites at the cherry
two attempts at something.

two bob
before decimal currency, the sum of two shillings or a coin of this value.
See also:
not the full two bob
not worth two bob
the full two bob
two-bob

two can play at that game
an assertion or threat of retaliation using similar tactics or behaviour.

two flags
(Australian Rules football) a goal.

two, four, six, eight, bog in, don't wait
jocular, mock grace said just before eating.

two heads are better than one
two people working together and combining their knowledge and minds probably have more chance of success or of solving a problem than one person alone.

two hoots
(see: give two hoots)

two left feet
(to have . . .) to be clumsy, awkward.

two men and a dog
very few people: e.g. The meeting was a failure — only two men and a dog turned up.

two of a kind
similar.

two shakes (of a dog's tail)
a very short time: e.g. I'll be there in two shakes.

two sides to a coin
(see: there's . . .)

two stuffs
(see: give . . .)

two wrongs don't make a right
advice given to someone about to perpetrate some form of revenge or illegal act as compensation.

two-bagger
ugly woman still viewed as a sex object.

two-be-four
(see: two-by-four)

two-bit
cheap; worthless; petty; small-time: e.g. He's nothing but a sleazy two-bit criminal.

two-bob
before decimal currency, the sum or value of two shillings — now used in many expressions of a derogatory nature.
See also:
like a two-bob watch
mad as a two-bob watch
put (one's) two-bob's worth in
silly as a two-bob watch
two bob

two-bob lair
flashy but cheap person; one who is extravagant in a cheap, gaudy, exhibitionistic manner.

two-bob millionaire
someone who has temporarily come into, or acquired, some money and who is considered not likely to have it for long.

two-by-four
a length of standard timber measuring 4 inches wide and 2 inches thick.

two-edged
ambiguous.

two-faced
insincere; deceitful; dishonest; hypocritical.

twopence
(see: tuppence)

twopenny
(also: tuppenny) cheap; worthless.

two-pot screamer
person who gets drunk very easily on very little alcohol.

two's company, three's a crowd
statement of romantic intent — that two people can indulge in romantic or sexual play whereas a third person would inhibit such activity.

two-timer
one who deceives, double-crosses or cheats another, especially by infidelity.

two-timing
deceit, especially by infidelity: e.g. He's been two-timing his wife with another girl on the side for years.

two-up
a gambling game whereby two coins are thrown in the air and bets laid as to whether they will land two heads or two tails.

tyke
1. (derog.) a Roman Catholic.
2. a naughty child.
3. a dog.

type
person (of specified character): e.g. He's not such a bad type.

uey
(see: U-turn)

UFO
Unidentified Flying Object — especially in the sense of objects, space-craft etc. that are not from Earth.

ug boot
a boot made of sheep-skin with the fleece on the inside lining.

ugh!
exclamation of distaste, displeasure, revulsion.

ugly as a hatful of arseholes

ugly as sin
(of a person) very ugly or unattractive.

ugly duckling
unattractive child who turns out more beautiful or admired than was thought possible.

uh-oh!
(also: oh-oh!) exclamation of surprised dismay, disappointment.

U-ie
(see: U-turn)

um and ah
1. to be indecisive.
2. to make misleading or evasive statements.

ump/umpie
umpire.

umpteen
many; an indefinite amount, usually large: e.g. I've told him umpteen times that he's not allowed to do that!
See also:
for the umpteenth time!

umpteen million times
very many times; repeatedly.

unable to scratch (oneself)
1. dead drunk; totally intoxicated.
2. very busy: e.g. I've had so much to do this week I haven't been able to scratch myself.

For other possible entries beginning with 'unable' see entries listed under 'can't'.

unattached
single; not married; having no romantic or family ties or commitments.

Uncle Sam
pertaining to the United States, and its government.

uncome-at-able
not attainable or accessible.

uncool
unsophisticated action or display of emotion: e.g. Farting at the dinner table was very uncool.

uncrowned king
an unofficial but recognised leader in a particular field: e.g. He's the uncrowned king of a national drug-smuggling syndicate.

uncut
1. (of drugs) pure; unadulterated: e.g. He smuggled millions of dollars worth of uncut heroin into the country.
2. (of a movie film) uncensored: e.g. This is the uncut version of the film.

under
(see: go under)

under a cloud
1. depressed; in a gloomy state; uncertain: e.g. His entire future is under a cloud until the outcome of the trial.
2. (Australian Rules football) doubtful player because of injury etc.

under fire
exposed to severe criticism: e.g. The present government is under fire for its failure to reduce the national debt.

under lock and key
1. secure; protected; locked, hidden away: e.g. The precious documents are under lock and key so there is no need to worry.

2. imprisoned: e.g. That criminal needs to be put under lock and key for the rest of his life to protect society.

under (one's) belt
in store; to (one's) credit; attributed to (oneself): e.g. He's got a lot of qualifications under his belt so he'd be a good choice for the job.

under (one's) breath
in a whisper; quietly: e.g. He swore at the headmaster under his breath.

under (one's) nose
in front of (one): e.g. The book you are looking for is right under your nose!

under (one's) own steam
without help; unaided: e.g. It's about time he learnt to do things under his own steam without the help of his parents all the time!

under (one's) roof
in (one's) home: e.g. There'll be no illegal gambling under my roof!

under (one's) wing
in (one's) loving, sympathetic and tender care: e.g. She seems to enjoy taking lonely people under her wing and giving them her friendship and confidence.

under (someone's) spell
under the influence of (someone); captivated, dominated by (someone).

under the affluence of inkahol
jocular spoonerism: under the influence of alcohol.

under the counter
illicitly; illegally; secretly: e.g. That shop sells pornographic magazines under the counter.

under the hammer
1. sold or to be sold at auction: e.g. That mansion is going under the hammer next weekend.
2. (Australian Rules football) about to be tackled.

under the influence
drunk; intoxicated: e.g. It is extremely dangerous to drive if one is under the influence.

under the lap
underhandedly; illicitly; illegally. (see: under the counter)

under the sun
anywhere on earth: e.g. My husband's the best beer-guzzler under the sun!

under the table
intoxicated; drunk: e.g. He always ends up under the table by the end of the night!
See also:
drink (someone) under the table

under the thumb
under (someone's) power, influence or domination: e.g. His wife really has him under the thumb!

under the weather
intoxicated; drunk: e.g. He's been under the weather all weekend!

under wraps
secret; confidential; not for public scrutiny: e.g. We're keeping our plans under wraps until the right time to make a public announcement.

underarm
(cricket) illegal, insulting delivery.

under-chunders
underpants.

under-cover
secret; highly confidential; not for public knowledge or scrutiny: e.g. He's an under-cover agent for the police.

underdaks
underpants.

under-dog
person, team etc. in a losing or inferior position, not favoured to win.

underfoot
1. in the way; of nuisance value: e.g. I'm sick of the children being underfoot all day!
2. oppressed; down-trodden: e.g. Dark-skinned people have always been underfoot compared with the light-skinned races.

underground
1. a railway system running through underground tunnels: e.g. The fastest way through the city is via the underground.
2. secret, illicit, such as an organisation, publication etc.: e.g. The authorities have captured the main leaders of an underground terrorist organisation.

underground ball/pass
(cricket) grubber; not quite a daisy cutter.

underground mutton
rabbit as food.

underhand/underhanded
deceptive; secret; illicit; sly: e.g. He won the election using underhanded tactics.

undersell (oneself)
to lack faith, confidence in (one's) abilities: e.g. He's always underselling himself, even though he's very good at what he does.

under-the-counter
(of goods) sold illicitly, illegally, secretly.

underworld
the criminal element within society: e.g. He's a well-known member of the underworld, but the police haven't been able to convict him yet.

undies
underpants.

undoing
cause of ruin, downfall: e.g. Alcohol was his undoing.

undone
brought to ruin, failure, destruction: e.g. He was finally undone when his drinking became an obsession.
See also:
bring (someone) undone
come undone

unearthly
unreasonably early: e.g. We had to wake up at the unearthly time of four in the morning!

unflappable
calm; dispassionate; imperturbable.

un-get-at-able
inaccessible: e.g. Too many politicians are un-get-at-able for the public who have legitimate complaints.

ungodly
outrageous: e.g. Four in the morning was an ungodly hour to have to get up!

unheard-of
outrageous.

unhinged
mentally unbalanced; upset; disordered: e.g. He's been a bit unhinged since the accident.

unholy
outrageous; dreadful: e.g. What an unholy, awful mess you've managed to get yourself into!

uni
university.

unit
1. any thing, piece of equipment or vehicle with a specific function: e.g. He spent thousands of dollars doing up that four-wheel-drive unit.
2. a person: e.g. He's a fucked unit since his wife left him.

unload
1. get rid of, dispose of, especially of an unwanted burden: e.g. Farmers had to unload their crops at give-away prices due to a glut on the market.
2. (Australian Rules football) pass the ball.

unmentionables
undergarments; personal items too embarrassing to mention: e.g. The customs officers went through all my things — including my unmentionables!

unreal
amazingly, unbelievably awful or wonderful, depending on the context of what is being discussed: e.g. 1. We saw an unreal accident on the way here — there were cars and bodies everywhere!
2.The concert last night was unreal — the best we've been to!

unsung hero
hero who is not celebrated or recognised.

unwind
relax: e.g. It takes me several hours to unwind after work.

unwritten law
custom; tradition or rule that is generally agreed upon or assumed rather than officially recorded: e.g. It's an unwritten law around here that the men help with the dishes.

up
1. wrong; amiss: e.g. Is anything up?
2. have sexual intercourse: e.g. He'll be up her like a rat up a drainpipe!
3. angry, annoyed with; scold, berate: e.g. 1. I'll get up him next time I see him! 2. She was up him for coming late.
4. winning, in front, having more money than one started with after gambling: e.g. We went to the casino last night, and I was a hundred dollars up by the end of the evening.
5. to increase, raise a previous wager or bet: e.g. I'll up you fifty dollars!
See also:
ace it up!; act up; add up; all broken up; all choked up; all cut up; all dolled up; all screwed up; all up; alley up; arse up; back up; bail up; balls up; belt up; blow (someone) up; blow up; bone up on; booze-up; break up; bring up; buck up; bugger (something) up; buggered up; bust-up; butter (someone) up; can't get it up; catch up; chat (someone) up; cheer up; clam up; clean up; clean-up; clock up; cock up; cock-up; come up; cook up; cover-up; crack up; cut up; dig up; dish up; do up; dog tied up; dolled up; done up; dredge up; dress up; drum up; dry up; face up to; fed up; feel (someone) up; feel up to; first up; fix (someone) up; foot up; fork up; foul up; frame-up; frig up; front up; fucked up; game's up; get (one's) Irish up; get the wind up; get up; get up (someone); get up to; get uppity; get-up; get-up-and-go; give up; go up in smoke; goof up; gum up; had up for; ham it up; hang-up; hard-up; high-up; hit (someone) up for; hit up; hole up; hot up; hung-up; hush up; jack up; jump up and down; jumped-up; keep (one's) chin up; keep (one's) end up; knock up; lap it up; let up; let-up; lit up; live it up; live up to; look up to; looking up; make up; mark up; measure up to;

mess up; mix up; mixed up with; mockered up; muff-up; nosh-up; notch up; nothing up top; oil (someone) up; on an upper; on the up and up; one up on (someone); open up; own up; pack up; pay up; pep up; perk up; pick up; pick-up; pick-me-up; pile up; pile-up; pin up; piss-up; play up; play up to (someone); psyched up; puffed up; punch-up; put (someone) up; put (someone) up to it; put up or shut up; put up with; rake up; rap-up; roar (someone) up; roll up; rough (someone) up; rub (someone) up the wrong way; run up; rustle up; scrape up; screw (something) up; send (someone) up; send-up; set (someone) up; set-up; settle up; sewn up; shake it up!; shoot up; show (someone) up; shut up; sign up; slap-up; slip up; slip-up; smash-up; snazzed up; soften (someone) up; soup up; split up; square up; stack-up; stand (someone) up; stand up for; stand up to; steamed up; step up in the world; stick up; stick-up; stood up; string (someone) up; stuck-up; stuff (something) up; stuff-up; sum (someone) up; take up with; tart up; things are looking up; throw up; tied up; tizz up; top-up; touch (someone) up; trip (someone) up; tune-up; turn it up!; turn up; two-up; wake up!; wake-up; warm up; washed-up; weigh up; what's up?; whistle up; whoop it up; who's up who?; wind up; wise up; word up; wrap-up; write-up; zap up

up a creek
(see: up shit creek)

up a gumtree
1. baffled; perplexed: e.g. Everyone's up a gumtree as far as this problem is concerned.
2. in difficulties; having problems; in trouble: e.g. He's up a gumtree good and proper this time!
3. confused; incorrect.

up against
confronted with: e.g. We'll be up against a lot of opposition this time.

up against a brick wall

up against it/the wall
in great difficulties with few or no options; in severe circumstances.

up and about
active after sleep or illness: e.g. He's up and about again after a long illness.

up and at it!
an exclamation of encouragement, motivation — get started! get moving! get working!

up and down like a honeymoon cock/nightie

up and down like a lavatory seat
1. repeatedly being performed, or taking place both upwards and downwards.
2. to be constantly getting up and sitting down.

up at sparrow fart
to rise, wake up very early: e.g. You'll have to be up at sparrow fart tomorrow if you want to come fishing with us.

up each other
1. behaving obsequiously, in a sycophantic manner towards each other.
2. arguing, fighting with each other: e.g. It's a wonder they still live together the way they're always up each other!

up for
appearing before court on some charge: e.g. He's up for drunken driving again.

up for grabs
available: e.g. That big house you said you'd like to buy is up for grabs as the owners are moving overseas.

up front
payment or paid in advance: e.g. He's not getting the goods until I get some money up front.

up here for thinking, down there for dancing
(pointing to the head and feet respectively) a statement of self-congratulation on a good idea or clever piece of thinking.

up 'im (up him)
1. fight, assault him: e.g. I'll up 'im if I ever see him again!
2. scornful remark of dismissal, contempt: e.g. Up 'im! I don't care what he said!

up in arms
in a state of agitation, anger: e.g. The entire town is up in arms over the proposed development of a tract of environmental park.

up in smoke
wasted, ruined, gone, lost — as of an opportunity, money, hard work, plans etc. — especially due to fire: e.g. Our entire future went up in smoke when the uninsured building burnt down.

up in the air
uncertain: e.g. The future of the project is up in the air until the next meeting.

up (one's) alley
entirely suited to (one's) ability, talents, knowledge: e.g. This new job is right up your alley.

up (one's) sleeve
pertaining to an undisclosed, secret tactic or advantage: e.g. Don't underestimate him as an opponent — he usually has something up his sleeve.

up (one's) street
favourable; pertaining to something (one) knows, likes or is familiar with (see: up one's alley): e.g. I think I'm going to like this job — it's right up my street.

up (oneself)
having an unjustifiably high opinion of (oneself); delude (oneself): e.g. He's up himself if he thinks people are going to vote for him!
See also:
so far up himself he's on the way down again

up shit creek

up shit creek in a barbed wire canoe without a paddle

up shit creek without a paddle
1. in difficulties; in dire straits; in extremely difficult circumstances.
2. (of a woman) pregnant and unmarried or deserted by the father of the child.

up (someone)
1. have sexual intercourse with (someone): e.g. You can bet he's up her by now!
2. fight, assault (someone): e.g. I'll up the bastard if he tells any more lies about me!

up the creek
(see: up shit creek)

up the donga/donger
out in the country as opposed to the city.

up the duff
1. pregnant: e.g. She's up the duff again!
2. broken; ruined; spoiled: e.g. Our television is up the duff.

up the garden path
(see: lead someone up the garden path)

up the pole/putt
1. confused; incorrect; muddled; wrong: e.g. Your thinking in this matter is up the pole!
2. broken down; ruined: e.g. This thing is up the putt again!

up the shit
1. troubled; in a state of turmoil, disorganisation, ruin: e.g. All our plans are up the shit.
2. in great difficulties; in dire straits; in extremely difficult circumstances; in trouble: e.g. He's really up the shit this time, as the bank has refused to extend his loan.
3. broken-down; ruined: e.g. This thing is up the shit again!

up the spout
1. pregnant: e.g. She's up the spout again!
2. ruined; spoiled; in a bad or hopeless situation: e.g. Our entire future is up the spout because the bank refused an extension on our loan and we need the money desperately.

up the wop
(see: up the spout, 2.)

up there Cazaly!
(Australian Rules football) a cry of encouragement (Roy Cazaly was a South Melbourne player in the 1920s and 1930s).

up to
1. capable of: e.g. He's not up to this job.
2. doing: e.g. What's he up to?

up to date
up to the present moment, time: e.g. Up to date, we've had no problems with this car.
See also:
bring (someone) up to date

up to dolly's wax
satisfied, full, up to the neck, such as with food.

up to it
capable of it: e.g. Do you think he's up to it?

up to mud
worthless.

up to no good
to have ill, evil, criminal intent: e.g. Those men look like they're up to no good to me.

up to (one's) armpits/ears/elbows/eyebrows/neck
1. inundated with; overwhelmed with: e.g. 1. He's up to his elbows with work this weekend. 2. He's up to his neck in debts.
2. completely and totally involved, implicated.

up to (one's) neck in shit
in very great difficulties; in dire trouble or circumstances: e.g. He's up to his neck in shit since the Taxation Department found out that he was avoiding paying tax.

up to par
(see: up to scratch)

up to putty
no good; worthless; broken down.

up to scratch
satisfactory; meeting requirements; good: e.g. A lot of training will be necessary before that horse is up to scratch.

up to something
doing, planning (something) in a secretive, devious or illicit manner: e.g. I don't know what it is yet, but I think he's up to something.

up to the elbows/eyeballs/eyebrows
(see: up to one's armpits)

up to the mark
at a required standard; satisfactory; very good: e.g. He failed because his assignments weren't up to the mark this term.

up with
1. informed; having knowledge about: e.g. Are you up with the latest news?
2. equal to.

up with the crows
awake, arise early: e.g. Farmers always have to be up with the crows.

up you!

up your arse/bum/bum chum/date mate/jumper/nose!

up your nose with a rubber hose! (and twice as far with a chocolate bar!)

up yours!
exclamation of scornful dismissal, rejection, insult, contempt, abuse to someone you are arguing with, or who has insulted you.

up-and-down
erratic; inconsistent: e.g. He's had such up-and-down moods these past few weeks.

up-and-coming
becoming well-known, famous or successful: e.g. He's an up-and-coming young athlete.

uphill battle/job
a difficult task all the way: e.g. It's going to be an uphill battle for him to give up drugs and booze.

up-market
pertaining to goods, commercialism, services etc. of superior quality: e.g. This new shopping centre will be very up-market.

upper
1. a stimulant drug: e.g. He takes uppers all the time in order to help overcome his severe bouts of depression.
2. a pleasant or stimulating experience.
See also:
on an upper

upper crust
the aristocracy; upper class; the very wealthy or powerful.

upper hand
the dominant position; advantage; mastery; control: e.g. As far as this battle is concerned, I have the upper hand.

upper-crust
posh; sophisticated; upper-class: e.g. That's a very upper-crust club with limited membership.

uppish/uppity
self-assertive; arrogant; snobbish.

upright
honest: e.g. He's an upright and decent man.

ups and downs
good and bad times, fortunes, experiences, moods etc.: e.g. Every marriage has its ups and downs.

upsadaisy
a term of encouragement to someone — especially a child — being lifted, helped up, climbing etc.

upset the apple-cart
throw into disorder, chaos; disturb; ruin: e.g. It will really upset the apple-cart if it rains this weekend.

upstage
divert attention from someone to oneself; steal the lime-light; do better than.

uptake
understanding; comprehension: e.g. She's a bit slow on the uptake when it comes to the ironic humour in some jokes.

uptight
1. tense; nervous; anxious; worried.
2. angry; bad-tempered; annoyed.

up-to-date
modern; fashionable; containing the latest news, information, improvements, innovations etc.: e.g. 1. She always wears up-to-date clothes. 2. Have you got an up-to-date map of the area?

up-to-the-minute
incorporating the latest news, information: e.g. We'll listen to an up-to-the-minute weather report before we take the boat out.

urge
1. desire to urinate: e.g. I hate getting the urge when I'm out shopping and can't find a toilet.
2. sexual desire: e.g. He gets the urge every night!

use
exploit a person for one's own selfish ends: e.g. He never loved her — he just used her all those years.

use a little elbow grease
apply oneself with energy and work hard: e.g. You'll have to use a little elbow grease to get that dirty stove clean!

use every trick in the book
try every means, avenue or method, either legal or illegal, licit or illicit: e.g. He used every trick in the book to get himself elected.

use (one's) head/loaf/noodle
1. think logically, clearly.
2. be clever, smart, enterprising: e.g. He used his loaf when he bought

all that land so cheaply — now it's worth a fortune.

used
selfishly exploited by someone for his own ends: e.g. I don't like being used!

used as a guinea-pig
1. used in an experimental manner.
2. selfishly exploited by someone without thought to one's safety.

useful/useless as a cunt full of cold water

useful/useless as a glass door on a dunny

useful/useless as a pocket on a singlet

useful/useless as a spare prick at a wedding

useful/useless as a submarine with screen doors

useful/useless as a witch's tit

useful/useless as an arsehole on a broom

useful/useless as an ashtray on a pushbike

useful/useless as the bottom half of a mermaid

useful/useless as tits on a bull
completely useless.

useful as four blocks away
to be so far-away as to be useless.

user
1. one who exploits people for his own selfish ends.
2. a drug-addict.

usual
(see: the usual)

ute
utility truck, car or vehicle.

U-turn
a turn that completely reverses the direction of travel in a car, vehicle.

vac
vacation.

vacuum
1. a vacuum cleaner.
2. to use a vacuum cleaner: e.g. I must vacuum the floor today.

Valium
drug used as a sedative and held in contempt as a cure-all prescribed by incompetent doctors.

vamoose
to depart quickly.

vamp
an unscrupulous flirt; woman who uses sexual charms to exploit men.

vampire's tea-bag
tampon used by menstruating women.

vanish into thin air
to disappear without trace.

vapours
tears; a fit of crying: e.g. She's got the vapours because she didn't get her own way.

varmint
scoundrel; annoying person or animal; pest.

VCR
video cassette recorder.

VD
venereal disease.

VDU
visual display unit, such as the screen that displays information for a computer.

Vee-dub
abbreviation of VW: Volkswagon car.

Vee-eight
(also: V8)
1. an internal combustion engine with two banks of four cylinders in a V formation.
2. a car with such an engine: e.g. He drives a V8.

Vee-wee
Volkswagon car.

Vegemite
dark brown vegetable extract used as a spread on bread and extremely popular in Australia (Trademark). The name can now be applied jocularly to people, especially children: e.g. Aren't you a clever little Vegemite!

vegetable
1. dull, boring person who leads an inactive and monotonous life.
2. person who is totally dependent on others or medical assistance for survival due to an accident that has severely impaired mental and physical activity.

vegetate
to live an inactive, unprogressive, unthinking or monotonous life: e.g. He's vegetating in that job — he should leave and try something more suited to his talents.

vegies
vegetables.

velvet
highly profitable, pleasant or advantageous position: e.g. Since winning all that money, he's been living in/on velvet.
See also:
black velvet

venom
spite; malice: e.g. His criticism was full of venom.

vent (one's) spleen
show, express (one's) anger: e.g. There's no need to vent your spleen on me just because you had a bad day at work!

verbal diarrhoea
ceaseless flow of talk (on the part of someone), often of little import.

very funny!
an interjection expressing displeasure, or that what has just occurred is not funny at all.

'Mark's missus told him to reduce th' number of beers he drinks. He's down to one a day!'

A man's wife — otherwise known as the ball and chain, better half, cheese and kisses, ever-lovin', good lady, little lady, little woman, boss, missus, old girl, old lady, old woman, other half, trouble-and-strife or 'er indoors — is often regarded as the thorn in his side when it comes to his drinking habits and his right to exercise them.

vet
1. veterinary surgeon.
2. war veteran.

VFL
Victorian Football League — Australian Rules football.

vibes
feelings aroused by the atmosphere of a place or by the people in it: e.g. 1. This place has bad vibes — I want to leave. 2. He gives off good vibes and I think he'll win the election.

vibrator
electronic vibrating massage instrument, often used for erotic stimulation.

vicious circle
a situation in which one difficulty leads to another, often exacerbating the first problem: e.g. It's a vicious circle where higher wages produce inflation, and inflation causes higher wage claims.

Victorian
prudish; old-fashioned; chaste.

village bike
promiscuous woman, girl of loose morals who is willing (or commonly believed) to have sex with anybody in town.

village idiot
well-known person considered to be the top fool, idiot.

vim
energy; vigour.

vinegar stroke
the point of climax — especially in sex.

Vinnies
St Vincent de Paul — a charitable organisation that manages second-hand shops for the needy.

vino
cheap wine.

V.I.P.
very important person: e.g. A lot of V.I.P.s are coming to this function.

virtually
almost: e.g. He did virtually all the work.

visiting card
any article or thing that is usually recognisable as the owner's.

visitors
pertaining to menstruation in women: e.g. I won't go swimming today as my visitors have arrived.

vital organ
the penis.

vital statistics
bust, waist and hip measurements of a woman, or measurement of any other sexual part of the body.

vitamiser
electronic blender for pulping food.

vitriol
highly offensive, caustic criticism.

vixen
an ill-tempered, spiteful and malicious woman.

vocab
vocabulary.

voice like a foghorn
(to have a . . .) to have a deep, loud, booming voice; to be outspoken.

volcanoes
pimples, acne.

vote
suggest, propose: e.g. I vote we all go in the same car.
See also:
donkey vote

vote with (one's) feet
to express (one's) disapproval by leaving.

V-sign
1. a gesture of victory, given by holding up the first and second fingers spread apart with palm facing outwards.
2. a rude gesture of contempt involving making upward-thrusting movements with the first and second fingers, palm facing inwards.

vulture
unscrupulous person who preys on others for his own gains.

wack/wacker
crazy, zany, irrational, peculiar, eccentric or amusing person.
(see also: whack)

wacko/wacky
crazy; insane; irrational.

waffle
1. nonsense; foolish, empty talk: e.g. His speech was a lot of waffle.
2. indulge in aimless, vague and lengthy talk or writing: e.g. He always waffles when he gets up to make a speech.

wag
1. a humorous, amusing person; practical joker.
2. (of children) to wilfully be absent from school: e.g. Some children wag school and spend their time in pin-ball parlours.

wagon
one's car or vehicle: e.g. My old wagon needs a tune-up.
See also:
fix (someone's) wagon
fuzz wagon
jump on the bandwagon
on the (water) wagon

wait hand and foot on
do everything for someone, completely look after someone; pamper: e.g. He's so lazy because his mother waited hand and foot on him all his life.

wait up
to remain awake; not to go to bed while waiting for someone to return: e.g. Don't wait up for me as I'll be home late.

wait-a-while
climbing wild vine (*Acacia colletioides*) with thorns that trap the clothing or skin of passers-by.

waiting game
the deferment of immediate action in the belief that the passage of time will present a better set of circumstances or advantage.

wake up!
an order to rouse from lethargy, inactivity or misunderstanding due to naivety or apathy: e.g. Wake up! The truth is obvious if you'd only care to think!

wake up to it
realise, understand (it); be aware of the true meaning or purpose: e.g. His wife meets a secret lover instead of going to bingo, but he hasn't woken up to it yet.

wake up to (oneself)
adopt a more realistic, sensible attitude: e.g. If he doesn't wake up to himself, he's going to be in a lot of trouble with the police in the future.

wake-up
one who is aware of the true meaning, purpose, significance of a situation and alert to possible deception: e.g. The police are definitely a wake-up to his criminal activities which he hides behind a veneer of respectability.

wakey-wakey
1. the time to wake up from sleep: e.g. Around here, wakey-wakey is at six in the morning!
2. a call to rise from bed, wake up from sleep: e.g. Wakey-wakey everybody — time to start work!

walk a tight-rope
be in a precarious, dangerous situation.

walk all over (someone)
exploit, abuse, insult, dominate (someone): e.g. How can you let your children walk all over you like that!

walk around with (one's) head in the clouds
1. be elated, happy, extremely pleased with (oneself).
2. be vague, unrealistic.

walk away with
1. to win easily: e.g. Our team walked away with the Grand Final.

2. to steal, pilfer: e.g. Some rotter walked away with my beer!

walk into
to encounter unwittingly: e.g. He walked right into my trap!

walk of life
occupation; way of life: e.g. There were people from all walks of life at the conference.

walk off with
(see: walk away with, 1. and 2.)

walk out
to leave as an expression of protest; go on strike; depart, especially suddenly or angrily.

walk out on (someone)
desert, abandon, jilt, leave (someone): e.g. The business went bust because my partner walked out on me.

walk the streets
be homeless, but especially to live the life of a prostitute: e.g. Many teenagers have turned to walking the streets as a last resort for supporting themselves.

walkabout
an Aborigine's period of nomadic wandering.
See also:
go walkabout

walkie-talkie
light radio device that combines transmitter and receiver and which can be carried about easily.

walking
(see: go walking)

walking a thin line
in a precarious, risky or dangerous situation.

walking disaster area
person who is prone to having unlucky accidents or mishaps: e.g. My son is a walking disaster area — he's always getting hurt.

walking on air
elated; very happy: e.g. He's been walking on air since he won the lottery.

walking papers/ticket
dismissal; the sack: e.g. He was given his walking papers because he was found stealing money from the till.

walkout
a walking out or leaving as an act of protest, such as a strike: e.g. The union has ordered a walkout if its demands aren't met.

walkover
1. an easily manipulated person: e.g. Don't worry about him — he's such a walkover that he'll be easily talked into agreeing with us.
2. an easy task; an unopposed or easy victory: e.g. Next week's game against the opposition will be a walkover.

walks as though (one) has a grass-seed between (one's) legs

walks as though (one) has a plum up (one's) bum

walks as though (one) is pinching sixpence
a mincing style of walking; pigeon-toed or knock-kneed.

wall
(see: back to the wall; climb up the wall; drive someone up the wall; go to the wall; if walls could speak; like talking to a brick wall; love to be a fly on the wall; nail someone to the wall; off the wall; screw someone to the wall; see the writing on the wall; up against a brick wall)

wall-flower
woman without a partner at a dance or social function.

wallop
1. thrash; beat; strike heavily.
2. a forceful impression: e.g. She really packed a wallop when she made her entry in the nude!
See also:
pack a wallop

walloper
1. a policeman.
2. the penis.

walloping
1. a sound defeat or beating: e.g. Our team got a walloping.
2. large, huge, very big: e.g. We had to hire a walloping truck just to move the junk out of the house!

walls have ears
beware of eavesdroppers: e.g. Watch what you say — walls have ears!

wally
stupid, foolish person.

Wally Grout
(rhyming slang) shout — turn to buy the round of drinks or bear the cost of something.

waltz
1. an easy task: e.g. That exam was a waltz!
2. walk quickly, haughtily: e.g. To everyone's amazement, she waltzed into the room and clobbered her husband!

waltz off with
take, win with ease: e.g. He waltzed off with first prize.

waltzing matilda
roaming aimlessly like a tramp.

wangle
1. a trick, scheme, swindle or act of deception.
2. bring about, accomplish, obtain, organise, manipulate, especially by indirect or scheming methods: e.g.

He knows so many people in high places that he can wangle things that would seems impossible to the average person.

wangler
a cheat or confidence trickster.

wank
1. funny, odd, amusing or eccentric person.
2. a person who deceives, deludes himself by refusing to see the truth or reality.
3. a person given to unproductive activity.
4. behaviour that is egotistical: e.g. What a wank that speech was!
5. to masturbate.
6. self-indulgence; over-indulgence: e.g. Having the conference in Hawaii was a bit of a wank.
See also:
load of wank

wank (oneself)
1. to deceive, delude (oneself): e.g. He's wanking himself if he thinks everyone will agree with his stupid and unrealistic ideas!
2. (. . . off) to masturbate.

wanker
(see: wank, 1., 2. and 3.)

wanna
contraction of want to: e.g. I don't wanna go!

want for
be short of; be in short supply of; need: e.g. She never wants for money as her family is very rich.

want (one's) bread buttered on both sides
to desire all options, possibilities; to desire two apparently opposing courses of action.

want (one's) head read
to show a need for psychiatric help; exhibit foolish tendencies, thoughts, actions: e.g. He wants his head read keeping on doing stupid things like that!

want out
to desire to withdraw from a commitment or responsibility that may have become difficult: e.g. I want out as I don't think this scheme is going to work any more.

want the earth/moon
to desire too much that cannot be attained.

want to have (one's) cake and eat it too
to desire all options, possibilities; to desire two apparently opposing courses of action.

want to talk to the butcher, not the block
1. derisive remark to one who butts in, interferes, offers unwanted advice.
2. to insist on seeing the boss or person in charge.

wanted
(of a criminal) sought by the police: e.g. He's wanted for murder.

war cry
group or political party catchword or slogan: e.g. Their latest war cry is 'Lower Taxes'.

war of nerves
psychological conflict using methods such as intimidation, fear, threats etc.

warhorse
veteran soldier or politician who is often aggressive.

warm
1. close to what is sought: e.g. The police are getting warm in their search for the murderer.
2. unpleasant; uncomfortable; embarrassing: e.g. All that talk about family scandals was a bit warm for me.

warm the cockles of (one's) heart
please (one); generate warm, pleasant, loving feelings in (one).

warm up
1. prepare for a performance by exercise or practice: e.g. The band is warming up for the concert with a jam session in the back rooms.
2. become more lively, active, enthusiastic: e.g. The party started to warm up after everybody had a few drinks.

warm-blooded
sexually ardent.

warm-hearted
affectionate; kind.

war-paint
cosmetics; make-up: e.g. That old lady looks awful with all that war-paint on!

warped
perverted; evil-minded.

warts and all
including defects, blemishes and unattractive faults: e.g. I want the portrait painted realistically — warts and all!

warwicks/warwick farms
(rhyming slang) arms: e.g. He grabbed me by the warwicks and held me down.

wash
bear investigation or scrutiny; convince: e.g. That excuse won't wash with the authorities.
See also:
come out in the wash

wash (one's) dirty linen in public
reveal scandalous, personal facts about (one's) private life in public.

wash (one's) hands of
decline responsibility for; refuse to have any more to do with.

wash (someone's) mouth out with soap and water
to severely reprimand (someone) for using bad language, swearing.

washed-out
exhausted; tired.

washed-up
failed; ruined or finished: e.g. He's washed-up after losing a fortune gambling.

washer
face-washer; flannel used for washing the face.

wash-out
1. unsuccessful person, thing or event; failure; fiasco.
2. sporting event that has been prematurely ended because of rain.

wasn't born yesterday
to be smarter, shrewder than given credit for: e.g. He tried to rip me off but I knew what he was up to — I wasn't born yesterday you know!

waspish
bad-tempered.

waste not, want not
an expression indicating the foolishness of wasting, discarding anything that may prove useful in the future; thrifty habits ensure that (one) will not become destitute.

waste (one's) breath
talk in vain without anyone heeding or paying serious attention.

waste (one's) time
expend (one's) energies and efforts fruitlessly, without effect.

waste (someone)
murder, kill (someone): e.g. The Mafia decided to waste him before he had a chance to talk to the police.
See also:
lay waste

wasted
1. (of a person) not used to full potential or capabilities; not occupied to the best of one's abilities.
2. exhausted, incapacitated as a result of excessive indulgence in alcohol or drugs: e.g. He was wasted for a week after taking that stuff!
3. killed: e.g. Those criminals had him wasted because he knew too much about their operations.

wasting (oneself)
not using (one's) potential, abilities etc. to the fullest.

watch it!
1. (a warning) look out! be careful! : e.g. Watch it! There's a big hole in front of you!
2. (a threat) cease one's present offensive behaviour or face the consequences! : e.g. Watch it, or I'll bash your face in!
3. be on guard; be alert; be very careful, cautious: e.g. I told her to watch it if she starts a business with him as a partner because he's let people down before!

watch (one's) mouth/p's and q's
be careful of what (one) says so that (one) does not offend, insult, swear or say the wrong thing.

watch (one's) step
be on guard; be alert; be very careful, cautious: e.g. You'd better watch your step if you get involved with him as he's a known criminal.

watch (one's) waist-line
to diet, take care not to put on any weight.

watch out
be on guard; be alert and careful.

watch over
protect; guard.

watch yourself!
(see: watch it!, 1., 2. and 3.)

watchdog
1. sentry; guard; inspector.
2. (joc.) guardian of morals: e.g. You're not my watchdog! I'll do as I please without any preaching from you!

watched pot never boils
impatience makes the waiting seem longer.

watch-springs
pubic hairs, especially those left in the toilet or bath.

water
(see: all above water; all wind and water; between wind and water; blood is thicker than water; bowels turn to water; fish out of water; get into hot water; get one's water cut off; go through fire and water for; go to water; hold water; in deep/hot water; keep one's head above water; like water; like water off a duck's back; of the first water; pour oil on troubled waters; spend it like water; still waters run deep; throw cold water on; troubled waters; weak as water; wet as water)

water down
make less extreme, forceful, unpleasant or horrifying: e.g. The authorities tried to water down the reports of the disaster to the public.

water has flowed under the bridge
many things have happened that have changed the situation irrevocably: e.g. Too much water has flowed under the bridge for them to ever be reconciled with each other.

water on the brain
(to have . . .) to be dumb, stupid, lacking in intelligence.

water the horse
to urinate: e.g. He's just gone to water the horse.

water under the bridge
in the past and cannot be changed or remedied: e.g. We must forget what happened in the past — it's all water under the bridge.

watered down
1. weakened; diluted; adulterated: e.g. This rum tastes like it's been watered down!
2. made less severe, extreme, unpleasant, horrifying: e.g. The official reports of the disaster were watered down.

Watergate
(U.S.A.) a scandal, usually involving corruption of political figures.

watering hole
pub; hotel; favourite drinking bar.

water-tight
unassailable; irrefutable; foolproof (as of an alibi or argument).

waterworks
1. tears: e.g. She always turns on the waterworks when she doesn't get her own way.
2. pertaining to the bladder: e.g. His waterworks aren't too good at the moment so he's going to see a specialist.
See also:
turn on the waterworks

wave
(see: don't make waves; make waves; new wave)

wave aside
dismiss as irrelevant or unimportant.

wavelength
a person's way of thinking or present mood: e.g. He's on a different wavelength to me at the moment.
See also:
on the same wavelength

wax
(children's language) take turns when kicking a football from end to end.

wax lyrical
to speak in an exaggerated, highly enthusiastic and supportive manner.

wax-head
a surfie — one who rides the waves on a surf-board.

way
(see: can't have it both ways; go a long way; go out of one's way; have/got a way with; in a bad way; in a big way; in the family way; look the other way; no two ways about it; no way!; nothing out of the way; pay one's own way; there are ways and there are ways)

way back
a long time ago.

way gone
1. completely intoxicated or under the influence of drugs: e.g. At the rate he's drinking, he'll be way gone by midnight!
2. ruined, damaged, useless beyond repair.

way of life
principles, habits, beliefs, circumstances governing one's actions or life-style.

way off
not close to the truth or facts: e.g. You're way off if you think that's what happened.

way off the beaten track
1. in a remote, sparsely populated area: e.g. He lives in the bush way off the beaten track.
2. not close to the truth or facts: e.g. The police are way off the beaten track in their search for the culprits, because I know who did it!

way to go!
expression of agreement, encouragement.

waylaid
accosted unexpectedly: e.g. I tried to avoid her all night, but she waylaid me in the carpark.

way-out
1. unusual; eccentric: e.g. They wear such way-out clothes now!
2. progressive; excellent; wonderful: e.g. What a way-out idea!

ways and means
methods of accomplishing a purpose.
See also:
there are ways and there are ways

WC
toilet (water-closet).

weak as cat's piss

weak as piss/shit/water
lacking in strength, power, influence, authority, effect, intelligence, moral resolution etc.

weak at the knees
emotionally drained from fear, excitement, infatuation, love etc.: e.g. 1. He's so handsome I go weak at the knees when I see him. 2. I go weak at the knees at the prospect of having to speak in front of a large audience.

weak bladder
(to have a . . .) to suffer from the need to frequently urinate.

weak link in the chain
the weakest, most vulnerable point.

weak shit
person who lacks courage, strength of character etc., is ineffectual.

weak spot
1. a flaw in one's personality, character: e.g. His biggest weak spot is his inability to make instant decisions.
2. fondness or liking for: e.g. I've got a weak spot for him even though he is a ratbag.

weaker sex
the female sex; women in general.

weakie
a coward; weak, irresolute person; person lacking in physical or moral strength.

weak-kneed
lacking in courage, resolution, strength of character.
See also:
weak at the knees

weakness
self-indulgent liking for someone or something: e.g. I've got a weakness when it comes to sweets so it's hard for me to diet.

wear
1. tolerate; put up with: e.g. I'm not going to wear any more of his abuse!
2. believe; accept as truth: e.g. I don't think the boss will wear that as an excuse for not going to work today.
See also:
can't wear (someone)
the worse for wear

wear and tear
deterioration through normal use, age.

wear (one's) fingers to the bone

wear (oneself) down to a frazzle/little thing

wear (oneself) down to the ground
toil, labour, work extremely hard and often to the point of exhaustion.

wear the pants in the family

wear the trousers
be the person in charge or authority; carry the most authority in a family: e.g. Mum wears the pants in our family.

wearing (one's) heart on (one's) sleeve
openly showing (one's) emotions.

wearing thin
exhausting the patience, tolerance, belief of; becoming unconvincing, monotonous, tiring, hackneyed: e.g. That excuse of his about why he has to work late so often is wearing thin with his wife.

wearing two (or more) hats
holding two (or more) titles, positions, offices.

weasel
a con-man, trickster, cheat.

weasel out
attempt to withdraw from or evade an obligation: e.g. He's been trying to weasel out of his promise.

weather
(see: keep a weather eye open; make heavy weather of; under the weather)

weather the storm
survive, endure difficulties.

wedgie
wedge-tailed eagle.

wedgies
women's shoes with a solid, wedge-shaped heel.

wee
1. urine: e.g. Is that wee between your legs or did you splash water on your trousers?
2. to urinate: e.g. I had to hide behind a tree to wee.
See also:
do wees

weed
1. marijuana: e.g. Do you know where we can get some weed?
2. cigarettes, cigars, tobacco.
3. thin, weak, insignificant or ineffectual person.

weed out
remove, eliminate the undesirable elements: e.g. If you want your business to pick up, you need to weed out the people who don't do their fair share of the work.

week in, week out
continually; incessantly: e.g. He complains about it week in, week out, but never does anything about it.

weekender
a holiday house or shack.

weenies
small cocktail frankfurts.

weeny
small; tiny: e.g. I'll just have a weeny slice of cake.

wee-pee
1. urine.
2. to urinate.

weepie
overly sentimental film that may reduce the audience to tears.

wee-wee(s)
1. urine.
2. to urinate.

weigh down
oppress; depress: e.g. I'm sick of being weighed down by everyone else's problems!

weigh into
1. physically or verbally attack: e.g. Mum really weighed into me when I got home so late.
2. begin with enthusiasm and energy: e.g. He really weighed into the food and drink.

weigh (one's) words
choose (one's) words carefully so as not to confuse (one's) meaning.

weigh up
1. form an estimate or opinion of after careful consideration: e.g. I've got him weighed up as a very clever con-man.
2. consider; ponder; estimate the value or importance of: e.g. Have you weighed up the consequences of an action like that?

weight
importance; influence: e.g. He has a lot of weight in that organisation.
See also:
carry a lot of weight
carry weight
pull (one's) weight
put (someone's) weights up
throw (one's) weight around
worth (one's) weight in gold

weird
queer; strange; incomprehensible.

weirdie/weirdo
strange, odd, eccentric, peculiar person.

welch
(see: welsh on)

well blow me down/fuck me dead!

well I never/I'll be!

well I'll be a monkey's uncle!

well I'll be blowed/buggered/darned/stuffed!
exclamation of surprise, astonishment, disbelief.

well in with
on good terms with; in a favourable position with: e.g. He won't get the sack — he's too well in with the boss.

well turned out
dressed smartly: e.g. Everyone was really well turned out for the fund-raising party.

well up (in the world)
in a secure, high, successful position.

well-endowed
1. (of a man) having large genitals.
2. (of a woman) having large breasts.

well-fixed/heeled
wealthy; prosperous.

well-hung
(of a man) having large genitals.

wellies
Wellington boots; gumboots.

well-in
well-connected; having influential friends: e.g. His is a very well-in family.

well-lined
(of the pocket, purse) having plenty of money.

well-off
wealthy; prosperous; affluent.

well-oiled
drunk; intoxicated.

well-preserved
maintaining a youthful appearance in advancing age: e.g. She's a well-preserved woman for seventy!

well-shod
(of a car) having very good tyres.

well-stacked
(of a woman) having large breasts.

well-to-do
wealthy; prosperous; affluent.

well-worn
hackneyed, trite through over-use: e.g. I'm sick of hearing all his well-worn jokes.

welsh on
1. to avoid paying back debts (especially in gambling); break an agreement or promise.
2. inform on; turn traitor; betray.

welsher
1. one who avoids paying back debts.
2. traitor.

wench
(joc.) young woman.

went A over T/arse over tit
fell head-over-heels; fell heavily: e.g. He went A over T coming down the stairs.

went blank
suffered a momentary memory failure: e.g. When I had to get up and speak in front of the audience, I went blank.

went down like a bag of spuds
fell heavily and clumsily: e.g. When I hit him, he went down like a bag of spuds.

went down like a lead balloon

went down like pork at a Jewish wedding
1. failed to have the desired effect; flopped; failed.
2. was received with hostility or lack of amusement.

went for a sixer
1. fell heavily and clumsily.
2. suffered a severe set-back.

went in one ear and out the other
was heard but either was ignored, or was not understood.

For other possible entries beginning with 'went' see entries listed under 'go', 'goes', 'going', 'gone'.

were you born in a tent?
a sarcastic comment made to someone who always forgets to close a door.

west
(see: go west)

western
film or book about frontier life in America, cowboys and Indians, etc.

westie
someone from the western suburbs of Sydney.

wet
1. weak; feeble; spiritless: e.g. What a wet party that was!
2. stupid; senseless: e.g. How wet can you get!
See also:
have/got a face as long as a wet week
silly as a wet hen
slow as a wet week
the Wet

wet area
any district having hotels and allowing the sale of alcohol.

wet as water
weak; feeble; spiritless; stupid.

wet behind the ears
naive; immature; inexperienced.

wet blanket
person who discourages and dampens enthusiasm.

wet dream
sexually exciting dream resulting in ejaculation for men and orgasm for women.

wet (one's) whistle
to have a drink.

wet (oneself)
receive a fright, shock: e.g. I wet myself when he jumped out from behind the bushes!

Wettex
a dishcloth. (Trademark)

whack
1. fair share of work, responsibility: e.g. He never does his whack!
2. share: e.g. I want my whack of the profits now!
3. attempt, try: e.g. I'll have a whack at it.
4. do, put etc.: e.g. 1. I'll be ready as soon as I whack a comb through my hair. 2. Whack the kettle on the stove.
See also:
getting a fair whack
out of whack

whack down
deposit, put down quickly, smartly.

whack it in
put (it) in; insert (it).

whack off
1. to masturbate.
2. to steal, pilfer: e.g. Who whacked off my beer!

whacked
1. drunk, intoxicated or drugged: e.g. I get whacked after three glasses of wine!
2. irrational; peculiar; crazy: e.g. He's whacked!
3. tired; exhausted: e.g. I'm whacked after all that work!

whacked out of (one's) brain
1. drunk; intoxicated.
2. under the influence of marijuana, drugs.

whacker
crazy, zany, irrational, peculiar, eccentric or amusing person.

whacking
1. very: e.g. He climbed to a whacking great height!
2. very large, big: e.g. I had to carry that whacking great parcel all by myself!

whacko!

whacko-the-did!

whacko-the-diddly-oh!
1. expression denoting surprised pleasure: e.g. Whacko! Look at what I just won on the lottery!
2. first-class; excellent: e.g. That new car is really whacko!

whacky
crazy, zany, irrational, peculiar, eccentric or amusing.

whale
a Murray River cod.

whale into
1. do, begin energetically.
2. attack physically or verbally.

whale of a time
an extremely enjoyable time.

whaling
beating; thrashing; sound defeating.

wham-bam-thank-you-ma'am!
1. pertaining to anything done in a perfunctory, superficial manner: e.g. That's the last time I'll hire that crew to repair anything — they came in wham-bam-thank-you-ma'am and left without doing the job correctly!
2. (of a man) performing the sexual act in a perfunctory, hurried or ungrateful manner.

whammy
a forceful effect or influence.

wharfie
wharf labourer.

what a beaut!
what an excellent idea, thing etc.!

what a bummer!
what an unfortunate, unlucky, sad, awful thing, happening or event!

what a corker!
1. what an excellent, amazing idea, thing etc.!
2. what an astounding, large, huge thing, object etc.!

what a dag!
1. what a ridiculous, stupid, old-fashioned, boring person!
2. what a funny, amusing, humorous person!

what a drag!
what a boring, dull, monotonous event, occasion, time etc.!

what a joke!
what a failure, fiasco; what a ridiculous idea!

what a load of wank/crap/rot!
what a lot of nonsense, lies, foolish and empty talk!

what a rip-off!
an exclamation of disgust at anything that is exorbitantly expensive, or obviously dishonest, excessive or deceitful.

what a ripper!
(see: what a corker, 1. and 2.)

what a turd!
what a despicable person!

what a wag!
what a funny, amusing person!

what a wank/wanker!
1. what a stupid, self-deluding person!
2. what a funny, amusing, eccentric person!
3. what an unproductive, lazy person!
4. what an egotistical person!
5. what a self-indulgent person!

what about . . .?
what do you say to the idea of . . .?: e.g. What about going to the movies tonight?

what about it?
1. what do you say to the idea of (it)?
2. a request for sexual intercourse.

what are ya (you)!
a curt remark to someone who has done something foolish, stupid, bungling.

what are you up to?
1. are you doing, planning anything suspicious, illegal, illicit?
2. what are you doing, planning etc.?: e.g. We're all going to the movies tonight — what are you up to?

what beats me
what amazes, astounds me: e.g. What beats me is the fact that she still loves him after all the awful things he's done!

what do you do for a crust?
how do you earn your living?; what is your job?

what do you know?
a form of greeting — hello.

what do you think this is — bush week?!
(see: bush week)

what doesn't fit in your mouth is a waste
pertaining to oral sexual practices and justifying small breasts or a small penis.

what else did you get for Christmas?
derisive, mocking retort to someone who has annoyed you with an action or a display of a possession.

what else's new?
1. what other news is there?
2. derisive, mocking retort to someone who mentions, tells about or reports a fact already known.

what for
1. severe punishment, scolding or treatment: e.g. I'll give him what for when he gets home!
2. sexual intercourse: e.g. I'd like to give her a bit of what for!
See also:
tell (someone) what for

what gives?
what's happening?; what's the explanation?

what it takes
the necessary skill, ability, talent: e.g. She's got what it takes to be a good actress.

what makes (one) tick
what motivates (one), causes (one) to behave the way (one) does: e.g. I wish I knew what makes him tick.

what makes (something) tick
what makes (something) work, operate: e.g. He's only ten but he already knows everything about what makes a car tick.

what next!
is there anything that could be more outrageous, stupid, ridiculous!

what of it!
an expression of scorn: what does it matter, it's none of your business anyway!

what racket are you in?
how do you earn your living?; what is your job, career?

what the fuck/heck/hell/shit!
exclamation of contempt, dismissal, exasperation; expression of an I-don't-care attitude.

what you don't hear/know/see won't hurt you
one's feelings are not injured, one's disgust is not aroused if one is ignorant of the unpleasantries.

what you lose on the swings you make up on the roundabouts
what is lost on one venture is gained or recovered on the next; the losses on one venture are negated by the experience, gains or advantages likely to occur on another.

what-cha-ma-call-it

what-d'ye-call-it
a term for something whose name one can't immediately remember: e.g. Pass me that what-cha-ma-call-it over there.

whatever
anything: e.g. I don't mind what you buy for dinner — whatever.

whatever tickles your fancy

whatever turns you on
1. anything that you like: e.g. Choose a present — you can have whatever tickles your fancy.
2. a derisive, mocking remark about someone else's likes or taste that you don't really agree with.

whatnot
term for an unspecified article, object; thing whose name one cannot immediately remember.

what's cooking?
what's happening, taking place, being planned?

what's eating (one/ someone)?
what's worrying (one/ someone)?: e.g. What's eating him? He hasn't said a word to anyone all day!

what's mine is yours
declaration of shared belongings.

what's that got to do with the price of eggs/fish?
derisive retort to someone who has just said something irrelevant.

what's the catch/hitch?
an expression of suspicion about something, such as a deal, offer etc., that appears too good to be true.

what's the matter with (someone)?
what is amiss, the trouble, upsetting (someone)?

what's the odds?
what difference does it make?; what does it matter?

what's the score?
what's the latest news or information?

what's the story?
1. what's the latest news or information?
2. what's the excuse, alibi?

what's up (doc)?
1. what's happening, being planned, occurring?
2. what's the problem?

what's what
what is the true situation, position; what are the facts: e.g. I know what's what — you don't have to tell me!
See also:
know what's what

what's with (someone)?
what's troubling (someone)?: e.g. What's with you? You look ill.

what's your beef?
what's your problem, complaint?

whatsaname
term for a person or thing whose name one cannot immediately remember: e.g. Is whatsaname coming with us?

what's-'is-face

what's-'is-name
person whose name one cannot immediately remember.

whatsit
(see: whatsaname)

wheel
(see: at the wheel; behind the wheel; big wheel; keep the wheels turning; put a spoke in someone's wheel; put one's shoulder to the wheel; set the wheels in motion; silly as a wheel)

wheel and deal
scheme, engineer, plot, instigate profitable transactions: e.g. He made his fortune through clever wheeling and dealing.

wheeler-dealer
a schemer, engineer, plotter, instigator of profitable business transactions.

wheelie
1. the noisy skidding of the drive wheels of a car or vehicle, made when either accelerating from a standing position or veering around a corner.
2. to manoeuvre a motorcycle or bicycle up on its back wheel.
See also:
drop a wheelie

wheels
car; vehicle; method of transport: e.g. You'll have to pick me up as I haven't got any wheels this week.

wheels within wheels
pertaining to a complicated situation in which many factors are involved; indirect or secret agencies; complicated motives and influences: e.g. It's going to be difficult for the authorities to investigate that organisation — it has so many wheels within wheels that no one really knows who runs it.

when all hell breaks loose
when the situation reaches its climax — usually disastrous.

when hell freezes over
never.

when I say 'jump', I want you to ask 'how high?'!
an expression demanding complete and immediate obedience.

when in Rome, do as the Romans do
follow the rules, behave the same as others when in a place with which one is unfamiliar.

when the chips are down
when the situation is grim.

when the crow shits
payday; the day one receives one's wages.

when the crunch comes
when the climax, crisis arrives: e.g. When the crunch comes, he won't know what to do.

when the heat's on
when pressure is brought to bear: e.g. When the heat's on at exam time, many students find themselves wishing they had studied more throughout the year.

when the shit hits the fan
when the climax, crisis, trouble arrives, is made public: e.g. When the shit hits the fan with this latest scandal, a lot of prominent business-men are going to be in plenty of trouble.

where have you been all my life?
jocular question to someone who is appealing, especially as a potential sexual partner.

where it hurts
(see: hit someone . . .)

where there's a will, there's a way
when one has hope and determination, a solution, method or means will be found.

where there's no sense, there's no feeling
a derisive or jocular remark to someone who has not been seriously injured, especially when hit or bumped on the head.

where there's smoke, there's fire
pertaining to the belief that where there is the hint, suggestion or suspicion of scandal or wrong-doing, closer investigation will provide facts and evidence to prove the suspicions.

where's the catch/hitch?
(see: what's the catch?)

wherewithal
means, especially money or finances, necessary for a purpose: e.g. He hasn't got the wherewithal to put his ideas into practice.

whew!
whistling sound expressing relief or surprise.

whichever way the wind blows/lies
whichever way the tendency is.

whiffy
having an offensive smell, odour.

while the cat's away, the mice will play
when the boss, leader, or person in authority is not present, people will do things they would otherwise not do, such as get up to mischief.

whimp
(also: wimp) ineffectual, complaining, simpering man.

whinge
complain, especially in an annoying way.

whingeing pom
the Englishman, commonly believed to always complain about his life in Australia.

whinger
person who always complains about everything.

whip
1. defeat soundly: e.g. Our team got whipped at the finals.
2. move, do or act quickly, suddenly, briskly: e.g. He whipped out his wallet and paid for the meal before anyone had a chance to complain.
See also:
crack the whip
fair crack of the whip!

whip it up, whip it in, whip it out and wipe it
(of a man) to perform sexual intercourse in a perfunctory, hurried, unemotional or ungrateful manner.

whip the cat
(joc.) to reproach oneself.
See also:
flog the cat

whip up
create, do in a hurried manner: e.g. Mum whipped up some scones when we arrived unexpectedly.

whipped
beaten; defeated.

whipper-snapper
young, impertinent person, child.

whipping boy
scapegoat; one made to take the blame for others.

whip-round
an informal appeal for donations towards a presentation, charitable purpose etc.

whips of
lots of: e.g. He always has whips of sour cream on his spuds.

whirl
attempt; try; a go: e.g. I'll have a whirl at it.
See also:
give it a whirl

whirly-bird
helicopter.

whisker
a very small margin: e.g. He won the race by a whisker.
See also:
by a (cat's) whisker
have/got whiskers on it

the cat's whiskers
thinks (he's/she's) the cat's whiskers

whistle
the penis.
See also:
blow the whistle on
clean as a whistle
wet (one's) whistle
wolf-whistle

whistle against/in the wind
protest vainly.

whistle and flute
(rhyming slang) suit.

whistle for
ask, seek, expect or wish for in vain.

whistle up
arouse enthusiasm, help etc.: e.g. I'll try to whistle up a few extra workers to help.

white
1. (of coffee) with cream or milk.
2. (of wine) light-coloured.
3. (of people) members of the pale-skinned, Caucasian races.
See also:
bleed (someone) white

white around the gills
upset; angry.

white as a ghost/lily/sheet
1. very white.
2. overcome with fear, terror, shock.

White Australia Policy
immigration policy designed to restrict the entry of coloured peoples into Australia.

white Christmas
Christmas in winter with snow.

white elephant
useless and burdensome possession.

white lady
methylated spirits as a drink, often mixed with other substances to make it more palatable.

white leghorn
1. woman — usually elderly — who plays lawn bowls and dresses in the required white clothes and hat.
2. (Australian Rules football) umpire.

white lie
a harmless fib usually told with good intentions.

white line fever
(sport) state of mind of a player who goes mad on the field.

white magic
magic used for good purposes.

white wedding
wedding in which the bride is a virgin.

white-ant
to seek to destroy or undermine from within.

white-collar
pertaining to professional, non-manual workers who traditionally used to wear a suit, white shirt and tie.

white-livered
cowardly.

whites
the eyes.

whitewash
to gloss over, attempt to hide, cover faults or defects: e.g. That press report tried to whitewash the government scandal.

whiz
smart, skilled, clever, brainy, intellectual: e.g. He's a whiz at mathematics.

whizkid
successful or brilliant young person.

who brung (her/him)!
derisive remark about someone at a party, social gathering etc. who is offensive or unpleasant.

who cares?!
so what?; what does it matter?

who flung dung?
a jocular request — who farted?

whodunit
a suspense novel, play or film involving murder and intrigue.

whole bang lot

whole box and dice
all of (it): e.g. He can buy a large pizza and eat the whole bang lot by himself!

whole hog
the lot; all; entirety; total commitment.
See also:
go the whole hog

whole kit and kaboodle
all of (it); the whole lot; entirety: e.g. Rather than buy a few items at a time, I bought the whole kit and kaboodle at once.

whole new ball game
situation in which the circumstances have changed, requiring a different approach.

whole shebang
the whole lot; all; the entire affair. (see: whole kit and kaboodle)

whole truth and nothing but the truth
entirely fact.

whole-hearted
sincere; earnest.

whomajigger
term for a person, object, thing whose actual name one cannot immediately remember.

whoop it up
enjoy oneself thoroughly and noisily; have a noisy party.

whoopee/whoopee-do!
shout of joy, exhilaration, excitement.
See also:
make whoopee

whoops/whoops-a-daisy!
exclamation of apology for an obvious error;

exclamation of mild dismay.

whop
1. thrash; beat; bash: e.g. I'll whop him next time I see him!
2. defeat soundly: e.g. Our team will whop the opposition.

whopper
1. something very large, huge, big: e.g. The fish he caught was a whopper!
2. an outrageous lie: e.g. Sounds like a whopper to me!

whopper-stopper
bottle-stopper, cork etc.

whopping
very large; huge; big: e.g. We had to hire a whopping great truck to shift our furniture.

who's he/she when he's/she's at home?!
scornful exclamation about someone who appears to have a very high opinion of him/herself.

who's milking this cat?!

who's robbing this coach?!
a curt reproach to someone who interferes or attempts to undermine one's authority; mind your own business!

who's running this show?!
an angry demand for co-operation, attention, obedience to the elected leader.

who's up who?
what are the alliances (of the members of a particular group)?; who is in control?

who's who
the important, influential people: e.g. This new book tells you who's who in the business and finance world.
See also:
know who's who

who's-a-whatsit
term for a person, object, thing whose actual name one cannot immediately remember.

whose shout?
whose turn is it to buy the round of drinks?

whose side are you on?!
an indignant remark to someone who appears to have betrayed you, or is not giving you the support you expected.

why go out for hamburger when you've got steak at home?
a sexual compliment to one's live-in partner in sex, love.

why keep a dog and bark oneself?
statement pointing out the unnecessary duplication of an activity or role; let jobs or functions be performed by those most suited.

whys and hows/wherefores
manner, method or ways of doing, working, operating: e.g. I'm not sure of the whys and hows with this gadget, but I know that it works!

wick
the penis.
See also:
dip (one's) wick
get on (one's) wick
short wick

wicket
(see: easy wicket; on a good wicket; on a sticky wicket; sticky wicket)

widdle
1. urine.
2. to urinate (especially of women).

wide enough to drive a coach and four through
very wide.

wide of the mark
not relevant; inaccurate; to have missed the point of a matter.

wide-awake
fully alert and aware of what is going on; shrewd: e.g. The police are wide-awake to his criminal activities and will eventually nail him.

wide-eyed
innocent; naive: e.g. There's no need to look wide-eyed — I know that you did it!

wide-on
(of a woman) sexually aroused; the equivalent of a man's hard-on: e.g. I think she's got a wide-on for you Alf!

widgie
a female bodgie, who follows the style of dress and behaviour made popular in the 1950s and 1960s.

widies
car tyres that have a wider tread than standard.

wife's best friend
the penis.

wifey
wife.

wigwam for a goose's bridle
(joc.) name given to an item that one can't or won't properly identify.

wig-warmer
a hat.

Wilcannia shower
dust storm (N.S.W.).

wild
1. very angry: e.g. Mum's going to be wild when she finds out what you've done!
2. excellent; wonderful; terrific: e.g. We had a wild time at his party.
See also:
go wild
like wildfire
run wild
sow (one's) wild oats

wild about
intensely enthusiastic about: e.g. Everyone's wild about that new movie.

wild and woolly
1. incoherent; mad; silly; stupid; unrealistic: e.g. He's always full of wild and woolly ideas!
2. rough; untidy; unrestrained; uncivilised: e.g. Those folks from the bush are a wild and woolly lot!
3. dangerous; risky; hair-raising: e.g. His driving is too wild and woolly for me!

wild blue yonder
far-away; a very remote place: e.g. He went off into the wild blue yonder and we never saw him again.

wild horses couldn't keep me away
I wouldn't miss that event, occasion etc. under any circumstances.

wildcat
a bad-tempered woman.

wildcat strike
an unofficial or unauthorised strike.

wild-goose chase
fruitless, foolish, hopeless quest or undertaking.

will of (its/one's) own
strong, uncanny power of assertion or independence: e.g. Most supermarket trolleys seem to have at least one wheel that has a will of its own, making it impossible to steer straight!

will wonders never cease?
facetious or jocular exclamation of surprise, disbelief.

Williamstown piers
(rhyming slang) ears.

willie
the penis.
See also:
chuck a willie

willies
feeling of fear, apprehension, uneasiness, revulsion: e.g. Walking alone at night in a deserted street gives me the willies.

willing horse
person who is a willing and capable worker.

willy-nilly
1. at random; uncontrollably.
2. whether it is desired or not.

willy-willy
a gusty, spiralling wind.

wimp
(also: whimp) ineffectual, complaining, simpering man.

win
(see: can't win; you can't win them all; you've got to be in it to win it)

win a heart
gain the affection, trust or allegiance of.

win fair and square
win honestly, justly.

win hands down
win easily, without effort.

win on points
to win on general performance rather than on one act.

win (someone)
gain the affection, trust, allegiance of (someone): e.g. His speech won the audience.

win the day
be victorious in battle or contest.

wind
1. empty talk; nonsense: e.g. Some politicians are full of wind.
2. gas generated in the bowels, stomach.
See also:
all wind and water
bag of wind
bend with the wind
between wind and water
break wind
full of wind
get (one's) second wind
get the wind up
get wind of
in the wind
piss into the wind
put the wind up (someone)
sail close to the wind
see how the wind blows
straw in the wind
take the wind out of (someone's) sails
three sheets to the wind
throw caution to the wind
whichever way the wind blows
whistle against/in the wind
wind-bag
windfall

wind down
1. to relax, especially after tension or hard work: e.g. After a hard day's work he likes to wind down by having a few beers.
2. diminish; lessen; taper off; decelerate.

wind (someone) up
excite (someone) to tension, over-activity, anger etc.

wind up
1. end up: e.g. You'll wind up in prison if you keep doing things like that!
2. finish, conclude a speech, action, affair etc.

wind-bag
person given to excessive, voluble and empty talk.

windfall
good luck or fortune — especially unexpected.

Windies
1. the West Indies cricket team.
2. people from the West Indies.

window-shopping
looking at goods in shop windows rather than buying.

wine and dine
to go out to a restaurant, night-club etc. for food and entertainment.

wine-bibber/dot
a heavy drinker of wine; a wino.

wing
the arm.
See also:
clip (someone's) wings
in the wings
take under (one's) wing

wing-ding
a wild, enjoyable, extravagant party or social occasion.

wing-dinger
an excellent example of its kind: e.g. The latest model of that car is a wing-dinger.

wingnuts
ears — especially protruding ones.

wink at
1. pretend not to notice: e.g. The police often wink at minor offences.
2. convey a message — often a sly or romantic one — by winking.

winkers
the eyes.

winkle-pickers
pointy-toed shoes — especially for men.

winner
something that is excellent, extremely good, successful: e.g. His new book is sure to be a winner.

winning streak
(see: on a . . .)

wino
alcoholic, drunkard — especially one addicted to wine.

wipe
1. to refuse to associate with or have anything to do with: e.g. People he thought were his friends have wiped him.
2. to eradicate, finish, destroy, eliminate: e.g. The council has decided to wipe that idea.

wipe (one's) hands of
to refuse to have anything to do with; terminate (one's) responsibility or obligation: e.g. He's let me down so often that I've decided to wipe my hands of him.

wipe (oneself) out
1. to become completely intoxicated, drunk or under the influence of drugs.
2. to lose control of a car and have an accident.

wipe out
1. destroy completely: e.g. The police have wiped out the criminal element in this town.
2. kill: e.g. The Mafia wipe out anyone who doesn't toe the line.

wipe (someone) out
1. completely defeat, demoralise, ruin, destroy (someone).
2. kill (someone).

wipe the floor with (someone)
completely and overwhelmingly defeat (someone) in a degrading, belittling manner.

wipe the grin off (someone's) face
(see: wipe the smile off someone's face)

wipe the slate clean
1. to forget about the past and start anew.
2. to pay back all one's debts.

wipe the smile off (someone's) dial/face
1. to threaten (someone) with a beating; to beat (someone) up.
2. to berate, denounce, upbraid, scold, belittle (someone).

wiped out
1. tired; exhausted: e.g. I'm wiped out after all that work!
2. completely under the influence of drugs; intoxicated.

wipe-out
a failure, fiasco: e.g. The party was a wipe-out because the beer didn't arrive.

wire
1. a telegraphic message or telegram.
2. (horse-racing) the finishing post.
3. to send a telegraphic message.
See also:
get (one's) wires crossed
pull wires

wire-tapping
secret and illicit listening to telephone conversations using electronic devices.

wiry
tough; sinewy; strong: e.g. He may be small but he's a wiry little bloke.

wise
alert; crafty; sly: e.g. That was a wise trick.
See also:
get wise
get wise with (someone)
none the wiser

wise as an owl
intelligent; shrewd; knowing.

wise guy
impertinent, cocky, self-assured, audacious person.

wise (someone) up
alert, inform (someone).

wise to
aware of; alert to; informed of: e.g. I think the police are wise to our hide-out.

wise up
1. learn about; become cognisant of, informed about.
2. face realities and facts of a situation: e.g. He'd

better wise up or else he'll end up in a lot of trouble.

wise-acre
an audacious know-all.

wise-crack
smart, witty, flippant or facetious remark.

wishful thinking
desires or belief based on fancy and hopes rather than fact.

wishy-washy
weak; ineffectual; feeble; lacking in strength or substance: e.g. I'm not going to listen to any more of his wishy-washy excuses!

witch-hunt
an emotional campaign, usually political and often based on doubtful evidence, to find or investigate people considered to be disloyal or unorthodox.

witching hour
midnight.

with
of the same mind, opinion, understanding, train of thought: e.g. 1. Are you with me? 2. I'm with you on this vote.
See also:
get with it
not with (someone)

with a bang
successfully; impressively: e.g. I want this party to go off with a bang!

with a capital . . . (any letter of the alphabet)
totally; absolutely: e.g. He's a bum with a capital B!

with a fine-tooth comb
painstakingly; thoroughly: e.g. The police searched the house with a fine-tooth comb and couldn't find a trace of the stolen money.

with a vengeance
extremely; to a great degree; with extreme effort.

with all (one's) heart
totally; willingly; enthusiastically; deeply: e.g. He loves her with all his heart.

with an eye to
with the purpose of.

with flying colours
easily; successfully: e.g. He passed his exams with flying colours.

with friends like that, who needs enemies?
a facetious remark about a friend or close associate who appears to be disloyal, untrustworthy, capable of doing harm.

with guns blazing
aggressively and with all one's resources and energy.

with me?
understand?; comprehend?

with one arm tied behind (one's) back
easily; without effort: e.g. I could beat him with one arm tied behind my back!

with (one's) eyes open
aware of the potential dangers, risks etc.

with (one's) pants down
surprised, caught unawares, off guard.

with (one's) tail between (one's) legs
in a defeated, dejected and humiliated manner: e.g. After causing all that trouble he came back with his tail between his legs to apologise.

with (one's) tongue hanging out
waiting with great anticipation.

with (one's) tongue in (one's) cheek
facetiously; in a satirical, teasing manner; ironically; mockingly.

with open arms
in total acceptance: e.g. She took him back with open arms.

with the naked eye
without the help of magnification instruments.

withdrawal symptoms
the distressing and painful effects occurring in a person denied a drug, alcohol etc. to which he is addicted.

wither on the vine
deteriorate through lack of use: e.g. His talents are withering on the vine.

within a bull's roar
anywhere near to or approaching: e.g. He didn't come within a bull's roar of winning.

within a hair's breadth/ stone's throw
nearby; within easy reach; very close to; almost.

within an inch of
very close to; almost: e.g. You came to within an inch of losing your life in that accident.

within cooee/spitting distance
1. in easy reach of; nearby: e.g. It feels very safe living within cooee of the police-station.
2. close to finishing a project or achieving an aim or goal.

with-it
1. fashionable; trendy; up-to-date: e.g. Her clothes are really with-it.
2. well-informed; knowledgeable; alert to the facts: e.g. He may look stupid but he's actually a very with-it person.
See also:
get with it

wiz
(see: whiz)

'All right, you can borrow it. But bring it back straight after th' grand final!'

Without a doubt, the Aussie ocker's favourite establishment is the pub, otherwise known as the bloodhouse, boozer, local, pisser, rub-a-dub-dub, rubbidy, rubbidy-dub or watering hole.

wizard
1. a clever and skilled person: e.g. He's a wizard at chess.
2. wonderful; excellent: e.g. That's a wizard idea!

wobbly
wallaby.
See also:
throw a wobbly

woe is me!
(joc.) exclamation of dismay, lamentation.

woeful
terrible; awful; very poor; bad; deplorable: e.g. That performance was woeful!

wog
1. influenza, a cold or similar disease or illness.
2. (derog.) an Italian, Greek, Arab or person of similar Mediterranean or Middle Eastern extraction.
3. small insect, bug: e.g. There are a million wogs in this water!
4. a germ.

wolf
1. man who pursues women for sexual exploitation; womaniser.
2. despicable, rapacious person.
See also:
cry wolf
keep the wolf from the door
left to the wolves
lone wolf
throw (someone) to the wolves

wolf in sheep's clothing
person who appears harmless but who has hostile intentions; hypocrite.

wolf (one's) food
eat greedily, ravenously.

wolf-whistle
two-toned whistle usually from a man expressing admiration at a woman.

woman
wife: e.g. Where's the woman tonight?
See also:
fallen woman
fancy woman
hell hath no fury like a woman scorned
kept woman
little woman
make an honest woman of
old woman
scarlet woman
the little woman
the old woman

woman of the world
sophisticated and knowing woman.

women's lib
women's liberation — a movement to free women from a subservient status and give them equal sexual and social rights with men.

women's libber
member of the women's liberation movement.

women's work
anything considered below the dignity of men to perform.

won me
convinced me; gained my allegiance, trust, approval: e.g. The idea sounds good — you've won me!

For other possible entries beginning with 'won' see entries listed under 'win'.

wonder what the poor people are doing today?
smug, facetious remark expressing pleasure at one's prosperity.

wonders never cease!
facetious or jocular remark of surprise (also: will wonders never cease!).

wonk
a homosexual man.

wonky
1. shaky; unsteady; unreliable; unsound: e.g. This bridge feels a bit wonky to me!
2. not well; ill: e.g. I felt wonky after the operation.
3. broken; out-of-order: e.g. This gadget's wonky!

won't have a bar of
have nothing to do with; refuse to associate oneself with: e.g. He won't have a bar of gambling.

For other possible entries beginning with 'won't' see entries listed under 'wouldn't', 'not' etc.

wood
(sport) the drop on; dominance over; a history of success against someone, a team etc.
See also:
can't see the wood for the trees
clean up the dead wood
come out of the woodwork
dead wood
have/got the wood on (someone)
knock on wood
neck of the woods
nigger in the woodpile
not out of the woods yet
out of the wood
put the wood in the hole
touch wood!

wood duck
1. a customer who is believed to have little likelihood of making a purchase — especially at a car salesyard.
2. naive customer who is easily duped, fooled, conned.

wooden spoon
1. the (fictitious) prize awarded for coming last or doing the worst.
2. kitchen spoon that is used to intimidate, subdue a naughty child.
See also:
born with a wooden spoon in (one's) mouth

woodenhead
1. dolt; fool; dimwit; stupid person.
2. umpire.

Woods/Woodsmen
Collingwood VFL football team.

woofer
a dog.

woofter
1. (rhyming slang) poofter; a homosexual man.
2. a dog.

wool
(see: all wool and a yard wide; dyed-in-the-wool; keep your wool!; lose one's wool; pull the wool over someone's eyes)

wool-gathering
absent-mindedness; day-dreaming; unrealistic thoughts.

woollies
1. warm, knitted woollen clothing.
2. (cap.) Woolworths supermarket. (also: Woolies)

woolly
unclear, clouded thinking: e.g. My memory of that time is a bit woolly.
See also:
wild and woolly

woolly woofter
(rhyming slang) poofter — a homosexual man.

Woop Woop
any remote, backward, sparsely populated area; a long way away (also: woop-woop): e.g. I had to drive out all the way to Woop Woop to find the right part for my car.

woops!
(see: whoops!)

woozy
1. slightly intoxicated.
2. dizzy; out of sorts; giddy.
3. muddled; confused; befuddled.

wop
(derog.) an Italian or anyone thought to look Latin in origin.
See also:
up the wop

wop-wops
any remote town or place: e.g. He lives out in the wop-wops.

word
1. promise; assurance: e.g. He gave me his word that he'd do it.
2. rumour: e.g. Word has it that she's pregnant again.
See also:
as good as (one's) word
break (one's) word
breathe a word to
can't get a word in edgeways
dirty word
drop the magic word
eat (one's) words
famous last words
four-letter word
go back on (one's) word
hang on every word
have a word with
have words with
high words
in a word
in so many words
just say the magic word
last word
magic word
make (someone) eat his words
man of his word
mark (one's) words
mince words
mum's the word
my word!
put in a good word for
put the hard/heavy word on (someone)
stuck for words
take (one) at (one's) word
take (someone's) word for it
take/took the words out of (one's) mouth
the last word
the magic word
twist (someone's) words
weigh (one's) words

word of honour
promise; assurance: e.g. He gave me his word of honour that he'd do it.

word of mouth
the passing, spreading of information verbally: e.g. He doesn't need to advertise as he gets all his customers by word of mouth.

word up
inform, alert, especially beforehand: e.g. Someone must have worded up the police about the gang's activities, because they were caught in the act.

words
an angry exchange of speech; quarrel: e.g. Those two are always having words in public!

work
(see: all work and no play makes Jack a dull boy; dirty work; have/got one's work cut out; make short work of; piece of work; wouldn't work in an iron lung)

work a ready
do an illegal, illicit act of deception, trickery.

work like a charm
work, turn out successfully, perfectly.

work like a Trojan

work like Jackie
to work very hard.

work of art
something done well, skilfully.

work off a dead horse
work to pay back a debt.

work (one's) fingers to the bone

work (one's) guts out/socks off
work very hard (often for very little reward).

work out
(of physical exercise, athletics) train or practise: e.g. I'm going to the gym today to work out.

work (someone) over
give (someone) a violent physical beating.

work to rule
as a form of protest, to follow the rules of one's occupation with pedantic precision in order to reduce efficiency.

workaholic
person considered to be 'addicted' to hard work.

worked up
1. excited; agitated.
2. angry; annoyed; irritated.
3. sexually aroused.

workhorse
a hard and efficient worker.

working girl
a prostitute, call-girl.

working-man's paradise
Australia.

work-out
period of practice or training in physical activity.

works
(see: have/got the works; spanner in the works; the works; throw a spanner in the works)

world
1. the public in general: e.g. You don't have to tell the whole world about it!
2. everything that is important: e.g. You mean the world to me.
3. a lot, great deal: e.g. He got into a world of trouble.
See also:
ask for the world
best of both worlds
bottom of (one's) world has dropped out
dead to the world
do the world of good
for all the world
for the world
have/got the world at (one's) feet
in a world of (one's) own
in another world
in the world
isn't it a small world!
it's a dog-eat-dog world
it's a man's world
it's a small world
make (one's) way in the world
money makes the world go round
move up in the world
no way in the world
not the end of the world
of the world
on top of the world
other world
out of this world
out to the world
set the world on fire
step up in the world
the end of the world
think the world of
underworld
wouldn't miss it for the world

world-beater
an exceptionally good person or thing.

worlds apart
differing in views, opinions, philosophies etc.

worm
contemptible person.
See also:
can of worms
open a can of worms
quiet/still the worms

worm (one's) way in
to insinuate, infiltrate, penetrate (oneself) into favour, a position etc. by devious means: e.g. He wormed his way into that job by bribing the officials.

worm (something) out of (someone)
to gain (such as information, a secret) by craft, persistence.

worm-eaten
antiquated; decrepit.

worn thin
(of an argument, point of view etc.) run out of tolerance, acceptance.

worn-out
exhausted; tired.

worrywart
constant worrier.

worse
(see: none the worse for; seen worse)

worse for wear
(the . . .) showing signs of decay, deterioration through use, age: e.g. It looks a bit the worse for wear but it still works perfectly.

worse luck!
unfortunately: e.g. I didn't win the raffle, worse luck!

worship the ground (someone) walks on
adore, love, respect (someone) a great deal.

worth
(see: for all one is worth; not worth . . .)

worth a few bob/a mint
expensive; worth a lot of money: e.g. That vintage car must be worth a few bob.

worth as much as a pinch of goatshit
worthless.

worth it
worthwhile: e.g. It was a lot of work but it was worth it.

worth (one's) salt

worth (one's) weight in gold
deserving merit, praise; reliable; dependable.

worth (one's) while
worth (one's) time, effort, expense etc.

wouldn't be in it
wouldn't have anything to do with it: e.g. I asked if he'd be a sponsor and get involved with the club, but he wouldn't be in it.

wouldn't be seen dead at/in/with
wouldn't have anything to do with; disassociate oneself from completely; refuse to have any contact or association with at all, whatsoever: e.g. I wouldn't be seen dead with him!

wouldn't budge
1. wouldn't move, shift.
2. wouldn't change an opinion or point of view: e.g. I tried to reason with him but he wouldn't budge.

wouldn't dream of it
wouldn't consider it.

wouldn't give you the sleeves out of his vest

wouldn't give you the steam off (his/her) shit
(of a person) extremely mean with money; lacking in generosity or compassion; niggardly; miserly.

wouldn't give you the time of day
(of a person) selfish; haughty; snobbish.

wouldn't have a clue
wouldn't have any knowledge about.

wouldn't in a pink fit
wouldn't under any circumstances: e.g. Mum and Dad wouldn't go to a topless nightclub in a pink fit!

wouldn't it!

wouldn't it rip/root you!

wouldn't it rot your socks!
expression of annoyance, frustration, dismay, disgust.

wouldn't know (one's) arse from a hole in a flower-pot

wouldn't know (one's) arse from a hole in the ground

wouldn't know (one's) arse from (one's) elbow
(of a person)
1. lacking in intelligence; stupid.
2. not informed; having no knowledge of; ignorant of.

wouldn't know (someone) from a bar of soap

wouldn't know (someone) from Adam

wouldn't know (someone) if I fell over (him/her)
wouldn't recognise or know (someone).

wouldn't lend you the harness off his nightmare
(see: wouldn't give you the sleeves out of his vest)

wouldn't miss it for the world
an assurance of one's intention to attend an event, occasion etc.

wouldn't piss down (someone's) throat if (his/her) guts were on fire

wouldn't piss on (someone) if (he/she) were on fire
1. declaration of contempt for (someone).
2. (of a person) extremely mean, lacking in generosity, compassion or desire to help.

wouldn't put it past (someone)
wouldn't doubt it of (someone): e.g. I wouldn't put it past him to steal from his friends.

wouldn't read about it
expression of incredulity: e.g. Fancy winning the lottery three times in a row — you wouldn't read about it!

wouldn't say boo to a goose
(of a person) extremely shy.

wouldn't say shit for a shilling
(of a person) wouldn't swear or use bad, vulgar language.

wouldn't shout if a shark bit (him/her)
(of a person) miserly; tight with money; parsimonious.

wouldn't stop a pig in a hallway/poke
pertaining to someone's bandy legs.

wouldn't that rip the crutch/fork out of your nightie!

wouldn't that rot your socks!
expression of annoyance, frustration, anger, dismay, disgust.

wouldn't touch it with a barge-pole

wouldn't touch it with a forty-foot/ten-foot pole
wouldn't have anything to do with it; wouldn't have any association with it whatsoever.

wouldn't trust (someone) as far as I could throw (him/her)
declaration of one's suspicion about or lack of trust in (someone).

wouldn't use (someone) for shark-bait
declaration of one's contempt for (someone).

wouldn't want (someone) to fart in my last pound of flour
statement about how fat (someone) is, or what a big behind, bum (someone) has.

wouldn't work in an iron lung
(of a person) lazy.

wound up
excited; agitated; anxious; angry.

wow
1. sensational success: e.g. We had a wow of a party.
2. exclamation of surprise, approval, admiration, astonishment.

wow (someone)
charm, impress, enchant (someone); win the admiration and approval of (someone).

wowser
1. person who doesn't drink alcohol or gamble; teetotaller.

2. spoilsport; killjoy; person who dampens enthusiasm.

wrap
enthusiastic recommendation or praise (also: rap): e.g. We got an excellent wrap in the newspaper.
See also:
under wraps

wrap (one's) laughing gear around (something)
1. to place (something) in (one's) mouth.
2. to eat: e.g. I'm going to wrap my laughing gear around a piece of that chocolate cake.

wrap up
conclude; finish; end; terminate: e.g. It's time to wrap up the meeting as it's getting late.

wrapped
delighted; pleased; enthusiastic about. (also: rapt)

wrapped in (somebody/something)
totally infatuated, in love with; wildly enthusiastic about (also: rapt in): e.g. 1. He's wrapped in that new girl. 2. I'm wrapped in that car.

wrapped up in
1. involved with; implicated in: e.g. Are you wrapped up in any of their illicit activities?
2. totally absorbed, engrossed in: e.g. He's so wrapped up in that new project that we hardly ever see him any more.

wrap-up
enthusiastic recommendation or praise: e.g. That was an excellent wrap-up the newspapers gave our club.

wreathed in smiles
to be beaming with laughter, smiles, pleasure.

wreck
1. person who is disabled, ill, ruined, dishevelled, in poor physical or mental health.
2. person suffering from over-indulgence in drink or drugs, or other excesses.

wrecked
1. exhausted.
2. drunk; intoxicated; under the influence of drugs.

wrecker
one who demolishes buildings or cars for a job.

wreckers
1. saleyard for parts from used cars.
2. saleyard for materials from building demolitions.

wriggle
cunningly, slyly, obsequiously insinuate oneself into a position of favour or advantage.
See also:
get a wriggle on

wriggle out of
attempt to evade responsibility or consequences: e.g. He tried to wriggle out of the blame by telling lies.

wring (one's) hands
show despair, grief, anxiety by clasping or squeezing (one's) hands together: e.g. Mum's been wringing her hands all night wondering where you've been!

wring (someone's) neck
threaten (someone) with violence; reprove, reproach (someone).

wring (something) out of (someone)
practise extortion; get money, a concession, a confession etc. from (someone) by exaction, by causing pain or distress.

wringing wet
very wet; soaked.

wrinkles
(see: iron out a few wrinkles; know all the wrinkles)

wrinklies
aged people.

write off
1. consider as a complete loss.
2. discard as an idea, project etc.; cancel.

write (oneself) off
1. to get very drunk or drugged.
2. to have a serious car accident.
3. to injure (oneself) seriously.
4. give a poor account of (oneself).

write (something) off (as a dead loss)
to treat, consider as an irretrievable loss, failure.

write-off
1. person who is an incompetent no-hoper.
2. (of a car, thing etc.) so badly damaged as to be not worth repairing.
3. (of a person) totally drunk or under the influence of drugs.

write-up
public written account of; laudatory description in a newspaper: e.g. There's a write-up about the event in today's papers.

writing is on the wall
the signs of approaching trouble are obvious: e.g. I'm afraid the writing is on the wall — there's going to be a war.
See also:
see the writing on the wall

written all over (one)
very obvious: e.g. His guilt was written all over his face even though he denied it.

wrong end of the stick
(get, given, got the . . .)
1. pertaining to a misunderstanding of the facts: e.g. You've got the wrong end of the stick — that's not what happened at all!
2. the worse deal; the worse part of the bargain.

wrong in the head
crazy; mad; insane.

wrong side of the tracks
pertaining to the lower class, inferior in social position: e.g. He's finding it difficult to be accepted because he was born on the wrong side of the tracks.

wrong time of the month
(of a woman) menstruation: e.g. It's the wrong time of the month for me to go swimming in the nude — I'd be embarrassed.

wrote (oneself) off
(see: write . . .)

wrung-out
tired, exhausted, especially mentally: e.g. I feel wrung-out after that funeral.

X
1. used in place of someone's name to maintain anonymity or secrecy: e.g. Madam X.
2. one's signature: e.g. Put your X on the dotted line.

x-amount
an unknown quantity; unspecified amount: e.g. Everybody has to outlay x-amount of dollars to make the project a success.

Xerox
to copy on a duplicating machine (Trademark): e.g. Can you Xerox a few copies off for me please?

XL
extra large — especially in clothing size.

Xmas
Christmas.

xox
symbols meaning 'kisses and hugs' placed at the end of a letter.

X-rated
sexually or obscenely pornographic, provocative.

xxx
symbols meaning 'kisses' placed at the end of a letter.

XXXX
Fourex — a favourite brand of Queensland beer.

ya
you: e.g. How are ya?

yabber
1. talk; palaver; chatter.
2. to talk, chat — especially indistinctly or too much.

yabbering
1. noisy chatter: e.g. There was so much yabbering that I couldn't hear the music.
2. talking, chatting noisily: e.g. What are they yabbering about?

yabbie
(also: yabby) Australian freshwater small crayfish.

yachtie
yachtsman; one who owns and enjoys sailing a yacht.

yack
(see: yak)

yacker
(also: yakka, yakker)
1. hard work or toil.
2. incessant talker.

yackety-yak/yackity-yak
any prolonged, idle, empty or pointless talk; to talk as such: e.g. Listen to the women — yackety-yak all night!

yahoo
1. an uncouth ruffian.
2. exclamation proclaiming success; a cheer.

yahooing
boisterous behaviour; behaving boisterously: e.g. 1. What's all that yahooing about? 2. The kids are yahooing around the place somewhere — I heard them.

yair
yes.

yair! yair!
(see: yeah! yeah!)

yak (also: yack)
1. idle talk, palaver, chatter: e.g. The girls are having a yak in the kitchen.
2. to talk, palaver, chat idly: e.g. What are they yakking about?

yakka/yakker
hard work, toil: e.g. That job must have taken a lot of hard yakka to finish. (also: yacker)

yakkety-yak/yakity-yak
(see: yackety-yak)

yak-yak-yak!
exclamation indicating the emptiness, pointlessness or excessive length of the talk, chatter that is going on.

yammer
1. talk quickly or in an agitated manner.
2. whinge, complain vociferously.

Yammy
Yamaha motorcycle.

yank
1. (often cap.) an American; pertaining to anything American.
2. a sharp tug, pull or jerk: e.g. Give it a yank — it might come loose!
3. tug, pull, jerk sharply: e.g. Don't yank so hard!

yank tank
a car of American make, and usually large and extravagant.

yap
1. the mouth: e.g. Shut your yap!
2. noisy, incessant talk: e.g. What's all that yapping about!
3. to talk noisily, foolishly, incessantly: e.g. He's always yapping about one thing or another.

yard of pump-water
(see: built like a . . .; skinny as a . . .; straight as a . . .)

yarn
1. story; tale; reminiscence: e.g. He tells some good yarns.
2. talk; chat; palaver; conversation: e.g. I need to have a yarn to him about a few things.
3. to talk, chat, tell stories or reminisce.
See also:
spin a yarn

yarra
mad; silly; crazy; insane.

Yarra-banker
soap-box orator — one who stands on a makeshift platform by the banks of the Yarra River in Melbourne and talks about a religious, political etc. subject to whoever will listen.

yawn
a tiresome, boring event, happening or occasion: e.g. That party was such a yawn!

yawp
talk, yell, cry loudly.

yea (big, tall, long etc.)
an unspecified but indicated size, height, length etc.

yea or nay
yes or no: e.g. I'm not sure whether he said yea or nay.

yeah
yes.

yeah! yeah!
interjection of mocking, sarcastic disbelief.

year in, year out
regularly, year after year.

yecch!
exclamation of disgust, revulsion.

yellow
cowardly: e.g. He's yellow.

yellow pages
the section of a telephone directory — often yellow — listing business and professional subscribers.

yellow peril
pertaining to the fear of invasion by Communist China: e.g. Many politicians think our northern shores are not sufficiently protected against the yellow peril.

yellow streak
trait of cowardice: e.g. I didn't realise he had a yellow streak (down his back).

yellow-bellied
cowardly; afraid.

yellow-belly
a coward.

yeo
ewe; female sheep.

yep
yes.

yes and no
maybe; perhaps.

yes-man
obsequious person; one who agrees with everything his superiors say.

yes-sir-no-sir-three-bags-full-sir
sarcastic remark, usually given after being ordered to do something by a superior.

Y-fronts
men's underpants, having overlapping folds of material in an inverted Y-shape to accommodate the penis for urination.

Yid
a Jew.

yike
a brawl; noisy fight.

yikes!
exclamation of surprise, astonishment, concern.

yippee!
exclamation of delight, success.

yippee-beans
drugs in tablet form, taken for giving a feeling of euphoria, to stay awake etc.

Y.M.C.A.
1. Young Men's Christian Association.
2. Yesterday's Muck Cooked Again — left-over food served again the next night.

yob/yobbo
1. uncouth ruffian; lout.
2. foolish, unsophisticated idiot.

yodel
to vomit: e.g. Someone yodelled all over the lawn!

yoicks!
exclamation of surprise, concern, dismay.

yonkers/yonks
ages; a long time: e.g. I haven't seen him for yonks.

yonnie
a stone, especially for throwing: e.g. I was hit on the head by a yonnie.

yoo-hoo!
a call to attract attention.

you
typical of; characteristic of; suitable: e.g. That red dress just isn't you!
See also:
up you!

you ain't seen nothin' yet!
exclamation that there is better to come.

you and what army?!
defiant exclamation when someone has threatened you with violence, a beating.

you beaut!
exclamation meaning: excellent! wonderful!
See also:
you-beaut

you bet!
certainly! emphatically yes!

you can bet your boots/bottom dollar/life
you can be certain, absolutely sure.

you can choose your friends but you can't choose your relatives
a form of justification for the relatives one may dislike but has no other choice but to tolerate.

you can say that again!
a statement of total agreement.

you can't talk!
a mocking rebuff to someone's false moralism,

saying in effect that he is guilty of the same thing.

you can't win them all!
flippant remark justifying some failure.

you could eat your dinner off the floor
declaration of how clean a house, floor is.

you could have cut the air with a knife!
declaration of how tense, unwelcoming the atmosphere was at a particular occasion.

you could have knocked me over with a feather!
declaration of one's complete surprise, astonishment, stunned bewilderment.

you don't say!
1. mocking statement declaring that one already knows about what has just been said.
2. is that so?; is that the truth?

you know (like)
these two (or three) words act as an intensifier, asking for agreement, and can be used extremely often in any one sentence.

you know what you can do with (something)!
a rude remark of contemptuous dismissal — and often followed by: shove it up your arse!

you know where you can go!
a rude remark of contemptuous dismissal — the insinuation being that 'you' can go to hell!

you little beaut/corker/ripper!
exclamation meaning: excellent! wonderful! success! you excellent, pleasing person or thing!

you made your bed, you lie in it
you were the cause of the present situation so therefore you must accept the consequences.

you must be kidding!
you can't be serious!

you said it!
exclamation of complete and positive agreement.

you scratch my back and I'll scratch yours
you do me a favour, and I'll do something for you in return.

you son of a gun!
exclamation of surprised admiration for or pleasure in someone.

you tell me and we'll both know!
declaration of one's ignorance, lack of knowledge.

you wouldn't read about it!
exclamation of incredulity, astonishment, surprise, wonder — often at some form of irony that has just occurred.

you-beaut
wonderful; excellent; amazing; admirable: e.g. He doesn't own that old bomb anymore — he drives a you-beaut sports-car now!

you'll get yours!
declaration or threat of vengeance: you'll suffer the consequences at a later date!

young and old
(rhyming slang) cold.
See also:
on for young and old

young blood
young people with fresh, new ideas: e.g. It's about time this organisation had some young blood on the committee.

youngie
a child; young person.

your guess is as good as mine
an admission that one does not know the answer any better than the next person.

your wish is my command
whatever you ask will be granted.

you're an angel
a statement of sincere thanks, appreciation to someone who has helped — especially in a time of urgent need.

you're kidding!
expression of astonishment, disbelief; you can't be serious!

you're not wrong!
an expression of total agreement with someone else's opinion or statement.

you're on!
declaration of acceptance of a wager, bet, gamble, or some difficult task.

yours truly
me, myself: e.g. As there was no one around at the time to help, can you guess who did the job alone? Yours truly!

youse
plural of you (considered to be poor use of English): e.g. What are youse all doing here?

you've done it now!
you've really made a mess of things! you're in a lot of trouble now!

you've got to be in it to win it
taking a chance, having a go, is necessary in order to be a contender for success.

you've got to be joking!
you can't be serious!

yow!
exclamation of pain, surprised dismay.

yowie
the Australian version of the Yeti — a mythical, large, ape-like man.

yo-yo
fool; idiot; dolt; dill.

yuck/yucky
1. exclamation of disgust, revulsion.
2. repulsive; disgusting; awful; distasteful; revolting: e.g. What a yuck meal that was!

yuck-yuck!
exclamation, interjection of scorn, pleasure, at someone else's expense: e.g. Yuck-yuck! That smart-aleck lost all his money on the roulette wheel.

yuk
(see: yuck)

yukered
(see: euchred)

yum! yum!
delicious!

yummy
1. delicious; tasty: e.g. That was a yummy meal.
2. excellent; very good; admirable; desirable: e.g. What a yummy dress!

yuppie
young, upwardly mobile, professional person: 1980s term (sometimes derog.) for a young, very trendy and successful urban professional.

Y.W.C.A.
Young Women's Christian Association.

zac/zack/zak
a coin to the value of sixpence (pre-decimal).
See also:
not worth a zac

zambuck
person who gives first-aid at a sporting event.

zap
1. attack; hit; kill.
2. do or make hastily.

zap off
1. fall asleep, especially in an exhausted state.
2. leave, depart in a hurry: e.g. We're out of milk — I'll zap off to the shop and get some.

zap up
1. make more interesting; inject with enthusiasm, life, energy: e.g. His arrival really zapped up that boring party!
2. make, erect, do hastily.

zapped
exhausted; tired; worn out.

zappy
lively; spirited; energetic.

zealot
religious fanatic.

zebra crossing
pedestrian crossing on a road, with marked broad stripes.

zeds
pertaining to sleep — zzz being the symbol for snoring.
See also:
push up zeds

zero hour
decisive, crucial moment or time.

zero in on
1. focus attention on.
2. approach a target etc. accurately.

ziff
a beard.

zigged when (one) should have zagged
to have made an error in judgement; to have moved one way, when (one) should have moved the other.

zilch
nothing: e.g. He got zilch for all his trouble and effort!

zillion
an unimaginable, large amount.

zing
vitality; vigour; energy; enthusiasm.

zinger
anything excellent, admirable, exciting.

zip
1. energy; vitality; vigour: e.g. That car has a lot of zip.
2. to move quickly and energetically: e.g. That car really zips along!

zip code
post-code.

zippy
fast; lively; energetic: e.g. That's a zippy little car!

zits
pimples — especially on the face.

zizz
a short sleep, nap.

zombie
dull, boring, witless person lacking in motivation.

zonk
1. fool; dolt; idiot; dill.
2. to hit, bash: e.g. I got zonked on the head by a flying can!

zonked
1. intoxicated or under the influence of drugs.
2. tired; exhausted.

zoom in on
focus attention on.

zoot-suit
finest, best clothes — especially a man's formal suit.

zot
1. bash; hit; kill: e.g. He's very accurate at zotting blow-flies with a rolled-up newspaper.
2. any quick action.

zot off
go, depart quickly.

zots
pimples — especially on the face.

zounds!
mild oath of anger, frustration etc.

zube/zubrick
(rhyming slang) prick — the penis.

zzz
zeds — the symbol for sleep and snoring.

Word lists

Australians have developed an extraordinarily large, varied and colourful vocabulary in all areas of vital national concern — such as sex and drink. The following lists are designed to demonstrate the main Australian preoccupations and Australians' ingenuity with words and phrases where these are concerned. As the 'Contracted expressions' and 'Diminutives' lists make clear, Aussies also have a predilection for using abbreviated words. The Australian ability to shorten a word, then add 'ie', 'y' or 'o' to it, seems infinite.

ALCOHOL, DRINKING AND INEBRIATION

Alcohol

amber
anotherie
black and tan
booze
bracer
brew
brownie
bubbly
champers
charge
chaser
coldie
drop
favourite poison
fire-water
fizz
frostie
goom
grin and chronic
grog
hair of the dog
hard stuff
heart-starter
hooch
hops
iron lung
Jimmy Woodser
jungle-juice
leg-opener
liquid amber
L.O.
longneck
malt
middy
moon-juice
moonshine
mother's ruin
mountain dew
nellie
piss
plonk
pony
pot
red
red ned
red-hot
rosiner
rot-gut
schooner
sheep dip
sherbet
shot
slops
snake juice
snifter
snort
tallie
ten-ounce sandwich
tube
turps
vino
white lady

Public drinking establishments, hotels

bloodhouse
boozer

local
pisser
rub-a-dub-dub
rubbidy (also: rubbity)
rubbidy-dub
rubby
watering hole

Heavy drinkers or alcoholics

alkie
barfly
booze artist
booze hound
boozer
dipso
guzzle-guts
guzzler
hard case
indulger
lush
piss-head
piss-pot
plonko
soak
souse
sponge
tippler
tosspot
two-pot screamer
wine-bibber
winedot
wino
write-off

To drink alcohol

(be) on a bender
(be) on it
(be) on the bottle/grog/piss/turps
(be) on the ran-tan
(be) on the shicker/slops
bend the elbow
down a few
drink like a fish
drink like it's going out of fashion
drink (someone) under the table
drink the piss from a brewer's horse
drink with the flies
give it a nudge
grog on
guzzle
have one for the road
have one too many
hit the booze/bottle/grog/slops
indulge
nudge the bottle/turps
piss on
sink a few
wet (one's) whistle

To be inebriated or under the influence of alcohol

(a) write-off
away with the birds/fairies/pixies
blasted
bleary-eyed
blind
blithered
blotto
bombed
boozed
canned
cock-eyed
corked
cut
dead to the world
drunk as a lord/owl/skunk
flaked out
full as a boot
full as a bull
full as a bull's bum
full as a fairy's phone-book
full as a fart
full as a footy final
full as a goog
full as a pommy complaint-box
full as a seaside shithouse on bank holiday
full as a state-school hat-rack
full as a tick
full as the family jerry/po/pot
gone
groggy
had a few
had a skinful
half a sheet to the wind
half shot
half-seas-over
high as a kite
history
hung-over
in the grip of the grape
inked
ironed-out
lit up
loaded
merry
mollo
molly the monk
off one's face

off the planet
out of it
out to it
out to the world
para
pickled
pie-eyed
pinko
pissed
pissed as a cricket
pissed as a fart
pissed as a newt
pissed as a parrot
pissed out of one's brain
pissed to the eyeballs
pissy
pissy-eyed
plastered
primed
ripe
ripped
rolling
rotten
rotten as a chop
sauced
screwed
shicker
shicky
shot
shot to the eyeballs
slewed
sloshed
smashed
soused
sozzled
spaced out
spastic
spiffed
spiflicated
squiffed
stewed
stewed to the gills
stinko
stoked
stoned
stonkered
stung
tanked
three parts gone
three sheets to the wind
tiddly
tight
tipsy
unable to scratch oneself
under the affluence of inkahol
under the influence
under the table
under the weather
wasted
well oiled
whacked
wiped out
woozy
wrecked
zonked

Vomit and vomiting

barf
bark at the lawn
berley
big spit
bring up
chuck
chunder
colourful yawn
cry Herb!/Ralph!/Ruth!
fetch up
go for the big spit
heave (one's) heart out
herk
hurl
laugh at the lawn
liquid laugh
long-distance call on the big white telephone
park (one's) tiger
perk up
puke
solid smile
spew
technicolour yawn
throw a seven
throw (one's) voice
throw up
turn up
yodel

ANGER AND HOSTILITY

To be angry or bad-tempered

berko
brassed off
browned off
cheesed off
crabby

cranky
crapped off
cross as two sticks
crotchety
dark
dirty
fed up (to the back teeth/eyeballs/gills/neck)
fit to be tied
foaming at the mouth
fuming
have/got (one's) arse in (one's) hands
have/got the pip/shits/tom-tits
het-up
hopping mad
hot and bothered
hot under the collar
huffy
in a huff
in a shit
like a bear with a sore head
livid
mad as a cut snake
mad as a hornet
mad as a maggot
mad as a meat-axe
maggoty
miffed
off (one's) block
off (one's) crumpet
off (one's) face
off (one's) head
off (one's) nana
off (one's) nut
off (one's) onion
off (one's) rocker
off (one's) scone
off (one's) tiles
off (one's) trolley
off the air
off the deep end
off the planet
on the rampage
on the warpath
pippy
pissed off
prickly
riled up
ropeable
scotty
shat off
shirty
shitty
shitty-livered
snaky
snitchy
snotty
sore
sour as a lemon
spitting chips
steamed up
stroppy
toey as a Roman sandal
touchy
uptight
worked up

To lose one's temper

blow a fuse
blow a gasket
blow (one's) cool
blow (one's) stack
blow (one's) top
blow up
bung on an act
chuck a mental
chuck a spas
chuck a willie
chuck a wobbly
climb up the wall
crack a darkie
crack a shitty
crawl up the wall
cut loose
cut up rough
do (one's) block
do (one's) bun
do (one's) cruet
do (one's) lolly
do (one's) nana
do (one's) nut
do (one's) onion
do (one's) quince
do (one's) scone
flip (one's) lid
flip out
fly off the handle
freak out
froth at the mouth
get dark
get off (one's) bike
get (one's) back up
get (one's) dander up
get (one's) hackles up
get (one's) Irish up
get (one's) knickers in a knot/twist
get (one's) tits in a tangle
get the gripes
get the pip
get the shits

get uppity
go bananas
go batty
go bonkers
go crackers
go crook
go mad
go nuts
go off (one's) brain
go off (one's) crumpet
go off (one's) head
go off (one's) nut
go off (one's) rocker
go off pop
go off the deep end
go off the rails
go through the roof
go to market
have kittens
(have) shit on the liver
hit the ceiling/roof
let fly
let rip
lose (one's) cool
lose (one's) head
lose (one's) wool
pack a shitty
pop (one's) cork
put on a turn
shit bricks
snap (one's) twig
sound off
tear (one's) hair out
throw a fit
throw a turn
throw a wobbly

To vent one's anger and hostility on someone

bawl (someone) out
blast hell out of (someone)
blow shit out of (someone)
blow (someone) up
bore it up (someone)
chew (someone) out
chew (someone's) ear
chew the arse off (someone)
come down on (someone)
cook (someone's) goose
dress (someone) down
fix (someone's) wagon
get stuck into (someone)
get up (someone)
give (someone) a blast
give (someone) a doing-over
give (someone) a dressing-down
give (someone) a piece of (one's) mind
give (someone) a serve
give (someone) a taste of (her/his) own medicine
give (someone) beans
give (someone) curry
give (someone) heaps/hell
give (someone) Larry Dooley
give (someone) the rounds of the kitchen
give (someone) what for
go butchers (hook) at
go off at (someone)
go to market
go to town on (someone)
gun for (someone)
hang, draw and quarter (someone)
haul (someone) over the coals
have a go at (someone)
have a shot at (someone)
have (someone's) balls
have (someone's) head
have words with (someone)
have/got an edge against (someone)
have/got it in for (someone)
hoe into (someone)
hop into (someone)
jump down (someone's) throat
lace into (someone)
lay into (someone)
let (someone) have it
light into (someone)
neck (someone)
pay out on (someone)
pin (someone's) ears back
rake (someone) over the coals
rip into (someone)
roar shit out of (someone)
roar (someone) up
roast (someone)
show (someone) a thing or two
snap (someone's) head off
take a piece out of (someone)
take it out on (someone)
tear into (someone)
tear strips off (someone)
tell (someone) off
tick (someone) off
turn on (someone)
up (someone)
weigh into (someone)
whale into (someone)
wipe the smile off (someone's) dial

Noisy fights and brawls

barney
battle royal
blow-up
blue
brush
bun fight
bust-up
ding-dong
domestic
donnybrook
dust-up
falling-out
fireworks
fisticuffs
flare-up
free-for-all
go-in
hassle
hooha(h)
kafuffle
Mexican stand-off
misunderstanding
mix-up
punch-up
rough-up
row
ruckus
rumble
run-in
scrap
scrape
set-to
shindig
slanging match
spat
stoush
turn-up
yike

To make hostile threats or take hostile action against someone

bean (someone)
beat the hell out of (someone)
beat the living daylights out of (someone)
beat the stuffing out of (someone)
belt (someone) one
brain (someone)
clobber (someone)
clock (someone)
clonk (someone)
cream (someone)
crown (someone)
deck (someone)
do (someone) (like a dinner)
give (someone) a doing-over
give (someone) a fat lip
give (someone) a thick ear
give (someone) one
hammer (someone)
hang a lefty on (someone)
hang one on (someone)
have a go at (someone)
have (someone)
have (someone) on
hop into (someone)
job (someone) one
jump (someone)
kick (someone's) head/teeth in
knock (someone's) block off
knock (someone) rotten
knock spots off (someone)
knock the stuffing out of (someone)
knuckle (someone)
lam into (someone)
lather (someone)
lay into (someone)
lay (someone) out
let (someone) have it
lick (someone)
light into (someone)
make custard/mince-meat out of (someone)
piss all over (someone)
pitch into (someone)
plant one on (someone)
plaster (someone)
plug (someone)
pulverise (someone)
punch shit out of (someone)
punch (someone's) head in
put in the boot
rearrange (someone's) face
rough (someone) up
screw (someone) to the wall
shit all over (someone)
sit (someone) on his arse
snot (someone) one
sock (someone) one
sort (someone) out
stand (someone) on (her/his) ear
straighten (someone) out
take a poke at (someone)
take on (someone)
take (someone) apart
take (someone) on
take (someone) to pieces
tan (someone's) hide
teach (someone) a thing or two
thrash (someone)

up (someone)
weigh into (someone)
whale into (someone)
whop (someone)
wipe the floor with (someone)
work (someone) over
wring (someone's) neck

Acts of violence

belt in the lug
belting
biff in the ear
bunch of fives
clip in the ear
clout in the earhole
doing-over
going-over
hiding
king-hit
knuckle sandwich
lefty
once-over
poke in the nose
shellacking
the old one-two
thick ear
thumping
towelling
what for

To be the recipient of anger and hostility

cop it
done like a dog's dinner
get a hammering
get a lift under the ear
get buckled
get done over
get the full treatment
hit for six

BROKEN, OUT OF ORDER

all screwed up
buggered
bung
busted
cactus
clagged the bag
clapped out
conked out
crook
done for
frigged
fucked
had it
had the dick
had the gong
had the Richard
had the ridgy-didge
had the sword
history
jiggered
kaput
on the blink
on the fritz
on the way out
onkus
play up
rat-shit
rooted
R.S.
stuffed
stukered
up the duff
up the pole
up the putt
up the shit
up the spout
up the wop
up to putty
wonky

CARS

beetle
black maria
black taxi
bomb
brm brm
bucket of nuts and bolts
buggy
bus
chaff-cutter
chariot
chevvy
crate
divvy-van
dumper
FJ
fuck-truck
fuzz-wagon
hack
heap
heap of shit
hot-rod
Jag
jalopy
kombi
lemon
limmo
Merc
micro oven
old girl
paddy-wagon
putt-putt
Q-car
rattle-trap
Roller
Rolls
Rolls Canardly
rust-bucket
set of wheels
shaggin' wagon

shit-heap
sin-bin
tank
tin lizzie
ute
Vee-dub
Vee-eight
Vee-wee
wagon
wheels
yank tank

CHEATING, DECEPTION AND TRICKERY

To be cheated, deceived or tricked

be sold a pup
been done
been had
been taken
been taken for a ride
bitten
brassed
chiselled
conned
crossed
diddled
done
done out of
double-crossed
dudded
fall for it (hook line and sinker)
fall into
fleeced
fucked
get conned
get done
get had
get screwed
get stung
get sucked in
get the rough end of the pineapple
gypped
had
had in
hoodwinked
hooked
ripped off
rooked
roped in
screwed
set on a bum steer
set up
shat on
short-changed
skinned
sold down the river
sold out
stabbed in the back
strung a line
stung
sucked in
taken
taken for a ride
taken in
touched

To cheat, deceive or trick someone

brass (someone)
chisel (one's) way in
come that with (someone)
come the raw prawn
come the uncooked crustacean
con
cross
diddle
do
do (someone) out of
double-cross
dud
fiddle
fix
fleece
fox
fuck
get at
give (someone) a bum steer
gyp
hand (someone) a line
have (someone)
have (someone) on
having a lend of (someone)
hoodwink
lead (someone) up the garden path
load the dice
play (someone) for a fool
pull a fast one
pull a fastie
pull a shifty
pull a swifty
pull (someone's) leg
pull the dirty
pull the wool over (someone's) eyes
put one across/over/past (someone)
put over a fast one
put over a fastie
rip (someone) off
rook (someone)
screw (someone)

sell (someone) down the river
sell (someone) out
set (someone) on a bum steer
set (someone) up
shit all over (someone)
short-change (someone)
skin (someone)
stab (someone) in the back
steal a march on (someone)
sting (someone)
string (someone) a line
suck in
swizzle (someone)
take (someone)
take (someone) down
take (someone) for a ride
touch (someone)
two-time (someone)
work a ready

Cheats and tricksters

cardsharp
chiseller
con artist/man
crook
diddler
double-crosser
fox
gyp
rat-bag
rat-fink
rip-off merchant
rook
shake-down merchant
share-pusher
shark
sharp
sheister
shicer
shrewdie
shyster
slick operator
slippery as a butcher's penis
slippery as an eel
snake in the grass
spieler
spiv
two-timer
wangler
weasel

Acts of cheating, deception or trickery

catch
con
dodge
double-cross
dud
fast one
fastie
fiddle
game
gyp
have
highway robbery
hitch
hocus-pocus
hokey-pokey
juggle
leg-pull
line
monkey business
put-up
ready
rip-off
rook
rort
set-up
shenanigan
shifty
shonk
slanter
slick trick
snow job
sting
swifty
swizzle
take
take-down
touch
wangle

Victims of cheating, deception or trickery

bunny
easy game
easy mark
easy take
easy target
easy touch
fall guy
galah
mug
patsy
pigeon
sitting duck
softy
sucker
turkey

CHILDREN

ankle-biters
beggars
billies
billy-lids
brat
bub
bubba
carpet grubs
horror
imp
junior
kid
kiddiewink
little buggers
little Johnny
little Vegemites
littlie
mite
monkey
monsters
nipper
perisher
pipsqueak
rug-rats
scone-gropers
terror
tiddler
toddler
tot
tyke
whipper-snapper
youngie

CLOTHES

Dressed in one's best clothes

all dolled up
all laired up
all mockered up
all ponced up
done up like a Christmas tree
done up like a dinner
done up like a pet lizard
done up like a pox-doctor's clerk
done up like a sore finger/toe
done up like an organ-grinder's monkey
done up to the nines
dressed in one's Sunday best
dressed to beat the band
dressed to kill
dressed up
full dress
pooned up
spiffed/spivved up
spruced up
tricked out
well turned out

Items of general clothing

Akubra (wide-brimmed felt hat)
almond rocks (socks)
bag of fruit (suit)
baggies (baggy trousers)
bathers (swimming costume)
beanie (close-fitting knitted cap)
bib and tucker (best suit or clothes)
birthday suit (the naked body)
bloomers (women's underpants)
boob-tube (women's elasticised summer top)
booties (knitted shoes for a baby)
bra (brassiere)
britches (trousers)
brothel boots (soft-soled shoes)
brunch coat (light dressing-gown for women)
civvies (ordinary clothes as opposed to uniform)
clobber (clothes in general)
clod-hoppers (shoes or boots)
cords (corduroy trousers)
cossie (swimming costume)
daks (trousers)
Dolly Varden (women's wide-brimmed hat)
duds (trousers; clothes in general)
fancy duds (good clothes)
flatties (flat-heeled shoes)
glad rags (good clothes)
grundies (underpants)
G-string (minimal covering for the genitals)
gummies (gumboots)
hotpants (sexy shorts for women)
iron underpants (control-briefs for women)
Jackie Howe (black or navy work singlet)
Japanese safety shoes (thongs)
jarmies (pyjamas)
knickers (underpants)
long johns (men's long underwear)
long'uns (long trousers)
middies (women's low-heeled shoes)
monkey suit (suit)
nightie (women's night-dress)
nut-chokers (men's underpants)
over-shoulder-boulder-holder (brassiere)
panties (women's underpants)
pants (trousers; underpants)
PJ's (pyjamas)
poop-catchers (loose-fitting, ankle-tight trousers)
rags (clothes in general)
reg grundies (undies)

reginalds (undies)
roll-ons (control-briefs for women)
runners (sand-shoes)
skidlid (safety helmet)
sling-shot (brassiere)
slip (petticoat)
sloppy joe (loose-fitting jumper)
slouch hat (Australian Army hat)
sneakers (soft-soled shoes)
step-ins (control-briefs for women)
stove-pipes (tight-fitting trousers)
strides (trousers)
Sunday best (best clothes)
swimmers (swimming costume)
tank top (garment resembling a singlet)
threads (clothes in general)
titfer (hat)
togs (swimming costume)
tux (tuxedo suit)
tweeds (trousers)
twin-set (matching jumper and cardigan)
ug boot (fleecy-lined sheepskin boot)
under-chunders (underpants)
underdaks (underpants)
undies (underpants)
unmentionables (underwear)
wedgies (shoes with wedge-shaped heels)
wellies (gumboots)
winkle-pickers (pointy toed shoes)
woollies (warm, woollen clothing)
Y-fronts (men's underpants)
zoot-suit (suit)

CONTRACTED EXPRESSIONS

betcha (bet you)
carn! (come on!)
dunno (don't know)
'em (them)
emma chisit? (how much is it?)
garn! (go on!)
g'day (good day)
gidday (good day)
gimme (give me)
gonna (going to)
gotcha! (got you!)
gotta (got to)
gunna (going to)
helluva (hell of a)
how ya goin' mate — orright? (how are you going mate — all right?)
on ya! (good on you!)
wanna (want to)
ya (you)

DEATH

To die or be killed

bite the dust
breathe (one's) last
buy it
cark it
cash in (one's chips)
chuck a seven
conk out
croak
curl up (one's) toes
die on (someone)
do a perish
drop off
get bumped off
get done in
get hers/his/yours
give up the ghost
go west
keel over
kick off
kick the bucket
lick the dust
meet (one's) Waterloo
pass away
pass in (one's) marble
peg out
pop off
snap (one's) twig
snuff it
throw a seven
toss in (one's) alley
turn up (one's) toes

Dead or killed

at rest
bought it
cactus
carried out feet first
caught it
clagged the bag
creamed
dead and buried
dead as a dodo/doornail/maggot
done for
dusted
gone
goner
had it
had the dick
had the gong
had the Richard
had the ridgy-didge
had the sword
history
jiggered
kaput
knocked off
pushing up daisies
rat-shit
rooted
R.S.
six foot under
stone-cold

stuffed
wasted

To kill

bump off
cream (someone)
do away with (someone)
do (someone) in
knock (someone) off
nail (someone)
rub (someone) out
take (someone) for a ride
waste (someone)
wipe (someone) out

DIMINUTIVES

aggro (aggressive))
alkie (alcoholic)
ammo (ammunition)
amp (amplifier)
anotherie (another one)
arvo (afternoon)
Aussie (Australian)
backy (tobacco)
baddie (bad, lawless person)
baggies (baggy, loose trousers)
barbie (barbecue)
barra (barramundi)
bickies (biscuits)
biggie (something big)
bikie (member of motorbike gang)
blowie (blowfly)
boatie (boat enthusiast)
bookie (bookmaker)
bottie (bottle; bottom)
brekkie (breakfast)
brickie (bricklayer)
Brissie (Brisbane)
budgie (budgerigar)
bundy (Bundaberg rum)
cabbie (cab, taxi driver)
carbie (carburettor)
cardie (cardigan)
carnie (carnival worker)
caulie (cauliflower)
chalkie (chalk user: teacher)
chappie (chap, fellow)
chewie/chewy (chewing-gum)
chockie (chocolate)
Chrissie (Christmas)
ciggie (cigarette)
civvies (civilian clothes or people)
cockie (cockroach; cockatoo)
coldie (cold beer)
comfy (comfortable)
commie (communist)
compo (worker's compensation)
conchie (conscientious objector)
condo (condominium)
cossie (swimming costume)
croc (crocodile)
crookie (broken-down, 'crook' item)
cuey/cuie/cuke (cucumber)
cuppa (cup of tea)
deli/dellie (delicatessen)
demo (demonstration)
dero (derelict, vagrant)
doley (person receiving the dole)
druggie (drug-addict)
Ekka (Brisbane's Agricultural Exhibition)
fastie (act of deception)
fibro (house made from fibro-cement — asbestos and cement sheet)
flattie (flathead fish; flat tyre)
folkie (player or follower of folk-music)
footy (Australian Rules football)
freebie (something free, for no payment)
frenchie (French letter, condom)
fridge (refrigerator)
frillie (frill-necked lizard)
frostie (cold, frosted-over can or bottle of beer)
galvo (galvanised iron)
garbo (garbage collector)
gastro (gastroenteritis: stomach upset)
genny (generator)
geri (old person, geriatric)
gladdie (gladiolus)
glam (glamorous)
goalie (goal-keeper)
goodie (ethical, good person)
goodies (good, desirable things, items, foods)
goosies (goose-bumps)
govie (government, governmental)
grannie (grandmother)
greenies (conservationists)
groupie (woman who follows rock groups and offers herself sexually to them)
gummies (gumboots)
hankie (handkerchief)
heavies ('heavy' body-guards etc.: those using strong-arm tactics)
hippo (hippopotamus)
hollies (holidays)
hols (holidays)

homo (homosexual)
hostie (air hostess)
hottie (hot-water bottle)
hyper (hyperactive)
hypo (hypodermic needle)
incog (incognito)
info (information)
intro (introduction)
jarmies (pyjamas)
jelly (gelignite: an explosive)
kero (kerosine)
kiddie (child)
kindy (kindergarten)
kooky (kookaburra)
lavvy (lavatory)
lecky (electric)
lesso (lesbian)
limmo (limousine)
lippie (lipstick)
littlie (young child)
lobbies (lobsters, crayfish)
lube (lubrication of a motor vehicle)
mag (magazine)
maggie (magpie)
marties (tomatoes)
meanie (mean, unkind, miserly person)
metho (methylated spirits)
milkie (milk vendor)
milko (milk vendor)
mo (moment)
mossie (mosquito)
muddie (Queensland mud-crab)
mushie (mushroom)
muso (musician)
myxo (myxomatosis: disease of rabbits)
nanas/narnas/narnies (bananas)
nasho (national service)
newie (new item)
nightie (women's night dress)
nitro (nitroglycerine: an explosive)
nympho (nymphomaniac)
obs (objections)
oldies (old people; parents)
physio (physiotherapy)
pickie (picture; photograph)
placky (plastic)
pokies (poker-machines)
pollies (politicians)
porno (pornography)
possie (position)
postie (postman, mail deliverer)
potty (chamber-pot)
prac (practice class)
preggers/preggie/preggo (pregnant)
premmie (premature infant)
prep (preparatory class in school)
pressie (present, gift)
promo (promotion)
prop (propeller)
quickie (quick act of sexual intercourse)
ref (referee)
rego (vehicle registration)
rellies (relatives)
rep (travelling representative, salesman)
repro (reproduction)
revs (revolutions of an engine)
Rocky (Rockhampton)
rollie (hand-rolled cigarette)
roughie (ruffian, lout)
sammie (sandwich)
sandie (Queensland sand-crab)
sarnies (sandwiches)
sax (saxophone)
secko (sexual pervert)
shrewdie (shrewd, astute person)
sickie (a day absent from work, whether the worker is sick or not)
smoko (break for a smoke etc., rest from work)
smoothie (smooth, flattering but insincere talker)
specs (spectacles)
speedo (speedometer)
stat dec (statutory declaration)
Straddie (Stradbroke Island, Queensland)
strawbs (strawberries)
stubbie/stubby (small, stubby bottle of beer)
subbie (sub-contractor)
sunnies (sunglasses)
swaggie (swagman, drifter, tramp)
tacho (tachometer)
taddie (tadpole)
Tassie (Tasmania)
tat (tattoo)
tatie (potato)
telly (television)
tinnie (beer in a tin, can; small aluminium boat)
townie (person from town, the city)
trannie (transistor radio; trans-sexual)
trashie (garbage — trash — collector)
truckie (truck-driver)
U-ie (U-turn in a vehicle)
umpie (umpire)
undies (underpants)
vegies (vegetables)
Vinnies (St Vincent de Paul, a charitable organisation)
vocab (vocabulary)
weakie (weakling, coward)

wedgies (women's shoes with wedge-shaped heel)
weepie (sad film that makes one weep)
weirdie/weirdo (weird, odd person)
wellies (Wellingtons: gumboots)
wharfie (wharf labourer)
wheelie (noisy skidding of the drive wheels of a vehicle)
Windies (West Indies cricket team)
wino (wine alcoholic)
Woolies/Woollies (Woolworths supermarket)
woollies (warm woollen clothing)
yachtie (yacht owner and enthusiast)
Yammy (Yamaha motorcycle)
youngie (young child)

DRUGS

Common terms

acid (LSD: an hallucinogenic drug)
angel dust (Phencyclidine: an hallucinogenic drug)
bag (a measure of marijuana)
bang/bhang (marijuana)
benny (Benzedrine tablet: an amphetamine)
blow (cocaine)
blue meanies (hallucinogenic mushrooms)
Bob Hope (dope: marijuana)
bomb (a pill or tablet)
bong (special water pipe for smoking marijuana)
Buddha stick (marijuana, originating in Asia, sold in pre-rolled stick)
coke (cocaine)
crack (highly addictive manufactured form of cocaine)
crank (mixture of cocaine and amphetamines which is highly lethal)
dakka (marijuana)
deal (a measure of marijuana)
dope (marijuana)
downer (tranquilliser or depressant)
ego food (cocaine)
fix (dose of narcotic drug, such as heroin)
ganja (marijuana)
gear (marijuana or other drugs)
glue-sniffing (inhalation of intoxicating vapours from glue, petrol etc.)
gold-tops (hallucinogenic mushrooms)
goof balls (amphetamines; stimulants)
grass (marijuana)
H (heroin)
hammer and tack (heroin)
hard stuff (dangerously addictive drugs)
hash (hashish: resinous extract from marijuana)
hash oil (hashish distilled to a viscous oil)
haze (LSD: an hallucinogenic drug)
heaven dust (cocaine)
hemp (marijuana)
herb (marijuana)
herb superb (marijuana)
hit (a dose of heroin or other drug that is injected)
hitting gear (heroin)
hog (Phencyclidine: an hallucinogenic drug)
homebake (heroin manufactured in the home)
hooch (marijuana)
horse (heroin)
J (marijuana)
joint (marijuana cigarette)
junk (narcotic drugs, especially heroin)
lady (cocaine)
Leb red (hashish)
line (thin line of cocaine prepared for snorting)
LSD (lysergic acid diethylamide: a powerful hallucinogenic drug)
magic mushroom (hallucinogenic mushroom)
mandies (Mandrax: barbiturates)
Maori's pyjamas (marijuana)
marry-you-later (marijuana)
Mary J/Jane (marijuana)
mesc (peyote: an hallucinogenic drug prepared from a Mexican cactus)
mescal buttons (peyote: an hallucinogenic drug prepared from a Mexican cactus)
meth (Methedrine)
microdot (small amount of hallucinogenic drug such as LSD)
morf (morphine)
morpho (morphine)
mull (marijuana, dried and prepared for smoking)
nose candy (cocaine)
number (marijuana cigarette)
pep pills (amphetamines; stimulants)
pot (marijuana)
puff (marijuana)

purple hearts (amphetamines)
reds (amphetamines)
reefer (marijuana cigarette)
roach (the butt end of a nearly smoked marijuana cigarette)
rush (amyl nitrate used as a stimulant)
scoob (marijuana cigarette)
shit (marijuana and related products; heroin)
shot (an injection of a drug, such as heroin)
skag (heroin)
smack (heroin)
snort (a sniff of cocaine)
snow (heroin; cocaine)
space base (highly addictive and lethal combination of crack and angel dust)
speed (amphetamines)
speedball (mixture of heroin and cocaine)
stash (hidden supply of drugs)
ticket (blotting paper impregnated with LSD)
toot (cocaine)
twang (opium)
uppers (amphetamines; stimulant tablets, drugs)
weed (marijuana)
yippee-beans (stimulant tablets)

Methods of use

bogarting (selfishly smoking a joint)
drop acid (to take LSD)
freebasing (the smoking of cocaine)
glue sniffing (to inhale intoxicating vapours)
hit up (to inject with a drug such as heroin)
mainline (to inject heroin directly into the veins)
shoot up (to inject with a drug such as heroin)
sniff (to inhale intoxicating vapours)
snort (to sniff cocaine)
toke (a puff on a marijuana cigarette)
tracks (scars: evidence of injecting drugs)
trip (to hallucinate under the influence of a drug)
trip out (to hallucinate, especially badly or in a frightening manner under the influence of a drug such as acid or marijuana)

Addicts or users

druggie
head
junkie
mainliner
shithead
smack-freak
user

To be under the influence of drugs

bombed
burgered out
cold turkey
come down
freak
freak out
high (as a kite)
loaded
OD
off (one's) face
(on a) downer
out of it
out of (one's) tree
psyched out
ripped
smashed
spaced out
spun out
stoked
stoned
trip out
wasted
whacked
wiped out
wrecked
zonked

EASY AND DIFFICULT

Easy

all beer and skittles
all cush
bang (something) over
bed of roses
breeze
child's play
cinch
cushy
do it on (one's) ear/head
do it standing on (one's) head
do it with one arm tied behind (one's) back
easy as falling off a log
easy as pie

home on the pig's back
kick-over
knock-over
like a greasy stick up a dead dog's arse
like shooting fish in a barrel
like taking candy from a baby
loaf
make short work of
no probs
no sweat
nothing to it
picnic
piece of cake
piece of piss
pushover
romp home
romp it in
shit it in (carrying a brick)
snack
snap
soda
steal
sweet (as a nut)
walkover
waltz

Difficult

bugger
devil's own job
easy as pushing shit uphill with a pointed stick/rubber fork
easy as shoving butter up a porcupine's bum with a knitting-needle on a hot day
easy as spearing an eel with a spoon
fair cow
fun and games
merry old time
murder
no picnic
tall order

EXCLAMATIONS OF WONDER, DISBELIEF AND ANGER

Surprise, wonder, amazement

blimey!
bloody hell!
bloody Nora!
blow me down!
boy!
boy-oh-boy!
brother!
bugger me dead!
by cripes!
by George!
by gum!
by jingo!
by jove!
can you beat that!
Christ!
Christ almighty!
cor!
could have knocked me down with a feather!
couldn't get over it!
crikes!
crikey!
cripes!
curl the mo!
egad!
far out!
fart a crowbar!
fuck!
fuck a duck!
fuck me dead!
gads!
gadzooks!
gee!
gee whiz!
glory be!
God!
God almighty!
golly!
good grief!
good lord!
goodness!
goodness gracious (me)!
gorblimey!
gosh!
gracious (me)!
great balls of fire!
great galloping goannas!
great Scott!
heavens (to Betsy)!
heck!
hell!
hell's bells!
hell's teeth!
holy Christ!
holy cow!
holy dooley!
holy hell!
holy mackerel!
holy Moses!

holy shit!
holy snapping duck shit!
hoo-boy!
hot-dog!
how about that!
hullo!
hush my mouth!
I ask you!
I say!
I'll be!
I'll be a monkey's uncle!
I'll be a son of a gun!
I'll be blowed!
I'll be buggered!
I'll be damned!
I'll be darned!
I'll be fucked!
I'll be hanged!
I'll be jiggered!
I'll be stuffed!
jeepers!
jeepers creepers!
jees!
Jesus (Christ)!
jiminy cricket!
jingoes!
leaping lizards!
lord, love a duck!
man!
man-oh-man!
mother!
my!
my! my!
my word!
my-oh-my!
now I've seen it all!
oh boy!
ripper!
shit a brick!
shiver me timbers!
shivers!
snakes alive!
starve the bardies!
starve the crows!
starve the lizards!
stone the crows!
strewth/struth!
strike!
strike a light!
strike me lucky!
strike me pink!
strike me roan!
stripe me pink!
stuff a duck!
sugar!
sweet Jesus!
too much!
well I never!
well blow me down!
well! well!
whew!
wonders never cease!
yikes!
you son of a gun!
you wouldn't read about it!

Doubt, disbelief

all my eye and Betty Martin!
arseholes!
balls!
baloney!
bull!
bulldust!
bullshit!
bullswool!
crap!
didn't come down in the last shower!
don't come that with me!
don't come the raw prawn!
don't come the uncooked crustacean!
don't make me laugh!
fiddlesticks!
garn!
get away!
get off the grass!
go on!
like buggery!
like fun!
likely story!
my foot!
oh yeah!
phooey!
pigs!
pig's arse/bum/ring-hole!
pigs can/might fly!
pish!
pull the other leg (it jingles/it's got bells on)!
sure!
tell that to the marines!
tell us anotherie!
that'll be the day!
that's a good one!
tosh!
try another one!
wasn't born yesterday!
yeah! yeah!

Anger, annoyance, frustration

arseholes!
blast!
bloody hell!
blow it!
blow that!
bugger!
bugger it!
bum!
cunt!
damn-bugger-bitch-bum!
darn!
dash!
drat/drats!
for crying out loud!
for fuck's sake!
for Pete's sake!
for the love of God/Mike!
fuck!
fuck it!
fuck me dead!
God!
God-damn!
God-damn-it!
hang it!
heck!
hell!
horror of horrors!
isn't that the living end!
mother!
oh-oh!
phooey!
phut!
pigs!
poo!
poo-bum-bugger-shit!
pooh!
rats!
really!
shit!
shivers!
shucks!
stiffen the crows!
stiffen the lizards!
stuff it!
sugar!
tarnation!
that's got whiskers on it!
that's the breaks!
that's the way it goes!
that's the way the ball bounces!
that's the way the cookie crumbles!
to heck with it!
tut-tut!
uh-oh!
what the fuck/heck/hell!
whoops!
whoops-a-daisy!
wouldn't it!
wouldn't it rip you!
wouldn't it root you!
wouldn't it rot your socks!
wouldn't that rip the crutch/fork out of your nightie!
yikes!
yoicks!
yow!
zounds!

Angry dismissal

bug off!
bugger off!
fuck off!
fuck you!
get fucked!
get knotted!
get lost!
get nicked!
get rooted!
get stuffed!
go fly a kite!
go jump!
go jump in the lake!
go to billyo/blazes/buggery/hell!
in your boot!
jump on your head!
kiss my arse!
may your chooks turn into emus and kick your dunny door down!
may your ears turn into arseholes and shit all over your shoulders!
naff off!
nick off!
nickywoop!
piss off!
piss off hairy legs!
poo to you too!
P.O.Q.
rack off noddy!
run away!
scat!
scram!
screw you!
shove it!
shove off!
sorf!
stick it!
stick it in your gob!

stick it up your arse!
stick it up your ginger!
stick it up your jumper!
stick that for a joke!
stick that in your pipe and smoke it!
stuff it!
take a long walk off a short pier!
take a running jump at yourself!
take a slow boat to China!
take a walk!
take it and shove it!
to heck with it!
to hell with it!
up 'im!
up you!
up your arse!
up your bum!
up your date mate!
up your nose with a rubber hose! (and twice as far with a chocolate bar!)
up yours!
what are ya!
what else did you get for Christmas!
you know where you can go!

FOOD

(That wonderful stuff that sticks to one's ribs.)

General terms

chow
din-dins
dinnies
feed
grub
monger
munchies
nibblies
nosh
num-nums
spread
tucker

Particular foods

bangers (sausages)
bardie (edible grub)
barra (barramundi)
binder (cheese)
brekkie (breakfast)
brunch (breakfast and lunch in the same meal)
bubble and squeak (left-over meat and vegetables)
bullocky's joy (treacle)
bum-nuts (eggs)
bunghole (cheese)
burnt offerings (burnt food)
cackleberry (egg)
caulie (cauliflower)
cheerio (small party sausage)
chew and spew (take-away food)
chewie/chewy/chuttie/chutty (chewing-gum)
chockies (chocolate)
chook (chicken)
cocky's joy (treacle)
cow juice (milk)
cuey/cuie/cuke (cucumber)
cuppa (cup of tea, refreshments)
dagwood sandwich (very large sandwich)
damper (type of outback bread)
dead horse (sauce)
dish-water (weak tea, coffee or soup)
dodger (bread; sausage)
dog's eye (pie)
drumstick (leg of chicken)
fart fodder (anything that causes flatulence)
flake (fillet of shark)
floater (pie in gravy)
fly cemetery (fruit slice)
flybog (jam)
goog (egg)
googy-egg (egg)
grannie (apple)
greasies (fish and chips or similar oily food)
greens (green vegetables)
gunk (unsavoury food)
henfruit (eggs)
husband-beater (long bread stick)
johnny-cake (type of small damper)
junk food (take-away food)
lamington (chocolate and coconut coated cake)
little boys (cocktail sausages)
lobbies (lobsters)
lolly-water (lemonade)
loop-the-loop (soup)
marge (margarine)
marties (tomatoes)
mash (mashed potato)
moo-juice (milk)
mountain oysters (testicles of lambs)
mousetrap (cheese)
muddie (Queensland mud-crab)

murphy (potato)
mushie (mushroom)
mystery bags (sausages)
nana/narna/narnie (banana)
parson's nose (tail-end of a chicken)
pav (pavlova)
reaper and binder (cheese)
sammie (sandwich)
sandie (Queensland sand-crab)
sanger (sandwich)
sarnies (sandwiches)
sav (saveloy)
sinker (pie)
smoko (refreshments during a work-break)
snag (sausage)
snarler (sausage)
snorker (sausage)
snot-log (custard-slice cake)
spud (potato)
strawbs (strawberries)
take-away (take-away food)
tater/tatie (potato)
tea (main evening meal)
tinned dog (any tinned meat)
underground mutton (rabbit)
Vegemite (a favourite spread made from vegetable extract)
vegies (vegetables)
weenies (small cocktail sausages)

Expressions of hunger, thirst or satiety

belly thinks me throat's cut!
chew the arse out of a rag doll
chew the crutch out of an Afghan camel-driver's jocks
could eat a baby's bum through a cane chair
could eat a horse and chase the rider
didn't touch the sides
dry as a bone
dry as a dead dingo's dong
dry as a medieval monk's manuscript
dry as a nun's nasty
dry as a pommy's towel
dry as a stone god
dry as a sun-struck bone
dry as a wooden chip/idol
empty
famished
fill the hole in (one's) stomach
full as a boot/bull/bull's bum
full as a fairy's phone-book/footy final
full as a goog
full as a pommie complaint-box
full as a seaside shithouse on bank holiday
full as a state-school hat-rack
full as a tick
full as the family jerry/po/pot
full up to dolly's wax
full up to pussy's bow
F.U.R.T.B.
get the munchies
hanging out for a nosebag
(have) hollow legs
hungry as a black dog
my stomach thinks me throat's cut
quiet the worms
still the worms

FOOLISHNESS AND LUNACY

Fools, idiots or lunatics

ass
basket case
berk
bimbo
bird-brain
blithering idiot
blob
blockhead
bloody galah
bloody nong
boob
booby
boofhead
bright spark
bunny
chucklehead
chump
clod
clot
clown
coot
cough drop
crackpot
cretin
dag
dead-head
dick
dick-head
dill
dillpot
dimwit
ding
dingaling
dingbat
ding-dong
dipstick
dodo
donkey
dope
drip
drongo
droob
dubbo
duffer

dumb-bell
dumb-bum
dumb-cluck
dumbo
dum-dum
dummy
dunce
dunderhead
fart
fathead
fruit
fruitcake
fruit-loop
fuck-wit
galah
galoot
gawk
gig
gink
git
goat
goof
goog
goon
goose
great ape
half-wit
hatter
hoon
jackass
jerk
jerk-off
klutz
knucklehead
lame-brain
log of wood
lolly
loon
loony
loop
lummox
meatball
melon
monkey
moo
moron
mug
muggins
Muldoon
mutt
mutton-head
nana
nerd
nig-nog
nincompoop
ning-nong
ninny
nit
nit-wit
noddy
nong
noodle
numb-skull
nut
nut case
nutter
pea-brain
pinhead
poon
psycho
pud
pudding
queer
rabbit
Richard Cranium
sap
schmo
schmuck
schnook
screwball
shit-wit
silly sausage
silly-billy
spas
spastic
thick-head
thump-wit
troglodyte
turkey
twerp
twit
village idiot
wally
woodenhead
yob
yobbo
yo-yo
zonk

Strange or eccentric

bird
geezer
hard case
kook
oddball
queer bird/card
raving idiot
scatterbrain
slow-coach
slow-poke
spook
wack
wacker
wag
wank
weirdie
weirdo
whacker

Lacking in intelligence, insane or silly

air between the ears
balmy/barmy
bananas
barmy as a bandicoot
bats
bats in the belfry
batty
bent
bent as a scrub tick
berko
bonkers
brick short of a load
broad between the ears
cottonwool between the ears
cracked
crackers
crazy
cuckoo
daffy
dead and won't lie down
dead from the neck up
dense
dingbats
dippy
doesn't know B from a bull's foot
doesn't know whether it's Pitt Street or Christmas
doesn't know whether it's Tuesday or Bourke Street
doesn't know whether (one) is Arthur or Martha
don't pick your nose or your head will cave in
dotty
empty-headed
far gone
fucked in the head
funny
ga-ga
gonzo
goofy

hare-brained
hasn't got a brain in (her/his) head
hasn't got enough brains to give (her/himself) a headache
have/got a few marbles missing
have/got a screw loose
have/got kangaroos in the top paddock
have/got only one oar in the water
have/got rocks in (one's) head
have/got shit for brains
have/got some lights out upstairs
haven't got enough sense to come in out of the rain
haven't got much grey matter
if brains were dynamite he wouldn't have enough to blow his nose
if brains were dynamite he wouldn't have enough to part his hair
if brains were shit he wouldn't have enough to soil his collar
if you had a brain it would be lonely
lights are on but there's nobody home
loco
loony
loopy
lose (one's) marbles
mad as a cut snake
mad as a gumtree full of galahs
mad as a hatter
mad as a March hare
mad as a two-bob watch
mental
muscle-bound between the ears
narrow between the ears
need (one's) head read
nineteen and six in the pound
no brains
non compos
not all (one's) dogs are barking
not all there
not playing with the full deck
not right in the head/skull
not the full packet of bickies
not the full quid
not the full quid's worth
not the full two bob
nothing between the ears
nothing up top
nuts
nutty as a fruitcake
off (one's) block
off (one's) crumpet
off (one's) face
off (one's) head
off (one's) nana
off (one's) nut
off (one's) onion
off (one's) pannikin
off (one's) rocker
off (one's) scone
off (one's) tiles
off (one's) trolley
off the air/beam/planet/rails/wall
only eighteen bob in the pound
original
out of (one's) cotton-picking mind
out of (one's) head
out of (one's) tree
over the edge
pea-brain
potty
psycho
queer
round the bend/twist
sandwich short of a picnic
sappy
screwy
see daylight through (someone's) ears
shingle short
shit for brains
short of a sheet of bark
short of a shingle
short of change
short of grey matter
silly as a cut snake
silly as a square wheel
silly as a tin of worms
silly as a two-bob watch
silly as a wet hen
silly as a wheel
silly-billy
simple
slow as a wet hen/wet week
slow off the mark
slow on the uptake
soft in the crumpet/head
starkers
strange
ten cents short of the dollar
thick as a brick
thick as two short planks
thick between the ears
thick-skulled
thick-witted
touched
troppo
unhinged-
up the pole
wacko
wacky
want (one's) head read
water on the brain
whacked
wouldn't know (one's) arse from a hole in a flower-pot
wouldn't know (one's) arse from a hole in the ground
wouldn't know (one's) arse from (one's) elbow
wrong in the head
yarra

GREETINGS AND FAREWELLS

Greetings

g'day
gidday
hi
hiya!
how are the bots biting?

how are you?
how are you keeping?
how would you be?
how ya goin' mate — orright?
how-de-do?
howdy
how's it going?
how's things?
how's tricks?
hullo
what do you know?

Farewells

catch you later
chin-chin
chip-chip
ciao
cop-you-later
hoo-ray
hoo-roo
love you and leave you
nightie-night
see you
see you in the soup
see you later alligator
so long
tally-ho
ta-ta
toodle-oo
toodle-pip

OCCUPATIONS

beak (policeman; magistrate; private investigator)
bluebottle (policeman)
bomber (parking officer)
bookie (horse-racing bookmaker)
bottle-oh (used-bottle merchant)
bouncer (one employed to evict trouble-makers)
boys in blue (policemen)
brickie (bricklayer)
brown bomber (parking officer)
bull (policeman)
bush carpenter (unqualified carpenter)
butcher (surgeon believed to use the knife unnecessarily)
cabbie (driver of taxi-cabs)
chalkie (teacher)
checkout chick (cash-register operator at a store)
chippie (carpenter)
chromo (prostitute)
chucker-outer (one employed to evict trouble-makers)
cleaner-upper (cleaner)
cop (policeman)
counter-jumper (clerk; salesperson; public servant)
cowbanger (dairy-farmer)
cow-cocky (dairy farmer)
D/dee (detective; federal policeman; policeman)
demon (motorcycle policeman; detective)
dick (detective)
dixie-bashing (the washing of dishes and pots in an army kitchen)
DJ (disc-jockey)
doc (doctor)
dogger (dingo hunter)
dowser (water diviner)
ducks and geese (police)
dumpie (garbage collector)
endless belt (prostitute)
fed (federal policeman)
fence (dealer in stolen goods)
fizz (police informer)
fizz-gig (police informer)
flatfoot (policeman)
forty (petty criminal)
fuzz (police)
garbo (garbage collector)
grease-monkey (motor mechanic)
greasy (outback cook; sheep shearer)
grey ghost/meanie (parking officer)
grunter (prostitute)
gun (top fruit-picker or shearer)
gyno (gynaecologist)
hatchet man (one employed to perform unpleasant tasks, such as dismissing people etc.)
headshrinker (psychiatrist)
heavy (detective or investigator)
hit-man (hired assassin)
hooker (prostitute)
hoop (jockey)
hostie (air-hostess)
jackeroo (male outback station-hand)
jilleroo (female outback station-hand)
john (policeman)
John Hop (policeman)
journo (journalist)
legal-eagle (lawyer; solicitor)
man in white (umpire at a sporting game)
man of God (clergyman; priest)
medic (doctor)
milkie (milk vendor)
milko (milk vendor)
minder (bodyguard)
muso (musician)
nark (federal policeman or investigator)
news-hawk (journalist)

oinker (policeman)
pen-pusher (one whose work entails much writing)
pig (policeman)
pollies (politicians)
postie (mail deliverer)
pox-doctor (venereal disease specialist)
pug (boxer)
quack (doctor)
rag-and-bone-man (second-hand dealer)
rep (travelling representative, salesman)
ringer (stockman; drover; station-hand)
roadie (manager of a travelling music group)
salt (experienced seaman)
sarge (policeman; sergeant)
saw-bones (surgeon)
schoolie (teacher)
shark (moneylender)
shiny-arse (office-worker; public servant)
shrink (psychiatrist)
sky-pilot (clergyman; priest)
slushy (kitchen or cook's assistant)
sod-buster (farmer)
sparkie (electrician)
speed-cop (policeman who enforces the road laws)
subbie (sub-contractor)
tar (sailor; seaman)
teach (teacher)
traps (policemen)
trashie (garbage collector)
truckie (truck-driver)
turd-strangler (plumber)
vet (veterinarian)
walloper (policeman)
wharfie (wharf labourer)
wrecker (demolisher of houses, cars)

PEOPLES AND NATIONALITIES

Abo (Aborigine)
Aussie (Australian)
Balt (one from Central or Eastern Europe)
binghi (Aborigine)
blackfellow (Aborigine; dark person)
Blacks (dark-skinned peoples)
Bolshie (Bolshevik)
boong (Aborigine; dark person)
Brit (Englishman)
Canuck (Canadian, especially French)
Chink (Chinese person)
chocko (dark-skinned person)
choom (Englishman)
Chow (Chinese person)
coon (dark-skinned person)
dago (person of Latin origin; any foreign person)
darkie (dark-skinned person)
Enzedder (New Zealander)
ethno/ethnic (New Australian; migrant)
eyetie (Italian)
fernleaf (New Zealander)
Frog (Frenchman)
fuzzy wuzzy (native of Papua New Guinea)
garlic muncher (Greek or Italian)
Geordie (Scotsman)
goori/goorie (Maori)
grease-ball (Greek)
greaser (Greek, Italian or person of other foreign origin)
Gyppo (Egyptian)
honky (white man — mainly U.S.)
Hun (German)
ikeymo (Jew)
Itie (Italian)
jackie (Aborigine)
Jap (Japanese)
jerry (German)
Jock (Scotsman)
jungle-bunny (dark-skinned person)
Kanaka (Pacific Islander)
kike (Jew)
kipper (Englishman)
Kiwi (New Zealander)
koori (Aborigine)
Kraut (German)
kuri (Maori)
leprechaun (Irish)
limey (Englishman)
Mick (Irishman)
nigger (negroid, dark-skinned person)
nig-nog (negroid, dark-skinned person)
Nip (Japanese)
nog/noggy (negroid, dark-skinned person)
Paddy (Irishman)
Pakis (Pakistanis)
pie-eater (Australian)
Polack (Pole)
pom/pommy (English person)
power-point (Oriental person)
redskin (U.S. Indian)
rock-ape (negroid, dark-skinned person)

Ruskie (Russian)
sambo (negroid, dark-skinned person)
Scottie (Scotsman)
seppo (U.S. citizen)
septic/septic tank (U.S. citizen)
skip (Australian)
slant-eye (Oriental person)
slope (Oriental person)
slopehead/slopey (Oriental person)
spade (negroid, dark-skinned person)
spag (Italian)
spaghett (Italian)
spaghetti bender/muncher (Italian)
spic (Spaniard; Latin)
spud (Irishman)
to and from (pom — Englishman)
Windies (West Indians)
wog (Italian; Greek; Arab)
wop (Italian; Latin)
yank (U.S. citizen)

Australians by State

banana-bender (Queenslander)
cabbage-patcher (Victorian)
cornstalk (New South Welshman)
croweater (South Australian)
groper (West Australian)
magpie (South Australian)
mainlander (Tasmanian)
Melburnian (someone from Melbourne, Victoria)
Mexican (Victorian — living 'south of the border', according to New South Welshmen)
mutton-bird (Tasmanian)
sandgroper (West Australian)
Sydneyite (someone from Sydney, New South Wales)
top-ender (someone from northern reaches of Northern Territory)
westie (someone from western suburbs of Sydney, New South Wales)

PLACES

Alice (Alice Springs)
Apple Isle (Tasmania)
Aus (Australia)
Aussie/Aussieland (Australia)
back country (remote area)
back o' Bourke (remote area)
back of beyond (remote area)
backblocks (remote area)
backwater (remote area)
backwoods (remote area)
Bamboo Curtain (China)
Banana Republic (Queensland)
Banana-land (Queensland)
Bazzaland (Australia)
Big Apple (New York)
big smoke (the city)
Black Stump (country; remote area)
Brissie (Brisbane)
burg (a city)
Coat Hanger (Sydney Harbour Bridge)
Dead Heart (Central Australia)
Down Under (Australia)
Enzed (New Zealand)
Freo (Fremantle)
Gabba (Queensland Cricket Association ground at Woollongabba)
Honkers (Hong Kong)
Lucky Country (Australia)
mainland (New Zealand; Tasmania)
mallee (remote bushland)
mulga (remote bushland)
never-never (remote or imaginary place)
Old Dart (England)
out here (Australia)
outback (remote central areas of Australia)
Oz (Australia)
Pig Islands (New Zealand)
Pommyland (England)
Quaky Isles (New Zealand)
Rocky (Rockhampton)
Shaky Isles (New Zealand)
Snake Gully (any unsophisticated country place)
Speewa (legendary outback station)
steak and kidney (Sydney)
Straddie (Stradbroke Island, Queensland)
Sufferer's Parasite (Surfer's Paradise, Queensland)
Sunshine State (Queensland)
Tas/Tassie (Tasmania)
the bush (remote bushland, backwoods)
the Centre (Central Australia)
the Cross (King's Cross, Sydney)
the Rock (Ayer's Rock)
the sticks (remote bushland, backwoods)
Timbuktu (somewhere far away)
Woop Woop/woop-woop (somewhere far away)
wop-wops (remote area)

RHYMING SLANG

The examples of rhyming slang in this dictionary represent only a small selection of some of the most common ones — an entire collection would form another book again!

An example of the use of rhyming slang in speech is: 'Hey china! Stick yer onkas in yer sky-rocket, grab some rifle-range and get a couple of red-hots — it's your Wally Grout!'. (Translation: 'Hey mate! Put your fingers in your pocket, grab some change and get a couple of pots of beer — it's your shout!'.)

after darks (sharks)
Al Capone (phone)
almond rocks (socks)
apples and pears (stairs)
aristotle (bottle)
arra (bottle)
babbler (cook)
bag of fruit (suit)
billy (bong for smoking marijuana)
billies/billy lids (kids)
billygoat (tote: TAB)
blood and blister (sister)
Bob Hope (soap; dope: marijuana)
bristols (boobs, tits)
butchers/butchers hook (look; crook)
Captain/Captain Cook (look)
china/china plate/chine (mate)
comic-cuts (guts)
country cousin (dozen)
Dad 'n' Dave (shave)
dead horse (sauce)
dickory dock (clock; cock)
dog's eye (pie)
dry rots (trots: diarrhoea)
ducks and geese (police)
eau de cologne (phone)
fiddly-dids (quids: dollars)
four-be-two (Jew)
frog and toad (road)
Germaine Greer (ear)
German band (hand)
Ginger Meggs (legs)
ginger-beer (ear; queer)
ham and eggs (legs)
hammer (hammer and tack: back)
hammer and tack (back; heroin)
hard hit (shit)
hey-diddle-diddle (middle; piddle)
hit-and-miss (piss)
hoffman brick (dick: penis)
horse and cart (fart)
horse's hoof (poof: homosexual)
I supppose (nose)
jam tart (heart)
Jimmy Britts (shits)
Jimmy Dancer (cancer)
Joe Blake (snake)
Joe Hunt (cunt)
John Hopper (copper: policeman)
King Richard the Third (turd)
lemon squash (wash)
Lionel Rose (nose)
loop-the-loop (soup)
mallee root (prostitute)
Mickey Fritt (shit)
Mickey Mouse (grouse)
mince pies (eyes)
mollo/molly the monk (drunk)
mystery bags (snags: sausages)
nanny-goat (tote: TAB)
Niagara Falls/niagaras (balls: testicles)
Noah/Noah's Ark (shark)
north-and-south (mouth)
now is the hour (shower)
on one's Pat Malone (alone)
on the Murray Cod (on the nod: on credit)
onka/onkaparinga (finger)
optic nerve (perve: a look)
orchestra stalls (balls: testicles)
Oxford scholar (dollar)
piccadilly (chilly, cold)
plates of meat (feet)
raspberry tart (fart; heart)
red-hot (pot of beer)
red-hots (trots: harness horse-racing; diarrhoea)
reg grundies (undies)
reginalds (undies, from reg grundies)
Rhodes scholar (dollar)
rifle-range (change)
Saint Louis Blues (shoes)
Sandy McNab (cab, taxi)
sausage/sausage roll (goal in VFL)
septic/septic tank (yank)
sky-rocket (pocket)
soldiers bold (cold)
steak and kidney (Sydney)
tea-leaf (thief)
this-an'-that (hat)
titfer (tit for tat: hat)

to and from (pom)
tom tits (shits)
trams and trains (brains; drains)
trouble-and-strife (wife)
Wally Grout (shout: one's turn to pay or buy)
warwicks (arms, from Warwick Farm: arm)
whistle and flute (suit)
Williamstown piers (ears)
woolly woofter (poofter: homosexual)
young and old (cold)
zubrick (prick: penis)

SEX

Sexual intercourse and lascivious play

afternoon delight
any
backscuttle
balling
bang
bat on a sticky wicket
be good — if you can't, be careful!
bed (someone)
between the sheets
bit
bit on the side
bonk
bump and grind
bury the bishop
canoodle
carry on
come across
crack it
crash on
curl up
daisy chain
deliver the goods
dip (one's) wick
dirty deed
dirty weekend
do it
doggie fashion
dud bash
exercise the ferret
extra-curricular activities
feature with (someone)
feel
feel (someone) up
finger
flash (one's) nasty
fool around
forbidden fruits
fuck
fucks like a rattlesnake
fun and games
funny business
gang bang/slash
gangie
get a bit
get a length
get carried away
get into (someone's) pants
get it
get it off with (someone)
get off on
get off with (someone)
get one
get (one's) end in
get (one's) rocks off
get screwed
get up (someone)
get with (someone)
getting any?
getting it?
give (someone) one
go all the way
go for the growler
go in off the red
go the grope
go through (someone)
golden shower
grope
had it
hanky-panky
have a pasho
have a session
have it off
have relations
hide the sausage
hole in one
how about it?
hump
in and out like a fiddler's elbow
in-and-out
in-out-in-out
it
itch
jollies
jump (someone)
kick a goal
knock
knock (someone) off
knocks like a Mack truck
laid
lay
lay in the hay
lie with (someone)
looking for a bit of skirt
lost weekend
love bite
love-making
lover's balls
make love
make out
make whoopee
mess around
missionary position
monkey business
morning glory
nasty
naughty
neck
nookie
on a promise
on a sure thing
on heat
on the con
on the make
on with
one in the bush is worth two in the hand
oomph
pash on
pearl necklace
play around
play footsies with (someone)
play up
pluck (someone's) cherry
poke
pound the mound

produce the goods
proposition
put the hard word on (someone)
put the heavies on (someone)
quickie
rasp
raspberry dip
ride (someone)
roll
roll in the hay
Roman hands and Russian fingers
romp in the hay
root
score
score a hole-in-one
scrape
screw
shaft
shag
show (someone) one's etchings
sink the sausage/sav
sit on my face
sixty-niner
slap-and-tickle
slip (someone) a length
spear the bearded clam
stuff
the old one-two
throw (oneself) at (someone)
tomfoolery
tool
turn the lights out and play hide the sausage
up (someone)
what about it?
what for

Sexual arousal, erection

bar-on
boner
bring (someone) on
crack a fat
fat
Foster's flop
fresh
frigid digit
frisky
get it up
get the hots for (someone)
hard-on
heat in the meat
horn
horny
hot
hot stuff
hot-blooded
hotpants
lover's balls
on heat
on the con
on the make
pole-vault
power of the pussy
raise one
randy as a bitch on heat
randy as a drover's dog
randy as a mallee bull
rigid digit
rod
stiff
tilt in his kilt
turn (someone) on
turned on
turn-on
wide-on
worked up

Masturbation

beat the meat
dicky-whacker
flip (oneself) off
frig
grow hairs on (one's) palms
jack off
jerk off
jerkin' the gherkin
Missus Palmer and her five daughters
play the organ
play with (oneself)
pull (oneself)
rod-walloper
toss off
twanging the wire
wank
whack off

Orgasm

baby batter
bring (someone) off
come
cream (one's) jeans
doves flying out of (one's) arse
get off at Redfern
gism
love juice
on the vinegar stroke
pearl necklace
shoot (one's) bolt/load
spoof
spunk
wet dream

Oral sex

blow-job
cut lunch
deep throat
dine at the Y
eat
fur-burger
fur-pie
give head
gnaw the nana
go down on (someone)
gobbler
hair pie
head-job
mickey-muncher
muff-diver
muff-muncher
sit on my face
sixty-niner
soixante-neuf
suck off
tongue-sandwich

Contraception

be good — if you can't be careful!
Dutch cap
franger
fred
French letter
frenchie
Frog
gumboot
loop
protection
raincoat
rhythm method
rubber
the pill

Homosexuality

backdoor bandit

bender
bimbo
bronzer
bum-bandit
butch
camp as a row of tents
chocolate bandit
closet queen
cocksucker
cream puff
dung-puncher
fag
faggot
fairy
fancypants
fruit
gay
ginger-beer
have/got counter-sunk shit
homo
horse's hoof
les-be-friends/lesbo/leso/
lesso/lezzy
pansy
pillow-biter
ponce
poof
poofter
poonce
pouffe
precious
queen
queer
shirt-lifter
shit-puncher
shit-stabber
that way inclined
tonk
turd-bandit
turd-burglar
turd-puncher
wonk
woofter
woolly woofter

Women as sex objects

all pink on the inside
bag over the head job
bang
bangs like a dunny door in a gale
bangs like a tappet
bit of arse
bit of crumpet
bit of fluff
bit of skirt
black velvet
crumpet
cunt
fluff
gash
paper-bag job
skirt
slashing line
snatch
tail
town bike
tush

SPOUSE

ball and chain (wife)
better half (wife or husband)
boss (wife)
cheese and kisses (wife)
'er indoors (wife)
ever-loving (wife or husband)
good lady (wife)
her indoors (wife)
his lordship (husband)
hubby (husband)
lady (wife)
little lady/woman (wife)
lord of the manor/roost (husband)
other half (wife or husband)
the missus (wife)
the old ball and chain (wife)
the old boy (husband)
the old girl (wife)
the old lady (wife)
the old man (husband)
the old woman (wife)
trouble-and-strife (wife)
woman (wife)

THE CALL OF NATURE

The toilet

bathroom
boghouse
brasco
can
comfort station
crapper
diddy
dunger
dunny
dyke
gents
jerry
john
kharsi
la-di-da
ladies
lav
lavvy
little boys'/girls' room
little house
loo
Mary's room
men's
outhouse
pisser
piss-pot
place where the big nobs hang out
powder room
privy
rest room
shithouse
shouse
throne
thunder-box

toot
twinkle-palace
wash room
WC

Urination

do wees
drain the dragon
drain the lizard
drain the spuds
flash fanny at the Fowlers
go for a snake's (hiss)
go to the bathroom
have a leak
hey-diddle-diddle
hit-and-miss
kill a snake
number one
pay a visit
pee
piddle
piss
point percy at the porcelain
powder (one's) nose
relieve oneself
see a man about a dog
see a star about a twinkle
shake hands with the unemployed
shake hands with the wife's best friend
slash
snake's hiss
splash (one's) boots
spray the bowl/porcelain
squat
squeeze a lemon
strain the potatoes
syphon the python
take a walk
take (one's) dog for a walk
train terrence at the terracotta
twinkle
water the horse
wee
wee-pee
wee-wees
widdle

Defecation

bog
break a bit off
business
cack
chase out a chocolate monster
choke a darkie
crap
drop a darkie
give birth to a politician
grogin
gruff nuts
hard hit
Jimmy Britt
job
King Richard the Third
lay a cable
lay an egg
number two
plop
poo
poop
punch out a nougat/steamer
relieve oneself
squitters
strangle a darkie
the shits
the trots
turd

A

A over H
(arse over head); (see main entry: A over T).

about right
absolutely correct (sometimes used ironically): e.g. That'd be about right, mate!

accidentally on purpose
planned but appearing to be spontaneous (sometimes used ironically): e.g. I know you always hated that vase — I bet it got broken accidentally on purpose!

ackers
acne or pimples: e.g. Boy! Check the ackers on his moosh!

Adrian Quist
(rhyming slang) pissed; intoxicated.

aggers/aggers to the max
aggressive; angry: e.g. What's he so aggers about?

airhead
a brainless, silly person.

and (all) that
and associated matters: e.g. How've his marriage problems and that been going?

aroonie
(in combination) used as an intensifier: e.g.
1. We got a real buzzaroonie out of that marijuana!
2. He's such a spazzaroonie!

arse-end of nowhere

arsehole of the world
any place considered despicable, dirty, uninteresting.

arvie
afternoon: e.g. What are you doing this arvie?

asshole
(see main entry: arsehole)

axe-mark
vagina.

ay
1. (as a question) pardon? What did you say?
2. (at the end of a sentence, used especially by Kiwis and Queenslanders) don't you agree?: e.g. Good weather, ay?

B

B.A.
bloody awful: e.g. After a night out on the booze, Carol felt B.A. the next morning.

baby boomer
a person who was born during the baby boom that followed the Second World War.

band-aid
superficial. e.g. Raising interest rates was a band-aid solution to serious economic ills.

barbed wire
(Northern Territory slang) XXXX beer.

barbie doll
girl or woman who resembles the Barbie Doll toy — one who looks artificial, with plenty of make-up and dyed blonde hair.

bark
cough: e.g. He barked all night even though we gave him some cough medicine.

barker's nest
pile of dog faeces.

bazookas/bazoomas
breasts; tits; boobs.

bean counter
an accountant.

beat the crap out of
(see main entry: beat the living daylights out of)

bet Anthony Hordern's to a bark hut
(see main entry: bet London to a brick)

big bucks
a lot of money: e.g. He is earning big bucks this year.

big words
technical or pretentious

words that are not generally understood by others.

big-nose
an over-inquisitive person.

bike/bike it
to ride a bicycle: e.g. We biked it up the mountain.

bimbo
1. (see main entry)
2. a girl or woman who is attractive but not very intelligent.

black hole
a place into which things disappear without a trace.

blanket toss
an informal appeal for donations, as by a charitable institution.

bless (someone's) little cotton socks
expression of approval, gratitude.

bless (someone's) little fart and hole
(rhyming slang — heart and soul) expression of approval, gratitude.

blimey teddy!
exclamation of surprise or amazement.

blimming
(see main entry: blooming)

blind mullet
floating faeces, such as effluent washed up on beaches or a large solid lump in the toilet bowl, which resists flushing.

blinder
1. (see main entry)
2. high-quality performance, such as a spectacular mark in football.

bloody marvel
an exasperating, displeasing or contemptible person: e.g. Look at the mess you've made! You're a bloody marvel, you are!

blow away
to shoot and kill: e.g. John Lennon was blown away by some looney.

blow-out
1. (see main entry)
2. a dramatic increase in expenditure or costs.

blurt
1. emission of wind from the anus; fart: e.g. He let off a loud blurt.
2. to fart: e.g. Did you just blurt?
3. backside; bum: e.g. He sits on his blurt all day doing nothing.

boardies
1. (see main entry: board-shorts)
2. people (especially youths) who ride surf-boards.

boff
(especially of men) to have sexual intercourse: e.g. Who's he been boffing lately?

bog it in
to do, achieve, win easily: e.g. Did we win? We bogged it in!

bogan
(teenage slang) a boring, ignorant or unfashionable person.

bog trotters
Irish people.

bomb
1. (see main entry)
2. to practise graffiti; to attack with a can of spray paint any surface that can sustain writing: e.g. It was our gang that bombed the side of the local train last night.

bomber
1. (see main entry)
2. young person who indulges in graffiti, especially on public property.

bone-head
a stupid, ignorant person.

booby-hatch
1. prison.
2. institution for the mentally ill.

boom-box
portable stereo radio-cassette player, ghetto-blaster.

bop (one's) baconey
(of a man) to masturbate.

boppy
lively and swinging, so that one feels like dancing: e.g. That's a really boppy night-club.

bosom buddy
a very close friend in whom one confides.

bottom line
the basic standard or requirement: e.g. That's the bottom line — he won't accept a penny less than ten grand!

bozo
an idiot, fool or simpleton.

brrr
onomatopoeic sound denoting cold.

brace and bit
(rhyming slang) shit.

brandy
children's game of tag, using a tennis ball.

break out the violins!
facetious response to exaggerated or trite emotion.

brownie points
(to earn/score . . .) to win favour or approval.

bubble-car
police-car with a blue 'bubble' light on its roof.

buckets
great amounts of: e.g. He's got buckets of money.

bug-zapper
an electronic device for killing insects.

bum!
1. (see main entry)
2. mild exclamation of frustration or annoyance.

bumf/bumph
1. written or printed material, especially when unwanted or in excess.
2. worthless talk, ideas, theories: e.g. His thesis on UFOs was a whole lot of bumf!

bums on seats
audience or market, especially in terms of the profitability of some enterprise.

bushman's hanky
(of men) the practice of holding one nostril closed and blowing snot from the other on to the ground.

business end
the end of something that has the main function or poses the most danger: e.g. He grabbed the snake by the business end in.tead of by the tail and consequently was bitten.

bust (one's) arse/bum/gut
try very hard: e.g. I had to bust my arse to get this typed in time!

buster
1. (see main entry)
2. (in combination) something superior, overpowering: e.g. chartbusters; pricebuster sale; ghostbusters.

busy as a blue-arsed fly/bluebottle in a strange dunny

busy as a cat in a tripe shop

busy as a one-armed brickie in Beirut
(see main entry: busy as a bee)

butcher's paper
large sheets of cheap, unbleached paper traditionally used by butchers or fishmongers to wrap their wares.

butterfly kisses
affectionate caress whereby one brushes another's cheek with the eyelashes.

buzz-word
popular or trendy term, saying; catch-phrase.

C

camp
1. (see main entry)
2. affected or exaggerated: e.g. camp humour.

canardly
(joc. contraction of: can hardly) a hat (canardly tell it from a stetson).

canary
an unroadworthy certificate for a vehicle (traditionally issued on yellow paper).

cardboard money
a carton of beer given as payment or as a tip, instead of cash: e.g. Just sling the garbos some cardboard money and they'll take away your empties.

carry on like a two-bob watch
behave in a foolish, erratic, fussing manner.

cat's hiss
(rhyming slang) piss.

changa
Chinese person.

chauve
chauvinist.

chicken and egg story
case in which it is difficult to decide which facts or events came first.

chill out
1. (as an exclamation) stop! cut it out! shut up!
2. calm down; be reasonable.

ching/ching-chong
Chinese person; Chinese.

chiro
chiropractor.

choice
1. (see main entry)
2. excellent; first-rate: e.g. That was a choice dinner!

chonga
Chinese person.

chonks
sweets; lollies: e.g. There's nothing like sitting down to a couple of videos and a big bag of chonks!

chopper
1. (see main entry)
2. penis.

chuck a spastic/spazzo
display sudden anger, bad temper.

chuck a spread
(of women) to spread the legs ready for sex; to be willing to have sexual intercourse: e.g. She'd chuck a spread for any Tom, Dick or Harry!

chuff
female pudendum; vagina.

clacker
bum
See also:
sitting right on (one's/someone's) clacker

clangers
testicles.

clumsy as a duck in a ploughed paddock
very clumsy or unco-ordinated.

cockroach
person held in low esteem or contempt.

come a right proper charlie
1. (see main entry: come a cropper/gutser)
2. get hit or have an accident.
3. behave in a manner that makes one look like a fool.

come up smelling of roses
to be found or seen to be innocent of some wrong-doing, especially after being accused.

cone-head
one addicted to smoking marijuana using a bong.

cop that!
1. look at that!
2. (facetiously) so there! that'll serve you right!

corporate cowboy
business leader who makes maverick, often extravagant, investment decisions.

cos
(abbrev.) because.

couch potato
inactive person who spends a great deal of unproductive, monotonous time sitting watching television or videos.

could swim to (somewhere) with a bag of cement before that!
facetious expression of confidence that one can get to (somewhere), do something much faster than has been arranged or suggested.

couldn't organise a fart in a Baked Bean factory

couldn't run out of sight on a dark night
(of a person) totally incompetent.

couple of cans/stubbies short of a six-pack
(to be a . . .) to be lacking in intelligence; stupid.

cow candy
pile of cow dung.

cowabunga dudes!
a form of greeting, especially among youth — made popular by the cartoon characters, the Teenage Mutant Ninja Turtles.

Craven A chorus
loud, rasping fit of coughing associated with smoking, especially when made by several people simultaneously upon waking.

cream
1. (see main entry)
2. semen.
3. (of women) to produce vaginal juices when sexually aroused: e.g. He got me so excited I could have creamed the streets of Sydney!

crud
1. (see main entry)
2. a despicable person.

crudface
a despicable person.

cuddles
affectionate nick-name for a loved one.

cunt-struck
(of a man) totally infatuated or in love with a woman.

D

damage the Doulton
to go to the lavatory, toilet.

dangler
penis.

Darwin pyjamas
(to wear . . .) to wear no pyjamas at all; to go to bed naked.

desperado
(generally of a man) person so eager to have sex that he/she will go out with a very unattractive person in order to achieve it.

Dickless Tracy
a police-woman.

diddle
1. (see main entry)
2. to urinate: e.g. I laughed so hard at that joke I diddled my pants!

dingo date
an ugly or unattractive woman taken out on a date by a man for the sole purpose of having sex.

dingo's breakfast
no breakfast at all (joc. defined as 'a drink of water, a piss and a quick look around').

dinkies/dinks
(acronym: *d*ouble *i*ncome *n*o *k*ids) young married couples who have no children and both work.

dinter
male homosexual.

dip
1. (see main entry)
2. petty thief, especially a pick-pocket.

disaster just waiting to happen
a person prone or exposed to trouble or misfortune: e.g. Perry's so clumsy he's a disaster just waiting to happen.

do
1. (see main entry)
2. arrest; charge with a felony: e.g. he got done last night for drink-driving.

do it with the lights out
have sex in complete darkness, especially to avoid seeing one's partner: e.g. She's so ugly you'd have to do it with the lights out!

docs/doccers
a brand of heavy, rubber-soled boots and shoes held in high esteem by teenagers. (Trademark: Dr. Martens)

dogs are barking
feet are tired and sore: e.g. Cripes my dogs are barking — I can't walk another step!

donger
1. (see main entry)
2. penis.

don't give me that!
don't talk such nonsense!

dooflickie
(see main entry: doobrie)

dopey Dora
a foolish, slow-witted or unintelligent woman.

dots one and carries five
walks with the aid of crutches.

double-decker dog
two dogs mating, copulating.

down the Mallee crutching bull-ants
said of someone whose whereabouts are unknown: e.g. Fred? Cripes, I haven't seen him for years — he's probably down the Mallee somewhere crutching bull-ants!

dream on!
contemptuous remark to someone who is boasting, exaggerating or talking fancifully.

dredge up
1. (see main entry)
2. disclose, especially something unpleasant: e.g. During the trial the prosecutor dredged up a lot of information about her past.

driving the porcelain bus
on one's knees clutching the toilet bowl (as if it were a steering wheel) and vomiting into it, especially after an over-indulgence in alcohol.

dry as a gum-digger's dog
very dry; very thirsty.

D.T.'s
1. (see main entry)
2. dick togs — a clinging, revealing men's swim-suit.

dude
any person, but especially a trendy.

dunny-diver
a plumber.

E

eeny-meeny-miny-mo
a chant of chance used to make a choice when one does not care particularly about the outcome.

elephants/elephant's trunk
(rhyming slang) drunk: e.g. Boy! Did I get elephants last night with Carol!

enough to make a saint swear
an exasperating, frustrating situation or person.

even Jack Hill the blind miner saw that one!
(see main entry: Blind Freddie)

evo
evening: e.g. Where are we dining this evo?

eyeball (someone)
to observe or stare at.

eyes stuck out like organ stops
(to have one's . . .) to show complete astonishment or wonder.

F

fang farrier
dentist

fart at both ends
(of a person) to be a conceited, know-all, loud-mouthed bore.

fart-arse
one who brags, although basically lacking most of the qualities boasted of.

fast-track
to speed up the progress of events.

fazzo
fabulous; wonderful: e.g. That concert was just fazzo!

filthy
1. (see main entry)
2. (teenage slang) excellent; first-rate.

fishface
term of endearment, friendship: e.g. G'day, fishface!

fist as a part
(facetious spoonerism — pissed as a fart); intoxicated.

fits like a bum in a bucket

fits like a stocking on a Jew's nose
an extremely tight fit; fits snugly.

flash as a rat with a gold tooth
(see main entry: suave as a rat with a gold tooth)

flat
1. (see main entry)
2. set of rooms used as accommodation, usually rented.
3. to share rented accommodation: e.g. Who's she flatting with?

flied lice
pseudo-Asian for: fried rice.

flog the lizard
(of a man) to urinate.

fluoro
fluorescent.

flyer
small advertising pamphlet: e.g. I'm sick of flyers stuck under my windscreen wipers every time I park at the supermarket!

flyshit
very small measure, amount: e.g. That was only a flyshit away from being a disastrous accident!

foodie
a gourmet, especially a pretentious one: e.g. The foodies were out in force at that new restaurant.

foof
(of hair) to plump up, give body and fullness: e.g. I never seem to be able to foof my hair like my hairdresser can!

Foster's fart
foul-smelling fart from one who has indulged in too much beer.

freckle-puncher
male homosexual.

freight
money: e.g. he lost all his freight at the trots last night.

Fridayitis
general lack of desire to work on a Friday, in anticipation of the weekend; a fictitious illness due to this.

frigging in the rigging
wasting time; procrastinaing: e.g. Quit frigging in the rigging and get on with the bloody job!

fuck (someone) off
irritate, anger (someone) extremely.

fuck (someone) over
cheat, deceive, swindle, betray (someone).

fuck (someone) silly

fuck the legs off (someone)
have vigorous sexual intercourse with (someone).

fuckable
sexually desirable: e.g. Even after twelve years I still think my hubby's most fuckable.

fucker
1. (see main entry)
2. an intensifier, usually meaning big, admirable or astounding, according to the context: You should have seen the size of the fucker!
2.This fucker came up from nowhere and won the race!

fuckface
despicable person; term of contempt used particularly when one is angry or annoyed.

fuck-head
stupid, unattractive or despicable person.

fucking A!
exclamation of approval.

full as a fowl
(see main entry: full as a boot)

full mush mode
overwhelmed by trite or extreme sentimentality: e.g. We were all in full mush mode after that sad movie.

G

G
a grand — one thousand dollars.

gabfest
prolonged discussion or gossip session.

gazumping
the illicit practice of the vendor of a property accepting an offer from a prospective buyer and then accepting a higher offer from someone else before contracts have been exchanged with the first party.

gazundering
the illicit practice of a prospective buyer trying to force down the price of a property, after having agreed on a figure, by threatening to withdraw from the sale on spurious grounds (such as a concocted survey).

geek
1. (see main entry)
2. a fool, especially a person willing to appear so in order to make money.

get a bag!
(cricket) abuse hurled at a player who has missed or dropped an easy catch.

get real!
stop talking nonsense! stop day-dreaming! be realistic!

ghetto-blaster
portable stereo radio-cassette player.

give away (one's) arsehole and shit through (one's) ribs
to be particularly generous, benevolent.

give (someone) shit
1. (see main entry)
2. to berate, criticise, tease or harass (someone): e.g. His friends always give him shit because he's so short.

give (someone) the flick
to dismiss (someone), usually with contempt.

give (someone) the mail
to give (someone) reliable information or advice.

glitterati
celebrities; the rich and famous, seen as a social set.

glitz
pretentious display of luxury.

glitzy
full of glitz.

glue factory
the mythical place where useless or slow horses are sent to be disposed of.

go the growl
to perform cunnilingus.

good grab
(Australian Rules football) spectacular mark or catch.

good on the fang
a hearty eater who always displays a large appetite: e.g. How come your kids are so good on the fang and mine are so fussy?

good riddance to bad rubbish!
expression of pleasure, relief at the departure of a person or thing that one holds in contempt.

googly
a ball that has been bowled crooked or foul.
See also:
make googly eyes at (someone)

grass
1. (see main entry)
2. an informant; one who betrays.
3. to betray, inform on: e.g. If you grass on those guys they'd kill you!

great leap forward
momentous progress or achievement: e.g. It was a great leap forward for women when they got the right to vote.

great stuff
anything deserving the highest praise. e.g. This book is great stuff!

green
pertaining to environmental causes or issues: e.g. green politics; green power.

greenhouse effect
the commonly held theory, supported by many world scientists, that the build-up of certain gases in the earth's atmosphere as the result of industrialisation and other human activities is causing the temperature of the atmosphere to rise — with potentially catastrophic consequences.

Gregory Peck
(rhyming slang) neck.

grenade
small twist-top beer bottle.

grommet
very young surfboard rider.

ground
1. land: e.g. How much ground does he own?
2. distance: e.g. He covers a lot of ground now he has that new sports car.

grunge
dirt; filth; scum.

grunt
1. a policeman.
2. a soldier, especially of the lower rank; infantryman.
3. sexual intercourse.
4. to have sexual intercourse.
5. person viewed as the object of sexual intercourse.

guaranteed to choke a brown dog
(of a meal) awful, tasteless, poorly prepared, burnt.

guaranteed to kill a germ at twenty paces
(of alcohol) very strong or potent.

gucci
fashionable, especially in a pretentious way; trendy: e.g. That's a very gucci restaurant.

gumbo
cheap wine or alcohol, often home-made.

gump
to limp, walk awkwardly.

gunner/gunnerdo
(contraction of: going to/going to do) one who procrastinates or claims to be 'going to do this or going to do that', but never does.

H

hairy-legs
term of endearment: e.g. Hey, g'day hairy-legs!

hairy-legs and floppy-tits brigade
women leading alternative life-styles; hippie types.

hand-job
the act of masturbation.

hands-on
pertaining to direct or practical involvement: e.g. He's well known for his hands-on approach to management.

hanging
(teenage slang) placing limbs or head out of the windows or doors of a speeding train, or otherwise acting dangerously.

happy as a cane-toad with a nine iron under its chin

happy as a horn toad in a bucket of piss
not happy at all.

hard tit/titty
bad luck! — usually conveying scorn or lack of sympathy.

have/got a verandah over his toyshop
(of a man) having a large, overhanging belly, usually as a result of excessive beer drinking.

have/got (one's) snout in the trough
to obtain financial benefit, usually from the public purse, by unfair or illicit means: e.g. According to the report, several members of the government had their snouts in the trough for years.

have/got/take the bull by the horns
face, tackle a situation or problem with courage.

have/got the bull by the tits
have the wrong grasp of a situation; tackle a task or problem incorrectly; have the wrong method of approach.

haven't got a pot to piss in
without any money; broke; destitute.

headlights
breasts; boobs; tits.

heat
1. (see main entry)
2. blame: e.g. I'll take

some of the heat for what's happened, but I won't take the whole rap!

heavy
1. (see main entry)
2. beer of standard alcoholic content (as opposed to 'light' — of reduced alcoholic content): e.g. He won't touch the lights — he only drinks the heavies.

heifer
young girl or woman.

here's looking at you sideways!
a salute or proposal for a toast.

hit the kapok
go to bed, sleep; retire.

holic/aholic
(in combination) person addicted to the substance or activity specified. e.g. a chocoholic; a workaholic.

horizontal folk-dancing
sexual intercourse and activity.

horse and trap
(rhyming slang) crap — to defecate.

howdja go?
(contraction of: how do/did you go?)
1. a form of greeting.
2. (used as an inquiry) — How did you get on? What was the outcome?

humungous
extremely big, large: e.g. What a humungous spider!

I

I dunno!
(contraction of: I don't know) an exclamation of exasperation or bewilderment, usually uttered at the beginning of a statement: e.g. I dunno! They fight so much I'm not sure what's to become of their marriage!

I mean ...
an intensifier, used at the beginning of a sentence: e.g. I mean ... you should've see her — she was so fat!

if he had soup for brains he wouldn't have enough to wet his plate

if his brains were made of elastic they wouldn't make a set of garters for a one-legged canary
(an insult) he is not very intelligent, smart or alert.

if I bought a kangaroo it wouldn't hop!

if it was raining virgins I'd be washed away with a poofter!
to be extremely unlucky.

if it were up to me
in my opinion.

in deep shit

in more trouble than a one-legged bullfrog in a snake-pit
in serious trouble.

in (one's) rocking boots
(to be ...) to be so under the influence of alcohol as to be unable to walk steadily.

intestinal tourist
male homosexual.

irontits
person (especially a female) who can withstand cold.

Ivans
Russian people.

J

Jewish piano
cash register.

jig
(teenage slang) to play truant: e.g. I can remember jigging, especially at High School during Geography classes.

jump the rattler
to avoid paying the fare for a train trip.

jumper
woollen or knitted jersey or sweater.

K

K
thousand: e.g. That car only cost me six K!

kangaroo short of a full paddock
(to be a ...) to be lacking in intelligence.

kangaroo the dunny seat
to stand on a toilet seat and squat, to avoid placing one's buttocks on a soiled seat.

kay-one-double-you-one
Kiwi — a New Zealander.

kick a goal
attain one's aim of sexual intercourse; to score.

kiff
the leaves of marijuana, with no flower heads and therefore not as potent: e.g. I could only afford a bag of kiff this week.

kinda
(contraction of: kind of) sort of; in some manner: e.g. Even though he's shy I think he's kinda nice.

L

Lady Macbeth
woman with an aversion to manual work: e.g. And Lady Macbeth here can help with the dishes!

lager bomb
foul-smelling fart from one who has indulged in too much beer.

laugh like a drain
laugh heartily.

lay out the lilo
make preparations to

accommodate an overnight guest.

leave (one's) run too late
to miss an opportunity through inaction or procrastination.

leave (one/someone) short
cause (one/someone) to be lacking in cash or available money: e.g That trip to Surfers left me short this week.

legless
extremely intoxicated, drunk or drugged: e.g. Boy! Did I get legless at Stan's fiftieth!

lemming
a Hitler-style moustache.

let's have a bit of shoosh!
a plea for quiet, usually just prior to or during a speech.

light
beer of reduced alcoholic content.

like . . .
an intensifier, used at the beginning of a sentence: e.g. Like . . . you should've seen this guy — like, I mean he was really weird!

like an all-night chemist
(of a person) one who never shuts up; person who talks incessantly.

like fuck
1. exclamation of denial, scorn, disbelief: e.g. Like fuck you can!
2. very fast, quickly: e.g. We'll have to work like fuck to finish on time.

like putting Dracula in charge of the Blood Bank
an unwise decision or course of action.

little silver bodgie
Bob Hawke, Australian Prime Minister.

log jam
confusing situation for which there is no apparent solution.

lounge lizard
1. (especially of a man) a sleazebag who frequents hotels, parties.
2. inactive person who spends a great deal of unproductive, monotonous time sitting around watching television or videos.

love glove
a condom.

love-muscle
penis.

lower than a duck's bum
(of a person) despicable; contemptible.

lughole/lug'ole
the ear.

lure of the hairy magnet
(of men) overwhelming desire for sex, to the extent that one will go to great lengths to achieve it.

M

maggots
children, especially young babies.

make a pavement pizza
to vomit, especially on the footpath upon leaving a pub or nightclub intoxicated.

make googly eyes at (someone)
cast seductive glances at (someone): e.g. Her husband's been making googly eyes at me all night!

map of Tasmania/Tassie
the characteristically triangular patch of pubic hair on a woman.

massage the clit
(of women) to masturbate.

mattress-muncher
male homosexual.

meathead
1. idiot; fool; incompetent person.
2. person considered to have more brawn than brain, such as a weight-lifter, bouncer, body-builder.

megafugly
(derog., generally used by men) an unattractive, ugly or unappealing woman.

milk, milk, lemonade, round the corner chocolate's made
children's rhyme denoting the sexual parts of the female body.

min
minute; a tick: e.g. Be with you in a min!

mine of useless information
person who offers a lot of information that is generally useless, irrelevant.

moo poo
1. cow dung.
2. (in rural areas) a form of fund-raising whereby a paddock is divided and marked into lots, all of which are sold. A cow is then set free in the paddock and the 'owner' of the lot on which the animal drops its first pile of dung wins a designated percentage of the takings, while the remainder goes to the fund-raisers.

mooch
1. (see main entry)
2. to behave affectionately, amorously; indulge in light sexual activity: e.g. The main reason I went to drive-in movies when I was young was to mooch in the back seat with my boyfriend.

mooning
the act of exposing one's buttocks in public.

mother of a (something)
an intensifier, denoting (something) big, outstanding: e.g. That was a mother of a fight they had last night!

mush out
to become intoxicated with heavy, trite or feeble sentimentality: e.g. That sad movie made everybody mush out!

mutt
(rhymes with: foot) female pudendum; genitals.

N

nah, forest fortnight!
stock response to the saying: What do you think this is — bush week?!

nappy valley
a suburban housing development populated principally by young families.

nectar of the gods
alcohol, especially one's favourite.

Ned Kelly
(rhyming slang) belly.

need a labrador/white cane
to fail to see the obvious — used especially of a sporting umpire who fails to detect an apparent infringement of rules.

never-never
1. (see main entry)
2. hire-purchase: e.g. We bought the car and the fridge on the never-never.

nimby syndrome
(acronym: *n*ot *i*n *m*y *b*ack *y*ard) the difficulty experienced by public authorities in locating new developments or facilities in residential areas, as the result of public protests.

no way José!
emphatically no! under no circumstances!

norgs
breasts; boobs; tits.

not for the faint-hearted
any situation or set of circumstances requiring courage, stamina.

not half bad
excellent; first-rate: e.g. This wine's not half bad!

not worth a tinker's damn
worthless; insignificant.

nother
another, separate: e.g. That's a whole nother thing you're talking about now!

O

old-timer's disease
(joc.) Alzheimer's disease.

only a mother could love (someone/something)
said of a person or thing that is extraordinarily ugly or unappealing.

only two bob in the dollar
(to be . . .) to be dull-witted; lacking in intelligence; stupid.

open (one's) lunch
to fart obviously in public.

out on the tiles
having a good time out; on a spree; e.g. We need a few quiet nights at home as we've been out on the tiles every night for the last week.

over the fence is six and out
a common rule in backyard or children's cricket games.

owyergoinmate–orright?
the Strine form of: How are you going mate — all right?; a popular form of greeting heard in pubs between mates and workers.

P

paint (oneself) into a corner
to manoeuvre (oneself) into a difficult or impossible situation.

park the prawn
(of a man) to achieve sexual intercourse: e.g. Did you manage to park the prawn last night?

pearl before the swine
(joc.) I'll go first.

perform
1. display bad temper or emotion: e.g. You should've seen the way her kids performed in the middle of the supermarket after not getting their own way!
2. accomplish with great success the act of sexual intercourse: e.g. Well! After all that beer he couldn't even raise one, let alone perform!

petrol-head
a car fanatic who spends a great deal of time and money on his/her vehicle.

pick-and-shovel man
labourer.

piles
1. (see main entry)
2. haemorrhoids.

piss in the same pot as (someone)
to behave in an obsequious manner toward (someone), in the hope of personal gain.

plagon
flagon (of wine) — coined from the supposed pronunciation of the word by Aborigines.

plastic money
any credit card or credit facility used instead of cash.

play (someone) along
cheat, deceive, fool (someone): e.g. He never really wanted to marry you — he's been playing you along all these years!

play stinkfinger
indulge in sexual activity using a finger.

plod
police: e.g. Something must have happened — the plod are all over the place tonight!

poo-jabber
male homosexual.

popular as a pork chop in a synagogue
not popular at all.

pork
(of men) to have sexual intercourse: e.g. Boy! I'd love to pork her!

pork out
to eat greedily or to excess.

pork-barrelling
the practice of allocating public money or funds inequitably, to further one's own political interests.

prairie oysters
testicles of castrated calves, considered a delicacy.

prat
1. (see main entry)
2. a foolish or contemptible person.

publics
children attending government schools (as opposed to those attending private schools).

punch in the pants
sexual intercourse: e.g. What she needs is a good punch in the pants or she'll turn out to be a sour old maid.

purple patch
a period or run of good luck, fortune: e.g. After being in debt for ages, our business has finally hit a purple patch.

pushbike
bicycle.

put a brick on (someone's) head
(joc.) try to arrest the sudden upward growth of a child or teenager: e.g. He's getting so tall now we'll have to put a brick on his head!

put down the two and carry one
walk with the aid of crutches, having either an injured leg or one leg only.

put (oneself)/(one's bum) on the line
to put (oneself) in a dangerous position or situation; to take a risk, especially a financial one.

put out for (someone)
have sexual intercourse with (someone): e.g. Did she put out for you last night?

Q

quiche eater
(usually scornful) a sensitive man.

R

rack
(teenage slang) to steal from shops: e.g. We all rack for thrills.

rad
1. radical: e.g. His ideas are so rad!
2. excellent; groovy: e.g. We had a really rad time last night!

randy as a three-legged grasshopper
(see main entry: randy)

rant and rave
to behave in a very angry, hostile manner.

rat (one's) kick
to rummage through (one's) pockets for money: e.g. Come on everybody — rat your kicks for a donation to this worthy cause!

rat-arsed
very drunk, intoxicated: e.g. We really got rat-arsed at the pub last night!

rat pack
a male clique.

rattler
train.

real doozie/doozy
excellent or first-rate.

rear (its/someone's) ugly head again
(of something disliked or unwanted) to reappear; to return to one's attention: e.g. The matter of corruption in government has reared its ugly head again.

red pussy
pertaining to menstruation: e.g. You won't get any tonight — she's got a red pussy.

red-back
the venomous red-back spider.

reffo
refugee.

remember — it's the second hole from the back of the neck!
(joc.) taunt directed at a man obviously pursuing a woman for the sole purpose of having sexual intercourse.

rev-head
fast driver of a car or motorcycle.

right, left and centre
everywhere; all over the place: e.g. When I dropped my handbag, all manner of embarrassing articles went right, left and centre!

right proper charlie
idiot; fool; dolt: e.g. You made a right proper charlie of yourself in front of everybody last night!

right smack dab in the middle
(see main entry: right

slap-bang in the hey-diddle-diddle)

ring jockey
male homosexual.

rock-spider
1. a paedophile; child molester.
2. any despicable, contemptible person.

root me rigid!

root my thong!
exclamation of amazement, wonder.

rough as hessian bags
(see main entry: rough as bags)

roundabout
1. playground equipment resembling a large cart-wheel that spins horizontally.
2. traffic-control device consisting of a central island at the intersection of several roads, around which traffic may move in one direction only.

roundeyes
Australians, Europeans, in the opinion of Asians.

rum, bum and gramophone
the navy equivalent of wine, women and song.

S

safe sex
any sexual practice (such as wearing a condom) considered to eliminate the possibility of one's contracting AIDS or any other sexually transmitted disease.

sambo
1. (see main entry)
2. sandwich.

sarky
bad-tempered; ill-mannered: e.g. What's that creep getting sarky with you for?

scab
1. (see main entry)
2. to borrow, cadge, with no real intention of paying back: e.g. Can I scab a fag?
3. person who does this: e.g. I'm not supplying that scab with another single freebie!

school of hard knocks
a life where experience and knowledge is gained the hard way: e.g. Nothing was handed to me on a silver platter — I got where I am through the school of hard knocks!

scratch
made up of whatever is available: e.g. She ransacked the fridge for the makings of a scratch meal.

screw
1. (see main entry)
2. a look: e.g. Have a screw at this!

scrummy
scrumptious; delicious.

scum of the earth
the lowest, most despicable type of person or people.

see straight
understand; think clearly: e.g. He's so upset he can't see straight at the moment.

see the colour of (someone's) money
to invite (someone) to support (his/her) boast, promise or wager with actual money, visible cash: e.g. Before I accept your bet I want to see the colour of your money!

see youse
(pronounced: seeyez) goodbye; see you later.

servo
service station; petrol station.

shaft (someone)
1. (see main entry)
2. to treat (someone) unfairly; to swindle.

shit before the shovel
(joc.) you go first.

shit doughnuts
(of a man) to be homosexual.

sicko
morally reprehensible person.

sit up like Jacky
be zealously attentive; to sit quietly and attentively.

sits down to piss
expression of contempt for a man considered pathetic, weak or effeminate.

sitting right on (one's/someone's) clacker
driving a vehicle dangerously close to the back of another: e.g. That bloody truck sat right on my clacker for miles!

six-pack
plastic-wrapped package of six stubbies or cans of beer.

skin and blister
(rhyming slang) sister.

slab
carton of beer that holds 24 stubbies or cans: e.g. Grab a couple of slabs on your way home for the barbie tonight.

slag
1. (see main entry)
2. a sleazy or sluttish woman.
3. to criticise.

sleazebag
despicable person of low character.

smiley
(teenage slang) a distinctive burn imposed on the wrist by a disposable cigarette lighter.

smoke
(see main entry) the term now also refers to the use of marijuana: e.g. Does he smoke?

snag short of a barbie
(to be . . .) to be stupid, lacking in intelligence.

snatch-and-grab
a take-away meal.

snorter
nose.

so full of shit that even his eyes are brown
expression of contempt for someone who brags or talks nonsense.

so mean he'd take a worm from a blind chook
(of a person) parsimonious; stingy.

so windy it'd blow a blue dog off its chain
(of weather) very windy, blowy.

soap-dodger
English person.

sofa spud
inactive person who spends a great deal of unproductive, monotonous time sitting watching television; couch potato.

so's Christmas/Easter/Father Christmas!
stock response to the saying: I'm coming!

spacies
arcade video-game machines.

spag bol
spaghetti bolognaise.

spare me the violins!
please don't waste your time trying to enlist my sympathy or pity.

sparrow-starver
street-sweeper.

speckie
1. a house built as a speculative investment.
2. (Australian Rules football) a spectacular mark, catch.

spin
1. (see main entry)
2. extra material added to a drug to make it last longer, such as tobacco with marijuana: e.g. Got any spin in this joint?

sprogs
young children.

squeeze
1. (see main entry)
2. partner in sex: e.g. Who's her latest squeeze?

stacks on the mill
(football) the action of many players jumping on the ball simultaneously.

stiff bickies!
(see main entry: stiff cheddar/cheese/shit!)

strap-hangers
commuters who, unable to find a vacant seat on a train, tram or bus, must stand and hold a suspended strap for support.

stressed out
feeling anxious, worried; under great strain.

stubbie short of a six-pack
(to be . . .) to be lacking in intelligence; stupid; dull-witted.

suck face
(teenage slang) kiss passionately: e.g. Those two have been sucking face in the back seat all night!

suitcase
(derog., used especially in the Northern Territory) a cask of wine, when carried by Aborigines.

sump-oil
thick, usually home-made, alcohol or liqueur.

supergrass
police informant whose evidence involves a large number of people or relates to large-scale crime.

surfboard
sanitary pad used by women during menstruation.

swan
to walk or move about idly, aimlessly, or with an air of superiority: e.g. He's been swanning around all day!

T

take a bath
to lose (especially money) on a deal.

take (something) on board
to accept or give serious consideration to: e.g. Unions have now taken child care on board as a political issue.

talk under water with a mouthful of marbles

talk under wet cement
1. to talk at great length, often boring the listener.
2. to be very persuasive, convincing.

tantalise the tassel
(of men) to masturbate.

tan-track specialist
male homosexual.

tarpaulin muster
an informal appeal for donations, money.

technicolour laugh/yodel
(see main entry: technicolour yawn)

the opera's not over till the fat lady sings
a warning not to expect or anticipate the outcome of events as things could quite conceivably turn out differently.

the Track
(Northern Territory) the Stuart Highway.

thick as Ayers Rock

thick as shit in the neck of a bottle
(see main entry: thick as a brick)

thinks he's hot bog but he's only a cold fart warmed up
to have a high opinion of

oneself that is not shared by others.

thrash
heavy metal music.

three-piece suite
male genitals; the penis and testicles.

three-sixty
a complete circle: e.g. We did a three-sixty twice at that roundabout before we made the right turn!

throw (one's) money around like a bloke with no arms
to be mean, parsimonious, stingy.

tight as a finger up a Jew's arsehole
1. an extremely tight fit.
2. mean; parsimonious; stingy.

tin-lid
(rhyming slang) kid; child.

tippety-run
(in backyard or children's cricket games) a rule whereby a run must be made every time the ball is hit.

tired and emotional
euphemism for being totally intoxicated or drunk: e.g. Mum was a bit tired and emotional at the pub last night!

tit over tail
(see main entry: A over T)

tit-puller
one who milks cows by hand: e.g. Mum's a better tit-puller than dad.

to the max
to the maximum, utmost; fully: e.g. We all got stoned to the max at the pub last night!

toffy drop
an exceptionally attractive woman.

tombowler/tommy
a large playing marble.

totally awesome
anything amazing, wonderful, excellent, worthy of special attention: e.g. You should have been there last night — the concert was totally awesome!

touch
1. (see main entry)
2. turn to pay for something: e.g. It's your touch for the next round of drinks.

trammie
tram-conductor.

Trots/Trotskyists
left-wing activists.

trumps
(of a person) admirable.

tummy-banana
penis.

turd-dinter
male homosexual.

U

up the bum of a black chook looking for white feathers
1. stock reply to the query 'What are you up to?', 'Where are you going?'.
2. involved in a fruitless, wasteful search or activity.

up the shute
(see main entry: up the pole)

up the stick
pregnant: e.g. Is she up the stick again?!

up your arse with a piece of glass!
rude dismissal, rebuke.

upperer
(in combination) denoting the doer of the stated activity: e.g. washer-upperer; cleaner-upperer.

us
me: e.g. Give us a drink please.

useful/useless as a bucket under a bull

useful/useless as a sore arse to a boundary rider

useful/useless as a third armpit

useful/useless as two knobs of billy-goat poop
(see main entry: useful/useless as a cunt full of cold water)

V

veg out
to spend time in an idle, unprogressive or monotonous manner: e.g. We're going to veg out in front of the telly watching footy all weekend.

vegied out
totally intoxicated, drunk, or under the influence of drugs.

vertical smile
vagina.

vice-versa
subtle reference to lesbianism: e.g. She likes her vice-versa.

virile member
penis.

visit the five-fingered widow
(of men) to masturbate.

W

wakey, wakey, hands off snakey!
jocular call to a man to get out of bed in the morning instead of masturbating.

wedding tackle
male genitals.

went down quicker than the first cold tinnie at the butcher's picnic
said of anything that happened very quickly or

suddenly, but especially of a man who is knocked down quickly in a fight.

westie
(see main entry) the term has now extended beyond Sydney and generally denotes someone from any western suburbs (traditionally a region of economic disadvantage), who is considered rustic, unsophisticated.

wet patch/spot
the damp area of semen or sexual juices in the bed following sexual activity.

whacky-tobaccy

whacko-tobacco
marijuana.

what do you expect — this is Australia/Queensland!
stock response by locals to criticism from new arrivals.

whatever you think's a fair thing
whatever you decide to do is OK by me.

when the golden eagle shits
(see main entry: when the crow shits)

where the crows fly backwards
in remote, uninhabitable, outback areas (the crows fly backwards presumably to keep the dust out of their eyes).

white-collar worker
man who ejaculates over his partner's neck, face.

whoopie-weed
marijuana.

who's fucking this pig anyway?
(see main entry: who's milking this cat?)

who's up who and who's paying the rent?
(see main entry: who's up who?)

woofy
smelly; having a distasteful odour: e.g. That shirt is a bit woofy under the armpits!

wouldn't know if a band was up him until he got the drum

wouldn't know if a bus was up him till the people got off

wouldn't know if a train was up him till the whistle blew

wouldn't know if a tram was up him till the bell rang

wouldn't know if the Salvation Army was up his arse playing the Dead March
(see main entry: wouldn't know (one's) arse from a hole in a flowerpot)

wouldn't use (someone) for ammo at a shit fight
declaration of one's contempt for (someone).

wuss
(rhymes with puss) wimp; ineffectual, simpering person: e.g. Don't be such a bloody wuss!

Y

yike
1. (see main entry)
2. complaint: e.g. Our biggest yike is that we pay too many taxes.

yo!
exclamation of approval, enthusiasm.

you can knock but nobody answers
(of a person) lacking in intelligence; dull-witted.

you don't have to be dead to be stiff
expression relating to one's exceedingly bad run of luck.

you don't look at the mantelpiece when you stoke the fire
(usually said by men of women) anyone is a possible sexual partner, no matter how ugly or unattractive.

you know what (someone) did/thought?
rebuff to anyone who says 'I thought . . . ', to which there are several stock answers, such as: 1. He thought he had a car but woke up with a horn! 2. He thought his bum was out of bed so he got out to shove it back in again!

young'un
child: e.g. Have they got any young'uns?